MW00574719

The Handbook of Culture and Biology

The Handbook of Culture and Biology

Edited by

José M. Causadias
Eva H. Telzer
Nancy A. Gonzales

This edition first published 2018

Registered Office(s)
John Wiley & Sons, Inc., 111 River Street, Hoboken, NJ 07030, USA

Editorial Office
9600 Garsington Road, Oxford, OX4 2DQ, UK

For details of our global editorial offices, customer services, and more information about Wiley products visit us at www.wiley.com.

Wiley also publishes its books in a variety of electronic formats and by print-on-demand. Some content that appears in standard print versions of this book may not be available in other formats.

Library of Congress Cataloging-in-Publication Data

Names: Causadias, José M.
Title: The handbook of culture and biology / José M. Causadias, Arizona State University, Eva H. Telzer, University of Illinois Urbana-Champaign, Nancy A. Gonzales, Arizona State University.
Description: First edition. | Hoboken, NJ : John Wiley & Sons, Inc., 2017. | Includes bibliographical references and index. |
Identifiers: LCCN 2017015694 (print) | LCCN 2017024899 (ebook) | ISBN 9781119181347 (pdf) | ISBN 9781119181354 (epub) | ISBN 9781119181323 (cloth)
Subjects: LCSH: Physical anthropology. | Sociobiology. | Evolutionary psychology.
Classification: LCC GN60 (ebook) | LCC GN60 .C38 2017 (print) | DDC 599.9–dc23
LC record available at https://lccn.loc.gov/2017015694

Cover Design: Wiley
Cover Images: (DNA and Brain icons) © steppeua/iStockphoto; (Male Silhouette) © nale/iStockphoto

Set in 11/14pt WarnockPro by Aptara Inc., New Delhi, India

Printed in Singapore by C.O.S. Printers Pte Ltd

10 9 8 7 6 5 4 3 2 1

Contents

Biographical Notes

Emma K. Adam is Professor of Human Development and Social Policy in the School of Education and Social Policy at Northwestern University. She examines stress and coping in adolescence and early adulthood, focusing on everyday social influences on stress hormones and sleep, and their implications for health and academic achievement. Her research has revealed, and explores the impacts of, racial/ethnic disparities in stress and stress biology.

R. Alexander Bentley is Chair of the Department of Comparative Cultural Studies at the University of Houston. His research interests are in modeling and understanding collective "herding" behavior in society and testing those models against real-world phenomena. A second, distinct area of research explores community diversity, kinship, and social complexity in prehistoric societies.

Jennifer Botting is a PhD student in the School of Psychology and Neuroscience at the University of St Andrews, researching social learning biases in wild vervet monkeys at the Inkawu Field Project, South Africa. Her research interests focus on social cognition in non-human primates.

Belinda Campos is an Associate Professor in the Department of Chicano/Latino Studies as well as an affiliate of the School of Medicine PRIME-LC Program and the Department of Psychology and Social Behavior at the University of California, Irvine. Her research examines the role of culture in shaping relationship experience and health. Her work shows that a cultural emphasis on prioritizing others before the self (as found in, for example, in Latino and East Asian cultures) can be beneficial for relationships and protective of health.

José M. Causadias is an Assistant Professor in the T. Denny Sanford School of Social and Family Dynamics at Arizona State University. His work is centered on promoting innovation in cultural research that can transform psychological and developmental sciences. With this aim in mind, he conducts research on culture and biology interplay, particularly in the field of cultural genomics.

Lucia Cavanagh is a doctoral student in the Counseling Psychology program at the University of Houston. She received a bachelor's degree in Psychology and English from the University of Florida. She is a member of the Hwemudua Addictions and Health Disparities Laboratory with research interests that center on biopsychosocial predictors of disease and drug use vulnerability, specifically focusing on psychoneuroimmunology, stress dysregulation, and neurocognition.

Adam B. Cohen is Associate Professor in the Department of Psychology at Arizona State University. His research focuses on the cultural and evolutionary psychology of religion. He is the editor of *Culture Reexamined* (American Psychological Association, 2014) and he was given the Margaret Gorman early career award by the American Psychological Association and the Godin prize by the International Association for the Psychology of Religion.

Saarang Deshpande is currently an undergraduate student at Cornell University and will be attending medical school after graduation. His research interests involve the intersection of neuroendocrinology, gene–environment interaction, and psychosocial intervention. He aims to focus on academic medical practice in neuropsychiatry.

Stacey N. Doan is a developmental health psychologist and Assistant Professor in the Department of Psychology at Claremont McKenna College. Her work focuses on understanding how social factors, such as socioeconomic practices, and cultural values and parenting practices influence health and well-being.

Leah D. Doane is an Associate Professor in the Department of Psychology at Arizona State University. She studies adolescent and emerging adult development, particularly with regard to identifying the psychophysiological mechanisms that underlie adolescent and young adult everyday stress experiences in naturalistic settings. Her most recent work uses culturally and genetically informed designs for studying daily associations among socio-emotional experiences, physiology and sleep in the prediction of subsequent health and academic achievement in Latino children and adolescents.

Gary W. Evans is Elizabeth Lee Vincent Professor in the Department of Human Development at Cornell University. He is interested in how the physical environment affects human health and well-being among children. His specific areas of expertise include the environment of childhood poverty, children's environments, cumulative risk and child development, environmental stressors, and the development of children's environmental attitudes and behaviors.

Ewune Ewane is a doctoral student in the Counseling Psychology program at the University of Houston. She received her master's degree in Community Counseling at Loyola University Chicago and her bachelor's degree in Psychology at Marquette University. She is a member of the Hwemudua Addictions and Health Disparities Laboratory (HAHDL) and has research interests in addictions, health disparities, identity development, and African/African-American psychology.

Nancy A. Gonzales is ASU Foundation Professor in the Department of Psychology at Arizona State University. She received her PhD in Clinical Psychology from the University of Washington. Her research examines cultural and contextual influences on child and family developmental processes across the lifespan. Her work has focused particularly on the study of meaningful aspects of culture at multiple levels to understand the interplay of culture with normative and maladaptive adaptation within diverse communities.

Ryan S. Hampton is a PhD student in the Department of Psychology at Arizona State University. His research focuses on cultural variations in neural responses involved in processes related to affect, including empathy, emotion regulation, and positive self-views.

LaBarron K. Hill is an Assistant Professor in the Department of Psychiatry and Behavioral Sciences at the Duke University School of Medicine. His research focuses on deciphering the interaction of the biobehavioral mechanisms implicated in cardiovascular disease disparities.

Lori S. Hoggard is a Postdoctoral Research Associate in the Department of Social Medicine at the University of North Carolina at Chapel Hill. Her research focuses on elucidating the unique consequences of racial discrimination as a stressor and identifying potential protective or vulnerability factors in this context.

Ummul-Kiram Kathawalla is a PhD student and National Science Foundation Graduate Research Fellow in the Department of Psychology at the University of Minnesota, Twin Cities. Her research interests focus on understanding how various interpersonal, societal, and personal factors influence minority identity development. She is particularly interested in how identity formation contributes to the development and persistence of psychological conditions and physiological well-being.

Kevin M. Korous is a PhD student and graduate research assistant in the T. Denny Sanford School of Social and Family Dynamics at Arizona State University. He received his bachelor's degree in Psychology from the University of Utah. His research interests include the role of biological processes, culture, and environmental stressors in shaping development, with a focus on cognition and well-being.

Kevin N. Laland is a Professor in the School of Biology at the University of St Andrews. His principal academic interests are in the general area of animal behavior and evolution, with a specific focus on animal social learning, cultural evolution, and niche construction. He is engaged in empirical studies of animal social learning and innovation, including experimental work with fish, birds, non-human primates, and humans.

Lynda C. Lin is a PhD student in the Department of Psychology at the University of Illinois Urbana Champaign. She is interested in using an interdisciplinary approach to understand the underlying neural mechanisms through which culture can influence behavior.

Ronda F. Lo is a graduate student in the Department of Psychology at York University. She is broadly interested in how culture influences a number of cognitive processes and social behaviors, such as attention, language use, sibling relationships, and the intersection of national, ethnic, religious, and linguistic identities.

Meghan L. Meyer is an Assistant Professor in the Department of Psychological and Brain Sciences at Dartmouth College. Her research integrates social and cognitive neuroscience to promote the understanding of what drives our tendency, ability, and need to think about the social world around us.

Stefanie B. Northover received a Bachelor of Arts degree in psychology at California State University, Long Beach, and a Master of Science degree in psychology at McMaster University. She is currently a graduate student in social psychology at Arizona State University. She is interested in the psychology of religion from evolutionary and cultural perspectives.

Ezemenari M. Obasi is an Associate Professor at the University of Houston in the Department of Psychological, Health, and Learning Sciences (PHLS). His current program of research focuses on addictions, health disparities that disproportionately affect the African-American community, psychoneuroimmunology, and cultural predictors of health behaviors. He is the director of the Hwemudua Addictions and Health Disparities Laboratory (HAHDL) and the director of the University of Houston's HEALTH Research Institute. He also has unique expertise in the study of African/African-American culture and mental health. This includes human laboratory studies, field data collections in the community, and large-scale longitudinal research designs.

Michael J. O'Brien is Professor of Anthropology and Dean of the College of Arts and Science at the University of Missouri. His research interests are in developing theory to increase our understanding of numerous anthropological and archaeological issues, including the colonization of the New World and the subsequent spread of populations eastward across North America.

Anthony D. Ong is Associate Professor of Human Development at Cornell University. His research aims to advance understanding of human development and plasticity across multiple levels of analysis, including emotion–cognition interactions, sociocultural processes, and neurobiological systems. A major focus of his recent work involves understanding the physiological mechanisms through which subtle forms of recurring bias and unfair treatment get under the skin to affect disease susceptibility.

Yang Qu is a postdoctoral scholar at Stanford University. He received his PhD in Developmental Psychology from the University of Illinois at Urbana-Champaign. He uses an interdisciplinary approach to examine how culture shapes emotion, motivation, and decision making among adolescents and adults.

Luke Rendell is a MASTS Lecturer in the School of Biology at the University of St Andrews, appointed in 2012 after receiving a PhD from Dalhousie University in 2003. His broad research interests are focused on the evolution of learning and communication, with a particular emphasis on cetaceans, and has published over 60 papers on these topics. He is co-author of *The Cultural Lives of Whales and Dolphins* (Chicago University Press, 2015).

Joni Y. Sasaki is an Assistant Professor and director of the Culture and Religion Lab in the Department of Psychology at York University. In her research, she integrates perspectives from psychology and biology to examine basic scientific questions about culture and religion.

Michael R. Sladek is a doctoral student in Developmental Psychology at Arizona State University. He is interested in stress and coping processes among adolescents and young adults. From a biopsychosocial perspective, his research has focused on stress and coping among students transitioning to the college context using multiple assessment methods (e.g., daily diaries, stress biomarkers, sleep). With greater attention to culture, his current work extends this approach to Latino and other historically underrepresented college students.

Charles T. Snowdon is Hilldale Professor Emeritus of Psychology and Zoology at the University of Wisconsin, Madison. His research has involved cooperatively breeding marmosets and tamarins, with work in captivity and in the field. He has studied the behavioral and neuroendocrine mechanisms involved in successful cooperative breeding as well as vocal and chemical signaling and social learning. He has served as an editor of *Animal Behaviour* and of the *Journal of Comparative Psychology.*

Moin Syed is an Associate Professor in the Department of Psychology at the University of Minnesota, Twin Cities. His research interests lie broadly in how adolescents and young adults from diverse ethnic, racial, and cultural backgrounds weave together their multiple identities to lead healthy, productive, and purposeful lives.

Eva H. Telzer is an Assistant Professor in the Department of Psychology and Neuroscience at the University of North Carolina at Chapel Hill. She received her PhD in Developmental Psychology from UCLA. Her research centers on adolescent development, social relationships, and the role the brain plays during this important transitional period. Her research takes a multi-method approach that includes the use of fMRI, daily diaries, and diurnal cortisol.

Erica van de Waal is a Society in Science–Branco Weiss Fellow at the Anthropological Institute and Museum of the University of Zurich and the research coordinator of the Inkawu Vervet Project in South Africa. She finished her PhD in 2010 and did four years of postdoctoral research at the University of St Andrews before taking up her current position. Her main research topic is animal cognition with a focus on primate social learning. She has co-authored a key paper on this last topic, "Potent social learning and conformity shape a wild primate's foraging decisions," published in *Science* (2013).

Michael E. W. Varnum is an Assistant Professor in the Department of Psychology at Arizona State University. His research focuses on the proximal biological mechanisms that underpin cultural variations in social cognition (using neuroscience techniques), as well as the role played by more distal ecological factors in patterns of cultural variation and cultural change. His research has been published in leading journals, including *PNAS, Psychological Science, Journal of Experimental Psychology: General,* and *NeuroImage.*

Shu-wen Wang is an Assistant Professor in the Department of Psychology at Haverford College. Her research examines stress, coping, and social behavior, with an emphasis on social support interactions. One branch of her work focuses on the cultural shaping of stress and coping processes, and has found that cultural values impact the use and experience of social support.

Kristin A. Wilborn is a postdoctoral research fellow at University of Houston. She received her doctoral degree in Experimental Psychology at the University of Texas at San Antonio, a master's degree in Health Psychology at Texas State University, and a bachelor's degree in Political Science at Furman University. She currently serves as the project manager in the Hwemudua Addictions and Health Disparities Laboratory (HAHDL), and has research interests in psychoneuroimmunology, health disparities, and quantitative methods.

David R. Williams is the Florence Sprague Norman and Laura Smart Norman Professor of Public Health at the Harvard T. H. Chan School of Public Health, and Professor of African and African American Studies and of Sociology at Harvard University. He is internationally recognized as a leading social scientist whose research is focused on the complex ways in which race, racism, socioeconomic status, stress, health behaviors, and religious involvement can affect physical and mental health.

Sandra Yan is a doctoral student in the Counseling Psychology program at University of Houston, where she received her bachelor's degree in Biology and Psychology. She is a member of the Hwemudua Addictions and Health Disparities Laboratory (HAHDL) and has research interests in addictions, psychoneuroimmunology, health disparities, and cultural psychology.

Foreword: On Culture and Biology

I recently found myself at an interdisciplinary workshop on the topic of human nature. The only biologist present, I argued strongly that the term "human nature" was inherently problematical and should be abandoned (Laland & Brown, in press). Curiously, I was followed by two anthropologists willing to defend the concept. That our presentations should have gone against the historical tendency for our respective disciplines says something about how far research has come in the cross-disciplinary investigation of the biology–culture relationship. It also hints at some of the challenges ahead. For researchers seeking to understand the interplay between biology and culture, these are exciting yet tortuous times.

We now live in an age in which attempts to separate "nature" from "nurture" or "biology" from "culture" are long discredited. Countless experimental studies show how genes take cues from environments, how learning relies on gene expression, and how all development is a dynamic interplay between internal and external factors. Science had taught us that many of the genes expressed in our body are themselves environmentally acquired. The human microbiome – a community of bacteria, archaea, fungi and protozoa that cohabit our body cavities, surfaces and tissues – are symbionts we inherit from our mothers (but not through transmission of genes), or else pick up from the external environment. We have around 20,000 genes of our own, but our bodies house more than 3 million genes belonging to other species, which play important roles in nutrient acquisition, metabolism, immune function and behavior. Human development is a multi-species project.

Indeed, characterizing what is human appears to be becoming increasingly difficult. A decade ago we might have found it straightforward to distinguish our species from other living animals. Today we recognize that this exercise would have been far more challenging 100,000 years ago, before the demise of other hominins. The fission–fusion nature of biological reality – for instance, the recently detected interbreeding of humans with Neanderthals and Denisovans (Green et al., 2010; Krause et al., 2010) – and the associated realization that even today's human populations have variant evolutionary histories, both in space and time, render any attempt to describe the "biological essence" or "defining characteristics" of humanity vulnerable to arbitrary judgments. A few years ago researchers discovered that the African elephant is actually two separate non-interbreeding species, now known as the forest and savannah elephants (Roca, Georgiadis, Pecon-Slattery, & O'Brien, 2001). The properties that allow species to be distinguished (forest elephants have slightly thinner tusks and rounder ears than savannah elephants) are typically quite different from those seem to capture their "biological essence" (their large size, their trunk, their long lives).

Equally, conceptions of "human nature" or "human biology" as umbrella terms for a package of universal, evolved human characteristics have long but increasingly troubled histories within the human evolutionary behavioral sciences. These days, were researchers to document a constellation of reliably developing human capacities that are more or less ubiquitous, and whose development seems to be well buffered against broad environmental fluctuations, we would have difficulty in attributing such traits to "nature" as opposed to "nurture," "culture," or "environment." Experimental findings are leading to a broadened conception of inheritance and the recognition that parent–offspring similarity results not solely from the transmission of genes from one generation to the next but also from the transfer of a wide variety of other resources, and through a variety of different pathways (epigenetic variants such as DNA methylation and small RNAs, antibodies, hormones, symbionts, ecological resources, and the social transmission of knowledge and skills). These data undermine the hitherto strict separation of development and heredity that followed August Weismann's famous delineation of germ line and soma.

Phenotypes are not well described as the output of genetic programs; rather, they self-assemble through a reciprocally caused process that comprises both "upward" and "downward" causation, and in which genes are far from being the only informational resource. We don't first develop a brain and then subsequently use it to perceive, learn and reason; rather, our perception, learning and reasoning fashion a thinking brain. Organisms are not passively molded by selection to suit a pre-existing environment: they part-construct the environments to which they adapt (Odling-Smee, Laland, & Feldman, 2003). Different developmental upbringings forge different brains, and alternative environmental conditions precipitate variant gene expression. Cultural experiences leave neurobiological traces, which in turn are expressed in complex behavior that shapes the cultural experiences of others. The products of such within- and between-individual interactions are society-specific traditions, which anthropological, genetic and mathematical analyses now reveal have modified the natural selection acting on humans (and other species) in richly interwoven gene–culture coevolutionary histories (Laland, Odling-Smee, & Myles, 2010). Whatever level of analysis we choose, organisms are dynamical systems, constantly responding to, and changing, their immediate surrounds.

In line with this rejection of nature/nurture and biology/culture dichotomies, behavioral scientists have established that the social transmission of knowledge and skills, traditional behavior, and society-specific conventions, are no longer the exclusive province of humanity. To the contrary, a wide variety of animals, from fruit flies and wood crickets to gorillas and sperm whales, acquire knowledge and skills through copying the behavior of others. Paradoxically, biologists have begun to take "culture" seriously at virtually the same time that many social scientists have abandoned the notion. Fortunately, these ostensibly opposing trends have more in common than is apparent at first sight. Anthropologists' disquiet with a monolithic conception of culture has much in common with my own troubles with "human nature." That is because setting "culture" in opposition to "nature" (which is how culture is conceived by many anthropologists) inherently suffers from broadly equivalent deficiencies as the reverse. It is no easier to describe the culture of a population than to describe its biological nature.

Biology and culture have refused to be pinned down fundamentally because they are in constant flux. There are no species, genes, cultures, or natures: these are illusions of "things," the traces of constancy in a network of dynamical interrelated processes. Yet that fluidity does not render the processes any less real or amenable to scientific investigation. Far from drowning in this sea of change and complexity, biology as an academic field has never been more vibrant, and investigations of the field's interplay with culture are imbued with no less vigor than other biological domains. Technological advances in genomics, epigenetics, neuroscience, and the computational analysis of big data, lend new resolution to our research. Oftentimes pragmatic stances and simplifying assumptions are necessary for progress to be made. A powerful combination of new tools and innovative thinking is opening up exciting new avenues to study.

More than anything, integrative methodologies are required that bridge and synthesize the domains historically separated as social and biological science. If reciprocal causation and feedback are organizing themes of development then effective psychological science demands initiatives that explore the bidirectional interplay between culture and biology, amalgamating theory and methods from fields such as cultural psychology, cognitive neuroscience, and genetics in innovative ways. If gene expression varies with internal and external environment, then psychological research needs to explore how cultural practices and beliefs differentially condition brain epigenetics, and the ramifications of this conditioning for brain functioning and individual experience, feeding back to culture. We perhaps need fewer dedicated geneticists, neuroscientists, psychologists, and anthropologists, and more neuroanthropologists, cultural neuroscientists, and gene–culture coevolutionists. We require researchers who set out to unravel the feedbacks between genes, brain, behavior, and culture without prejudicing the direction of causality. The real action – and some of the most exciting science – are at the interface.

Dichotomous thinking still pervades the biological and social sciences, but it is being eroded by sound experimentation and rich interdisciplinary theory. I heartily commend the articles in this collection as examples of the innovative science at the nexus of (those processes somewhat inadequately labeled) "culture" and (those processes equally unsatisfactorily called) "biology."

Kevin N. Laland
St Andrews, UK
September, 2016

References

Green, R. E., Krause, J., Briggs, A. W., Maricic, T., Stenzel, U., Kircher, M., … & Pääbo, S. (2010). A draft sequence of the Neandertal genome. *Science, 328*(5979), 710–722. doi:10.1126/science.1188021

Krause, J., Fu, Q., Good, J. M., Viola, B., Shunkov, M. V., Derevianko, A. P., & Pääbo, S. (2010). The complete mitochondrial DNA genome of an unknown hominin from southern Siberia. *Nature, 464*(7290), 894–897. doi:10.1038/nature08976

Laland, K. N., & Brown, G. R. (in press). The social construction of human nature. In T. Lewens & B. Hannon (Eds.), *Why we disagree about human nature.* Oxford: Oxford University Press.

Laland, K. N., Odling-Smee, F. J., & Myles, S. (2010). How culture has shaped the human genome: Bringing genetics and the human sciences together. *Nature Reviews Genetics, 11,* 137–148. doi:10.1038/nrg2734

Odling-Smee, F. J., Laland, K. N., & Feldman, M. W. (2003). *Niche construction: The neglected process in evolution.* Monographs in Population Biology, 37. Princeton, NJ: Princeton University Press.

Roca, A. L., Georgiadis, N., Pecon-Slattery, J., & O'Brien, S. J. (2001). Genetic evidence for two species of elephant in Africa. *Science, 293*(5534), 1473–1477. doi:10.1126/science.1059936

Preface: Why Culture *and* Biology?

This handbook is the product of a series of discoveries, conversations, and collaborations that started back in 2012. I was tasked with formulating a novel and significant theoretical contribution as a curricular capstone in my graduate training at the Institute of Child Development at the University of Minnesota, Twin Cities. I proposed a roadmap for integrating culture and developmental psychopathology. The outcome of this effort was an article (Causadias, 2013), and an amazing discovery: three groups of scientists from different disciplines were making similar arguments to advance the study of culture and biology. But these groups were segregated by academic and geographical barriers.

The first group is leading the "St Andrews revolt," a movement rebelling against the constraints of the modern evolutionary synthesis (Huxley, 1942; Mayr & Provine, 1998), and advocating an extended evolutionary synthesis (see Laland et al., 2014, 2015). It is led by scientists working or trained at the University of St Andrews in Scotland, including Kevin Laland, Andrew Whitten, and Alex Mesoudi. By emphasizing reciprocal causation and an inclusive view of inheritance that gives greater emphasis to culture, they have shown how humans and animal are not merely the product of their environments, but make their environments a product of themselves by building new niches.

At the other side of the Atlantic, pioneer scholars such as Eva Telzer, Joan Chiao, Heejung Kim, and Joni Sasaki championed the new field of cultural neuroscience. Emboldened by advances in theory and methods in neurosciences, they pursued interdisciplinary investigations on the relationship between cultural, neural, and psychological processes. This new research illustrates, among other things, the pivotal role of culture in shaping brain functioning, going beyond the exploration of brain differences across ethnic groups to advance our understanding of behavior, cognition, and development.

The third group is made up of a network of innovative psychologists working at Arizona State University, who are taking new perspectives on culture by examining how cultural processes develop over time (e.g., Nancy Gonzales, Adriana Umaña-Taylor), the link between religion and evolution (e.g., Adam Cohen), and how cultural experiences affect neuroendocrine functioning (e.g., Leah Doane). This spirit of innovation and discovery has made Arizona State a unique niche for research on culture and biology, and it is the main reason I did not hesitate when I had the opportunity to join its faculty in 2015.

These three groups share a passion for new paradigms that can incorporate recent advances in theory and methods, emphasize interdisciplinarity to tackle the complexity of cultural and biological systems, and reconsider culture in novel and improved ways. But the fact that academic and geographic barriers facilitated a relative disconnection among them led to the realization that we needed to integrate them into one metaparadigm: culture and biology interplay.

The next step in this journey was starting a conversation. I contacted two of the leading scholars working in these areas: Eva Telzer and Nancy Gonzales. Together, we organized a symposium on culture and biology interplay at the 2014 biennial meeting of the Society of Research on Adolescence. We were encouraged by the enthusiastic response we got from our colleagues. This discussion soon provided us with the insight that we had more questions than answers, and that we needed to bring scholars from these three groups into the conversation. In response to these challenges, we decided to launch the Culture and Biology Initiative, a collective effort aimed at generating new models, methods, and research questions. So far, this initiative has produced a special section on culture and biology in the journal *Cultural Diversity and Ethnic Minority Psychology* (see Causadias, Telzer, & Lee, 2017), roundtables in research conferences, new courses and teaching seminars, and the formulation of novel collaborative research projects. This handbook is the pinnacle of this initiative.

The aim of this handbook is ambitious. The tensions between cultural and biological explanations are at the heart of psychology and, in a way, of all behavioral sciences. Psychology has been a hybrid discipline since its inception, oscillating throughout its history between the social and the biological dimensions (Schwartz, Lilienfeld, Meca, & Sauvigné, 2016). This bidimensional nature can be best understood by approaching psychology as a two-headed eagle: one head looks at culture, the social sciences, arts and humanities, qualitative methods, and nurture, while the other looks at biology, the hard sciences, quantitative methods, and nature. Reconciling these two traditions and balancing these two poles is a major challenge in our quest of understanding human behavior, cognition, and development. It is also the major goal of this handbook.

This handbook is not the first attempt at pursuing the theoretical, methodological, and empirical integration of culture and biology, but is part of an illustrious tradition and has built upon it (see Kitayama & Uskul, 2011; Li, 2003; Mesoudi, Whiten, & Laland, 2006; Overton, 2010; Super & Harkness, 1986). Culture and biology are indivisible. That is why this handbook centers on culture *and* biology, not culture *or* biology. Their inseparable nature has been documented repeatedly (see Laland's foreword to this volume). But in academia they are often divided. For the most part, the study of culture and biology has evolved into different disciplines, subdisciplines, and even schools within subdisciplines. So rather than reifying this polarity, the goal of this handbook is to showcase cutting-edge research that aspires to integrate culture and biology in a meaningful and balanced way. Hence, this handbook is a true hybrid. It approaches culture and biology from multiple perspectives, levels of analysis, theoretical traditions, and epistemologies. It showcases the work of scholars from diverse disciplines, including biology, anthropology, neurosciences, as well as clinical, cultural, developmental, and social psychology.

We organized this handbook into five parts: an introductory part on general issues, and four parts centered on different domains of culture and biology interplay: animal culture, cultural genomics, cultural neurobiology, and cultural neuroscience. Each part is spearheaded by an introductory chapter that provides a general overview of the theory, research, and methods of each domain.

First, Part I, on the main issues in culture and biology, is intended as a discussion of general themes, including an introduction to the field (chapter 1, Causadias, Telzer, & Gonzales), conceptual clarifications and recommendations (chapter 2, Syed & Kathawalla), and a discussion of religion from cultural and biological perspectives (chapter 3, Northover & Cohen).

Part II, on animal culture, is devoted to a domain of research that has generated significant debate and attention in recent years (Laland, 2008; Laland & Janik, 2006), but has had little impact in psychology: how animals create, employ, and transmit knowledge from one generation to the next. Because psychology has benefited greatly from research with animals, we hope future psychological research on culture will also be informed by investigations on animal culture. The part includes an introduction (chapter 4, Snowdon), an examination of research on primate and cetacean culture (chapter 5, Botting, van de Waal, & Rendell), and a discussion of primate communication, parenting, and cognition (chapter 6, Snowdon).

Part III, on cultural genomics, details the multiple ways in which cultural experiences are influenced by, affect, and covary with the genome and the environment to shape behavior and cognition at the social, developmental, and evolutionary levels. The interplay of culture and genes has recently been studied as part of cultural neurosciences (see Chiao, Cheon, Pornpattananangkul, Mrazek, & Blizinsky, 2013), given the intimate link between neural and genomic systems. However, we decided to carve a unique niche for this domain, given (1) the accelerated growth in recent years of genomic, cultural, and evolutionary research, and (2) the rising complexity of theory, methods, and evidence in culture and genomics. This part is composed of an introduction (chapter 7, Causadias & Korous), an examination of dual-inheritance theory, cultural transmission, and niche construction (chapter 8, O'Brien & Bentley), and a discussion of the relation between religion, culture, and genetics (chapter 9, Lo & Sasaki).

Part IV, on cultural neurobiology, focuses on the domain of culture and biology that examines transactions among cultural processes and central and peripheral stress-sensitive neurobiological systems. This is one of the most exciting and fast-growing domains of inquiry, and its explosive progression is well represented in this handbook by several chapters targeting different ways in which cultural experiences – adverse or normative – get under the skin. This part includes an introduction (chapter 10, Doane, Sladek, & Adam), and examinations of the relations between poverty, stress, and allostatic load (chapter 11, Doan & Evans), the biological consequences of unfair treatment (chapter 12, Ong, Deshpande, & Williams), the effects of cultural experiences, social ties, and stress on the HPA axis (chapter 13, Wang & Campos), cultural influences on parasympathetic activity (chapter 14, Hill & Hoggard), and the neurobiology of stress and drug use vulnerability (chapter 15, Obasi, Wilborn, Cavanagh, Yan, & Ewane).

Finally, Part V focuses on cultural neuroscience, perhaps the most robust and consolidated domain of research on culture and biology interplay. This part includes an introduction (chapter 16, Lin & Telzer), and discussions on the causes and consequences of cultural differences in social cognition (chapter 17, Meyer), culture and self–other overlap (chapter 18, Varnum & Hampton), and culture, brain, and development (chapter 19, Qu & Telzer).

I want to acknowledge all the people that made this handbook possible. First and foremost, I want to thank my co-editors, Eva Telzer and Nancy Gonzales. This volume would have not been possible without them for several reasons. Not only have they enriched the content of this handbook with their own contributions, but they were critical in identifying, convincing, and bringing on board authors that ultimately wrote landmark chapters. I am also incredibly grateful to Eva and Nancy for their nuanced and thoughtful support in editing the chapters, providing feedback to authors, and navigating the uniquely demanding tasks of providing coherence across chapters while making them accessible to psychologists and other behavioral scientists.

I also want to thank Dante Cicchetti, Moin Syed, and Alan Sroufe, my graduate school advisers, mentors, and friends at the University of Minnesota, Twin Cities. I am grateful to Dante for putting me in contact with Wiley, providing guidance in writing the handbook proposal, and supporting me in this project, something most mentors would not encourage a junior scholar right out of graduate school to pursue, and for good reasons! I want to acknowledge Dante and Alan's vision in building developmental psychopathology as a field of inquiry that encourages meaningful examination of multiple levels of analysis in the study of development. Their attention to complexity and dynamic systems is an inspiration for the field of culture and biology interplay. I also want to thank Moin for introducing me to the world of multicultural psychology and for agreeing to write a chapter that lays out critical conceptual and methodological issues that will require attention in future culture and biology research.

I also want to thank everyone at Wiley that believed in this project, and worked with us through this process, including Danielle Descoteaux, Amy Minshul, Emily Corkhill, Darren Reed, and Silvy Achankunju. Their generous support, feedback, and guidance have cemented the quality of this volume.

I want to express my deepest gratitude to all the authors for their unique and thoughtful contributions that made this handbook possible. I am especially grateful to Kevin Laland for writing the foreword and putting me in contact with Michael O'Brien, who wrote a superb chapter with Alexander Bentley. I am thankful to Charles Snowdon for writing two authoritative chapters that make up the bulk of the animal culture section. I want to acknowledge the leading role of Leah Doane, who agreed to write a chapter with Michael Sladek and Emma Adam on a new field, and took it upon herself to contact the other authors in the cultural neurobiology section and read their chapters in advance. Lastly, I want to thank two graduate students working in my lab, Kevin Korous and Annabelle Atkin, for their meticulous assistance in editing some of the chapters.

José M. Causadias, PhD
Phoenix, AZ
November, 2016

References

Causadias, J. M. (2013). A roadmap for the integration of culture into developmental psychopathology. *Development and Psychopathology, 25*(4pt2), 1375–1398. doi:10.1017/S0954579413000679

Causadias, J. M., Telzer, E. H., &, Lee, R. M. (2017). Culture and biology interplay: An introduction. *Cultural Diversity and Ethnic Minority Psychology, 23*(1), 1–4. doi:10.1037/cdp0000121

Chiao, J. Y., Cheon, B. K., Pornpattananangkul, N., Mrazek, A. J., & Blizinsky, K. D. (2013). Cultural neuroscience: Progress and promise. *Psychological Inquiry, 24*(1), 1–19. doi:10.1080/1047840X.2013.752715

Huxley, J. (1942). *Evolution: The modern synthesis.* London: Allen & Unwin.

Kitayama, S., & Uskul, A. K. (2011). Culture, mind, and the brain: Current evidence and future directions. *Annual Review of Psychology, 62*, 419–449. doi:10.1146/annurev-psych-120709-145357

Laland, K. N. (2008). Animal cultures. *Current Biology, 18*, 366–370. doi:10.1016/j.cub.2008.02.049

Laland, K. N., & Janik, V. (2006). The animal cultures debate. *Trends in Ecology and Evolution, 21*, 542–547. doi:10.1016/j.tree.2006.06.005

Laland, K., Uller, T., Feldman, M., Sterelny, K., Müller, G. B., Moczek, A., … & Futuyma, D. J. (2014). Does evolutionary theory need a rethink? *Nature, 514*(7521), 161–164. doi:10.1038/514161a

Laland, K. N., Uller, T., Feldman, M. W., Sterelny, K., Müller, G. B., Moczek, A., … & Odling-Smee, J. (2015). The extended evolutionary synthesis: Its structure, assumptions and predictions. *Proceedings of the Royal Society B, 282*, 20151019. doi:10.1098/rspb.2015.1019

Li, S. C. (2003). Biocultural orchestration of developmental plasticity across levels: The interplay of biology and culture in shaping the mind and behavior across the life span. *Psychological Bulletin, 129*(2), 171–194. doi:10.1037/0033-2909.129.2.171

Mayr, E., & Provine, W. B. (1998). *The evolutionary synthesis: Perspectives on the unification of biology.* Cambridge, MA: Harvard University Press.

Mesoudi, A., Whiten, A., & Laland, K. N. (2006). Towards a unified science of cultural evolution. *Behavioral and Brain Sciences, 29*(4), 329–347. doi:10.1017/S0140525X06009083

Overton, W. F. (2010). Life-span development: Concepts and issues. In R. M. Lerner (Editor-in-chief) and W. F. Overton (Vol. Ed.), *Handbook of life-span development. Volume 1: Cognition, biology, and methods across the lifespan* (pp. 1–29). Hoboken, NJ: Wiley.

Schwartz, S. J., Lilienfeld, S. O., Meca, A., & Sauvigné, K. C. (2016). The role of neuroscience within psychology: A call for inclusiveness over exclusiveness. *American Psychologist, 71*(1), 52–70. doi:10.1037/a0039678

Super, C. M., & Harkness, S. (1986). The developmental niche: A conceptualization at the interface of child and culture. *International Journal of Behavioral Development, 9*(4), 545–569. doi: 10.1177/016502548600900409

[illegible]

[illegible] and V. F. [illegible] *Handbook of* [illegible]

Sch[illegible] S. J. [illegible] of measuring [illegible] [illegible]

[illegible]

Part I

General Issues in Culture and Biology Interplay

1

Introduction to Culture and Biology Interplay

José M. Causadias, Eva H. Telzer, and Nancy A. Gonzales

The relationship between culture and biology, and the issues that arise with it, have been at the forefront of psychology since its origin. Pioneers in the field, with different degrees of success, sought to explain human behavior, cognition, and development using both biological and cultural arguments. For instance, while Darwin (1872) emphasized the evolutionary significance of emotions by connecting animal and human behavior, Freud (1930) examined the impact of culture in the etiology of neurosis, as well as the role of hard-wired drives in conditioning human behavior. But perhaps the strongest evidence of how this relationship has shaped the history of psychology lies in the emergence and persistence of the nature-versus-nurture debate, introduced by Galton (1869, 1874), which in a way exemplifies the tension between innate-biological influences and social-cultural processes (Rutter, 2006). Psychology has often oscillated between these two poles, emphasizing the role of biological influences in some periods and environmental and cultural forces in others (see Schwartz, Lilienfeld, Meca, & Sauvigné, 2016).

Several scholars have argued that we are witnessing a period in psychology of growing emphasis on the role of biological processes (see Eisenberg, 2014; Kitayama & Uskul, 2011). Technical and methodological innovations in biological research in the last decades, as well as the improved understanding of the brain and the genome they have afforded, have opened new opportunities to elucidate their role in shaping psychological processes (Miller, 2010). Importantly, these advances improve our ability not only to explain behavior, but also to predict it. For example, a recent study suggests that using a joint clinical and genomic risk assessment can substantively advance our ability to predict suicidality (Niculescu et al.,

The Handbook of Culture and Biology, First Edition. Edited by José M. Causadias, Eva H. Telzer and Nancy A. Gonzales.

2015). Furthermore, a new generation of scientists have begun to integrate biologically informed methods into their psychological research on culture, offering new insights on how experiences of racial discrimination can affect diurnal cortisol rhythm among African Americans (Fuller-Rowell, Doan, & Eccles, 2012) and Mexican Americans (Zeiders, Doane, & Roosa, 2012) and examining how dopamine polymorphisms are related to cultural differences in independent versus interdependent social orientation (Kitayama et al., 2014) and how cultural processes are associated with distinct patterns of brain functioning (Chiao & Ambady, 2007; Telzer, Masten, Berkman, Lieberman, & Fuligni, 2010).

Obstacles to the Integration of Culture and Biology

Despite these recent advances, there are several obstacles to achieving a more meaningful integration of cultural and biological methods that can substantially improve our understanding of human nature (Causadias, Telzer, & Lee, 2017). First, scholars who conduct research on social and cultural processes are well aware of the challenges associated with conveying the complexity of subjective experiences, so they might be skeptical about simplistic approaches that can potentially limit rich behavioral and symbolic human expressions to an image reflecting brain activity (see Syed & Kathawalla, chapter 2 in this volume). There is a growing concern with the idea that brain- or gene-based processes will ultimately explain everything and eventually render psychology useless (Lilienfeld, 2007; Satel & Lilienfeld, 2013; Schwartz et al., 2016). These new arguments echo the pushback experienced by previous attempts to infuse biology into social sciences like sociobiology, that were condemned for the use of inappropriate reductionism (see Wilson, 2000).

Second, some scholars are predisposed against the use of these biological methods in cultural research, because biologically infused pseudoscience has in the past been employed to justify social and racial hierarchies (Hartigan, 2015), to rationalize group differences regarding intelligence (Sternberg, Grigorenko, & Kidd, 2005), and even to vindicate ethnic cleansing and genocide in the name of social Darwinism and the "survival of the fittest" (see Allen et al., 1975). Likewise, poorly designed and conducted studies of genes and culture that rely on incomplete data, deficient statistics, or logical fallacies are especially problematic and have been criticized from anthropological and biological perspectives (see Creanza & Feldman, 2016; Feldman, 2014; Guedes et al., 2013; Rosenberg & Kang, 2015).

Examples include studies that conclude that lower genetic diversity in the Americas and greater genetic diversity in Africa both lead to poverty, while the intermediate level of genetic diversity in Europe is favorable to economic prosperity (Ashraf & Galor, 2013), and studies that argue for a genetic basis to racial differences in wealth, intelligence, and social institutions (Wade, 2014). However, racial ideologies preceded scientific attempts to justify them, or, as Coates (2015) argued, "race is the child of racism, not the father. And the process of naming 'the people' has never been a matter of genealogy and physiognomy so much as one of hierarchy" (p. 7). Thus, severe scrutiny is necessary to avoid invalid conclusions that run the risk of providing pseudoscientific ammunition for those attempting to justify ethnic cleansing, the systematic mistreatment of immigrants and minorities, or the stopping of humanitarian aid (Creanza & Feldman, 2016).

Third, the scientific exploitation of disenfranchised groups by unscrupulous biomedical researchers also has negative repercussions for the field. Past examples include the experiments conducted with African-American men in Alabama and with prisoners in Guatemala in which individuals were purposely infected with syphilis, as well as the diabetes project with the Havasupai Tribe in which participants' DNA was used for other studies without their consent. These cases have contributed to resistance among some communities to participating in biologically informed studies, and have diminished trust in scientists (see Freimuth et al., 2001).

Fourth, there are not many conceptual models available to researchers in psychology that can account for the multiple ways in which these two processes relate and shape normal and abnormal development, with some noteworthy exceptions (see Fischer & Boer, 2016; Li, 2003; Mesoudi, Whiten, & Laland, 2006). Arguably, there are several theories on culture and biology interplay formulated by evolutionary biologists and population geneticists, including sociobiology (Wilson, 1975), gene–culture coevolutionary theory (Cavalli-Sforza & Feldman, 1981) and dual-inheritance theory (Boyd & Richerson, 1985). However, these models have had limited impact on current research on culture and biology in psychology, partly because of interdisciplinary barriers. With some possible exceptions, like molecular anthropology (Goodman, Tashian, & Tashian, 1976), behavioral research in the fields of culture and biology has evolved into different traditions and veered towards hyper-specialization, resulting in separate conceptual and methodological niches that favor intellectual insularity. This is reflected in graduate and postgraduate training. Scientists are socialized through research training into very distinct subgroups, often concentrating on a limited set of assumptions, values, algorithms, and priorities that condition research decisions (Cicchetti & Richters, 1997). Thus, training programs that focus on culture frequently emphasize models and methods closer to the humanities and social sciences than to neurosciences, while psychological programs specialized in genetics traditionally gravitate more towards life and biological sciences, and less towards cultural issues (Causadias et al., 2016).

In sum, justified skepticism about reductionist approaches, predisposition against biological explanations of social issues, distrust among ethnic minority communities of biomedical research, the disconnection between research fields and diverging training traditions all contribute to a paucity of research that meaningfully integrates cultural and biological levels of analysis to help us advance our understanding of behavior, cognition, and development. The most detrimental consequence of the current lack of integration of culture and biology is a biased, incomplete, and, most importantly, bipolar perspective that overemphasizes either the biological or cultural dimensions, thus perpetuating the nature versus nurture dichotomy and severely limiting our understanding of human nature.

The Field of Culture and Biology Interplay

In order to overcome these obstacles and the resulting schism between these two dimensions, we introduce the field of culture and biology interplay. In this chapter, we define its basic principles, describe the importance of conducting research using this paradigm, provide an overview of its history, and examine different types, levels, and domains of research in culture and biology interplay. We close by presenting some conclusions and future directions.

Culture and biology interplay is the field of study that centers on how these two processes have evolved together, how culture, biology, and environment influence each other, and how they shape behavior, cognition, and development among humans and animals across multiple levels, types, timeframes, and domains of analysis (Causadias et al., 2016). The field of culture and biology interplay was introduced as a promising avenue to integrate culture into developmental psychopathology, another hybrid field that emphasizes complex and dynamic relationships among various areas of functioning (Causadias, 2013). Culture and biology interplay functions as a meta-paradigm, gathering under the same roof separate domains of research that have traditionally functioned separately (e.g., animal culture, cultural neuroscience), and bringing together other lines of research that have not been recognized as such (e.g., cultural genomics, cultural neurobiology). Rather than reducing cultural processes to biological indicators, research on culture and biology interplay can advance our understanding by illuminating how we have evolved to develop complex cultural systems, such as religions (see Northover & Cohen, chapter 3 in this volume).

We define culture as a shared system of behaviors (and cognitions) that are transmitted from one generation to the next. This system serves a function within a group that has a shared history (geographical, social), which informs traditions, beliefs, conduct, and institutions (Cohen, 2009). Culture has a wide-ranging impact in a myriad of domains of psychological functioning, and operates at an individual and social level (Kitayama & Uskul, 2011). Evidence suggests that humans and animals possess behavioral culture, while symbolic culture is believed to be exclusive to humans (Whiten, Hinde, Laland, and Stringer, 2011). We also approach biology from a systems perspective, as living creatures are themselves organized and composed of different structures, ranging from individual cells to superorganisms (Hölldobler & Wilson, 2009). In the case of humans and animals, we function as the result of an interconnected network of biological systems, such as the nervous, endocrine, and immune systems. Importantly, culture and biology are the two major systems of inheritance. While cultural inheritance is composed of the behavioral and symbolic systems, biological inheritance is constituted by the genetic and epigenetic systems (see Jablonka & Lamb, 2014). The term "interplay" is very suitable for conceptualizing the relationship between culture and biology for several reasons. According to the arguments formulated by Rutter (2006, 2007, 2013), "interplay" (or "interdependence") is less restrictive than terms like "interaction" because it conveys a variety of ways in which two processes affect each other, and is not limited to statistical relations.

Principles for the Study of Culture and Biology

Culture and biology interplay is informed by an interdisciplinary, multiple-levels-of-analysis perspective (Cicchetti & Dawson, 2002) that incorporates theory and research from the fields of psychology, anthropology, evolutionary biology, population genetics, neuroscience, and neurobiology of stress. Ultimately, behavior and cognition are approached as the result of the interdependence, codetermination, and simultaneous influence of multiple processes (Sroufe, 2007). Moreover, cultural and biological processes are recognized as equally important and mutually influential. Thus, no component, subsystem, or level of analysis has causal privileges over the other (Cicchetti & Cannon, 1999).

One of the most detailed examinations of principles for the study of culture and biology was formulated by Overton (2007, 2010). One of the quintessential examples of fundamental split dichotomies, typical of Cartesian dualistic epistemologies and false dichotomies, is culture versus biology (Overton, 2010). However, from a relational epistemology this separation between culture and biology is only nominal, as both dimensions are in constant interpenetration, coaction, and reciprocal bidirectionality or multidirectionality (Overton, 2010). The relational epistemological perspective has taken hold of fields like physics (Smolin, 1997), anthropology (Ingold, 2000), and biology (Robert, 2004). Relationism is a metatheory that incorporates contextualism and organicism to approach scientific problems from four major principles (Overton, 2010).

First, the *holism* principle indicates that the meaning and significance of any given phenomenon depends on the relational context in which it is embedded (Overton, 2010). In the cases of culture and biology, holism invites us to acknowledge that even if we focus on just one component of each system – a single gene, a single cultural trait – we also need to recognize that these units must be contextualized because they operate as part of systems that function as wholes (e.g., genome, brain, cultural self, organism, community, population).

Second, the *identity of opposites* principle "establishes the *identity among parts* of a whole by casting them not as exclusive contradictions as in the split epistemology but as differentiated polarities (i.e., coequals) of a unified (i.e., indissociable), inclusive matrix – as a relation" (Overton, 2010, p. 14, emphasis in original). According to this principle, culture is biology and biology is culture: they are coequal and inseparable. Both are part of the matrix of evolution, adaptation, and transformation. Culture and biology are constantly engaged in a co-constructing feedback loop, in a reciprocal codetermination (Overton & Reese, 1973), that we are only beginning to understand. "[T]he fact that a behavior implicates activity of the biological system does not imply that it does not implicate activity of the cultural system, and the fact that the behavior implicates activity of the cultural system does not imply that it does not implicate activity of the biological system. In other words, the identity of opposites establishes the metatheoretical rationale for the theoretical position that biology and culture (like culture and person, biology and person, etc.) operate in a truly *interpenetrating* manner" (Overton, 2010, p. 15, emphasis in original).

Third, the *opposites of identity* principle aims at establishing a bedrock for inquiry by moving to a second moment of analysis – after the identity of opposites – in which the law of contradiction is restated and categories again exclude each other (Overton, 2010). Hence, next we should consider that culture is not biology, as each system is given a unique identity that differentiates it. This principle provides a platform in which these new opposites – culture and biology – become standpoints, points of view, lines of sight (Latour, 1993), or levels of analysis (Overton, 2010). "[A]lthough explicitly recognizing that any behavior is 100% biology and 100% culture, alternative points-of-view permit the scientist to analyze the behavior from a *biological* or from a *cultural standpoint.* Biology and culture no longer constitute competing alternative explanations; rather, they are two points-of-view on an object of inquiry that has been created by and will be fully understood only through multiple viewpoints" (Overton, 2010, pp. 15–16).

Finally, the *synthesis of wholes* principle functions as a third moment of analysis in the dialectical undertaking of relational epistemology, as it proposes a resolution to the bipolar tension of the opposites of identity by moving away from this conflict to formulate a new system that integrates the two poles (Overton, 2010). For instance, the person can function as a supra-ordinate system that coordinates, synthesizes, and resolves the tension between culture and biology by regulating and organizing them within the self (Magnusson & Stattin, 1998). In this synthesis, a standpoint provides a stable base for future research (Overton, 2010). From the person standpoint we can examine how the relation between culture and biology shapes individual differences in development. From the biology standpoint, we can investigate the relation between culture and the person by focusing on correlates of brain functioning. From the cultural standpoint, we can inquire into the relation between person and biology by centering on cultural variation in a given domain. In sum, Overton's (2010) relational epistemology provides a invaluable set of guiding principles for the study of culture and biology.

History of Culture and Biology Interplay

The interplay of culture and biology is rooted in evolution, as natural selection has favored the transmission of a predisposition to cooperate and participate in cultural communities (Tomasello, 1999). There is a long tradition of applying evolutionary mechanisms to understand the nature and function of cultural change (see Whiten, Hinde, Stringer, & Laland, 2012), beginning with Darwin's (1859, 1871) observation of the similarities between language and biological evolution. According to Darwin (1871), "[w]e find in distinct languages striking homologies due to community of descent, and analogies due to a similar process of formation. The manner in which certain letters or sounds change when others change is very like correlated growth. We have in both cases the reduplication of parts, the effects of long-continued use, and so forth. The frequent presence of rudiments, both in languages and in species, is still more remarkable" (pp. 59–60). These notions were further elaborated in the work of Pitt-Rivers (1906), Steward (1955), White (1959), Huxley (1955), Sahlins and Service (1960), and Campbell (1965). But research on the interplay of culture and biology has truly gained momentum in the last decades with the irruption of three landmark conceptual models: Wilson's (1975) sociobiology, Cavalli-Sforza and Feldman's (1981) gene–culture coevolutionary theory, and Boyd and Richerson's (1985) dual-inheritance theory.

E. O. Wilson (1975) formulated sociobiology in an attempt to explain the role of evolution in the emergence of complex social behaviors in animals and humans, such as culture, altruism, eusociality, violence, and caregiving. For instance, using his work with social insects, Wilson (1975, 2000) discussed the evolutionary implications of slavery in ants (i.e., dulosis), arguing that it benefits ant colonies, thus maximizing natural selection. Sociobiology was widely criticized (Wilson, 2000), but the most scathing diatribe came from those who argued that it justified the oppression of disadvantaged groups throughout history by explaining social processes purely on the basis of evolutionary mechanisms (see Allen et al., 1975).

Another important antecedent of research in culture and biology interplay is gene–culture coevolutionary theory. Cavalli-Sforza and Feldman (1981) examined how evolutionary mechanisms (e.g., natural selection, mutation, migration, and genetic drift) can also explain the process of cultural transmission and evolution. Two of the most compelling innovations of this model are the delineation of the role of social learning as the main process of cultural transmission, and the introduction of highly detailed mathematical models of vertical (e.g., parent–child, teacher–student) and horizontal (e.g., peer–peer) cultural transmission. Cultural traits play a crucial role in evolution by increasing adaptive fitness in the population, and a parallel role to genetic inheritance (for further discussion, see O'Brien & Bentley, chapter 8 in this volume).

The third major theoretical antecedent of culture and biology interplay is dual-inheritance theory. Boyd and Richerson (1985) proposed that the evolution of genes and culture as inheritance systems is shaped by natural selection and that these two systems are engaged in a dynamic competition to influence the phenotype of individuals. However, these two systems differ in the way they are transmitted. While culture is continuously transmitted by either genetically related or unrelated individuals, genes are passed only once by parents. Furthermore, while parents might not contribute equally in the transmission of culture to their offspring, their genetic contribution is equal (Richerson & Boyd, 1978). One of the most noteworthy features of this model is the consideration of cultural processes as a second inheritance system that operates in dynamic interplay with genes, the first inheritance system. More recently, Mesoudi and colleagues (2006) proposed a unified theory of evolution that attempted to synthesize biological, social, and behavioral sciences, but this formulation was met with fierce criticism (see Ingold, 2007), and was followed by further disagreements (see Acerbi & Mesoudi, 2015; Morin, 2016).

In psychology, there is also a tradition of research in this field, as scholars have employed biological metaphors to account for the role of culture in child development (e.g., developmental niche, Super & Harkness, 1986). In addition, Li (2003) formulated a biocultural model to approach cognitive and behavioral development across the lifespan. Li (2003) proposed a triarchic perspective that approached culture as ongoing social processes (e.g., interpersonal interactions, social situations) that operate in the present time, as relevant for the development (e.g., cognitive) of individuals throughout their lives, and as socially inherited resources (e.g., tools, knowledge, values) that have accumulated throughout human evolution. We delineate different levels of culture and biology interplay by employing these three perspectives of biocultural analysis formulated by Li (2003).

Levels of Culture and Biology Interplay

The interplay of cultural and biological processes takes place at the social, developmental, and evolutionary levels (for other discussions of levels of analysis in culture and biology, see Causadias & Korous, and Doane, Sladek, & Adam, chapters 7 and 10 in this volume). First, the social level of interplay encompasses scenarios in which cultural and biological processes are influencing each other in social situations in the present time. For instance, enculturation into individualistic social orientations is associated with differential activation of the prefrontal cortex, in contrast to individuals exposed to collectivistic cultural values (Chiao et al., 2009). In contrast, some cultural practices can have distinctly positive biological effects, as research suggests that prenatal behaviors among first-generation Mexican-American mothers are the healthiest in comparison to other ethnic groups (Fuller & García Coll, 2010).

Second, the developmental level includes scenarios in which early experiences can set up probabilistic trajectories that shape future outcomes in the lifespan of an organism (i.e., ontogenetic history). For instance, repeated negative social experiences can have important biological effects: research conducted by Chae and colleagues (2014, 2016) has shown that African Americans subjected to chronic discrimination internalize bias, and are more likely to later experience telomere erosion, mental illness, and shortened lifespans. Also, cultural experiences can account for differences in developmental trajectories of autonomic nervous system functioning between European Americans and African Americans (Fuller-Rowell et al., 2013).

Third, the evolutionary level exemplifies scenarios in which culture and biology have influenced each other over centuries and shaped the adaptation of populations of organisms (i.e., phylogenetic history). The role of agriculture in evolution leads to one of the prototypical examples of how cultural changes increase our evolutionary fitness and shape the genome, because it led the development of adult lactose tolerance. In most mammals, the activity of the enzyme lactase, responsible for the digestion of lactose in milk, is dramatically reduced after weaning. However, among human populations with traditions of dairy farming there is a high percentage of individuals who continue to produce lactase (they are lactose-tolerant), in contrast with populations without this cultural practice (see Aoki, 1986; Feldman & Cavalli-Sforza, 1989). The evolutionary level illustrates one of the unique features of culture–biology interplay, in that human beings are capable of using their own cultural capital (e.g., science, technology, medicine) to offset selective environmental pressures (e.g., disease survival, life expectancy), thereby shaping their own biological evolution (Li, 2003). This idea is so revolutionary that it generated a debate between evolutionary scientists that place natural selection as the pre-eminent mechanism of population change, and those who argue in favor of reciprocal causation and the role of alternative mechanisms, such as niche construction (see Laland et al., 2014). Niche construction is the process by which some species modify their own environment and act as co-directors of their own evolution (Laland, Odling-Smee, & Myles, 2010), as is the case with human agriculture (O'Brien & Laland, 2012). Importantly, niche construction builds upon and enhances our traditional views of inheritance, incorporating a third component in addition to genes and culture: the constructed niche or ecosystem (for a more detailed discussion of niche construction, see O'Brien & Bentley, chapter 8 in this volume).

Types of Culture and Biology Interplay

In addition to the social, developmental, and evolutionary levels, there are different types of culture and biology interplay. Using Rutter's (2006, 2007, 2013) distinction, we can examine different ways in which these two processes relate. First, culture can affect biological processes (*C→B*) at the developmental level, through the effects of sociocultural experiences like racial discrimination on neurobiological functioning (Zeiders et al., 2012), and at the evolutionary level, as in the case of the emergence of the lactose-tolerance genotype among some populations as a result of the invention of dairy farming (Aoki, 1986; Feldman & Cavalli-Sforza, 1989). Second, biological processes can shape culture (*B→C*), as evidence suggests that individuals with certain dopamine genotypes may be more likely to engage in reward-seeking behavior and migrate (Chen, Burton, Greenberger, & Dmitrieva, 1999). Third, there are culture and biology interactions (*CxB*) at the developmental level: some studies have found that certain genetic variations moderate the link between racial discrimination and the development of conduct problems (Brody et al., 2011) and criminal arrests (Schwartz & Beaver, 2011). Fourth, culture and biology correlations (*rCB*) are similar to *B→C*, and refer to biological influences on variations of exposure to particular cultural environments (Richerson, Boyd, & Henrich, 2010). *rCB* can be approached at the evolutionary level to represent gene–culture covariation. For instance, recent research on the association between phonemes (i.e., the smallest units of speech capable of being perceived), genes, and geography has shown that both genetic distance and phonemic distance between populations were significantly correlated with geographic distance, suggesting historical migration and recent population contact (Creanza et al., 2015). In contrast, at the social and developmental level, research on *rCB*s has shown how genetic and neighborhood influences contribute to youth aggressive or non-aggressive antisocial behavior (Burt, Klump, Gorman-Smith, & Neiderhiser, 2016). Fifth, in culture–biology–environment interactions (*CxBxE*) genetic, cultural, and ecological inheritance work together to produce certain outcomes: studies have shown how genetics, ethnic heterogeneity, and neighborhoods shape aggression among adolescents (Hart & Marmorstein, 2009), and how neighborhood disadvantage and genetics shape antisocial behavior (Burt et al., 2016). For an examination of gene–culture–niche interplay research (*GxCxN*), see Causadias and Korous, chapter 7 in this volume. Finally, there are developmental approaches to culture and biology interplay, including research on developmental cultural neuroscience (see Qu & Telzer, chapter 19 in this volume) and on the developmental effects of gene–environment on culture (*dcGE*; see Causadias & Korous, chapter 17 in this volume).

However, it is critical to acknowledge that these types of culture–biology interplay illustrate associations in a simplistic way in order to convey their variety and isolate mechanisms. In reality, many of these interrelations occur simultaneously. It is also important to approach these types under Overton's (2010) relational epistemology principles. Furthermore, cause-and-effect relationships in biology are not easy to determine for multiple reasons, including the extreme complexity of highly integrated systems, the randomness of some events, the uniqueness of biological entities, and the emergence of new qualities (Mayr, 1961). Therefore, these types of interplay are suggestive of the influence of one system on another at a given moment, rather than strict models of cause and effect.

Domains of Culture and Biology Interplay Research

The study of culture and biology interplay can be organized into different domains that focus on the relationship between cultural processes and one particular biological level of analysis, including animal culture, cultural genomics, cultural neurobiology and cultural neuroscience (see Figure 1.1). These domains provide the structure for this handbook.

Animal Culture

Research on animal culture has grown exponentially in the last decades, advancing our understanding of variation in social learning and traditions, as well as the crucial role culture plays in animal communities (Whiten et al., 2011). Evidence of animal culture can be seen in the documented ability of different populations of chimpanzees (*Pan troglodytes*) in Africa to use small stones as hammers and large stones as anvils to extract nuts from their shells, as well as in the training involved in teaching their offspring how to use these tools so the skill can be passed on to the next generation (for an introduction, see Snowdon, chapter 4 in this volume). Comparative

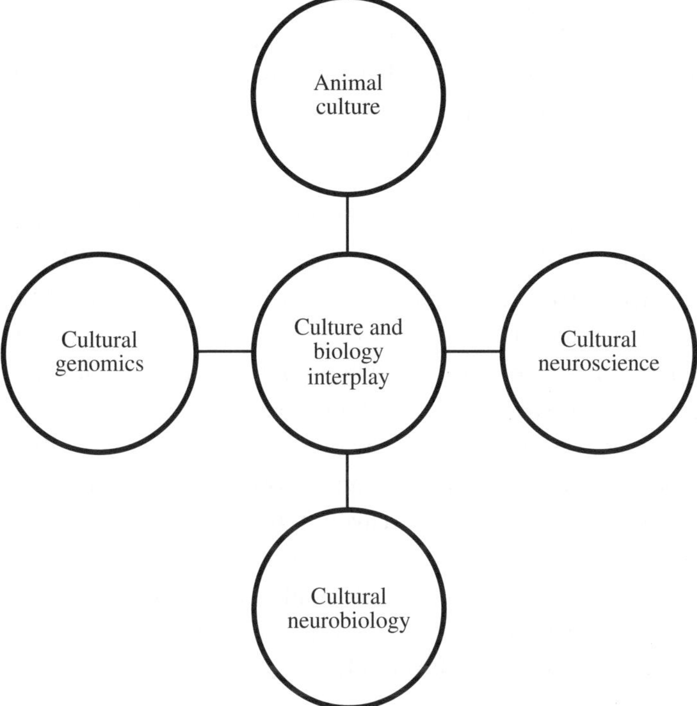

Figure 1.1 Domains of research in culture and biology interplay

research on animal culture can also improve our understanding of evolution and adaptation, for instance by comparing and contrasting primate and cetacean culture (see Botting, van de Waal, & Rendell, chapter 5 in this volume). Primate communication and the biological basis of caregiving constitute another key line of animal culture research, which explores the multiple ways in which cultural processes and natural selection influence each other (see Snowdon, chapter 6 in this volume).

The notion that animals create and re-create culture is truly revolutionary in two ways. First, it dignifies the animal kingdom because it allows us to further appreciate the enormous complexity, sophistication, and meaning of non-human behavior and social systems. Second, it keeps us from claiming that culture is exclusively human, while at the same time it allows us to see connections with other social creatures. New research has shown that animals also have culture, although debate exists over its precise nature. Whereas there is wide consensus that animals are incapable of creating rich symbolic systems similar to human innovations (Laland & Janik, 2006), of radically shaping their environment to the degree humans have (Laland, Atton, & Webster, 2011), or of transmitting and accumulating cultural capital (see O'Brien & Bentley, chapter 8 in this volume), recent evidence calls into question the notion that animals are incapable of symbolic culture. A recent study, for example, documented that in chimpanzee behavior there may be evidence of primitive rituals unconnected to food or status (Kühl et al., 2016).

Nevertheless, we recognize the existence of culture in animals when it is approached not with a rigid anthropocentric bias but as the transmission of skills and knowledge from one generation to the next (Laland, 2008), and when we recognize that these behaviors are learned and not merely explained by genetic inheritance, that they are restricted to specific communities, and that there are important variations between animal communities of the same species. Perhaps one way of settling the animal culture debate is by reframing the question. Instead of forcing the debate to be about whether culture is or is not exclusively human, which is possibly a false dichotomy, we can approach it as a non-hierarchical, horizontal continuum that ranges from behavioral to symbolic culture. We could place fish and insects at one end of the spectrum, great apes and cetaceans further down the line, and humans at the other end.

Cultural Genomics

Cultural genomics studies the interplay of genes, cultures, and environments, or the multiple ways in which cultural experiences affect, are influenced by and covary with the genome and the environment to shape behavior and cognition at the social, developmental, and evolutionary levels (see Causadias & Korous, chapter 7 in this volume). Cultural genomics also approaches the interplay of genes, culture and environment at three levels: the social, developmental, and evolutionary levels (for a more detailed discussion of the evolutionary level of gene–culture interplay, see O'Brien & Bentley, chapter 8 in this volume). The social level of gene–culture interplay represents day-to-day scenarios in which these processes affect each other. For example, some individuals with certain genetic variants might be more susceptible to particular cultural experiences, such as racial discrimination and prejudice (Brody et al., 2011; Sales et al., 2015). At the developmental level of analysis, the study of gene–culture interplay examines how genes, or culture, or both, trigger probabilistic trajectories that lead to adaptive or maladaptive outcomes. For instance, evidence suggests that continuity in cultural development is related to decreases in depressive symptoms in individuals who carry specific genetic variants

(Dressler, Balieiro, Ribeiro, & Santos, 2009). At the evolutionary level, cultural genomics examines the cumulative effect of gene–culture interplay in natural selection and adaptation of humans over centuries. Agriculture, for instance, epitomizes how we not only adapt to our environment, but build new niches to fit our needs. In turn, cultural innovations in agriculture have eventually led to changes in the human genome (see O'Brien & Laland, 2012).

Researchers in cultural genomics can inform our comprehension of the importance of studying the joint influence of nature and nurture, for instance by investigating religion, culture, and genetics (see Lo & Sasaki, chapter 9 in this volume). Cultural genomics is one of the least studied domains of culture and biology interplay in psychology, and most of the studies employ a *CxB* approach by examining gene-by-culture interactions. Also, while most research on this domain of culture and biology interplay focuses on single genetic variants, such as 5-HTTLPR, there is an increased awareness of the importance of using alternative approaches that can provide a more compelling picture, including polygenic models, genome-wide association analyses, and twin, family and adoption studies (see Causadias & Korous, chapter 7 in this volume).

Cultural Neurobiology

Cultural neurobiology, or the neurobiology of cultural experiences (Causadias et al., 2016), encompasses moment-to-moment, day-to-day, year-to-year or ontological transactions among cultural processes and central and peripheral stress-sensitive neurobiological systems, including the autonomic nervous system (ANS), the hypothalamic-pituitary adrenal (HPA) axis, and immune mechanisms (for an introduction, see Doane, Sladek, & Adam, chapter 10 in this volume). For instance, stereotype threat has been associated with increases in blood pressure and cardiovascular reactivity, sympathetic activation, and cortisol levels (John-Henderson, Rheinschmidt, Mendoza-Denton, & Francis, 2014), while lifelong subjection to racial discrimination, as well as discrimination in the form of threats or actual aggression, has been found to inversely predict heart rate variability (Hill et al., 2017).

Cultural neurobiology is one of the domains of culture and biology interplay that have received most recent attention: a growing number of lines of study have examined the relationship between poverty, stress, and allostatic load (see Doan & Evans, chapter 11 in this volume), the biological consequences of unfair treatment (see Ong, Deshpande, & Williams, chapter 12 in this volume), the effects of cultural experiences, social ties and stress on the HPA axis (see Wang & Campos, chapter 13 in this volume), cultural influences on parasympathetic activity (see Hill & Hoggard, chapter 14 in this volume), and stress reactivity and drug use vulnerability in culturally diverse communities (see Obasi, Wilborn, Cavanagh, Yan, & Ewane, chapter 15 in this volume). Importantly, most of the literature in cultural neurobiology focuses on $C \rightarrow B$ effects. Similarly to cultural genomics, research on this domain of culture and biology interplay often employs a single marker of the neurobiological effects of stress, such as measures of cortisol. There is an increasing awareness of the need to utilize comprehensive indexes that provide a most comprehensive picture of the affected systems, such as allostatic load (for a discussion, see Doan & Evans, chapter 11 in this volume).

Cultural Neuroscience

Cultural neuroscience is an emerging interdisciplinary field that integrates theories and methods from cultural and social psychology, anthropology, and social and cognitive neuroscience to investigate the interactions between culture and the brain at different timescales (for an introduction, see Lin & Telzer, chapter 16 in this volume). Cultural neuroscience studies sociocultural variations in cognitive and social processes and how they are represented in the brain. It aims to uncover how repeated engagement in different sociocultural environments might have influences on the brain (Kitayama & Uskul, 2011). Cultural neuroscience does not necessarily look at neural similarities and differences between races and nationalities but rather between and within cultures (Chiao & Ambady, 2007; Chiao et al., 2010). Studies in this field have shown that Latino adolescents who reported greater family obligation values showed decreased activation in reward regions during risk taking and increased activation in cognitive control regions during behavioral inhibition (Telzer, Fuligni, Lieberman, & Gálvan, 2013), underscoring how cultural values can shape the brain. Importantly, these neural systems predict long-term adjustment (Telzer, Fuligni, Lieberman, & Gálvan, 2014), further highlighting that culture shapes neural processing, which impacts behaviors over time.

Cultural neuroscience is perhaps the most established domain of research in culture and biology interplay, with an emerging literature on the causes and consequences of cultural differences in social cognition (see Meyer, chapter 17 in this volume), culture and self–other overlap (see

Varnum & Hampton, chapter 18 in this volume), and culture, brain, and development (see Qu & Telzer, chapter 19 in this volume). As a testament to this growth, the last decade has seen special issues and handbooks devoted to cultural neuroscience, and even a new journal (*Culture and Brain*). Notably, most of the literature in cultural neuroscience focuses on $C \rightarrow B$ effects.

Conclusions and Future Directions

There are possible aids to overcoming obstacles in future culture and biology research (see Table 1.1). First, we should avoid reductionism and determinism in the employment of increasingly sophisticated biological methods in behavioral science in order to overcome well-founded skepticism (Schwartz et al., 2016). To do so, we should aspire to develop models and methods that reflect the complexity of human and animal culture, as well as conducting research on the intersection of multiple types, levels, and domains of culture and biology. Following Overton's (2010) principles will be key in this endeavor. They provide a stable base for inquiry – not an absolute fixity or absolute relativity, but a relative relativity (Latour, 1993). Admittedly, creating a grand theory of the field might not be attainable in the short term, so in the meanwhile we can focus on "patchy reductions" in which sections of a causal network are elucidated, progressively leading to a better understanding of the whole system (see Kendler, 2005; Schaffner, 1994).

Second, instead of using biomedical and genetic methods to justify social and racial hierarchies, we should employ these methods to document the effects of social injustice and inequality. For instance, we can use novel

Table 1.1 Obstacles and solutions in culture and biology interplay research

Obstacles	Solutions
Reductionism and determinism	Complexity and "patchy reductions"
Justification of social hierarchies	Documenting the effects of injustice and inequality
Unethical biomedical research	Community participatory research
Disconnection between fields	Interdisciplinary research approaches

biologically informed methods to provide further evidence of the deleterious effects of racial discrimination and unfair treatment on the nervous system (see Hill & Hoggard, and Ong, Deshpande, & Williams, chapter 12 in this volume) and on genes (Chae et al., 2014, 2016). Similarly, by appreciating the complexity of animal culture we might be persuaded to promote conservation efforts for endangered species of apes and other mammals, which are rapidly losing their cultural heritage through poaching and habitat loss (see Yong, 2015).

Third, to overcome the legacy of unethical biomedical research with underprivileged communities, and the mistrust that it has engendered, we should develop community participatory research approaches that make individuals and groups active partners in research designs, and incorporate their needs and legitimate demands into the proposed outcomes (see Minkler & Wallerstein, 2008). This would not only help advance science, but hopefully generate interventions and applied solutions to community challenges that arise from the intersection of culture and biology.

Fourth, in order to address the disconnection between scientific fields and avoid intellectual insularity, it is necessary to promote new hybrid training programs, interdisciplinary research groups, grant opportunities, and peer-reviewed journals that can truly carve a new niche for this emerging discipline. Along these lines, we have created the Culture and Biology Initiative, an effort aimed at generating innovative models, studies, and questions. This initiative includes this handbook, which showcases some of the most ground-breaking thinking and research in this field, a special section on culture and biology in the journal *Cultural Diversity and Ethnic Minority Psychology* (see Causadias et al., 2016), symposiums in research conferences, new courses and teaching seminars, and the formulation of novel collaborative research projects.

In this chapter, we began by examining some obstacles preventing the integration of culture and biology in behavioral sciences. To overcome these obstacles and their consequences, we introduced the field of culture and biology interplay, defining its basic principles and providing an overview of its history. We examined different types, levels, and domains of research in culture and biology interplay. The chapters that follow offer varied examples that illustrate the breadth of the disciplines and methods that are giving shape to this emerging field. We hope this collection will illustrate how insights that cut across disciplines, across biological systems and conceptualizations of culture, and even across species, may facilitate a better understanding of what it means to have culture, and the evolutionary significance of culture and biology as integrated systems of adaptation.

Acknowledgment

We want to thank Michael O'Brien and Kevin Korous for their feedback on an earlier version of this manuscript.

References

Acerbi, A., & Mesoudi, A. (2015). If we are all cultural Darwinians what's the fuss about? Clarifying recent disagreements in the field of cultural evolution. *Biology and Philosophy, 30*(4), 481–503. doi:10.1007/s10539-015-9490-2

Allen, E., Beckwith, B., Beckwith, J., Chorover, S., Culver, D., Duncan, M., … & Schreier, H. (1975, November). Against sociobiology. *New York Review of Books.*

Aoki, K. (1986). A stochastic model of gene–culture coevolution suggested by the "culture historical hypothesis" for the evolution of adult lactose absorption in humans. *Proceedings of the National Academy of Sciences of the USA, 83*(9), 2929–2933.

Ashraf, Q., & Galor, O. (2013). The "Out of Africa" hypothesis, human genetic diversity, and comparative economic development. *American Economic Review, 103*(1), 1–46. doi:10.1257/aer.103.1.1

Boyd, R., & Richerson, P. J. (1985). *Culture and the evolutionary process.* Chicago, IL: Chicago University Press.

Brody, G. H., Beach, S. R., Chen, Y. F., Obasi, E., Philibert, R. A., Kogan, S. M., & Simons, R. L. (2011). Perceived discrimination, serotonin transporter linked polymorphic region status, and the development of conduct problems. *Development and Psychopathology, 23*(2), 617–627. doi:10.1017/S0954579411000046

Burt, S. A., Klump, K. L., Gorman-Smith, D., & Neiderhiser, J. M. (2016). Neighborhood disadvantage alters the origins of children's nonaggressive conduct problems. *Clinical Psychological Science, 4*(3), 511–526. doi:10.1177/2167702615618164

Campbell, D. T. (1965). Variation and selective retention in socio-cultural evolution. In H. R. Barringer, G. I. Blanksten, & R. W. Mack (Eds.), *Social change in developing areas: A reinterpretation of evolutionary theory* (pp. 19–49). Cambridge, MA: Schenkman.

Causadias, J. M. (2013). A roadmap for the integration of culture into developmental psychopathology. *Development and Psychopathology: A Vision Realized, 25*(4pt2), 1375–1398. doi:10.1017/S0954579413000679

Causadias, J. M., Telzer, E. H., & Lee, R. M. (2017). Culture and biology interplay: An introduction. *Cultural Diversity and Ethnic Minority Psychology, 23*(1), 1–4. 10.1037/cdp0000121

Cavalli-Sforza, L. L., & Feldman, M. W. (1981). *Cultural transmission and evolution: A quantitative approach* (Monographs in population biology, 16). Princeton, NJ: Princeton University Press.

Chae, D. H., Epel, E. S., Nuru-Jeter, A. M., Lincoln, K. D., Taylor, R. J., Lin, J., … & Thomas, S. B. (2016). Discrimination, mental health, and leukocyte telomere length among African American men. *Psychoneuroendocrinology, 63,* 10–16. doi:10.1016/j.psyneuen.2015.09:002

Chae, D. H., Nuru-Jeter, A. M., Adler, N. E., Brody, G. H., Lin, J., Blackburn, E. H., & Epel, E. S. (2014). Discrimination, racial bias, and telomere length in African-American men. *American Journal of Preventive Medicine, 46*(2), 103–111. doi:10.1016/j.ampre.2013.10.020

Chen, C., Burton, M., Greenberger, E., & Dmitrieva, J. (1999). Population migration and the variation of dopamine D4 receptor (DRD4) allele frequencies around the globe. *Evolution and Human Behavior, 20*(5), 309–324. doi:10/1016/s1090-5138(99)00015-x

Chiao, J. Y., & Ambady, N. (2007). Cultural neuroscience: Parsing universality and diversity across levels of analysis. In S. Kitayama & D. Cohen (Eds.), *The handbook of cultural psychology* (pp. 237–254). New York: Guilford Press.

Chiao, J. Y., Harada, T., Komeda, H., Li, Z., Mano, Y., Saito, D., Parrish, T. B., … & Iidaka, T. (2009). Neural basis of individualistic and collectivistic views of self. *Human Brain Mapping, 30*(9), 2813–2820. doi:10.1002/hbm.20707

Chiao, J. Y., Hariri, A. R., Harada, T., Mano, Y., Sadato, N., Parrish, T. B., & Iidaka, T. (2010). Theory and methods in cultural neuroscience. *Social Cognitive and Affective Neuroscience, 5*(2–3), 356–361. doi:10.1093/scan/nsq063

Cicchetti, D., & Cannon, T. D. (1999). Neurodevelopmental processes in the ontogenesis and epigenesis of psychopathology. *Development and Psychopathology, 11*(3), 375–393. doi:10.1017/s0954579499002114

Cicchetti, D., & Dawson, G. (2002). Editorial: Multiple levels of analysis. *Development and Psychopathology, 14*(3), 417–420. doi:10.1017/s0954579402003012

Cicchetti, D., & Richters, J. E. (1997). Examining the conceptual and scientific underpinnings of research in developmental psychopathology. *Development and Psychopathology, 9,* 189–191.

Coates, T. N. (2015). *Between the world and me*. New York: Spiegel & Grau.

Cohen, A. B. (2009). Many forms of culture. *American Psychologist, 64*(3), 194–204. doi:10.1037/a0015308

Creanza, N., & Feldman, M. W. (2016). Worldwide genetic and cultural change in human evolution. *Current Opinion in Genetics and Development, 41*, 85–92. doi:10.1016/j.gde.2016.08.006

Creanza, N., Ruhlen, M., Pemberton, T. J., Rosenberg, N. A., Feldman, M. W., & Ramachandran, S. (2015). A comparison of worldwide phonemic and genetic variation in human populations. *Proceedings of the National Academy of Sciences, 112*(5), 1265–1272. doi:10.1073/pnas.1424033112

Darwin, C. (1859). *The origin of species by means of natural selection*. London: John Murray.

Darwin, C. (1871). *The descent of man and selection in relation to sex*. London: John Murray.

Darwin, C. (1872). *The expression of the emotions in man and animals*. London: John Murray.

Dressler, W. W., Balieiro, M. C., Ribeiro, R. P., & Santos, J. E. D. (2009). Cultural consonance, a 5HT2A receptor polymorphism, and depressive symptoms: A longitudinal study of gene × culture interaction in urban Brazil. *American Journal of Human Biology, 21*(1), 91–97. doi:10.1002/ajhb.20823

Eisenberg, N. (2014). Is our focus becoming overly narrow? *APS Observer*, September. Retrieved from https://www.psychologicalscience.org/index.php/publications/observer/2014/september-14/is-our-focus-becoming-overly-narrow.html (accessed 30 March 2017).

Feldman, M. (2014). Echoes of the past: Hereditarianism and *A Troublesome Inheritance*. *PLoS Genetics, 10*(12), e1004817. doi:10.1371/journal.pgen.1004817

Feldman, M. W., & Cavalli-Sforza, L. L. (1989). On the theory of evolution under genetic and cultural transmission with application to the lactose absorption problem. In M. W. Feldman (Ed.), *Mathematical evolutionary theory* (pp. 145–173). Princeton, NJ: Princeton University Press.

Fischer, R., & Boer, D. (2016). Values: The dynamic nexus between biology, ecology and culture. *Current Opinion in Psychology, 8*, 155–160. doi:10.1016/j.copsyc.2015.12.009

Freimuth, V. S., Quinn, S. C., Thomas, S. B., Cole, G., Zook, E., & Duncan, T. (2001). African Americans' views on research and the Tuskegee Syphilis Study. *Social Science and Medicine, 52*(5), 797–808. doi:10.1016/s0277-9536(00)00178-7

Freud, S. (1930). *Civilization and its discontents* (J. Riviere, trans.). London: Hogarth Press.

Fuller, B., & García Coll, C. (2010). Learning from Latinos: Contexts, families, and child development in motion. *Developmental Psychology, 46*(3), 559–565. doi:10.1037/a0019412

Fuller-Rowell, T. E., Doan, S. N., & Eccles, J. S. (2012). Differential effects of perceived discrimination on the diurnal cortisol rhythm of African Americans and Whites. *Psychoneuroendocrinology, 37*(1), 107–118. doi:10.1016/j.psyneuen.2011.05.011

Fuller-Rowell, T. E., Williams, D. R., Love, G. D., McKinley, P. S., Sloan, R. P., & Ryff, C. D. (2013). Race differences in age-trends of autonomic nervous system functioning. *Journal of Aging and Health, 25*, 839–862. doi:10.1177/0898264313491427

Galton, F. (1869). *Hereditary genius: An inquiry into its laws and consequences.* London: Macmillan.

Galton, F. (1874). On men of science, their nature and their nurture. *Proceedings of the Royal Institution of Great Britain, 7*, 227–236.

Goodman, M., Tashian, R. E., & Tashian, J. H. (Eds.) (1976). *Molecular anthropology: Genes and proteins in the evolutionary ascent of the primates.* New York: Plenum Press.

Guedes, J. D. A., Bestor, T. C., Carrasco, D., Flad, R., Fosse, E., Herzfeld, M., … & Patterson, N. (2013). Is poverty in our genes? *Current Anthropology, 54*(1), 71–79. doi:10.1086/669034

Hart, D., & Marmorstein, N. R. (2009). Neighborhoods and genes and everything in between: Understanding adolescent aggression in social and biological contexts. *Development and Psychopathology, 21*(3), 961–973. doi:10.1017/s0954579409000510

Hartigan, J. (2015). *Race in the 21st century. Ethnographic approaches.* New York: Oxford University Press.

Hill, L. K., Hoggard, L. S., Richmond, A. L., Gray, D. L., Williams, D. P., & Thayer, J. F. (2017). Examining the association between perceived discrimination and heart rate variability in African Americans. *Cultural Diversity and Ethnic Minority Psychology, 23*(1), 5–14.

Hölldobler, B., & Wilson, E. O. (2009). *The superorganism: The beauty, elegance, and strangeness of insect societies.* New York: W.W. Norton.

Huxley, J. S. (1955). Guest editorial: Evolution, cultural and biological. *Yearbook of Anthropology*, 2–25.

Ingold, T. (2000) Evolving skills. In H. Rose & S. Rose (Eds.), *Alas, poor Darwin: Arguments against evolutionary psychology* (pp. 273–297). New York: Harmony Books.

Ingold, T. (2007). The trouble with "evolutionary biology." *Anthropology Today, 23*(2), 13–17.

Jablonka, E., & Lamb, M. J. (2014). *Evolution in Four Dimensions: Genetic, Epigenetic, Behavioral, and Symbolic Variation in the History of Life.* Cambridge, MA: MIT Press.

John-Henderson, N. A., Rheinschmidt, M. L., Mendoza-Denton, R., & Francis, D. D. (2014). Performance and inflammation outcomes are predicted by different facets of SES under stereotype threat. *Social Psychological and Personality Science, 5*(3), 301–309. doi:10.1177/1948550613494226

Kendler, K. S. (2005). Toward a philosophical structure for psychiatry. *American Journal of Psychiatry, 162*(3), 433–440. doi:10.1176/appi.ajp.162.3.433

Kitayama, S., King, A., Yoon, C., Tompson, S., Huff, S., & Liberzon, I. (2014). The dopamine D4 receptor gene (DRD4) moderates cultural difference in independent versus interdependent social orientation. *Psychological Science, 25*(6), 1169–1177. doi:10.1177/0956797614528338

Kitayama, S., & Uskul, A. K. (2011). Culture, mind, and the brain: Current evidence and future directions. *Annual Review of Psychology, 62*, 419–449. doi:10.1146/annurev-psych-120709-145357

Kühl, H. S., Kalan, A. K., Arandjelovic, M., Aubert, F., D'Auvergne, L., Goedmakers, A., … & Boesch, C. (2016). Chimpanzee accumulative stone throwing. *Scientific Reports, 6*:22219. Online first. doi:10.1038/srep22219

Laland, K. N. (2008). Animal cultures. *Current Biology, 18*, 366–370. doi:10.1016/j.cub.2008.02.049

Laland, K. N., Atton, N., & Webster, M. M. (2011). From fish to fashion: Experimental and theoretical insights into the evolution of culture. *Philosophical Transactions of the Royal Society B, 366*, 958–968. doi:10.1098/rstb.2010.0328

Laland, K. N., & Janik, V. (2006). The animal cultures debate. *Trends in Ecology and Evolution, 21*, 542–547. doi:10.1016/j.tree.2006.06.005

Laland, K. N., Odling-Smee, J., & Myles, S. (2010). How culture shaped the human genome: Bringing genetics and the human sciences together. *Nature Reviews Genetics, 11*(2), 137–148. doi:10.1038/nrg2734

Laland, K. N., Uller, T., Feldman, M., Sterelny, K., Müller, G. B., Moczek, A., … & Futuyma, D. J. (2014). Does evolutionary theory need a rethink? *Nature, 514*(7521), 161–164. doi:10.1038/514161a

Latour, B. (1993). *We have never been modern.* Cambridge, MA: Harvard University Press.

Li, S. C. (2003). Biocultural orchestration of developmental plasticity across levels: The interplay of biology and culture in shaping the mind and behavior across the life span. *Psychological Bulletin, 129*(2), 171–194. doi:10.1037/0033-2909.129.2.171

Lilienfeld, S. O. (2007). Cognitive neuroscience and depression: Legitimate versus illegitimate reductionism and five challenges. *Cognitive Therapy and Research, 31*, 263–272. doi:10.1007/s10608-007-9127-0

Magnusson, D., & Stattin, H. (1998). Person–context interaction theories. In R. M. Lerner (Ed.), *Handbook of child psychology. Volume 1: Theoretical models of human development,* (5th ed., Editor-in-chief W. Damon, pp. 685–760). New York: John Wiley & Sons.

Mayr, E. (1961). Cause and effect in biology: Kinds of causes, predictability, and teleology are viewed by a practicing biologist. *Science, 134*(3489), 1501–1506. doi:10.1126/science.134.3489.1501

Mesoudi, A., Whiten, A., & Laland, K. N. (2006). Towards a unified science of cultural evolution. *Behavioral and Brain Sciences, 29*(4), 329–347. doi:10.1017/S0140525X06009083

Miller, G. A. (2010). Mistreating psychology in the decades of the brain. *Perspectives on Psychological Science, 5*, 716–743. doi:10.1177/1745691610388774

Minkler, M., & Wallerstein, N. (Eds.). (2008). *Community-based participatory research for health: From process to outcomes.* San Francisco, CA: Jossey-Bass.

Morin, O. (2016). Reasons to be fussy about cultural evolution. *Biology and Philosophy, 31*(3), 447–458. doi:10.1007/s10539-016-9516-4

Niculescu, A. B., Levey, D. F., Phalen, P. L., Le-Niculescu, H., Dainton, H. D., Jain, N., … & Graham, D. L. (2015). Understanding and predicting suicidality using a combined genomic and clinical risk assessment approach. *Molecular Psychiatry, 20*(11), 1266–1285. doi:10.1038/mp.2015.112

O'Brien, M. J., & Laland, K. N. (2012). Genes, culture, and agriculture. *Current Anthropology, 53*(4), 434–470. doi:10.1086/666585

Overton, W. F. (2007). A coherent metatheory for dynamic systems: Relational organicism–contextualism. *Human Development, 50*(2–3), 154–159. doi:10.1159/000100944

Overton, W. F. (2010). Life-span development: Concepts and issues. In W. F. Overton (Vol. Ed.), *Handbook of life-span development. Volume 1: Cognition, biology, and methods* (Editor-in-chief R. M. Lerner, pp. 1–29). Hoboken, NJ: Wiley.

Overton, W. F., & Reese, H. W. (1973). Models of development: Methodological implications. In J. R. Nesselroade & H. W. Reese (Eds.), *Life-span developmental psychology: Methodological issues* (pp. 65–86). New York: Academic Press.

Pitt-Rivers, A. H. L. F. (1906). *The evolution of culture and other essays.* Oxford: Clarendon Press.

Richerson, P. J., & Boyd, R. (1978). A dual inheritance model of the human evolutionary process I: Basic postulates and a simple model. *Journal of Social and Biological Structures, 1*(2), 127–154. doi:10.1016/s0140-1750(78)80002-5

Richerson, P. J., Boyd, R., & Henrich, J. (2010). Gene–culture coevolution in the age of genomics. *Proceedings of the National Academy of Sciences, 107*(2), 8985–8992. doi:10.1073/pnas.0914631107

Robert, J. S. (2004). *Embryology, epigenesis, and evolution: Taking development seriously.* Cambridge: Cambridge University Press.

Rosenberg, N. A., & Kang, J. T. (2015). Genetic diversity and societally important disparities. *Genetics, 201*(1), 1–12. doi:10.1534/genetics.115.176750/-/DC1

Rutter, M. (2006). *Genes and behavior: Nature–nurture interplay explained.* Malden, MA: Blackwell Publishing.

Rutter, M. (2007). Gene–environment interdependence. *Developmental Science, 10*(1), 12–18. doi:10.1111/j.1467-7687.2007.00557.x

Rutter, M. (2013). Developmental psychopathology: A paradigm shift or just a relabeling? *Development and Psychopathology, 25*(4pt2), 1201–1213. doi:10.1017/s0954579413000564

Sahlins, M. D., & Service, E. R. (eds.) (1960). *Evolution and culture.* Ann Arbor: University of Michigan Press.

Sales, J. M., Brown, J. L., Swartzendruber, A. L., Smearman, E. L., Brody, G. H., & DiClemente, R. (2015). Genetic sensitivity to emotional cues, racial discrimination and depressive symptoms among African–American adolescent females. *Frontiers in Psychology, 6*, 1–10. doi:10.3389/fpsyg.2015.00854

Satel, S., & Lilienfeld, S. O. (2013). *Brainwashed: The seductive appeal of mindless neuroscience.* New York: Basic Books.

Schaffner, K. F. (1994). Psychiatry and molecular biology: Reductionistic approaches to schizophrenia. In J. Z. Sadler, O. P. Wiggins, and M. Schwartz (Eds.), *Philosophical perspectives on psychiatric diagnostic classification* (pp. 279–294). Baltimore, MD: Johns Hopkins University Press.

Schwartz, J. A., & Beaver, K. M. (2011). Evidence of a gene × environment interaction between perceived prejudice and MAOA genotype in the prediction of criminal arrests. *Journal of Criminal Justice, 39*(5), 378–384. doi:10.1016/j.jcrimjus.2011.05.003

Schwartz, S. J., Lilienfeld, S. O., Meca, A., & Sauvigné, K. C. (2016). The role of neuroscience within psychology: A call for inclusiveness over exclusiveness. *American Psychologist, 71*(1), 52–70. doi:10.1037/a0039678

Smolin, L. (1997). *The life of the cosmos.* New York: Oxford University Press.

Sroufe, L. A. (2007). The place of development in developmental psychopathology. In A. Masten (Ed.), *Multilevel dynamics in developmental psychopathology: Pathways to the future* (Minnesota symposia on child psychology, 34, pp. 285–299). Mahwah, NJ: Lawrence Erlbaum Associates.

Sternberg, R. J., Grigorenko, E. L., & Kidd, K. K. (2005). Intelligence, race, and genetics. *American Psychologist, 60*(1), 46–59. doi:10.1037/0003-066x.60.1.46

Steward, J. H. (1955). *Theory of culture change.* Urbana: University of Illinois Press.

Super, C. M., & Harkness, S. (1986). The developmental niche: A conceptualization at the interface of child and culture. *International Journal of Behavioral Development, 9*(4), 545–569. doi:10.1177/016502548600900409

Telzer, E. H., Fuligni, A. J., Lieberman, M. D, & Gálvan, A. (2013). Meaningful family relationships: Neurocognitive buffers of adolescent risk taking. *Journal of Cognitive Neuroscience, 25*, 374–387. doi:10.1162/jocn_a_00331

Telzer, E. H., Fuligni, A. J., Lieberman, M. D, & Gálvan, A. (2014). Neural sensitivity to eudaimonic and hedonic rewards differentially predict adolescent depressive symptoms over time. *Proceedings of the National Academy of Sciences, 111*, 6600–6605. doi:10.1073/pnas.1323014111

Telzer, E. H., Masten, C. L., Berkman, E. T., Lieberman, M. D., & Fuligni, A. J. (2010). Gaining while giving: An fMRI study of the rewards of family assistance among White and Latino youth. *Social Neuroscience, 5*(5–6), 508–518. doi:10.1080/17470911003687913

Tomasello, M. (1999). *The cultural origins of human cognition.* Cambridge, MA: Harvard University Press.

Wade, N. (2014). *A troublesome inheritance: Genes, race and human history.* New York: Penguin.

White, L. A. (1959). *The evolution of culture.* New York: McGraw-Hill.

Whiten, A., Hinde, R. A., Laland, K. N., & Stringer, C. B. (2011). Culture evolves. *Philosophical Transactions of the Royal Society B, 366*(1567), 938–948. doi:10.1098/rstb.2010.0372

Whiten, A., Hinde, R. A., Stringer, C. B., & Laland, K. N. (Eds.) (2012). *Culture evolves.* New York: Oxford University Press.

Wilson, E. O. (1975). *Sociobiology: The new synthesis.* Cambridge, MA: Belknap Press of Harvard University Press.

Wilson, E. O. (2000). *Sociobiology: The new synthesis* (25th anniversary ed.). Cambridge, MA: Belknap Press of Harvard University Press.

Yong, E. (2015, December). How poaching destroys elephant wisdom. *The Atlantic,* 17 December. Retrieved from http://www.theatlantic.com/science/archive/2015/12/can-elephant-daughters-fill-the-holes-left-by-their-poached-mothers/420741/ (accessed March 30, 2017).

Zeiders, K. H., Doane, L. D., & Roosa, M. W. (2012). Perceived discrimination and diurnal cortisol: Examining relations among Mexican American adolescents. *Hormones and Behavior, 61*(4), 541–548. doi:10.1016/j.yhbeh.2012.01.018

2

Integrating Culture and Biology in Psychological Research: Conceptual Clarifications and Recommendations

Moin Syed and Ummul-Kiram Kathawalla

Psychological research that integrates cultural and biological perspectives has become increasingly prevalent in the last decade (see reviews by Causadias, 2013; Han et al., 2013; Kim & Sasaki, 2014; Mrazek, Harada, & Chiao, 2015). Despite the apparent impressiveness of the scope and methods of this work, psychological research integrating cultural and biological processes remains very much in its infancy. This fledgling status leads to great excitement about the new questions that can be asked and answered; very little has been addressed empirically, and thus the sky is seemingly the limit for the future of the field. At the same time, its nascence demands that we take stock of how the field approaches conceptualization and measurement, before we get too deep, too rooted in one way of doing things.

The purpose of this chapter is to provide such a reflection. The primary goal of our chapter is to raise what we view as some of the most substantial conceptual and methodological issues of which researchers in the field should be aware. This chapter is by no means intended to serve as an exhaustive review of the field, nor is it intended to address all critical issues in this area of research. Rather, it is meant to provide a broad introduction to the types of thinking that we feel researchers interested in culture and biology interplay would benefit from engaging in.

To facilitate our goals, the chapter is organized into two broad sections. In the first section we address the question, *what is cultural psychology?* Within this discussion we highlight the critical need for researchers studying culture and biology to carefully conceptualize the nature of cultural groups, and pay special attention to the supposed biological basis of race. We adopt a broad view of culture that involves shared meanings, values,

The Handbook of Culture and Biology, First Edition. Edited by José M. Causadias, Eva H. Telzer and Nancy A. Gonzales.

and practices within and among groups (Cohen, 2009; Rogoff, 2003; Shweder, 2000). We do not offer a companion section on *what is biological psychology?* The conceptualization of biological psychology is not nearly as diffuse and contested as is that of cultural psychology. "Biological psychology" generally refers to linking genetics or activities of the nervous system to behavior and mental process. Numerous specific approaches are subsumed under this broad header, including behavior genetics, cognitive/affective/social neuroscience, and physiological psychology. We do not treat these separately in this chapter, as the issues we raise are broadly applicable across different levels of analysis. It is also important to note that, although we use the phrasing "culture and biology" throughout this chapter, and often discuss them as independent levels of analysis, we do so with full recognition that the two are not so easily separable.

In the second broad section of this chapter we provide some specific recommendations for future researchers who wish to pursue a rigorous scientific approach to understanding the interplay of culture and biology. The ultimate goal of this chapter is to encourage researchers to engage in deeper thinking about conceptual and methodological issues that have the potential to compromise their work.

What Is Cultural Psychology?

The term "cultural psychology" refers to a broad family of approaches dedicated to understanding human diversity in psychological processes. Understanding that cultural psychology is broad, subsuming many different approaches, is critical in the context of this chapter, as there may be different concerns associated with each of the different cultural approaches.

Shweder (2000) articulated the nature and relations of the "three psychologies": cultural psychology, cross-cultural psychology, and indigenous psychology. Each of these represents an approach to conducting research on the cultural nature of behavior and mental processes. *Cultural psychology* assumes psychological pluralism – that cultures and societies around the world exhibit different mentalities that define their psychological experience (see also Hammack, 2008; Rogoff, 2003). The emphasis of cultural psychology tends to be on the meanings that people make of their existence, from their own perspective. Importantly, cultural psychology does not reject the idea that there are universal or common processes among groups of people. Indeed, most cultural psychologists subscribe to the idea that while general psychological processes might be universal (e.g., developing a sense of identity), the specific instantiations of those processes (e.g., the content of the identity) will vary by culture. *Indigenous psychology*, according to Shweder (2000), is more or less the same as cultural psychology in its emphasis on local psychological meanings. However, indigenous psychology often originates from within the culture that is being studied (rather than from an outside researcher studying a different cultural community), makes greater use of culture-specific folk concepts, and may be less concerned than cultural psychology with the implications of the findings outside of the context in which they were generated. In contrast, *cross-cultural psychology* is largely an extension of "mainstream" or non-cultural psychological research (Segall, Lonner, & Berry, 1998). Cross-cultural psychologists are generally more concerned with establishing human universals in psychological processes and contents, and thus are oriented towards testing the generalizability of existing findings or establishing cross-cultural measurement invariance of established constructs (Matsumoto, 2003). This orientation towards generalization is a very different focus from that of cultural psychology and its focus on local meanings that may or may not generalize.

Shweder's (2000) description of these three psychologies is clear and important, yet also incomplete in two primary ways. The first is that his analysis does not fully articulate the diversity of approaches *within* the cultural psychology framework. There are three general approaches we will expand on here. First, there is the cultural-developmental work falling under the umbrella of sociocultural theory, which is largely based on the writings of Vygotsky (1978) and Leont'ev (1978). This approach places a strong emphasis on development as culturally situated and mediated through tool usage (e.g., language and communication), and thus frequently consists of analyses of psychological phenomena embedded in activities (Rogoff, 2003). A somewhat similar approach, most clearly linked to the cognitive approach of Bruner (1990), Harré (2015), and others, focuses heavily on culture as meaning, as discussed by Shweder (2000), but places greater emphasis on meaning constructions in naturally occurring conversations. This discursive approach to psychology takes a stronger stance on power dynamics than sociocultural theory, seeking to understand how contexts can constrain cultural expressions (Durrheim & Dixon, 2010). Finally, a third approach to cultural psychology, found mostly in social psychology, may be most recognizable to readers. This work is strongly based in Hofstede's (1980) cultural dimension of individualistic versus collectivistic values and Markus and Kitayama's (1991) corresponding theory of independent versus interdependent self-construals. This very large body of research is a good example of comparative cultural psychology (see the handbook by Kitayama & Cohen, 2010); that is, although group comparisons are foundational to this approach, the goal is not generalization of psychological processes across cultures. In fact, the goal is often the opposite: to demonstrate that cultures are quite different in some fundamental psychological process (what they value, how they understand the self), and that these differences have major ramifications for how people think about and behave in the world. Thus, cultural psychology itself, even within Shweder's (2000) restricted definition, is quite diverse.

In a related vein, the second aspect lacking in Shweder's (2000) presentation is *ethnic minority psychology* (Cauce, Coronado, & Watson, 1998). Ethnic minority psychology is concerned with the psychological experiences of ethnic minorities within a specific nation, and can focus on a single ethnic group or examine the similarities and differences among various ethnic groups (Cauce et al., 1998). The critical component of ethnic minority psychology is the focus on the *minority*. Ethnic minority research is always situated within the context of power differentials and access to societal resources, and seeks to understand individuals' psychological experiences by examining the barriers minorities face and the strengths they draw upon to overcome them (García Coll et al., 1996; Cooper, 2011). This is clearly a different project from cultural or cross-cultural psychology, as defined by Shweder (2000). Because of the ethnic diversity in the United States and Canada, the vast majority of ethnic minority research is conducted in these two countries, although significant research also comes out of the Netherlands (Verkuyten, 2005), the United Kingdom (Gaines et al. 2010), Sweden (Gyberg, Syed, Frisén, Wängqvist, & Svensson, 2016) and Israel (Seginer & Mahajna, 2004), among many other countries.

When we think about research on culture and biology, we find many different broad approaches to culture in which the investigation may be situated. It is important to be aware of these different approaches and to be explicit about which one guides the study. Existing research on culture and biology is not evenly distributed across these different forms; there is more research within the social-psychological approach to cross-cultural psychology (e.g., Chiao & Blizinsky, 2010), and essentially none within the culture-as-meaning approach. Moreover, given the historical factors and power dynamics, research on culture and biology may be received differently within these different approaches, both by researchers and by the communities they study. For example, studying the genetic factors underlying mental health among African Americans may call for different conceptualizations and safeguards than studying the same topic among White Americans (see Snowden, 2012). The need to think about how research might be differentially executed with different groups raises the vexing issue of how to conceptualize groups, an issue to which we now turn.

On Terminology Used in Cultural Psychology

The need to think about how to conceptualize groups may be one of the most pressing issues for the future of culture and biology research. Moreover, as we will discuss, taking the nature of group definition seriously poses a major threat to the validity of past research, as well as to its ability to serve as the necessary cumulative foundation. Conceptualization of groups is critical to culture and biology because groups represent the starting point in any conceptual model: whether a study is focused on one specific group or compares multiple groups, some boundaries for inclusion or exclusion from each group have been set *a priori*. What processes do researchers use to set these boundary conditions? What criteria are used to determine the nature of the group definition?

The answer to these questions is, essentially, *none*. Rather than using specific processes or criteria, the great majority of research in culture and biology relies on colloquial understandings of groups, many of which are potentially misleading. To be fair, this problem is by no means limited to the domain of culture and biology. The challenge of defining and conceptualizing groups has a long history in psychology that continues to this day (Anastasi, 1937; García Coll, Akerman, & Cicchetti, 2000; Gjerde, 2004).

The terms race, ethnicity, culture and nation are difficult to define. Each has a separate meaning, although there is ongoing debate about what those meanings are. Moreover, there is considerable overlap among the terms, which renders it nearly impossible to conceptualize them as orthogonal. Nevertheless, any inquiry situated within the phenomena captured by these terms should be clear as to the meaning that will be used. We briefly do that here.

The terms race and ethnicity may have the most contentious definitions and may be the most difficult to disentangle. Despite this, there is growing consensus among social scientists about how best to understand and use these terms (see Umaña-Taylor et al., 2014). Race is considered a socially constructed system of power and dominance. Although debate continues, most researchers agree that there is little evidence of a biological basis for race (more on this issue below). Thus, rather than being considered a characteristic of the individual, race is conceptualized as a system of power that confers and sustains dominance upon those with access to social and cultural power and marginalization upon those who do not enjoy such access.

Ethnicity is also a historically and socially informed construct but tends to have a closer conceptual connection to culture than does race (Syed & Mitchell, 2013). Ethnicity generally corresponds to the history, beliefs, and practices of a relatively homogeneous group. If this definition sounds similar to what a definition of culture might look like, that's because it is. There are, however, important distinctions between the two. Culture is a system of shared beliefs, practices, and ways of living. Ethnic groups share a cultural background, but cultural groups may or may not share an ethnic background (e.g., American culture comprises many ethnic groups). In this way, culture can be thought of as a broader, higher-order construct that encompasses ethnicity.

Nations can encompass many races, ethnicities, and cultures, and thus may be the least specific of the terms. Some nations comprise highly diverse races, ethnicities, and cultures, particularly in the context of colonialism and imperial nation-building (e.g., Iraq) and large-scale immigration (e.g., the United States). "Nation" does, of course, have meaning, but it does not often have the meaning that many believe it does in psychological research; that is, nation is not the same thing as culture (see Matsumoto, 1999). There can be a "national culture" that has psychological relevance, but it must be understood that the national culture overlies many distinct cultures that may or may not resemble the national one (McLean & Syed, 2015). For this reason, cross-national studies are often difficult to interpret because it is unclear which culture is represented in the data.

To put the different definitions in the simplest possible terms, *race* pertains to social groups formed within a system of power, *ethnicity* pertains to social groups who share a cultural background, *culture* itself is a system of beliefs, practices, and behaviors, and *nation* refers to the country in which individuals live. Shared characteristics contribute to ongoing deliberations about the distinctiveness of the terms within psychological research (Cokley, 2007; Helms, Jernigan, & Mascher, 2005). Moreover, race and ethnicity can be particularly difficult to separate in the context of actual research practice. For this reason, many have adopted a hybrid term, "race/ethnicity," to acknowledge that the terms are distinct but that it is not really possible to separate race and ethnicity (Syed & Mitchell, 2013; Umaña-Taylor et al., 2014).

On the Supposed Biological Basis of Race and the Justified Skepticism of Culture and Biology Research

There are many reasons for cultural psychologists to be concerned, and even skeptical, about the increasing integration of biological factors in cultural research. Indeed, there is a long history of biological arguments being used to advance racial superiority (Graves, 2001). In-depth analyses of biological theories of race through history are available elsewhere, and the interested reader is encouraged to consult those texts (e.g., Graves, 2001; Smedley & Smedley, 2005). The genetic basis of intelligence is the substantive domain that has certainly been the focus of the most controversy and scholarly dispute, and thus serves as a good example. To be clear, there is certainly strong evidence for the heritability of intelligence, indicating a clear genetic contribution (Neisser et al., 1996). At the same time, there is strong evidence for environmental contributions to intelligence (e.g., Turkheimer, Haley, Waldron, D'Onofrio, & Gottesman, 2003). The genetic basis of intelligence is an unsurprisingly sensitive topic for many, given that race and racial differences have been at the center of the discussion. From the eugenics movement in the late nineteenth and early twentieth centuries, to Rushton's research on race, brain size, and intelligence (Rushton & Jensen, 2005; but see Cain & Vanderwolf, 1990), to the publication of *The Bell Curve* (Herrnstein & Murray, 1994), genetics, race, and intelligence have been the subject of academic and popular debate.

A central question vis-à-vis the context of this chapter is the nature of the groups being compared. A snapshot of American history highlights the tenuous and shifting nature of race. Around the beginning of the twentieth century, European immigrants from Irish, Italian, and Jewish backgrounds were not considered White, but of a different "race" of their own (Hochschild, 2005). Over time, with the changing economic and immigrant contexts, these groups have been absorbed into the broader White "racial" group, although vestiges of their recent minority status remain (Lipsitz, 1998). More recently, in the wake of the September 11th attacks on the US, Muslims have become *racialized*. That is, a single historical event created a racial group from a highly diverse group of approximately 1.6 billion people (in 2010) who live all around the world (Lipka, 2015). The process is best described as racialization because a power structure has been enacted in the US and other countries around the world that enables racial profiling, hate crimes, and restrictions on religious freedoms (Meer & Modood, 2009). Latinos in the US also present a curious case. According to the federal government, Latinos (or Hispanics[1]) are not a race but an ethnicity (Humes, Jones, & Ramirez, 2010). However, Latinos have also been racialized, particularly in the context of immigration and bilingual education (Solis, 2003). This historical dynamism of race makes it difficult to derive a single definition, and is one of the arguments for a social constructivist versus a biological view on race (Helms et al., 2005).

The belief in racial taxonomies as "natural" is evident all around in psychological research. In response to the media's discussion and portrayal of *The Bell Curve*, a group of 52 researchers contributed to a *Wall Street Journal* editorial, "Mainstream science on intelligence" (see Gottfredson, 1997 for the editorial and some background). The statement consisted of 25 brief points that cover general issues of what intelligence is, how it can be measured, its genetic basis, and racial variation. On this latter issue, point 7 reads, in part, "Members of all racial-ethnic groups can be found at every IQ level ... but groups often differ in where their members tend to cluster along the IQ line" (Gottfredson, 1997, p. 14). On the basis of this statement, they took as fact that the particular racial groups identified could be reliably and meaningfully classified. It is not until point 24 that they write, "Because research on intelligence relies on self-classification into distinct racial categories ... its findings likewise relate to some unclear mixture of social and biological distinctions among groups (no one claims otherwise)" (Gottfredson, 1997, p. 15). Thus, appropriately, they cast doubt on the accuracy and meaningfulness of the categories, the same categories that, in several earlier points in the list, they made reference to in regard to reliable and valid group differences in intelligence. Rather than putting it at the end of the list, it would have been more appropriate to begin with the problems of racial categorization and highlight how such problems render all subsequent points regarding race tenuous. Indeed, there is currently great consensus across numerous disciplines that the evidence for a biological basis of race is severely lacking (Bonham, Warshauer-Baker, & Collins, 2005; Caulfield et al., 2009; Teo, 2009; but see Risch, Burchard, Ziv, & Tang, 2002). Indeed, there is agreement that any racial variations in genetic patterns can be attributed to geographic regional origins, and not to race (for example, sickle-cell anemia, often considered a "Black disease," is an adaptive genetic mutation found in malaria-prevalent areas, including India, the Caribbean, and sub-Saharan Africa; Rees, Williams, & Gladwin, 2010; Serre & Pääbo, 2004).

A great deal of ink has been devoted to discussing the challenges and perils of racial classification and the definition of groups (Bhopal, 2004; Gjerde, 2004; Hochschild, 2005). One way to think about all of this is that a supposed, but incorrect, biological model of groups serves as the foundation for how we think about groups. We then examine how these groups differ in biological functions. However, this tautological approach rests on a false premise. Indeed, there is great irony in lauding their rigorous "scientific" approach to their research when they take racial groups as givens, not seriously questioning the origins of how the groups were constructed (see

Lipsitz, 1998 for a fascinating account of the creation of "Whites" in the US, and Teo, 2009, on the origins and problems of the term "Caucasian"). The following section provides some suggestions for what a scientific study of culture and biology ought to be.

The Path Forward: Recommendations for a Sensible Science of Culture and Biology

Despite the emphasis heretofore on questions and criticisms associated with culture and biology research, the integration of these two broad levels of analysis is important for the future of psychology. Indeed, there are many exciting programs of research that have struck a proper balance between innovation and rigor (e.g., Neblett & Roberts, 2013; Obasi et al., 2015), and building upon these exemplars will be important in the development of a credible knowledge base. In this section, we provide recommendations and considerations for scholars engaging in culture and biology research.

Assess the Psychological Process Underlying Group Differences

It is essential that studies conceptualize, measure, and analyze the psychological processes that underlie any purported group-based phenomenon. This is especially important for cultural comparative work, in which two or more cultural groups are compared on some process. At this point in our knowledge of cultural processes, methodologies, and interpretive pitfalls, there is little justifiable reason to compare groups analytically and leave interpretation up to speculation. For example, if "Asians" and "Westerners" are compared on some outcome, interpretation will often rely on differences in interdependent versus independent self-construals, respectively (see Matsumoto, 1999). That people from such cultural groups align with these self-construals, however, is a point of serious contention in the literature (Gjerde, 2004; Matsumoto, 1999; Oyserman, Coon, & Kemmelmeier, 2002; Syed & Mitchell, 2013; Takano & Osaka, 1999). Illustrating this approach, Kitayama and colleagues (2015) compared the association between expressions of anger and biological health risk (a composite of four inflammation and cardiovascular malfunction biomarkers) among a sample of Japanese and American adults. They purported to assess how "culture" moderated the association between expressions of anger and biological health risk, but they did not actually include any measure of culture. Rather, they used national origin of the participants as a proxy for culture, and then interpreted the findings in the context of cultural differences in independent and interdependent self-construals (which were not assessed in the study). Again, this analytic approach has been roundly criticized for what should be obvious reasons (Gjerde, 2004; Matsumoto, 1999; Tamis-LeMonda et al., 2008).

Rather than relying on contested cultural stereotypes, researchers must test the putative psychological mechanism underlying group differences (Helms et al., 2005). This may lead to surprises. Chiao and colleagues (2009) conducted a study that examined whether activation in the medial prefrontal cortex (MPFC) during a self-relevant judgment task was associated with participant ratings of individualism and collectivism among a sample of White Americans and Japanese. The primary finding was that MPFC activation was greater when participants identifying as individualistic described themselves in general terms and when participants identifying as collectivistic described themselves in contextual terms. The importance of actually assessing the cultural values is clear: Using a categorical procedure,[2] they found that the Japanese participants were more likely than Americans to be classified as individualistic (58% versus 25%) and thus conversely the Americans were more likely than the Japanese to be classified as collectivistic (75% versus 42%). Thus, consistently with past research (e.g., Takano & Osaka, 1999), self-construal did not map onto national origin as is repeatedly asserted in the literature (e.g., Kitayama et al., 2015). Importantly, this study relied on a very small sample ($N = 24$), so any findings should either be considered tenuous or be regarded with extreme skepticism. Indeed, as will be discussed next, there are many critical methodological issues that must be attended to in research on culture and biology.

Clue in to the Myriad Discussions of Methods Reforms in the Wake of the "Reproducibility Crisis"

For the most part, cultural psychologists have been noticeably absent from the conversations about reforming the science of psychology (see John, Loewenstein, & Prelec, 2012; Open Science Collaboration, 2015). This could be, in part, because many of the issues arose out of experimental social psychology, an approach used by only a small slice of cultural psychologists. Researchers in biological psychology, in contrast, have been very involved in the debate, particularly those in behavior and molecular genetics and social cognitive neuroscience. It is worth considering these areas in some detail.

Much of the existing research on cultural genetics takes a candidate gene approach, often in the context of a genetic x environmental (GxE) design (Beach et al., 2014; Obasi et al., 2015; see Kim & Sasaki, 2014, for a review). GxE models examine how the association between an environmental factor and a given outcome depends on the presence of particular genetic polymorphism (Duncan, Pollastri, & Smoller, 2014). Arguably the most well-known of these types of analyses is Caspi and colleagues' (2003) study of stressful life events and depression, in which they found that the presence of the short allele on the 5-HTT serotonin transporter resulted in a stronger association between stress and depression. In other words, the genetic polymorphism moderated the association between stress and depression, providing clues about why some people are more impacted by life stress than others.

Despite the prevalence and apparent appeal of the candidate gene GxE designs, they have several major limitations. First, there is ongoing debate about the replicability of the findings. For example, Caspi and colleagues' (2003) study of 5-HTT and depression has been subject to numerous replications and meta-analyses that have left the verisimilitude of the finding unresolved (e.g., Clarke, Flint, Attwood, & Munafò, 2010; Risch et al., 2009). Similarly, a major challenge to interpreting this line of research is that, like many areas of psychology, it likely suffers from extreme publication bias (Ferguson & Heene, 2012). *Not finding* that a genetic polymorphism moderates a psychological association may be very difficult to publish – especially if it has not previously been identified in the literature. Moreover, the candidate gene approach isolates a single genetic variant as responsible for the observed psychological outcomes, when in nearly all instances multiple genes operate in conjunction to contribute to such a result (e.g., the multifactorial polygenic model; Gottesman & Shields, 1982). Finally, analysis of a candidate gene requires researchers to identify and develop hypotheses about that specific gene, leading to a strong likelihood that other important genetic variants will be overlooked (Hirschhorn & Daly, 2005). For these reasons and more, some researchers in behavior genetics have increasingly made use of genome-wide association studies (GWAS), which involve genotyping a large portion of the genome using very large samples (> 100,000) to identify common genetic variants (Hirschhorn & Daly, 2005; but see Visscher, Brown, McCarthy, & Yang, 2012, for some criticisms of the GWAS approach).

When taking these developments into consideration, consumers of cultural genetics research should be skeptical of existing genetic studies. It is critical to investigate the replicability of the association and properly assess the potential of publication bias toward statistically significant associations before taking such findings seriously. As discussed in more detail below, these cautions are not limited to research on cultural genetics, but, given the historical context and interpretive affordances of this work, extra care may be called for.

The field of cultural neuroscience has enjoyed tremendous growth in recent years (Kim & Sasaki, 2014), riding the broader wave of neuroscience perspectives that are permeating all areas of psychology (Schwartz, Lilienfeld, Meca, & Sauvigné, 2016). In social cognitive neuroscience, however, arguably the biggest threat to reproducibility is underpowered studies (Yarkoni, 2009). In part because of the resources involved (time and cost), social neuroscience studies tend to have very small samples. Conventional wisdom held that it was impressive to detect an effect with a small sample, suggesting that the effect is "large." One of the most important revelations in recent years is that rather than detecting an effect *in spite of* a small sample, it is much more likely that the effect was detected *because* of the small sample. The unreliability associated with the small sample, the bias introduced by questionable research practices (e.g., optional stopping in data collection, selective use of covariates) and the analytic procedures that inflate Type 1 errors work together to seriously bring into question the reproducibility of the original findings (John et al., 2012; Simmons, Nelson, & Simonsohn, 2011).

Again, these issues dovetail with prior assertions that we use extra care in our theory and conceptualization when doing work at the interface of culture and biology. Many studies rely on very small samples – much too small – and results from such studies should at best be interpreted with extreme skepticism and at worst be disregarded altogether. Finally, it is important to note that behavioral neuroscience researchers are working on solutions to the problem of small samples due to resource constraints (see Mar, Spreng, & DeYoung, 2013, for an excellent example).

Be Especially Attentive to Effect Sizes versus *p*-Values

By now it seems so redundant as to be trite, but it is imperative that researchers put stronger interpretive weight on the observed effect sizes to understand the nature of any effect or association, rather than the binary interpretive framework enabled by *p*-values (at least within the context of null hypothesis significance testing). Effect sizes give greater interpretive information to the *strength* of the association, rather than the mere *presence* of an association afforded by *p*-values (Cumming, 2013). In cross-national, cross-cultural, or race-comparative designs this is especially critical, because "statistically significant" differences between groups can be interpreted as "completely non-overlapping." Unfortunately, researchers will, at times, provide interpretations that facilitate this way of thinking. Matsumoto, Grissom, and Dinnel's (2001) analysis of effect sizes in cultural research, which they called "cultural effect sizes," poignantly illustrated how the lack of effect size reporting can lead to faulty interpretations. And yet, despite such pleas, some researchers continue to omit effect sizes in their reports (e.g., Kitayama et al., 2015). Fortunately, effect sizes can be calculated *ex post facto* provided that sufficient information is included in the report: Cohen's d and Pearson's r can be calculated from the t-statistic and associated degrees of freedom (df). Calculation of effect sizes for the Kitayama et al. (2015) study indicates that they are quite small (for simple effects all ds < .14 and all rs < .09). These data are not consistent with their conclusion (effect sizes added by us) that "[t]his pattern was quite robust for the expressive facet of anger [ds = .13–.15, rs = .06–.08], but weak for anger suppression [ds = .06–.11, rs = .03–.06] and negligible for trait anger and anger control" (p. 216). To be clear, we are certainly not picking on this one paper: the lack of reporting of effect sizes is widespread in cultural psychology, both biological and otherwise (e.g., Mathur, Harada, & Chiao, 2012; Meisel, Ning, Campbell, & Goodie, 2015). This practice must stop.

Be Skeptical of "Established" Measures of Culture

Another major issue in this line of research is the conceptualization and measurement of culture itself, a point that has been made by researchers in cultural and biological psychology (Caspi, Hariri, Holmes, Uher, & Moffitt, 2010; Causadias, 2013; Matsumoto, 1999). The Hofstede (1980) index of individualism–collectivism is arguably the most widely recognized and used measure of cultural values. We have found that few researchers actually know how the Hofstede indexes were generated, this despite their ubiquity in the field. The original work was based on pre-existing data collected from over 100,000 employees of the large multinational corporation International Business Machines (IBM) from 66 countries between 1968 and 1973. This brief description should raise several red flags and causes for concern. Moreover, despite the large sample, the sample sizes were not evenly distributed across the different countries (e.g., there were only 107 respondents in Pakistan). These were the data that were used to generate the index scores that are so widely used and taken as fact in some cultural-biological research (e.g., Chiao & Blizinksy, 2010; Fincher, Thornhill, Murray, & Schaller, 2008). We recommend McSweeney's (2002) critical review of the Hofstede indexes as required reading for any producers or consumers of cultural research, as it highlights a number of threats to the validity of a large body of research. Moreover, Hofstede's approach treats individualism–collectivism as a single continuum and a static aspect of culture (Chiao & Blizinksy, 2010; Fincher et al., 2008). Tamis-LeMonda et al.'s (2008) explication of a "dynamic" way to implement these constructs as contextualized processes linked to developmental goals is also required reading. In short, studying cultural processes is messy, and researchers should be highly skeptical of overly parsimonious approaches.

These Issues Are Not Limited to Culture and Biology

Many of the issues raised in this chapter are, of course, not limited to culture and biology research. Issues of group definition and the need to examine underlying psychological process are just as relevant to cultural psychology on its own as they are to culture and biology research (see Helms et al., 2005; Matsumoto, 1999; Syed & Mitchell, 2013). Similar issues are at play for research on gender and biology (Fine & Fidler, 2015; Rippon, Jordan-Young, Kaiser, & Fine, 2014) and for educational neuroscience (Bowers, 2016). One of the reasons that we highlight group conceptualization in this chapter is that, in the context of biological processes, the stakes are much higher. Evidence for biological processes can be interpreted as though the evidence is natural and immutable (Gould & Heine, 2012). At the same time, the current zeitgeist of valuing biological processes in psychological research means that cultural work that includes a biological component may have a greater chance of receiving grant funding and getting published in high-visibility journals (Schwartz et al., 2016). This confluence of factors suggests that great care must be taken with conceptualization issues when doing research on culture and biology.

Check Assumptions, Break Barriers, and Seek Collaboration

Rigorous research on culture and biology requires expertise in both cultural and biological processes. This is a relatively rare, although not impossible, combination of expertise for an individual investigator, and there are few training programs that would adequately prepare researchers to go it alone. A fruitful path forward is to develop collaborations among researchers with differing perspectives. One barrier to doing this is simply getting these researchers in the same room. Psychology is such a fractured field, in which subdisciplines effectively operate as separate disciplines. Moreover, there needs to be greater understanding of the fact that many researchers may be interested in integrating cultural and biological perspectives, but assumptions about the interests of other researchers get in the way. In conclusion, we are all interested in human psychological functioning, and all levels of human functioning are linked to some degree, so we should pursue collaborations that can expand our understandings.

Conclusions and Future Directions

We conclude with a cautionary tale. Increasingly, cultural psychologists are looking to move beyond the traditional focus on understanding variation in self, identity, and corresponding outcomes, and towards "larger" perspectives that signal evolutionary or otherwise biological significance. In 2014, a study published in *Science* linking self-construals to agricultural practices received quite a bit of media and scholarly attention (Talhelm et al., 2014). The authors argued that the labor and cooperation required for rice farming lead to greater levels of interdependent self-construals than wheat farming, which can be carried out relatively autonomously and is thus associated with greater independent self-construals. This move is consistent with other large-scale theories, namely the modernization hypothesis (Inglehart & Baker, 2000) and the pathogen prevalence theory (Fincher et al., 2008), that seek to understand population-level causes for cultural variation in psychological processes. In general, this is a very good thing for the field, and if you read Talhelm and colleagues' paper, it appears rather convincing.

Despite the appeal and apparent rigor of Talhelm and colleagues' (2014) study, several published critiques very quickly surfaced, focusing on a range of conceptual and methodological issues, some of which are quite substantial (Hu & Yuan, 2015; Roberts, 2015; Ruan, Xie, & Zhang, 2014). Whether or not rice and wheat production are related to psychological phenomena remains an open question: there are simply not enough available data from which to draw conclusions with any certainty. It is worth reading these articles, and the others on this topic, as there are many general lessons to learn from them. One lesson in particular serves well as a parting thought. As we all seek to expand the scope and significance of our research, including greater linkage between cultural and biological processes, we must be careful and measured in our studies and conclusions, and how we disseminate them. In other words, by all means let us integrate cultural and biological perspectives when we seek to understand psychological phenomena, but let us also demonstrate the appropriate caution as we do so.

Notes

1 The term 'Hispanic' itself is an interesting case story in race. The term was popularized by Richard Nixon's administration as a way to classify a group of diverse people for social and political purposes. Because of this, and because of the link to their Spanish colonizers, many prefer the term Latino, which is what we use in this chapter. However, there is wide geographical variation in what is considered an acceptable term, with Hispanic being much more acceptable on the US East Coast than on the West Coast.

2 This approach, it should be noted, is not advised, as individualism and collectivism are more properly conceptualized as two continuous value orientations than as the ends of a single continuum (Tamis-LeMonda et al., 2008).

References

Anastasi, A. (1937). *Differential psychology*. New York: Macmillan.

Beach, S. R., Brody, G. H., Lei, M. K., Kim, S., Cui, J., & Philibert, R. A. (2014). Is serotonin transporter genotype associated with epigenetic susceptibility or vulnerability? Examination of the impact of socioeconomic status risk on African American youth. *Development and Psychopathology, 26*(2), 289–304. doi:10.1017/S0954579413000990

Bhopal, R. (2004). Glossary of terms relating to ethnicity and race: For reflection and debate. *Journal of Epidemiology and Community Health, 58*(6), 441–445. doi:10.1136/jech.2003.013466

Bonham, V. L., Warshauer-Baker, E., & Collins, F. S. (2005). Race and ethnicity in the genome era: The complexity of the constructs. *American Psychologist, 60*(1), 9. doi:10.1037/0003-066X.60.1.9

Bowers, J. S. (2016). The practical and principled problems with educational neuroscience. *Psychological Review*. Online first. doi:10.1037/rev0000025

Bruner, J. (1990). Culture and human development: A new look. *Human Development, 33*(6), 344–355. doi:10.1159/000276535

Cain, D. P., & Vanderwolf, C. H. (1990). A critique of Rushton on race, brain size and intelligence. *Personality and Individual Differences, 11*(8), 777–784. doi:10.1016/0191-8869(90)90185-T

Caspi, A., Hariri, A. R., Holmes, A., Uher, R., & Moffitt, T. E. (2010). Genetic sensitivity to the environment: The case of the serotonin transporter gene and its implications for studying complex diseases and traits. *American Journal of Psychiatry, 167*(5), 509–527. doi:10.1176/appi.ajp.2010.09101452

Caspi, A., Sugden, K., Moffitt, T. E., Taylor, A., Craig, I. W., Harrington, H., … & Poulton, R. (2003). Influence of life stress on depression: Moderation by a polymorphism in the 5-HTT gene. *Science, 301*(5631), 386–389. doi:10.1126/science.1083968

Cauce, A. M., Coronado, N., & Watson, J. (1998). Conceptual, methodological, and statistical issues in culturally competent research. In M. Hernandez & M. R. Isaacs (Eds.), *Promoting cultural competence in children's mental health service: Systems of care for children's mental health* (pp. 305–329). Baltimore, MD: Paul H. Brookes.

Caulfield, T., Fullerton, S. M., Ali-Khan, S. E., Arbour, L., Burchard, E. G., Cooper, R. S., … & Daar, A. S. (2009). Race and ancestry in biomedical research: Exploring the challenges. *Genome Medicine, 1*(1), 1–8. doi:10.1186/gm8

Causadias, J. M. (2013). A roadmap for the integration of culture into developmental psychopathology. *Development and Psychopathology, 25*(4pt2), 1375–1398. doi:10.1017/S0954579413000679

Chiao, J. Y., & Blizinsky, K. D. (2010). Culture–gene coevolution of individualism–collectivism and the serotonin transporter gene. *Proceedings of the Royal Society B, 277*(1681), 529–537. doi:10.1098/rspb.2009.1650

Chiao, J. Y., Harada, T., Komeda, H., Li, Z., Mano, Y., Saito, D., … & Iidaka, T. (2009). Neural basis of individualistic and collectivistic views of self. *Human Brain Mapping, 30*(9), 2813–2820. doi:10.1098/rspb.2009.1650

Clarke, H., Flint, J., Attwood, A. S., & Munafò, M. R. (2010). Association of the 5-HTTLPR genotype and unipolar depression: A meta-analysis. *Psychological Medicine, 40*(11), 1767–1778. doi:10.1017/S0033291710000516

Cohen, A. B. (2009). Many forms of culture. *American Psychologist, 64*(3), 194–204. doi:10.1037/a0015308

Cokley, K. (2007). Critical issues in the measurement of ethnic and racial identity: A referendum on the state of the field. *Journal of Counseling Psychology, 54*(3), 224–234. doi:10.1037/0022-0167.54.3.224

Cooper, C. R. (2011). *Bridging multiple worlds: Cultures, identities, and pathways to college.* New York: Oxford University Press. doi:10.1093/acprof:oso/9780195080209.001.0001

Cumming, G. (2013). The new statistics: Why and how. *Psychological Science, 25*, 7–29. doi:10.1177/0956797613504966

Duncan, L. E., Pollastri, A. R., & Smoller, J. W. (2014). Mind the gap: Why many geneticists and psychological scientists have discrepant views about gene–environment interaction (G×E) research. *American Psychologist, 69*(3), 249–268. doi:10.1037/a0036320

Durrheim, K., & Dixon, J. (2010). Racial contact and change in South Africa. *Journal of Social Issues, 66*(2), 273–288. doi:10.1111/j.1540-4560.2010.01645.x

Ferguson, C. J., & Heene, M. (2012). A vast graveyard of undead theories: Publication bias and psychological science's aversion to the null. *Perspectives on Psychological Science, 7*(6), 555–561. doi:10.1177/1745691612459059

Fincher, C. L., Thornhill, R., Murray, D. R., & Schaller, M. (2008). Pathogen prevalence predicts human cross-cultural variability in individualism/collectivism. *Proceedings of the Royal Society B, 275*(1640), 1279–1285. doi:10.1098/rspb.2008.0094

Fine, C., & Fidler, F. (2015). Sex and power: Why sex/gender neuroscience should motivate statistical reform. In J. Clausen & N. Levy (Eds.), *Handbook of neuroethics* (pp. 1447–1462). Dordrecht: Springer. doi:10.1007/978-94-007-4707-4_156

Gaines, S. O., Jr, Bunce, D., Robertson, T., & Wright, B. with Goossens, Y., Heer, D., … & Minhas, S. (2010). Evaluating the psychometric properties of the Multigroup Ethnic Identity Measure (MEIM) within the United Kingdom. *Identity, 10*(1), 1–19. doi:10.1080/15283481003676176

García Coll, C., Akerman, A., & Cicchetti, D. (2000). Cultural influences on developmental processes and outcomes: Implications for the study of development and psychopathology. *Development and Psychopathology, 12*(3), 333–356. doi:10.1017/S0954579400003059

García Coll, C., Lamberty, G., Jenkins, R., McAdoo, H. P., Crnic, K., Wasik, B. H., & Garcia, H. V. (1996). An integrative model for the study of developmental competencies in minority children. *Child Development, 67*, 1891–1914. doi:10.2307/1131600

Gjerde, P. F. (2004). Culture, power, and experience: Toward a person-centered cultural psychology. *Human Development, 47*(3), 138–157. doi: 10.1159/000077987

Gottesman, I. I., & Shields, J. (1982). *Schizophrenia: The epigenetic puzzle.* Cambridge: Cambridge University Press.

Gottfredson, L. S. (1997). Mainstream science on intelligence: An editorial with 52 signatories, history, and bibliography. *Intelligence, 24*(1), 13–23. doi:10.1016/S0160-2896(97)90011-8

Gould, W. A., & Heine, S. J. (2012). Implicit essentialism: Genetic concepts are implicitly associated with fate concepts. *PloS One, 7*(6), e38176. doi:10.1371/journal.pone.0038176

Graves, J. L. (2001). *The Emperor's new clothes: Biological theories of race at the millennium*. New Brunswick, NJ: Rutgers University Press.

Gyberg, F., Syed, M., Frisén, A., Wängqvist, M., & Svensson, Y. (2016). "Another kind of Swede": Ethnic identity in contemporary Sweden. Manuscript submitted for publication.

Hammack, P. L. (2008). Narrative and the cultural psychology of identity. *Personality and Social Psychology Review, 12*, 222–247. doi:10.1177/1088868308316892

Han, S., Northoff, G., Vogeley, K., Wexler, B. E., Kitayama, S., & Varnum, M. E. (2013). A cultural neuroscience approach to the biosocial nature of the human brain. *Annual Review of Psychology, 64*, 335–359. doi:10.1146/annurev-psych-071112-054629

Harré, R. (2015). The person as the nexus of patterns of discursive practices. *Culture & Psychology, 21*(4), 492–504. doi:10.1177/1354067X15615808

Helms, J. E., Jernigan, M., & Mascher, J. (2005). The meaning of race in psychology and how to change it: A methodological perspective. *American Psychologist, 60*(1), 27. doi:10.1037/0003-066X.60.1.27

Herrnstein, R., & Murray, C. (1994). *The bell curve*. New York: Free Press.

Hirschhorn, J. N., & Daly, M. J. (2005). Genome-wide association studies for common diseases and complex traits. *Nature Reviews Genetics*, 6(2), 95–108. doi:10.1038/nrg1521

Hochschild, J. L. (2005). Looking ahead: Racial trends in the United States. *Daedalus, 134*(1), 70–81. doi:10.1162/0011526053124343

Hofstede, G. (1980). *Culture's consequences: International differences in work-related values*. Beverly Hills, CA: Sage.

Hu, S., & Yuan, Z. (2015). Commentary: "Large-scale psychological differences within China explained by rice vs. wheat agriculture." *Frontiers in Psychology*. 6(489). doi:10.3389/fpsyg.2015.00489

Humes, K. R., Jones, N. A., & Ramirez, R. R. (2011). Overview of race and Hispanic origin: 2010. *2010 Census Briefs*. US Census Bureau. Retrieved from http://www.census.gov/prod/cen2010/briefs/c2010br-02.pdf (accessed 31 March 2017).

Inglehart, R., & Baker, W. E. (2000). Modernization, cultural change, and the persistence of traditional values. *American Sociological Review, 65*(1), 19–51. doi:10.2307/2657288

John, L. K., Loewenstein, G., & Prelec, D. (2012). Measuring the prevalence of questionable research practices with incentives for truth telling. *Psychological Science, 23*, 524–532. doi:10.1177/0956797611430953

Kim, H. S., & Sasaki, J. Y. (2014). Cultural neuroscience: Biology of the mind in cultural contexts. *Annual Review of Psychology, 65*, 487–514. doi:10.1146/annurev-psych-010213-115040

Kitayama, S., & Cohen, D. (Eds.). (2010). *Handbook of cultural psychology*. New York: Guilford Press.

Kitayama, S., Park, J., Boylan, J. M., Miyamoto, Y., Levine, C. S., Markus, H. R., … & Ryff, C. D. (2015). Expression of anger and ill health in two cultures: An examination of inflammation and cardiovascular risk. *Psychological Science, 26*(2), 211–220. doi:10.1177/0956797614561268

Leont'ev, A. N. (1978). *Activity, consciousness, and personality*. Englewood Cliffs, NJ: Prentice-Hall.

Lipka, M. (2015). Muslims and Islam: Key findings in the U.S. and around the world. *Facttank*, 27 February. Pew Research Center. Retrieved from http://www.pewresearch.org/fact-tank/2015/12/07/muslims-and-islam-key-findings-in-the-u-s-and-around-the-world/ (31 March 2017).

Lipsitz, G. (1998). *The possessive investment of whiteness: How white people profit from identity politics*. Philadelphia, PA: Temple University Press.

Mar, R. A., Spreng, R. N., & DeYoung, C. G. (2013). How to produce personality neuroscience research with high statistical power and low additional cost. *Cognitive, Affective, and Behavioral Neuroscience, 13*, 674–685. doi:10.3758/s13415-013-0202-6

Markus, H. R., & Kitayama, S. (1991). Culture and the self: Implications for cognition, emotion, and motivation. *Psychological Review, 98*(2), 224. doi:10.1037/0033-295X.98.2.224

Mathur, V. A., Harada, T., & Chiao, J. Y. (2012). Racial identification modulates default network activity for same and other races. *Human Brain Mapping, 33*(8), 1883–1893. doi:10.1002/hbm.21330

Matsumoto, D. (1999). Culture and self: An empirical assessment of Markus and Kitayama's theory of independent and interdependent self-construals. *Asian Journal of Social Psychology, 2*(3), 289–310. doi:10.1111/1467-839X.00042

Matsumoto, D. (2003). Cross-cultural research. In S. Davis (Ed.), *Handbook of research methods in experimental psychology* (189–208). Oxford: Blackwell. doi:10.1002/9780470756973.ch9

Matsumoto, D., Grissom, R. J., & Dinnel, D. L. (2001). Do between-culture differences really mean that people are different? A look at some measures of cultural effect size. *Journal of Cross-Cultural Psychology, 32*(4), 478–490. doi:10.1177/0022022101032004007

McLean, K. C., & Syed., M. (2015). Personal, master, and alternative narratives: An integrative framework for understanding identity development in context. *Human Development, 58*, 318–349. doi:10.1159/000445817

McSweeney, B. (2002). Hofstede's model of national cultural differences and their consequences: A triumph of faith – a failure of analysis. *Human Relations, 55*(1), 89–118. doi:10.1177/0018726702551004

Meer, N., & Modood, T. (2009). The multicultural state we're in: Muslims, "multiculture" and the "civic re-balancing" of British multiculturalism. *Political Studies, 57*(3), 473–497. doi:10.1111/j.1467-9248.2008.00745.x

Meisel, M. K., Ning, H., Campbell, W. K., & Goodie, A. S. (2015). Narcissism, overconfidence, and risk taking in US and Chinese student samples. *Journal of Cross-Cultural Psychology, 47*(3), 385–400. doi:10.1177/0022022115621968

Mrazek, A. J., Harada, T., & Chiao, J. Y. (2015). Cultural neuroscience of identity development. In K. C. McLean and M. Syed (Eds.), *The Oxford handbook of identity development* (pp. 423–436). New York: Oxford University Press. doi:10.1093/oxfordhb/9780199936564.013.22

Neblett, E. W., & Roberts, S. O. (2013). Racial identity and autonomic responses to racial discrimination. *Psychophysiology, 50*(10), 943–953. doi:10.1111/psyp.12087

Neisser, U., Boodoo, G., Bouchard, T. J., Jr, Boykin, A. W., Brody, N., Ceci, S. J., … & Urbina, S. (1996). Intelligence: Knowns and unknowns. *American Psychologist, 51*(2), 77–101. doi:10.1037/0003-066X.51.2.77

Obasi, E. M., Shirtcliff, E. A., Brody, G. H., MacKillop, J., Pittman, D. M., Cavanagh, L., & Philibert, R. A. (2015). The relationship between alcohol consumption, perceived stress, and CRHR1 genotype on the hypothalamic–pituitary–adrenal axis in rural African Americans. *Frontiers in Psychology, 6*, 37–44. doi:10.3389/fpsyg.2015.00832

Open Science Collaboration (2015). Estimating the reproducibility of psychological science. *Science, 349*(6251), aac4716. doi:10.1126/science.aac4716

Oyserman, D., Coon, H. M., & Kemmelmeier, M. (2002). Rethinking individualism and collectivism: Evaluation of theoretical assumptions and meta-analyses. *Psychological Bulletin, 128*(1), 3–72. doi:10.1037/0033-2909.128.1.3

Rees, D. C., Williams, T. N., & Gladwin, M. T. (2010). Sickle-cell disease. *The Lancet, 376*(9757), 2018–2031. doi:10.1016/S0140-6736(10)61029-X

Rippon, G., Jordan-Young, R., Kaiser, A., & Fine, C. (2014). Recommendations for sex/gender neuroimaging research: Key principles and implications for research design, analysis, and interpretation. *Frontiers in Human Neuroscience, 8*, 1–13. doi:10.3389/fnhum.2014.00650

Risch, N., Burchard, E., Ziv, E., & Tang, H. (2002). Categorization of humans in biomedical research: Genes, race and disease. *Genome Biology, 3*(7), 1–12. doi:10.1186/gb-2002-3-7-comment2007

Risch, N., Herrell, R., Lehner, T., Liang, K. Y., Eaves, L., Hoh, J., … & Merikangas, K. R. (2009). Interaction between the serotonin transporter gene (5-HTTLPR), stressful life events, and risk of depression: a meta-analysis. *JAMA, 301*(23), 2462–2471. doi:10.1001/jama.2009.878

Roberts, S. G. (2015) Commentary: Large-scale psychological differences within China explained by rice vs. wheat agriculture. *Frontiers in Psychology, 6*, article 950, 1–4. doi:10.3389/fpsyg.2015.00950

Rogoff, B. (2003). *The cultural nature of human development*. New York: Oxford University Press.

Ruan J., Xie Z., & Zhang X. (2014). Does rice farming shape individualism and innovation? A response to Talhelm et al. (2014). *International Food Policy Research Institute (IFPRI) Discussion Paper* 01389.

Rushton, J. P., & Jensen, A. R. (2005). Thirty years of research on race differences in cognitive ability. *Psychology, Public Policy, and Law, 11*(2), 235–294. doi:10.1037/1076-8971.11.2.235

Schwartz, S. J., Lilienfeld, S. O., Meca, A., & Sauvigné, K. C. (2016). The role of neuroscience within psychology: A call for inclusiveness over exclusiveness. *American Psychologist, 71*(1), 52–70. doi:10.1037/a0039678

Segall, M. H., Lonner, W. J., & Berry, J. W. (1998). Cross-cultural psychology as a scholarly discipline: On the flowering of culture in behavioral research. *American Psychologist, 53*(10), 1101–1110. doi:10.1037/0003-066X.53.10.1101

Seginer, R., & Mahajna, S. (2004). How the future orientation of traditional Israeli Palestinian girls links beliefs about women's roles and academic achievement. *Psychology of Women Quarterly, 28*(2), 122–135. doi:10.1111/j.1471-6402.2004.00129.x

Serre, D., & Pääbo, S. (2004). Evidence for gradients of human genetic diversity within and among continents. *Genome Research, 14*(9), 1679–1685. doi:10.1101/gr.2529604

Shweder, R. A. (2000). The psychology of practice and the practice of the three psychologies. *Asian Journal of Social Psychology, 3*(3), 207–222. doi:10.1111/1467-839X.00065

Simmons, J. P., Nelson, L. D., & Simonsohn, U. (2011). False-positive psychology: Undisclosed flexibility in data collection and analysis allows presenting anything as significant. *Psychological Science, 22*(11), 1359–1366. doi:10.1177/0956797611417632

Smedley, A., & Smedley, B. D. (2005). Race as biology is fiction, racism as a social problem is real: Anthropological and historical perspectives on the social construction of race. *American Psychologist, 60*(1), 16–26. doi:10.1037/0003-066X.60.1.16

Snowden, L. R. (2012). Health and mental health policies' role in better understanding and closing African American–White American disparities in treatment access and quality of care. *American Psychologist, 67*(7), 524–531. doi:10.1037/a0030054

Solis, J. (2003). Re-thinking illegality as a violence *against*, not *by* Mexican immigrants, children, and youth. *Journal of Social Issues, 59*(1), 15–31. doi:10.1111/1540-4560.00002

Syed, M., & Mitchell, L. L. (2013). Race, ethnicity, and emerging adulthood: Retrospect and prospects. *Emerging Adulthood, 1*(2), 83–95. doi:10.1177/2167696813480503

Takano, Y., & Osaka, E. (1999). An unsupported common view: Comparing Japan and the US on individualism/collectivism. *Asian Journal of Social Psychology, 2*(3), 311–341. doi:10.1111/1467-839X.00043

Talhelm, T., Zhang, X., Oishi, S., Shimin, C., Duan, D., Lan, X., & Kitayama, S. (2014). Large-scale psychological differences within China explained by rice versus wheat agriculture. *Science, 344*(6184), 603–608. doi:10.1126/science.1246850

Tamis-LeMonda, C. S., Way, N., Hughes, D., Yoshikawa, H., Kalman, R. K., & Niwa, E. Y. (2008). Parents' goals for children: The dynamic coexistence of individualism and collectivism in cultures and individuals. *Social Development, 17*(1), 183–209. doi:10.1111/j.1467-9507.2007.00419.x

Teo, T. (2009). Psychology without Caucasians. *Canadian Psychology/Psychologie canadienne, 50*(2), 91. doi:10.1037/a0014393

Turkheimer, E., Haley, A., Waldron, M., D'Onofrio, B., & Gottesman, I. I. (2003). Socioeconomic status modifies heritability of IQ in young children. *Psychological Science, 14*(6), 623–628. doi:10.1046/j.0956-7976.2003.psci_1475.x

Umaña-Taylor, A. J., Quintana, S. M., Lee, R. M., Cross, W. E., Rivas-Drake, D., Schwartz, S. J., … & Seaton, E. (2014). Ethnic and racial identity during adolescence and into young adulthood: An integrated conceptualization. *Child Development, 85*(1), 21–39. doi:10.1111/cdev.12196

Verkuyten, M. (2005). Ethnic group identification and group evaluation among minority and majority groups: Testing the multiculturalism hypothesis. *Journal of Personality and Social Psychology, 88*(1), 121. doi:10.1037/0022-3514.88.1.121

Visscher, P. M., Brown, M. A., McCarthy, M. I., & Yang, J. (2012). Five years of GWAS discovery. *American Journal of Human Genetics, 90*(1), 7–24. doi:10.1016/j.ajhg.2011.11.029

Vygotsky, L. S. (1978). *Mind in society.* Cambridge, MA: Harvard University Press.

Yarkoni, T. (2009). Big correlations in little studies: Inflated fMRI correlations reflect low statistical power – Commentary on Vul et al. (2009). *Perspectives on Psychological Science, 4*(3), 294–298. doi:10.1111/j.1745-6924.2009.01127.x

3

Understanding Religion from Cultural and Biological Perspectives

Stefanie B. Northover and Adam B. Cohen

We present a synthesized cultural and biological explanation of the origin of religious beliefs and behaviors. Any phenomenon is the effect of multiple causes (Mayr, 1961), but we will pay special attention to cultural and biological causes. Specifically, we will propose that religious beliefs first appeared as byproducts of evolved cognitive adaptations, that these byproducts may be adaptive or functional, and that cultural learning largely determines the details of one's religious beliefs and behaviors and partly determines the degree of one's religiosity. In all we discuss religion as a product of a complex interplay of culture and biology.

First, we note that it is not easy to discuss what features religions do and do not have in common, or even what a religion is. As Cohen (2009) noted, religion is a fuzzy set, comprised of religious traditions with very different features. Nonetheless, all religions involve moral codes, rituals, community, and beliefs about supernatural agents (Atran & Norenzayan, 2004; Saroglou, 2011). While these commonalities are important, some liberties must be taken in considering certain features to be common across religions (for example, considering both Buddha and the Jewish God to be supernatural agents), while also acknowledging the unique cultural instantiations of religions.

Where Religions Come From

There is no way of knowing exactly when religion emerged, but certain behaviors among non-human primates, such as chimpanzee accumulative stone throwing, share features with human rituals (Kühl et al., 2016).

The Handbook of Culture and Biology, First Edition. Edited by José M. Causadias, Eva H. Telzer and Nancy A. Gonzales.

Precursors of religious beliefs and behaviors might, therefore, have emerged in our pre-human ancestors. Humans are equipped with evolved psychological mechanisms for solving problems of survival and reproduction that recurred over evolutionary history. Many religious representations have been explained as byproducts of these adaptive cognitive systems. Religious concepts may flow naturally from intuitive mental systems such as teleology (Kelemen, 2004), person permanence (Bering, 2011), dualism (Bloom, 2005), agency detection, anthropomorphism, and theory of mind. We will focus on the last three.

Supernatural Agents

Supernatural agents play a large role in religion (Atran & Norenzayan, 2004; Barrett, 2000; Boyer, 2003; Guthrie, 1993). An agent is an animal, person, or other being that reacts to others and can move of its own accord (Barrett, 2004; Boyer, 2001, 2003). Belief in supernatural agents, including gods, spirits, ancestors, ghosts, demons, angels, and jinn, is culturally universal (Pyysiäinen, 2009; Whitehouse, 2004).

Humans possess a cognitive mechanism for detecting agency. This ability to recognize agents goes beyond mere object recognition, as demonstrated by New, Cosmides, and Tooby (2007). Participants were shown images of scenes, such as an African savannah or a desk, and then, a moment later, shown the images again with an object, person, or animal missing. Participants more quickly and accurately detected changes in people and animals (i.e., agents) than in inanimate objects. For example, participants did a better job of spotting a distant gray elephant on a fairly gray background than they did of spotting a red van on a green background, even though the image of the van was larger than that of the elephant.

We can be reasonably certain that agency detection has always been adaptive. Throughout human evolutionary history, people and animals have afforded opportunities and imposed costs (New et al., 2007). Agency detection allows adaptive responding, for example avoiding or defending against threatening agents (such as predatory animals and human enemies) and approaching beneficial agents (such as food animals and caretakers).

Our agency detection mechanism is highly sensitive, frequently over-inferring the presence of agents (Atran & Norenzayan, 2004; Barrett, 2000; Guthrie, 1993). Agency detection may be triggered by non-agentic stimuli such as rustling grass or simple geometric shapes moving on a screen (Bloom & Veres, 1999; Heider & Simmel, 1944). The threshold may be set low because failing to notice a dangerous agent can be deadly.

Many have hypothesized that belief in supernatural agents is a byproduct of our adaptation for detecting agents (Atran & Norenzayan, 2004; Barrett, 2000). Empirical evidence is somewhat lacking, however. Tests of this hypothesis have revealed no correlation between religious belief and illusory agent detection (van Elk, 2013) and no effect of supernatural agent primes on agency detection (van Elk, Rutjens, van der Pligt, & van Harreveld, 2016).

Anthropomorphism

Supernatural agents are often conceptualized as humanlike (Boyer, 2001). Anthropomorphism, the interpretation of non-human beings or traits as humanlike (Guthrie, 1980), is found in every culture (Brown, 1991; Guthrie, 1996) and can be understood as an adaptation for group living. Humans are highly social animals who depend on each other for survival (by providing each other with mating opportunities, protection, resources, and so on) but also impose costs on each other. Therefore, humans possess evolved cognitive mechanisms for perceiving other humans, mechanisms that allow the recognition of other humans, human behavior, and the consequences of human behavior (Guthrie, 1993). These mechanisms may err on the side of perceiving ambiguous stimuli as human or caused by humans. For instance, people often see humanlike faces in clouds, smoke, and geological features, or hear voices in the wind (Atran & Norenzayan, 2004; Schick & Vaughn, 2005).

Theologies often contain ideas about superhuman supernatural agents; however, people often think of supernatural agents in simpler and intuitive – humanlike – ways (Barrett, 2000; Barrett & Keil, 1996; Boyer, 2001; Gervais, 2013b). In one classic study, participants heard or read stories about God and then answered questions about or paraphrased the content of the stories. Participants who endorsed a theologically correct description of God (as omnipotent, omniscient, omnipresent, etc.) on a separate questionnaire nonetheless frequently projected human limitations on God when recalling the stories, even though the stories left God's abilities open to interpretation. For example, the following line comes from a story about a boy who gets his leg stuck between two rocks in a river and prays to God to save him from drowning: "Though God was answering another prayer in another part of the world when the boy started praying, before long God responded by pushing one of the rocks so the boy could get his leg out" (Barret & Keil, 1996, p. 224). Participants often indicated that God answered the prayer in another part of the world before answering the boy's prayer – doing one task after another, as a human would – rather than answering two prayers at the same time. Hindus in India responded similarly (Barrett, 1998). This study is often cited as an example of a cognitive constraint on religious concepts. This interpretation has received criticism, however. Westh (2014) argued that participants anthropomorphized God at least in part because the language of the stories strongly implied an anthropomorphic version of God. Westh (2014) also suggested that the universality of religious anthropomorphic concepts is due to the universality of story-telling.

Further evidence for a link between anthropomorphism and religion comes from a study in which religious believers perceived more faces in images of scenery than skeptics did (Riekki, Lindeman, Aleneff, Halme, & Nuortimo, 2013). On the other hand, Norenzayan, Hansen, and Cady (2008) found no relationship between participants' belief in religious supernatural agents and their tendency to anthropomorphize a tree and a volcano.

Theory of Mind

Supernatural beings are often endowed with humanlike minds; in fact, Boyer (2001) claims that the mind is the only humanlike trait supernatural agents are always believed to possess. Perceiving the minds of others is referred to as mentalizing, and someone with the ability to mentalize possesses a theory of mind. Individuals with a theory of mind understand that other people have thoughts, desires, intentions, memories, and knowledge, and that these may differ from their own (Premack & Woodruff, 1978).

Theory of mind is critical for a species as socially sophisticated as humans; it allows individuals to interpret and predict the behavior of others, to accurately determine what other people know (or what they *think* they know, as their representations may be incorrect), and to read between the lines (for example, sometimes "I'll call you" means "Get lost"). Humans often err on the side of mind over-perception. Both adults and children have attributed mental states to stimuli as varied as robots, action figures, blobs, and animated shapes on screens (Abell, Happé, & Frith, 2000; Csibra, Gergely, Bíró, Koós, & Brockbank, 1999; Gergely, Nádasdy, Csibra, & Bíró, 1995; Morewedge, Preston, & Wegner, 2007).

Some support for the idea that belief in supernatural agents is a byproduct of theory of mind comes from a comparison of men and women. On average, women are more religious than men, and they also perform better on theory of mind tasks than men do (Baron-Cohen, Knickmeyer, & Belmonte, 2005; Baron-Cohen, Wheelwright, Hill, Raste, & Plumb, 2001;

Stiller & Dunbar, 2007). This gender difference is apparently driven to some extent by women's greater mentalizing abilities (Norenzayan, Gervais, & Trzesniewski, 2012; Rosenkranz & Charlton, 2013). Furthermore, individuals diagnosed with autism, a developmental disorder characterized by a deficit in mentalizing abilities, tend to report less belief in God than neurotypical individuals, and the relationship between autism and belief is mediated by mentalizing (Norenzayan, Gervais and Trzesniewski, 2012). Finally, functional magnetic resonance imaging (fMRI) studies have found that the brain regions associated with theory of mind activate when religious participants pray to or think about God (Kapogiannis et al., 2009; Schjoedt, Stødkilde-Jørgensen, Geertz, & Roepstorff, 2009).

Evidence and Conclusions

We have described three cognitive biases: agency detection, anthropomorphism, and theory of mind. All of these are intuitive mental systems, and there is evidence that religious belief is related to intuitive thinking generally. Participants who favor intuitive thinking or have been put into an intuitive state of mind report stronger belief in God than participants who favor analytical thinking or have been put into an analytical state of mind (Gervais & Norenzayan, 2012; Pennycook, Cheyne, Seli, Koehler, & Fugelsang, 2012; Shenhav, Rand, & Greene, 2012).

According to one point of view, religious representations are byproducts of evolved cognitive mechanisms for adaptively detecting and understanding animals and people. This may help to explain the ubiquity of religion across cultures. Furthermore, it seems that anthropomorphism, mentalizing abilities, and intuitive thinking can explain some of the variance in religious belief. In our view there is less empirical support for agency detection as underpinning religion. Some researchers have argued that intuitive cognitive biases are not a cause of religious beliefs, but account for which features of religious beliefs are easy to mentally represent (Gervais & Najle, 2015). From this perspective, anthropomorphism, for example, does not cause belief in supernatural agents, but explains why supernatural agents tend to be anthropomorphic.

From Byproducts to Adaptive Religion

Some scholars have promoted the view that religion can be adaptive. Rather than seeing religion as either a byproduct or an adaptation, we think it is possible that religious beliefs and behaviors began as byproducts, and some of these then provided useful functions. Thus, some religious beliefs and behaviors may be *exaptations* – useful features not developed by natural selection for their current function (Gould & Vrba, 1982).

Researchers have long noted a connection between religion and cooperation, and religion may be an adaptation (or exaptation) to promote intragroup cooperation (e.g., Irons, 2001; Wilson, 2002; Xygalatas et al., 2013). Evolutionary theories of kin selection, reciprocal altruism, and indirect reciprocity are inadequate to explain the high level of cooperation demonstrated by humans, particularly in the context of interactions between genetically unrelated people, because individuals are tempted to free-ride on the efforts of others (Dawkins, 1976). Here we discuss two theories of how religious behaviors and beliefs have served to promote intragroup cooperation: supernatural punishment and commitment signaling.

Supernatural Punishment

One prominent theory is that people cooperate because they fear punishment from supernatural agents or impersonal cosmic forces (e.g., karma) for violating norms and moral codes (Bering & Johnson, 2005; D. Johnson, 2015; D. Johnson & Krüger, 2004; Norenzayan, 2013). Misfortunes, such as illness, death, or scarcity, are frequently interpreted as punishment from supernatural agents (Bering, 2011; Boehm, 2008; Froese & Bader, 2010; Hartberg, Cox, & Villamayor-Tomas, 2014; Hartland, 1924; Murdock, 1980; Swanson, 1960). Furthermore, many cultures believe that supernatural punishment extends to the transgressor's family and friends (Aten et al., 2008; Bering & Johnson, 2005; Hartberg et al., 2014) and to the afterlife. World Values Survey data collected from 2010 to 2014 revealed that about 60% of people worldwide believe in Hell (D. Johnson, 2016, p. 63).

Fear of supernatural punishment is possibly a multilevel adaptation. First, individuals who are caught cheating others suffer negative consequences such as loss of reputation and punishment from group members. With the emergence of language came greater risk of discovery, as those who bore witness to transgressive behavior could spread the word. Individuals who feared supernatural punishment were probably less likely to violate cooperative norms and, therefore, less likely to get *caught* violating cooperative norms. Fear of supernatural punishment profited individual believers by sparing them from the costs (e.g., punishment, revenge) group members imposed on those caught breaking rules. Second, within a group, widespread fear of supernatural punishment for cheating and other antisocial behaviors that erode trust may increase intragroup cooperation

(D. Johnson & Krüger, 2004) and reduce the amount of costly sanctioning that must be carried out (D. Johnson, 2016). Thus, fear of supernatural punishment might have conferred fitness benefits on individuals as well as groups (D. Johnson, 2015, 2016; D. Johnson & Bering, 2006; D. Johnson & Krüger, 2004).

Evidence for Supernatural Punishment

Two experiments found that belief in the presence of supernatural agents deterred cheating among children (Piazza, Bering, & Ingram, 2011) and adults (Bering, McLeod, & Shackelford, 2005). It is unclear, however, whether the participants anticipated punishment from the supernatural agents (an invisible princess in the former and a ghost in the latter). People do intuitively attribute morally relevant knowledge to God, however. Participants in a study conducted by Purzycki and colleagues (2012) responded more quickly to questions about God's knowledge of moral transgressions (e.g., "Does God know that Adam cheats on his taxes?") than to those about morally irrelevant information ("Does God know how many pickles Stefanie has in her refrigerator?") even though people explicitly claim that God's omniscience means he knows absolutely everything. The results were the same when God was replaced with a fictional omniscient agent, as long as the agent punished moral transgressions. Furthermore, in Burkina Faso, entrepreneurs had a greater tendency to play an economic game fairly when they were first reminded of supernatural punishment (Hadnes & Schumacher, 2012).

As its name implies, the supernatural punishment hypothesis focuses on punishment rather than reward. Research suggests that punishment is more conducive than reward to cooperation (Gürerk, Irlenbusch, & Rockenbach, 2006; D. Johnson, 2016). An investigation of 67 societies revealed a negative correlation between crime rate and belief in Hell, but a *positive* correlation between crime rate and belief in Heaven (Shariff & Rhemtulla, 2012). In a lab study, participants who reported that God was vengeful and punishing cheated less on a task than participants who reported that God was forgiving and compassionate (Shariff & Norenzayan, 2011). Finally, in a series of economic games, participants more frequently believed that people, rather than computers or chance, caused negative outcomes, but not positive outcomes. That is, unfavorable events were more likely to be seen as caused by agents than favorable events were (Morewedge, 2009).

The studies discussed so far put forth substantial, though not completely unambiguous, evidence that belief in supernatural punishment reduces antisocial behavior. Two experimental studies suggest that fear of supernatural punishment can also increase prosocial behavior (Hadnes & Schumacher, 2012; Yilmaz & Bahçekapili, 2016). Furthermore, supernatural punishment is frequently involved in the cooperative management of shared natural resources such as water, forests, and fisheries (Hartberg et al., 2014; Snarey, 1996). Currently, there is indirect evidence to support the hypothesis that belief in supernatural punishment increases intragroup cooperation.

It should be noted that belief in supernatural punishment is not a perfect mechanism for good. Belief in supernatural punishment increases compliance with group norms but these norms may not be good for every individual, and may even be considered morally repugnant by other groups. For example, various misfortunes have been explained as divine punishment for homosexuality (Tashman, 2011), feminism (Goodstein, 2001), weaving on the wrong day of the week (Boehm, 2008), and failure to practice the "correct" religion (*USA Today*, 2012; Tashman, 2016; Wood, 2010). Belief in supernatural punishment is associated with aggression (K. Johnson, Li, Cohen, & Okun, 2013), victim blaming (Strömwall, Alfredsson, & Landström, 2013), and justification of inequality (Cotterill, Sidanius, Bhardwaj, & Kumar, 2014). All that said, societal coordination and cooperation often depend on people being able to send and receive signals of their intentions and trustworthiness. For that reason, we next discuss theories about religious signals of cooperative intent.

Costly Signals

Animals sometimes display phenotypic traits or behaviors that are difficult to understand from an evolutionary perspective, because they are costly. Perhaps the best-known example is the extravagant train of a peacock. Peacock trains are metabolically costly and should hinder escape from danger. Springboks and gazelles provide another example (Sosis & Alcorta, 2003). These animals may vigorously jump into the air, or *stot*, when predators are nearby, drawing the attention of predators and expending precious energy moments before they may have to run for their lives. According to costly signaling theory, costly physiological traits and behaviors are designed to signal some underlying, unobservable trait (Sosis, 2003). An extravagant train may be a reliable signal of a peacock's genetic quality and health. This costly signal may attract mates or scare off rivals and predators. For a gazelle, stotting may be a reliable signal of swiftness. A stotting gazelle may benefit by signaling to predators that she is not worth chasing, as she will probably escape. The costliness of these signals is what makes them reliable; only healthy, fit individuals can bear the cost of stotting or growing an extravagant train.

Strange as it may seem, such ideas have been applied to religion. Previously, we discussed the difficulty of achieving cooperation within groups. Individuals often stand to gain the most by free-riding on the cooperative efforts of others (Sosis, 2003). Costly signaling is perhaps a method of solving the problem of free-riding. Group members wish to discriminate between those who will cooperate and those who will attempt to free-ride; individuals who are committed to the group's values signal that commitment with costly religious behaviors (Sosis, 2003). Religious behaviors may cost time (e.g., time spent praying and attending services) and resources (e.g., tithing, sacrificing animals). The true cost of religious behaviors may be the same for those who are committed to the values of a group and those who are not. However, those who are committed to religious values perceive fewer costs and greater benefits than those who are not committed, because they believe religious ideas about supernatural rewards (e.g., Heaven) for religious behaviors and punishments (e.g., Hell) for breaking religious rules (Bulbulia, 2004; Sosis, 2003). Therefore, individuals who are not committed to the values of the group are less likely to participate in costly religious behaviors and can thus be identified and avoided. Costly signaling theory proposes that the tendency to display costly signals is an evolved adaptation; costly signalers gain the trust and acceptance of group members and therefore benefit from group membership (Bulbulia, 2004; Irons, 2001; Wilson, 2002). Moreover, because costly signaling promotes cooperation within groups, it may be adaptive at the group level.

Hard-to-Fake Signals and CREDs

Some researchers argue that signals of commitment do not have to be costly. Emotions elicited by religious situations may reliably signal group commitment because they are hard to fake (Bulbulia, 2008; Schloss, 2008). Religious emotional behavior includes speaking in tongues, crying, laughing, singing, fainting, trembling, going into a trance, and spontaneous bleeding (Schloss, 2008). An individual expressing hard-to-fake religious emotion is probably committed to his or her religion.

Another signaling theory is that of credibility-enhancing displays, or CREDs (Henrich, 2009). This theory proposes that humans have an evolved cognitive mechanism for evaluating the degree of others' commitments to the values, beliefs, and ideologies they say they are committed to. Talk is cheap, so cultural learners seek credibility-enhancing displays – reliable signals of sincerity and commitment. A model's religious behaviors, which may or may not be costly, are displays that enhance the credibility of the model's claims of commitment to the shared values and beliefs of the religious in-group.

Evidence for Signals

In an analysis of nineteenth-century American communes, Sosis (2000) found that religious communes lasted longer than secular communes. Assuming that commune longevity is a reliable index of cooperation, this suggests religious beliefs promote intragroup cooperation. On average, religious communes imposed more than twice as many costly requirements on their members as secular communes (Sosis & Bressler, 2003). Furthermore, among religious communes, there was a positive correlation between the number of costly constraints and commune longevity. Experimental studies have also found a relationship between costly signaling and in-group cooperation. In one such study, members of Israeli kibbutzim played an economic game with other members of their kibbutz (Sosis & Ruffle, 2003, 2004). When several factors were controlled for, such as the degree to which participants predicted their game partners would cooperate, men who attended synagogue daily (i.e., costly signalers) were more cooperative than other participants.

A similar study was conducted by Orbell, Goldman, Mulford, and Dawes (1992), who compared cooperation among residents of Logan, Utah with cooperation among residents of Eugene-Springfield, Oregon. Church attendance was positively correlated with cooperation, but only for Mormons in Logan, where over 75% of the population are members of the Church of Latter-Day Saints. These data suggest that church attendance increases cooperation among in-group members, but perhaps not cooperation generally (i.e., parochially but not universally).

Finally, Christian undergraduates rated costly signaling religious individuals as more trustworthy than their non-signaling counterparts, even when the costly signals were performed by people from a different religion (Hall, Cohen, Meyer, Varley, & Brewer, 2015). If we make the reasonable assumption that trust facilitates cooperation (Acedo-Carmona & Gomila, 2014), these results are consistent with the hypothesis that costly signaling fosters cooperation.

Evidence and Conclusions

It is important to note that traits that were adaptive in the past are not always adaptive today. Religious beliefs and behaviors might have been adaptive to our ancestors long ago without necessarily providing adaptive value now. Even if religion is or ever was adaptive, it did not necessarily emerge or evolve because of its functional nature (Gould & Lewontin, 1979). Religion most likely emerged as a byproduct of evolved cognitive adaptations for navigating an environment teeming with agents. Still, we do think that religious beliefs and behaviors can increase intragroup cooperation today. However, there are secular routes to cooperation as well. Some of the most cooperative, trusting, and peaceful countries in the world are also the least religious (Norenzayan, 2013; Zuckerman, 2008). Less than one-third of Danes and Swedes believe in God (Gervais, 2013a), yet Denmark and Sweden have some of the lowest rates of violent crime and corruption in the world, and have strong economies and high-quality educational systems (Zuckerman, 2008). Perhaps these nations have developed intragroup cooperation in part because of highly trusted secular institutions such as police force and courts of law (Norenzayan, 2013). Consistently with this, secular law-enforcement primes seemingly increase prosocial behavior to a similar extent as religious primes do (Shariff & Norenzayan, 2007).

We have discussed how religious beliefs and behaviors may foster intragroup cooperation. The other side of the coin is that religiosity can promote intergroup conflict. A strong religious identity can be associated with racism (Hall, Matz, & Wood, 2010); religious service attendance is related to support for religious martyrdom attacks (e.g., suicide bombing) and hostility toward out-group members (Ginges, Hansen, & Norenzayan, 2009); and greater religious infusion predicts prejudice, discrimination, and violence between groups (Neuberg et al., 2014).

Culture

Humans are not just biological beings. We dually inherit a biological endowment (shaped by biological evolution) and a cultural endowment (shaped by cultural evolution; Richerson & Boyd, 2005). Although there is evidence of some features of culture in a few non-human animals (Whiten et al., 1999), human cultures are exceptionally rich and diverse. Cultural learning mechanisms apparently evolved to allow humans to obtain ideas, beliefs, values, preferences, and practices from other humans (Henrich, 2009; Mesoudi, 2016). Such cultural learning is particularly adaptive when it allows people to obtain knowledge or skills they are incapable of obtaining on their own (Mesoudi, 2016). Cultural learning allows for learned improvements to pass on to future generations, resulting in substantial improvement in tools and information over generations (Richerson & Boyd, 2005).

Cultural learning is partly responsible for the existence of religious beliefs. A study of more than 50 cultures spread around the world (Gervais & Najle, 2015) found that whether someone was raised to be religious had a large impact on their likelihood of believing in a god (or gods). Above and beyond the effect of religious upbringing, the likelihood that someone believed in gods was strongly influenced by the frequency of religious attendance by other people in the society. Cultural learning is also largely responsible for the details of religious beliefs (e.g., what supernatural agents people from a specific cultural group believe in) and practices (e.g., what rituals they perform). Indeed, because of cultural learning, it seems religious beliefs and practices may outlive the original ecological features that gave rise to them. For example, many Ultra-Orthodox Jewish men, whose ancestors dealt with long, cold winters in eastern Europe, wear thick fur hats today in the hot Jerusalem desert (Sosis, 2006).

Cultural evolution deals with how cultures change over time. As in any evolutionary process, some cultural beliefs and practices spread while others disappear. One process by which this may happen is intergroup competition. When groups compete for resources, more competitive groups replace less competitive groups. The members of the defeated group may be killed, but they may also disperse or be assimilated into the winning group. Beliefs and practices may also spread through emulation of members of successful groups (Henrich & Gil-White, 2001; Richerson & Boyd, 2005). It has been proposed that beliefs and practices that foster intragroup cooperation, such as fear of supernatural punishment and commitment signaling, have spread and multiplied via these mechanisms (Henrich, 2004; Richerson & Boyd, 2005). Beliefs and behaviors may also propagate because the group that sustains them increases in number. Two methods by which a religious group may grow are the production and indoctrination of children, and proselytism. Despite sharing a common religious origin, Jews, members of a religion that does not proselytize, make up about 0.2% of the world population, whereas Christians and Muslims, members of proselytizing religions, make up 31% and 23% of the population, respectively (Pew Research Center, 2015).

Conclusions and Future Directions

Previously, we described religion as the result of the interplay of culture and biology. At the risk of oversimplifying, one might think of biology as forming the framework of religion and culture as filling in the details. Religious beliefs and behaviors vary from one culture to another, but that variation is constrained by biology. For example, individuals from different religious traditions share a belief in supernatural agents, and this belief is likely a byproduct of biological mental systems for adaptively navigating a social world. The specific characteristics of supernatural agents vary from one religious tradition to another, however, and individuals learn about these characteristics from their culture. In addition to the details of religion, cultural learning affects the degree and even the likelihood of religiosity.

Not only is religion a product of biology and culture, but biology and culture are in turn products of religion. Religious traditions may affect biology, for instance by promoting a high-fertility lifestyle (McQuillan, 2004; Weeden, Cohen, & Kenrick, 2008; Westoff & Jones, 1979; Zhang, 2008) or, alternatively, a low-fertility lifestyle (Coşgel, 2000; Hoodfar & Assadpour, 2000; Skirbekk et al., 2015). The relationship between religion and health provides another example: although we can't be certain of a cause-and-effect relationship, people who are high in religious involvement live longer than people who are low in religious involvement (McCullough, Hoyt, Larson, Koenig, & Thoresen, 2000).

Protestant individualism in the United States provides an example of religious influence on culture. Protestant Christianity views each individual as having a direct relationship with God. Thus, religion is more individualistic for Protestants than it is for Catholics and Jews, and it has been hypothesized that Protestant individualism is at least partially responsible for the individualistic nature of American culture (Cohen & Hill, 2007). Veiling practices in Turkey provide another instance of a religious influence on culture. In the last few decades, it has become increasingly popular for Turkish women to cover their hair and most of their bodies in a way that is encouraged by certain traditions within Islam. This growing trend has resulted in a veiling fashion industry (Sandikci & Ger, 2010).

If religion is so robustly a byproduct of universal psychological modules, and religion might help promote cooperation, why are some societies and people more religious than others? And why does religion take so many different forms? The capacity for different behaviors, including religious repertoires of behaviors, could all be in our genes, and facultatively elicited by different environments (Cosmides & Tooby, 1992; Kenrick et al., 2002). Therefore, religions may depend to some extent on selection pressures in the environment. For example, in places with a lot of disease, religions might be concerned with purity and contagion, with what you eat, and with whom you are allowed to have sex (K. Johnson, Li, & Cohen, 2015; K. Johnson, White, Boyd, & Cohen, 2011). All of these religious strictures could help to contain the spread of disease. In environments with unpredictable or inconsistent resources, cultures may evolve harsher, more punishing concepts of gods, as such gods would punish people for taking more than their fair share of resources (Snarey, 1996). While surely not all of religion's complexities can be explained by features of the ecology, the effect of ecological variables on religious features is a promising area for future research, one which has received very little attention to date. The study of religion would also benefit from more empirical testing of the theories described in this chapter.

We have discussed how religious beliefs may be byproducts of evolved psychological mechanisms for detecting and understanding animals and people, how religious commitment signaling and fear of supernatural punishment may be functional, and how these processes are further shaped by cultural factors. Culture and biology interact to produce the multifaceted phenomenon we think of as religion.

References

Abell, F., Happé, F., & Frith, U. (2000). Do triangles play tricks? Attribution of mental states to animated shapes in normal and abnormal development. *Cognitive Development, 15*, 1–16. doi:10.1016/S0885-2014(00)00014-9

Acedo-Carmona, C., & Gomila, A. (2014). Personal trust increases cooperation beyond general trust. *PLoS One, 9*, e105559. doi:10.1371/journal.pone.0105559

Aten, J., Moore, M., Denney, R., Bayne, T., Stagg, A., Owens, S., … Jones, C. (2008). God images following hurricane Katrina in south Mississippi: An exploratory study. *Journal of Psychology and Theology, 36*, 249–257.

Atran, S., & Norenzayan, A. (2004). Religion's evolutionary landscape: Counterintuition, commitment, compassion, communion. *Behavioral and Brain Sciences, 27*, 713–770. doi:10.1017/S0140525X04000172

Baron-Cohen, S., Knickmeyer, R., & Belmonte, M. (2005). Sex differences in the brain: Implications for explaining autism. *Science, 310*, 819–823. doi:10.1126/science.1115455

Baron-Cohen, S., Wheelwright, S., Hill, J., Raste, Y., & Plumb, I. (2001). The "reading the mind in the eyes" test revised version: A study with normal adults, and adults with Asperger syndrome or high-functioning autism. *Journal of Child Psychology and Psychiatry, 42*, 241–252. doi:10.1017/S0021963001006643

Barrett, J. (1998). Cognitive constraints on Hindu concepts of the divine. *Journal for the Scientific Study of Religion, 37*, 608–619. doi:10.2307/1388144

Barrett, J. (2000). Exploring the natural foundations of religion. *Trends in Cognitive Science, 4,* 29–34. doi:10.1016/S1364-6613(99)01419-9

Barrett, J. (2004). *Why would anyone believe in God?* Oxford: AltaMira Press.

Barrett, J., & Keil, F. (1996). Conceptualizing a non-natural entity: Anthropomorphism in god concepts. *Cognitive Psychology, 31,* 219–247. doi:10.1006/cogp.1996.0017

Bering, J. (2011). *The belief instinct: The psychology of souls, destiny, and the meaning of life* (1st American ed.). New York: W.W. Norton.

Bering, J., & Johnson, D. (2005). "O Lord … you perceive my thoughts from afar": Recursiveness and the evolution of supernatural agency. *Journal of Cognition and Culture, 5,* 118–142. doi:10.1163/1568537054068679

Bering, J., McLeod, K., & Shackelford, T. (2005). Reasoning about dead agents reveals possible adaptive trends. *Human Nature, 16,* 360–381. doi:10.1007/s12110-005-1015-2

Bloom, P. (2005). *Descartes' baby: How the science of child development explains what makes us human.* New York: Basic Books.

Bloom, P., & Veres, C. (1999). The perceived intentionality of groups. *Cognition, 71,* B1–B9. doi:10.1016/S0010-0277(99)00014-1

Boehm, C. (2008). A biocultural evolutionary exploration of supernatural sanctioning. In J. Bulbulia, R. Sosis, E. Harris, R. Genet, C. Genet, & K. Wyman (Eds.), *The evolution of religion: Studies, theories, and critiques* (pp. 143–152). Santa Margarita, CA: Collins Foundation Press.

Boyer, P. (2001). *Religion explained.* New York: Basic Books.

Boyer, P. (2003). Religious thought and behaviour as by-products of brain function. *Trends in Cognitive Sciences, 7,* 119–124. doi:10.1016/S1364-6613(03)00031-7

Brown, D. (1991). *Human universals.* Philadelphia, PA: Temple University Press.

Bulbulia, J. (2004). Religious costs as adaptations that signal altruistic intention. *Evolution and Cognition, 10,* 19–42. Retrieved from http://www.kli.ac.at/evolution-and-cognition (accessed April 1, 2017).

Bulbulia, J. (2008). Free love: Religious solidarity on the cheap. In J. Bulbulia, R. Sosis, E. Harris, R. Genet, C. Genet, & K. Wyman (Eds.), *The evolution of religion: Studies, theories, and critiques* (pp. 153–160). Santa Margarita, CA: Collins Foundation Press.

Cohen, A. (2009). Many forms of culture. *American Psychologist, 64,* 194–204. doi:10.1037/a0015308

Cohen, A., & Hill, P. (2007). Religion as culture: Religious individualism and collectivism among American Catholics, Jews, and Protestants. *Journal of Personality, 75,* 709–742. doi:10.1111/j.1467-6494.2007.00454.x

Coşgel, M. (2000). The family in Utopia: Celibacy, communal child rearing, and continuity in a religious commune. *Journal of Family History, 25,* 491–503. doi:10.1177/036319900002500403

Cosmides, L., & Tooby, J. (1992). Cognitive adaptations for social exchange. In J. H. Barkow, L. Cosmides, & J. Tooby (Eds.), *The adapted mind* (pp. 163–228). New York: Oxford University Press.

Cotterill, S., Sidanius, J., Bhardwaj, A., & Kumar, V. (2014). Ideological support for the Indian caste system: Social dominance orientation, right-wing authoritarianism and karma. *Journal of Social and Political Psychology, 2,* 98–116. doi: 10.5964/jspp.v2i1.171

Csibra, G., Gergely, G., Bíró, S., Koós, O., & Brockbank, M. (1999). Goal attribution without agency cues: The perception of "pure reason" in infancy. *Cognition, 72,* 237–267. doi:10.1016/S0010-0277(99)00039-6

Dawkins, R. (1976). *The selfish gene.* Oxford: Oxford University Press.

Froese, P., & Bader, C. (2010). *America's four gods: What we say about God – & what that says about us.* New York: Oxford University Press.

Gergely, G., Nádasdy, Z., Csibra, G., & Bíró, S. (1995). Taking the intentional stance at 12 months of age. *Cognition, 56,* 165–193. doi:10.1016/0010-0277(95)00661-H

Gervais, W. (2013a). In godlessness we distrust: Using social psychology to solve the puzzle of anti-atheist prejudice. *Social and Personality Psychology Compass, 7,* 366–377. doi:10.1111/spc3.12035

Gervais, W. (2013b). Perceiving minds and gods: How mind perception enables, constrains, and is triggered by belief in gods. *Perspectives on Psychological Science, 8,* 380–394. doi:10.1177/1745691613489836

Gervais, W., & Najle, M. (2015). Learned faith: The influences of evolved cultural learning mechanisms on belief in gods. *Psychology of Religion and Spirituality, 7,* 327–335. doi:10.1037/rel0000044

Gervais, W., & Norenzayan, A. (2012). Analytic thinking promotes religious disbelief. *Science, 336,* 493–496. doi:10.1126/science.1215647

Ginges, J., Hansen, I., & Norenzayan, A. (2009). Religion and support for suicide attacks. *Psychological Science, 20,* 224–230. doi:10.1111/j.1467-9280.2009.02270.x

Goodstein, L. (2001, September 15). After the attacks: Finding fault; Falwell's finger-pointing inappropriate, Bush says. *New York Times.* Retrieved from http://www.nytimes.com/2001/09/15/us/after-attacks-finding-fault-falwell-s-finger-pointing-inappropriate-bush-says.html (accessed April 1, 2017).

Gould, S., & Lewontin, R. (1979). The spandrels of San Marco and the Panglossian paradigm: A critique of the adaptationist programme.

Proceedings of the Royal Society B, 205, 581–598. doi: 10.1098/rspb.1979.0086

Gould, S., & Vrba, E. (1982). Exaptation – a missing term in the science of form. *Paleobiology, 8,* 4–15. doi:10.1017/s0094837300004310

Gürerk, Ö., Irlenbusch, B., & Rockenbach, B. (2006). The competitive advantage of sanctioning institutions. *Science, 312,* 108–111. doi: 10.1126/science.1123633

Guthrie, S. (1980). A cognitive theory of religion. *Current Anthropology, 21,* 181–203. doi:10.1086/202429

Guthrie, S. (1993). *Faces in the clouds: A new theory of religion.* New York: Oxford University Press.

Guthrie, S. (1996). Religion: What is it? *Journal for the Scientific Study of Religion, 35,* 412–419. doi:10.2307/1386417

Hadnes, M., & Schumacher, H. (2012). The gods are watching: An experimental study of religion and traditional belief in Burkina Faso. *Journal for the Scientific Study of Religion, 51,* 689–704. doi:10.1111/j.1468-5906.2012.01676.x

Hall, D., Cohen, A., Meyer, K., Varley, A., & Brewer, G. (2015). Costly signaling increases trust, even across religious affiliations. *Psychological Science, 26,* 1368–1376. doi:10.1177/0956797615576473

Hall, D., Matz, D., & Wood, W. (2010). Why don't we practice what we preach? A meta-analytic review of religious racism. *Personality and Social Psychology Review, 14,* 126–139. doi:10.1177/1088868309352179

Hartberg, Y., Cox, M., & Villamayor-Tomas, S. (2014). Supernatural monitoring and sanctioning in community-based resource management. *Religion, Brain and Behavior.* doi:10.1080/2153599X.2014.959547

Hartland, E. (1924). *Primitive law.* London: Methuen.

Heider, F., & Simmel, M. (1944). An experimental study of apparent behavior. *American Journal of Psychology, 57,* 243–259. doi:10.2307/1416950

Henrich, J. (2004). Cultural group selection, coevolutionary processes and large-scale cooperation. *Journal of Economic Behavior and Organization, 53,* 3–35. doi:10.1016/S0167-2681(03)00094-5

Henrich, J. (2009). The evolution of costly displays, cooperation and religion: Credibility enhancing displays and their implications for cultural evolution. *Evolution and Human Behavior, 30,* 244–260. doi:10.1016/j.evolhumbehav.2009.03.005

Henrich, J., & Gil-White, F. (2001). The evolution of prestige: Freely conferred deference as a mechanism for enhancing the benefits of cultural transmission. *Evolution and Human Behavior, 22,* 165–196. doi:10.1016/S1090-5138(00)00071-4

Hoodfar, H., & Assadpour, S. (2000). The politics of population policy in the Islamic Republic of Iran. *Studies in Family Planning, 31*, 19–34. doi:10.1111/j.1728-4465.2000.00019.x

Irons, W. (2001). Religion as a hard-to-fake sign of commitment. In R. Nesse (Ed.), *Evolution and the capacity for commitment* (pp. 292–309). New York: Russell Sage Foundation.

Johnson, D. (2015). Big gods, small wonder: Supernatural punishment strikes back. *Religion, Brain and Behavior, 5*, 290–298. doi:10.1080/2153599X.2014.928356

Johnson, D. (2016). *God is watching you: How the fear of God makes us human*. New York: Oxford University Press.

Johnson, D., & Bering, J. (2006). Hand of God, mind of man: Punishment and cognition in the evolution of cooperation. *Evolutionary Psychology, 4*, 219–233. doi:10.1177/147470490600400119

Johnson, D., & Krüger, O. (2004). The good of wrath: Supernatural punishment and the evolution of cooperation. *Political Theology, 5*, 159–176. doi:10.1558/poth.2004.5.2.159

Johnson, K., Li, Y., & Cohen, A. (2015). Fundamental motives and the varieties of religious experience. *Religion, Brain and Behavior, 5*, 197–231. doi:10.1080/2153599x.2014.918684

Johnson, K., Li, Y., Cohen, A., & Okun, M. (2013). Friends in high places: The influence of authoritarian and benevolent god-concepts on social attitudes and behaviors. *Psychology of Religion and Spirituality, 5*, 15–22. doi:10.1037/a0030138

Johnson, K., White, A., Boyd, B., & Cohen, A. (2011). Matzo, meat, milk, and mana: A psychological analysis of religious cultural food practices. *Journal of Cross-Cultural Psychology, 42*, 1421–1436. doi:10.1177/0022022111412528

Kapogiannis, D., Barbey, A., Su, M., Zamboni, G., Krueger, F., & Grafman, J. (2009). Cognitive and neural foundations of religious belief. *Proceedings of the National Academy of Sciences, 106*, 4876–4881. doi:10.1073/pnas.0811717106

Kelemen, D. (2004). Are children "intuitive theists"? Reasoning about purpose and design in nature. *Psychological Science, 15*, 295–301. doi:10.1111/j.0956-7976.2004.00672.x

Kenrick, D., Maner, J., Butner, J., Li, N., Becker, D., & Schaller, M. (2002). Dynamic evolutionary psychology: Mapping the domains of the new interactionist paradigm. *Personality and Social Psychology Review, 6*, 347–356. doi:10.1207/s15327957pspr0604_09

Kühl, H., Kalan, A., Arandjelovic, M., Aubert, F., D'Auvergne, L., Goedmakers, A., ... & Boesch, C. (2016). Chimpanzee accumulative stone throwing. *Scientific Reports, 6*:22219. doi:10.1038/srep22219

Mayr, E. (1961). Cause and effect in biology: Kinds of causes, predictability, and teleology are viewed by a practicing biologist. *Science, 134*(3489), 1501–1506. doi:10.1126/science.134.3489.1501

McCullough, M., Hoyt, W., Larson, D., Koenig, H., & Thoresen, C. (2000). Religious involvement and mortality: A meta-analytic review. *Health Psychology, 19*, 211–222. doi:10.1037/0278-6133.19.3.211

McQuillan, K. (2004). When does religion influence fertility? *Population and Development Review, 30*, 25–56. doi:10.1111/j.1728-4457.2004.00002.x

Mesoudi, A. (2016). Cultural evolution: Integrating psychology, evolution and culture. *Current Opinion in Psychology, 7*, 17–22. doi:10.1016/j.copsyc.2015.07.001

Morewedge, C. (2009). Negativity bias in attribution of external agency. *Journal of Experimental Psychology: General, 138*, 535–545. doi:10.1037/a0016796

Morewedge, C., Preston, J., & Wegner, D. (2007). Timescale bias in the attribution of mind. *Journal of Personality and Social Psychology, 93*, 1–11. doi:10.1037/0022-3514.93.1.1

Murdock, G. (1980). *Theories of illness: A world survey*. Pittsburgh, PA: University of Pittsburgh Press.

Neuberg, S., Warner, C., Mistler, S., Berlin, A., Hill, E., Johnson, J., ... & Schober, J. (2014). Religion and intergroup conflict: Findings from the Global Group Relations Project. *Psychological Science, 25*, 198–206. doi:10.1177/0956797613504303

New, J., Cosmides, L., & Tooby, J. (2007). Category-specific attention for animals reflects ancestral priorities, not expertise. *Proceedings of the National Academy of Sciences, 104*, 16598–16603. doi:10.1073/pnas.0703913104

Norenzayan, A. (2013). *Big gods: How religion transformed cooperation and conflict*. Princeton, NJ: Princeton University Press.

Norenzayan, A., Gervais, W., & Trzesniewski, K. (2012). Mentalizing deficits constrain belief in a personal god. *PLoS One, 7*, e36880. doi:10.1371/journal.pone.0036880

Norenzayan, A., Hansen, I., & Cady, J. (2008). An angry volcano? Reminders of death and anthropomorphizing nature. *Social Cognition, 26*, 190–197. doi:10.1521/soco.2008.26.2.190

Orbell, J., Goldman, M., Mulford, M., & Dawes, R. (1992). Religion, context, and constraint toward strangers. *Rationality and Society, 4,* 291–307. doi:10.1177/1043463192004003004

Pennycook, G., Cheyne, J., Seli, P., Koehler, D., & Fugelsang, J. (2012). Analytic cognitive style predicts religious and paranormal belief. *Cognition, 123,* 335–346. doi:10.1016/j.cognition.2012.03.003

Pew Research Center (2015). The future of world religions: Population growth projections, 2010–2050. *Religion and Public Life,* 2 April. Washington, DC: Author. Retrieved from http://www.pewforum.org/2015/04/02/religious-projections-2010-2050/ (accessed April 1, 2017).

Piazza, J., Bering, J., & Ingram, G. (2011). "Princess Alice is watching you": Children's belief in an invisible person inhibits cheating. *Journal of Experimental Child Psychology, 109,* 311–320. doi:10.1016/j.jecp.2011.02.003

Premack, D., & Woodruff, G. (1978). Does the chimpanzee have a theory of mind? *Behavioral and Brain Sciences, 1,* 515–526. doi:10.1017/S0140525X00076512

Purzycki, B., Finkel, D., Shaver, J., Wales, N., Cohen, A., & Sosis, R. (2012). What does God know? Supernatural agents' access to socially strategic and non-strategic information. *Cognitive Science, 36,* 846–869. doi:10.1111/j.1551-6709.2012.01242.x

Pyysiäinen, I. (2009). *Supernatural agents: Why we believe in souls, gods, and buddhas.* New York: Oxford University Press.

Richerson, P., & Boyd, R. (2005). *Not by genes alone: How culture transformed human evolution.* Chicago, IL: University of Chicago Press.

Riekki, T., Lindeman, M., Aleneff, M., Halme, A., & Nuortimo, A. (2013). Paranormal and religious believers are more prone to illusory face perception than skeptics and non-believers. *Applied Cognitive Psychology, 27,* 150–155. doi:10.1002/acp.2874

Rosenkranz, P., & Charlton, B. (2013). Individual differences in existential orientation: Empathizing and systemizing explain the sex difference in religious orientation and science acceptance. *Archive for the Psychology of Religion, 35,* 119–146. doi:10.1163/15736121-12341255

Sandikci, Ö, & Ger, G. (2010). Veiling in style: How does a stigmatized practice become fashionable? *Journal of Consumer Research, 37,* 15–36. doi:10.1086/649910

Saroglou, V. (2011). Believing, bonding, behaving, and belonging: The big four religious dimensions and cultural variation. *Journal of Cross-Cultural Psychology, 42,* 1320–1340. doi:10.1177/0022022111412267

Schick, T., Jr., & Vaughn, L. (2005). *How to think about weird things.* New York: McGraw-Hill.

Schjoedt, U., Stødkilde-Jørgensen, H., Geertz, A., & Roepstorff, A. (2009). Highly religious participants recruit areas of social cognition in personal prayer. *Social Cognitive and Affective Neuroscience, 4,* 199–207. doi:10.1093/scan/nsn050

Schloss, J. (2008). He who laughs best: Involuntary religious affect as a solution to recursive cooperative defection. In J. Bulbulia, R. Sosis, E. Harris, R. Genet, C. Genet, & K. Wyman (Eds.), *The evolution of religion: Studies, theories, and critiques* (pp. 197–207). Santa Margarita, CA: Collins Foundation Press.

Shariff, A., & Norenzayan, A. (2007). God is watching you: Priming god concepts increases prosocial behavior in an anonymous economic game. *Psychological Science, 18,* 803–809. doi:10.1111/j.1467-9280.2007.01983.x

Shariff, A., & Norenzayan, A. (2011). Mean gods make good people: Different views of God predict cheating behavior. *International Journal for the Psychology of Religion, 21,* 85–96. doi:10.1080/10508619.2011.556990

Shariff, A., & Rhemtulla, M. (2012). Divergent effects of beliefs in heaven and hell on national crime rates. *PLoS One, 7,* e39048. doi:10.1371/journal.pone.0039048

Shenhav, A., Rand, D., & Greene, J. (2012). Divine intuition: Cognitive style influences belief in God. *Journal of Experimental Psychology: General, 141,* 423–428. doi:10.1037/a0025391

Skirbekk, V., Stonawski, M., Fukuda, S., Spoorenberg, T., Hackett, C., & Muttarak, R. (2015). Is Buddhism the low fertility religion of Asia? *Demographic Research, 32,* 1–28. doi:10.4054/demres.2015.32.1

Snarey, J. (1996). The natural environment's impact upon religious ethics: A cross-cultural study. *Journal for the Scientific Study of Religion, 35,* 85–96. doi:10.2307/1387077

Sosis, R. (2000). Religion and intragroup cooperation: Preliminary results of a comparative analysis of utopian communities. *Cross-Cultural Research, 34,* 70–87. doi:10.1177/106939710003400105

Sosis, R. (2003). Why aren't we all Hutterites? Costly signaling theory and religious behavior. *Human Nature, 14,* 91–127. doi:10.1007/s12110-003-1000-6

Sosis, R. (2006). Religious behaviors, badges, and bans: Signaling theory and the evolution of religion. In P. McNamara (Ed.), *Where God and science meet: How brain and evolutionary studies alter our understanding of religion. Volume 1: Evolution, genes, and the religious brain* (pp. 61–86). Westport, CT: Praeger.

Sosis, R., & Alcorta, C. (2003). Signaling, solidarity, and the sacred: The evolution of religious behavior. *Evolutionary Anthropology, 12,* 264–274. doi:10.1002/evan.10120

Sosis, R., & Bressler, E. (2003). Cooperation and commune longevity: A test of the costly signaling theory of religion. *Cross-Cultural Research, 37,* 211–239. doi:10.1177/1069397103037002003

Sosis, R., & Ruffle, B. (2003). Religious ritual and cooperation: Testing for a relationship on Israeli religious and secular kibbutzim. *Current Anthropology, 44,* 713–722. doi:10.1086/379260

Sosis, R., & Ruffle, B. (2004). Ideology, religion, and the evolution of cooperation: Field experiments on Israeli kibbutzim. *Research in Economic Anthropology, 23,* 89–117. doi:10.1016/s0190-1281(04)23004-9

Stiller, J., & Dunbar, R. (2007). Perspective-taking and memory capacity predict social network size. *Social Networks, 29,* 93–104. doi:10.1016/j.socnet.2006.04.001

Strömwall, L., Alfredsson, H., & Landström, S. (2013). Blame attributions and rape: Effects of belief in a just world and relationship level. *Legal and Criminological Psychology, 18,* 254–261. doi:10.1111/j.2044-8333.2012.02044.x

Swanson, G. (1960). *The birth of the gods: The origin of primitive beliefs.* Ann Arbor: University of Michigan Press.

Tashman, B. (2011). Joyner: Hurricane Katrina was God's judgment for homosexuality. *Right Wing Watch,* June 29. Retrieved from http://www.rightwingwatch.org/content/joyner-hurricane-katrina-was-gods-judgment-homosexuality (accessed July 13, 2017).

Tashman, B. (2016, February 12). Rick Wiles: Zika virus God's punishment for "worshiping death." *Right Wing Watch.* Retrieved from http://www.rightwingwatch.org/post/rick-wiles-zika-virus-gods-punishment-for-worshiping-death/

USA Today (2012, 2 November). Some Muslim clerics say Sandy is God's punishment. Retrieved from http://www.usatoday.com/story/news/world/2012/11/02/america-hurricane-sandy-muslim/1676683/ (accessed April 1, 2017).

van Elk, M. (2013). Paranormal believers are more prone to illusory agency detection than skeptics. *Consciousness and Cognition, 22,* 1041–1046. doi:10.1016/j.concog.2013.07.004

van Elk, M., Rutjens, B., van der Pligt, J., & van Harreveld, F. (2016). Priming of supernatural agent concepts and agency detection. *Religion, Brain and Behavior,* 6, 4–33, doi:10.1080/2153599X.2014.933444

Weeden, J., Cohen, A., & Kenrick, D. (2008). Religious attendance as reproductive support. *Evolution and Human Behavior, 29,* 327–334. doi:10.1016/j.evolhumbehav.2008.03.004

Westh, P. (2014). Anthropomorphism in god concepts: The role of narrative. In A. Geertz (Ed.), *Origins of religion, cognition and culture* (pp. 396–414). Abingdon, UK: Routledge.

Westoff, C., & Jones, E. (1979). The end of "Catholic" fertility. *Demography, 16,* 209–217. doi:10.2307/2061139

Whitehouse, H. (2004). *Modes of religiosity: A cognitive theory of religious transmission.* Walnut Creek, CA: AltaMira Press.

Whiten, A., Goodall, J., McGrew, W., Nishida, T., Reynolds, V., Sugiyama, Y., … & Boesch, C. (1999). Cultures in chimpanzees. *Nature, 399,* 682–685. doi:10.1038/21415

Wilson, D. (2002). *Darwin's cathedral: Evolution, religion, and the nature of society.* Chicago, IL: University of Chicago Press.

Wood, J. (2010). Between God and a hard place. *New York Times,* 23 January. Retrieved from http://www.nytimes.com/2010/01/24/opinion/24wood.html (accessed April 1, 2017).

Xygalatas, D., Mitkidis, P., Fischer, R., Reddish, P., Skewes, J., Geertz, A., … & Bulbulia, J. (2013). Extreme rituals promote prosociality. *Psychological Science, 24,* 1602–1605. doi: 10.1177/0956797612472910

Yilmaz, O., & Bahçekapili, H. G. (2016). Supernatural and secular monitors promote human cooperation only if they remind of punishment. *Evolution and Human Behavior, 37,* 79–84. doi:10.1016/j.evolhumbehav.2015.09.005

Zhang, L. (2008). Religious affiliation, religiosity, and male and female fertility. *Demographic Research, 18,* 233–262. doi:10.4054/DemRes.2008.18.8

Zuckerman, P. (2008). *Society without God: What the least religious nations can tell us about contentment.* New York: New York University Press.

Part II

Animal Culture

4

Introduction to Animal Culture: Is Culture Uniquely Human?

Charles T. Snowdon

Consider whether the following are examples of culture:

1) Archaeologists can identify clear assemblages of tools at various sites, and by dating the tools and examining the skills needed to create the tools they can identify specific ancient cultures and distinguish between different hominid species according to the typicality of the tools used. These cultural artifacts are important clues to understanding our ancestors as well as understanding the evolution of our own species.
2) Different populations in Africa feed on nuts from palm or panda trees. However, not all populations feed on the same species of nuts and some populations do not eat these nuts at all, even though they are very abundant. Extracting the edible portions of these nuts takes considerable skill, and youngsters may take several years to master the techniques to open these nuts. In some parts of Africa a large stone serves as an anvil and a smaller stone as a hammer.
3) In South America also there are populations that use stone tools to crack open nuts, but there are also several other populations where nuts are not eaten and stone tool use has not been observed.
4) In parts of Australia and New Guinea, males can attract mates by constructing large artistic-seeming works made of wood, stone, feathers, and moss and other vegetation. These constructions vary in different locations, with different shapes and styles, different building materials and different colors of materials. Males tend these structures carefully, cleaning up debris, and the structures persist across generations. However, within a given population there is consistency in style among neighbors.

The Handbook of Culture and Biology, First Edition. Edited by José M. Causadias, Eva H. Telzer and Nancy A. Gonzales.

5) In the United States there are different regional dialects, with clearly different patterns in North Carolina, Texas, Indiana and South Dakota. Studies indicate that females tend to prefer as mates males who share the same dialect. However, especially attentive males from other regions can use subtle feedback from females to change their dialects to match the preferences of females and thus become successful suitors.

In each of the above cases we have evidence of culture defined thus: "Culture is a shared system of behaviors (and cognitions) that are transmitted from one generation to the next. This shared system of behavior serves a function within the group and applies to a group that has a shared history (geographical, social)" (see Causadias, Telzer, & Gonzales, chapter 1 in this volume). In each case the behavior patterns described (1) are limited to specific groups or populations, (2) show some evidence of continuity across generations, (3) vary across different groups or populations but are consistent within each group, (4) show evidence of being to at least some degree learned; that is, the behaviors cannot be explained purely by genetic inheritance. I think most of us could accept these vignettes as evidence of culture.

Now what will you think if I tell you that only example 1 is from human beings, that example 2 is from chimpanzees (*Pan troglodytes*), that example 3 is from brown capuchin monkeys (*Cebus libidinosis*), that example 4 is from bowerbirds (family *Ptilonorhynchidae*) and that example 5 is from cowbirds (*Molothrus ater*)? Will you still accept these as examples of culture? If you are skeptical about these examples, what is the difference between human animals and non-human animals that leads you to reject the idea of culture? Many definitions of culture include language, but this automatically leads to the exclusion from consideration of any non-human, and any non-linguistic human. A good operational definition should be able to produce testable hypotheses through experiments or careful observational data of actual behavior. A good operational definition cannot be "speciesist," that is, only applicable to our own species. Our editors' definition allows us to at least consider the idea of culture in non-human species, and indeed this part of the book will provide several intriguing examples of culture (or tradition) in non-human species.

However, even among researchers on animal behavior there is considerable controversy over whether to assert that animals have culture or not (see reviews in Laland & Janik, 2006; Laland & Galef, 2009). Researchers trained in anthropology and some trained in psychology see an important difference between human culture and traditions that may appear in non-human animals. In their views human culture is cumulative: one innovation builds on another (consider the development of long-distance communication from Pony Express and telegraph to airmail and the telephone and to cell phones and the internet). Cultural traits have symbolic aspects that help identify a population and define it as separate from others. Although some species of non-human animals have group norms, they do not appear to have the identifying symbolism that team colors or a certain dress style or preferred musical style have for humans. Finally, skeptics argue that it is only through true imitation learning that a cultural pattern can be transmitted with fidelity. Only recently have these researchers accepted that imitation has been shown in some non-human species.

At the other end of the spectrum of the animal culture debates are the enthusiasts, often trained in biology, who see value in documenting evolutionary continuity, rather than finding human uniqueness. These researchers vary in the criteria they use for culture, but some argue that any behavioral pattern that is transmitted by social learning could qualify as culture. This criterion brings a wide array of behaviors and non-human species into the picture, as illustrated by the examples that began this chapter.

In the rest of this chapter, I will first consider the several criteria that are considered necessary for culture, excluding language and symbolic constructs, and how these can be applied to non-human animals. It might be interesting to reflect on how many of these criteria can be met for patterns considered cultural in humans. Then I will consider potential mechanisms for cultural transmission from one generation to another, specifically social learning and teaching and the social climate that promotes these behaviors. Finally, I will discuss gene–cultural evolution, including some recent work on epigenetics that addresses how culture can change genes and gene expression. All of these points have relevance to making the case for culture in non-human species.

Criteria for Culture

Primatologist William McGrew (1992) developed a set of criteria for evaluating the presence of culture in wild chimpanzees that was based on writing by the cultural anthropologist Alfred Kroeber (1928) about his observations of captive chimpanzees. Kroeber developed six operational criteria for recognizing culture in other species; McGrew added two others, and I will add two more (see Table 4.1). Let me consider each of these in turn.

Table 4.1 Criteria for culture (in humans and other animals)

Characteristic	Criterion
Innovation	A new behavioral pattern must appear
Dissemination	The pattern cannot be unique to the innovator but must be seen in others
Standardization	The pattern should be consistent across individuals
Durability	The pattern should appear without the presence of the demonstrator
Diffusion	The pattern should transfer to other social groups
Tradition	The pattern should occur over generations and outlive the innovator
Independence of subsistence	The pattern should not be directly related to subsistence, though it can relate to ways of processing subsistence resources
Naturalness	The pattern should arise within the species without human influence
Independence of ecology and genetics	Differences in behavior must be independent of genetic or ecological differences between populations
Social learning	The pattern should be transmitted through some social interaction with the demonstrator rather than by trial-and-error learning

Source: Adapted and modified from McGrew, 1992

Innovation

A novel behavioral pattern must be observed. This is perhaps the most difficult criterion to meet, since it is likely to be rare for an observer to see an innovation develop and persist across generations. In a review of innovation in non-human primates Reader and Laland (2001) noted that older males were the most likely to show novel behaviors, but they were rarely followed by others and thus their innovations rarely spread to other group members. Innovations often arise in times of scarcity of food or other resources and are more common among low-ranking animals with less access to resources, supporting the adage that "necessity is the mother of invention" (Reader & Laland, 2003). An innovation that is not adopted by others has no future as culture. Innovation might be inferred when one observes a problem which has multiple possible solutions being solved in different ways by different populations or groups. Innovation may also be promoted in captive animals by providing a novel task which has different possible solutions.

An example from captive common marmosets (*Callithrix jacchus*) is that one individual learned to use its mouth to remove the lid on a film canister to obtain food and other marmosets imitated the innovator (Voelkl & Huber, 2000). A second example of experimenter-induced innovation is by Aplin and colleagues (2015), who created an automated puzzle box, with two alternative solutions, for use by wild great tits (*Parus major*). Two males in each of five sub-populations were trained in one solution, and within 20 days 75% of the birds in these sub-populations were solving the puzzle, the majority of solutions matching those of the trained males.

There are a few examples from natural populations with minimal human influence. The first is of stone play in Japanese macaques (*Macaca fuscata*); Huffman (1984) first observed this in a single individual in 1979 at Arashiyama near Kyoto and has subsequently tracked the spread of stone play to the entire population, and to multiple populations throughout Japan (Leca, Gunst, & Huffman, 2007). Another example, described by Van Leeuwen, Cronin, and Haun (2014), concerns chimpanzees at a sanctuary in Zambia: an innovation of placing a blade of grass in the ear developed and spread throughout one group, but not to any of the other groups at the sanctuary. Sapolsky and Share (2004) describe the emergence of a pacific culture among wild olive baboons (*Papio anubis*) that developed after the deaths of the most aggressive males in the group. The non-aggressive culture persisted even after the death or migration of all the males present at the time of the innovation. Incoming males are shaped by resident females to be less aggressive. It is rare to directly observe innovation in natural populations, and yet culture differences must at some level be due to innovation.

Dissemination

An innovation cannot become a cultural trait unless others pick up and adopt the same behavior. Novel behavior must spread throughout a group or population and be adapted by most individuals. As with innovation, the process of dissemination is also rarely and fortuitously observed, but dissemination can be inferred if most, or all, members of a group show the behavior. McGrew (1992) distinguishes between dissemination – the transmission of a novel behavior within a population – and "diffusion" – the transmission of behaviors between populations, but more recent papers have used "diffusion" synonymously with "dissemination." I will discuss

McGrew's (1992) idea of diffusion later. Whiten, Caldwell, and Mesoudi (2016) provide a current review of dissemination.

There are some observations of dissemination. Observations of potato washing and stone play in Japanese macaques have shown that the behavior spreads horizontally to peers and then vertically to mothers. The innovators of potato washing and stone play were juvenile females, and the behaviors spread first to other juveniles and then to their mothers. In this matriarchal species, adult males were the last to acquire the behavior, and generally only those males who engaged in the behavior as juveniles acquired the behavior. Males who were adult at the time of the innovation failed to acquire the task (Kawai, 1965).

In an experimental study van de Waal, Borheaud, and Whiten (2013) provided several groups of vervet monkeys (*Chlorocebus aethiops*) with maize kernels that were artificially colored; one color had been made noxious through a bitter taste, the other had not. Four to six months after the initial training the same-colored kernels were again presented, but with no bitter taste to either. Monkeys continued to eat the kernels whose color was associated with palatable taste. All of the infants born into a group ingested kernels of the color ingested by their mothers, and males migrating into a group from groups where the alternative color had been palatable adapted to the color preference of their new group.

The actual mechanisms of acquisition are difficult to discern in a wild population, but newly developed methods of network-based diffusion analysis have been used with lobtail feeding in humpback whales (*Megaptera novaeangliae*) (Allen, Weinrich, Hoppitt, & Rendell, 2013), transmission of a novel foraging task in great tits (Aplin et al., 2015) and transmission of a novel tool use method in chimpanzees (Hobaiter, Poisot, Zuberbühler, Hoppitt, & Gruber, 2014). In all three studies a model that includes some form of social transmission accounted for a much higher proportion of dissemination than models based on individual learning. Although these studies demonstrate that social transmission is involved, they beg the question of exactly how the social transmission occurs. This will be discussed in the section on mechanisms later in the chapter.

Standardization

If a behavior is to be identified as cultural, there must be some sort of standardization or conformity among group members. An individually idiosyncratic behavior cannot be considered an example of culture. On the other hand, a behavior that is similar in all groups and populations of a species is unlikely to be considered as culture. Thus there must be some differentiation between populations but standardization or conformity within a population. Through observations, one can assess the degree to which all members of a group share the same behavior, and one can observe whether newcomers to a group, be they immigrants or infants, acquire the behavior. In the study on vervet monkeys, both newly immigrant males and newborn infants showed the group preference for the color of kernels, suggesting clear mechanisms for conformity (van de Waal et al., 2013; Botting, van de Waal, & Rendell, chapter 5 in this volume). In chimpanzees, where females migrate to new groups after puberty, Luncz and Boesch (2014) reported that different communities within their population at Tai Forest in Ivory Coast had different preferences for the material and size of hammers used for nut cracking. Observations of females transferring from one community to another over a 35-year period found that immigrant females adopted the material and hammer size of their new community, rather than using the materials of their natal community. Detailed observations of one immigrant female found that, although her behavior differed from that of the new community during her first year of residence, she had conformed to the group behavior by her second year of residence. In another example, Gunhold, Massen, Schiel, Souto, and Bugnyar (2014) trained groups of wild common marmosets to solve a foraging task in one of two ways and then retested the groups three years later. They found that infants and juveniles that had been born into the group since the initial training, as well as new immigrants to the group, maintained the group-specific method of solving the task. Kendal and colleagues (2015) found that chimpanzees copied the behavior of dominant and knowledgeable individuals, a pattern that leads to greater conformity or standardization but also decreases innovation. Thus, there is considerable evidence for standardization and conformity.

Durability

Cultural traits must persist beyond the presence of the innovator and beyond the presence of the demonstrator for an individual learner. Cultural behavior should not be something that occurs idiosyncratically but should instead be stable over a considerable period of time relative to the lifespan of the individuals showing it. Several studies have demonstrated durability. Aplin and colleagues (2015) tested great tits a year after initial training and after the removal of the foraging devices, and found that the birds showed the same degree of fidelity to the originally trained solution as they had in the first weeks after training. Gunhold and Bugnyar (2014) found that common marmosets tested three years after initial exposure to a specific mode of performing a foraging task persisted in using the same solution. Luncz and Boesch (2014) reported that over a 25-year period the community-specific preferences for material and size of hammers for nut cracking remained consistent, and Sapolsky and Share (2004) reported the persistence of pacific behavior among male baboons even after the death or dispersal of all of the original males.

Perhaps the most impressive evidence for durability comes from archaeological excavations in Ivory Coast, where behaviorally modified anvil stones have been dated to 4,300 years ago (Mercader et al., 2007). Many of these stones contain residues of starch, which suggests that they were actually used for opening nuts. Furthermore, the age of these stones predates any settled human habitations in the area, making it highly likely that these stones were used by ancient chimpanzees in much the same way as modern chimpanzees in the same area. (Stone tool use may have been reinvented at a later time, but it is more parsimonious to assume continuity.) Across a range of species and time, there is clear evidence for durability of cultural behavior.

Diffusion

As noted earlier, McGrew (1992) defined diffusion as a spread of behavior from one community or population to another, whereas contemporary authors have used the term "diffusion" synonymously with McGrew's term of "dissemination." There is a logical problem in seeking diffusion across populations or communities if at the same time cultural behaviors are defined as population-specific with a long duration. McGrew cites an example of diffusion of the use of termite fishing from one community to another in the Mahale Mountain population in Tanzania (Takahata, 1982). However, other studies suggest a resistance to acquiring a behavior from outside the community: immigrants generally acquire the behavior of the resident community. This has been shown in chimpanzees (Luncz & Boesch, 2014), vervet monkeys (van de Waal et al., 2013), baboons (Sapolsky & Share, 2004) and common marmosets (Gunhold et al., 2014). Thus, diffusion (*sensu* McGrew) appears to be relatively rare, and yet examples of diffusion from one group to another can also serve as a marker of innovation for the group that does not yet show the behavior.

Tradition

Given that chimpanzees in Ivory Coast have been using the same hammer and anvil methods to crack nuts for more than four millennia it is clear that some transmission across generations has occurred, leading to a tradition. Other recent studies have found that infants born after training on a novel foraging device acquire the behavior demonstrated to the group (chimpanzees, Luncz & Boesch, 2014; vervet monkeys, van de Waal et al., 2013; savannah baboons, Sapolsky & Share, 2004; common marmosets, Gunhold et al., 2014). The potato-washing behavior initially shown by one Japanese macaque has continued after her death, and most of the early innovators of stone play as documented by Huffman (1984) are unlikely to be alive. Thus, we have both direct evidence through experimental manipulation and indirect evidence through naturalistic observation that tradition is a component of cultural behavior in non-human animals.

Non-Subsistence

This criterion and the next were added by McGrew (1992) to the initial list from Kroeber (1928). Both are important criteria for evaluating the natural history of cultural behavior. The early and famous work on potato washing and tossing wheat kernels into water (where sand sinks and wheat floats) in Japanese macaques (Kawai, 1965) has been criticized, since these monkeys were provisioned by humans who may have shaped their behavior through selective reinforcement of behavioral tendencies already seen in Japanese macaques (Galef, 1992). Supporting this idea is that population-specific food calls in Japanese macaques were likely to have been reinforced by humans provisioning the monkeys (Green, 1975; Masataka, 1992). These critiques can be answered in the case of Japanese macaques by the discovery of stone play in the same species (Huffman, 1984), which behavior cannot be explained in terms of provisioning by humans.

The majority of the studies described so far, both experimental and observational, have involved food of some sort. The majority of cultural behaviors described for chimpanzees (Whiten et al., 1999) are subsistence-related. In fact, necessity has been named the mother of animal innovation and tradition (Reader & Laland, 2003). However, there are some cases of non-subsistence behaviors in non-human animals. Chimpanzees in the Mahale Mountains in Tanzania have a grooming handclasp behavior, in which each animal holds on to the hand or arm of its partner with one hand while they groom each other with the other hand (McGrew & Tutin,

1978). In the same population males tear up leaves in front of females as part of a courtship display. Van Leeuwen and colleagues (2014) describe other non-subsistence behaviors in sanctuary-housed chimpanzees, and Perry and colleagues (2003) have described several non-subsistence behaviors in capuchin monkeys (*Cebus apella*).

Naturalness

Naturalness is important, since cultural behavior should have developed in the absence of intervention by human experimenters or observers. In the majority of chimpanzee field sites, early researchers used food provisioning as a way to rapidly habituate animals to observation. Thus we do not know to what degree culture-like behaviors were shaped inadvertently by provisioning or are natural. Although many of the criteria for cultural patterns cannot be observed directly and experimental interventions are required to demonstrate them, a true cultural behavior in non-human animals must be something that is independent of human intervention. At the time McGrew (1992) was writing, only the chimpanzee site at Tai Forest in Ivory Coast had never had any provisioning, and thus all behaviors seen in that population could be considered natural. Fortunately, this is one of the sites that have shown impressive tool use to open palm and panda nuts (Boesch & Boesch-Achermann, 2000), is the location of the archaeological material suggesting this type of tool use has been going on for millennia and pre-dates human settlement in the area (Mercader et al., 2007), and is the site that demonstrates variation between adjacent communities and best demonstrates standardization, durability and transmission (Luncz & Boesch, 2014).

Independence of Ecology and Genetics

There are two additional criteria that I think are quite important. First, if nut-cracking chimpanzees were only found in areas where stones and hard-to-open palm nuts were found, it would be difficult to advance culture as an explanation of behavioral variation when ecological variation would be a more parsimonious explanation. Fortunately, for the case of stone tools and nut cracking (and many other cultural behaviors in chimpanzees) there is clear evidence that stones and palm nuts are abundant in areas where chimpanzees have not been observed to use stone tools or to crack nuts. Nonetheless, it is wise to rule out ecological explanations before concluding that a behavior is cultural. Mitani, Hasegawa, Gros-Louis, Marler, and

Byrne (1992) have demonstrated variation in the structure of chimpanzee pant-hoots (a conspicuous long-distance vocalization at different sites in East Africa). While it is tempting to conclude that differing vocal structures are cultural, alternative explanations could include genetic drift due to long separations of populations or variations in habitat structure that might constrain call structure (Mitani, Hunley, & Murdoch, 1999). Habitat differences may constrain the distance over which a call can travel or may lead to degradation of some components of a call and thus shape call variation. The same concerns can be applied to the variation that exists between different populations of various bird species. However, for migrating birds who may not return to the same breeding location each year and change their song to match other males in the new breeding area in which they settle (e.g. Payne & Payne, 1997), genetic drift can be ruled out as a mechanism, and the habitats in which birds of a given species are likely to breed successfully are unlikely to differ enough to impose change on song structure (but this latter point is a speculation).

One of the major arguments for culture in chimpanzees has been ant-dipping behavior, in which chimpanzees in East Africa use long sticks to collect biting ants and collect ants on their hand to ingest them, whereas at Tai Forest in West Africa chimpanzees use short sticks and pass the ants directly to their mouth. However, Humle and Matsuzawa (2002) found both techniques being used in another West African population; here, chimpanzees used longer sticks with a more aggressive species of ant and shorter sticks with a less aggressive species, which shows the difficulty of completely controlling for potential ecological differences. This study is often used to disparage notions of cultural behavior in chimpanzees. Nonetheless, some sort of cultural behavior could still be present (with many of the criteria listed above being met), but the behavior would simply be more complex and differentiated by micro-ecological variation.

Social Learning

Almost all researchers agree that behavior indicative of culture requires some sort of social transmission. If each organism discovered the behavioral pattern on its own with no influence from other group members, we would be unlikely to consider it cultural. Both skeptics and enthusiasts of animal culture agree that social learning is critical, although they may differ on the type of social learning that is necessary and sufficient, and skeptics would say that although social learning is necessary, it is not sufficient to establish culture. The types of social learning and how it relates to culture will be discussed in greater detail below.

Mechanisms of Cultural Transmission

The preceding section described several criteria that can be used to determine whether cultural behavior can be inferred in a non-human species. In this section I want to describe some of the social mechanisms for cultural transmission. Novel behaviors might appear and become stable within a population if somehow the environment provides a means for each individual to acquire a behavior on its own through trial-and-error learning. However, such a mechanism would be inefficient and would be likely to lead to several alternative behaviors within the same population. An important component of culture is social transmission among individuals. Social transmission is highly efficient and assures a great deal of behavioral conformity that would be unlikely to occur with individual trial-and-error learning. First I will discuss social tolerance as a basis for social learning. Then I will discuss different types of social learning, including teaching.

Social Tolerance

A key component that encourages social learning is social tolerance and a relative lack of hierarchy. Coussi-Korbel and Fragaszy (1995) provided a theoretical argument for the conditions under which social learning would be optimized. To be successful a naïve individual must be able to closely observe the behavior of a knowledgeable individual and the knowledgeable individual must tolerate the close presence and attention of the naïve individual. Species vary widely in the degree to which organisms tolerate the close presence of others, and across different breeding systems the individuals who can be close to others may vary. Thus, in hierarchical societies of macaques, baboons and chimpanzees, mothers and offspring will tolerate each other and allow the close observation needed to acquire a behavioral skill more than, say, a dominant male and subordinate females. Thus in hierarchical species, social transmission might be maximized among mother–offspring pairs and among peers with similar social status. In cooperatively breeding species such as marmosets and tamarins, in which behavioral hierarchies are minimal, social learning might be expected to occur more readily and among almost all group members. Coussi-Korbel and Fragaszy (1995) would predict faster social learning among relatively egalitarian species, and these species might be a better place to look for cultural transmission than among more hierarchical species such as chimpanzees.

However, there is considerable within-species variation in social tolerance. Cronin, van Leeuven, Vreeman, and Haun (2014) have described variation in what they call "social climate" in groups of sanctuary-housed chimpanzees living in identical feeding and ecological conditions, some groups being more willing to share resources as well as showing greater social tolerance. The groups with greater social tolerance would be predicted to show more rapid social learning and thus a more rapid spread of any innovation.

Types of Social Learning and Teaching

Whiten and Ham (1992) compiled a taxonomy of mechanisms by which behavior can be altered through social processes. They distinguish between social influence, in which animal B's behavior is influenced by the behavior of A but B does not learn directly from A, and social learning, where B is learning some aspect of behavior directly from its interaction with A. Whiten and Ham (1992) consider the following: social contagion, whereby an action by A stimulates a similar action by B; exposure, where, by virtue of being close to A, B is exposed to a similar learning environment; social support, where the presence of A has an effect on B's motivation and thus its ability to learn; and matched dependent learning, where B uses an act of A that is similar to its own as a stimulus for making similar responses.

However, direct social learning is of more interest for cultural transmission. Whiten and Ham (1992) described four categories. The first is stimulus or local enhancement. An observer's attention is drawn to something produced by a demonstrator and by trial-and-error learning acquires the same solution as the demonstrator, although without mimicking the actions involved. The second is observational conditioning: an animal learns not only about attention to something in the environment but also about its significance. For example, Mineka, Davidson, Cook, and Keir (1984) showed that captive-born monkeys rapidly acquired a fear of snakes by watching a caught wild monkey reach fearfully toward the snake. The third category is imitation. This takes place when B is learning some form of behavior by its observations of A. Thus a young male songbird listening to the songs of adult birds in a given location will produce the exact form of the song when it becomes an adult, or an ape will copy the exact form of the behavior that a demonstrator uses to solve a task. Initially this was considered to be the epitome of social learning as it appeared to require from the observer a deep understanding of the intentions of the demonstrator, something perhaps only a human being could do (Tomasello, 1990). However, the discovery of mirror neurons in macaques (Di Pellegrino, Fadiga, Fogassi, Gallese, & Rizzolatti, 1992) and subsequently in other species showed that imitation did not require complex cognition as originally thought, and in recent years imitation has been demonstrated in a variety of species. The final mechanism is goal emulation, which occurs when organism B learns which goal A is pursuing and pursues the same goal, without necessarily imitating the actions of A. Because emulation does not require precise following of actions, it has been thought to be of less value to culture than imitation, but recent work by Whiten, McGuigan, Marshall-Pescini, and Hopper (2009) shows the involvement of both imitation and emulation in the acquisition of novel skills in children and chimpanzees, with children engaging in over-imitation (and thus not finding the most efficient solution to a problem). However, chimpanzees are in general more conservative and conforming, whereas children showed cumulative learning ability.

Many of these definitions of social processes may appear to be fairly arbitrary and hair-splitting, and indeed many pages have been devoted to arguing whether a given study of non-human animals has or has not shown one of these mechanisms. However, I think it is valuable to consider all of these mechanisms as potential ways in which an innovative behavior might be passed on to others and become stable within a population. Acquiring a particular novel skill from others may, in reality, involve aspects of social contagion, local enhancement, observational learning and emulation. For example, a young chimpanzee learning to use stone tools to crack open nuts is attracted to other group members, especially its mother and peers, becomes interested in the stones used, may scavenge bits of nuts remaining after another has opened a nut, may emulate the goal of opening a nut and may finally develop specific motor skills to be as successful as its mother.

There remains one final mechanism that is more rarely discussed than these others, namely teaching. Teaching is a highly effective method that humans use to transfer behavioral skills to others. Can we find or even define teaching in non-human animals? Caro and Hauser (1992) provided three criteria to demonstrate if teaching exists in non-human animals. A teacher must behave differently with naïve individuals than with experienced individuals. There must be a cost to the teacher and there must be a change in the behavior of the naïve animal as a result. The clearest evidence of teaching has been seen in cooperatively breeding mammals; this will be discussed in greater detail in chapter 6, on culture in cooperatively breeding animals. Teaching has been observed in feeding contexts in meerkats (*Suricata suricatta*) (Thornton & McAuliffe, 2006), and in food sharing in marmoset and tamarin monkeys (Rapaport, 2011). In striking contrast to the teaching behavior seen in meerkats, marmosets, and tamarins, chimpanzee mothers feeding on dangerous biting army ants show no evidence of teaching or any form of assistance to their infants (Humle, Snowdon, & Matsuzawa, 2009).

Gene–Culture Coevolution and Epigenetics

After arguing that culture should not have a genetic component I now want to argue that genes and culture may interact closely. I will first present a brief summary of gene–culture coevolution with some examples and then explore the relatively new field of epigenetics, which shows that various types of experience can permanently or transiently alter gene expression, leading to non-genomic transmission of behavior from one generation to another.

Gene–Culture Coevolution

In an attempt to synthesize the influences of genetics and of culture several biologists have attempted modeling that involved both genetics and culture (e.g. Cavalli-Sforza & Feldman, 1981). Key concepts are that cultural evolution can be slow and genetic evolution can occur rapidly, and that humans (and other species) have the capacity to construct their own ecological niches, which may influence changes in the genome. By constructing nests or other shelters, and adopting novel food-processing techniques and the like, organisms can alter the environmental influences that influence natural selection. Thus, cultural changes might lead to genetic changes. A key example used to describe this idea is the coincidence of dairy cattle with the ability of adult humans to break down lactose. The raising of dairy cattle in Africa is thought to be coincident with areas without the tsetse fly, which transmits sleeping sickness. Subsequently, in order to utilize dairy products more fully, adults retained the lactase enzyme, which breaks down lactose into simple sugars. Thus, the development of dairy farming has led to a genetic change in some human populations to allow adults to metabolize milk sugar (Simoons, 1969, 1976). Since yogurt and some forms of cheese contain reduced lactose, the development of these dairy products may have allowed the gradual adaptation to milk in some human populations. There are few examples as well developed among non-human animals, but one can imagine how the construction of a new niche coupled with rapid genetic change could lead to gene–culture coevolution in other species. For a general introduction to this topic see Laland and Brown (2011).

Epigenetics

The idea of epigenetics is closely related to gene–culture coevolution and provides a mechanism for how environmental (or cultural) change can effect gene expression. The term "epigenetics" was first used by Kuo (1967) to describe how seemingly innate behaviors in animals might be influenced through processes occurring *in utero* or *in ovo*. Kuo (1967) studied the behavior of chickens and reported that the pecking response developed *in ovo* and was determined by the fetal heartbeat moving the head and neck in a pattern that essentially trained the chick's pecking responses before it hatched. Modern epigenetics has taken a different approach to determining how environmental factors shape gene expression.

Perhaps the best-known example of epigenetics is research on maternal licking behavior in rodents. Mothers vary in the amount of licking and grooming they give their pups, and pups that experience a high amount of maternal licking have lower levels of the stress hormone corticosterone and are behaviorally more resistant to stress. Daughters groom their infants in the way their mothers groomed them. Thus daughters of mothers with high rates of maternal licking will do the same to their infants and so on. Francis, Diorio, Liu, and Meaney (1999) cross-fostered pups born to high-licking mothers with low-licking mothers and vice versa, and showed that this transgenerational effect was not transmitted genetically but as a result of behavior, since cross-fostered infants acquired the behavior of their foster mothers. High rates of maternal grooming led to the expression of oxytocin receptors in females and vasopressin receptors in males (Francis, Young, Meaney, & Insel, 2002). Oxytocin increases feelings of trust and vasopressin influences positive social behavior in males. Finally, this effect has been shown to be mediated through methylation of the estrogen receptor (Champagne, 2008). The addition of a methyl group to a strand of DNA blocks its ability to produce messenger RNA and thus blocks transcription of the protein encoded by that gene.

In another example of epigenetics, Bester-Meredith and Marler (2001) cross-fostered two species of deer mice. The California mouse (*Peromyscus californicus*) is strictly monogamous (Ribble, 1991) and territorial, and paternal care is common. The white-footed mouse (*Peromyscus leucopus*) is promiscuous, non-territorial, and non-paternal. Bester-Meredith and Marler (2001) found an epigenetic transmission of territorial aggression, paternal care, and vasopressin activity in cross-fostered compared with in-fostered mice. Paternal behavior, territorial aggression, and immunoreactive staining of vasopressin in the bed nucleus of the stria terminalis were all reduced in cross-fostered California mice compared with in-fostered mice. Cross-fostering also led to increased aggression in white-footed mice compared with in-fostering. Thus, cross-fostering changed behavior and the expression of vasopressin in the brain. Frazier, Trainor, Cravens, Whitney, and Marler (2006) looked at which variables led to behavioral change. Male offspring of either species developed the paternal care and territorial aggression patterns of California mice only if fathers were present in the families. More specifically, the number of paternal retrievals when infants left the nest was the main variable that explained variation in paternal behavior, territorial aggression, and staining of vasopressin neurons in the brain. Thus, it is the behavior of the fathers before weaning takes place that shapes the subsequent behavior of the offspring he cares for. In effect, fathers are creating a cultural pattern of paternal care and territorial defense through the way in which they interact (or do not interact) with infants.

Many other examples of epigenetics are emerging. In rats the presence of estrogen at the neonatal stage of development leads to masculinization of play and mounting behavior in males. Injections of estrogen into female neonates also masculinize their behavior, but, remarkably, so do injections of dopamine into the brain (A. P. Auger, 2001). Since dopamine is associated with motivation and reward, this suggests that other processes that increase brain dopamine levels could also influence sex-typical behavior. However, epigenetic effects do not occur only early in development, but can also be seen in adults and be reversible. For example, C. A. Auger, Coss, A. P. Auger, and Forbes-Lorman (2011) found that castrating an adult male rat led to methylation of the testosterone receptor and demethylation of the estrogen receptor. Replacing testosterone in castrated males reversed the process, leading to methylation of the estrogen receptor and demethylation of the testosterone receptor.

One more example comes from non-human primates. Rhesus macaques, like humans, have two forms of the serotonin transponder gene, and monkeys with two long forms of the gene show normal behavior. Some monkeys with short alleles demonstrated increased impulsivity and alcohol intake and decreased alertness as neonates, but this was dependent on rearing condition. Monkeys with short alleles and stressful rearing conditions exhibited deficits but monkeys with short alleles reared normally did not (Barr et al., 2003; Bennett et al., 2002; Champoux et al., 2002).

While the studies to date may not seem to bear directly on the issue of culture, what emerges is the suggestion that what an individual experiences (as either an infant or an adult) can modify gene expression, which in turn affects the influence that individual has on others, which leads to a long-lasting behavioral change. It is not too far-fetched to think that the socially tolerant groups of chimpanzees studied by Cronin and colleagues (2014) or the newly pacific baboon groups of Sapolsky and Share (2004) might continue into the future because a combination of behavioral and epigenetic effects has created a lasting social culture. It is also tempting to speculate that many species differences in behavior may be initiated by seemingly random variations in behavioral development that can produce lasting effects.

Conclusions and Future Directions

Some forms of culture (or tradition) can develop in non-human species, and the criteria advanced for evaluating whether culture exists in non-human animals can provide a rigorous standard for evaluating human culture as well. It is easy to assume that we know what culture is in humans, but our assumptions may not always be accurate. The extensive work that has been done on social transmission of behavior in non-human animals also provides some rigorous methods for understanding how human culture is transmitted. Although animal researchers have developed a taxonomy of social mechanisms, it is important to recognize that multiple mechanisms may be involved simultaneously in the transfer of information from one organism to another. The recent emergence of modern epigenetics suggests a novel mechanism whereby cultural experiences can modify gene expression, and thus illustrates a close interaction of genes and the environment.

For psychologists there is value in at least thinking about cultural phenomena in non-human animals. The culture-in-animals debates have led to more careful definitions of what might constitute culture, and the methods of combining rigorous experimentation (common in psychology) with naturalistic observations (not so common in psychology) might be very useful in studying the presence and development of cultural traits in humans. The putative differences between humans and animals, such as symbols, group identification, and the presence of cumulative cultural traits, may lead to new ways of studying such phenomena in both human and non-human animals. As a biological psychologist, I think it is important to understand the differences as well as the similarities between our own and other species. It is especially important to consider a broader range of species than great apes, since other species may have different developmental processes and different degrees of social tolerance and helpfulness that can provide diverse models to researchers on human culture.

Two areas are of particular importance for future research. The first is expanding work on the notions of social tolerance and putative teaching. If social learning is facilitated and predicted by patterns of social tolerance, then chimpanzees with less social tolerance than some other species may not be the best models. Studying species with different degrees of social tolerance should lead to the discovery of different degrees of social learning and culture-like behavior as a function of social tolerance. However, the findings that a pacifist culture can develop in baboons (Sapolsky & Share, 2004) and that social climate can vary among different groups of chimpanzees (Cronin et al., 2014) raise interesting predictions that social transmission (and the emergence of culture-like phenomena) should be more evident in these groups than in other groups of the same species.

The second is understanding the implications of epigenetics for all forms of social behavior. The results with rodents suggest that early experiences (and possibly even adult experiences) may play an important role in regulating gene expression. The degree to which epigenetics lead to permanent or at least long-lasting behavioral change that can cross generational boundaries has major implications for understanding not only culture, but virtually every aspect of human psychology.

The subsequent chapters in this part will go into greater detail about cultural phenomena, and it is hoped that the phenomena they describe will be convincing. Nonetheless, although strong claims can be made for culture in non-human species, the cultural phenomena described fall far short of what we know about human cultures. Any non-human species might exhibit one or a few culture-like phenomena, but no other species has the richness of cultural phenomena seen in our species, and there appears to be no evidence to date of cumulative culture, where one cultural phenomenon builds upon others. This is perhaps most clearly illustrated by language, which has provided a grounding upon which many other cultural phenomena can develop.

References

Allen, J., Weinrich, M., Hoppitt, W., & Rendell, L. (2013). Network-based diffusion analysis reveals cultural transmission of lobtail feeding in humpback whales. *Science, 340,* 485–448. doi:10.1126/science.1231976

Aplin, L. M., Farine, D. R., Morand-Ferron, J., Cockburn, A., Thornton, A., & Sheldon, B. C. (2015). Experimentally induced innovations lead to persistent culture via conformity in wild birds. *Nature, 518*(7540), 538–541. doi:10.1038/nature13998

Auger, C. J., Coss, D., Auger, A. P., & Forbes-Lorman, R. M. (2011). Epigenetic control of vasopressin expression is maintained by steroid hormones in the adult male rat brain. *Proceedings of the National Academy of Sciences, 108,* 4242–4247. doi:10.1073/pnas.1100314108

Auger, A. P. (2001). Ligand-independent activation of progestin receptors: Relevance to female sexual behavior. *Reproduction, 122,* 847–855. doi:10.1530/rep.0.1220847

Barr, C. S., Newman, T. K., Becker, M. L., Champoux, M., Lesch, K. P., Suomi, S. J., … & Higley, J. D. (2003). Serotonin transporter gene variation is associated with alcohol sensitivity in rhesus macaques exposed to early-life stress. *Alcoholism: Clinical and Experimental Research, 27,* 812–817. doi:10.1097/01.ALC.0000067976.62827.ED

Bennett, A. J., Lesch, K. P., Heils, A., Long, J. C., Lorenz, J. G., Shoaf, S. E., … & Higley, J. D. (2002). Early experience and serotonin transporter gene variation interact to influence primate CNS function. *Molecular Psychiatry, 7,* 118–122. doi:10.1038/sj.mp.4000949

Bester-Meredith, J. K., & Marler, C. A. (2001).Vasopressin and aggression in cross-fostered California mice (*Peromyscus californicus*) and white-footed mice (*Peromyscus leucopus*). *Hormones and Behavior, 40,* 51–64. doi:10.1006/hbeh.2001.1666

Boesch, C., & Boesch-Achermann, H. (2000). *The chimpanzees of the Tai Forest: Behavioral ecology and evolution.* Oxford: Oxford University Press.

Caro, T. M., & Hauser, M. D. (1992). Is there teaching in nonhuman animals? *Quarterly Review of Biology, 67,* 151–174. doi:10.1086/417553

Cavalli-Sforza, L. L., & Feldman, M. W. (1981). *Cultural transmission and evolution: A quantitative approach.* Princeton, NJ: Princeton University Press.

Champagne, F. A. (2008). Epigenetic mechanisms and the transgenerational effects of maternal care. *Frontiers of Neuroendocrinology, 29,* 286–297.

Champoux, M., Bennett, A., Shannon, C., Higley, J. D. Lesch, K. P., & Suomi, S. J. (2002). Serotonin transporter gene polymorphism, differential early rearing, and behavior in rhesus monkey neonates. *Molecular Psychiatry, 7,* 1058–1063. doi:10.1038/sj.mp.4001157

Coussi-Korbel, S., & Fragaszy, D. M. (1995). On the relation between social dynamics and social learning. *Animal Behaviour, 50,* 1441–1453. doi:10.1016/0003-3472(95)80001-8

Cronin, K. A., van Leeuwen, E. J. C., Vreeman, V., & Haun, D. B. M. (2014). Population-level variability in the social climate of four chimpanzee societies. *Evolution and Human Behavior, 35,* 389–396. doi:10.1016/j.evolhumbehav.2014.05.004

Di Pellegrino, G., Fadiga, L., Fogassi, L., Gallese, V., & Rizzolatti, G. (1992). Understanding motor events: A neurophysiological study. *Experimental Brain Research, 91,* 176–180. doi:10.1007/BF00230027

Francis, D., Diorio, J., Liu, D, & Meaney, M. J. (1999). Nongenomic transmission across generations of maternal behavior and stress responses in the rat. *Science, 286,* 1155–1158. doi:10.1126/science.286.5442.1155

Francis, D. D., Young, L. J., Meaney, M. J., & Insel, T. R. (2002). Naturally occurring differences in maternal care are associated with the expression of oxytocin and vasopressin (v1a) receptors: Gender differences. *Journal of Neuroendocrinology, 14,* 349–353. doi:10.1046/j.0007-1331.2002.00776.x

Frazier, C. R. M., Trainor, B. C., Cravens, C. J., Whitney, T. K., & Marler, C. A. (2006). Paternal behavior influences development of aggression and vasopressin expression in male California mouse offspring. *Hormones and Behavior, 50,* 699–707. doi:10.1016/j.yhbeh.2006.06.035

Galef, B. G., Jr. (1992). The question of animal culture. *Human Nature, 3,* 157–178. doi:10.1007/BF02692251

Green, S. (1975). Dialects in Japanese monkeys: Vocal learning and cultural transmission of locale-specific behavior? *Zeitschrift für Tierpsychologie, 38,* 304–314. doi:10.1111/j.1439-0310.1975.tb02006.x

Gunhold, T., & Bugnyar, T. (2014). Long-term fidelity of foraging techniques in common marmosets (*Callithrix jacchus*). *American Journal of Primatology, 77,* 264–270. doi:10.1002/ajp.22342

Gunhold, T., Massen, J. J. M., Schiel, N., Souto, A., & Bugnyar, T. (2014). Memory, transmission and persistence of alternative foraging techniques in wild common marmosets. *Animal Behaviour, 91,* 79–91. doi:10.1016/j.anbehav.2014.02.023

Hobaiter, C., Poisot, T., Zuberbühler, K., Hoppitt, W., & Gruber, T. (2014). Social network analysis shows direct evidence for social transmission of tool use in wild chimpanzees. *PLoS Biology, 12,* e1001960.

Huffman, M. A. (1984). Stone play of *Macaca fuscata* in Arashiyama B troop: Transmission of a non-adaptive behavior. *Journal of Human Evolution, 13,* 725–735. doi:10.1016/S0047-2484(84)80022-6

Humle, T., & Matsuzawa, T. (2002). Ant-dipping among the chimpanzees at Bossou, Guinea, and some comparisons with other sites. *American Journal of Primatology, 58,* 133–148. doi:10.1002/ajp.10055

Humle, T., Snowdon, C. T., & Matsuzawa, T. (2009). Social influences on the acquisition of ant-dipping among the wild chimpanzees (*Pan troglodytes verus*) of Bossou, Guinea, West Africa. *Animal Cognition, 12,* S37–S48. doi:10.1007/s10071-009-0272-6

Kawai, M. (1965). Newly-acquired pre-cultural behavior of the natural troop of Japanese macaques at Koshima Islet. *Primates, 6,* 1–30. doi:10.1007/BF01794457

Kendal, R., Hopper, L. M., Whiten, A., Brosnan, S. F., Lambeth, S. P., Schapiro, S. J., & Hoppitt, W. (2015). Chimpanzees copy dominant and knowledgeable individuals: Implications for cultural diversity. *Evolution and Human Behavior, 36,* 65–72. doi:10.1016/j.evolhumbehav.2014.09.002

Kroeber, A. L. (1928). Subhuman cultural beginnings. *Quarterly Review of Biology, 3,* 325–342. doi:10.1086/394308

Kuo, Z.-Y. (1967). *The dynamics of behavior development: An epigenetic view.* New York: Random House.

Laland, K. N., & Brown, G. R. (2011) *Sense and nonsense: Evolutionary perspectives on human behaviour.* Oxford: Oxford University Press.

Laland, K. N., & Galef, B. G. (eds.) (2009). *The question of animal culture.* Cambridge, MA: Harvard University Press.

Laland, K. N., & Janik, V. M. (2006). The animal cultures debate. *Trends in Ecology and Evolution, 21,* 542–547. doi:10.1016/j.tree.2006.06.005

Leca, J.-B., Gunst, N., & Huffman, M. A. (2007). Japanese macaque cultures: Inter- and intra-troop behavioural variability of stone handling patterns across 10 troops. *Behaviour, 144*(3), 251–281. doi:10.1163/156853907780425712

Luncz, L. V., & Boesch, C. (2014). Tradition over trend: Neighboring chimpanzee communities maintain differences in cultural behavior despite frequent immigration of adult females. *American Journal of Primatology, 76,* 649–657. doi:10.1002/ajp.22259

Masataka, N. (1992). Attempts by animal caretakers to condition Japanese macaque vocalizations result inadvertently in individual specific calls. In T. Nishida, W. C. McGrew, P. Marler, M. Pickford, & F. de Waal (Eds.), *Topics in primatology,* vol. *1* (pp. 271–278). Tokyo: University of Tokyo Press.

McGrew, W. C. (1992). *Chimpanzee material culture: Implications for human evolution.* Cambridge: Cambridge University Press. doi:10.1017/CBO9780511565519

McGrew, W. C., & Tutin, C. E. G. (1978). Evidence for a social custom in wild chimpanzees? *Man, 14,* 234–251.

Mercader, J., Barton, H., Gillespie, J., Harris, J., Kuhn, S, Tyler, R., & Boesch, C. (2007). 4,300-year-old chimpanzee sites and the origins of percussive stone technology. *Proceedings of the National Academy of Sciences, 104*(9), 3043–3048. doi:10.1073/pnas.0607909104

Mineka, S., Davidson, M., Cook, M., & Keir, R. (1984). Fear of snakes in wild and lab-reared rhesus monkeys. *Journal of Abnormal Psychology, 93,* 355–372. doi:10.1037/0021-843X.93.4.355

Mitani, J. C., Hasegawa, T., Gros-Louis, J., Marler, P., & Byrne, R. (1992). Dialects in wild chimpanzees? *American Journal of Primatology, 27,* 233–243. doi:10.1002/ajp.1350270402

Mitani, J.C., Hunley, K. L., & Murdoch, M. E. (1999). Geographic variation in the calls of wild chimpanzees: A re-assessment. *American Journal of Primatology, 47,* 133–152. doi:10.1002/(SICI)1098-2345(1999)47: 2%3C133::AID-AJP4%3E3.0.CO;2-I

Payne, R. B., & Payne, L. L. (1997). Field observations, experimental design and the time and place of learning bird songs. In C. T. Snowdon & M. Hausberger (Eds.), *Social influences on vocal development* (pp. 57–84). Cambridge: Cambridge University Press.

Perry, S., Baker, M., Fedigan, L., Gros-Louis, J., Jack, K., MacKinnon, K. C., … & Rose, L. (2003). Social conventions in wild white-faced capuchin monkeys: Evidence for traditions in a neotropical primate. *Current Anthropology, 44,* 241–268. doi:10.1086/345825

Rapaport, L. G. (2011). Progressive parenting behavior in wild golden lion tamarins. *Behavioral Ecology, 22*(4), 745–754. doi:10.1093/beheco/arr055

Reader, S. M., & Laland, K. N. (2001). Primate innovation: Sex, age and social rank differences. *International Journal of Primatology, 22*(5), 787–805. doi:10.1023/A:1012069500899

Reader, S. M., & Laland, K. N. (2003). Animal innovation: An introduction. In S. M. Reader & K. N. Laland (Eds.), *Animal Innovation* (pp. 3–35). Oxford: Oxford University Press.

Ribble, D. O. (1991). The monogamous mating system of *Peromyscus californicus* as revealed by DNA fingerprinting. *Behavioral Ecology and Sociobiology, 29,* 161–166. doi:10.1007/BF00166397

Sapolsky, R. M., & Share, L. J. (2004). Pacific culture among wild baboons: Its emergence and transmission. *PLoS Biology, 2,* 534–541.

Simoons, F. J. (1969). Primary adult lactose intolerance and the milking habit: A problem in biological and cultural interrelations. I. Review of medical research. *American Journal of Digestive Diseases, 14*, 819–836. doi:10.1007/BF02233204

Simoons, F. J. (1976). New light on ethnic differences in adult lactose intolerance. *American Journal of Digestive Diseases, 18*, 595–611. doi:10.1007/BF01072224

Takahata, Y. (1982). Termite fishing observed in the M group chimpanzees. *Mahale Mountains Chimpanzee Research Project Ecological Report*, 18.

Tomasello, M. (1990). Cultural transmission in the tool use and communicatory signaling of chimpanzees? In S. T. Parker & K. R. Gibson (Eds.), *Language and intelligence in monkeys and apes* (pp. 274–311). Cambridge: Cambridge University Press.

Thornton, A., & McAuliffe, K. (2006). Teaching in wild meerkats. *Science, 313*, 227–229. doi:10.1126/science.1128727

van de Waal, E., Borheaud, C., & Whiten, A. (2013). Potent social learning and conformity shapes a wild primate's foraging decisions. *Science, 340*, 483–485. doi:10.1126/science.1232769

van Leeuwen, E. J. C., Cronin, K. A., & Haun, D. B. M. (2014). A group-specific arbitrary tradition in chimpanzees (*Pan troglodytes*). *Animal Cognition, 17*, 1421–1425. doi:10.1007/s10071-014-0766-8

Voelkl, B., & Huber, L. (2000). True imitation in marmosets. *Animal Behaviour, 60*, 195–202. doi:10.1006/anbe.2000.1457

Whiten, A., Caldwell, C. A., & Mesoudi, A. (2016). Cultural diffusion in humans and other animals. *Current Opinion in Psychology, 8*, 15–21. doi:10.1016/j.copsyc.2015.09.002

Whiten, A., Goodall, J., McGrew, W. C., Nishida, T., Reynolds, V., Sugiyama, Y., Tutin, C. E. G., Wrangham, R. W., & Boesch, C. (1999). Cultures in chimpanzees. *Nature, 399*, 682–685. doi:10.1038/21415

Whiten, A., & Ham, R. (1992). On the nature and evolution of imitation in the animal kingdom: Reappraisal of a century of research. *Advances in the Study of Behavior, 21*, 239–283. doi:10.1016/S0065-3454(08)60146-1

Whiten, A., McGuigan, N., Marshall-Pescini, & Hopper, L. M. (2009). Emulation, imitation, over-imitation and the scope of culture for child and chimpanzee. *Philosophical Transactions of the Royal Society B, 364*, 2417–2428. doi:10.1098/rstb.2009.0069

5

Comparing and Contrasting Primate and Cetacean Culture

Jennifer Botting, Erica van de Waal, and Luke Rendell

As humans, culture is an intrinsic part of our lives, evident in our language, technology and rituals, and has long been viewed as a defining feature of human uniqueness. However, the last few decades have seen a growing debate about the role of cultural process in non-humans. When we are investigating the evolution of human culture, it seems a natural step to look to our closest relatives, the primates, for evidence of the roots of cultural capacity. What we have found has surprised many: a plethora of cultural behaviors and abilities that were previously thought of as uniquely human. Yet what is arguably more surprising is that another group of animals shows a remarkable propensity for cultural behaviors: whales and dolphins, collectively known as cetaceans. While separated by millions of years of evolution, it seems that both taxa have evolved forms of culture as an adaptive response to their vastly different environments. But what form do these cultures take? How comparable are they to each other? Have they evolved along similar lines for similar functions? In recent years these questions have prompted the unearthing of some fascinating data.

Before proceeding, we must define exactly what we mean by culture. Culture can be a divisive topic, with academics often in disagreement about what this term actually means. Certainly, it is only in fairly recent history that the term culture has been used to describe animal behaviors (Kawai, 1965). For us, the best definition is the one that is the most useful from a scientific point of view. If by definition culture excludes all species but humans, *ipso facto* it cannot be a topic of comparative research, which at the same time excludes a very powerful scientific approach and leads to a profound rejection of Darwinian continuity in the evolution of culture. Thus, for the rest of the chapter, when we discuss culture, we use the

The Handbook of Culture and Biology, First Edition. Edited by José M. Causadias, Eva H. Telzer and Nancy A. Gonzales.

broad definition suggested by Hoppitt and Laland (2013), "group-typical behavior patterns shared by members of a community that rely on socially learned and transmitted information" (p. 4). While we argue for an inclusive definition of culture, it is obvious to all that human culture is different to that in non-humans: the intricacies of our language and customs as well as our technological advancement are plain to see. Tomasello, Kruger, and Ratner (1993) suggested that this difference lies in the cumulative properties of human culture, in the ability to build upon the work of others and end up with a product that is too complex to be innovated by a single individual. Tomasello and colleagues (1993) called this cumulative culture. Researchers have yet to find any convincing evidence for cumulative culture in a non-human species (Dean, Kendal, Schapiro, Thierry, & Laland, 2012). What is accumulating, however, is a stockpile of evidence of culture in multiple non-human species.

What can we learn from comparing the cultures of primates and cetaceans? What does it mean for human cultural evolution to find culturally transmitted behaviors in these distantly related taxa? This chapter aims to explore how evolution has operated convergently and divergently in these taxa with respect to culture. We outline the pivotal role that environment, physiology and social structure can play in the shaping of culture, the mechanisms though which culture operates, and the adaptive role that culture plays in the survival of each taxon. By comparing cultural behaviors within functional domains (communication, foraging, and so forth) we can begin to investigate why these cultural behaviors have emerged in both taxa.

Social Systems, Ecology, and Culture

Are the capability of acquiring and transmitting culture, and the cultural content itself, adaptions to specific social and physical environments? As we know, adaptive explanations cannot necessarily be assumed (Gould & Lewontin, 1979), and just what evolves when a species (or an individual for that matter) becomes able to acquire and transmit cultural knowledge is a matter of considerable topical debate (Enquist, Eriksson, & Ghirlanda, 2007; Heyes, 2012; Heyes & Pearce, 2015; Mesoudi, Chang, Dall, & Thornton, 2016; Rendell, Fogarty, & Laland, 2010). We obviously do not propose to definitively answer this question here, but note that it is self-evident, in the case of human societies, that whatever has allowed us to generate cumulative cultural processes is both extraordinarily adaptive, at least in the geological short term, and capable of producing cultural traits that are adaptively neutral, or even maladaptive, in specific circumstances (see e.g. Lindenbaum, 2008). It is also self-evident from human ethnography that both social structure and physical environment have major effects on what forms of culture emerge. If we are to understand the evolution of culture in any species, these factors must loom large in our thinking. Obviously cetaceans and primates occupy vastly different habitats, which impose very different constraints. For example, because of the physical properties of water, sound appears to play a much more pivotal role in cetacean communication than in that of primates (Whitehead & Rendell, 2014), and, as a result of their natural environment and foraging challenges, the physiology of apes may make them more adept at tool use than cetaceans.

It is not only the physical environment that has formative effects upon the culture expressed within a species; the social structure of a species or even a population (a group of organisms, all of the same species, that live together and reproduce; Gotelli, 1995) is also important. A similarity between these two taxa is that individuals from both spend extended periods of their early lives in close proximity to their mothers; several examples of culture from both taxa seem to be transmitted primarily from mother to infant, from learning migratory routes in whales (Valenzuela, Sironi, Rowntree, & Seger, 2009) to nut-cracking in chimpanzees (Matsuzawa, Biro, Humle, Inoue, & Tonooka, 2001).

Culture is also passed on by "horizontal" transmission through social learning between group members outside parental relations. Necessarily, then, the group composition and structure will have important influences on how cultures evolve. For example, field experiments have shown that immigrating male vervet monkeys show strong conformity towards their new group's food color preferences, overriding existing individually learned preferences (van de Waal, Borgeaud, & Whiten, 2013, see Figure 5.1). A similar effect was seen in an immigrant female chimpanzee whose nut-cracking behavior became more like her new group's behavior throughout her first year after immigration (Luncz & Boesch, 2014); these authors suggest that this conformity maintains the distinct between-group traditions in chimpanzees. Therefore, it follows that the social structure of the species beyond the mother–infant relationship is important for how culture evolves and is maintained in each group.

Within these taxa, groups can range from relatively solitarily living individuals such as blue whales and orangutans to larger groups, such as oceanic dolphins and baboons, and including species such as killer

Figure 5.1 Experimental set-up illustrating preferential foraging. A photograph from the follow-up experiments of van de Waal et al. (2013) showing a group of vervets crowding around their preferred colour of corn (pink, left) and avoiding the other (blue, right)

whales and sperm whales who live in hierarchical social structures forming "groups within groups" (Bigg, Olesiuk, Ellis, Ford, & Balcomb, 1990; Whitehead, 2003). Differences in how time is spent within these groups will naturally affect cultural transmission. Some species live in fission–fusion societies in which the group may temporarily divide into subgroups (e.g. chimpanzees and bottlenose dolphins), whereas others maintain more stable groupings (e.g. sperm whales and gibbons), leading to variation in the models and frequencies of behaviors observed. As we will see, these differences in social structure are associated with stark differences in cultural behaviors both between and within taxa. To explore this variation, we will organize our brief review into three behavioral domains: foraging, vocal communication, and social and play behaviors.

Culture in Foraging

Foraging is a critical part of any animal's behavioral activities, and consequently some of the best evidence we have for culture in primates and cetaceans comes from foraging behaviors (Allen, Weinrich, Hoppitt, &

Rendell, 2013; Whiten et al. 1999). Indeed, the first documented example of cultural behavior in primates was a foraging behavior: a Japanese macaque named Imo began washing pieces of sweet potato in the river before eating them. Following this, several members of her group copied this behavior, resulting in the attribution of "pre-culture" to these macaques (Kawai, 1965). While the evidence for social transmission has since been questioned in this case (Galef, 1992), it was the spark that ignited the study of cultural behaviors in non-human primates.

In the decades that followed, several researchers put forth cases for potential cultural behaviors in chimpanzees (Goodall, 1986; McGrew & Tutin, 1978). Then, in 1999, Whiten and colleagues published a seminal paper detailing behavioral traditions in chimpanzees which collated data from seven long-term field sites. Researchers were asked to list the frequency with which certain behaviors occurred in chimpanzees at their field sites, resulting in the identification of 39 behaviors that were customary or habitual at some sites, while being absent from others. Of these 39, almost half were related to foraging (Whiten et al. 1999), including nut hammering and termite fishing. For example, populations in West Africa used stone hammers and anvils to crack nuts, whereas East African populations did not, thus indicating a social spread of behavior (Whiten et al. 1999). Following this, evidence was revealed of cultural behaviors in wild orangutans, some of which were also in the foraging domain (van Schaik et al., 2003). Later research lent further support to a cultural hypothesis for this behavioral variation by examining the roles of genetics and ecology in the behaviors and finding that while ecology played a significant role, the analyses pointed at social learning as the likely basis of the behaviors (Krützen, Willems, & van Schaik, 2011). Nut-cracking behaviors are also seen in wild capuchins, where the patterns of acquisition are again consistent with a cultural hypothesis (Ottoni & Izar, 2008).

Many of these behaviors in the wild have been examined with the "method of exclusion" (Krützen, van Schaik, & Whiten, 2007). This requires elimination of potential genetic and direct environmental causes of the behavioral variation, the assumption being that if these factors could not explain the presence of a behavior at one site and its absence at another, the behavior must be transmitted through social learning (Whiten et al., 1999). While this method has been useful in identifying a number of cultural variants, critics of the method highlight the danger that its uncritical use will result in both Type I and II errors (Laland & Janik, 2006; Langergraber et al., 2010). For example, Type I errors could result from missing subtle ecological differences that might account for behavioral variation (Laland & Hoppitt, 2003) and Type II errors from incorrectly rejecting a cultural hypothesis if the behavioral variation aligns with genetic population structure (Langergraber et al., 2010). Indeed, research with primates and cetaceans alike has shown that ecology does play a major role in shaping culture (Allen et al., 2013; Krützen et al., 2011), and it self-evidently does in humans, if one considers only for a moment the different lifestyles of indigenous peoples in the Amazon and the Arctic. Thus, the method of exclusion is not without limitations.

More recently, however, by charting the emergence and spread of two novel foraging behaviors, moss sponging and leaf-sponge reuse in a wild group of chimpanzees, and lobtail feeding in a population of humpback whales, researchers have managed to demonstrate the role of social learning in the acquisition of foraging behavior via methods other than exclusion (Allen et al., 2013; Hobaiter, Poisot, Zuberbühler, Hoppitt, & Gruber, 2014). In both cases researchers used a statistical technique called network-based diffusion analysis (NBDA; Franz & Nunn, 2009; Hoppitt, Boogert, & Laland, 2010), which quantifies the influence of social networks on behavioral diffusion within a given population. Hobaiter and colleagues (2014) used NBDA to compare the spread of a behavior through individuals in a group with the number of times each individual witnessed another individual performing the novel behavior. The analysis found that social learning explained the spread of the behavior significantly better than did individual learning: the more often the chimpanzees saw the behavior, the more likely they were to perform it. This is an important finding as it provides us with direct evidence of social learning in wild chimpanzees, rather than requiring that alternative explanations be excluded. It also highlights the difficulties of comparing primate and cetacean culture: the authors recognize that this level of analysis requires total habituation, constant observation and individual identification, requirements that are all but impossible with wild cetaceans. Despite these difficulties, we also have convincing evidence for cultural foraging behaviors in cetaceans.

NBDA was also used to analyze the spread of a unique foraging technique in humpback whales (Allen et al., 2013; see Figure 5.2). In lobtail feeding a whale first slaps or agitates the surface of the water with its tail, then dives below to begin a bubble-net feeding event. It was first seen in just one whale off the waters of Cape Cod in 1980 (Hain, Carter, Kraus, Mayo, & Winn, 1982), before spreading to nearly half the observed feeders by the mid-2000s. The strength of this example rests partly upon the speed with which the behavior spread through the population: it spread too fast to be attributed solely to genetics (Whitehead & Rendell, 2014). To analyze this

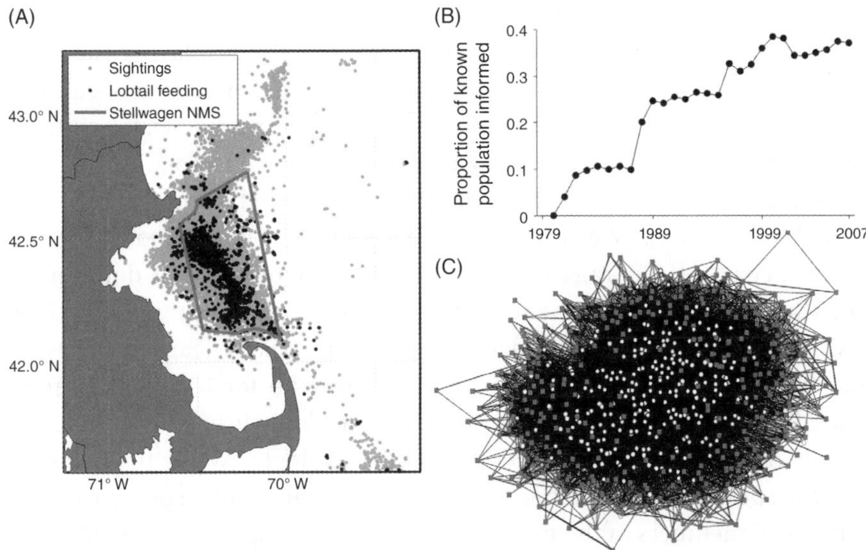

Figure 5.2 The spread of lobtail feeding in a humpback whale population. (A) Map of spatial distribution of lobtail feeding events and sightings data. (B) The proportion of the known population each year that have also been seen lobtail feeding at least once in the study and were thus considered to be informed about the behavior. (C) The social network of whales sighted at least 20 times. White nodes are individuals observed lobtail feeding, gray nodes are those never observed lobtail feeding. The network is laid out by spring-embedding. *Source*: Allen et al. (2013: 485). Reproduced with permission AAAS

further, NBDA was employed to chart the spread in relation to the social network of the population, which had been well characterized over several decades by observers working on whale-watch vessels. This static method is slightly different from that used by Hobaiter and colleagues (2014) in that it compares the spread of behavior with social associations rather than with direct observations of the behavior.

These findings provided strong evidence of a role of social learning: whales who associated more often with lobtail feeders were much more likely to exhibit this behavior than those who associated less (Allen et al., 2013). These analyses show us that the same statistical techniques can be used for primates and cetaceans to reveal that the diffusion of novel behaviors follows similar patterns in both taxa. As has also been shown in captive studies, the social network of each species appears to be an integral aspect of cultural transmission: for example, individuals more central to the network acquire information more rapidly (Claidière, Messer, Hoppitt, & Whiten, 2013). Importantly, Allen and colleagues (2013) also found that use of this distinctive foraging technique (lobtailing) was strongly related to the abundance of sand lance in the area, thereby displaying the joint roles that social network and ecology can play in the emergence of cultural behaviors and the dangers inherent in excluding all candidates for cultural behaviors that can be partially explained by ecological factors.

Another strong candidate for a cultural foraging behavior also provides us with one of the few examples of material culture in cetaceans. On the western coast of Australia in Shark Bay live a population of dolphins, a small subset of whom can be seen at the surface carrying sponges on their rostrums. Scientists hypothesize that this is a socially learned behavior that functions to protect their noses as they grub for fish in the sandy seabed (Krützen et al., 2005), although frustratingly it has never actually been witnessed because of a lack of visibility at depth. While the majority of these spongers are members of the same matriline, one sponger is not, and not all members of the matrilines engage in sponging. This, combined with evidence from another, genetically distinct, population of spongers (Ackermann, 2008) in a different area, makes it hard to rule out the role of culture in this fascinating behavior (although see Laland & Janik, 2007 for a critique).

As we have seen, social learning appears to be very beneficial to both taxa when it comes to foraging strategies, and gives rise to foraging traditions that can persist across generations. However, there is another domain which provides an equally fascinating insight into the evolution of cultural capacities in non-humans and especially in cetaceans.

Vocal Communication

Species adapt to the environments that they inhabit, and primates and cetaceans inhabit very different worlds. The reason we find such strong evidence of vocal culture in cetaceans is that sound is the most effective form of underwater communication (Whitehead & Rendell, 2014). Sounds travel through water around four times faster than through air and are less attenuated by water, and thus the sounds of marine mammals can be heard at far greater distances than mammals on land (Tyack & Miller, 2002). This is an excellent example of the environment shaping physiology and behavior, and thus culture. As we shall see, there are many candidates for culture within cetacean vocal communication, but we shall start with the best-known and arguably the most persuasive example: the song of the humpback whale.

The songs that humpbacks sing are long, loud, and complex; the songs are structured hierarchically and are repeated in cycles, traveling at least 15 km under water (Whitehead, 2009; Payne, 2000). It is only the males who sing and only during their migrations and in the breeding months (Glockner & Venus, 1983; McSweeney, Chu, Dolphin, & Guinee, 1989). Females do not sing, strongly suggesting that the songs are involved in mating, although it is still unclear exactly how (Whitehead & Rendell, 2014). The migrations of these animals can span several hundred kilometers across vast oceans. Yet, despite this vast range, researchers have found that all male humpbacks in a population sing the same song at the same time (Payne, 2000). This may not be so remarkable – if song is based purely on genetics, one might find the same pattern – but there is another key feature of humpback songs which immediately suggests culture: they change. Each song evolves over time to include a different arrangement of its units (Payne, 2000). This change is important because it is not a generational change but a constant evolution of the song, and, most importantly, the songs of all members of a population change in the same way. Indeed, there have been examples of songs changing completely in less than a year, ostensibly due to some stray whales from a neighboring population introducing their different, and apparently favored, song to the existing population (Noad, Cato, Bryden, Jenner, and Jenner, 2000). No mechanism we know of other than culture could produce the observed swift, synchronous changes in song.

A key study by Garland and colleagues (2011) examined a decade's worth of recordings across the Southern Pacific and found repeated eastbound "waves" in the evolution of the song. Entire songs spread eastward through the various discrete breeding populations between Australia and French Polynesia. The songs sung by the whales off the eastern Australian coast were heard a year later off the Cook Islands and then a year after that in French Polynesia, by which time the eastern Australian whales were singing a new song. As far as we know, there is no comparable phenomenon in the northern hemisphere. Instead, all populations sing the same song at the same time across a vast area (Cerchio, Jacobsen, & Norris, 2001). A plausible reason for this difference is that the northern-hemisphere whales come closer together to feed in the Arctic than do the southern-hemisphere whales in the Antarctic, where they may hear each other and synchronize their songs (Whitehead & Rendell, 2014).

While the song of the blue whale is much simpler and less well known than that of the humpback, it is equally intriguing. Researchers have documented 11 song types across the world, which are linked to populations

(McDonald, Mesnick, & Hildebrand, 2006; Frank & Ferris, 2011). Similarly to humpbacks, all of the whales within a population sing the same song, with some amount of individual variation. However, in all of the different, widespread populations the songs have been lowering in pitch over time (McDonald, Hildebrand, & Mesnick, 2009). While the authors failed to find an explanation that satisfactorily explained these changes, this situation can perhaps be likened to cultural drive in humans (Whitehead & Rendell, 2014), whereby trends move, seemingly arbitrarily, in one direction over time. While we do not currently know what is causing this shift of frequency, the fact that all blue whales are adjusting their songs at the same rate strongly indicates social learning and perhaps suggests a role for conformist transmission.

Researchers have also found evidence of vocal cultures in two other cetacean species: killer whales and sperm whales. Killer whales live in matrilines, within pods, within clans, within communities (Bigg et al., 1990). However, they mate with partners outside of their own pod, or even clan (an important point to remember when considering non-cultural explanations for certain behaviors). Amongst other vocalizations, killer whales emit stereotyped pulsed calls, which can be complex, containing both low- and high-frequency voicings. Ford (1991) discovered that each pod has its own distinct repertoire of pulsed calls, and that these calls can be shared between groups within clans, but never between clans. Additionally, it has been revealed that, like humpback song, these pulsed calls change over time, so that a given call can change structure gradually over time, but all members of the pods using the call conform to the "current" version (Deecke, Ford, & Spong, 2000). Such changes can only occur if the animals are updating their calls by listening to each other.

Finally, sperm whales make codas, stereotyped click sequences that are hypothesized to be used for social bonding (Rendell & Whitehead, 2003; Schulz, Whitehead, Gero, & Rendell, 2008). In the Pacific, sympatric whales can be grouped into distinct vocal "clans" according to differences in these codas, and membership of a vocal clan correlates with differences in feeding success and thus potentially reproduction rates. While we currently lack data on changes over time, females occasionally move between clans, and vocal clans do not map onto genetic population structure, which makes genetic explanation of dialects difficult (Rendell, Mesnick, Dalebout, Burtenshaw, & Whitehead, 2012).

We have several strong examples of vocal variation that can only, sensibly, be attributed to cultural transmission, and others for which culture is the likely explanation, but others cannot be ruled out yet (see Whitehead & Rendell, 2014, for a full review of these behaviors). It is immediately clear that there is far more evidence for vocal cultures in the cetaceans than in the primates. After initial studies of geographical variation in chimpanzee pant-hoots, it was thought that evidence of vocal cultures had been found (Mitani, Hasegawa, Gros-Louis, Marler, & Byrne, 1992). However, researchers revisiting these results later suggested that genetic and ecological differences might well account for these differences (Mitani, Hunley, Murdoch, & Arbor, 1999). Nevertheless, there is some evidence for different "call cultures" in orangutans that are seemingly not attributable to genetic or ecological differences (Wich et al., 2012). Researchers found differences in four types of calls made across five different field sites. These different call cultures can be compared to the vocal clans of the sperm whales, in that they consist of different dialects, not different accents, as was suggested for the chimpanzees.

A study of captive chimpanzees has also provided tentative evidence for social learning of vocalizations. In 2011, a group of chimpanzees was moved from the Netherlands to Edinburgh Zoo to be integrated with an existing group of chimpanzees. Researchers recorded food calls for apples from both groups at the start of the integration and then yearly as the integration of the two groups progressed (Watson et al., 2015). Analysis of the food calls indicated that while the "resident" group of Edinburgh chimpanzees did not show much change, the calls of the Dutch chimps gradually became more similar to the Edinburgh chimps. Researchers suggested this was a form of "vocal conformity": the Dutch chimps were conforming to the vocal culture of their new group. This can be compared to the food color conformity seen in the migrating male vervets and the case study of tool conformity in a female immigrant chimpanzee (Luncz & Boesch, 2014; van de Waal et al., 2013). This could be somewhat comparable to signature whistle convergence in bottlenose dolphins. Dolphins have signature whistles which are unique and appear to be learned (Janik, 1999; King & Janik, 2013). Studies have shown that males within alliances have more similar whistles than those without (Watwood, Tyack, & Wells, 2004), and that the males converge on a common signature whistle rarely produced by any of them before the alliance was formed (Smolker & Pepper, 1999). While this differs from the chimpanzee example in that it does not involve "immigrants" conforming to their new group's existing vocal culture, but rather individuals converging on a new whistle, it still suggests that these signature whistles are socially learned and therefore good candidates for vocal culture.

To summarize the data collected so far, it appears that, compared with that for the vocal culture of cetaceans, the evidence for a vocal culture in primates is weak. It is perhaps not surprising that we should find such plentiful evidence of vocal cultures in cetaceans, given the properties of sound in water. However, the lack of vocal culture in primates is more surprising given their close phylogenetic relationship to humans. The importance of vocal learning in humans and cetaceans, as well as in birds and bats, but not in our closest primate relatives, remains to be adequately explained.

Social, Play, and "Fad" Behaviors

While the majority of cultural traditions in both cetaceans and primates have emerged in domains crucial for the animals' survival, the functions of some remain unclear. Within both taxa it is these "arbitrary" behaviors that provide some of the best examples of cultural transmission, perhaps because it is harder to invoke ecological variation as an explanation for variation in arbitrary behavior.

Two of the best-known examples of primate cultural behaviors fall into this rather broad category: hand-clasp grooming (HCG) in chimpanzees and the finger-poking "games" of the capuchins of Costa Rica. Both appear to function to strengthen social bonds. In hand-clasp grooming (McGrew and Tutin, 1978) the two participants clasp hands while grooming each other. This custom was found in several, but not all, of the studied populations of wild chimpanzees (Whiten et al., 1999). More in-depth analyses have revealed that differences in form during HCG predict group membership, and thus further cement HCG's place as a cultural behavior (van Leeuwen, Cronin, Haun, Mundry, & Bodamer, 2012).

In 2003, Perry and colleagues described a number of hand-sniffing and finger-poking games seen in wild capuchins. Each of a pair of capuchins in turn poked its fingers into the mouth or up the nose of its partner. The authors hypothesize that these games could serve a social function, helping to strengthen bonds between partners. Not all individuals participated in these games, and they were present in only some of the studied groups, suggesting that these behaviors are socially learned and thus could be described as traditions (Perry et al., 2003).

The emergence of stone-handling behavior in semi-captive Japanese macaques is another important example, since researchers have been able to track its spread and diversification (Huffman, 1996). More recently, the discovery of stone-throwing behaviors in chimpanzees could indicate a socially learned behavior, given its distribution, which is limited to certain populations in West Africa (Kühl et al., 2016). The chimpanzees throw stones at or into hollow trees, and although the function of the behavior is currently unclear, it is probably related to male displays.

One example of ephemeral culture is salmon balancing in killer whales. A member of the southern resident community off Vancouver Island was seen carrying a dead salmon on top of her head. Within weeks, this "fad" had spread to the two other pods within the community, but it died out quickly, with only a few cases being seen the next year and then no more (Whitehead, Rendell, Osborne, & Würsig, 2004). The speed of transmission of this behavior rules out genetics, and the ephemeral nature of the behavior can easily be compared to short-lived human fads (Whiten, Horner, Litchfield, & Marshall-Pescini, 2004).

Additionally, there is the case of "tail-walking" in a community of bottlenose dolphins. In this case, a wild female dolphin was housed with trained dolphins at an aquarium during rehabilitation. After the dolphin's release, scientists monitoring her progress observed her performing one of the trained dolphins' tricks, "tail-walking," despite her never receiving any of the training required to produce this behavior (Whitehead & Rendell, 2014). Furthermore, four other female dolphins began performing the same trick and several calves appeared to be attempting to replicate it. This phenomenon is not ephemeral like the salmon balancing – it has persisted some 25 years so far – and is an excellent example of a spread of behavior that cannot plausibly be explained by anything other than social learning.

Social Learning Experiments

Thus far we have detailed from each taxon observations of behaviors in the wild that either must be, or are very likely to be, reliant on social learning and shared by a community. To be cultural, these behaviors must rely on social learning, and a question that has long motivated researchers is how to understand the learning processes involved. It was initially suggested that culture could only be transmitted via mechanisms which allowed high-fidelity copying, namely imitation and teaching (Galef, 1992). Therefore the last two decades have seen a huge research effort concentrated on understanding imitative or teaching abilities in non-humans (or the lack thereof). However, there are a number of other processes through which an animal may learn from another. One is emulation: whereas imitation means copying the bodily actions of another, emulation means copying the end-state of the action; it does not result in such high-fidelity copying

(Tomasello, Camak, & Bard, 1987). Another comprises the perhaps cognitively simpler processes of stimulus and local enhancement (Heyes, 1994). Contrary to the arguments originally put forth, we have evidence to suggest that chimpanzees are capable of both imitation and emulation (Hopper, Lambeth, Schapiro, & Whiten, 2008; Horner & Whiten, 2005) (which one they use often depends upon context), and that they avoid the imitation of causally irrelevant actions. However, the extent to which chimpanzees can imitate truly novel actions is still under debate (Tennie, Call, & Tomasello, 2012). More recently a field experiment provided information about how primates learn socially in the wild. Van de Waal, Claidiere, and Whiten (2015) presented groups of wild vervet monkeys with baited boxes which could be opened in two different ways using the same door, and trained a model in each group to demonstrate a particular method. By revealing that the method shown by the demonstrator was the one used significantly more in each group, and by virtue of the fact that the opening mechanism was in the same location on the box for each method, the authors showed that the monkeys must be using either emulation or imitation.

Here we come to another great divide between the primate and cetacean literature: it is far easier to conduct captive experiments with primates than with cetaceans. The logistical, financial and ethical barriers to keeping a humpback or sperm whale in captivity are likely to remain insurmountable in our lifetimes. So, as an obvious result of these logistical differences, our understanding of primate social learning mechanisms, while far from complete, is at least a lot clearer than it is for the cetaceans. However, a small number of studies have examined imitative abilities in dolphins and killer whales, with some striking results. The first anecdotal report of imitation came from observers of a captive dolphin that appeared to be copying the actions of a human diver who cleaned the windows in the tank, and which even used a range of objects to do so (Taylor & Saayman, 1973). Following this came experimental studies of imitation in dolphins. Researchers separated two dolphins, who had been trained to perform certain bodily actions, by a partition which allowed them to see each other, but not each other's human trainers. The dolphins were then asked via hand signals to mimic the behavior of the other dolphin, and succeeded in mimicking behaviors already known in their repertoires after a relatively small number of trials (Herman, 2002). More impressively, however, they also had some success when asked to copy a novel behavior performed by the other, trained dolphin. While they did not successfully copy all of these behaviors, they still displayed some ability to imitate novel actions. A small number of additional studies have also shown that dolphins can perform actions in pairs when told just to perform any behavior that they had not performed in that session (Herman, 2002), and that they can copy humans and other dolphins even when blindfolded (Jaakkola, Guarino, & Rodriguez, 2010). Killer whales have also demonstrated the ability to readily generalize a "mimic" concept and use it to copy behaviors which they had not previously been trained to do or seen being performed, with impressive apparent ease (Abramson, Hernández-Lloreda, Call, & Colmenares, 2013).

While it may be argued, as it has been for primates (Buttelmann, Carpenter, Call, & Tomasello, 2007), that these skills may be a product of enculturation, the extraordinary synchronization abilities of cetaceans, displayed during foraging and also apparently for social purposes (Connor, 2007; Connor, Smolker, & Bejder, 2006; Hastie, Wilson, Tufft, & Thompson, 2003), do somewhat refute this suggestion. There is much less evidence for both taxa when it comes to teaching; there are just two reports of teaching in wild chimpanzees (Boesch, 1991) and they have failed to show evidence for teaching in captivity (Dean et al. 2012). However, there is some tentative evidence that killer whale mothers may assist their young to learn the foraging technique of "beaching," by pushing them on and off the beach and towards prey (Guinet & Bouvier, 1995). While we cannot, from this evidence alone, claim that cetaceans are capable of teaching, it is an intriguing report.

Conclusions and Future Direction

Using a broad definition of culture, we find that there are many behaviors that meet the criteria of this definition in primates and cetaceans. While some behaviors, such as hand-clasp grooming in chimpanzees and humpback whale song, provide extremely strong evidence for culture, the role of cultural transmission in other behaviors remains more contested. However, social transmission is not an easy thing to demonstrate outside of controlled laboratory conditions. As a result there is inevitably a suite of additional behaviors that many researchers think are culturally transmitted, but for which transmission they cannot yet provide direct evidence.

Future research directions should focus on new techniques such as NBDA and on observing technologies such as animal-borne telemetry loggers (Krause et al., 2013), which offer the hope of overcoming this impasse more readily in the future. In addition, field experiments have given us valuable data while removing some of the problems of ecological validity incurred with captive work, and are likely to continue to do so in the future. Of course, these advances will not be confined to cetaceans and primates

(Aplin et al., 2015; Aplin, Farine, Morand-Ferron, & Sheldon, 2012; Farine, Aplin, Sheldon, & Hoppitt, 2015), and as long as a broad concept of culture is considered useful we must cast a wide taxonomic net if we are to fully realize the power of the comparative method to explain the evolutionary roots of human culture. By examining these non-human species, we can hope to elucidate both the selection pressures and the transmission mechanisms that have led to their cultural repertoires. In turn, we can more fully understand the emergence of human culture and the mechanisms that have led to the gulf we see between our own complex cultures and those of non-human animals.

There are some obvious differences between the taxa in the examples of culture that we have set forth here, related to environment, physiology and social structure. Vocal cultures appear far more prevalent in cetaceans, whereas traditions involving tool use and manipulation of objects in the environment occur much more often in the primate family. However, there are also some similarities. The occurrence of social and play-based traditions in both taxa might suggest that traditions are important for strengthening social bonds between group members. Evidence from wild chimpanzees, captive monkeys and humpback whales has also shown the importance of the social network, as well as the mother–infant bond, in the spread of behavior.

To conclude, it is clear from a comparison of the cultural behaviors of cetaceans and primates that each species has a repertoire of cultural behaviors adapted to suit its physiology, social structure and physical environment, all three of these being intrinsically linked to culture and to the others. However, one final comparison must be made between these two taxa, namely the impact of our own culture upon them both. Both cetaceans and primates are experiencing massive habitat pollution and destruction at the hands of humans. If this destruction continues, we will lose not only these remarkable animals, but also their distinct cultural repertoires and the ability to study these in the hope of unveiling the processes by which they have emerged. If we are to gain any further understanding of the evolution of culture, we must take action to ensure that these animals are permitted to continue exhibiting their fascinating and captivating cultural behaviors in the wild.

Acknowledgments

JB was supported by the John Templeton Foundation. LR was supported by the Marine Alliance for Science and Technology for Scotland pooling initiative, which is funded by the Scottish Funding Council (HR09011) and contributing institutions. EW was supported by the Swiss National Science Foundation (P300P3_151187) and Society in Science – The Branco Weiss Fellowship.

References

Abramson, J. Z., Hernández-Lloreda, V., Call, J., & Colmenares, F. (2013). Experimental evidence for action imitation in killer whales (*Orcinus orca*). *Animal Cognition, 16*(1), 11–22. http://doi.org/10.1007/s10071-012-0546-2

Ackermann, C. (2008). Contrasting vertical skill transmission patterns of a tool use behaviour in two groups of wild bottlenose dolphins (*Tursiops* sp.), as revealed by molecular genetic analyses. MSc thesis, University of Zurich.

Allen, J., Weinrich, M., Hoppitt, W., & Rendell, L. (2013). Network-based diffusion analysis reveals cultural transmission of lobtail feeding in humpback whales. *Science, 340*(6131), 485–488. http://doi.org/10.1126/science.1231976

Aplin, L. M., Farine, D. R., Morand-Ferron, J., Cockburn, A., Thornton, A., & Sheldon, B. C. (2015). Experimentally induced innovations lead to persistent culture via conformity in wild birds. *Nature, 518*(7540), 538–541. http://doi.org/10.1038/nature13998

Aplin, L. M., Farine, D. R., Morand-Ferron, J., & Sheldon, B. C. (2012). Social networks predict patch discovery in a wild population of songbirds. *Proceedings of the Royal Society B, 279*(1745), 4199–4205. http://doi.org/10.1098/rspb.2012.1591

Bigg, M. A., Olesiuk, P. F., Ellis, G. M., Ford, J. K. B., & Balcomb, K. C. (1990). Social organization and genealogy of resident killer whales *(Orcinus orca*) in the coastal waters of British Columbia and Washington State. *Report of the International Whaling Commission, Special, 12*, 383–405.

Boesch, C. (1991). Teaching among wild chimpanzees. *Animal Behaviour, 41*(3), 530–532.

Buttelmann, D., Carpenter, M., Call, J., & Tomasello, M. (2007). Enculturated chimpanzees imitate rationally. *Developmental Science, 10*(4), 31–38.

Cerchio, S., Jacobsen, J. K., & Norris, T. F. (2001). Temporal and geographical variation in songs of humpback whales, *Megaptera novaeangliae*: Synchronous change in Hawaiian and Mexican breeding assemblages. *Animal Behaviour, 62*(2), 313–329. http://doi.org/10.1006/anbe.2001.1747

Claidière, N., Messer, E. J. E., Hoppitt, W., & Whiten, A. (2013). Diffusion dynamics of socially learned foraging techniques in squirrel monkeys. *Current Biology, 23*(13), 1251–1255. http://doi.org/10.1016/j.cub.2013.05.036

Connor, R. C. (2007). Dolphin social intelligence: Complex alliance relationships in bottlenose dolphins and a consideration of selective environments for extreme brain size evolution in mammals. *Philosophical Transactions of the Royal Society B, 362*(1480), 587–602. http://doi.org/10.1098/rstb.2006.1997

Connor, R. C., Smolker, R., & Bejder, L. (2006). Synchrony, social behaviour and alliance affiliation in Indian Ocean bottlenose dolphins, *Tursiops aduncus. Animal Behaviour, 72*(6), 1371–1378. http://doi.org/10.1016/j.anbehav.2006.03.014

Dean, L. G., Kendal, R. L., Schapiro, S. J., Thierry, B., & Laland, K. N. (2012). Identification of the social and cognitive processes underlying human cumulative culture. *Science, 335*(6072), 1114–1118.

Deecke, V., Ford, J., & Spong, P. (2000). Dialect change in resident killer whales: Implications for vocal learning and cultural transmission. *Animal Behaviour, 60*(5), 629–638. http://doi.org/10.1006/anbe.2000.1454

Enquist, M., Eriksson, K., & Ghirlanda, S. (2007). Critical social learning: A solution to Rogers's paradox of nonadaptive culture. *American Anthropologist, 109*(4), 727–734.

Farine, D. R., Aplin, L. M., Sheldon, B. C., & Hoppitt, W. (2015). Interspecific social networks promote information transmission in wild songbirds. *Proceedings of the Royal Society B, 282*(1803), doi:10.1098/rspb.2014.2804

Ford, J. K. B. (1991). Vocal traditions among resident killer whales (*Orcinus orca*) in coastal waters of British Columbia. *Canadian Journal of Zoology, 69*(6), 1454–1483.

Frank, S. D., & Ferris, A. N. (2011). Analysis and localization of blue whale vocalizations in the Solomon Sea using waveform amplitude data. *Journal of the Acoustical Society of America, 130*(2), 731–736.

Franz, M., & Nunn, C. L. (2009). Network-based diffusion analysis: A new method for detecting social learning. *Proceedings of the Royal Society B, 276*(1663), 1829–1836.

Galef, B. G. (1992). The question of animal culture. *Human Nature, 3*(2), 157–178. http://doi.org/10.1007/BF02692251

Garland, E. C., Goldizen, A. W., Rekdahl, M. L., Constantine, R., Garrigue, C., Hauser, N. D., … & Noad, M. J. (2011). Dynamic horizontal cultural transmission of humpback whale song at the ocean basin scale. *Current Biology, 21*(8), 687–691.

Glockner, D. A., & Venus, S. C. (1983). Identification, growth rate, and behavior of humpback whale (*Megaptera novaeangliae*) cows and calves in the waters off Maui, Hawaii, 1977–1979. In R. Payne (Ed.), *Communication and behavior of whales* (pp. 223–258). Boulder, CO: Westview Press.

Goodall, J. (1986). *The chimpanzees of Gombe: Patterns of behavior.* Cambridge, MA: Belknap Press of Harvard University Press.

Gotelli, N. J. (1995). *A primer of ecology*. Sunderland, MA: Sinauer Associates.

Gould, S. J., & Lewontin, R. C. (1979). The spandrels of San Marco and the Panglossian paradigm: A critique of the adaptationist programme. *Proceedings of the Royal Society B, 205*(1161), 581–598.

Guinet, C., & Bouvier, J. (1995). Development of intentional stranding hunting techniques in killer whale (*Orcinus orca*) calves at Crozet Archipelago. *Canadian Journal of Zoology, 73*(1), 27–33.

Hain, J. H. W., Carter, G. R., Kraus, S. C., Mayo, C. A., & Winn, H. E. (1982). Feeding-behavior of the humpback whale, *Megaptera novaeangliae*, in the western North Atlantic. *Fishery Bulletin, 80*(2), 259–268.

Hastie, G. D., Wilson, B., Tufft, L. H., & Thompson, P. M. (2003). Bottlenose dolphins increase breathing synchrony in response to boat traffic. *Marine Mammal Science, 19*(1), 74–84. http://doi.org/10.1111/j.1748-7692.2003.tb01093.x

Herman, L. H. (2002). Vocal, social, and self-imitation by bottlenosed dolphins. In K. Dautenhahn & C. L. Nehaniv (Eds.), *Imitation in animals and artifacts* (pp. 63–108). Cambridge, MA: MIT Press.

Heyes, C. M. (1994). Social learning in animals: Categories and mechanisms. *Biological Reviews of the Cambridge Philosophical Society, 69*(2), 207–31.

Heyes, C. (2012). What's social about social learning? *Journal of Comparative Psychology, 126*(2), 193–202.

Heyes, C., & Pearce, J. M. (2015). Not-so-social learning strategies. *Proceedings of the Royal Society B, 282*(1802), doi:10.1098/rspb.20141709

Hobaiter, C., Poisot, T., Zuberbühler, K., Hoppitt, W., & Gruber, T. (2014). Social network analysis shows direct evidence for social transmission of tool use in wild chimpanzees. *PLoS Biology, 12*(9), e1001960. http://doi.org/10.1371/journal.pbio.1001960

Hopper, L. M., Lambeth, S. P., Schapiro, S. J., & Whiten, A. (2008). Observational learning in chimpanzees and children studied through "ghost" conditions. *Proceedings of the Royal Society B, 275*(1636), 835–840. http://doi.org/10.1098/rspb.2007.1542

Hoppitt, W., Boogert, N. J., & Laland, K. N. (2010). Detecting social transmission in networks. *Journal of Theoretical Biology, 263*(4), 544–555. http://doi.org/10.1016/j.jtbi.2010.01.004

Hoppitt, W., & Laland, K. N. (2013). *Social learning: An introduction to mechanisms, methods, and models*. Princeton, NJ: Princeton University Press.

Horner, V., & Whiten, A. (2005). Causal knowledge and imitation/emulation switching in chimpanzees (*Pan troglodytes*) and children (*Homo sapiens*). *Animal Cognition, 8*(3), 164–181. http://doi.org/10.1007/s10071-004-0239-6

Huffman, M. A. 1996. Acquisition of innovative cultural behaviors in nonhuman primates: A case study of stone handling, a socially transmitted behavior in Japanese macaques. In C. M. Heyes and B. G. Galef (Eds.), *Social learning in animals* (pp. 267–289). San Diego, CA: Academic Press.

Jaakkola, K., Guarino, E., & Rodriguez, M. (2010). Blindfolded imitation in a bottlenose dolphin (*Tursiops truncatus*). *International Journal of Comparative Psychology, 23*(4), 671–688.

Janik, V. M. (1999). Origins and implications of vocal learning in bottlenose dolphins. In H. O. Box & K. R. Gibson (Eds.), *Mammalian social learning: Comparative and ecological perspectives* (pp. 308–326). Cambridge: Cambridge University Press.

Kawai, M. (1965). Newly-acquired pre-cultural behavior of the natural troop of Japanese monkeys on Koshima Islet. *Primates, 6*(1), 1–30.

King, S. L., & Janik, V. M. (2013). Bottlenose dolphins can use learned vocal labels to address each other. *Proceedings of the National Academy of Sciences, 110*(32), 13216–13221.

Krause, J., Krause, S., Arlinghaus, R., Psorakis, I., Roberts, S., & Rutz, C. (2013). Reality mining of animal social systems. *Trends in Ecology and Evolution, 28*(9), 541–551. http://doi.org/10.1016/j.tree.2013.06.002

Krützen, M., Mann, J., Heithaus, M. R., Connor, R. C., Bejder, L., & Sherwin, W. B. (2005). Cultural transmission of tool use in bottlenose dolphins. *Proceedings of the National Academy of Sciences, 102*(25), 8939–8943.

Krützen, M., van Schaik, C., & Whiten, A. (2007). The animal cultures debate: Response to Laland and Janik. *Trends in Ecology and Evolution, 22*(1), 6.

Krützen, M., Willems, E. P., & van Schaik, C. P. (2011). Culture and geographic variation in orangutan behavior. *Current Biology, 21*(21), 1808–1812.

Kühl, H. S., Kalan, A. K., Arandjelovic, M., Aubert, F., D'Auvergne, L., Goedmakers, A., … & Ton, E. (2016). Chimpanzee accumulative stone throwing. *Scientific Reports, 6*, 22219.

Laland, K. N., & Hoppitt, W. (2003). Do animals have culture? *Evolutionary Anthropology: Issues, News, and Reviews, 12*(3), 150–159.

Laland, K. N., & Janik, V. M. (2006). The animal cultures debate. *Trends in Ecology and Evolution, 21*(10), 542–547. http://doi.org/10.1016/j.tree.2006.06.005

Laland, K. N., & Janik, V. M. (2007). Response to Krützen *et al.*: Further problems with the "method of exclusion." *Trends in Ecology and Evolution, 22*(1), 7.

Langergraber, K. E., Boesch, C., Inoue, E., Inoue-Murayama, M., Mitani, J. C., Nishida, T., … & Vigilant, L. (2010). Genetic and "cultural" similarity in wild chimpanzees. *Proceedings of the Royal Society B, 278*, 408–416. http://doi.org/10.1098/rspb.2010.1112

Lindenbaum, S. (2008). Understanding kuru: The contribution of anthropology and medicine. *Philosophical Transactions of the Royal Society B, 363*(1510), 3715–3720.

Luncz, L. V., & Boesch, C. (2014). Tradition over trend: Neighboring chimpanzee communities maintain differences in cultural behavior despite frequent immigration of adult females. *American Journal of Primatology, 76*(7), 649–657.

Matsuzawa, T., Biro, D., Humle, T., Inoue, N., & Tonooka, R. (2001). Emergence of culture in wild chimpanzees: Education by master-apprenticeship. In T. Matsuzawa (Ed.), *Primate origins of human cognition and behavior* (pp. 557–574). New York: Springer.

McDonald, M., Hildebrand, J., & Mesnick, S. (2009). Worldwide decline in tonal frequencies of blue whale songs. *Endangered Species Research, 9*, 13–21. http://doi.org/10.3354/esr00217

McDonald, M., Mesnick, S., & Hildebrand J. (2006). Biogeographic characterization of blue whale song worldwide: Using song to identify populations. *Journal of Cetacean Research and Management, 8*(1), 55–65.

McGrew, W. C., & Tutin, C. E. (1978). Evidence for a social custom in wild chimpanzees? *Man*, n.s. *13*(2), 234–251.

McSweeney, D. J., Chu, K. C., Dolphin, W. F., & Guinee, L. N. (1989). North Pacific humpback whale songs: A comparison of southeast Alaskan feeding ground songs with Hawaiian wintering ground songs. *Marine Mammal Science, 5*(2), 139–148.

Mesoudi, A., Chang, L., Dall, S. R., & Thornton, A. (2016). The evolution of individual and cultural variation in social learning. *Trends in Ecology and Evolution, 31*(3), 215–225.

Mitani, J. C., Hasegawa, T., Gros-Louis, J., Marler, P., & Byrne, R. (1992). Dialects in wild chimpanzees? *American Journal of Primatology, 27*, 233–243.

Mitani, J. C., Hunley, K. L., Murdoch, M. E., & Arbor, A. (1999). Geographic variation in the calls of wild chimpanzees: A reassessment. *American Journal of Primatology, 151*, 133–151.

Noad, M. J., Cato, D. H., Bryden, M. M., Jenner, M. N., & Jenner, K. C. S. (2000). Cultural revolution in whale songs. *Nature, 408*(6812), 537–537.

Ottoni, E. B., & Izar, P. (2008). Capuchin monkey tool use: Overview and implications. *Evolutionary Anthropology, 17*, 171–178. http://doi.org/10.1002/evan.20185

Payne, K. (2000). The progressively changing songs of humpback whales: A window on the creative process in a wild animal. In N. L. Wallin & B. Merker (Eds.), *The origins of music* (pp. 135–150). Cambridge, MA: MIT Press.

Perry, S., Baker, M., Fedigan, L., Gros-Louis, J., Jack, K., Mackinnon, K. C., ... & Rose, L. (2003). Social conventions in wild white-faced capuchin monkeys. *Current Anthropology, 44*(2), 241–269.

Rendell, L., Fogarty, L., & Laland, K. N. (2010). Roger's paradox recast and resolved: Population structure and the evolution of social learning strategies. *Evolution, 64*(2), 534–548.

Rendell, L., Mesnick, S. L., Dalebout, M. L., Burtenshaw, J., & Whitehead, H. (2012). Can genetic differences explain vocal dialect variation in sperm whales, *Physeter macrocephalus*? *Behavior Genetics, 42*(2), 332–43. http://doi.org/10.1007/s10519-011-9513-y

Rendell, L. E., & Whitehead, H. (2003). Vocal clans in sperm whales (*Physeter macrocephalus*). *Proceedings of the Royal Society, B, 270*, 225–231. http://doi.org/10.1098/rspb.2002.2239

Schulz, T. M., Whitehead, H., Gero, S., & Rendell, L. (2008). Overlapping and matching of codas in vocal interactions between sperm whales: Insights into communication function. *Animal Behaviour, 76*(6), 1977–1988. http://dx.doi.org/10.1016/j.anbehav.2008.07.032

Smolker, R., & Pepper, J. W. (1999). Whistle convergence among allied male bottlenose dolphins (*Delphinidae, Tursiops sp.*). *Ethology, 105*(7), 595–617.

Tayler, C. K., & Saayman, G. S. (1973). Imitative behaviour by Indian Ocean bottlenose dolphins (*Tursiops aduncus*) in captivity. *Behaviour, 44*, 286–298.

Tennie, C., Call, J., & Tomasello, M. (2012). Untrained chimpanzees (*Pan troglodytes schweinfurthii*) fail to imitate novel actions. *PLoS One, 7*(8), e41548.

Tomasello, M., Camak, L., & Bard, K. (1987). Observational learning of tool-use by young chimpanzees. *Human Evolution, 2*(1982), 175–183.

Tomasello, M., Kruger, A. C., & Ratner, H. H. (1993). Cultural learning. *Behavioral and Brain Sciences, 16*(03), 495–511.

Tyack, P. L., & Miller, E. H. (2002). Vocal anatomy, acoustic communication and echolocation. In A. R. Hoelzel (Ed.), *Marine mammal biology: An evolutionary approach* (pp. 142–184). Oxford: Blackwell Science.

Valenzuela, L. O., Sironi, M., Rowntree, V. J., & Seger, J. (2009). Isotopic and genetic evidence for culturally inherited site fidelity to feeding grounds in southern right whales (*Eubalaena australis*). *Molecular Ecology, 18*(5), 782–791. http://doi.org/10.1111/j.1365-294X.2008.04069.x

van de Waal, E., Borgeaud, C., & Whiten, A. (2013). Potent social learning and conformity shape a wild primate's foraging decisions. *Science, 340*(6131), 483–485. http://doi.org/10.1126/science.1232769

van de Waal, E., Claidière, N., & Whiten, A. (2015). Wild vervet monkeys copy alternative methods for opening an artificial fruit. *Animal Cognition, 18*(3), 617–627.

van Leeuwen, E. J. C., Cronin, K. A, Haun, D. B. M., Mundry, R., & Bodamer, M. D. (2012). Neighbouring chimpanzee communities show different preferences in social grooming behaviour. *Proceedings of the Royal Society B, 279*(1746), 4362–4367. http://doi.org/10.1098/rspb.2012.1543

van Schaik, C. P., Ancrenaz, M., Borgen, G., Galdikas, B., Knott, C. D., Singleton, I., … & Merrill, M. (2003). Orangutan cultures and the evolution of material culture. *Science, 299*(5603), 102–105. http://doi.org/10.1126/science.1078004

Watson, S. K., Townsend, S., Schel, A., Wilke, C., Wallace, E., Cheng, L., … & Slocombe, K. (2015). Vocal learning in the functionally referential food grunts of chimpanzees. *Current Biology, 25*(4), 495–9. http://doi.org/10.1016/j.cub.2014.12.032

Watwood, S. L., Tyack, P. L., & Wells, R. S. (2004). Whistle sharing in paired male bottlenose dolphins, *Tursiops truncates. Behavioral Ecology and Sociobiology, 55*(6), 531–543. http://doi.org/10.1007/s00265-003-0724-y

Whitehead, H. (2003). *Sperm whales: Social evolution in the ocean.* Chicago: University of Chicago Press.

Whitehead, H. (2009). Estimating abundance from one-dimensional passive acoustic surveys. *Journal of Wildlife Management, 73*(6), 1000–1009.

Whitehead, H., & Rendell, L. (2014). *The cultural lives of whales and dolphins.* Chicago, IL: University of Chicago Press.

Whitehead, H., Rendell, L., Osborne, R. W., & Würsig, B. (2004). Culture and conservation of non-humans with reference to whales and dolphins: Review and new directions. *Biological Conservation, 120*(3), 431–441. http://doi.org/10.1016/j.biocon.2004.03.017

Whiten, A., Goodall, J., McGrew, W. C., Nishida, T., Reynolds, V., Sugiyama, Y., ... & Boesch, C. (1999). Cultures in chimpanzees. *Nature, 399*(6737), 682–685. http://doi.org/10.1038/21415

Whiten, A., Horner, V., Litchfield, C. A., & Marshall-Pescini, S. (2004). How do apes ape? *Learning & Behavior, 32*(1), 36–52.

Wich, S. A., Krützen, M., Lameira, A. R., Nater, A., Arora, N., Bastian, M. L., ... & van Schaik, C. P. (2012). Call cultures in orang-utans? *PloS One, 7*(5), e36180. http://doi.org/10.1371/journal.pone.0036180

6

Cultural Phenomena in Cooperatively Breeding Primates

Charles T. Snowdon

This chapter reviews culture-like phenomena in cooperatively breeding species, mainly in marmoset and tamarin monkeys. The anthropologist Sarah Blaffer Hrdy (2009) has argued that humans are cooperative breeders, meaning that human mothers, unlike other ape mothers, cannot rear infants without help. For humans and other cooperative breeders, assistance from individuals other than the mother is critical for successful infant rearing. Most human cultures are organized around families as the basic social unit, as are cooperatively breeding monkeys. Cooperatively breeding species share a family-like breeding system similar to that of humans that requires a high degree of social tolerance, clear communication to allow multiple caregivers to coordinate infant care, and cooperative social interactions, which are not as readily seen in more closely related non-human primates, such as chimpanzees (*Pan* sp.), baboons (*Papio* sp.) and macaques (*Macaca* sp.). Because of their evolutionary distance from humans (the separation was approximately 35 million years ago), marmosets and tamarins are often thought to be of little relevance to understanding human behavior in comparison with more closely related primates such as apes and Old World primates. However, given the similarities of social organization and family life between humans and cooperatively breeding monkeys, these monkeys may be of interest because they contribute to our understanding of convergent evolutionary processes.

Several authors have pointed to the differences between humans and other apes – tailless primates such as chimpanzees (*Pan troglodytes*), bonobos (*Pan paniscus*), orangutans (*Pongo* sp.) and gorillas (*Gorilla* sp.) – with respect to cooperation and prosocial behavior, which are likely to be precursors of culture. For example, Wilson (2012) sees parallels between

The Handbook of Culture and Biology, First Edition. Edited by José M. Causadias, Eva H. Telzer and Nancy A. Gonzales.

human social organization and eusocial insects, and regards this social structure as what has allowed humans to be so dominant. Tomasello (2009) finds few parallels in cooperation and prosocial behavior between humans and chimpanzees, and attributes this lack to cognitive differences. Humans display better social coordination and communication skills, engaging in joint attention, and humans also have higher levels of mutual tolerance and trust than do chimpanzees. Tomasello (2009) sees these factors as critical for the development of culture. De Waal and colleagues (Brosnan, Schiff, & de Waal, 2005; de Waal & Suchak, 2010), in contrast, have proposed that variation in social relationships can predict prosocial behavior: individuals that have close social relationships with each other are more likely to share food and tolerate inequity than those that have distant relationships.

As will be shown, cooperatively breeding marmosets and tamarins have close social relationships within groups, exhibit great tolerance and trust, and in sharing food with, and teaching, their young show many of the features that Tomasello (2009) sees as unique to humans. There is more evidence of rapid social learning, imitation, and active teaching in these species than in our closest ape relatives and in other monkeys. Evidence of culturally transmitted phenomena is seen in the long-term maintenance and intergenerational transmission of novel foraging methods and of directed teaching behavior with scaffolding as a naïve learner becomes more skillful, and, possibly, in the transmission of population-specific vocal dialects. Experimental laboratory studies and field observations suggest that food preferences and aversions can be transmitted socially and have long-lasting effects, and that there may be a cultural component to paternal care skills.

As illustrated in the introductory chapter to this part on animal culture (see chapter 4 in this volume), the mechanisms of cultural transmission are thought to include social learning, imitation and direct teaching, and for these mechanisms to be effective several things are necessary. Coussi-Korbel and Fragaszy (1995) have outlined the relationship between social dynamics and social learning, and the characteristics that they describe are seen most clearly in cooperative breeders. First, Coussi-Korbel and Fragaszy note that there must be a stimulus that attracts the attention of the learner and that this may be an affective, a physical or an action stimulus. Second, coordination in space and time is needed between the demonstrator and the learner, and this may be complementary, as in the case of teacher and learner or parent and child, or dominant and subordinate, or isomorphic, as when the behavior of one individual channels that of another to act on the same stimulus in the same way. This coordination is critical if imitation is to occur. Third, the identity of the demonstrator may be important: a learner is more likely to direct attention to influential individuals than to others. Directed attention may lead to within-group differentiation of behavior and to increased efficiency of transmission. Coussi-Korbel and Fragaszy (1995) predict that one will see both more extensive and more frequent coordination of behavior in groups or species that have an egalitarian social structure and that have a highly tolerant style of social dynamics. Furthermore, a greater number of individuals within an egalitarian group should lead to more individuals being salient for social learning. They conclude that social learning (including imitation and teaching) and the types of information that can be transmitted socially are more likely to be functions of social dynamics than of phylogeny. According to this logic, cooperatively breeding primates could be more relevant for our understanding of the social learning processes that underlie culture than our closest ape relatives.

Recently authors have argued that socially transmitted knowledge should be more evident in cooperative breeders than in species with other forms of social organization (Burkart, Hrdy, & van Schaik, 2009; Burkart & van Schaik, 2010; Snowdon, 2001). Burkart and colleagues (2009) distinguished between the cognitive preconditions for human mental capacities that can be seen in great apes and Old World primates and the psychological preconditions that promote the cooperative and prosocial processes that lead individuals to infer the mental states of others and to the shared intentionality that promotes cumulative culture and language. These psychological processes, they argue, have emerged from the cooperative breeding system that is uniquely human among apes. Human cognition and culture represent a melding of the cognitive precursors seen in apes with the cooperative processes that derive from cooperative breeding. Thus, to truly understand human social and physical cognition, one needs to study not only our closest relatives, the apes, but also those primate species that share our cooperative breeding system, the marmosets and the tamarins.

Tests of the cooperative breeding hypothesis involve the provision of similar tasks for a range of species that have different breeding systems: it is predicted that tests of physical cognition will be solved best by species phylogenetically close to humans, whereas tests of prosocial behavior will be solved best by cooperatively breeding species. Burkart and van Schaik (2011) developed a group service paradigm. A tray placed outside a cage with a handle that could pull the tray close to the cage had two positions for placing food, one from which the animal pulling the handle could obtain the food and another from where the one pulling the tray could not obtain food but other group members could. The initial study compared Japanese macaques (*Macaca fuscata*), among which mothers do most of the infant care, capuchin monkeys (*Cebus apella*), an intermediate species, and common marmosets (*Callithrix jacchus*), which are cooperative breeders. Measures of social tolerance (how close animals could be to each other when food was present) found greater tolerance among capuchins and marmosets than among macaques, but only the marmosets readily provided food to other group members.

A subsequent extension of this paradigm to 24 different groups from 15 different species (Burkart et al., 2014) found that successful performance in the prosocial task was related to the presence of heterosexual pair bonds and social tolerance and inversely related to brain size. However, the greatest amount of variance was explained by the amount of allomaternal care (helping by non-mothers). Tamarins (*Saguinus oedipus* and *Leontopithecus chrysomelas*) and humans had the greatest degree of allomaternal care and the greatest proportion of prosocial behavior in the tests. Since monogamy and strong pair bonds are prerequisites for paternal care (Lukas & Clutton-Brock, 2013), and trust and social tolerance are required for the shared care of infants, it is not surprising that these variables also show strong correlations with prosocial behavior.

Social tolerance, allomaternal care and prosocial actions that benefit other group members should also promote the development of culture or pre-cultural phenomena, since these phenomena depend upon close observation, social learning and even tutoring, which arise more readily in socially tolerant, prosocial animals that coordinate behavior with each other. The other chapters in this part illustrate cultural processes in vervet monkeys, apes and other primate species, so the characteristics of cooperative breeding are not necessary for cultural phenomena to appear. However, cultural processes may be more likely to emerge in cooperative breeders. The rest of this chapter reviews results from cooperatively breeding primates that show rapid social learning, imitation, and teaching, which are all mechanisms involved in cultural transmission; it will then review three areas of potential culture, namely communication, food preferences, and paternal care.

Rapid Social Learning

Tolerance of other group members and the ability to coordinate actions in space and time should lead to rapid social learning. Moscovice and Snowdon (2006) trained one cotton-top tamarin (*Saguinus oedipus*) in a mated pair to locate food in an apparatus which contained five food locations, obscured by differently colored circular metal doors. The tamarin had to learn a novel motor task, to rotate the door with one hand while removing the food with the other. Food was placed behind each of the five doors so that odor cues would be constant, but four of the doors were locked so that a tamarin could only obtain food from one container. The monkeys were allowed to explore the apparatus, and some solved the problem by trial and error over eight sessions of two trials each. However, most monkeys needed additional guidance. After all the monkeys reached criterion, the naïve mate of each was introduced at the same time, and the number of trials the mate needed to solve the problem was recorded. The naïve monkeys closely followed the demonstrator and all learned to open the container within the first two or three sessions. However, although they demonstrated learning of the task, the naïve animals received few rewards, since they were usually following behind the demonstrator (which ate the food after opening the container). In the fourth session (trials 7–8) naïve observers were tested alone; they readily opened the correct location and obtained food. From this point onwards, both naïve and experienced animals rapidly found food. A control group of mated animals tested together with the same apparatus over the same number of sessions failed to learn the correct location and received no food. When demonstrator tamarins and their social learning companions were tested 17 months later with no sessions in between, both groups solved the problem with few errors and a short latency, meeting the durability criterion for a cultural behavior. In contrast, research with chimpanzees (*Pan troglodytes*) has shown that they learn a task much faster under competitive than under cooperative social conditions (Hare & Tomasello, 2004). Furthermore, whereas the tamarins nearly always chose the correct location (out of five choices), chimpanzees in a two-choice apparatus responded only at chance levels under cooperation and at 72% in the competitive regime, a performance well below that of tamarins, thus showing superior social learning abilities in tamarins compared to chimpanzees.

Although Galef and Giraldeau (2001) showed that birds and many mammals socially learn to avoid noxious foods by observing conspecifics, there has been little evidence of social learning to avoid noxious foods in nonhuman primates. For example, Visalberghi and Addessi (2000) presented capuchin monkeys (a non-cooperatively breeding species) with a familiar and preferred food, mozzarella cheese, that had been flavored with white pepper to make it aversive. Capuchin monkeys learned individually to avoid this food, but failed to learn from observing other monkeys responding to the food. In contrast, Snowdon and Boe (2003) presented cotton-top tamarins with a highly preferred food, tuna fish, also made noxious by the addition of white pepper. Of the 42 monkeys in eight social groups that were tested, only a third of the animals ever tasted the tuna, while the other two-thirds avoided it. After three presentations of the tuna (one each week) no one was sampling the tuna. In the fourth week, tuna was presented without pepper, and only two-thirds of the animals ate it. Some of the remaining monkeys failed to eat tuna for up to a year afterwards, even though they had never tasted the noxious tuna. This is a powerful, and for some animals a long-lasting, change in diet brought about through social learning. Why did tamarins show rapid avoidance learning from others, whereas capuchin monkeys did not? One important difference was that tamarins that sampled the pepper-laced tuna gave alarm calls and displayed facial reactions of disgust, whereas the capuchin monkeys produced no communication signals that might have helped naïve animals learn.

Imitation

The first convincing demonstrations of imitation were seen in common marmosets. Bugnyar and Huber (1997) presented marmosets with a simple two-action feeding device. Food could be obtained by either pushing a Plexiglas door or lifting it up. A demonstrator in one group was trained to lift the door and one in another group to push the door, and the rest of the group members imitated the action of the demonstrator. In another study Voelkl and Huber (2000) presented food in film canisters. One group opened the canisters using their hands and the other group had a demonstrator that used its mouth to open the canister. None of the animals that observed the hand-opening demonstrator opened lids with their mouths, whereas those which observed the mouth-opening method used both their hands and their mouths to open canisters.

Building on the push–pull apparatus of Bugnyar and Huber (1997), Gunhold, Range, Huber, and Bugnyar (2015) exposed groups of captive marmosets to either the pull or push method and then tested the same animals three years later; they found that the marmosets retained the technique to which they were initially exposed. Animals born into the group since the initial training and testing acquired the same method of obtaining the food as others in the group. Gunhold, Massen, Schiel, Souto, and Bugnyar (2014) took the same apparatus into a wild population of marmosets in Brazil and again found long-term memory for the initial solution within each group; they found as well that new immigrants and animals born into the group since the initial training also acquired the group-typical solution. In a subsequent study Gunhold, Whiten, and Bugnyar (2014) found that wild common marmosets could also learn to imitate a task solution merely by watching videotapes of a captive animal solving the problem. Thus, through imitation, marmosets learned a novel foraging task that spread throughout the entire group. The behavior persisted over several years in the absence of further testing, and animals that joined the group acquired the same behavior as other group members. These studies clearly meet several of the criteria for culture described in chapter 4 of this volume, including dissemination, standardization, tradition, naturalness, and social learning. In addition, the small brain size of marmosets compared to chimpanzees and humans suggests that culture-like behaviors are possible in the absence of large, complex brains.

Food Preferences

In the previous section I described a study on social learning to avoid noxious food (tuna laced with white pepper). Unlike many other primate species, for which there is no evidence of social learning when noxious foods are involved, cotton-top tamarins rapidly learned to avoid tainted food without actually tasting it (Snowdon & Boe, 2003). In some cases animals did not sample the tuna again even several months after normal tuna was again presented. Thus, many individual tamarins learned to avoid a previously preferred food for a long time, and since these individuals were clustered within groups one could speak of group-specific cultural preferences (or avoidance) of food.

A second example of potential cultural differences in food preferences comes from pygmy marmosets in five populations in the Ecuadoran Amazon. Pygmy marmosets have specialized teeth for creating holes in the bark of trees, and the exudate that flows into these holes is a major source of nutrition. Yepez, de la Torre, and Snowdon (2005) recorded the species of trees used for exudate by each group of marmosets in each of the five populations. Each population had a preferred tree species that was used for exudate feeding, and the preference varied across populations. One explanation for this is that marmosets simply select the tree species that is most abundant in their environment, since eventually an exudate feeding tree becomes used up and monkeys need to find a new tree. However, all five preferred exudate species were found in each of the five populations and in no case was the preferred exudate tree the most abundant tree within that population. Thus marmosets are selecting exudate trees on some basis other than abundance. Given the rapid social learning to avoid noxious food in captive tamarins and the extensive food sharing with young animals, it is not far-fetched to think that the selection of exudate species is socially transmitted across generations, leading to cultural preferences for food.

Teaching

Teaching may be the ultimate form of cultural transmission. An experienced instructor provides guidance to a naïve learner, and through instruction the learner acquires new skills more readily than it would on its own through trial-and-error learning. In the introductory chapter to this part I reviewed how Caro and Hauser (1992) developed an operational definition of teaching that could be applied to non-human animals. A teacher must behave differently with naïve individuals than with experienced individuals. There must be a cost to the teacher and there must be a change in the behavior of the naïve animal as a result. I would add an additional criterion, that the teacher will change its behavior as the naïve animal acquires skills.

To date the evidence for teaching in our closest ape relatives has been scant. In one report two chimpanzee mothers were reported to engage one time each in teaching young to crack nuts using anvils and hammers. In one case the mother demonstrated the correct positioning of a nut on an anvil and her son successfully opened the nut. In the second case the mother slowly and with apparent deliberation rotated the hammer to a position where it could be used successfully and her daughter subsequently imitated that position and was successful (Boesch, 1991). However, these two examples were the only examples seen in hundreds of hours of direct observation and have not been reported by researchers at other sites.

Humle, Snowdon, and Matsuzawa (2009) observed interactions of mothers and infants during ant-dipping. Chimpanzees eat biting ants, and adults have specific methods of stripping leaves from a stick and adjusting the length of the stick and the method of collecting ants for ingestion according to the aggressiveness of the ants. This would appear to be a prime situation for teaching to occur, yet no evidence was seen of mothers deliberately modeling behavior for their young, helping young prepare a stick of appropriate length, or showing any other behavior that might help their offspring learn faster.

In contrast, the best evidence for teaching comes from cooperatively breeding animals. In most species of marmosets and tamarins there is active food sharing between adults and offspring at the time of weaning, which creates opportunities for teaching. In cotton-top tamarins food sharing is accompanied by a very rapid sequence of food calls given by an adult who will share food (Joyce & Snowdon, 2007). These are the same syllables as in food calls made between adults, but in food-sharing contexts many more calls are given at a much more rapid rate than when adults feed (Joyce & Snowdon, 2007; Roush & Snowdon, 2001). Young tamarins can usually obtain food only if an adult gives these rapid calls. Thus, there is an alteration of behavior by adults in the context of food sharing. Since the adults are calling at a more rapid rate as well as giving up food, there is a cost to them. Young tamarins acquire the ability to obtain solid food on their own more quickly, and begin giving adult-like food calls sooner, if food sharing starts at an earlier age, which suggests that their behavior has been altered by the interaction. Food sharing begins about the third month of life and peaks in the fourth month, after which adults reduce the amount of food sharing (Joyce & Snowdon, 2007), suggesting that adult teachers are responding to the skills of the learners.

Further evidence of this is seen in a study done with juvenile tamarins by Humle and Snowdon (2008). By seven months of age tamarins are completely independent in feeding and never receive food from their parents. However, Humle and Snowdon (2008) trained each parent of a family in one of two alternative solutions to a novel foraging task. After the adults had mastered the methods in which they were trained, one twin juvenile was tested alone over several weeks with a parent. (Each juvenile in a family was exposed to a different solution.) Parents began to give food calls again and to share food with juveniles during tests with the novel apparatus, but not during sessions when the apparatus was not present. As soon as a juvenile solved the novel task once, the parents ceased food calling and sharing. We also observed times when the adult would deliberately hold open the foraging apparatus and wait until the juvenile came to take the food. This suggests that more than coaching is involved and that adults adjust their behavior to the changes in skill level of their offspring, a behavior known as "scaffolding" (e.g., Wood, Bruner, & Ross, 1976). Thus, cotton-top tamarins show all of the criteria for teaching.

Similar results have been obtained in a series of field and captive studies by Rapaport and colleagues on lion tamarins (*Leontopithecus* spp.). Lion tamarins were more likely to share with infants food that was novel or difficult to extract than food already familiar to them (Rapaport, 1999). In field studies, when young tamarins have difficulty in foraging, especially for insects, adults will continue to share insects with them well into their adolescence, and show clear evidence of scaffolding behavior as the young tamarins acquire more skills (Rapaport, 2006; Rapaport & Ruiz Miranda, 2002, 2006). Among several examples observed by Rapaport and Ruiz Miranda (2002) was a mother who gave food calls that attracted her son to where she was sitting. She did not offer food to her son; instead, he looked into a hole in the trunk of a nearby tree and extracted prey.

Stick weaving is a behavior seen in some captive cotton-top tamarins. In environments in which branches were provided for travel and enrichment some individual tamarins began spontaneously to pick off pieces of the branches and weave them into the mesh of the cage. The process involves breaking off a twig, biting it sufficiently to allow it to be bent but without breaking it, and then weaving the stick in and out of the enclosing mesh. All stick weavers were either descendants of two of the 16 founding breeders in the colony or mates of the descendant. Once we had observed one animal in a group weaving sticks, we found that others in the group who had not previously shown the behavior would imitate and begin weaving sticks as well. In a few cases we observed an adult appearing to deliberately slow its behavior when a young animal was nearby; eventually the young animal began to stick-weave (Snowdon & Roskos, 2017). The spread of stick weaving within a group represents a novel form of cultural transmission that does not involve any nutritional reward, but it does provide an example of innovation in cooperative breeders.

Teaching is not restricted to primates but is seen in other cooperatively breeding species. Meerkats (*Suricata suricatta*) are cooperatively breeding mammals that feed on a variety of insects, including scorpions which have a neurotoxic venom and large pinchers (Thornton & McAuliffe, 2006). Helpers typically kill or disable (by removing the stinger) scorpions before presenting them to pups. Helpers are more likely to kill and disable scorpions than non-toxic prey. They reduce the proportion of prey killed or disabled with the increasing age of pups, and present more live prey. Helpers spent more time monitoring young with live prey than with dead or disabled prey, and this monitoring time decreased with increasing pup age. Helpers nudged rare prey toward pups more often than common prey, and as pups aged they became more successful in handling live prey on their own. Thornton and McAuliffe (2006) also played back calls of young pups to helpers with older pups present and found helpers disabled more prey than when calls of older pups were presented. Conversely, helpers did less killing and disabling of prey for young pups when calls from older pups were played back. Thus helpers do not appear to track the skills of individual pups but used vocal cues of age to determine whether to disable scorpions or not. Young pups took significantly longer to handle prey than older pups, but it is unclear whether this is simply due to physical maturation or to the teaching-like behavior of helpers.

Communication

Several authors have argued that vocal learning does not occur in non-human primates, in striking contrast to the results from birds (e.g. Hammerschmidt & Fischer, 2008; Janik & Slater, 1997, 2000). Vocal communication, especially the development of song in birds, is a clear example of cultural aspects in communication. In passerine birds (most songbirds), as well as in birds of the parrot family, young must learn song from adult models, and the song that birds of at least some species are exposed to during a sensitive period is the song that bird will sing as an adult (Catchpole & Slater, 2008). In other species adults may change their song when they encounter birds with different songs or dialects, as they return from migration or enter new social groups (e.g. Farabaugh, Linzenbold, & Dooling, 1994; Hausberger, Richard, Henry, Lepage, & Schmidt, 1995; Mundinger, 1970; Nowicki, 1989; Payne & Payne, 1993). Although these birds are not cooperative breeders, they are biparental: that is, the parents share the care of the chicks. Thus, many of the pressures that lead to rapid social learning and proto-cultural behavior apply to birds as well.

However, among cooperatively breeding monkeys there is increasing evidence of group- or pair-specific features of calls, of dialects or population-level vocal variation, and of parental coaching of vocal development in young. Two studies of pygmy marmosets (*Cebuella pygmaea*) found vocal convergence. The first found convergence among entire groups of marmosets when two colonies were merged: all the marmosets modified the pitch and band-width of their trill vocalizations to create a common trill for the merged colonies (Elowson & Snowdon, 1994). The second found it when individuals were paired and pair members changed their trill structure as they converged on a common, pair-specific trill. In follow-up studies three years later, although some trill parameters had changed, the pair still had similar trills (Snowdon & Elowson, 1999). Similar results were found in marmosets by Jorgenson and French (1998).

In a study of wild pygmy marmosets, de la Torre and Snowdon (2009) described population-level differences in trills and J-calls (each a form of within-group contact call). The study populations ranged across a 200 km east–west transect and a 100 km north–south transect in the Ecuadoran Amazon, and the population-level variation in vocal structure was evident even though there were also individual and pair differences in trill structure within each population. There are several possible reasons for population-level variation. Genetic differences in each population may have led to different vocal structure, or differences in habitat acoustics may have shaped the structure of vocalizations for maximum clarity in the habitat of each population. However, playbacks, followed by re-recordings of calls in each habitat, and measurements of ambient noise suggest that differences in habitat acoustic structure could not explain the acoustic differences found (de la Torre & Snowdon, 2009). Genetic explanations have not yet been ruled out. Nonetheless, the fact that captive adult marmosets can adjust vocal signatures to accommodate new groups or to match a new mate suggests that some cultural processes may also be involved.

Despite the arguments that vocal learning does not occur in non-human primates, data from marmosets and tamarins suggest that learning and possibly teaching do occur. Infant pygmy marmosets engage in much vocal activity, which has been labeled "babbling" because of its similarities to human infant babbling (Elowson, Snowdon, & Lazaro-Perea, 1998). Babbling begins early in life and can go on for long periods. Babbling is seemingly random: many sounds are repeated in contexts that are not relevant to adult behavior. Many of the forms of adult calls appear in babbling, although they are not fully formed. Most importantly, adults respond to infant babbling behavior with social contact. In research on the ontogeny of the trill call in pygmy marmosets, Elowson, Snowdon, and Sweet (1992) reported that trill structure was not innate, since it changed over development, but the rate of developmental change differed between twins and other infants, which suggests that changes were not due to simple maturation. In a follow-up to the original babbling report Snowdon and Elowson (2001) reported that the development of trill calls was related to the amount and diversity of babbling shown by an infant: more babbling and greater diversity of calls in the first month of babbling correlated with a more adult-like trill structure at five months of age. However, fully formed adult-like trills did not appear until the marmosets reached puberty.

A recent study of vocal development in common marmosets shows the importance in development of parental responsiveness to infant calls. Takahashi and colleagues (2015) studied the development of the "phee" call, a frequent call given when marmosets are separated from one another, and found that the phee calls of infant marmosets became more stereotyped over the first two months: they had increased duration, decreased central frequency, and decreased entropy. The authors found four discrete clusters of calls in neonatal marmosets, but these had reduced to one or two clusters by two months of age. At first glance this reduction may seem to support a simple maturational model of vocal development. However, changes in phee structure were not correlated with age, body weight, or the physiological development of the respiratory system. Takahashi and colleagues (2015) recorded infants both when they were alone and when they were in vocal contact with one of their parents. Parents generally respond to infant calls with well-formed adult phees. The rates of parental responsiveness to infants correlated directly with the age at which infants began producing well-formed phees of their own, suggesting that parental responsiveness to infant cries directly influences an infant's trajectory toward an adult call. Although the studies on babbling in infant pygmy marmosets reported that parents responded to infant babbling with increased social contact, the results from Takahashi and colleagues (2015) suggest a direct connection between parental reinforcement (coaching) and infant vocal competence.

Similar processes influence vocal development in cotton-top tamarins as well. Adult tamarins produce eight different types of chirp vocalizations in different contexts (mild alarm, strong alarm, mobbing, response to hearing strangers, social contact and feeding; Cleveland & Snowdon, 1982). Castro and Snowdon (2000) experimentally created contexts for eliciting several of these chirp types and showed that adults responded with the predicted chirp type in each of the contexts. Then, when infants had been born, Castro and Snowdon (2000) presented the same contexts to family groups over the first months of infant development. In most tests, infants gave a sequence of two to three chirp calls that were not differentiated by context. However, in occasional tests an infant did give a chirp appropriate to the context, but in no context did all infants give an appropriate chirp, and no infant gave an appropriate chirp in all contexts. Furthermore, once an infant gave a chirp in an appropriate context, the likelihood of it giving the chirp again in a later test was very low. These results also support the idea that vocal structures are not innate in cotton-top tamarins. However, in the section on teaching above, it was noted that adults produce rapid sequences of food chirps when they share food with infants, and the one context in which the most infants gave an appropriate chirp and had the highest probability of repeating the call in future tests was feeding. It is likely that adults, by giving intense food calls and then sharing food, are shaping the vocal development of their infants, just as the marmoset parents did in Takahashi and colleagues (2015).

Roush and Snowdon (1994) found that young tamarins gave imperfect versions of food calls, and produced other types of calls in feeding contexts, and that this did not change with age, persisting well past puberty. In a subsequent study Roush and Snowdon (1999) monitored food calls when young tamarins were living in a helper role in their family groups, and then paired them with a novel mate. Soon after pairing, these tamarins began producing adult-like calls in feeding contexts, with none of the extraneous vocalizations seen earlier. This is similar to pygmy marmosets not producing fully adult trills until after pairing. Since helpers in cooperative breeding species do not breed and have subordinate status, even though vocal development is assisted by parents full expression of adult call structure may be delayed until animals are no longer subordinate helpers but have become breeding adults.

Paternal Care

In chapter 4 I described how epigenetic factors, some of which might result from cultural processes, could influence gene expression. One of the examples was paternal behavior in the California mouse (*Peromyscus californicus*) and its close relative, the white-footed mouse (*Peromyscus leucopus*). California mice are monogamous and highly territorial, and males engage in paternal care, whereas white-footed mice are promiscuous and non-territorial and show no paternal care. When Bester-Meredith and Marler (2001) cross-fostered pups between species, they found that cross-fostered pups acquired many of the behaviors of their foster parents and also showed species-novel brain distribution of arginine vasopressin activity. This study shows that the early environmental experience an infant receives can change not only behavior, but also brain function. In a subsequent study Frazier, Trainor, Cravens, Whitney, and Marler (2006) showed that it was the behavior of the father that determined these differences. Males of either California mice or cross-fostered mice developed patterns of territorial aggression and paternal care only if fathers were present, most of the variance in paternal care and aggression being determined by the rate of paternal retrieval when pups left the nest. Thus, in monogamous mice, the behavior of males toward pups creates a culture of paternal care.

One of the biggest problems in understanding the evolution of cooperative breeding is working out why some animals forgo their own reproduction in order to care for infants that are not their own. Many caregivers are related to the offspring they care for, and kinship can explain many cases of alloparental care. However, in the wild there are also many examples of unrelated animals that are involved in infant care. Some authors have suggested that male parental care has no direct adaptive value other than to make that male more likely to be able to mate with the mother when she ovulates again (e.g., Smuts & Gubernick, 1992). However, there is another reason why serving as a helper can be adaptive: it provides an opportunity to learn paternal care skills. Surveys of infant survival in marmoset and tamarin colonies have shown near-zero survival rates for infants born to parents that had no previous infant care experience (e.g., Tardif, Richter, & Carson, 1984). In experimental studies of response to infant vocal cues, experienced males reacted to and retrieved infants readily, even unrelated infants, whereas males who had no prior infant care experience were unresponsive to infant cues (Zahed, Prudom, Snowdon, & Ziegler (2008). Thus, learning infant care skills by taking care of someone else's infants is essential for tamarins and marmosets to be successful parents themselves. Male cotton-top tamarins which carried infants more in their family groups also spent more time carrying their own infants when they became fathers ($R_S = 0.786$, $N = 7$, $P = 0.036$; Zahed, Kurian, & Snowdon, 2010), although for females there was no relationship between infant carrying time in the natal group and subsequent parenting when they were mothers. Older infants showed extensive interest when new infants were born, although adults prevented them from carrying infants until the new infants were at least four weeks old (Achenbach & Snowdon, 1998). At least for males, infant care is a behavior that develops through experience with other infants and, given the intense interest in newborns coupled with the lack of access to infants for several weeks, suggests a possibility of social learning or imitation of infant care skills.

Conclusions and Future Directions

Cooperative breeding species represent one end of a parental care continuum that ranges from a mother providing all (or the majority) of the parental care, as is seen in many other monkeys and apes, to several group members cooperating in the care of infants. Shared parental care requires close attention and coordination among group members as well as social tolerance and prosocial behavior. These characteristics facilitate rapid social learning, imitation and teaching behavior. Culture-like processes are seen in acquisition of food preferences and aversions, in vocal communication and in the acquisition of parenting skills. The family life of cooperative breeders appears to facilitate the behaviors that are crucial for the development of culture. However, these features are not necessary for the emergence of culture, since culture is seen in species with other social systems as well.

However, this review has focused primarily on cooperatively breeding primates, and there are other cooperatively breeding mammals, such as wolves, mongooses, and meerkats, as well as cooperatively breeding birds. At present we know little about rapid social learning, imitation and teaching ability in these species, other than from the study on teaching in meerkats (Thornton & McAuliffe, 2006) and a study on rapid social learning in Florida scrub jays (*Aphelocoma coerulescens*) by Midford, Hailman, and Woolfenden (2000). If the theory presented here is correct – that socially tolerant and cooperative species should be more likely to show social learning, imitation and teaching – then one should expect these other species to demonstrate more aspects of cultural behavior as well. One important future direction would be to look for rapid social learning, imitation and teaching behavior in these other species. Comparative research on pairs of related species, of which one is cooperatively breeding and the other is not, would be very useful, since phylogenetic status would be controlled. Some good examples would be comparing wolves (*Canis lupus*) with dogs (*Canis lupus familiaris*), and cooperatively breeding Florida scrub jays with blue jays (*Cyanocitta cristata*).

A related direction for future research is that many species engage in biparental care, in which fathers and mothers, but not other group members, take part in infant care. Among these species are songbirds, whose cultural patterns of song learning and transmission across generations are well established, and many non-human primate species. These species have not been well studied with respect to rapid social learning, imitation and teaching, and we have little knowledge of any culture-like phenomena beyond birdsong. It would be fruitful to expand the range of species studied to include biparental species.

Finally, no non-human species, not even the chimpanzee, has met all of the criteria described in the chapter introducing this section (see chapter 4 in this volume), and no non-human species displays the cultural range and flexibility seen in human primates. A more thorough understanding of cultural processes is needed to explain what differentiates human culture from that of other primates, and why. This is an important task for the future.

References

Achenbach, G. G., & Snowdon, C. T. (1998). Response to sibling birth in juvenile cotton-top tamarins (*Saguinus oedipus*). *Behaviour, 135*, 845–862. doi:10.1163/156853998792640369

Bester-Meredith, J. K., & Marler, C. A. (2001).Vasopressin and aggression in cross-fostered California mice (*Peromyscus californicus*) and white-footed mice (*Peromyscus leucopus*). *Hormones and Behavior, 40*, 51–64. doi:10.1006/hbeh.2001.1666

Boesch, C. (1991). Teaching among wild chimpanzees. *Animal Behaviour, 41*, 530–532. doi:10.1016/S0003-3472(05)80857-7

Brosnan, S. F., Schiff, H. C., & de Waal, F. B. M. (2005). Tolerance for inequity may increase with social closeness in chimpanzees. *Proceedings of the Royal Society B, 272*, 253–258. doi:10.1098/rspb.2004.2947

Bugnyar, T., & Huber, L. (1997). Push or pull: An experimental study of imitation in marmosets. *Animal Behaviour, 54*, 817–831. doi:10.1006/anbe.1996.0497

Burkart, J. M., Allon, O, Amici, F., Fichtel, C., Finkenwirth, C., Heschl, A., … & van Schaik, C. P. (2014). The evolutionary origin of human hyper-cooperation. *Nature Communications, 5*, article 4747. doi:10.1038/ncomms5747

Burkart, J. M., Hrdy, S. B., & van Schaik, C. P. (2009). Cooperative breeding and human cognitive evolution. *Evolutionary Anthropology, 18*, 175–186.

Burkart, J. M., & van Schaik, C. (2010). Cognitive consequences of cooperative breeding in primates. *Animal Cognition, 13*, 1–19. doi:10.1002/evan.20222

Burkart, J. M., & van Schaik, C. (2011). Group service in macaques (*Macaca fuscata*), capuchins (*Cebus apella*) and marmosets (*Callithrix jacchus*): A comparative approach to identifying prosocial motivations. *Journal of Comparative Psychology, 127*, 212–225. doi:10.1037/a0026392

Caro, T. M., & Hauser, M. D. (1992). Is there teaching in nonhuman animals? *Quarterly Review of Biology, 67*, 151–174. doi:10.1086/417553

Castro, N. A., & Snowdon, C. T. (2000). Development of vocal responses in infant cotton-top tamarins. *Behaviour, 137*, 629–646. doi:10.1163/156853900502259

Catchpole, C. K., & Slater, P. J. B. (2008). *Bird song: Biological themes and variations*. Cambridge: Cambridge University Press. doi:10.1017/CBO9780511754791

Cleveland, J., & Snowdon, C. T. (1982). The complex vocal repertoire of the adult cotton-top tamarin (*Saguinus oedipus oedipus*). *Zeitschrift für Tierpsychologie, 58*, 231–270. doi:10.1111/j.1439-0310.1982.tb00320.x

Coussi-Korbel, S., & Fragaszy, D. M. (1995). On the relation between social dynamics and social learning. *Animal Behaviour, 50,* 1441–1453. doi:10.1016/0003-3472(95)80001-8

de la Torre, S., & Snowdon, C. T. (2009). Dialects in pygmy marmosets? Population variation in call structure. *American Journal of Primatology, 71,* 333–342. doi:10.1002/ajp.20657

De Waal, F. B. M., & Suchak, M. (2010). Prosocial primates: Selfish and unselfish motivations. *Philosophical Transactions of the Royal Society B, 365,* 2711–2722. doi:10.1098/rstb.2010.0119

Elowson, A. M., & Snowdon, C. T. (1994). Pygmy marmosets, *Cebuella pygmaea,* modify vocal structure in response to changed social environment. *Animal Behaviour, 47,* 1267–1277. doi:10.1006/anbe.1994.1175

Elowson, A. M., Snowdon, C. T., & Lazaro-Perea, C. (1998). Infant "babbling" in a nonhuman primate: Complex sequences of vocal behavior. *Behaviour, 135,* 643–664. doi:10.1163/156853998792897905

Elowson, A. M., Snowdon, C. T., & Sweet, C. S. (1992). Ontogeny of trill and J-call vocalizations in pygmy marmosets, *Cebuella pygmaea. Animal Behaviour, 43,* 703–715. doi:10.1016/S0003-3472(05)80195-2

Farabaugh, S. M., Linzenbold, A., & Dooling, R. J. (1994). Vocal plasticity in budgerigars (*Melopsittacus undulatus*): Evidence of social factors in the learning of contact calls. *Journal of Comparative Psychology, 108,* 81–92. doi:10.1037/0735-7036.108.1.81

Frazier, C. R. M., Trainor, B. C., Cravens, C. J., Whitney, T. K., & Marler, C. A. (2006). Paternal behavior influences development of aggression and vasopressin expression in male California mouse offspring. *Hormones and Behavior, 50,* 699–707. doi:10.1016/j.yhbeh.2006.06.035

Galef, B. G., & Giraldeau, L. A. (2001). Social influences on foraging in vertebrates: Causal mechanisms and adaptive functions. *Animal Behaviour, 61,* 3–15. doi:10.1006/anbe.2000.1557

Gunhold, T., Massen, J. J. M., Schiel, N., Souto, A., & Bugnyar, T. (2014). Memory, transmission and persistence of alternative foraging techniques in wild common marmosets. *Animal Behaviour, 91,* 79–91. doi:10.1016/j.anbehav.2014.02.023

Gunhold, T., Range, F., Huber, L., & Bugnyar, T. (2015). Long-term fidelity of foraging techniques in common marmosets (*Callithrix jacchus*). *American Journal of Primatology 77*(3), 264–270. doi:10.1002/ajp.22342

Gunhold, T., Whiten, A., & Bugnyar, T. (2014). Video demonstrations seed alternative problem-solving techniques in wild common marmosets. *Biology Letters, 10*(9), 20140439. doi:10.1098/rsbl.2014.0439

Hammerschmidt, K., & Fischer, J. (2008). Constraints on primate vocal production. In D. K. Oller & U. Griebel (Eds.), *Evolution of communicative flexibility* (pp. 93–119), Cambridge, MA: MIT Press.

Hare, B., & Tomasello, M. (2004). Chimpanzees are more skillful in competitive than in cooperative cognitive tasks. *Animal Behaviour, 68*(3), 571–581. doi:10.1016/j.anbehav.2003.11.011

Hausberger, M., Richard, M. A., Henry, L., Lepage, L., & Schmidt, S. (1995). Song sharing reflects the social organization in a captive group of European starlings (*Sturnus vulgaris*). *Journal of Comparative Psychology, 109*, 222–241. doi:10.1037/0735-7036.109.3.222

Hrdy, S. B. (2009). *Mothers and others: The evolutionary origins of mutual understanding.* Cambridge, MA: Belknap Press of Harvard University Press.

Humle, T., & Snowdon, C. T. (2008). Socially biased learning in the acquisition of a complex foraging task in juvenile cottontop tamarins, *Saguinus oedipus. Animal Behaviour, 75*(1), 267–277. doi:10.1016/j.anbehav.2007.05.021

Humle, T., Snowdon, C. T., & Matsuzawa, T. (2009). Social influences on the acquisition of ant dipping among the wild chimpanzees (*Pan troglodytes verus*) of Bossou, Guinea, West Africa. *Animal Cognition, 12*, S37–S48. doi:10.1007/s10071-009-0272-6

Janik, V. M., & Slater, P. J. B. (1997). Vocal learning in mammals. *Advances in the Study of Behavior, 26*, 59–99. doi:10.1016/S0065-3454(08)60377-0

Janik, V. M., & Slater, P. J. B. (2000). The different roles of social learning in vocal communication. *Animal Behaviour, 60*, 1–11. doi:10.1006/anbe.2000.1410

Jorgenson, D. D., & French, J. A. (1998). Individuality but not stability in marmoset long calls. *Ethology, 104*, 729–742. doi:10.1111/j.1439-0310.1998.tb00107.x

Joyce, S. M., & Snowdon, C. T. (2007). Developmental changes in food transfers in cotton-top tamarins (*Saguinus oedipus*). *American Journal of Primatology, 69*, 955–965. doi:10.1002/ajp.20393

Lukas, D., & Clutton-Brock, T. H. (2013). The evolution of social monogamy in mammals. *Science, 341*, 526–529. doi:10.1126/science.1238677

Midford, P. E., Hailman, J. P., & Woolfenden, G. E. (2000). Social learning of a novel foraging patch in families of free-living Florida scrub-jays. *Animal Behaviour, 59*, 1199–1207. doi:10.1006/anbe.1999.1419

Moscovice, L. R., & Snowdon, C. T. (2006). The role of social context and individual experience in novel task acquisition in cotton-top tamarins

(*Saguinus oedipus*). *Animal Behaviour, 71,* 933–943. doi:10.1016/j.anbehav.2005.09.007

Mundinger, P. C. (1970). Vocal imitation and individual recognition of finch calls. *Science, 168,* 480–482. doi:10.1126/science.168.3930.480

Nowicki, S. (1989). Vocal plasticity in captive black-capped chickadees: The acoustic basis and rate of call convergence. *Animal Behaviour, 37,* 64–73. doi:10.1016/0003-3472(89)90007-9

Payne, R. B., & Payne, L. L. (1993). Song copying and cultural transmission in indigo buntings. *Animal Behaviour, 46,* 1045–1065. doi:10.1006/anbe.1993.1296

Rapaport, L. G. (1999). Provisioning of young in golden lion tamarins (Callitrichidae, *Leontopithecus rosalia*): A test of the information hypothesis. *Ethology, 105,* 619–636. doi:10.1046/j.1439-0310.1999.00449.x

Rapaport, L. G. (2006). Provisioning in wild golden lion tamarins: Benefits to omnivorous young. *Behavioral Ecology, 17,* 212–221. doi:10.1093/beheco/arj016

Rapaport, L. G., & Ruiz-Miranda C. R. (2002). Tutoring in wild golden lion tamarins. *International Journal of Primatology, 23,* 1063–1070. doi:10.1023/A:1019650032735

Rapaport, L. G., & Ruiz-Miranda, C. R. (2006). Ontogeny of provisioning in two populations of wild golden lion tamarins (*Leontopithecus rosalia*). *Behavioral Ecology and Sociobiology, 60,* 724–735. doi:10.1007/s00265-006-0216-y

Roush, R. S., & Snowdon, C. T. (1994). Ontogeny of food-associated calls in cotton-top tamarins. *Animal Behaviour, 47*(2), 263–273. doi:10.1006/anbe.1994.1038

Roush, R. S., & Snowdon, C. T. (1999). The effects of social status on food-associated calls in captive cotton-top tamarins. *Animal Behaviour, 58*(6), 1299–1305. doi:10.1006/anbe.1999.1262

Roush, R. S., & Snowdon, C. T. (2001). Food transfer and development of feeding behavior and food-associated vocalizations in cotton-top tamarins. *Ethology, 107,* 415–429. doi:10.1046/j.1439-0310.2001.00670.x

Smuts, B. B., & Gubernick, D. J. (1992). Male–infant relationships in nonhuman primates: Paternal investment or mating effort? In B. S. Hewlett (Ed.), *Father–child relations: Cultural and biosocial contexts* (pp. 1–30). New York: Aldine de Gruyter.

Snowdon, C. T. (2001). Social processes in communication and cognition in callitrichid monkeys: A review. *Animal Cognition, 4*(3), 247–257. doi:10.1007/s100710100094

Snowdon, C. T., & Boe, C. Y. (2003). Social communication about unpalatable foods in tamarins. *Journal of Comparative Psychology, 117,* 142–148. doi:10.1037/0735-7036.117.2.142

Snowdon, C. T., & Elowson, A. M. (1999). Pygmy marmosets modify vocal structure when paired. *Ethology, 105,* 893–908. doi:10.1046/j.1439-0310.1999.00483.x

Snowdon, C. T., & Elowson, A. M. (2001). "Babbling" in pygmy marmosets: Development after infancy. *Behaviour, 138,* 1235–1248. doi:10.1163/15685390152822193

Snowdon, C. T., and Roskos, T. R. (2017). Stick-weaving: innovative behavior in tamarins (Saguinus oedipus). *Journal of Comparative Psychology, 131*(2), 174–178. doi: 10.1037/com0000071

Takahashi, D. Y., Fenley, A. R., Teramoto, Y., Narayanan, D. Z., Borjon, J. I., Holmes, P., & Ghazanfar, A. A. (2015). The developmental dynamics of marmoset monkey vocal production. *Science, 349,* 734–738. doi:10.1126/science.aab1058

Tardif, S. D., Richter, C. B., & Carson, R. L. (1984). Effects of sibling-rearing experience on future reproductive success in two species of callitrichidae. *American Journal of Primatology,* 6(4), 377–380. doi:10.1002/ajp.1350060408

Thornton, A., & McAuliffe, K. (2006). Teaching in wild meerkats. *Science, 313,* 227–229. doi:10.1126/science.1128727

Tomasello, M. (2009). *Why we cooperate.* Cambridge, MA: MIT Press.

Visalberghi, E., & Addessi, E. (2000). Response to changes in food palatability in tufted capuchin monkeys, *Cebus apella. Animal Behaviour, 59,* 231–238. doi:10.1006/anbe.1999.1297

Voelkl, B., & Huber, L. (2000). True imitation in marmosets. *Animal Behaviour, 60,* 195–202. doi:10.1006/anbe.2000.1457

Wilson, E. O. (2012). *The social conquest of earth.* New York: Liveright.

Wood, D., Bruner, J., & Ross, G. (1976). The role of tutoring in problem solving. *Journal of Child Psychology and Psychiatry and Allied Disciplines, 17,* 89–100. doi:10.1111/j.1469-7610.1976.tb00381.x

Yépez, P., de la Torre, S., & Snowdon, C. T. (2005). Interpopulation differences in exudate feeding of pygmy marmosets in Ecuadorian Amazonia. *American Journal of Primatology,* 66(2), 145–158. doi:10.1002/ajp.20134

Zahed, S. R., Kurian, A. V., & Snowdon, C. T. (2010). Social dynamics and individual plasticity of infant care behavior in cooperatively breeding cotton-top tamarins. *American Journal of Primatology, 72*(4), 296–306. doi:10.1002/ajp.20782

Zahed, S. R., Prudom, S. L., Snowdon, C. T., & Ziegler, T. E. (2008). Male parenting and response to infant stimuli in the common marmoset (*Callithrix jacchus*). *American Journal of Primatology, 70*(1), 84–92. doi:10.1002/ajp.20460

Part III

Cultural Genomics

7

How Are Genes Related to Culture? An Introduction to the Field of Cultural Genomics

José M. Causadias and Kevin M. Korous

The relation between genetics and culture has the doubtful privilege of being one of the most widely studied and best-documented cases of culture and biology interplay in the natural sciences, while being one of the less understood and scarcely studied cases of culture and biology interplay in behavioral sciences. For instance, while the first essays by evolutionary biologists (e.g., Huxley, 1955) and quantitative research by population geneticists (e.g., Cavalli-Sforza, 1962) on the interplay of genes, cultures, and environments appeared decades ago, it is only recently that this association has been examined in essays (Li, 2003) and empirical studies (Chiao & Blizinsky, 2010) by psychologists. Moreover, since about 2010 there has been a substantial growth in the number of studies on culture and genes in psychology (e.g., Brody et al., 2011; Chae et al., 2014; Chiao & Blizinsky, 2010; Schwartz & Beaver, 2011), research in this field remains scarce and mostly focused on a single candidate gene (for exceptions, see LeClair, Janusonis, & Kim, 2014; Lei, Simons, Edmond, Simons, & Cutrona, 2014). The goals of this chapter are to introduce the field of cultural genomics, examine its levels of analysis, discuss types of studies and provide some examples of each, elaborate on some of the issues with current research, and provide some conclusions and future directions. It is beyond the scope of this chapter to provide a systematic review of all published research on cultural genomics. Thus, we only discuss some landmark studies and illustrative examples, mostly using molecular genetic approaches.

The Handbook of Culture and Biology, First Edition. Edited by José M. Causadias, Eva H. Telzer and Nancy A. Gonzales.

What Is Cultural Genomics?

Before we define cultural genomics, it is important to disclose what we mean by culture, genes, genomics, and environment. Culture can be defined as a system of behaviors (and cognitions) that is shared and transmitted in a community, that is subject to change and evolves over time, that serves a concrete, adaptive, or symbolic purpose, and that has important repercussions in multiple domains of functioning (Causadias, Telzer, & Gonzales, chapter 1 in this volume; Causadias, 2013). Although there is lack of consensus on the definition of culture among behavioral scientists, there is a growing agreement about some of its common features, including the idea that culture originates in and is shared by a community: it is transmitted from one generation to the next and is susceptible to change, shapes behavior, cognition, and development by promoting and creating values, ideas, and worldviews, and is located both in the social world and within individuals (Cohen, 2009). Culture is commonly associated with other concepts – such as ethnicity, race, and nationality – that are frequently used as proxies of cultural processes.

Environments are all the natural and human-made physical surroundings that have important effects on culture and genomes, including houses, neighborhoods, schools, prisons, and cities. Although environments and culture share some features (for example, they are transmitted intergenerationally and subject to change), they also differ in several ways. First, while "culture" refers to social-level processes that often define interpersonal interactions (e.g., community participation, acculturation, racial discrimination), human-made environments are created through niche construction (see O'Brien & Bentley, chapter 8 in this volume), and are the physical embodiment of the cultural values, tools and practices of a particular group. For example, communities create neighborhoods with architectural features that reflect their cultural values and practices, such as churches. Second, culture and environments can be consonant but also dissonant, as illustrated by instances in which displaced or exiled cultural groups come to inhabit niches that reflect the values of local groups, from which they differ.

Genes are an ordered sequence of nucleotides located in a certain position on a precise chromosome that encode a specific functional product, such as proteins (Feero, Guttmacher, & Collins, 2010). Genes are important in behavioral and biological sciences because they are the essential physical and functional units of heredity. While a genotype is the complete collection of genes carried by an individual, a phenotype is the recognizable traits of an individual person that are shaped by the genotype and the environment (Feero et al., 2010). Many psychological studies that incorporate genes focus on single-nucleotide polymorphisms (SNPs) or on common variations in the genetic sequence. The genome is the complete set of genetic instructions found in a cell, consisting of 23 pairs of chromosomes in humans (Feero et al., 2010).

Behavioral genetics is a field of research that investigates the environmental and genetic influences on behavior. There are several methods within this field, including twin/family studies, adoption studies, and molecular genetic studies. For instance, twin/family studies are frequently employed to establish and pinpoint the strength of a genetic component by comparing monozygotic and dizygotic twins without necessarily genotyping them. Adoption studies are similar, as they disentangle environmental and genetic influences by comparing adoptive families (environment) and biological parents (genetics). On the other hand, in molecular genetic studies gene variants are measured and identified. While studies vary in focus, ranging from analyses of one gene (e.g., the candidate gene approach) or several genes (e.g., polygenic scores; see Purcell et al., 2009) to examinations of the whole genome (e.g., genome-wide association studies), most of the literature on cultural genomics uses a single candidate gene approach in which attention is centered on the role of certain SNPs or common variations in the genetic sequence that are conceptualized as especially sensitive to the environment (such as *5-HTTLPR*, *DRD4*, *MAOA*), though there are some exceptions (see Burt, Klump, Gorman-Smith, & Neiderhiser, 2016). With the advancement of microarrays that allow researchers to genotype a multitude of DNA variants cheaply and quickly, research is steering towards genome-wide associations (GWAs) as they are replicable and not limited to specific candidate genes (Plomin, 2013).

Cultural genomics examines the interplay of genes, cultures, and environments, and the multiple ways in which cultural experiences are influenced by, affect, and covary with the genome and the environment to shape behavior and cognition at the social, developmental, and evolutionary levels (see Causadias, Telzer, & Lee, 2017; Moya & Henrich, 2016). Importantly, this field focuses on genomics, not genetics. The difference is that while genetics centers on the study of heredity and the role of specific genes, genomics is more complex and focuses on the study of the entire genome, its functions, and how it is interrelated with the environment. Cultural genomics is informed by several conceptual frameworks, including gene–culture coevolution theory, dual inheritance theory, the extended evolutionary synthesis, and developmental psychopathology (for an overview of approaches to the interplay of genes, cultures, and environments, see Mesoudi, Whiten, & Laland, 2006). Gene–culture coevolutionary theory posits that traditional evolutionary mechanisms, such as natural selection, can also explain the process of cultural transmission and evolution, and that social learning is the main mechanism of cultural transmission (Cavalli-Sforza & Feldman, 1981; Mesoudi, 2016). Dual-inheritance theory argues that genes and culture are constantly competing to shape individuals' phenotypes (Boyd & Richerson, 1985; Henrich & McElreath, 2007). The extended evolutionary synthesis underscores reciprocal depictions of causation and the role of constructive mechanisms (e.g., niche construction) in development and in the direction and range of evolution (Laland et al., 2015). After all, "the organism influences its own evolution, by being both the object of natural selection and the creator of the conditions of that selection" (Levins & Lewontin, 1985: 106). Guided by these three frameworks, cultural genomics understands both genetic and cultural processes as a dual helix, evolving together over time and intimately embraced.

Influenced by developmental psychopathology theory (Cicchetti & Cannon, 1999; Sroufe, 2007), cultural genomics approaches behavior and cognition as the outcomes of the interdependence, codetermination, and concurrent influence of genes, cultures, and environments. Although they are equally important, they function under different sets of principles. For instance, while genetic transmission is usually vertical (parents to offspring), cultural transmission through teaching and learning can be vertical, horizontal (peer to peer), or oblique (teacher to student; see Cavalli-Sforza, 2001). Furthermore, while changes in human culture can occur rapidly in the same generation, changes in the human genome happen over multiple generations, although there are important exceptions of rapid genotypic change that leads to speciation (Gavrilets, 2010). It is noteworthy that some scholars have criticized the idea that culture and genes are transmitted somewhat similarly (Claidière & André, 2012).

Cultural genomics research is important for the future of behavioral sciences for several reasons. First, it can advance our understanding of individual differences in responses towards exposure to cultural experiences (e.g., racial discrimination) and participation in cultural communities (e.g., enculturation and acculturation) by, for instance, uncovering how individuals with certain genotypes might be more susceptible to particular cultural experiences or interventions, how some genotypes could evoke certain cultural behaviors (evocative gene–culture correlation), or whether some cultural behaviors are based more on inherited genotypes (passive gene–culture correlation). Second, cultural genomics research can inform our understanding of the complex processes that shape behavior and cognition, advancing our theoretical knowledge within social, developmental, and evolutionary paradigms. For example, this research can lead to the formulation of new, or adaptations of current, theoretical models to account for the intricate nature of human development across the lifespan.

In this chapter, we review some cultural genomics studies that have employed SNPs associated with sensitivity to social experiences, including *5-HTTLPR*, *MAOA*, and *DRD4*. We exclude from this review the G (versus A) allele of the oxytocin receptor gene (*OXTR*) polymorphism rs53576, which has been extensively examined in relation to culture (see Kim, Sherman, Mojaverian et al., 2011; Kim, Sherman, Sasaki et al., 2010; Luo & Han, 2014), because this research is discussed in detail by Lo and Sasaki in chapter 9 of this volume. The promoter region of the human serotonin transporter gene (*SLC6A4*, also referred to as *5-HTT* and *5-HTTLPR*) is the most widely researched genetic variant in psychiatry, psychology and neuroscience (Caspi, Hariri, Holmes, Uher, & Moffitt, 2010). The significance of this gene lies in the well-documented evidence that variations in *5-HTT* affect how humans, primates and other animals respond to stressful events in their environments (Caspi et al., 2010). Most research on humans focuses on those carrying at least one short allele "s" related to heightened sensitivity to adverse experiences (Belsky & Pluess, 2009). However, the role of this serotonin transporter gene has been subject to controversy, with some meta-analyses showing that it has trivial effects (e.g., Risch et al., 2009), while others have supported its role in the stress response (van IJzendoorn, Belsky, & Bakermans-Kranenburg, 2012).

The *uVNTR* variation of the *MAOA* gene is related to differences in expression of the monoamine oxidase A (*MAOA*) enzyme that breaks down neurotransmitters like serotonin (Way & Lieberman, 2010). The *uVNTR-MAOA* has been related to heightened response to social injustice (Way & Lieberman, 2010), differential susceptibility to the environment (Belsky & Pluess, 2009), and increased likelihood of developing antisocial behaviors after experiencing adversity (Schwartz & Beaver, 2011). Finally, the dopamine receptor D4 gene (*DRD4*) seven- and second-tandem repeat alleles affect transmission in the neural pathways that are involved in numerous important psychological processes, including attention, learning, motivation, and reward-seeking behavior (Kitayama et al., 2014). Furthermore, *DRD4* has also been widely studied in psychiatry, psychology, and neuroscience, and has been associated with increased sensitivity to the environment (Belsky & Pluess, 2009).

Levels of Analysis of Cultural Genomics

Using Li's (2003) perspectives of biocultural analysis, we can delineate three levels of the interplay of genes, cultures and environments: the social, developmental, and evolutionary levels. (For a more detailed discussion of the evolutionary level of the interplay of genes, cultures, and environments, see O'Brien and Bentley, chapter 8 in this volume.) These three levels reflect, to some degree, Tinbergen's (1963) questions about behavior patterns. The social level of the interplay of genes, cultures, and environments is represented by day-to-day scenarios in which these processes affect each other. For instance, individuals with certain genotypes might be more sensitive to cultural experiences, such as racial discrimination and prejudice (Brody et al., 2011; Sales et al., 2015). The developmental level of analysis represents situations in which genes, or culture, or both, have an effect in an organism that triggers probabilistic trajectories that lead to the development, over years and decades, of adaptive or maladaptive outcomes (i.e., ontogenetic history). For example, evidence suggests that stability in cultural consonance in family life over two years, the degree to which an individual perceives their family as corresponding to a cultural model of the prototypical family, is related to differences in depressive symptoms for individuals who carry specific SNPs (Dressler et al., 2009). The interplay of genes, cultures, and environments at the evolutionary level represents the cumulative effect of this relation in natural selection and adaptation of humans over centuries (i.e., phylogenetic history). Many organisms not only adapt to their environment, but change their environment to fit their needs through niche construction and transmission. The foremost example among humans is the link between genes, culture, and agriculture, in which cultural innovations in agriculture have eventually led to changes in the human genome (see O'Brien & Laland, 2012).

Types of Gene–Culture–Environment Interplay

Cultural genomics focuses on several forms of the interplay of genes, cultures and environments. The term "interplay" is very suitable for conceptualizing the relation between culture and biology for several reasons (Causadias, 2013). For instance, Rutter (2006, 2007, 2013) argued that the concept of interplay – or interdependence – is broader than terms like "interaction" because it conveys a variety of scenarios in which two processes affect each other. Furthermore, while interplay represents conceptual interrelations that take place at the biological and evolutionary levels, interactions are often discussed purely in statistical terms. Some types of the interplay of genes, cultures and environments include cultural effects on genes or cultural epigenomics (*C→G*), genetic effects on culture (*G→C*), gene–culture interactions (*GxC*), gene–culture correlations (*rGC*), gene–culture–niche interplay (*GxCxN*), and developmental effects of gene–environment on culture (*dcGE*). Here we describe each type of interplay and provide some examples. It is worth noting that a single study can report different types of the interplay of genes, cultures, and environments.

First, cultural effects on genes (*C→G*), or cultural epigenomics, centers on how repeated exposure to cultural experiences and participation in cultural traditions affect the genome at the social, developmental, and evolutionary levels (see Laland, Odling-Smee, & Myles, 2010). For instance, at the long-term evolutionary level, the invention of agriculture favored the emergence of lactose-tolerant genotypes (Aoki, 1986; Feldman & Cavalli-Sforza, 1989). At the developmental level, a growing body of research has employed the *C→G* approach to understand how racial bias, prejudice, and discrimination influence the genome. Chae and colleagues (2014) tested the impact of racial discrimination and internalized racial bias among African-American men on leukocyte telomere length (LTL), a marker of chronic diseases associated with aging, and found that high levels of racial discrimination were significantly related to shorter LTL among participants who held stronger implicit anti-Black bias. In a follow-up study, Chae and colleagues (2016) examined the role of depressive symptoms in the relation between racial discrimination and telomere length. Shorter LTL was related to higher levels of racial discrimination in males who reported fewer depressive symptoms. Altogether, the work of Chae and colleagues (2014, 2016) shows that cultural experiences may affect the genome, contribute to cellular aging, and explain racial health disparities.

Second, genetic effects on culture (*G→C*) represent scenarios in which genotypes can affect cultural behavior (Richerson, Boyd, & Henrich, 2010). A growing body of evidence suggests that there is an association between certain dopamine genotypes and cultural outcomes, such as language learning differences (Wong, Morgan-Short, Ettlinger, & Zheng, 2012), cultural learning (Kitayama et al., 2014), and sensitivity to cultural norms (Kitayama, King, Hsu, Liberzon, & Yoon, 2016). At the evolutionary level it has been argued that some dopamine genotypes, like DRD4, might be involved in long-distance group migration (Chen, Burton, Greenberger, & Dmitrieva, 1999). For instance, Kitayama and colleagues (2010, 2014) argued that carriers of the seven-tandem repeat allele (7R) of *DRD4*, because of their genetically increased reward sensitivity, might be encouraged to migrate, or have more favorable likelihoods of survival and reproduction in challenging frontier environments. This evidence suggests that, to a certain extent, cultural behavior can be partly explained by individual differences in genomic variants.

Third, gene–culture interactions (*GxC*), perhaps the most widely studied form of the interplay of genes, cultures, and environments, characterize instances in which the effects of a cultural experience on a behavioral, cognitive, or developmental outcome are moderated by a certain SNP, or vice versa. Importantly, like other forms of gene-by-environment interactions, *GxC* takes place at the biological and social levels, and should not be confused with mere statistical terms (see Rutter, 2006). Some studies have investigated the interaction between racial discrimination and *5-HTTLPR* in predicting behavior problems among African-American adolescents. One study reported that male African-American adolescents who carried one or two short alleles of the *5-HTTLPR* reported higher rates of conduct problems when they perceived high levels of racial discrimination than did male youth who perceived low levels of racial discrimination (Brody et al., 2011). Another study found that the short allele of *5-HTTLPR* moderated the association between racial discrimination and depressive symptoms among African-American adolescent females (Sales et al., 2015). Similarly, Schwartz and Beaver (2011) investigated the effects of perceived prejudice and MAOA gene on criminal arrests, and reported that a *GxC* interaction between perceived levels of prejudice and MAOA predicted criminal arrests, but only among males. Other *GxC* studies have also examined the role of genetic variations on developing intergroup biases (see Cheon, Livingston, Chiao, & Hong, 2015; Cheon, Livingston, Hong, & Chiao, 2013). In sum, these studies illustrate how certain genes moderate the association between experiences of prejudice, discrimination, and bias with several outcomes, advancing our comprehension of individual differences in response to adverse cultural experiences.

Fourth, gene–culture correlations (*rGC*) represent covariation between genes and cultural processes. However, while most *rGC* studies conducted recently focus on the social and developmental levels of analysis, the pioneer investigations in cultural genomics focused on *rGC* at the evolutionary level (see O'Brien & Bentley, chapter 8 in this volume). In addition, cultural genomic researchers use "*rGC*" with different meanings and theoretical implications. For example, while some studies in cultural genomics use "*rGC*" to refer to the correlation coefficients of genetic variability estimates and scores in cultural measures, other studies use this term to represent more complex developmental processes (see Burt et al., 2016). This latter approach is informed by behavioral genetics theory, for which gene–environment correlations reflect differential exposure of genotypes to environments, including "passive," "active," and "evocative" effects (Plomin, DeFries, & Loehlin, 1977). In passive genotype–environment correlations, parents give their children both genes and environments that are conducive to the development of a trait, independent of children's choices (Plomin et al., 1977). Applied to cultural genomics, these correlations refer to cases in which parents provide their children with genetic, cultural, and environmental influences. For instance, first-generation immigrants may provide their children with genotypes in which certain dopamine polymorphisms associate with reward-seeking behavior (Kitayama et al., 2010, 2014), as well as socialize them into their culture of origin (i.e., enculturation), and raise them in a particular environment or niche (e.g., neighborhoods). Active gene–environment correlations reflect the fact that children are not passive recipients of their environment, but actively engage and select environments that fit their genetic predispositions (Plomin et al., 1977). In cultural genomics, these correlations are exemplified in cases in which individuals pursue environments and cultural experiences that match their genetic propensities. For instance, some individuals may actively seek cultural communities aligned with their own political ideology by applying for admission to universities with liberal or conservative orientations. Evocative (or reactive) gene–environment correlations represent scenarios in which individuals with certain genotypes and phenotypes elicit different social responses (Plomin et al., 1977). In terms of cultural genomics, phenotypic traits such as sex and skin color can trigger different cultural responses, ranging from privilege to prejudice.

Some studies have employed an *rGC* approach to examine the interplay of genes, cultures, and environments in cultural orientation, particularly by documenting significant *rGC* between the *5-HTTLPR* variant and several cultural phenomena, including collectivism (Chiao & Blizinsky, 2010), strong social norms and a low tolerance for deviant behavior (Mrazek, Chiao, Blizinsky, Lun, & Gelfand, 2013), external threat of invasion, disease prevalence, and expenditure on food (Fisher & Vernes, 2015), and national neuroticism and long-term orientation, but not individualism or power distance (Minkov, Blagoev, & Bond, 2014). Additional studies have documented *rGC* between collectivism and the *5-HTTLPR* and MAOA polymorphisms (Way & Lieberman, 2010). However, other studies have not replicated these results. Bisso-Machado and colleagues (2013) examined the *5-HTTPLR* allele frequency of individuals of Native South

Amerindian ancestry and did not find an association between cultural orientation and the serotonin-transporter polymorphism. Finally, Brown and colleagues (2013) sampled participants from different Taiwan regions and found a significant *rGC* between music and genes, even after controlling for the geographical distance between the regions. They suggested the correlation indicates that genes, and music, a cultural trait, coevolve through shared ancestry instead of geographical distance. In conclusion, *rGC* studies exemplify how covariation of culture and genomes shapes unique behavioral outcomes. However, most of these studies do not examine *rGC* in terms of passive, active, or evocative types.

Fifth, in gene–culture–niche interplay (*GxCxN*) the three levels of inheritance are engaged in shaping behavior and cognition at the social, developmental, and evolutionary levels. Although often confused, cultural and niche (or ecological) inheritance are systems that are deeply intertwined, but nevertheless different (see Odling-Smee & Laland, 2011), as seen when genes, cultural processes, and neighborhood effects are involved in shaping an outcome (Burt et al., 2016). This pattern of associations can be approached statistically as three-way interactions, but also by examining how patterns of *GxC* differ across environments or niches. Several studies have used the *GxCxN* approach to examine the association between neighborhood characteristics, *MAOA*, *DRD4*, and *5-HTTLPR* variants, and antisocial and risky behavior. One study found that the MAOA polymorphism interacted with the concentration of children within a neighborhood to predict levels of adolescent aggression among males (Hart & Marmorstein, 2009). Lei and colleagues (2014) reported that the effect of disadvantaged neighborhoods and social ties on antisocial behavior among adult African-American females was moderated by the presence of *DRD4* and *5-HTTLPR* polymorphisms. Cho and Kogan (2015) investigated the role of *DRD4*, parenting, and goals in the effects of community disadvantage on African-American adolescents' risky behavior. Protective parenting increased future orientation only for youth with the long (seven or more tandem repeats) *DRD4* allele, shielding against risky behavior, whereas protective parenting had no effect on youth who did not carry the variant. In sum, these studies increase our understanding of the myriad of pathways in which genes, culture and environments shape behavior, cognition, and development.

Sixth, the developmental effects of gene–environment on culture (*dcGE*) involve instances in which the genetic or environmental contribution to a certain cultural trait changes over time. For example, it has been well documented that heritability of intelligence increases over time (Plomin &

Spinath, 2004). Applied to cultural genomics, longitudinal studies examining *dcGE* can help elucidate how genetic and environmental contributions to the development of cultural processes like acculturation can increase or decrease over time. We are not aware of any study that has used this approach, but we believe it is a promising research direction.

Problems (and Solutions) in Cultural Genomics Research

Problems in cultural genomics research can be divided into two kinds: issues that arise from outside the field and problems that arise from within (see Table 7.1). Some issues external to the field are common to culture and biology research in general (e.g., cultural neurobiology, cultural neuroscience), including skepticism towards biological methods, the lasting effects of the nature versus nurture debate, and institutional and educational barriers. For another discussion of issues in culture and biology

Table 7.1 Summary of problems (and solutions) in cultural genomic research

Problems	Solutions
Outside of cultural genomics	
Skepticism about using genes in cultural research	Understanding the intimate relation between culture and genes
Graduate training that emphasizes genes *or* culture	Graduate training that emphasizes genes *and* culture
Genetic determinism	Approaching individuals as active agents in their development
The persistence of the nature-versus-nurture debate	Recognition of the importance of nature and nurture
Within cultural genomics	
Using demographic proxies to infer culture	Measuring cultural processes directly
Not reporting tests of Hardy–Weinberg Equilibrium	Testing and reporting Hardy–Weinberg Equilibrium
Use of small samples	Use of larger samples
Overreliance on single candidate gene approaches	Employing polygenic, twin/family, and adoption studies
The internal–external validity paradox	Balancing sample size and measurement depth

interplay, see Syed and Kathawalla, chapter 2 in this volume. First, scholars investigating culture, ethnicity and race are understandably suspicious of methods that may diminish the richness of cultural processes and reduce them to biomarkers (see Causadias et al., 2017). Also, the nature-versus-nurture debate has facilitated a dichotomous understanding of behavior and cognition, in which some processes are viewed as determined by culture, while others are regarded as influenced by genes. In reality, genes and culture are intimately related, and both shape all levels of human behavior and cognition, although in different ways. Furthermore, graduate training and research programs can become barriers to the advancement of the field, as they often promote the accumulation of skills and resources for conducting research on either culture or genes, but rarely on both (Causadias et al., 2017).

Additional problems that arise from outside the field are unique to research on cultural genomics, including genetic determinism and fallacies about inheritance. Many scholars are wary of conceptualizations that reinforce or subscribe to genetic determinism, the idea that we are governed by our genomes (Wilson, 2000). There are also widespread misconceptions about inheritance, particularly the belief that an inherited trait is not subject to change or sensitive to environmental influences (see Lilienfeld, Lynn, Ruscio, & Beyerstein, 2011). Most complex behavioral and psychological traits are influenced by genetic inheritance and social experiences, intelligence for example (see Plomin & Spinath, 2004). There are notable exceptions, however, like some single-gene or Mendelian disorders like cystic fibrosis (for a review, see Antonarakis & Beckmann, 2006). Moreover, it is important to recognize that neither genes nor experiences are destiny: personal agency plays a major role in development because individuals actively shape their own cultural and genetic development.

Other problems in cultural genomics research are internal to the field. They are determined by the methodological and conceptual intricacies of integrating multiple levels of analysis while safeguarding scientific rigor without violating conceptual and statistical assumptions. First, there are several issues with the quality of measurement of culture and genes in the overviewed research in cultural genomics. For instance, many studies do not measure cultural processes directly, but make inferences based on demographic proxies (e.g., nationality, race, ethnicity) or group comparisons. Instances of this are country-level analyses of the effects of gene–culture interplay on the global prevalence of pathogens and mental health disorders (Chiao & Blizinsky, 2010) and on ecological threat (Mrazek et al., 2013). However, this approach has been severely criticized (see Eisenberg & Hayes, 2011). The problem of inferring culture from group membership has been addressed extensively and repeatedly in the literature (see Betancourt & López, 1993; Campbell, 1961; Matsumoto & Yoo, 2006). The employment of demographic characteristics as substitutes for the careful and validated assessment of culture is concerning, because these proxies have restricted construct validity and often function as a black box that reveals little about the underlying mechanisms that account for different effects (see Priem, Lyon, & Dess, 1999).

On the other hand, rarely do many of the reviewed studies in cultural genomics report tests of Hardy–Weinberg equilibrium (HWE), the expectation that genotype frequencies at any locus are a function of allele frequencies in large and randomly mating human populations (Hosking et al., 2004; Wigginton, Cutler, & Abecasis, 2005). HWE is a principle that has been utilized for more than a century to better appreciate the genetic characteristics of populations (Wittke-Thompson, Pluzhnikov, & Cox, 2005). HWE is not simply an idea of conceptual relevance, but also a test with major implications. Deviations or departures from HWE often suggest problems with genotyping or population structure (Salanti, Amountza, Ntzani, & Ioannidis, 2005; Wigginton et al., 2005), as violations of HWE can seriously compromise the central inferences of any genetic study (Salanti et al., 2005). Not surprisingly, testing for HWE is widely used as a test of measurement quality, because it is one of the most efficient ways to detect non-random errors in genotyping unrelated individuals (Wittke-Thompson et al., 2005). Errors in genetic data originate from a variety of sources, including sample mishandling and problems with the genotyping process (Hosking et al., 2004), and evidence supports the notion that several molecular genetic studies have substantial deficiencies in design, analysis, and reporting (Salanti et al., 2005). However, these shortcomings can be aggravated in cultural genomics research, because many studies are not subjected to the often more stringent quality tests imposed by molecular genetic journals. In sum, while measurement error is a recurring issue in psychological and biological assessment, and any large dataset is expected to contain some errors, cultural genomic researchers should do everything in their power to increase the precision and validity of their estimates by conducting and reporting tests of HWE.

In addition to measurement problems, most cultural genomics research is faced with other issues that are inherent to *GxE* designs. For instance, *GxE* studies frequently rely on small samples that lack the power to detect interactions (Duncan & Keller, 2011), often employ samples of individuals of European ancestry while other groups remain understudied (Oquendo, Canino, Lehner, & Licinio, 2010), and report findings that are subsequently not replicated (Duncan, Pollastri, & Smoller, 2014; Hewitt, 2012). The high false-positive rate is often, but not exclusively, a result of poor transparency in research procedures, an absence of specification or registration of the statistical analyses before the study, and, ultimately, a lack of limits to researchers' degrees of freedom (Simmons, Nelson, & Simonsohn, 2011). One strategy to tackle some of these challenges is the use of *the new statistics*, which emphasizes the preregistration of studies before analyses are conducted in order to restrict researchers' degrees of freedom, the complete disclosure of the research procedure (in this case, gene selection strategy), and moving away from null hypothesis significance testing (NHST) to focus on effect sizes and confidence intervals (Cumming, 2012, 2013).

While these issues affect most *GxE* studies, cultural genomic research has additional burdens that are unique to investigations of culture. While quality *GxE* research in molecular genetics pursues external validity by using large samples that provide optimal power to detect effects (Duncan & Keller, 2011), quality cultural research in psychology pursues internal validity by relying on careful, time-consuming, multi-trait, multi-method assessments of cultural processes through ethnographies, observations, experiments, interviews, and self-reports that convey the complexity of human cultural experiences (Causadias, 2013). Thus, cultural genomic researchers that aspired to the highest scientific standard found themselves between the Scylla of having to recruit large samples to detect genetic effects and the Charybdis of having to measure culture in depth (see Figure 7.1). This internal/external validity paradox implies that researchers

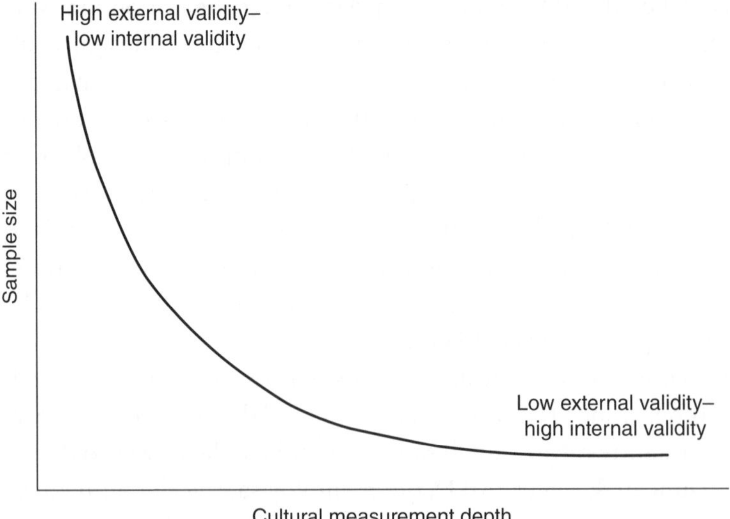

Figure 7.1 The internal/external validity paradox in cultural genomic research

need to balance sample size and cultural measurement depth. Collectively, this challenge requires new initiatives, such as the creation of new research consortiums and special grant programs that recognize the unique challenges of cultural genomics.

Finally, another problem in the field of cultural genomics is the overreliance on molecular genetics methods (e.g., candidate genes) and the lack of research using other behavioral genetic approaches. More research using polygenic and genome-wide models, as well as twin and family designs (e.g., Burt et al., 2016) and adoption studies, is necessary to understand how culture and genes are inherited, and to what extent environmental and genetic influences shape the development of certain cultural traits.

Conclusions and Future Directions

In this chapter, we have introduced the emergent field of cultural genomics, described the importance of conducting research in this area, examined its different levels of analysis, outlined several types of interplay of genes, cultures, and environments, illustrated these types with recent studies, and discussed some of the problems with current research. The field of cultural genomics has grown rapidly since Chiao and Blizinsky's (2010) pioneer study. However, there are several important challenges and future research directions. Most studies have used a single candidate gene *GxE* approach, and those that included multiple genes did not assess how genes interact with each other (epistasis) to shape culture. Although most *GxC* research focuses on individual cultural processes and single candidate genes, at the biological level *GxC* involves the interrelations between the whole genome and all cultural influences. For this reason, future cultural genomic research should go beyond the use of the candidate gene approach and explore other methods, including behavioral genetic designs, polygenic sensitivity scores, gene-by-gene interplay or epistasis, and genome-wide association analyses (GWAS). Testing and reporting HWE is another crucial safeguard for quality cultural genomic research, as is attention to issues of power, diversity and replication. Also, quantitative reviews of cultural genomic research (i.e., meta-analyses) are instrumental in generating a cumulative discipline and discerning the overall size of these associations.

Researchers should also move away from country-level analysis, group comparisons, and demographic information as proxies for culture, and invest in more rigorous and substantial cultural measurement. After all, *GxE* effects cannot be detected if the quality of the measures of environment is suboptimal (Caspi et al., 2010). Importantly, future cultural genomic research should pay more attention to theoretical models from evolutionary biology (e.g., gene–culture coevolution), avoid confounding statistical effects with conceptual terms (e.g., gene–environment correlations), and apply novel ideas, such as differential susceptibility hypothesis, to the study of culture (Causadias & Syed, 2015). Because experiments and interventions are useful tests of genetic theories (Bakermans-Kranenburg, van IJzendoorn, Pijlman, Mesman, & Juffer, 2008), future cultural genomic research should employ randomized controlled trials to examine how the effects of interventions aimed at cultural change are shaped by the genome.

In addition, researchers should purposely seek out different ethnic groups in their cultural genomics research. This is particularly relevant because in our review of the research we discovered that many studies that focused on adverse cultural experiences and environments employed African-American samples. For example, the studies we identified on genes and racial discrimination (Brody et al., 2011; Chae et al., 2014, 2016; Sales et al., 2015; Schwartz & Beaver, 2011) and neighborhood or community disadvantage (Cho & Kogan, 2015; Lei et al., 2014; Windle et al., 2015) focused almost exclusively on African-American samples. In contrast, the studies we identified on normative cultural processes and genes frequently employed samples of Asian ancestry. For instance, most studies examining genes and cultural orientation (Kitayama et al., 2014), self-expression and cultural norms (LeClair et al., 2014) and social support seeking (Kim et al., 2010) used Asian or Asian-American samples, or both. It is vital to address this trend because Asians also experience adversity, and African Americans also go through normative developmental processes. Moreover, the external validity of the field is conditional on the inclusion of representative samples from all ethnic and national backgrounds.

Finally, future cultural genomic research should examine the role of personal agency in the interplay of genes, cultures, and environments. Some findings can give the impression that individuals are passive witnesses of their cultural experiences and passive heirs of their genomes, when in fact humans play a crucial role as active agents in their own cultural and genetic development and evolution (see, e.g., Sameroff, 2009). As illustrated by active gene–environment correlations, not only are individuals unidirectionally shaped by their environment, but they actively construct their own niches, choose to participate in cultural communities, move to neighborhoods, and even migrate to specific areas that fit their own cultural preferences. Likewise, individuals make decisions that affect their genomes, through either diet or exposure to certain environments. Future studies should also consider how individuals play a starring role in their own genetic and cultural development, rather than how they are affected by the interplay of genes, cultures, and environments.

References

Antonarakis, S. E., & Beckmann, J. S. (2006). Mendelian disorders deserve more attention. *Nature Reviews Genetics, 7*(4), 277–282. doi:10.1038/nrg1826

Aoki, K. (1986). A stochastic model of gene–culture coevolution suggested by the "culture historical hypothesis" for the evolution of adult lactose absorption in humans. *Proceedings of the National Academy of Sciences, 83,* 2929–2933. doi:10.1073/pnas.83.9.2929

Bakermans-Kranenburg, M. J., van IJzendoorn, M. H., Pijlman, F. T., Mesman, J., & Juffer, F. (2008). Experimental evidence for differential susceptibility: Dopamine D4 receptor polymorphism (DRD4 VNTR) moderates intervention effects on toddlers' externalizing behavior in a randomized controlled trial. *Developmental Psychology, 44,* 293–300. doi:10.1037/0012-1649.44.1.293

Belsky, J., & Pluess, M. (2009). Beyond diathesis stress: Differential susceptibility to environmental influences. *Psychological Bulletin, 135*(6), 885–908. doi:10.1037/a0017376

Betancourt, H., & López, S. R. (1993). The study of culture, ethnicity, and race in American psychology. *American Psychologist, 48*(6), 629–637. doi:10.1037/0003-066x.48.6.629

Bisso-Machado, R., Ramallo, V., Tarazona-Santos, E., Salzano, F. M., Bortolini, M. C., & Hünemeier, T. (2013). Brief communication: 5-HTTLPR genetic diversity and mode of subsistence in Native Americans. *American Journal of Physical Anthropology, 151*(3), 492–494. doi:10.1002/ajpa.22286

Boyd, R., & Richerson, P. J. (1985). *Culture and the evolutionary process.* Chicago, IL: Chicago University Press.

Brody, G. H., Beach, S. R., Chen, Y. F., Obasi, E., Philibert, R. A., Kogan, S. M., & Simons, R. L. (2011). Perceived discrimination, serotonin transporter linked polymorphic region status, and the development of conduct problems. *Development and Psychopathology, 23*(2), 617–627. doi:10.1017/S0954579411000046

Brown, S., Savage, P. E., Ko, A. M.-S., Stoneking, M., Ko, Y.-C., Loo, J.-H., & Trejaut, J. A. (2013). Correlations in the population structure of music, genes and language. *Proceedings of the Royal Society B, 281*(20132072), 1–7. doi:10.1098/rspb.2013.2072

Burt, S. A., Klump, K. L., Gorman-Smith, D., & Neiderhiser, J. M. (2016). Neighborhood disadvantage alters the origins of children's nonaggressive conduct problems. *Clinical Psychological Science, 4*(3), 511–526. doi:10.1177/2167702615618164

Campbell, D. T. (1961). The mutual methodological relevance of anthropology and psychology. In F. L. Hsu (Ed.), *Psychological anthropology* (pp. 333–352). Homewood, IL: Dorsey.

Caspi, A., Hariri, A. R., Holmes, A., Uher, R., & Moffitt, T. E. (2010). Genetic sensitivity to the environment: The case of the serotonin transporter gene and its implications for studying complex diseases and traits. *Focus, 8*(3), 398–416. doi:10.1176/foc.8.3.foc398

Causadias, J. M. (2013). A roadmap for the integration of culture into developmental psychopathology. *Development and Psychopathology, 25*(4), 1375–1398. doi:10.1017/S0954579413000679

Causadias, J. M., & Syed, M. (2015). Is there differential susceptibility to acculturation? How culture and genes shape the adaptation of Filipino- and Mexican-American adolescents. Unpublished manuscript.

Causadias, J. M., Telzer, E. H., & Lee, R. M. (2017). Culture and biology interplay: An introduction. *Cultural Diversity and Ethnic Minority Psychology, 23*(1), 1–4. doi:10.1037/cdp0000121

Cavalli-Sforza, L. L. (1962). The distribution of migration distances: Models, and applications to genetics. In J. Sutter (ed.), *Les Déplacements humains: Aspects méthodologiques de leur mesure* (pp. 139–166). Monaco: Éditions Sciences Humaines.

Cavalli-Sforza, L. L. (2001). *Genes, peoples, and languages.* Berkeley: University of California Press.

Cavalli-Sforza, L. L., & Feldman, M. W. (1981). *Cultural transmission and evolution: A quantitative approach* (Monographs in population biology 16). Princeton, NJ: Princeton University Press.

Chae, D. H., Epel, E. S., Nuru-Jeter, A. M., Lincoln, K. D., Taylor, R. J., Lin, J., … & Thomas, S. B. (2016). Discrimination, mental health, and leukocyte telomere length among African American men. *Psychoneuroendocrinology, 63,* 10–16. doi:10.1016/j.psyneuen.2015.09.001

Chae, D. H., Nuru-Jeter, A. M., Adler, N. E., Brody, G. H., Lin, J., Blackburn, E. H., & Epel, E. S. (2014). Discrimination, racial bias, and telomere length in African-American men. *American Journal of Preventive Medicine, 46*(2), 103–111. doi:10.1016/j.amepre.2013.10.020

Chen, C., Burton, M., Greenberger, E., & Dmitrieva, J. (1999). Population migration and the variation of dopamine D4 receptor (DRD4) allele frequencies around the globe. *Evolution and Human Behavior, 20,* 309–324. doi:10.1016/s1090-5138(99)00015-x

Cheon, B. K., Livingston, R. W., Chiao, J. Y., & Hong, Y.-Y. (2015). Contribution of serotonin transporter polymorphism (5-HTTLPR) to automatic racial bias. *Personality and Individual Differences, 79,* 35–38. doi:10.1016/j.paid.2015.01.019

Cheon, B. K., Livingston, R. W., Hong, Y.-Y., & Chiao, J. Y. (2013). Gene × environment interaction on intergroup bias: The role of 5-HTTLPR and perceived outgroup threat. *Social Cognitive and Affective Neuroscience, 9*(9), 1268–1275. doi:10.1093/scan/nst111

Chiao, J. Y., & Blizinsky, K. D. (2010). Culture–gene coevolution of individualism–collectivism and the serotonin transporter gene. *Proceedings of the Royal Society B, 277*(1681), 529–537. doi:10.1098/rspb.2009.1650

Cho, J., & Kogan, S. M. (2015). Parent and youth dopamine D4 receptor genotypes moderate multilevel contextual effects on rural African American youth's risk behavior. *Development and Psychopathology,* 1–13. doi:10.1017/S0954579415000565

Cicchetti, D., & Cannon, T. D. (1999). Neurodevelopmental processes in the ontogenesis and epigenesis of psychopathology. *Development and Psychopathology, 11*(3), 375–393. doi:10.1017/s0954579499002114

Claidière, N., & André, J.-B. (2012). The transmission of genes and culture: A questionable analogy. *Evolutionary Biology, 39*(1), 12–24. doi:10.1007/s11692-011-9141-8

Cohen, A. B. (2009). Many forms of culture. *American Psychologist, 64,* 194–204. doi:10.1037/a0015308

Cumming, G. (2012). *Understanding the new statistics: Effect sizes, confidence intervals, and meta-analysis.* New York: Routledge.

Cumming, G. (2013). The new statistics: Why and how. *Psychological Science, 25,* 7–29. doi:10.1177/0956797613504966

Dressler, W. W., Balieiro, M. C., Ribeiro, R. P., & Santos, J. E. D. (2009). Cultural consonance, a 5HT2A receptor polymorphism, and depressive symptoms: A longitudinal study of gene × culture interaction in urban Brazil. *American Journal of Human Biology, 21*(1), 91–97. doi:10.1002/ajhb.20823

Duncan, L. E., & Keller, M. C. (2011). A critical review of the first 10 years of candidate gene-by-environment interaction research in psychiatry.

American Journal of Psychiatry, 168(10), 1041–1049. doi:10.1176/appi.ajp.2011.11020191

Duncan, L. E., Pollastri, A. R., & Smoller, J. W. (2014). Mind the gap: Why many geneticists and psychological scientists have discrepant views about gene–environment interaction (G×E) research. *American Psychologist, 69*(3), 249–268. doi:10.1037/a0036320

Eisenberg, D. T., & Hayes, M. G. (2011). Testing the null hypothesis: Comments on "Culture–gene coevolution of individualism–collectivism and the serotonin transporter gene." *Proceedings of the Royal Society B, 278*, 329–332. doi:10.1098/rspb.2010.0714

Feero, W. G., Guttmacher, A. E., & Collins, F. S. (2010). Genomic medicine – an updated primer. *New England Journal of Medicine, 362*(21), 2001–2011. doi:10.1056/nejmra0907175

Feldman, M. W., & Cavalli-Sforza, L. L. (1989). On the theory of evolution under genetic and cultural transmission with application to the lactose absorption problem. In M. W. Feldman (Ed.), *Mathematical evolutionary theory* (pp. 145–173). Princeton, NJ: Princeton University Press. doi:10.1515/9781400859832-009

Fisher, S. E., & Vernes, S. C. (2015). Genetics and the language sciences. *Annual Review of Linguistics, 1*(1), 289–310. doi:10.1146/annurev-linguist-030514-125024

Gavrilets, S. (2010). High-dimensional fitness landscapes and speciation. In M. Pigliucci & G. B. Müller (Eds.), *Evolution: The extended synthesis.* Cambridge, MA: MIT Press. doi:10.7551/mitpress/9780262513678.003.0003

Hart, D., & Marmorstein, N. R. (2009). Neighborhoods and genes and everything in between: Understanding adolescent aggression in social and biological contexts. *Development and Psychopathology, 21*(3), 961–973. doi:10.1017/s0954579409000510

Henrich, J., & McElreath, R. (2007). Dual-inheritance theory: The evolution of human cultural capacities and cultural evolution. In R. I. M. Dunbar & L. Barrett (Eds.), *Oxford handbook of evolutionary psychology* (pp. 555–570). New York: Oxford University Press.

Hewitt, J. K. (2012). Editorial policy on candidate gene association and candidate gene-by-environment interaction studies of complex traits. *Behavior Genetics, 42*(1), 1–2. doi:10.1007/s10519-011-9504-z

Hosking, L., Lumsden, S., Lewis, K., Yeo, A., McCarthy, L., Bansal, A., … & Xu, C. F. (2004). Detection of genotyping errors by Hardy–Weinberg equilibrium testing. *European Journal of Human Genetics, 12*(5), 395–399. doi:10.1002/gepi.20086

Huxley, J. S. (1955). Guest editorial: Evolution, cultural and biological. *Yearbook of Anthropology*, 2–25.

Kim, H. S., Sherman, D. K., Mojaverian, T., Sasaki, J. Y., Park, J., Suh, E. M., & Taylor, S. E. (2011). Gene–culture interaction: Oxytocin receptor polymorphism (OXTR) and emotion regulation. *Social Psychological and Personality Science, 2*(6), 665–672. doi:10.1177/1948550611405854

Kim, H. S., Sherman, D. K., Sasaki, J. Y., Xu, J., Chu, T. Q., Ryu, C., ... & Taylor, S. E. (2010). Culture, distress, and oxytocin receptor polymorphism (OXTR) interact to influence emotional support seeking. *Proceedings of the National Academy of Sciences, 107*(36), 15717–15721. doi:10.1073/pnas.1010830107

Kitayama, S., Conway, L. G., III, Pietromonaco, P. R., & Park, H. (2010). Ethos of independence across regions in the United States. *American Psychologist, 65*, 559–574. doi:10.1037/a0020277

Kitayama, S., King, A., Hsu, M., Liberzon, I., & Yoon, C. (2016). Dopamine-system genes and cultural acquisition: The norm sensitivity hypothesis. *Current Opinion in Psychology, 8*, 167–174. doi:10.1016/j.copsyc.2015.11.006

Kitayama, S., King, A., Yoon, C., Tompson, S., Huff, S., & Liberzon, I. (2014). The dopamine D4 receptor gene (*DRD4*) moderates cultural difference in independent versus interdependent social orientation. *Psychological Science, 25*(6), 1169–1177. doi:10.1177/0956797614528338

Laland, K. N., Odling-Smee, J., & Myles, S. (2010). How culture shaped the human genome: Bringing genetics and the human sciences together. *Nature Reviews Genetics, 11*(2), 137–148. doi:10.1038/nrg2734

Laland, K. N., Uller, T., Feldman, M. W., Sterelny, K., Müller, G. B., Moczek, A., ... & Odling-Smee, J. (2015). The extended evolutionary synthesis: Its structure, assumptions and predictions. *Proceedings of the Royal Society B, 282*(1813), 20151019. doi:10.1098/rspb.2015.1019

LeClair, J., Janusonis, S., & Kim, H. S. (2014). Gene–culture interactions: A multi-gene approach. *Culture and Brain, 2*(2), 122–140. doi:10.1007/s40167-014-0022-8

Lei, M.-K., Simons, R. L., Edmond, M. B., Simons, L. G., & Cutrona, C. E. (2014). The effect of neighborhood disadvantage, social ties, and genetic variation on the antisocial behavior of African American women: A multilevel analysis. *Development and Psychopathology, 26*(4), 1113–1128. doi:10.1017/s0954579414000200

Levins, R., & Lewontin, R. C. (1985). *The dialectical biologist*. Cambridge, MA: Harvard University Press.

Li, S. C. (2003). Biocultural orchestration of developmental plasticity across levels: The interplay of biology and culture in shaping the mind and behavior across the life span. *Psychological Bulletin, 129*(2), 171–194. doi:10.1037/0033-2909.129.2.171

Lilienfeld, S. O., Lynn, S. J., Ruscio, J., & Beyerstein, B. L. (2011). *50 great myths of popular psychology: Shattering widespread misconceptions about human behavior*. Malden, MA: Wiley-Blackwell.

Luo, S., & Han, S. (2014). The association between an oxytocin receptor gene polymorphism and cultural orientations. *Culture and Brain, 2*(1), 89–107. doi:10.1007/s40167-014-0017-5

Matsumoto, D., & Yoo, S. H. (2006). Toward a new generation of cross-cultural research. *Perspectives on Psychological Science, 1*, 234–250. doi:10.1111/j.1745-6916.2006.00014.x

Mesoudi, A. (2016). Cultural evolution: Integrating psychology, evolution and culture. *Current Opinion in Psychology, 7*, 17–22. doi:10.1016/j.copsyc.2015.07.001

Mesoudi, A., Whiten, A., & Laland, K. N. (2006). Towards a unified science of cultural evolution. *Behavioral and Brain Sciences, 29*(4), 329–347. doi:10.1017/s0140525x06009083

Minkov, M., Blagoev, V., & Bond, M. H. (2014). Improving research in the emerging field of cross-cultural sociogenetics: The case of serotonin. *Journal of Cross-Cultural Psychology, 46*(3), 336–354. doi:10.1177/0022022114563612

Moya, C., & Henrich, J. (2016). Culture–gene coevolutionary psychology: Cultural learning, language, and ethnic psychology. *Current Opinion in Psychology, 8*, 112–118. doi:10.1016/j.copsyc.2015.10.001

Mrazek, A. J., Chiao, J. Y., Blizinsky, K. D., Lun, J., & Gelfand, M. J. (2013). The role of culture–gene coevolution in morality judgment: Examining the interplay between tightness–looseness and allelic variation of the serotonin transporter gene. *Culture and Brain, 1*(2–4), 100–117. doi:10.1007/s40167-013-0009-x

O'Brien, M. J., & Laland, K. N. (2012). Genes, culture, and agriculture. *Current Anthropology, 53*(4), 434–470. doi:10.1086/666585

Odling-Smee, J., & Laland, K. N. (2011). Ecological inheritance and cultural inheritance: What are they and how do they differ? *Biological Theory, 6*(3), 220–230. doi:10.1007/s13752-012-0030-x

Oquendo, M. A., Canino, G., Lehner, T., & Licinio, J. (2010). Genetic repositories for the study of major psychiatric conditions: What do we know about ethnic minorities' genetic vulnerability? *Molecular Psychiatry, 15*, 970–975. doi:10.1038/mp.2010.11

Plomin, R. (2013). Child development and molecular genetics: 14 years later. *Child Development, 84*(1), 104–120. doi:10.1111/j.1467-8624.2012.01757.x

Plomin, R., DeFries, J. C., & Loehlin, J. C. (1977). Genotype–environment interaction and correlation in the analysis of human behavior. *Psychological Bulletin, 84*, 309–322. doi:10.1037/0033-2909.84.2.309

Plomin, R., & Spinath, F. M. (2004). Intelligence: Genetics, genes, and genomics. *Journal of Personality and Social Psychology, 86*(1), 112–129. doi:10.1037/0022-3514.86.1.112

Priem, R. L., Lyon, D. W., & Dess, G. G. (1999). Inherent limitations of demographic proxies in top management team heterogeneity research. *Journal of Management, 25*(6), 935–953. doi:10.1177/014920639902500607

Purcell, S. M., Wray, N. R., Stone, J. L., Visscher, P. M., O'Donovan, M. C., Sullivan, P. F., … & O'Dushlaine, C. T. (2009). Common polygenic variation contributes to risk of schizophrenia and bipolar disorder. *Nature, 460*(7256), 748–752. doi:10.1038/nature08185

Richerson, P. J., Boyd, R., & Henrich, J. (2010). Gene–culture coevolution in the age of genomics. *Proceedings of the National Academy of Sciences, 107*(2), 8985–8992. doi:10.1073/pnas.0914631107

Risch, N., Herrell, R., Lehner, T., Liang, K. Y., Eaves, L., Hoh, J., … & Merikangas, K. R. (2009). Interaction between the serotonin transporter gene (5-HTTLPR), stressful life events, and risk of depression: A meta-analysis. *Journal of the American Medical Association, 301*(23), 2462–2471. doi:10.1001/jama.2009.878

Rutter, M. (2006). *Genes and behavior: Nature–nurture interplay explained.* Malden, MA: Blackwell Publishing.

Rutter, M. (2007). Gene–environment interdependence. *Developmental Science, 10*(1), 12–18. doi:10.1111/j.1467-7687.2007.00557.x

Rutter, M. (2013). Developmental psychopathology: A paradigm shift or just a relabeling? *Development and Psychopathology, 25*(4pt2), 1201–1213. doi:10.1017/s0954579413000564

Salanti, G., Amountza, G., Ntzani, E. E., & Ioannidis, J. P. (2005). Hardy–Weinberg equilibrium in genetic association studies: An empirical evaluation of reporting, deviations, and power. *European Journal of Human Genetics, 13*(7), 840–848. doi:10.1038/sj.ejhg.5201410

Sales, J. M., Brown, J. L., Swartzendruber, A. L., Smearman, E. L., Brody, G. H., & DiClemente, R. (2015). Genetic sensitivity to emotional cues, racial discrimination and depressive symptoms among African–American adolescent females. *Frontiers in Psychology, 6*, 1–10. doi:10.3389/fpsyg.2015.00854

Sameroff, A. (2009). The transaction model. In A. Sameroff (Ed.), *The transactional model of development: How children and contexts shape each other* (pp. 3–21). Washington, DC: American Psychological Association. doi:10.1037/11877-001

Schwartz, J. A., & Beaver, K. M. (2011). Evidence of a gene × environment interaction between perceived prejudice and MAOA genotype in the prediction of criminal arrests. *Journal of Criminal Justice, 39*(5), 378–384. doi:10.1016/j.jcrimjus.2011.05.003

Simmons, J. P., Nelson, L. D., & Simonsohn, U. (2011). False-positive psychology: Undisclosed flexibility in data collection and analysis allows presenting anything as significant. *Psychological Science, 22*, 1359–1366. doi:10.1177/0956797611417632

Sroufe, L. A. (2007). The place of development in developmental psychopathology. In A. Masten (Ed.), *Multilevel dynamics in developmental psychopathology: Pathways to the future* (pp. 285–299) (Minnesota Symposia on Child Psychology, 34). Mahwah, NJ: Lawrence Erlbaum Associates.

Tinbergen, N. (1963). On aims and methods of ethology. *Zeitschrift für Tierpsychologie, 20*(4), 410–433. doi:10.1111/j.1439-0310.1963.tb01161.x

van IJzendoorn, M. H., Belsky, J., & Bakermans-Kranenburg, M. J. (2012). Serotonin transporter genotype 5HTTLPR as a marker of differential susceptibility: A meta-analysis of child and adolescent gene-by-environment studies. *Translational Psychiatry, 2*, e147.

Way, B. M., & Lieberman, M. D. (2010). Is there a genetic contribution to cultural differences? Collectivism, individualism and genetic markers of social sensitivity. *Social Cognitive and Affective Neuroscience, 5*(2–3), 203–211. doi:10.1093/scan/nsq059

Wigginton, J. E., Cutler, D. J., & Abecasis, G. R. (2005). A note on exact tests of Hardy–Weinberg equilibrium. *American Journal of Human Genetics, 76*(5), 887–893. doi:10.1086/429864

Wilson, E. O. (2000). *Sociobiology: The new synthesis* (25th anniversary edition). Cambridge, MA: Belknap Press of Harvard University Press.

Windle, M., Kogan, S. M., Lee, S., Chen, Y.-F., Lei, K. M., Brody, G. H., … & Yu, T. (2015). Neighborhood × serotonin transporter linked polymorphic region (5-HTTLPR) interactions for substance use from ages 10 to 24 years using a harmonized data set of African American children. *Development and Psychopathology, 28*(2), 415–431. doi:10.1017/s095457941500053x

Wittke-Thompson, J. K., Pluzhnikov, A., & Cox, N. J. (2005). Rational inferences about departures from Hardy–Weinberg equilibrium. *American Journal of Human Genetics, 76*(6), 967–986. doi:10.1086/430507

Wong, P., Morgan-Short, K., Ettlinger, M., & Zheng, J. (2012). Linking neurogenetics and individual differences in language learning: The dopamine hypothesis. *Cortex, 48*(9), 1091–1102. doi:10.1016/j.cortex.2012.03.017

8

Dual Inheritance, Cultural Transmission, and Niche Construction

Michael J. O'Brien and R. Alexander Bentley

As the behavioral sciences increasingly turn to explanatory models of cultural evolution based on a Darwinian perspective, three topics – dual inheritance, cultural transmission, and, more recently, niche construction – have assumed prominent positions on the analytical landscape. Until the early 1980s, the behavioral sciences in general tended to draw a sharp distinction between biologically based (innate) behavioral traits and cultural traits, the former being a reflection of one's genotype and the latter the result of learning. This is a false dichotomy (Mesoudi, Whiten, & Laland, 2006). "Biological" means living; thus, all human behavior is biological. Further, "innate" behaviors typically include cultural components, both innate and learned. Learning a language, for example – a quintessential cultural trait – requires transmission, but it also requires the appropriate mental facilities, which result from the interaction between an individual's genes and the environment (Nettle, 2006).

This is in no way meant to imply that before the 1980s behavioral scientists were uninterested in such things as cultural evolution, cultural transmission, and human niches. Note, for example, what Franz Boas, often identified as the "father" of American anthropology, pointed out with respect to cultural transmission: "We must investigate the innumerable cases of transmission that happen under our very eyes and try to understand how transmission is brought about and what are the conditions that favor the grouping of certain new elements of an older culture" (Boas, 1911: 809). This was an excellent identification of the problem, but here, as throughout so much of anthropology, common sense substituted for rigorous models of cultural transmission (Lyman & O'Brien, 2003).

The Handbook of Culture and Biology, First Edition. Edited by José M. Causadias, Eva H. Telzer and Nancy A. Gonzales.

That lack of rigor began to be addressed in the late 1970s through the mathematical-modeling work of Luca Cavalli-Sforza, a population geneticist, and Marcus Feldman, a theoretical biologist (e.g., Cavalli-Sforza & Feldman, 1981). The innovative aspect of their approach, which they labeled "gene–culture coevolutionary theory," was that they not only modeled the differential transmission of genes between generations but also incorporated cultural information into the analysis, which allowed the evolution of the two systems to be mutually dependent (Laland & Brown, 2011). Cavalli-Sforza and Feldman's work was followed by that of Robert Boyd and Peter Richerson, whose book *Culture and the Evolutionary Process* (Boyd & Richerson, 1985) laid the foundation for what they labeled "dual-inheritance theory," which we view as synonymous with Cavalli-Sforza and Feldman's "gene–culture coevolutionary theory."

With respect to the role that the human niche played in early anthropological thought, Hardesty's (1972) review is instructive. As he makes clear, the concept of the ecological niche was inconsistently used in early anthropological and ecological studies. Some researchers used it more in terms of a geographic location or habitat. Barth (1956: 1079), for example, defined it as "the place of a group in the total environment, its relation to resources and competitors," and Flannery (1965) defined it as a microenvironment in which a species is concentrated. Conversely, Odum (1959: 27) defined the niche as the functional role of an organism "within its community and ecosystem resulting from the organism's structural adaptations, physiological responses, and specific behavior." Odum (1959) made the well-known distinction between habitat and niche, the former being an organism's address and the latter its profession, or occupation.

Even today, when there is more of a consensus over what a niche entails, there is still a conventional perspective that although organisms, humans included, construct niches and modify environmental states, such behaviors are consequences of prior selection and not the causes of evolutionary change. This conventional perspective downplays the active role that organisms play in the evolutionary process as co-causes and co-directors of their own evolution and that of other species. The conceptual leap that niche construction theory brings is to regard niche construction as an evolutionary process in its own right – an initiator of evolutionary change rather than merely the end product of earlier selection. Although this position remains controversial even in the biological sciences (see, e.g., Scott-Phillips, Laland, Shuker, Dickins, & West, 2014), there is an abundance of evidence that niche construction is evolutionarily consequential (Laland & O'Brien, 2012; Laland, Odling-Smee, & Myles, 2010; Odling-Smee, Laland, & Feldman, 2003).

Here we discuss niche construction, dual inheritance, and cultural transmission as separate processes, more or less as modern biology texts contain separate chapters on selection, drift, mutation, and Mendelian inheritance. We cannot overemphasize, however, that all three processes act in tandem to shape and reshape human behavior in evolutionarily significant ways (O'Brien & Laland, 2012). Our goal is to provide behavioral scientists with enough background to make the various issues that emanate from these processes accessible. We begin with a discussion of dual inheritance and then turn to cultural transmission and finally to niche construction.

Dual-Inheritance Theory

Dual-inheritance theory is a branch of theoretical population genetics that incorporates cultural traits into models of the transmission of genes from one generation to the next (Boyd & Richerson, 1985; Cavalli-Sforza & Feldman, 1981; Durham, 1991; Richerson & Boyd, 2005). Anthropologists have long known the power that culture exerts in shaping the human condition, but it is becoming increasingly clear that the interactions of genes and culture – literally, their coevolution – offer a faster and stronger mode of human evolution than either by itself (Laland et al., 2010; Richerson & Boyd, 2005; Richerson, Boyd, & Henrich, 2010). The two inheritance systems cannot be treated independently, because what an individual learns may depend on his or her genotype expressed throughout development. Further, selection acting on the genetic system may be generated or modified by the spread of a cultural trait. This should not be contentious, particularly with respect to such things as agriculture, food production, and dietary habits. There is now strong empirical evidence that genotype affects acquired behavior (Laland et al., 2010; Richerson et al., 2010). Here, "culture" is defined as the "ability to acquire valuable knowledge and skills from other individuals through social learning and teaching, and to build on this reservoir of shared knowledge, iteratively, generation after generation, building ever more efficient solutions to life's challenges" (Laland, Atton, & Webster, 2011: 958).

Culturally derived selection pressures can be stronger than non-cultural ones. This means that culture can be just as powerful as nature when it comes to shaping organisms and their behaviors. There are at least two reasons for this. First, there is highly reliable transmission of cultural information between individuals. Although reliability differs among kinds of traits, culturally modified selective environments can produce unusually strong natural selection that is directionally consistent over time (Bersaglieri et al.,

2004). Second, cultural innovations typically spread more quickly than genetic mutations because social learning operates at a much faster rate than does biological evolution (Feldman & Laland, 1996). If cultural practices modify selection on human genes, then the more individuals exhibit a trait, the greater the intensity of selection will be on a gene (Laland et al., 2010). The rapid spread of a particular cultural practice often leads to maximum intensity of selection on the advantageous genetic variant or variants. Gene–culture coevolutionary models repeatedly demonstrate more rapid responses to selection than conventional population-genetic models. This underscores the fact that culture has accelerated human evolution (Cochran & Harpending, 2009; Hawks, Wang, Cochran, Harpending, & Mayzis, 2007; Laland et al., 2010; Richerson et al., 2010).

Those who study gene–culture interactions are not trying to model how entire cultures change over time, but rather to explore some of the general properties of gene–culture coevolution and to predict patterns of change in certain specific traits (Laland & Brown, 2006). Examples include investigations of the evolution of altruism and cooperation (Gintis, 2003) and the coevolution of female-biased infanticide and sex-ratio-distorter genes (Kumm, Laland, & Feldman, 1994). The study of gene–culture coevolution has associated with it a formal discipline and a progressive theoretical research program, and we would be among the first to admit that formal gene–culture models are technical and mathematical and often difficult to appreciate. The greater concern, however, is not with mathematical modeling but with the degree of fit between expectations derived from dual-inheritance theory and select aspects of the empirical record. Here, even those with little knowledge of mathematics can make significant contributions (Laland & O'Brien, 2010, 2012) by developing theory and finding empirical case studies that appear to substantiate hypotheses that stem directly from that theory.

Cultural Transmission

If Mayr (1973) is correct that behavior is perhaps the strongest selection pressure operating in the animal kingdom, then we need to take it all the more seriously when the animals are humans (O'Brien & Lyman, 2000). Cultural transmission is a primary determinant of behavior, and there is little doubt that it is one of the most effective means of evolutionary inheritance that nature could ever create. Gene–culture theorists model cultural transmission as a Darwinian process in which there is selective retention of favorable cultural variants, with concomitant effects on biological fitness, recognizing that other, non-selective processes such as mutation (invention, innovation), spread (diffusion), and drift (random change) play significant roles as well (Bentley, Hahn, & Shennan, 2004). Many other animals exhibit culture (Boesch, 2012; Laland et al., 2011; Whiten, 2011), but it is the fact that human culture evolves quickly and is cumulative that makes it an exceptional case. By this we mean that one generation does things in a certain way, and the next generation, instead of starting from scratch, does them in more or less the same way, except that perhaps it adds a modification or improvement. The succeeding generation learns the modified version, which persists across generations until further changes are made (Tennie, Call, & Tomasello, 2009). Human cultural transmission is thus characterized by the so-called "ratchet effect," in which modifications and improvements stay in the population until further changes ratchet things up again (Tomasello, Kruger, & Ratner, 1993), although there is nothing inevitable about progress and no guarantee that any "improvements" will be fitness-enhancing.

We can think of the actual units of transmission as *cultural traits* (O'Brien, Lyman, Mesoudi, & VanPool, 2010) – more or less what Dawkins (1989) had in mind with the concept of the *meme*. These units spread and create *traditions* – patterned behaviors that exist in identifiable form over extended periods of time. As with genes, cultural traits are subject to recombination, copying error, and the like and thus can serve as the foundation for the production of new traits. In other words, cultural traits can be both *inventions* – new creations – and *innovations* – inventions that spread because of some utility, regardless of whether that utility is immediately perceived or not (Erwin & Krakauer, 2004). To put it in a slightly different way, innovations are successful inventions, with "success" measured in terms of their having spread. Because they can exist at various scales of inclusiveness and can exhibit considerable flexibility, cultural traits have many of the characteristics of Hull's (1981) "replicators," or entities that pass on their structure directly through replication (Williams, 2002). Once transmitted, cultural traits serve as units of replication in that they can be modified as part of an individual's cultural repertoire through processes such as recombination (new associations with other cultural traits), loss (forgetting), and partial alteration (incomplete learning, personal experience, or overlooking select components) within an individual's mind (Eerkens & Lipo, 2005). In this regard, cultural traits are analogous to genes in that organisms replicate them, but they are also replicators in their own right. However, the transmission of these units is behavioral, and it uses mutually understandable spoken or written language, physical imitation, or some combination.

No one has ever seen a unit of transmission, either behavioral or genetic, although we can observe the effects of transmission. Genes and behavioral traits become units of transmission only in specific environmental contexts, meaning that although one can talk abstractly about them, their definition in analytically useful units depends on environmentally specific elements. Fortunately, such units are manifest in artifacts, features, and other components of the ethnographic and archaeological records, and they serve as proxies for studying the transmission (and modification) of cultural traits between people in an evolutionary process of descent with modification (Leonard & Jones, 1987; O'Brien & Holland, 1995).

As it does among animals that exhibit culture, learning drives cultural transmission. How could it be otherwise? If nothing is learned, nothing can be transmitted. The key question is, how was a particular behavior learned? Did an individual learn it on his or her own or from others? If the latter, from whom did the individual learn it, and how? Through copying? Through a prolonged apprenticeship? And how did the individual decide to do one or another? As a starting point for addressing these questions, we find it useful to do what other behavioral scientists have done and make a distinction between *individual learning* and *social learning.*

Individual Learning

In individual learning, an individual modifies existing behaviors through trial and error to suit his or her own needs. Perhaps a learner obtains the basic behavior from a parent or master and then begins to tinker with it with no influence from other people. He or she then passes the behavior on to others. Boyd and Richerson (1985) refer to this as "guided variation." The guided-variation model shows that, in the absence of selection for a particular trait, a population will move toward whichever trait is favored by people's individual-learning biases. This occurs even when guided variation is weak (Mesoudi, 2011).

This form of learning is called "unbiased" (Boyd & Richerson, 1985; Henrich, 2001), because at the population level it approximates the distribution of behaviors in the previous generation. After acquiring a behavior or a tool, an individual might obtain environmental information about the relative payoffs of alternative skills or tools. If the difference in payoffs is clear, the individual adopts the behavior indicated by the environmental information. If not, the individual sticks with the behavior acquired through unbiased cultural transmission (Henrich, 2001). Thus, Boyd and Richerson's (1985) "guided variation" has two equally important components: unbiased transmission and environmental (individual) learning. Henrich (2001) uses the term "environmental learning model" to include both the individual-level learning process, which may occur many times per generation, and its transgenerational counterpart, guided variation (unbiased transmission and individual learning).

Social Learning

Many animals use social learning – defined as learning by observing, or interacting with, others (Heyes, 1994) – for any number of adaptive purposes (Hoppitt & Laland, 2013), but humans excel at it. If we accept that large brains evolved through selection for complex social abilities (Dunbar & Shultz, 2007), it follows that behaviors usually become popular in human communities by means of social learning. Humans learn their language, morals, technology, how to behave socially, what foods to eat, and most ideas, from other people. This process is the basis of human culture, organizations, and technology (Whiten, Hinde, Laland, & Stringer, 2011). Much of the time, social learning is an effort to replicate another's behavior accurately without embellishment. It is a powerful adaptive strategy that allows others to risk failure first (Henrich, 2001): Let others filter behaviors for you and pass along those that have the highest payoff (Rendell et al., 2011). The benefits of copying apply equally to inventors and commercial firms interested in maximizing profits and to prehistoric potters attempting to make functional vessels. Copying others is itself a set of competing strategies, in that one might preferentially copy by identifying skill level as the main criterion (copy those who are better at something than you are, copy good social learners, copy those who are successful), whereas others might base their decisions on social criteria (copy the majority, copy kin or friends, copy older individuals).

It's Not Always One or the Other

We cannot imagine a situation in which one does only one kind of learning all one's life. Rather, humans both experiment *and* copy, depending on the circumstances. What is important is the composition of the population in terms of the number of social learners versus individual (asocial) learners there are at any given moment. We can think of individual learners as information producers, and social learners as information scroungers.

In one important study, Mesoudi (2008) found that populations of flexible learners outperform both individual learners and mixed populations of individual learners and social learners. And even if individuals are going to learn socially, how will they do it? There can be significant differences in the effects of copying based on selection for knowledge or a skill level and copying based on random social interaction. An excellent example of this difference comes from the computer-mediated tournament of learning algorithms held at St Andrews University in 2009 (Rendell et al., 2011). Before the tournament, many expected the winning strategy to be a combination of majority individual learning and some social learning. In fact, the most successful strategies relied almost exclusively on social learning, even when the environment was changing rapidly. The winning strategy, labeled "discountmachine," copied often and was biased in favor of copying the most recent successful behavior it observed.

This is consistent with how we view the world – as a highly interconnected and distributed collection of minds, the power of which for social transmission is only now becoming apparent (Bentley, O'Brien, & Brock, 2014). Our view mirrors that of Rendell et al. (2011): Copying confers an adaptive plasticity on populations, which allows them to draw on deep knowledge bases in order to respond to changing environments rapidly. High-fidelity copying leads to an exponential increase in the retention of cultural knowledge, the "ratcheting effect" mentioned above. There is a caveat, however: Even in the most successful strategies that came out of the tournament of learning algorithms held at St Andrews, where copying predominated, there had to be a source of new variation present, through either copying error or occasional innovation (Rendell et al., 2011). Without any individual learners to constantly sample the environment – to produce information useful to the group – social learners cannot track environmental change. They are simply "buying" whatever happens to be on the shelf and will eventually copy themselves into stasis.

A Simple Map of Learning

Several years ago we devised a two-dimensional map (Figure 8.1) that plots not only the kind of learning involved (east–west axis) in a particular context but the degree of transparency in terms of the costs and benefits of the kind of learning involved (north–south axis) (Bentley et al., 2014). Along the western edge of the map, agents are purely individual learners: they use no information from others in making decisions. Along the eastern edge, agents are purely social learners: their decisions are based solely on

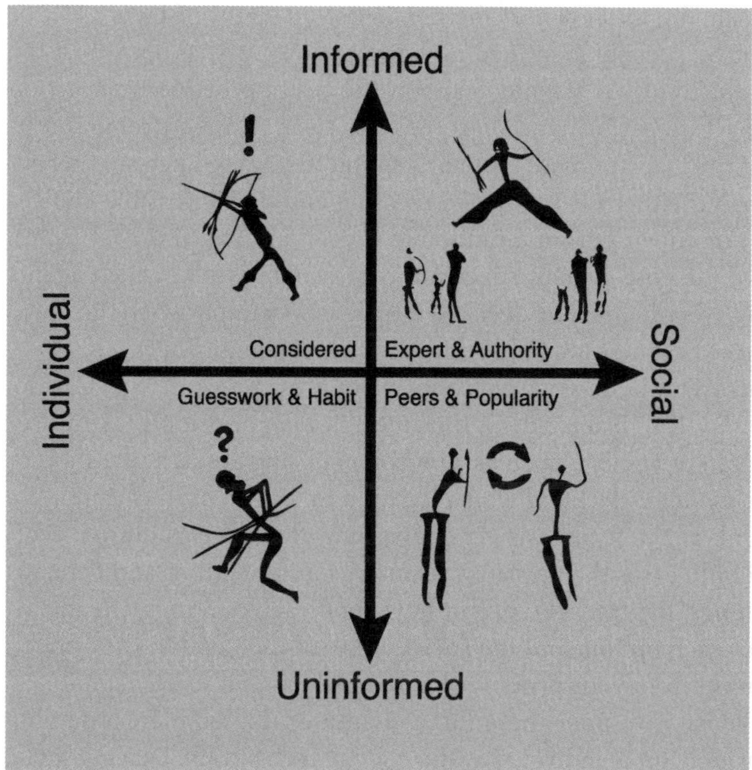

Figure 8.1 A four-quadrant map for understanding different domains of human decision making, based on whether a decision is made individually or socially (horizontal axis) and the transparency of options and payoffs that inform a decision (vertical axis) (from O'Brien et al. 2016). Reproduced with permission of Springer

copying, verbal instruction, imitation, or other, similar, social processes. In between the extremes is a balance between the two, a flexible measure of the agents represented. The midpoint could represent, for example, a population of half social learners and half individual learners, or a number of individuals giving a 50% weight to their own experience and the same amount to that of others. Location along the east–west axis may not always affect the equilibrium towards which each behavior evolves, but it will undoubtedly affect the dynamics by which that equilibrium is approached.

We can compare the kinds of learning with the costs and benefits related to that knowledge. The farther north on the map we go, the more attuned agents' decisions will be to the potential costs and payoffs of their decisions. A projectile-point manufacturer, for example, might quickly learn that a certain shape of base makes a point susceptible to catastrophic failure, and so would probably change the design. Such a decision might be made individually, as shown in the northwest quadrant of Figure 8.1, or there might be socially identified authoritative experts, as shown in the northeast quadrant. As we move south, the relation between an action and its impact on performance becomes less clear. At the extreme southern edge of the map are cases that correspond to total indifference, where choice is based either on randomly guessing among all possible choices (lower left) or copying from a randomly chosen individual (lower right). This area of the cost–benefit spectrum represents cases in which agents are perhaps overwhelmed by decision fatigue, for example when the number of choices becomes too large to be processed economically.

Here is an example, drawn from some of our previous work (e.g., Caiado, Brock, Bentley, & O'Brien, 2016). Imagine a human decision-making scenario, modern or ancient, such as a person choosing a watch in a shop or a prehistoric hunter deciding which location to visit to hunt caribou. We tend to think of the former as economics and the latter as human ecology, but in both cases the decision has many similar options and depends on three things: the transparency of how good each option is, the intrinsic utility of each option, and the social utility of each option (how much benefit you get from your peers – what sociologists call social capital).

The challenge is to infer these three quantities indirectly by observing only the proportion of individuals who choose each option. Leaving social influence aside for a moment, consider just the transparency of the intrinsic utility. If the intrinsic utility of each choice is highly transparent, as in the northwest quadrant of our map, the probability distribution of decisions ought to peak sharply at the highest-utility option. As transparency decreases – as we move southward on the map – the probability distribution flattens, as utility differences can no longer be discerned among the different options. At zero visibility, along the southern edge of the map, the probability distribution approaches a uniform distribution, and we effectively have random choice among indistinguishable options.

Now add social utility, which draws us eastward on the map. For example, a shopper chooses the brand that she has just seen someone else choose, or perhaps a novice hunter follows the most experienced hunter to track caribou. Then aggregate those decisions over time or people, or both. If social utility is transparent – if, for example, the lead hunter is indeed the best expert – the group's choice will probably be the best choice. If social utility is not transparent, however – for example, you see online that a certain technology product is popular – herding effects are more likely, and the most popular option among the aggregated observations need not have the highest utility. Indeed, if social utility is high and intrinsic transparency low, as in the southeast quadrant, the distributions of choice probability and intrinsic utility among the options could differ significantly.

Here is another example, from Atkisson, O'Brien, & Mesoudi (2012). Think of a woman who has married into a patrilocal society and her new community has a different kind of specialization from that of her home location. In fact, her new community is one of the few in the world where women rather than men are responsible for making stone arrowheads. This woman can enhance her new family's survival prospects by creating arrowheads that not only help her husband kill more game but can be traded to other communities. As she goes about learning the task of arrowhead making, she has several pathways to success. She could engage exclusively in individual learning (northwest quadrant of our map), where she tries to figure out how to make arrowheads entirely on her own. Given that projectile-point technology evolved culturally over tens of thousands of years through the efforts of countless generations of innovators, each making small improvements on what went before, her chances of reinventing projectile-point technology from scratch, using purely individual learning, are slim. Instead, she will probably fare much better through social learning, either by copying the object itself, if it is simple, or, more likely, copying how others are making their arrowheads.

In this example, social learning is superior to individual learning because of the high costs of the latter. One does not become a flint knapper, let alone an accomplished one, overnight. Instead of trying to reinvent the wheel, it is more cost-effective to just copy. The question then becomes what or whom to copy. Our learner could attempt to make arrowheads the way most women seem to be making them, which would place her in the southeast quadrant. As she doesn't yet know those women, conformity will be a challenging task: she would need to survey the whole group to determine the most frequently used technique. So although our novice flint knapper is learning socially, she has no clue as to social utility. It is as if she took a look around, pointed to another flint knapper, and said, "I'll make what she's making." Here her behavior is in the southeast quadrant.

Our novice flint knapper, however, sees another way to gather information quickly. The first thing she noticed when she started making arrowheads was that whenever someone had difficulty with the steps involved, that person always sought out a specific woman in the community for help. Perhaps the master flint knapper was someone older and presumably more knowledgeable, although our learner could not know this for sure, having no direct access to the hunting success of this woman's husband. All she knows is that everyone in the community pays this woman more attention and generally confers upon her more respect than they do upon other women. From this, our novice decides that she, too, should pay special attention to this other woman. Thus she is able to learn the intricacies of successful arrowhead creation, allowing her husband to kill more game and herself to receive more in trade for her arrowheads. Here, our agent is in the northeast quadrant of the map, where intrinsic utility is unclear to her but, apparently, *not* to the woman whom she chooses as a model. In essence, she is using the model as a proxy for decision making.

Niche Construction

Niche construction is the process whereby organisms, through their activities and choices, modify their own niche as well as those of other organisms. Niche construction theory (NCT) takes this a step further in that it places emphasis on the capacity of organisms to modify *natural selection* in their environment and thereby act as co-directors of their own evolution as well as that of others. Although it had its origin in population genetics, NCT has become a multidisciplinary movement, involving evolutionary biologists, ecologists, psychologists, anthropologists, archaeologists, computer scientists, philosophers, and others (Kendal, Tehrani, & Odling-Smee, 2011; Laland & O'Brien, 2012, 2015). This perspective contrasts with the conventional view of evolution as a straight-line process in which species, through natural selection, come to exhibit those characteristics that best enable them to survive and reproduce in their particular environments. Although environmental change may trigger bouts of selection, from the standard evolutionary perspective it is always changes in organisms, rather than changes in environments, that are held responsible for generating the organism–environment match that is commonly described as "adaptation." Organisms are generally perceived as being molded by selection to become better suited to their environments. Under this perspective, "adaptation is always asymmetrical; organisms adapt to their environment, never vice versa" (Williams, 1992: 484).

From the niche-construction perspective, "organisms do not adapt to their environments; they construct them out of the bits and pieces of the external world" (Lewontin, 1983: 280). In so doing, organisms co-direct their own evolution, often but not exclusively in a manner that suits their genotypes, in the process modifying patterns of selection that affect not only them but also other species that inhabit their environment. Niche construction thus provides a second evolutionary route to establishing the adaptive fit, or match, between organism and environment. From the niche-construction perspective, such matches need not be treated as products of a one-way process, exclusively involving the responses of organisms to environmentally imposed problems. Instead, they should be thought of as the dynamical products of a two-way process that involves organisms both responding to "problems" posed by their environments and solving some of those problems, as well as setting themselves some new problems by changing their environments through niche construction (Lewontin, 2000).

Numerous mathematical models have been developed to explore the evolutionary ramifications of niche construction (e.g., Brock, O'Brien, & Bentley, 2016; Odling-Smee et al., 2003), and all have concluded that niche construction is evolutionarily consequential. Populations evolving in response to features of the environment modified by their ancestors exhibit lag effects, such as continuing to evolve in the same direction after selection has stopped or reversed or has had a delayed evolutionary response to selection for a number of generations (Laland & Brown, 2006). With respect to humans, mathematical models suggest that niche construction resulting from cultural processes is likely to be even more potent than gene-based niche construction (Odling-Smee et al., 2003). Furthermore, such models establish that cultural niche construction can plausibly modify selection on human genes and actually drive evolutionary events (Feldman and Laland, 1996; Gerbault et al., 2011).

In terms of evolution, niche construction modifies selection not only at the genetic level but at the ontogenetic (developmental) and cultural levels as well. This facilitates learning and mediating cultural traditions, with consequences that not only feed back to the population engaged in niche construction but also modify selection for other organisms. For example, the construction of towns and cities created new health hazards associated with large-scale human aggregation, such as the rapid and large-scale spread of disease, resulting in epidemics. Humans may respond to this novel selection pressure exclusively or in combination, (1) through biological evolution, with selection of resistant genotypes, (2) at the ontogenetic level, for example by developing antibodies that confer some immunity, or (3) through cultural evolution, perhaps by creating hospitals, medicines and vaccines. Future research will establish the prevalence of these different types of response and delineate rules specifying when each occurs (Laland & O'Brien, 2015).

The capacity for technology and culture clearly underlies the potency of human niche construction: Culture is the human ecological niche

(Hardesty, 1972). Agriculture, for example, was not independently invented by each farmer, nor is its presence an unlearned maturational outcome of human gene expression. A well-researched case of gene–culture coevolution is the coevolution of the gene for lactose absorption and dairy farming in prehistory (Durham, 1991; O'Brien & Laland, 2012). Dairy farming spread before the allele for lactose absorption, generating a selection pressure favoring this gene in some human pastoralist societies (Burger, Kirchner, Bramanti, Haak, & Thomas, 2007). Another example is provided by a population of Kwa-speaking yam cultivators in West Africa (Durham, 1991), who cut clearings in forests to grow crops, with a cascade of consequences. The clearings increased the amount of standing water, which provided better breeding grounds for mosquitoes and increased the prevalence of malaria. This modified natural selection pressures in favor of an increase in the frequency of the sickle-cell (*HbS*) allele because, in the heterozygous condition, the *HbS* allele confers protection from malaria. The fact that other Kwa speakers, whose agricultural practices are different, do not show the same increase in the *HbS* allele frequency supports the conclusion that cultural practices can drive genetic evolution (Durham, 1991). It is not just yam cultivation that generates this pattern of selection: Modern Asian tire manufacturing is having the same effect, as mosquitoes infest pools of rainwater that collect in tires stored outside, and tire export contributes to the spread of malaria and dengue (Hawley, Reiter, Copeland, Pumpuni, & Craig, 1987).

These particular examples are familiar to anthropologists and archaeologists, but NCT brings the perspective, now well supported with hard data, that they are manifestations of a wider general pattern (Laland et al., 2010). Recent analyses of human genetic variation reveal that hundreds of genes have been subject to recent positive selection, often in response to human niche-constructing activities. The lactose absorption allele (*LCT*), for example, is just one of several genes now thought to have been selected over recent millennia in response to culturally generated changes in diet. Another compelling example of a human culture-initiated selective sweep concerns the evolution of the human amylase gene (Perry et al., 2007). Starch consumption is a feature of agricultural societies and hunter–gatherers in arid environments, whereas other hunter–gatherers and some pastoralists consume much less starch. This behavioral variation raises the possibility that different selective pressures have acted on amylase, the enzyme responsible for starch hydrolysis. Perry et al. (2007) found that the copy number of the salivary amylase gene (*AMY1*) is positively correlated with salivary amylase protein level and that individuals from populations with high-starch diets have, on average, more *AMY1* copies than those with traditionally low-starch diets. Higher *AMY1* copy numbers and protein levels are thought to improve the digestion of starchy foods and may buffer against the fitness-reducing effects of intestinal disease.

The important point here is that theoretical frameworks such as NCT channel thinking, encouraging researchers to embrace certain processes and explanations and to neglect others. NCT is heuristically valuable precisely because it draws our attention to a range of phenomena that are both important and easy to overlook using only standard perspectives, a point made even by critics of NCT (e.g., Wallach, 2016). Because it extends and builds on traditional dual-inheritance (genetic and cultural) models of cultural evolution that, as we pointed out earlier, have provided significant insights into human behavior, NCT is sometimes referred to as "triple-inheritance theory" (genetic, cultural, and ecological inheritance) (Odling-Smee et al., 2003).

Conclusions and Future Directions

Taken together, the three evolutionary processes discussed here – gene–culture coevolution, cultural transmission, and niche construction – are the underpinnings of what it means to be human. Humans are far from alone in their capacity to learn socially or to modify the environment in significant ways, but no animal comes close in its ability to radically change the world around it. This is what human culture brings to the table. As Laland et al. (2011: 958) point out, other animals are capable of social learning and creating behavioral traditions, but "the fact remains that humans alone have sequenced genomes, built satellites and Large Hadron Colliders, written plays and novels and composed moonlight sonatas, while the most culturally accomplished non-human animals sit naked in the jungle cracking nuts."

Not to defame chimpanzees and bonobos, but it is the ability to learn rapidly from one another, to build and maintain non-kinship-based alliances and to exert pressure on genes through cultural behaviors that makes humans the "ultimate niche constructors" (Odling-Smee et al., 2003: 28). For example, 70,000 years ago, humans dispersed from East Africa, first to Eurasia, then to Southeast Asia and eventually, around 45,000 years ago, to Australia and Tasmania. In northern latitudes, humans spread eastward through Siberia and, around 14,000 years ago, completed the settlement of the globe by spreading into the Americas by way of a land bridge that connected eastern Asia and western North America. This success story was made possible by their ability to modify environments to compensate for different climatic regimes and other challenges – by manufacturing clothes and shelters, controlling fire and making complex stone and bone tools and, later, by devising agricultural practices and domesticating livestock. The basis for human success as a species is not only an inordinately high capacity for learning but, we suspect, the ability to cooperate to an extraordinary degree with those to whom one is not closely related, if at all (Marean, 2015).

What will dual inheritance, cultural transmission, and human niche construction look like in the future? We can make a few educated guesses. Demographically, fertility is generally declining, median age is increasing, and the majority of the world's population live in cities (Mace, 2008). Not coincidentally, more people mean more inventions, innovation and cumulative cultural evolution (Malakoff, 2013). Indeed, urban population density shows elegant scaling relationships with numbers of patents, gross domestic product, income and other measures, which are the results of efficiencies of communication and transport (Bettencourt & West, 2010).

As communication and transport have become increasingly global and face-to-face conversation declines in many contexts, population density may come to matter less than the networks through which social learning occurs, physically or virtually. As technology changes how knowledge is stored and retrieved, it is less obvious how social learning is changed as a general process. For example, in the past, experts in particular skills such as fishing would be well known (Henrich & Broesch, 2011), and community leaders would be trusted on a range of topics (Banerjee, Chandrasekhar, Duflo, & Jackson, 2013). In the online world, by contrast, the competition for followers or attention involves algorithmic use of global popularity statistics and metadata (number of views, followers, recent purchases) collected and directed by large organizations. This suggests a shift on the spectrum toward more social learning and less transparency, as individuals rely less on their own knowledge and more on remembering where knowledge is stored. True, people have long "stored" knowledge in other people, but in simpler, kin-based societies, this was guided variation – effectively, individual learning – in which cultural recipes were passed down over generations, and modification was slow.

These are fascinating issues that will engage behavioral scientists well into the future. Keeping the analytical focus squarely on the three core evolutionary processes discussed here – gene–culture coevolutionary theory, cultural transmission, and niche construction – will allow research into such enormous change to stay objective, disciplined, and productive. It will also allow the behavioral sciences to play an even larger role in what has come to be known as the "extended evolutionary synthesis," which, while retaining the fundamentals of evolutionary theory, differs in its emphasis both on the role of constructive processes in development and evolution and on reciprocal portrayals of causation (Laland et al., 2015).

Acknowledgments

We thank José Causadias, Eva Telzer, and Nancy Gonzales for asking us to contribute to this volume and Matt Boulanger for producing the figure. MJO thanks Kevin Laland for his considerable intellectual views on niche construction as it applies to humans.

References

Atkisson, C., O'Brien, M. J., & Mesoudi, A. (2012). Adult learners in a novel environment use prestige-biased social learning. *Evolutionary Psychology, 10*, 519–538. http://dx.doi.org/10.1177/147470491201000309

Banerjee, A., Chandrasekhar, A. G., Duflo, E., & Jackson, M. O. (2013). The diffusion of microfinance. *Science, 341*, 1236498. http://dx.doi.org/10.1126/science.1236498

Barth, F. (1956). Ecological relations among ethnic groups in Swat, North Pakistan. *American Anthropologist, 58*(6), 1079–1089.

Bentley, R. A., Hahn, M. W., & Shennan, S. J. (2004). Random drift and culture change. *Proceedings of the Royal Society B, 271*, 1443–1450. http://dx.doi.org/10.1098/rspb.2004.2746

Bentley, R. A., O'Brien, M. J., & Brock, W. A. (2014). Mapping collective behavior in the big-data era. *Behavioral and Brain Sciences, 37*, 63–119. http://dx.doi.org/10.1017/S0140525X13000289

Bersaglieri, T., Sabeti, P. C., Patterson, N. Vanderploeg, T. Schaffner, S. F., Drake, … & Hirschhorn, J. N. (2004). Genetic signatures of strong recent positive selection at the lactase gene. *American Journal of Human Genetics, 74*, 1111–1120. http://dx.doi.org/10.1086/421051

Bettencourt, L., & West, G. W. (2010). A unified theory of early living. *Nature, 467*, 912–913.

Boas, F. (1911). Review of "Methode der Ethnologie" by F. Graebner. *Science, 34*(884), 804–810.

Boesch, C. (2012). *Wild cultures: A comparison between chimpanzee and human cultures.* Cambridge: Cambridge University Press. http://dx.doi.org/10.1017/CBO9781139178532

Boyd, R., & Richerson, P. J. (1985). *Culture and the evolutionary process.* Chicago: University of Chicago Press.

Brock, W. A., O'Brien, M. J., & Bentley, R. A. (2016). Validating niche-construction theory through path analysis. *Archaeological and Anthropological Sciences, 8*(4), 819–837. http://dx.doi.org/10.1007/s12520-015-0257-0

Burger, J., Kirchner, M., Bramanti, B., Haak, W., & Thomas, M. G. (2007). Absence of the lactase-persistence-associated allele in early Neolithic Europeans. *Proceedings of the National Academy of Sciences, 104,* 3736–3741. http://dx.doi.org/10.1073/pnas.0607187104

Caiado, C. C. S., Brock, W. A., Bentley, R. A., & O'Brien, M. J. (2016). Fitness landscapes among many options under social influence. *Journal of Theoretical Biology, 405,* 5–16. http://dx.doi.org/10.1016/j.jtbi.2015.12.013

Cavalli-Sforza, L. L., & Feldman, M. W. (1981). *Cultural transmission and evolution: A quantitative approach.* Princeton, NJ: Princeton University Press.

Cochran, G., & Harpending, H. (2009). *The 10,000 year explosion: How civilization accelerated human evolution.* New York: Basic Books.

Dawkins, R. (1989). *The selfish gene* (2nd ed.). Oxford: Oxford University Press.

Dunbar, R. I. M., & Shultz, S. (2007). Evolution in the social brain. *Science, 317,* 1344–1347. http://dx.doi.org/10.1126/science.1145463

Durham, W. H. (1991). *Coevolution: Genes, culture, and human diversity.* Stanford, CA: Stanford University Press.

Eerkens, J. W., & Lipo, C. P. (2005). Cultural transmission, copying errors, and the generation of variation in material culture and the archaeological record. *Journal of Anthropological Archaeology, 24,* 316–334. http://dx.doi.org/10.1016/j.jaa.2005.08.001

Erwin, D. H., & Krakauer, D. C. (2004). Insights into innovation. *Science, 304,* 1117–1119.

Feldman, M. W., & Laland, K. N. (1996). Gene–culture co-evolutionary theory. *Trends in Ecology and Evolution, 11,* 453–457.

Flannery, K. V. (1965). The ecology of early food production in Mesopotamia. *Science, 147,* 1247–1256.

Gerbault, P., Liebert, A., Itan, Y., Powell, A., Currat, M., Burger, J., ... & Thomas, M. G. (2011). Evolution of lactase persistence: An example of human niche construction. *Philosophical Transactions of the Royal Society B, 366,* 863–877. http://dx.doi.org/10.1098/rstb.2010.0268

Gintis, H. (2003). The hitchhiker's guide to altruism: Gene–culture coevolution and the internalization of norms. *Journal of Theoretical Biology, 220,* 407–418.

Hardesty, D. L. (1972). The human ecological niche. *American Anthropologist, 74,* 458–466.

Hawks, J., Wang, E. T., Cochran, G. M., Harpending, H. C., & Mayzis, R. K. (2007). Recent acceleration of human adaptive evolution. *Proceedings of the National Academy of Sciences, 104,* 20753–20758. http://dx.doi.org/10.1073/pnas.0707650104

Hawley, W. A., Reiter, P., Copeland, R. S., Pumpuni, C. B., & Craig, G. B. (1987). *Aedes albopictus* in North America: Probable introduction in used tires from northern Asia. *Science, 236,* 1114–1116. http://dx.doi.org/10.1126/science.3576225

Henrich, J. (2001). Cultural transmission and the diffusion of innovations: Adoption dynamics indicate that biased cultural transmission is the predominate force in behavioral change. *American Anthropologist, 103,* 992–1013.

Henrich, J., & Broesch, J. (2011). On the nature of cultural transmission networks: Evidence from Fijian villages for adaptive learning biases. *Philosophical Transactions of the Royal Society B, 366,* 1139–1148. http://dx.doi.org/10.1098/rstb.2010.0323

Heyes, C. M. (1994). Social learning in animals: Categories and mechanisms. *Biological Reviews, 69,* 207–231. http://dx.doi.org/10.1111/j.1469-185X.1994.tb01506.x

Hoppitt, W., & Laland, K. N. (2013). *Social learning: An introduction to mechanisms, methods, and models.* Princeton, NJ: Princeton University Press. http://dx.doi.org/10.1515/9781400846504

Hull, D. L. (1981). Units of evolution: A metaphysical essay. In U. J. Jenson & R. Harré (Eds.), *The philosophy of evolution* (pp. 23–44). New York: St. Martin's Press.

Kendal, J., Tehrani, J. J., & Odling-Smee, J. (2011). Human niche construction in interdisciplinary focus. *Philosophical Transactions of the Royal Society B, 366,* 785–792. http://dx.doi.org/10.1098/rstb.2010.0306

Kumm, J., Laland, K. N., & Feldman, M. W. (1994). Gene–culture coevolution and sex ratios – the effects of infanticide, sex-selective abortion, sex selection and sex-biased parental investment on the evolution of sex ratios. *Theoretical Population Biology, 46,* 249–278.

Laland, K. N., Atton, N., & Webster, M. M. (2011). From fish to fashion: Experimental and theoretical insights into the evolution of culture. *Philosophical Transactions of the Royal Society B, 366*, 958–968. http://dx.doi.org/10.1098/rstb.2010.0328

Laland, K. N., & Brown, G. R. (2006). Niche construction, human behavior, and the adaptive-lag hypothesis. *Evolutionary Anthropology, 15*, 95–104. http://dx.doi.org/10.1002/evan.20093

Laland, K. N., & Brown, G. R. (2011). *Sense and nonsense* (2nd ed.). Oxford: Oxford University Press.

Laland, K. N., & O'Brien, M. J. (2010). Niche construction theory and archaeology. *Journal of Archaeological Method and Theory, 17*, 303–322. http://dx.doi.org/10.1007/s10816-010-9096-6

Laland, K. N., & O'Brien, M. J. (2012). Cultural niche construction: An introduction. *Biological Theory, 6*, 191–202. http://dx.doi.org/10.1007/s13752-012-0026-6

Laland, K. N., & O'Brien, M. J. (2015). Niche construction: Implications for human sciences. In R. A. Scott & S. M. Kosslyn (Eds.), *Emerging trends in the social and behavioral sciences: An interdisciplinary, searchable, and linkable resource*. Hoboken, NJ: John Wiley & Sons. http:dx.10.1002/9781118900772.etrds0242

Laland, K. N., Odling-Smee, F. J., & Myles, S. (2010). How culture shaped the human genome: Bringing genetics and the human sciences together. *Nature Reviews Genetics, 11*, 137–148. http://dx.doi.org/10.1038/nrg2734

Laland, K. N., Uller, T., Feldman, M. W., Sterelny, K., Müller, G. B., Moczek, A., … & Odling-Smee, J. (2015). The extended evolutionary synthesis: Its structure, assumptions and predictions. *Proceedings of the Royal Society B, 282*(1813), 20151019. http://dx.doi.org/10.1098/rspb.2015.1019

Leonard, R. D., & Jones, G. T. (1987). Elements of an inclusive evolutionary model for archaeology. *Journal of Anthropological Archaeology, 6*, 199–219. http://dx.doi.org/10.1016/0278-4165(87)90001-8

Lewontin, R. C. (1983). Gene, organism and environment. In D. S. Bendall (ed.), *Evolution from molecules to men* (pp. 273–285). Cambridge: Cambridge University Press.

Lewontin, R. C. (2000). *The triple helix: Gene, organism, and environment.* Cambridge, MA: Harvard University Press.

Lyman, R. L., & O'Brien, M. J. (2003). Cultural traits: Units of analysis in early twentieth-century anthropology. *Journal of Anthropological Research, 59*, 225–250. http://dx.doi.org/10.1086/jar.59.2.3631642

Mace, R. (2008). Reproducing in cities. *Science, 319*, 764–766. http://dx.doi.org/10.1126/science.1153960

Malakoff, D. (2013). Are more people necessarily a problem? *Science, 333,* 544–46. http://dx.doi.org/10.1126/science.333.6042.544

Marean, C. (2015). The most invasive species of all. *Scientific American, 331*(2) (August), 32–39. http://dx.doi.org/10.1038/scientificamerican0815-32

Mayr, E. (1973). *Populations, species, and evolution.* Cambridge, MA: Harvard University Press.

Mesoudi, A. (2008). An experimental simulation of the "copy-successful-individuals" cultural learning strategy: Adaptive landscapes, producer–scrounger dynamics, and informational access costs. *Evolution and Human Behavior, 29,* 350–63.

Mesoudi, A. (2011). *Cultural evolution: How Darwinian evolutionary theory can explain human culture and synthesize the social sciences.* Chicago, IL: University of Chicago Press. http://dx.doi.org/10.7208/chicago/9780226520452.001.0001

Mesoudi, A., Whiten, A., & Laland, K. N. (2006). Towards a unified science of cultural evolution. *Behavioral and Brain Sciences, 29,* 329–383. http://dx.doi.org/10.1017/S0140525X06009083

Nettle, D. (2006). Language: Costs and benefits of a specialized system for social information transmission. In J. K. Wells, S. Strickland, & K. Laland (Eds.), *Social information transmission and human biology* (pp. 137–152). Boca Raton, FL: CRC Press. http://dx.doi.org/10.1201/9781420005837.ch8

O'Brien, M. J., Boulanger, M. T., Buchanan, B., Bentley, R. A., Lyman, R. L., Lipo, C. P, … & Eren, M. I. (2016). Design space and cultural transmission: Case studies from eastern Paleoindian North America. *Journal of Archaeological Method and Theory, 23*(2), 692–740. http://dx.doi.org/10.1007/s10816-015-9258-7

O'Brien, M. J., & Holland, T. D. (1995). Behavioral archaeology and the extended phenotype. In J. M. Skibo, W. H. Walker, & A. E. Nielsen (Eds.), *Expanding archaeology* (pp. 143–161). Salt Lake City: University of Utah Press.

O'Brien, M. J., & Laland, K. N. (2012). Genes, culture and agriculture: An example of human niche construction. *Current Anthropology, 53,* 434–470. http://dx.doi.org/10.1086/666585

O'Brien, M. J., & Lyman, R. L. (2000). *Applying evolutionary archaeology: A systematic approach.* New York: Plenum.

O'Brien, M. J., Lyman, R. L., Mesoudi, A., & VanPool, T. L. (2010). Cultural traits as units of analysis. *Philosophical Transactions of the Royal Society B, 365,* 3797–3806. http://dx.doi.org/10.1098/rstb.2010.0012

Odling-Smee, F. J., Laland, K. N., & Feldman, M. W. (2003). *Niche construction: The neglected process in evolution* (Monographs in Population Biology, 37). Princeton, NJ: Princeton University Press. http://dx.doi.org/10.1515/9781400847266

Odum, E. (1959). *Fundamentals of ecology* (2nd ed.). Philadelphia, PA: Saunders.

Perry, G. H., Dominy, N. J., Claw, K. G., Lee, A. S., Fiegler, H., Redon, R., … Stone, A. C. (2007). Diet and the evolution of human amylase gene copy number variation. *Nature Genetics, 39,* 1256–1260. http://dx.doi.org/10.1038/ng2123

Rendell, L., Boyd, R., Enquist, M., Feldman, M. W., Fogarty, L., & Laland, K. N. (2011). How copying affects the amount, evenness and persistence of cultural knowledge: Insights from the Social Learning Strategies Tournament. *Philosophical Transactions of the Royal Society B, 366,* 1118–1128. http://dx.doi.org/10.1098/rstb.2010.0376

Richerson, P. J., & Boyd, R. (2005). *Not by genes alone.* Chicago, IL: Chicago University Press. http://dx.doi.org/10.7208/chicago/9780226712130.001.0001

Richerson, P. J., Boyd, R., & Henrich, J. (2010). Gene–culture coevolution in the age of genomics. *Proceedings of the National Academy of Sciences, 107,* 8985–8992. http://dx.doi.org/10.1073/pnas.0914631107

Scott-Phillips, T. C., Laland, K. N., Shuker, D. M., Dickins, T. E., & West, S. A. (2014). The niche construction perspective: A critical appraisal. *Evolution, 68,* 1231–1243. http://dx.doi.org/10.1111/evo.12332

Tennie, C., Call, J., & Tomasello, M. (2009). Ratcheting up the ratchet: On the evolution of cumulative culture. *Philosophical Transactions of the Royal Society B, 364,* 2405–2415. http://dx.doi.org/10.1098/rstb.2009.0052

Tomasello, M., Kruger, A. C., & Ratner, H. H. (1993). Cultural learning. *Behavioral and Brain Sciences, 16,* 495–511. http://dx.doi.org/10.1017/S0140525X0003123X

Wallach, E. (2016). Niche construction theory as an explanatory framework for human phenomena. *Synthese, 193*(8), 2595–2618. http://dx.doi.org/10.1007/s11229-015-0868-0

Whiten, A. (2011). The scope of culture in chimpanzees, humans and ancestral apes. *Philosophical Transactions of the Royal Society B, 366,* 997–1007. http://dx.doi.org/10.1098/rstb.2010.0334

Whiten, A., Hinde, R. A., Laland, K. N., & Stringer, C. B. (2011). Culture evolves. *Philosophical Transactions of the Royal Society B, 366,* 938–48. http://dx.doi.org/10.1098/rstb.2010.0372

Williams, G. C. (1992). Gaia, nature worship and biocentric fallacies. *Quarterly Review of Biology, 67*(4), 479–486. http://dx.doi.org/10.1086/417796

Williams, P. A. (2002). Of replicators and selectors. *Quarterly Review of Biology, 77*, 302–306.

9

How the Study of Religion and Culture Informs Genetics and Vice Versa

Ronda F. Lo and Joni Y. Sasaki

In some places, cultural and religious practices may be considered distinct parts of life that individuals can choose according to personal preferences. In others, the boundary between culture and religion may be blurred in such a way that being a part of a culture may necessarily include affiliating with a certain religion. Yet what seems shared in many places is the idea that culture and religion are part of the learned environment. Just as a child may learn that fireworks signal the start of the new year, she may also learn that prayer can send messages to a being she cannot see. While laypeople may generally agree that the study of culture and the study of religion have some common ground, when they are asked whether culture and religion have anything to do with genes the answer is likely to be "no." As part of the environment, culture and religion are perceived to be socially transmitted and subject to change. Genes, on the other hand, are rooted in the biological makeup of an individual, and are perceived to be fixed and unmalleable. These two sources of influence are thought to be incompatible with each other, reflecting a larger assumption that nature is incompatible with nurture. Although long-accumulating scientific evidence suggests that behavior is shaped by both nature *and* nurture, the idea that culture and religion are separate and independent from genes is still deeply rooted in lay beliefs about the origins of human behavior.

These lay beliefs also parallel common practices in academic communities. How culture and religion influence human behavior has long been studied within the social science disciplines of anthropology, sociology, and psychology, and have remained relatively independent of the field of genetics. Perhaps there is an underlying assumption that the field of

The Handbook of Culture and Biology, First Edition. Edited by José M. Causadias, Eva H. Telzer and Nancy A. Gonzales.

genetics has nothing to gain from culture and religion research, and vice versa. Yet, more recently, there has been an emergence of multidisciplinary fields, such as cultural neuroscience, that have attempted to piece together the biological and environmental influences that shape human behavior and thought. Given the importance of culture and religion for a complete understanding of the human mind (Baumeister, 2002; Shweder, 1995), it seems crucial to study how these learned environmental influences, together with genes, jointly shape psychological processes.

In this chapter, our goal is to discuss foundational research on the influence of culture, religion, and genes on behavior while highlighting recent advances in this area. We first summarize psychological research on culture and religion, focusing on how these concepts in psychology can be studied alongside genetics. Next we explain how existing theoretical frameworks can be used to integrate research on culture and religion with genetics, followed by a review of empirical studies in genetics that examine the heritability of religiosity and genetic correlates of religious beliefs and behaviors, evidence of gene–culture coevolution in relation to morality, and gene–environment interaction research on prosocial behavior, immoral behavior, coping, and well-being. In the final section we provide suggestions for future research integrating culture, religion, and genes.

The Study of Culture and Religion in Psychology

People are necessarily cultural beings. Herskovits (1948) defined culture as the human-made part of the environment. Culture is a shared system of beliefs, ideas, and values passed down over generations that continuously informs people how to live their lives appropriately and meaningfully. From a cultural-psychological perspective, culture fundamentally changes how the mind perceives and manipulates environmental input (Shweder, 1995), leading to systematic differences in psychological processes across different cultures.

Beyond conventional conceptualizations of "culture" as synonymous with nationality or ethnicity, there are other forms of culture that may share similar definitional features to these but are not necessarily associated with a single country or ethnic group. Cohen (2009) states that there are other forms of culture, such as religion and social class, which can bind and impact groups of people in psychologically important ways. Religion, in particular, shares many key characteristics with national or ethnic culture. Religion and culture[1] both involve a set of passed-down beliefs and ideas about how to live one's life appropriately, and both function as resources for making sense of the world. Religion plays a significant role across many cultures (Bloom, 2012; Manuti, Scardigno, & Mininni, 2016), and different religious traditions emphasize certain patterns of behavior or thought, just as culture does. For example, Cohen and Rozin (2001) examined differences in religious groups and found that Protestant Christians were more likely than Jews to condemn immoral thoughts. This finding probably stems from Protestant traditions that emphasize that immoral thoughts inevitably lead to immoral behavior, whereas Jewish traditions do not believe the two are equivalent (Cohen & Rozin, 2001). Other research has included non-Western religious comparisons by examining Buddhists and Christians in the United States. In one study, Tsai, Miao, and Seppala (2007) found that American Christians valued high arousal positive states (e.g., excitement) more than American Buddhists, whereas American Buddhists valued low arousal positive states (e.g., calm) more than American Christians. It is clear that religion can be as influential as more commonly studied forms of culture, such as ethnic and national culture. Understanding religion as a form of culture requires conceptualizing it as a mutually constituted part of the human mind, not just as non-shared individual difference or as "noise." Religion may fundamentally change how people conceptualize their world, and thus it may be useful to study religion as a meaningful form of the sociocultural environment.

Even though the cultural-psychological perspective can be used to study different forms of culture, each culture has unique features that should be highlighted. Religion, unlike other forms of culture, is uniquely centered on the supernatural. Specifically, religion draws from beliefs about sacred items, rituals, and the divine to derive a fundamental understanding of the world based in spirituality[2] (Silberman, 2005). Relatedly, an emphasis on morality, or beliefs about what is right or wrong, is often central to religion. For some, religion is an important source of moral guidance, explicitly prescribing appropriate ways to think or behave (Cohen & Rozin, 2001), and morality seems particularly emphasized in relation to the divine in general, via sacred order, sanctity, and purity (Bloom, 2012). This emphasis on purity is particularly reflected in beliefs and rituals about sex and food (Johnson, White, Boyd, & Cohen, 2011). Religious teachings often focus on specific aspects of morality, explicitly claiming to know what is moral and immoral concerning issues such as abortion and homosexuality (Bloom, 2012). Religion is also unique in that religious membership varies in how it is perceived to be acquired, from membership by birth (e.g., Judaism) to personal faith (e.g., Protestant Christianity; Cohen, Siegel, & Rozin, 2003).

These different aspects of religion may have a unique influence on behavior, above and beyond other forms of culture.

Recent evidence suggests that the effect of religion, as a unique form of culture, can change depending on the broader national culture. The same religious affiliation across different cultures may encourage different strategies to achieve similar goals. Individualistic cultures, such as the North American, emphasize that the self is unique, relatively stable, and distinctly separate from others, whereas collectivist cultures, such as the East Asian, emphasize that the self is inherently connected with close others, and maintenance of social obligations and harmony are highly valued (Markus & Kitayama, 1991). Sasaki and Kim (2011) examined the effects of religion (mainly Christianity) across American and East Asian cultural contexts, focusing on the religiously informed strategies used in each culture to cope with distressing situations. Using multiple methods, they found that religion within American culture promoted the use of more secondary control to cope (e.g., adjustment of the self to the situation, personal spiritual growth), reflecting the focus on the self in individualistic cultures, whereas religion within East Asian culture promoted more social affiliative strategies to cope (e.g., seeking support from religious communities, such as fellowships), reflecting the emphasis on social relationships in collectivist cultures. It is likely that certain teachings born of religion become valued and emphasized more than others over time, and that culture (at the ethnic or national level) is a meaning system that can change which aspects of religion are promoted. Because religion always exists within a greater cultural context, it is important to consider the interaction of religion and culture.

Whether or not religion is studied as a unique form of culture, it is clearly a prominent influence in some people's social environment. Studying religion as a systematic, meaningful aspect of the environment may also have important implications for the integration of research on religion with approaches perceived as very disparate, such as biology or genetics. In addition to the crucial influences of culture and religion on psychology, biological features of the body also need to be considered for a complete understanding of the human mind.

Integrating Culture and Religion with Genetics

Religion is often assumed to be irrelevant or counter to scientific knowledge (e.g., Rios, Cheng, Totton, & Shariff, 2015). Yet, regardless of whether or not religious beliefs are valid, an understanding of human behavior may be incomplete without studying religion. Although the number of scientific investigations of religion has grown since around the early 2000s, there are still many gaps in basic scientific knowledge about religion and its effects on thoughts and behaviors. Especially when it comes to more "basic" scientific investigations such as biology, relatively few studies use approaches from, for instance, genetics to understand religion. Even though lay beliefs may typically keep religion from being studied together with genes, ironically these are exactly the sorts of investigations that hold the most promise for answering basic questions about how religion influences people, and why.

In the next section, we review research on the heritability and genetic correlates of religious beliefs and behaviors. We then discuss gene–culture coevolution theory by reviewing research on correlations between genetic variations and cultural norms at the societal level. Last, we review research on the interaction of genes with culture and religion, discussing how findings in this area may be relevant for understanding religion as a form of culture with unique features.

The Heritability of Religiosity and the Behavioral Correlates of Religion

What leads people to become more or less religious has often been thought of as a difference of family environment. In other words, religion is perceived to be learned from and socialized by the family at a young age and then carried throughout the lifetime. However, religiosity, or level of self-reported religiousness as indicated by factors such as religious values and attendance, may also be influenced by genes. In addition to providing evidence of the heritability of religiosity, research suggests that genes may also play a part in the etiology of religiosity over the lifespan and in other related constructs such as spirituality and meaning in life.

In a study by Koenig, McGue, Krueger, and Bouchard (2007), monozygotic (N = 165) and dizygotic (N = 100) adult male twins filled out a questionnaire on retrospective religiosity, current religiosity, antisocial behavior, and prosocial behavior. They found that prosocial behavior was positively correlated with both retrospective and current religiosity (r = .24) and antisocial behavior was negatively correlated with both retrospective (r = −.15) and current (r = −.23) religiosity. There was also shared genetic and environmental variability between religiosity and both prosocial and antisocial behavior. Prosocial behavior and religiosity shared most of their genetic variability and about half of their environmental variability. Antisocial behavior and religiosity, however, shared nearly all of their genetic variability (indicated with a near-perfect negative multiple genetic correlation of $R = 1.0$), with a small, but significant amount of shared environmental variability). These results suggest a significant, common genetic component underlying religiosity and prosocial and antisocial behavior.

To examine how genes may play a role in religious affiliation, behavior, and attitudes, D'Onofrio, Eaves, Murrelle, Maes, and Spilka (1999) recruited a large US sample of monozygotic and dizygotic twins (N = 14,781) from the Virginia Twin Registry and the American Association of Retired People. Participants filled out a questionnaire, including religious affiliation (65.8% Protestant, 15.5% Catholic, 3.9% Jewish, and 10.3% unspecified), a church attendance scale, and a 5-item subset from a larger inventory measuring social attitudes associated with the "Religious Right." Twin correlations among monozygotic and dizygotic twins on religious affiliation were not significantly different, suggesting an environmental influence underlying religious affiliation. In contrast, when it comes to religious behavior and attitudes, twin correlations were significantly smaller for dizygotic twins than for monozygotic twins. This reduction suggests that the factors underlying religious behavior and attitudes may have a genetic component.

Similarly, there is research that examines whether genetic factors play a role in how religiosity changes across the lifespan. Button, Stallings, Rhee, Corley, and Hewitt (2011) investigated genetic and environmental influences on religious values and attendance in a 5-year, longitudinal twin study in which they sampled monozygotic ($N = 685$) and dizygotic twins ($N = 739$) at two time points (ages ranged from 12 to 18 at wave 1, and 17 to 29 at wave 2). Religious values and attendance were both measured using a subset of items from Jessor's Adolescent Health and Behavior Questionnaire (Jessor & Jessor, 1977). They found that the heritability, or variability of phenotypic expression due to genetic variability of a trait in a population, of religious values and attendance was lower in adolescence and higher in early adulthood. The heritability of religious values, specifically, increased by only a small amount from adolescence, suggesting that religious values are relatively stable. However, the heritability of religious attendance increased significantly from adolescence to early adulthood. During adolescence, shared family environment between twins influenced religious attendance more than genetic factors did. This pattern of results is consistent with previous research (Koenig, McGue, & Iacono, 2009), and is expected, because religious attendance while living with the family is often controlled by parents. Yet in early adulthood, when young adults gain independence from their parents, genetic factors are likely to predispose them to embrace religious values, which then increases the likelihood that they will attend religious services because of personal religiosity rather than because of parental control in the environment. These findings on the heritability of religious attendance over time are consistent with the findings of D'Onofrio and colleagues (1999) that religious behavior is more similar between monozygotic than dizygotic twins, highlighting the role of genes that underlie religious behaviors.

Button and colleagues (2011) also examined the factors that contribute to the stability of religious values and attendance over time. Shared environmental influences contributed the most to the stability of religious values and attendance for both younger and older adolescents, but there was a significant genetic influence for older adolescents as well. This is in line with the previous finding that the heritability of religiosity increases from adolescence to young adulthood, as well as with previous research that has found a decrease in environmental, and an increase in genetic, influence on religiosity over the lifespan (Kandler & Rieman, 2013; Koenig, McGue, & Iacono, 2008).

Steger, Hicks, Krueger, and Bouchard (2011) examined the relationship between religiosity and two other related concepts: meaning in life and spirituality. The similarity of these three concepts is derived from their common desire for meaning, but distinctions can be made. Meaning in life refers to a person's understanding and realization of the significance and role of his or her life in the greater world (Steger et al., 2011). Using an adult twin sample ($N = 343$), Steger and colleagues collected responses on the Expressions of Spirituality Inventory (the Religiousness and the Cognitive Orientations Towards Spirituality subscales for the religiosity and spirituality constructs, respectively) (MacDonald, 2000) and the Meaning in Life questionnaire (the Presence for Meaning and Search for Meaning subscales were both included) (Steger, Frazier, Oishi, & Kaler, 2006). They found, through biometric modeling, that there were moderate genetic correlations between the Presence of Meaning subscale and the Religiousness ($r = .38$) and Cognitive Orientations Towards Spirituality ($r = .42$) subscales. These results seem to suggest that religiosity, spirituality, and meaning in life share considerable underlying genetic influence. An interesting possibility proposed by Steger and colleagues (2011) is that these three related concepts may be specific features of a broader function that compels humans to seek reasons for their existence, the significance of their roles in the greater world, and the overall meaning of life itself.

Previous research has also found evidence of genes interacting with some behavioral correlates of religion, such as cooperation. Schroeder, McElreath, and Nettle (2013) tested whether the mere possibility of punishment changes how people with different variants of the serotonin transporter gene (SLC6A4) and the serotonin 2A receptor gene (HTR2A) contribute in a cooperative economic game. They examined two variants of each of these genes within the serotonergic system, because they have been linked with an increased sensitivity to environmental and social threat cues and an increased tendency to experience negative affect (Hariri et al., 2002; Way & Taylor, 2010). In their study, participants (N = 184) played two versions (with or without punishment) of the Public Goods Game, a standard game used in experimental economics in which participants are given a certain amount of money and privately choose how much money to contribute to a collective pool that multiplies and is later split amongst the group. The version with no punishment in the current study was always played before the version with the punishment, and punishment was to be given by fellow group members. Results showed that SH2 homozygotes of SLC6A4 (SH2 was classified as having a short allele at 5-HTTLPR and a 10-repeat allele at serotonin transporter intron 2 variable number of tandem repeats (STin2 VNTR)) contributed less money to the pool in every round than SH1 homozygotes and heterozygotes (SH1 was classified as having a short allele at 5-HTTLPR and a 12-repeat allele at STin2 VNTR) in the no-punishment version, but in the presence of punishment they increased their contribution to about the level of SH1 homozygotes and heterozygotes. Overall, SH1 homozygotes and heterozygotes consistently contributed more money to the pool than SH2 homozygotes, which suggests that SH1 carriers internalized the group's norms and felt more social pressure from fellow group members to contribute. However, the difference in contributions between SH2 homozygotes and SH1 homozygotes and heterozygotes diminished once there was punishment. Interestingly, HH1 homozygotes and heterozygotes of HTR2A (HH1 was classified as G and C alleles at reference single nucleotide polymorphism rs6311 and rs6313) did not differ from HH2 homozygotes (HH2 classified as A and T alleles at rs6311 and rs313) in amount of contributions when playing the version with no punishment. However, the mere presence of punishment was enough to increase the contributions of those with HH1 compared with those homozygous for HH2, suggesting HH1 individuals were highly sensitive to potential punishment. This research raises the question of whether the differences in genotypes that led to smaller group-level behaviors could have bigger consequences in large populations that differ in these genotypes, especially in religious communities that create pressures for punishment avoidance.

Taken together, these results suggest that religiosity and its behavioral correlates may be at least partially influenced by genes, and a consistent pattern seems to be that heritability of religious traits increases over time. While high heritability of traits highlights the importance of genes, it is also important to understand that genetic influence is not necessarily fixed. Genes often interact with the surrounding environment to lead to changes in traits and behaviors over the course of the lifespan. Thus, a possible explanation for the increase in heritability of religious traits may come from mutual influences between genes and the environment. Certain genes may predispose an individual to embrace religious values, which influence individuals to choose and shape the environment around them to suit and reinforce their predisposition. In the following sections, we discuss different theories and frameworks that have examined this gene–environment interplay.

Gene–Culture Coevolution

Although a number of studies suggest that there may be genetic predispositions for stable traits, such as religiosity, or for morally relevant behaviors, there is no evidence of one-to-one mapping between specific genes and religiosity. Like many complex social behaviors, "religion" is unlikely to be reduced to a single gene or set of genes. It is also important to recognize that most traits and behaviors are influenced by a complex interplay of genetic and environmental factors. Basing their research on the idea that cultural norms and genetic predispositions in a population can influence each other via processes of cultural and genetic selection (dual-inheritance theory, Boyd & Richerson, 1985; gene–culture coevolution theory, Chiao & Blizinsky, 2010; Feldman & Laland, 1996), Mrazek and colleagues (2013) examined whether gene–culture coevolution may account for differences in morality judgments across nations. Using preexisting data from 21 countries, researchers in this study found, first, that the level of historical ecological threats predicted greater tightness (versus looseness) in a culture, which is characterized by more cautious behavior or preference for structure (Gelfand et al., 2011). It is theorized that normative behaviors related to tightness may have been adaptive as a response to ecological threats, such as the prevalence of disease. Second, cultural tightness–looseness covaried with the proportion of s allele carriers of 5-HTTLPR, a polymorphic region on the serotonin transporter gene, which has been related to harm avoidance in previous findings (Munafo, Clark, & Flint, 2005). This finding crucially suggests that cultural norms surrounding harm avoidance are also reflected in dominant genetic predispositions in a population, perhaps because of processes of gene–culture coevolution. Finally, this study showed that the proportion of 5-HTTLPR s alleles in a population and cultural tightness–looseness predicted whether people justified a series of morally relevant behaviors from the World Value Survey, including divorce, prostitution, evading taxes, and avoiding a fare on public transit. Mediation analyses demonstrated that population-level s allele frequency predicted a lower likelihood that these morally relevant behaviors would be justified in a culture, and this association was explained by the degree to which a culture endorsed tight (versus loose) norms (Mrazek et al., 2013). In other words, it seems that normative endorsement of morally relevant beliefs, such as whether it is justifiable to evade taxes, may be linked to dominant genotypes in a population and culturally shared beliefs about avoiding harm. Genetic tendencies and cultural norms may mutually influence each other over time via gene–culture evolutionary processes, and both genes and culture may be ecologically influenced, for example by the historical threat of disease. This research is one of only a few studies that have examined how morality may be influenced by a complex set of macroevolutionary processes involving genes and culture.

Gene–Environment Interactions

While gene–culture coevolution theory aims to uncover the more macro-level processes that underlie cultural and genetic influence, the gene–culture interaction framework (G × C) is a complementary model that focuses on the more micro-level processes of gene–culture interplay. G × C is based on the broader framework of gene–environment interactions (G × E), demonstrating that the same environment may lead to different outcomes according to differences in genes, and, similarly, that the same genetic predisposition may lead to different outcomes according to differences in the environment (Caspi et al., 2003). Some recent research has used the G × E framework to conceptualize religion and culture as important aspects of the environment that may interact with genes. A few studies have investigated how genetic predispositions interact specifically with different aspects of religion, whether it be the salience of the concept of religion, religious affiliation, or the level of religiosity, to predict different behavioral outcomes. These different ways of studying religion – as a form of culture with unique features (Sasaki et al., 2013), as a group identity with shared norms (Jiang, Bachner-Melman, Chew, & Ebstein, 2015), and as a level of involvement that can interact with other forms of culture (Sasaki & Kim, 2011) – can all be incorporated with genetics research in fruitful ways.

Implications for Prosocial Behavior

In one of the first experiments to directly examine a gene–religion interaction, Sasaki and colleagues (2013) found that genes may interact with religious information in the environment to influence prosocial behavior. In this study ($N = 178$), participants completed a sentence scramble task designed to implicitly prime concepts (that is, they were asked to make sentences from a string of words); about half the participants were exposed to religion-relevant words (e.g., God, spirit, divine, prophet, and sacred) and the other half were exposed to neutral words that formed no coherent theme (e.g., shoes, sky, holiday, worried; Shariff & Norenzayan, 2007). After the sentence scramble task was completed, the dependent variable – prosocial behavior – was measured in an ostensibly unrelated study. Participants read about a number of actual organizations which supported the environment on their college campus (e.g., the Green Campus Program), and prosocial behavior was measured by asking participants to complete a checklist to indicate whether they would like to get involved. They could indicate their wish to get involved by asking for more information about an organization, asking to be added to an organization's mailing list, and volunteering to get involved in organizational projects. Higher scores ("yes" responses) on the checklist indicated greater behavioral intentions to help society in general by volunteering their time to help these prosocial causes. This study showed that people with 2- or 7-repeat allele variants of a dopamine receptor gene (DRD4) were more prosocial when they were exposed to a religion prime than when exposed to a neutral prime. However, people without the 2-/7-repeat allele variant were not significantly influenced by the religion prime. Using an experimental manipulation of religious salience, this study was able to demonstrate that thinking about religion may causally influence prosocial behavior but that this effect crucially varies according to genetic predisposition. Given that the 2-/7-repeat allele of DRD4 may be linked to reward sensitivity, it is notable that people with this DRD4 variant were the most likely to act prosocially when there seemed to be a compelling reason to behave in this way (that is, when they were given an implicit reminder of God, which has been shown in past studies to increase prosocial behavior: Shariff & Norenzayan, 2007; see Shariff, Willard, Andersen, & Norenzayan, 2016 for meta-analysis), yet those with this same variant were also the least likely to behave prosocially when there was no particular motivator present. Importantly, in this study participants with the 2-/7-repeat allele of DRD4 did not differ from those without it in baseline religiosity or in self-reported level of religiousness, yet they changed their level of prosocial behavior if they were reminded of religion.

A similar gene–religion interaction was found in a correlational study comparing different religious affiliations (only among men; Jiang et al., 2015). This study included a sample of 2,288 Han Chinese participants who identified as Buddhist/Tao, Christian, or without religious affiliation. Altruism was measured using a resource-allocation task (the Andreoni–Miller Dictator Game; Andreoni & Miller, 2002) in which participants were classified according to their sharing behavior in the task. Results showed that among men with more reward-sensitive variants of DRD4 (i.e., mostly 2-repeat alleles given the East Asian sample), Christians demonstrated more altruistic giving behavior than non-Christians. Specifically, Christians with this genotype were more likely to increase fair behavior (splitting resources equally) and deviate from selfish behavior (keeping all resources for themselves) than non-Christians with the same genotype. Among men with less reward-sensitive DRD4 variants (i.e., two 4-repeat alleles), however, there was no difference in giving behavior between Christians and non-Christians. Interestingly, this pattern of results seemed to hold only for Christians versus non-Christians and not Buddhists/Taoists versus non-Christians. These findings suggest that the content of religious beliefs may play an important role in promoting prosocial behavior, and that some behavioral implications of religious (versus non-religious) beliefs may only emerge among people with particular genetic predispositions. What are the possible explanations for this G × E effect on prosocial behavior? The DRD4 2-/7-repeat allele variant may be linked to lower baseline dopamine signaling, which may translate to a greater motivation to increase dopamine to reach "normal" levels of cAMP reduction. Therefore, people with this genotype may be more likely to seek external motivators for their prosocial behavior because, for them, this maximizes their feelings of reward. For people without the DRD4 2-/7-repeat allele variant, who have higher baseline dopamine signaling and less motivation to increase dopamine, external motivators such as religion may not be as necessary for them to behave prosocially. Differences in motivation may explain why people with and without the 2-/7-repeat allele variant of DRD4 respond differently to religion in their environment. An interesting and as yet untested possibility is that people with different variants of DRD4 are all capable of behaving prosocially, but they do so for different reasons. People with the 2-/7-repeat allele may behave prosocially because they are motivated by the feelings associated with the reward that they might receive externally, while for people without the 2-/7-repeat allele the act itself may feel good enough.

Implications for Immoral Behavior

As mentioned previously, one of the features unique to religion is its emphasis on morality. Given that morality is an important feature of religion in certain contexts, it may be useful to consider research that has looked at the relationship between morality, culture, and genetics. Kong (2014) used a gene–environment perspective to examine relationships among corporate corruption, wealth, cultural endorsement of self-protective leadership, and 5-HTTLPR genotypes across cultures. Previous research has found that those with at least one s allele (s/s or s/l genotypes of 5-HTTLPR) attend more to negative affect and threat than those without the s allele (l/l genotypes of 5-HTTLPR) (Fox, Ridgewell, & Ashwin, 2009; Karg, Burmeister, Shedden, & Sen, 2011). Kong (2014) found that although low wealth increases corporate corruption in general (as low wealth leads to an environmental need to engage in self-protective behavior, such as corporate corruption), 5-HTTLPR moderated the relationship between wealth and corporate corruption. Societies with high 5-HTTLPR s allele frequencies tend to experience greater amounts of corporate corruption than societies with low 5-HTTLPR s allele frequencies. In addition, Kong (2014) found that wealth had a stronger relationship with cultural endorsement of self-protective leadership in societies with low 5-HTTLPR s allele frequencies than in societies with high 5-HTTLPR s allele frequencies. This research suggests that population genetics may interact with social and economic factors in ways that go above and beyond the individual influences of genes and the environment, and that, furthermore, these interactive effects may be linked with moral behavior at the societal level.

Implications for Coping and Well-Being

Some gene–religion studies have also demonstrated implications for coping behaviors and well-being. Sasaki, Mojaverian, and Kim (2015) examined the extent to which the DRD4-by-religion interaction found previously (Sasaki et al., 2013) was specific to prosocial behavior as an outcome. If people with the susceptibility variant of DRD4 are sensitive to any environmental input, perhaps they would just be more impacted by the religion prime in general, and any pre-existing relationship between religion and an outcome would be strongest among those with environmental susceptibilities, such as those with the 2-/7-repeat allele of DRD4. This recent investigation (Sasaki et al., 2015) put participants in a mildly distressing situation and tested whether the effect of religion priming on their coping behavior, which has been found in previous research in European-American samples (Sasaki & Kim, 2011), would be stronger among people who are supposedly more susceptible to the environment than those who are not. This was not the case. European Americans in this study were more likely to exhibit control-related coping behaviors, such as inhibiting their negative affect in front of the experimenter, when they were primed with religion versus not, replicating the initial finding (Sasaki & Kim, 2011); however, this effect of the religion prime on coping behavior was not moderated by the DRD4 genotype. But, interestingly, when a gene that is more relevant to socio-emotional sensitivity as a motivator of behavior was examined, a gene-by-religion interaction emerged. The G (vs. A) allele of the oxytocin receptor gene (OXTR) polymorphism rs53576 has been linked to more sensitive parenting (Bakermans-Kranenburg & van IJzendoorn, 2008) and greater empathy (Rodrigues, Saslow, Garcia, John, & Keltner, 2009). Sasaki and colleagues (2015) found that the effect of the religion prime on coping behavior was moderated by OXTR in such a way that among people with the G allele, who tend to be more socio-emotionally oriented, the religion prime increased their control-related coping behavior (that is, they inhibited their negative affect). However, among people with the A allele, who tend to be less socio-emotionally oriented, the religion prime did not influence their control-related coping (Sasaki et al., 2015). It is informative to consider these results together with the earlier findings on prosocial behavior (Sasaki et al., 2013), because it shows that it does not seem to be the case that one gene interacts with any environment indiscriminately to affect any psychological outcome. Instead it seems more likely that when people think about religion (versus not), people with certain predispositions to reward motivations may be impacted psychologically in a way that is relevant to reward, while people with other predispositions linked to socio-emotional motivations may be influenced in a way that is relevant to expressing emotions in social interactions.

Most of the studies so far have examined how genes interact with culture (Kim et al., 2010) or with religion (Sasaki et al., 2013), but in this next study researchers integrated gene–environment interactions with perspectives on both culture and religion (Sasaki & Kim, 2011) to examine how the interaction of religion, culture, and genes has implications for well-being. Previous research has shown that religiosity seems to be generally associated with greater well-being (McCullough, Hoyt, Larson, Koenig, & Thoresen, 2000, but see Diener, Tay, & Myers, 2011 for evidence of nation- and state-level moderation of this effect), and that one of the key mechanisms explaining this relationship may be social affiliation, or spending time and interacting with close others (Thoits, 1995; Wills, 1998). The extent to which religion encourages social affiliation, however, may vary depending on the broader cultural context. In North American culture, religion tends to encourage social affiliation less than in East Asian culture (Sasaki & Kim, 2011), where social relationships with others are highly emphasized (Markus & Kitayama, 1991). Therefore, research suggests that the link between religiosity and well-being may be moderated by culture, so that it is stronger in East Asia than in North America because of the greater emphasis on social relationships in East Asia. In order to utilize a G × E perspective, a study ($N = 242$) examined whether the predicted cultural difference in the link between religiosity and well-being would emerge only among people who are predisposed to care about social relationships (Sasaki, Kim, & Xu, 2011). Religiosity in this study was measured by the Religious Commitment Inventory (Worthington et al., 2003). Well-being was indexed by lower scores on a composite of two psychological distress measures: the Brief Symptoms Inventory (BSI; Derogatis & Spencer, 1982) and the Perceived Stress Scale (PSS; Cohen, Kamarck, & Mermelstein, 1983). Results indeed showed that for people with the G/G genotype of OXTR, who should be more motivated to care about social connectedness, religiosity predicted greater well-being (or lower psychological distress) among East Asians, but this same relationship between religiosity and well-being did not occur for European Americans. In fact, among European Americans, religiosity predicted lower well-being for people with G/G genotypes. However, for people with A/G or A/A genotypes, who should be less motivated to care about social connectedness, there was no cultural difference in the link between religiosity and well-being. Overall, this study demonstrates that religiosity may predict greater well-being only when the broader cultural context supports greater social affiliation in religious groups, and this matters more for people who are predisposed to care about social relationships in the first place.

Conclusions and Future Directions

Culture and religion, at first glance, may seem irrelevant to genetics. However, this lay assumption is unwarranted. There is increasing evidence that genes influence and interact with different cultures and religions. Our initial goal in this chapter was to familiarize the reader with how culture, religion and genetics research can be integrated with each other, and why this integration is important.

Although relatively few studies examine culture, religion and genes together, there is a growing awareness of the benefits of this type of cross-disciplinary research. There are a number of promising perspectives that can frame future research questions in this area. Gene–culture coevolution theory can examine whether dominant genetic tendencies in a population are linked to cultural norms (Chiao & Blizinsky, 2010), and the gene–culture interaction model can test whether genetic tendencies at the individual level can change according to differences in the cultural context (Kim et al., 2010). The broader gene–environment interaction framework (Caspi et al., 2003) can be used to test potential interactions between genetic tendencies and religious influences (Sasaki et al., 2013) by conceptualizing religion as a form of culture (Cohen, 2009) with a unique emphasis on the supernatural. The cultural shaping of religion (Sasaki & Kim, 2011) can also be examined simultaneously with the gene–culture interaction model to examine culture, religion, and genes together (Sasaki et al., 2011).

We offer this chapter as a way to provide the initial foundation for an understanding of gene–culture interactions, as well as to demonstrate how this framework can benefit culture and religion research by uncovering the underlying biological mechanisms of cultural and religious influence. Discoveries of gene–culture interactions can also benefit the field of genetics by showing that shared, complex social environments such as cultural and religious contexts can have significant downstream effects on behavior via their interaction with the biological body. We hope this not only informs future research in this area, but also encourages other seemingly unrelated areas to consider gene–environment interactions as a broader framework for explaining important processes in psychology.

Notes

1 Here, and later in the chapter, we use "culture" in the more conventionally understood way, to mean national or ethnic culture.

2 While religiosity and spirituality are both concerned with the pursuit of the sacred, the former is guided by existing communities and contextualized rituals, and the latter is often self-driven and individualized (Hill et al., 2000).

References

Andreoni, J., & Miller, J. (2002). Giving according to GARP: An experimental test of the consistency of preferences for altruism. *Econometrica, 70*(2), 737–753. doi:10.1111/1468-0262.00302

Bakermans-Kranenburg, M. J., & van IJzendoorn, M. H. (2008). Oxytocin receptor (OXTR) and serotonin transporter (5-HTT) genes associated with observed parenting. *Social Cognitive and Affective Neuroscience, 3*(2), 128–134. doi:10.1093/scan/nsn004

Baumeister, R. F. (2002). Religion and psychology: Introduction to the special issue. *Psychological Inquiry, 13*(3), 165–167. doi:10.1207/S15327965PLI1303_01

Bloom, P. (2012). Religion, morality, evolution. *Annual Review of Psychology, 63*, 179–199. doi:10.1146/annurev-psych-120710-100334

Boyd, R., & Richerson, P. J. (1985). *Culture and the evolutionary process.* Chicago, IL: University of Chicago Press.

Button, T. M. M., Stallings, M. C., Rhee, S. H., Corley, R. P., & Hewitt, J. K. (2011). The etiology of stability and change in religious values and religious attendance. *Behavior Genetics, 41*(2), 201–210. doi:10.1007/s10519-010-9388-3

Caspi, A., Sugden, K., Moffitt, T. E., Taylor, A., Craig, I. W., Harrington, H., … & Poulton, R. (2003). Influence of life stress on depression: Moderation by a polymorphism in the 5-HTT gene. *Science, 301*(563), 386–389. doi:10.1126/science.1083968

Chiao, J. Y., & Blizinsky, K. D. (2010). Culture–gene coevolution of individualism–collectivism and the serotonin transporter gene (5-HTTLPR). *Proceedings of the Royal Society B, 277*(1681), 529–537. doi:10.1098/rspb.2009.1650

Cohen, A. B. (2009). Many forms of culture. *American Psychologist, 64*(3), 194–204. doi:10.1037/a0015308

Cohen, A. B., & Rozin, P. (2001). Religion and the morality of mentality. *Journal of Personality and Social Psychology, 81*(4), 697–710. doi:10.1037//0022-3514.81.4.697

Cohen, A. B., Siegel, J. I., & Rozin, P. (2003). Faith versus practice: Different bases for religiosity judgments by Jews and Protestants. *European Journal of Social Psychology, 33*(2), 287–295. doi:10.1002/ejsp.148

Cohen, S., Kamarck, T., & Mermelstein, R. (1983). A global measure of perceived stress. *Journal of Health and Social Behavior, 24*(4), 385–396. doi:10.2307/2136404

Derogatis, L. R., & Spencer, P. M. (1982). *Brief Symptom Inventory: Administration, scoring, and procedures manual-I.* Baltimore, MD: Clinical Psychometric Research.

Diener, E., Tay, L., & Myers, D. G. (2011). The religion paradox: If religion makes people happy, why are so many dropping out? *Journal of Personality and Social Psychology, 101*(6), 1278–1290. doi:10.1037/a0024402

D'Onofrio, B. M., Eaves, L. J., Murrelle, L., Maes, H. H., & Spilka, B. (1999). Understanding biological and social influences on religious affiliation, attitudes, and behaviors: A behavior genetic perspective. *Journal of Personality, 67*(6), 953–984. doi:10.1111/1467-6494.00079

Feldman, M. W., & Laland, K. N. (1996). Gene–culture coevolutionary theory. *Trends in Ecology and Evolution, 11*(11), 453–457. doi:10.1016/0169-5347(96)10052-5

Fox, E., Ridgewell, A., & Ashwin, C. (2009). Looking on the bright side: Biased attention and the human serotonin transporter gene. *Proceedings of the Royal Society B, 276*(1663), 1747–1751. doi:10.1098/rspb.2008.1788

Gelfand, M. J., Raver, J. L., Nishii, L., Leslie, L. M., Lun, J., Lim, B. C., … & Yamaguchi, S. (2011). Differences between tight and loose cultures: A 33-nation study. *Science, 332*(6033), 1100–1104. doi:10.1126/science.1197754

Hariri, A. R., Mattay, V. S., Tessitore, A., Kolachana, B., Fera, F., Goldman, D., … & Weinberger, D. R. (2002). Serotonin transporter genetic variation and the response of the human amygdala. *Science, 297*(5580), 400–403. doi:10.1126/science.1071829

Herskovits, M. J. (1948). *Man and his works: The science of cultural anthropology.* New York: Knopf.

Hill, P. C., Pargament, K. I., Hood, R. W., Jr, McCullough, M. E., Swyers, J. P., Larson, D. B., … & Zinnbauer, B. J. (2000). Conceptualizing religion and spirituality: Points of commonality, points of departure. *Journal for the Theory of Social Behavior, 30*(1), 51–77. doi:10.1111/1468-5914.00119

Jessor, R., & Jessor, S. L. (1977). *Problem behavior and psychological development: A longitudinal study of youth.* New York: Academic Press.

Jiang, Y., Bachner-Melman, R., Chew, S. H., & Ebstein, R. P. (2015). Dopamine D4 receptor gene and religious affiliation correlate with dictator game altruism in males and not females: Evidence for gender-sensitive gene × culture interaction. *Frontiers in Neuroscience, 9*, 338. doi:10.3389/fnins.2015.00338

Johnson, K. A., White, A. E., Boyd, B. M., & Cohen, A. B. (2011). Matzah, meat, milk, and mana: Psychological influences on religio-cultural food practices. *Journal of Cross-Cultural Psychology, 42*(8), 1421–1436. doi:10.1177/0022022111412528

Kandler, C., & Rieman, R. (2013). Genetic and environmental sources of individual religiousness: The roles of individual personality traits and perceived environmental religiousness. *Behavior Genetics, 43*(4), 297–213. doi:10.1007/s10519-013-9596-8

Karg, K., Burmeister, M., Shedden, K., & Sen, S. (2011). The serotonin transporter promoter variant (5-HTTLPR), stress, and depression meta-analysis revisited: Evidence of genetic moderation. *Archives of General Psychiatry, 68*(5), 444–454. doi:10.1001/archgenpsychiatry.2010.189

Kim, H. S., Sherman, D. K., Sasaki, J. Y., Xu, J., Chu, T. Q., Ryu, C., … & Taylor, S. E. (2010). Culture, distress and oxytocin receptor polymorphism (OXTR) interact to influence emotional support seeking. *Proceedings of the National Academy of Sciences, 107*(36), 15717–15721. doi:10.1073/pnas.1010830107

Koenig, L. B., McGue, M., & Iacono, W. G. (2008). Stability and change in religiousness during emerging adulthood. *Developmental Psychology, 44*(2), 532–543. doi:10.1037/0012-1649.44.2.532

Koenig, L. B., McGue, M., & Iacono, W. G. (2009). Rearing environmental influences on religiousness: An investigation of adolescent adoptees. *Personality and Individual Differences, 47*(6), 652–656. doi:10.1016/j.paid.2009.06.003

Koenig, L. B., McGue, M., Krueger, R. F., & Bouchard, T. J. (2007). Religiousness, antisocial behavior, and altruism: Genetic and environmental mediation. *Journal of Personality, 75*(2), 265–290. doi:10.1111/j.1467-6494.2007.00439.x

Kong, D. T. (2014). An economic-genetic theory of corporate corruption across cultures: An interactive effect of wealth and the 5HTTLPR-SS/SL frequency on corporate corruption mediated by cultural endorsement of self-protective leadership. *Personality and Individual Differences, 63*, 106–111.

MacDonald, D. A. (2000). Spirituality: Description, measurement, and relation to the five factor model of personality. *Journal of Personality, 68*(1), 153–197. doi:10.1111/1467-6494.00094

Manuti, A., Scardigno, R., & Mininni, G. (2016). Me, myself, and God: Religion as a psychocultural resource of meaning in later life. *Culture & Psychology, 22*(1), 3–34.doi:10.1177/1354067X14551294

Markus, H. R., & Kitayama, S. (1991). Culture and the self: Implications for cognition, emotion and motivation. *Psychological Review, 98*(2), 224–253. doi:10.1037//0033-295X.98.2.224

McCullough, M. E., Hoyt, W. T., Larson, D. B., Koenig, H. G., & Thoresen, C. (2000). Religious involvement and mortality: A meta-analytic review. *Health Psychology, 19*(3), 211–222. doi:10.1037//0278-6133.19.3.211

Mrazek, A. J., Chiao, J. Y., Blizinsky, K. D., Lun, J., & Gelfand, M. J. (2013). The role of culture–gene coevolution in morality judgment: Examining the interplay between tightness–looseness and allelic variation of the serotonin transporter gene. *Culture and Brain, 1*, 100–117. doi:10.1007/s40167-013-0009-x

Munafo, M. R., Clark, T., & Flint, J. (2005). Does measurement instrument moderate the association between the serotonin transporter gene and anxiety-related personality traits? A meta-analysis. *Molecular Psychiatry, 10*(4), 415–419. doi:10.1038/sj.mp.4001627

Rios, K., Cheng, Z. H., Totton, R. R., & Shariff, A. F. (2015). Negative stereotypes cause Christians to underperform in and disidentify with science. *Social Psychological and Personality Science, 6*(8), 959–967. doi:10.1177/1948550615598378

Rodrigues, S. M., Saslow, L. R., Garcia, N., John, O. P., & Keltner, D. (2009). Oxytocin receptor genetic variation relates to empathy and stress reactivity in humans. *Proceedings of the National Academy of Sciences, 106*(50), 21437–21441. doi: 10.1073/pnas.0909579106

Sasaki, J. Y., & Kim, H. S. (2011). At the intersection of culture and religion: A cultural analysis of religion's implications for secondary control and social affiliation. *Journal of Personality and Social Psychology, 101*(2), 401–414. doi:10.1037/a0021849

Sasaki, J. Y., Kim, H. S., Mojaverian, T., Kelley, L. D., Park, I., & Janušonis, S. (2013). Religion priming differentially increases prosocial behaviour among variants of dopamine D4 Receptor (DRD4) gene. *Social Cognitive and Affective Neuroscience, 8*(2), 209–215.doi:10.1093/scan/nsr089

Sasaki, J. Y., Kim, H. S., & Xu, J. (2011). Religion and well-being: The moderating role of culture and the oxytocin receptor (OXTR) gene. *Journal of Cross-Cultural Psychology, 42*(8), 1394–1405. doi:10.1177/0022022111412526

Sasaki, J. Y., Mojaverian, T., & Kim, H. S. (2015). Religion priming and an oxytocin receptor gene (OXTR) polymorphism interact to affect self-control in a social context. *Development and Psychopathology, 27*(1), 97–109. doi:10.1017/S0954579414001321

Schroeder, K. B., McElreath, R., & Nettle, D. (2013). Variants at serotonin transporter and 2A receptor genes predict cooperative behavior differentially according to presence of punishment. *Proceedings of the National Academy of Sciences, 110*(10), 3955–3960. doi:10.1073/pnas.1216841110

Shariff, A. F., & Norenzayan, A. (2007). God is watching you: Priming God concepts increases prosocial behavior in an anonymous economic game. *Psychological Science, 18*(9), 803–809. doi:10.1017/S1461145709990290

Shariff, A. F., Willard, A. K., Andersen, T., & Norenzayan, A. (2016). Religious priming: A meta-analysis with a focus on prosociality. *Personality and Social Psychology Review, 20*(1), 27–48. doi:10.1177/1088868314568811

Shweder, R. (1995). Cultural psychology: What is it? In N. R. Goldberger & J. B. Veroff (Eds.), *The culture and psychology reader* (pp. 41–86). New York: New York University Press.

Silberman, I. (2005). Religion as a meaning system: Implications for the new millennium. *Journal of Social Issues, 61*(4), 641–663. doi:10.1111/j.1540-4560.2005.00425.x

Steger, M. F., Frazier, P., Oishi, S., & Kaler, M. (2006). The meaning in life questionnaire: Assessing the presence of and search for meaning in life. *Journal of Counseling Psychology, 53*(1), 80–93. doi:10.1037/0022-0167.53.1.80

Steger, M. F., Hicks, B. M., Krueger, R. F., & Bouchard, T. J. (2011). Genetic and environmental influences and covariance among meaning in life, religiousness, and spirituality. *Journal of Positive Psychology, 6*(3), 181–191. doi:10.1080/17439760.2011.569172

Thoits, P. A. (1995). Identity-relevant events and psychological symptoms: A cautionary tale. *Journal of Health and Social Behavior, 36*(1), 72–82. doi:10.2307/2137288

Tsai, J. L., Miao, F. F., & Seppala, E. (2007). Good feelings in Christianity and Buddhism: Religious differences in ideal affect. *Personality and Social Psychology Bulletin, 33*(3), 409–421. doi:10.1177/0146167206296107

Way, B. M., & Taylor, S. E. (2010). The serotonin transporter promoter polymorphism is associated with cortisol response to psychosocial stress. *Biological psychiatry, 67*(5), 487–492. doi:10.1016/j.biopsych.2009.10.021

Wills, T. A. (1998). Social support. In E. A. Blechman & K. D. Brownell (Eds.), *Behavioral medicine and women: A comprehensive handbook* (pp. 118–128). New York: Guilford Press.

Worthington, E. L., Wade, N. G., Hight, T. L., Ripley, J. S., McCullough, M. E., Berry, J. W., … & O'Connor, L. (2003). The Religious Commitment Inventory–10: Development, refinement, and validation of a brief scale for research and counseling. *Journal of Counseling Psychology, 50*(1), 84–96. doi:10.1037//0022-0167.50.1.84

Part IV

Cultural Neurobiology

10

An Introduction to Cultural Neurobiology: Evidence from Physiological Stress Systems

Leah D. Doane, Michael R. Sladek, and Emma K. Adam

Changing immigration and demographic patterns have led to the emergence of increasingly diverse and multicultural global communities. In the United States (US), census projections estimate that "ethnic minorities" will collectively become the majority group within the next 20 years (Colby & Ortman, 2014). For example, individuals of Latino/Hispanic descent now comprise 17% of the nation's population and are expected to account for almost 30% by 2060. There has also been steady growth in the number of biracial and multiracial individuals in the US (Colby & Ortman, 2014). This increasing racial/ethnic diversity precipitates increasing interpersonal and social interactions across multiple cultural traditions within families, neighborhoods, schools, and workplaces. Research in the field of psychobiology has long considered the implications of interpersonal and social interactions for stress-sensitive biological processes but has been traditionally slow to recognize the role of culture. Psychobiological researchers, however, are increasingly beginning to examine racial/ethnic and cultural processes, and researchers focusing on culture are beginning to incorporate psychobiological and neurobiological measures. In the current chapter, we provide a broad overview of the newly emerging field of cultural neurobiology.

Although definitions of "culture" may vary, most acknowledge that culture comprises values, traditions, and beliefs that influence the behaviors of a particular social group (American Psychological Association, 2003; Rogoff, 2003). Researchers from a variety of disciplines (e.g., psychology, sociology, anthropology) have garnered a wealth of knowledge through

The Handbook of Culture and Biology, First Edition. Edited by José M. Causadias, Eva H. Telzer and Nancy A. Gonzales.

the scientific study of culture and its influences on cognition, emotion, and behavior (Cooper & Denner, 1998), but less research has focused on the interplay between culture and biology (Causadias, 2013). Historically, culture has been considered a "macro" construct transmitted through the action of broad social and contextual influences on individuals within particular communities, whereas biology has been considered an "unchangeable" individual quality that is static over time (Rogoff, 2003). As a result of this theoretical distance between cultural and biological processes, empirical research on relations between them has remained relatively underdeveloped (Causadias, Telzer, & Lee, 2017). However, accumulating theory and evidence have emphasized the changeability of biological processes and their sensitivity to social and cultural contexts (Adam, Klimes-Dougan, & Gunnar, 2007; Sterling, 2004). Indeed, culture and biology dynamically interact across multiple time frames (e.g., Li, 2003): from moment to moment as individuals react to acute experiences (Smart Richman, Pek, Pascoe, & Bauer, 2010), from day to day as individuals adapt to varying social demands (Sladek & Doane, 2015), over years as individuals develop in changing sociocultural contexts (Adam et al., 2015), and both ontogenetically and intergenerationally as culture and biology are transmitted through shared environments and genetic and epigenetic pathways (D'Anna-Hernandez et al., 2012; see Causadias, Telzer, & Gonzales, chapter 1 in this volume).

We propose that the term *cultural neurobiology* should be used to encompass the transactions among cultural processes and central and peripheral aspects of neurobiology across the said multiple timeframes. We present a review of the literature supporting the emerging field of cultural neurobiology, and focus on literature that has examined transactions between culture and stress-sensitive neurobiological systems, including the autonomic nervous system (ANS), the hypothalamic-pituitary-adrenal (HPA) axis and immune mechanisms, for several reasons. First, biological indicators of these stress-sensitive systems can be measured outside the laboratory, in naturalistic settings where cultural processes actually occur (Luecken & Gallo, 2008). Second, these systems are commonly hypothesized to be mechanisms that underlie associations between racial/ethnic group membership, race-related psychological stress and health (Myers, 2009), and, more recently, racial/ethnic disparities in academic attainment (Levy, Heissel, Richeson, & Adam, 2016). In addition to focusing on the ANS, the HPA axis, and immune and inflammatory system functioning, we highlight more recent work incorporating multiple stress-sensitive biological indicators, including allostatic load (e.g., McEwen, 1998) and multisystem approaches (e.g., Bauer, Quas, & Boyce, 2002).

Although researchers have investigated cultural and identity-formation processes among majority-group members (e.g., White, European Americans in the US; Devos & Banaji, 2005; Helms, 1994), most research in the US on the cultural constructs described below in relation to neurobiology has been conducted with racial/ethnic minority or multiracial/-ethnic populations. We do, however, highlight instances when research was conducted with majority-group members. Further, it is worth noting that biological anthropologists (e.g., DeCaro & Worthman, 2008; McDade, Stallings, & Worthman, 2000) have examined interactions between culture and biology in many international contexts (e.g., Flinn & England, 1997; McDade & Worthman, 2004). While a detailed review of international and cross-national studies is beyond the scope of our brief introduction, we acknowledge their influence on the development of cultural neurobiology (e.g., McDade, 2005; Worthman & Costello, 2009).

In this chapter we first review important theoretical perspectives relevant to cultural neurobiology. Next, we briefly describe the function, measurement and health-relevance of the ANS, the HPA axis, immune/inflammatory systems, and allostatic load. We then provide definitions of key cultural constructs from extant literature and present examples of cultural neurobiological studies. In the final section, we highlight adaptive cultural processes and additional biomarkers that hold promise for informing our understanding of transactions between culture and biology.

Culturally Informed Theory

Early endeavors in psychology and related disciplines considered culture simply as a demographic or social grouping factor (i.e., they inferred culture from racial/ethnic categorizations; see García Coll, Akerman, & Cicchetti, 2000). More recently, researchers have argued that culture should be conceptualized as a major influence on individual and group processes rather than as a cursory background variable (García Coll et al., 1996). Here, we follow the lead of our colleagues who consider culture to be both a *context* in which biological processes unfold and a collection of *processes* that change over time. A widely used framework in the study of culture focuses on differences between groups (e.g., citizens of different nations, racial/ethnic groups) as broad constellations of values and practices termed individualistic (self-focused) or collectivistic (other-focused) (Triandis, 1995). Other researchers have focused on more specific processes that carry particular salience for certain groups with shared sociocultural histories, such as the collectivistic value of familism (feelings of loyalty, reciprocation, and solidarity among family members) among Latinos (Sabogal, Marín, Otero-Sabogal, Marín, & Perez-Stable, 1987). Disciplines such as anthropology use intensive ethnography as well as more quantitative techniques (e.g., cultural consensus modeling) to identify the values, behaviors, traditions, and markers of status important to particular groups living in particular locations at particular points in time, rather than assuming that values are constant and broadly shared among members of an ethnic or racial group (Dressler & Bindon, 2000; Flinn & England, 1997).

García Coll and colleagues (1996) proposed an integrative model of normative development for racial/ethnic-minority youth that considers the unique ecological circumstances of people of color growing up in the US. Based in social stratification theory, the model suggests that observed racial/ethnic differences represent legitimate adaptations to contextual demands embedded within historical and current systems of oppression (e.g., racism, segregation). García Coll et al. (1996) proposed that the experiences of individuals and their families within inhibiting and promoting environments result in *adaptive cultures*, or social systems defined by sets of goals, values, and attitudes that differ from the dominant culture and influence developmental competencies over time. Following this framework, it is important to acknowledge that many minorities are routinely exposed and must respond to daily challenges generated by a racially stratified society (e.g., discrimination, segregated housing).

Given the challenging nature of many everyday experiences for racial/ethnic minorities in the US, much research and theory thus far has focused on racial/ethnic or culturally based stressors that disproportionately affect these groups (American Psychological Association, 2016). However, it is also important to acknowledge that considerable cultural resources and strengths influence transactions between culture and neurobiology. Guided by classic stress and coping theory (Lazarus & Folkman, 1984), we argue that future work must examine the cultural ecology of coping (e.g., Gonzales & Kim, 1997) in cultural neurobiology, including both promotive cultural resources that directly benefit all youth and protective cultural resources that enable some racial/ethnic minorities to achieve positive outcomes despite facing marginalization, discrimination and socioeconomic inequalities (e.g., Causadias, 2013; Neblett, Rivas-Drake, & Umaña-Taylor,

2012). Throughout this chapter, we attempt to highlight such adaptive cultural resources, and their role in neurobiology.

Neurobiological Stress Systems

Here we provide an overview of autonomic nervous system (ANS) activity, the hypothalamic pituitary adrenal (HPA) axis, and immune/inflammatory function, and describe measures of these systems commonly used in behavioral research (for a comprehensive review of physiological stress and methods, see Luecken & Gallo, 2008).

The ANS

The ANS responds rapidly to stressors through a coordination of sympathetic and parasympathetic nervous system activity (SNS and PNS respectively). The SNS response provokes the secretion of epinephrine from the adrenal medulla and norepinephrine from both the adrenal medulla and the sympathetic nerve terminals. Epinephrine, through hormonal effects, and norepinephrine, through a combination of neurotransmitter and hormonal effects, widely influence peripheral organs and tissues (Lovallo & Thomas, 2000). Key effects include increased heart rate and respiratory output, which prepare the body for active responses to physical and psychosocial threats. The polyvagal theory (Porges, 2007) and the neurovisceral integration model (Thayer & Lane, 2000) suggest that the PNS also plays an integral role in the stress response by modulating both SNS and HPA activity. When engaged, the PNS helps to maintain lower heart rate and internal homeostasis, supporting social engagement (Porges, 2007). In contrast, when someone is facing a challenging or stressful situation, PNS activity decreases, releasing the "brakes" this system normally maintains on sympathetic activity and allowing the body to quickly mobilize fight-or-flight responses (Porges, 2007).

Several key measures of ANS activity include cardiovascular reactivity, heart rate variability (HRV) and respiratory sinus arrhythmia (RSA). The most common measures of *cardiovascular reactivity* are blood pressure and heart rate, which have been used in both laboratory and naturalistic settings to measure stress-related changes in cardiovascular function. *Heart rate variability* (HRV) is measured using an electrocardiogram and quantifies changes in beat-to-beat intervals caused by PNS modulation of SNS. Finally, *RSA* is an indicator of HRV that occurs at the frequency of spontaneous respiration. Researchers have focused on both baseline RSA, measured at rest, and RSA change in response to a particular stressor. High baseline RSA has been theorized to be adaptive, allowing individuals to attend to and engage with their environment quickly (Porges, 2007). Decreases in RSA ("withdrawal") have also been theorized to reflect optimal regulation or vagal flexibility, allowing greater cardiac output and thus more active responses to stress (Muhtadie, Koslov, Akinola, & Mendes, 2015).

The HPA Axis

Through a cascade of hormone events beginning in the brain, activation of the HPA axis results in the release of cortisol into the bloodstream, which helps to provide adaptive behavioral responses during stressful situations. Psychological stressors, particularly those involving lack of control and social evaluation, activate the HPA axis (Dickerson & Kemeny, 2004). While most commonly measured in saliva, cortisol can also be measured in blood, urine and hair. Cortisol peaks in saliva approximately 21-40 minutes after a discrete stressor, but may take up to one hour to return to baseline. Both elevated and blunted cortisol reactivity are associated with poor mental and physical health (Hagan, Roubinov, Mistler, & Luecken, 2014; Phillips, Ginty, & Hughes, 2013).

In addition to its role in stress reactivity, cortisol is released throughout the day in a typical diurnal pattern characterized by relatively high levels at waking, a dramatic increase approximately 30 minutes after waking, then a general decrease across the day with the lowest levels occurring in the late evening hours (Adam & Kumari, 2009; Pruessner et al., 1997). The three metrics most commonly used to index daily HPA axis activity include the cortisol awakening response (CAR, the increase in cortisol levels that typically occurs 30–45 minutes after waking; Clow, Hucklebridge, Stalder, Evans, & Thorn, 2010), the diurnal slope (the linear rate of decline in cortisol levels from waking to bedtime; Adam, Hawkley, Kudielka, & Cacioppo, 2006) and the diurnal area under the curve with respect to ground (AUCg, the total daily output; Pruessner, Kirschbaum, Meinlschmid, & Hellhammer, 2003). Variations in cortisol diurnal patterns have been used as indices of early exposure to adversity or chronic stress (for a review see Ehrlich, Miller, & Chen, 2016), biological susceptibility to environmental influences (Boyce & Ellis, 2005) and exposure to recent acute stressors (for a review see Adam, 2012). Recent research, however, has found that short-term elevations in cortisol provide subsequent reductions in fatigue and short-term "boosts" in both energy and positive emotional states (Adam et al., 2006; Hoyt, Zeiders, Ehrlich, & Adam, 2016).

Immune Markers

While the ANS and the HPA axis mobilize resources for a response to a challenge or a threat, the immune system provides defense and repair in the face of injury or infection. The immune system identifies cells that are "self" or "other" through innate and acquired immunity. Innate immunity is the body's immediate response to a pathogen: it includes the direct responses of macrophages and natural killer cells, which attack an infection; this attack leads to *inflammation*. Inflammation is the process by which cells of the immune system, primarily cytokines, aggregate at the point of infection. Acquired immunity occurs through a secondary cascade of events that results in the proliferation of lymphocytes; these attack infectious agents (T-cells) and then prepare the body against future infections by creating antibody-mediated immunity (e.g., the ability to recognize the agent in the future). The immune system indicators most often incorporated into behavioral research are measures of cytokines and their related proteins, which play an important role in cell signaling (for a review of stress and the immune response see Glaser & Kiecolt-Glaser, 2014). The most frequently measured inflammatory biomarkers are C-reactive protein, IL-6, IL-12, TNF-α, IFN-γ, and IL1-β.

Much of the immune response is activated by direct connections between the brain and the tissues that produce the immune response. Studies have linked psychosocial stressors and contextual influences with immune system activity and related endocrine processes by using both laboratory and naturalistic paradigms (Glaser & Kiecolt-Glaser, 2005; Kirschbaum & Hellhammer, 1989; McEwen, 1998). Exposure to social stressors in both laboratory and naturalistic settings is associated with elevated inflammatory activity (Dickerson, Gable, Irwin, Aziz, & Kemeny, 2009; Fuligni et al., 2009). There are additional communication pathways in the body between autonomic, HPA, and immune systems (e.g., immune-suppressive or enhancing effects), all of which contribute to illness and disease vulnerability. The HPA and ANS responses to stress can influence immune function either directly, through binding of the hormone to receptors (e.g., glucocorticoid receptors), or indirectly, through suppression or overproduction of cells that send vital signals to cytokines (Glaser & Kiecolt-Glaser, 2005; Padgett & Glaser, 2003; Webster, Tonelli, & Sternberg, 2002).

Allostatic Load and Multisystem Approaches

One approach to studying how psychosocial stressors influence multiple biological systems is to use a quantitative additive indicator – allostatic load (AL), a concept pioneered by McEwen (1998). Under normal circumstances, the body adjusts biological responses to match acute environmental demands, a process called allostasis (McEwen, 1998, 2000; McEwen & Seeman, 1999; Sterling & Eyer, 1988). Under conditions of ongoing stress, however, dysregulation of multiple biological systems may occur as a result of cumulative "wear and tear" (i.e., chronic over- or underactivation). Measures of AL summarize dysregulation across multiple systems, including those responsible for immune, endocrine, metabolic, and cardiovascular function. Measures of AL have been used as outcomes of chronic stress (e.g., Dich, Lange, Head, & Rod, 2015) as well as predictors of disease (e.g., Mattei, Demissie, Falcon, Ordovas, & Tucker, 2010).

Many have suggested that studies should move beyond one-to-one associations between psychosocial constructs and single indicators of biology (Bauer, Quas, & Boyce, 2002; McEwen, 2000; Quas et al., 2014). Biological systems may work independently to inhibit or enhance each other's functions, or together in response to stress (e.g., Laurent, Lucas, Pierce, Goetz, & Granger, 2016). Thus, *multisystem* approaches emphasize the importance of including multiple indicators of interacting biological systems to elucidate connections between psychological experience and physical and mental health and disease.

Evidence of Relations between Culture and Neurobiology

The second aim of this chapter is to introduce research contributions that have already been made to our understanding of cultural neurobiology. Racial/ethnic minorities face more and different stressors from majority group members. For example, in a national US survey (American Psychological Association, 2016), Black, Latino, Asian, and American Indian/Alaska Native adults reported more everyday discrimination than did non-Hispanic White adults, across most examples of unfair treatment (for example, being treated with less respect, not being hired for a job). Extensive research has contrasted the biological profiles of different racial/ethnic groups in the US, showing differences in stress biology, and assuming that such differences are due to varying cultural processes or stress experiences. Such comparisons have mostly shown that racial/ethnic minorities exhibit altered ANS, HPA and immune function, which reflects the dysregulation of stress-sensitive systems compared with those of non-Hispanic Whites (e.g., Chapman et al., 2009; Cohen et al., 2006; Geronimus, Hicken, Keene, & Bound, 2006; Mozaffarian et al., 2016). However, some studies have not found such differences, and many have struggled to separate out effects unique to racial/ethnic group membership, given the complex overlap between socioeconomic status and race/ethnicity (Kaufman, Cooper, & McGee, 1997). Rather than reviewing research that shows differences purely by racial/ethnic category, we focus on research in which culturally relevant processes have been directly measured and modeled in relation to stress biology, including perceived discrimination, stereotype threat, ethnic and racial identity, acculturation, and family processes (for a discussion of the effects of poverty on neurobiological systems, see Doan & Evans, chapter 11 in this volume).

Perceived Discrimination

One proximal mechanism or experience used to explain *why* stress biology may differ between racial/ethnic majority and minority group members is perceived racial/ethnic discrimination (the perception of being treated unfairly due to one's race or ethnicity).[1] These perceptions of discrimination experiences operate at multiple levels, from *systemic racism* or *chronic discrimination* to *microaggressions* (commonplace racial slights and insults; Sue et al., 2007). Meta-analyses suggest that perceived discrimination has significant detrimental effects on physical and mental health, including depression, anxiety, hypertension, obesity, and substance use (Pascoe & Smart Richman, 2009), with recent evidence pointing to the role of neurobiological stress mechanisms (see Ong, Deshpande, & Williams, chapter 12, and Hill & Hoggard, chapter 14, in this volume).

Perceived racial discrimination has been associated with higher blood pressure (Brondolo et al., 2008), lower HRV (Hill et al., 2017), hypertension (Dolezsar, McGrath, Herzig, & Miller, 2014), and increased risk of cardiovascular disease (Lewis, Williams, Tamene, & Clark, 2014). However, some variation based on racial/ethnic group (e.g., Hispanic, Black) and sex (Lewis et al., 2014; Williams, Neighbors, & Jackson, 2003) has been reported, and longitudinal research on cardiovascular function is rare (Brondolo, Rieppi, Kelly, & Gerin, 2003). Cross-sectional studies of ethnic minority and majority (e.g., European-American) populations have also linked perceived discrimination with HPA-axis activity, including flatter diurnal cortisol slopes and greater cortisol reactivity to laboratory and everyday stressors (Doane & Zeiders, 2014; Smart Richman & Jonassaint, 2008; Zeiders, Hoyt, & Adam, 2014). Further, there is now evidence of *cumulative effects and sensitive-period effects of discrimination* on cortisol regulation. Perceived racial discrimination measured over 20 years was associated with flatter diurnal cortisol slopes in adulthood among both Blacks and Whites, and perceived discrimination in adolescence accounted for most of this association (Adam et al., 2015).

Evidence from experimental, cross-sectional and longitudinal research suggests similar adverse effects of perceived discrimination on immune function, with most studies focusing on IL-6 or C-reactive protein (CRP). For example, everyday discrimination was associated with higher levels of CRP in older African-American adults (Lewis, Aiello, Leurgans, Kelly, & Barnes, 2010). However, effects vary by sex or race/ethnicity. Results from the Multi-Ethnic Study of Atherosclerosis (MESA) study indicated that both everyday and lifetime discrimination were associated with elevated IL-6 in women, but only everyday discrimination was associated with elevations in men, across all ethnic groups (Kershaw et al., 2016). In a different epidemiological sample, Cunningham and colleagues (2012) found that perceived discrimination was negatively associated with CRP levels in Black men and women but positively associated with CRP in White women.

While some cross-sectional studies have identified perceived discrimination as a key pathway between race/ethnicity and composites of AL (e.g., Tomfohr, Pung, & Dimsdale, 2016), to our knowledge only one study has examined *prospective* relations of perceived discrimination with an AL index. In a longitudinal study of African-American youth, Brody and colleagues (2014) found that perceived discrimination during adolescence was associated with increased AL (cortisol, epinephrine, norepinephrine, blood pressure, CRP, and body mass index (BMI)) in young adulthood, but not for those who reported high levels of emotional support from parents and peers. This study identifies the harmful effects of cumulative discrimination experiences over time, while highlighting the importance of culturally relevant protective processes in the prediction of stress biology.

Stereotype Threat

Beyond the stress of perceiving unfair treatment, researchers have focused on the stress associated with unfair expectations, stereotypes or assumptions regarding one's group, a concept called "stereotype threat" (Steele & Aronson, 1995). In situations where known group stereotypes are activated, such as when racial/ethnic-minority individuals face a testing situation believing that they are expected to perform poorly because of their race, the attentional demands and stress posed by the threat of that stereotype impair performance (Gonzales, Blanton, & Williams, 2002; Jaramillo, Mello, & Worrell, 2016; Spencer, Logel, & Davies, 2016). Stereotype threat also has biological consequences (Levy et al., 2016; Mendes & Jamieson, 2011), having been linked to increases in blood pressure reactivity, cardiovascular reactivity, HRV, sympathetic activation, cortisol levels, and IL-6 levels (John-Henderson, Rheinschmidt, Mendoza-Denton, & Francis, 2014; see Mendes & Jamieson, 2011, for a review). To our knowledge, stereotype threat has not yet been examined in relation to allostatic load. Past neurobiological stereotype-threat studies have focused on acute activation of stress biology in the context of testing or performance situations; whether repeated stereotype threat is sufficiently biologically aversive to represent a chronic stressor that predicts long-term changes in stress biology remains to be examined.

Ethnic and Racial Identity

The multidimensional construct of ethnic and racial identity (ERI) includes the beliefs and attitudes individuals have about their racial/ethnic group memberships as well as the processes by which these beliefs and attitudes develop over time (Umaña-Taylor et al., 2014). The extent to which racial/ethnic minorities have explored, and made a commitment regarding, their identity as members of their racial/ethnic group, and to which they have positive feelings about their racial/ethnic group membership (known as private regard), is generally associated with positive psychological adjustment (Sellers, Copeland-Linder, Martin, & Lewis, 2006; Umaña-Taylor, Yazedjian, & Bámaca-Gómez, 2004). The salience of ERI formation and how it relates to adjustment among majority-group members is less clear (Helms, 1994; Phinney, 1989). Some evidence indicates that ERI is associated with self-esteem to a lesser degree for Whites than for racial/ethnic minorities (Umaña-Taylor et al., 2004). Researchers have theorized that ERI also buffers racial/ethnic minorities from the adverse effects of discrimination on health and well-being (see Brondolo, Brady Ver Halen, Pencille, Beatty, & Contrada, 2009, for a review).

Some empirical evidence indicates that the protective effect of ERI processes operates through stress biology, particularly ANS reactivity. For example, African Americans with higher private regard exhibited lower RSA reactivity after viewing a racism vignette which showed a White perpetrator than those with lower private regard (Neblett & Roberts, 2013). Higher private regard has also been associated with lower overall cardiac output during race-related stressors (Clark & Gochett, 2006). Other studies have found that greater internalization of Black identity was associated with *elevated* resting systolic blood pressure in the laboratory, *greater* systolic blood pressure reactivity to race-related stressors, and *elevated* ambulatory blood pressure (e.g., Thompson, Kamarck, & Manuck, 2002; Torres & Bowens, 2000). These seemingly contradictory findings might suggest that greater racial/ethnic salience actually heightens (rather than attenuates) stress reactivity, an adaptive result for individuals who must routinely be prepared to contend with race-related stressors (Sellers et al., 2006). Available neurobiological research has focused almost exclusively on the racial identity of Blacks and ANS activity; future work might consider ERI across other racial/ethnic groups and other neurobiological stress systems.

Acculturation

An emerging literature has started to document differences in stress biology among immigrant groups who vary in levels of acculturation, or the process by which individuals engage in and adapt to a new culture (Ferguson, 2013). Immigrants partly construct their environments by selecting the ethnic heritage traditions or values they prefer to maintain from their countries of origin (*enculturation*), while adapting to traditions of the new mainstream culture (*acculturation*). The psychological stress associated with this dual-cultural adaptation process has been called *acculturative* or *enculturative stress* (Gonzales, Germán, & Fabrett, 2012).

Acculturative and enculturative stressors have been linked with alterations to several neurobiological stress systems. A recent meta-analysis found that immigrants' acculturation to the US and to European countries was associated with increases in both systolic and diastolic blood pressure, independently of other known risk factors (e.g., high body mass index; Steffen, Smith, Larson, & Butler, 2006). Evidence from longitudinal multi-ethnic epidemiological samples has also shown that recent immigrants experience the fastest declines in cardiovascular health (Lê-Scherban et al., 2016). In a series of studies of Mexican-American adults, Mangold and colleagues (2010, 2012) found that greater Anglo orientation (adopting mainstream cultural views and practices) was associated with smaller CARs (a pattern linked with chronic fatigue and "burnout"). Other research on Mexican-American women and their infants has suggested that maternal cortisol during the prenatal and postpartum period may mediate associations between acculturation and adverse infant outcomes (D'Anna-Hernandez et al., 2012; Ruiz, Pickler, Marti, & Jallo, 2013). Similarly, time spent in the US was associated with the absence of a protective cytokine (IL-10), which subsequently predicted the odds of preterm birth in a sample of Mexican-American pregnant women (Wommack et al., 2013).

Finally, studies of Mexican immigrants and their families have shown that cumulative experiences in the US (for example years living in the US, adapting to mainstream culture) were associated with increased AL, including indicators of blood pressure, glucose, cholesterol and immune function (e.g., McClure et al., 2015). Peek and colleagues (2010) found that US-born individuals of Mexican descent had higher AL scores than their counterparts who had been born in Mexico, but this was *not* accounted for by English language use, social integration or cultural assimilation. This finding suggests that it could be the loss of culturally specific protective factors that explains how acculturation gets under the skin to influence neurobiological function.

Family Processes

Cultural neurobiology research with an emphasis on human development has focused much attention on the family (Fuligni & Telzer, 2013) and other close social ties. Research on *familism* among Latinos, *communalism* among African Americans and *filial piety* among Asian Americans has examined whether these society- and family-centric values are associated with adaptive outcomes for children and families (Schwartz et al., 2010). Family values, such as feeling obligated to help family members, may be protective (Schwartz et al., 2010), whereas some family expectations, such as daily assistance behaviors, may be sources of vulnerability (Fuligni et al., 2009). For example, the values of family unity and support generally promote positive outcomes for Mexican-origin youth (Fuligni, Tseng, & Lam, 1999; Suárez-Orozco & Suárez-Orozco, 1995), but youth who feel responsible for helping their families financially may be significantly burdened by providing assistance in a variety of ways (e.g., translating for family members, childcare).

Perceived availability of social support, particularly from family, may buffer individuals from chronic activation of neurobiological stress activity (e.g., Brody et al., 2014). In contrast, providing for family members (e.g., by undertaking caretaking responsibilities) can have direct, adverse effects on stress biology (Kiecolt-Glaser et al., 2003), or can moderate or exacerbate the negative effects of other risk factors (e.g., chronic family stress; Marin, Chen, Munch, & Miller, 2009). For example, in a sample of African-American adults, greater cultural consonance was associated with lower systolic and diastolic blood pressure when these adults also perceived greater family support (Dressler & Bindon, 2000). Many studies of racial/ethnic-minority and -majority populations have also indicated that perceived availability of social support, particularly from family, buffers against HPA-axis dysregulation, activation of immune pathways, and AL (e.g., Brody et al., 2014; Doane & Zeiders, 2014; Guan et al., 2016; Jewell, Luecken, Gress-Smith, Crnic & Gonzales, 2015; Seeman, Gruenewald, Cohen, Williams, & Matthews, 2014). Other studies have found that family assistance behaviors are associated with a risk of dysregulated neurobiological stress systems (Chiang et al., 2016; Fuligni et al., 2009; see Fuligni & Telzer, 2013 for a review). For example, family assistance behaviors were associated with *higher* levels of immune markers, including sIL-6r and CRP (Fuligni et al., 2009). Interestingly, this association was attenuated among youth with high levels of family obligation values, highlighting the protective role of traditional family-based cultural values.

Conclusions and Future Directions

The following chapters in this part represent exciting extensions of cultural neurobiology research across the various biological systems introduced here. In addition to the pioneering work conducted and reviewed by our colleagues in the following chapters, we offer four categories as central candidates for future work, with an emphasis on *positive or protective cultural processes*: (1) supportive family processes, (2) biculturalism or multiculturalism, (3) cultural experiences and identities in majority groups, and (4) additional neurobiological markers that hold promise for future culturally informed research.

Supportive Family Processes

From various studies that have explored the supportive role of family processes (e.g., Fuligni & Telzer, 2013), it is clear that more family-centered values and greater perceptions of available family support have the potential to promote enhanced neurobiological stress regulation and protect individuals from the risk of neurobiological dysfunction when they face stressful conditions. Future research is needed to explore more nuance in family processes (particularly if putatively supportive family influences can become sources of risk) and the corresponding effects on neurobiological systems.

Biculturalism or Multiculturalism

Although research has found that maintaining ties to one's traditional ethnic culture is protective, those who are able to interact effectively within both their ethnic-heritage *and* mainstream cultural contexts garner various psychosocial benefits (García Coll et al., 1996; Nguyen & Benet-Martínez, 2012). Future research should consider biculturalism (or multiculturalism) as a potentially promotive or protective cultural process in relation to neurobiological stress systems. Do highly bicultural individuals benefit from enhanced biological regulation under stress, compared to individuals oriented more exclusively towards either their ethnic-heritage culture or mainstream culture?

Cultural Experiences and Identities for Majority-Group Members

As communities become increasingly diverse with respect to race, ethnicity and the intersection of multiple cultural traditions, it will be critical for cultural neurobiology research to consider the values, attitudes, and identities of those with majority status (e.g., White, European Americans in the US). Our review revealed that most research has focused on culture and biology interplay among racial/ethnic minorities. We encourage future cultural neurobiology research to draw from rich conceptual frameworks that have also considered the salience of these processes for those in the racial/ethnic majority. For example, Helms (1994) argued that White, European Americans develop racial identity through a process that requires them to recognize and abandon internalized White privilege and to create a non-racist, self-defining White identity. Some researchers have already started to examine such processes in relation to stress biology, showing that White Americans' concerns about appearing prejudiced were associated with heightened cortisol responses during interracial encounters in a laboratory and alterations in diurnal cortisol rhythms over a year (Trawalter, Adam, Chase-Lansdale, & Richeson, 2012). More work is needed to consider measured cultural processes among majority-group members that may support the function and regulation of stress-sensitive neurobiological systems.

Additional Biological Markers of Cultural Relevance

This review, to a large extent reflecting the literature, has focused on stress biology. Many positive aspects of culture may not only serve as buffers against the activation of stress biology, but also relate more directly to biological systems that are involved in positive emotion, social affiliation and motivation. For example, hormones such as dehydroepiandosterone (DHEA) are thought to play a role in coping with stress, and oxytocin is thought to play a role in affiliation and attachment. Researchers are now beginning to consider biomarkers of these systems in cultural neurobiology research. For example, researchers are examining interactions between oxytocin polymorphisms and cultural norms regarding support seeking and emotion regulation (Chiao, 2015; Kim et al., 2010). More research is needed on the positive neurobiology of culture.

Conclusions

We are pleased to highlight research that is exploring a new frontier of cultural neurobiology. Researchers who study social and cultural processes may have little incentive to incorporate neurobiological measures into their work. Of course, the opposite is likely to be true as well: researchers who traditionally focus on neurobiology may not be motivated to draw from the conceptual complexity of cultural theory. As we develop this emerging field, it will be increasingly important to bring these disciplines together. It is also essential to move beyond the study of cultural risk factors and stressors to identify cultural strengths, and how they are interwoven with complex biological systems that regulate everyday psychological and social functioning. Doing so will help us better understand the role of biology not only in disease processes, but in the health, well-being, and thriving of individuals from all cultural backgrounds.

Note

1 We use the term "perceived discrimination" to follow empirical research in the fields of psychology and human development. Perceptions of discrimination across many time courses (past, current or anticipatory) activate the physiological stress processes described in this chapter.

References

Adam, E. K. (2012). Emotion–cortisol transactions occur over multiple time scales in development: Implications for research on emotion and the development of emotional disorders. *Monographs of the Society for Research in Child Development, 77*(2), 17–27. doi:10.1111/j.1540-5834.2012.00657.x

Adam, E. K., Hawkley, L. C., Kudielka, B. M., & Cacioppo, J. T. (2006). Day-to-day dynamics of experience–cortisol associations in a population-based sample of older adults. *Proceedings of the National Academy of Sciences, 103*(45), 17058–17063. doi:10.1073/pnas.0605053103

Adam, E. K., Heissel, J. A., Zeiders, K. H., Richeson, J. A., Ross, E. C., Ehrlich, K. B., … & Malanchuk, O. (2015). Developmental histories of perceived racial discrimination and diurnal cortisol profiles in adulthood: A 20-year prospective study. *Psychoneuroendocrinology, 62*, 279–291. doi:10.1016/j.psyneuen.2015.08.018

Adam, E. K., Klimes-Dougan, B., & Gunnar, M. R. (2007). Social regulation of the adrenocortical response to stress in infants, children and adolescents: Implications for psychopathology and education. In D. Coch, G. Dawson & K. Fischer (Eds.), *Human Behavior, Learning, and the Developing Brain: Atypical Development* (pp. 264–304): New York: Guilford Press.

Adam, E. K., & Kumari, M. (2009). Assessing salivary cortisol in large-scale, epidemiological research. *Psychoneuroendocrinology, 34*(10), 1423–1436. doi:10.1016/j.psyneuen.2009.06.011

American Psychological Association (2003). Guidelines on multicultural education, training, research, practice, and organizational change for psychologists. *American Psychologist, 58*, 377–402. doi:10.1037/0003-066X.58.5.377

American Psychological Association (2016). *Stress in America: The impact of discrimination.* Stress in America™ Survey. Retrieved from http://www.apa.org/news/press/releases/stress/2015/impact-of-discrimination.pdf (10 April 2017).

Bauer, A., Quas, J., & Boyce, W. (2002). Associations between physiological reactivity and children's behavior: Advantages of a multisystem approach. *Journal of Developmental and Behavioral Pediatrics, 23*(2), 102–113. doi:10.1097/00004703-200204000-00007

Boyce, W. T., & Ellis, B. J. (2005). Biological sensitivity to context: I. An evolutionary–developmental theory of the origins and functions of stress reactivity. *Development and Psychopathology, 17*(2), 271–301. doi:10.1017/S0954579405050145

Brody, G. H., Lei, M. K., Chae, D. H., Yu, T., Kogan, S. M., & Beach, S. R. (2014). Perceived discrimination among African American adolescents and allostatic load: A longitudinal analysis with buffering effects. *Child Development, 85*(3), 989–1002. doi:10.1111/cdev.12213

Brondolo, E., Brady Ver Halen, N., Pencille, M., Beatty, D., & Contrada, R. J. (2009). Coping with racism: A selective review of the literature and a theoretical and methodological critique. *Journal of Behavioral Medicine, 32*(1), 64–88. doi:10.1007/s10865-008-9193-0

Brondolo, E., Libby, D. J., Denton, E.-g., Thompson, S., Beatty, D. L., Schwartz, J., ... Gerin, W. (2008). Racism and ambulatory blood pressure in a community sample. *Psychosomatic Medicine, 70*(1), 49–56. doi:10.1097/PSY.0b013e31815ff3bd

Brondolo, E., Rieppi, R., Kelly, K. P., & Gerin, W. (2003). Perceived racism and blood pressure: A review of the literature and conceptual and methodological critique. *Annals of Behavioral Medicine, 25*(1), 55–65. doi:10.1207/S15324796ABM2501_08

Causadias, J. M. (2013). A roadmap for the integration of culture into developmental psychopathology. *Development and Psychopathology, 25*, 1375–1398. doi:10.1017/S0954579413000679

Causadias, J. M., Telzer, E. H., & Lee, R. M. (2017). Culture and biology interplay: An introduction. *Cultural Diversity and Ethnic Minority Psychology, 23*(1), 1–4. doi:10.1037/cdp0000121

Chapman, B. P., Khan, A., Harper, M., Stockman, D., Fiscella, K., Walton, J., ... & Moynihan, J. (2009). Gender, race/ethnicity, personality, and interleukin-6 in urban primary care patients. *Brain, Behavior, and Immunity, 23*(5), 636–642. doi:10.1016/j.bbi.2008.12.009

Chiang, J. J., Tsai, K. M., Park, H., Bower, J. E., Almeida, D. M., Dahl, R. E., ... & Fuligni, A. J. (2016). Daily family stress and HPA axis functioning during adolescence: The moderating role of sleep. *Psychoneuroendocrinology, 71*, 43–53. doi:10.1016/j.psyneuen.2016.05.009

Chiao, J. Y. (2015). Current emotion research in cultural neuroscience. *Emotion Review, 7*(3), 280–293. doi:10.1177/1754073914546389

Clark, R., & Gochett, P. (2006). Interactive effects of perceived racism and coping responses predict a school-based assessment of blood pressure in black youth. *Annals of Behavioral Medicine, 32*(1), 1–9. doi:10.1207/s15324796abm3201_1

Clow, A., Hucklebridge, F., Stalder, T., Evans, P., & Thorn, L. (2010). The cortisol awakening response: More than a measure of HPA axis function. *Neuroscience and Biobehavioral Reviews, 35*(1), 97–103. doi:10.1016/j.neubiorev.2009.12.011

Cohen, S., Schwartz, J. E., Epel, E., Kirschbaum, C., Sidney, S., & Seeman, T. (2006). Socioeconomic status, race and diurnal cortisol decline in the coronary artery risk development in young adults (CARDIA) study. *Psychosomatic Medicine, 68,* 41–50. doi:10.1097/01.psy.0000195967.51768.ea

Colby, S. L., & Ortman, J. M. (2014). Projections of the size and composition of the U.S. population: 2014 to 2060 (Current population reports, P25-1143). US Census Bureau. Retrieved from https://www.census.gov/content/dam/Census/library/publications/2015/demo/p25-1143.pdf (accessed April 10, 2017).

Cooper, C. R., & Denner, J. (1998). Theories linking culture and psychology: Universal and community-specific processes. *Annual Review of Psychology, 49,* 559–584. doi:10.1146/annurev.psych.49.1.559

Cunningham, T. J., Seeman, T. E., Kawachi, I., Gortmaker, S. L., Jacobs, D. R., Kiefe, C. I., & Berkman, L. F. (2012). Racial/ethnic and gender differences in the association between self-reported experiences of racial/ethnic discrimination and inflammation in the CARDIA cohort of 4 US communities. *Social Science & Medicine, 75*(5), 922–931. doi:10.1016/j.socscimed.2012.04.027

D'Anna-Hernandez, K. L., Hoffman, M. C., Zerbe, G. O., Coussons-Read, M., Ross, R. G., & Laudenslager, M. L. (2012). Acculturation, maternal cortisol, and birth outcomes in women of Mexican descent. *Psychosomatic Medicine, 74*(3), 296–304. doi:10.1097/PSY.0b013e318244fbde

DeCaro, J. A., & Worthman, C. M. (2008). Culture and the socialization of child cardiovascular regulation at school entry in the US. *American Journal of Human Biology, 20*(5), 572–583. doi:10.1002/ajhb.20782

Devos, T., & Banaji, M. R. (2005). American = white? *Journal of Personality and Social Psychology, 88*(3), 447–466. doi:10.1037/0022-3514.88.3.447

Dich, N., Lange, T., Head, J., & Rod, N. H. (2015). Work stress, caregiving, and allostatic load: Prospective results from the Whitehall II cohort study. *Psychosomatic Medicine, 77*(5), 539–547. doi:10.1097/PSY.0000000000000191

Dickerson, S. S., Gable, S. L., Irwin, M. R., Aziz, N., & Kemeny, M. E. (2009). Social-evaluative threat and proinflammatory cytokine regulation: An experimental laboratory investigation. *Psychological Science, 20,* 1237–1244. doi:10.1111/j.1467-9280.2009.02437.x

Dickerson, S. S., & Kemeny, M. E. (2004). Acute stressors and cortisol responses: A theoretical integration and synthesis of laboratory research. *Psychological Bulletin, 130,* 355–391. doi:10.1037/0033-2909.130.3.355.

Doane, L. D., & Zeiders, K. H. (2014). Contextual moderators of momentary cortisol and negative affect in adolescents' daily lives. *Journal of Adolescent Health, 54*, 536–542. doi:10.1016/j.jadohealth.2013.10.007.

Dolezsar, C. M., McGrath, J. J., Herzig, A. J., & Miller, S. B. (2014). Perceived racial discrimination and hypertension: A comprehensive systematic review. *Health Psychology, 33*(1), 20–34. doi:10.1037/a0033718

Dressler, W. W., & Bindon, J. R. (2000). The health consequences of cultural consonance: Cultural dimensions of lifestyle, social support and arterial blood pressure in an African American community. *American Anthropology, 102*, 244–260. doi:10.1525/aa.2000.102.2.244

Ehrlich, K. B., Miller, G. E., & Chen, E. (2016). Childhood adversity and adult physical health. In D. Cicchetti (Ed.), *Developmental Psychopathology* (3rd ed., pp. 1–42). Hoboken, NJ: John Wiley & Sons.

Ferguson, G. M. (2013). The big difference a small island can make: How Jamaican adolescents are advancing acculturation science. *Child Development Perspectives, 7*(4), 248–254. doi:10.1111/cdep.12051

Flinn, M. V., & England, B. G. (1997). Social economics of childhood glucocorticoid response and health. *American Journal of Physical Anthropology, 102*, 33–53. doi:10.1002/(SICI)1096-8644(199701)102:1<33::AID-AJPA4>3.0.CO;2-E

Fuligni, A. J., & Telzer, E. H. (2013). Another way family can get in the head and under the skin: The neurobiology of helping the family. *Child Development Perspectives, 7*(3), 138–142. doi:10.1111/cdep.12029

Fuligni, A. J., Telzer, E. H., Bower, J., Cole, S. W., Kiang, L., & Irwin, M. R. (2009). A preliminary study of daily interpersonal stress and C-reactive protein levels among adolescents from Latin American and European backgrounds. *Psychosomatic Medicine, 71*(3), 329–333. doi:10.1097/PSY.0b013e3181921b1f

Fuligni, A. J., Tseng, V., & Lam, M. (1999). Attitudes toward family obligations among American adolescents with Asian, Latin American, and European backgrounds. *Child Development, 70*(4), 1030–1044. doi:10.1111/1467-8624.00075

García Coll, C., Akerman, A., & Cicchetti, D. (2000). Cultural influences on developmental processes and outcomes: Implications for the study of development and psychopathology. *Development and Psychopathology, 12*(3), 333–356.

García Coll, C., Lamberty, G., Jenkins, R., McAdoo, H. P., Crnic, K., Wasik, B. H., & Vázquez García, H. (1996). An integrative model for the study of competencies in minority children. *Child Development, 67*(5), 1891–1914. doi:10.2307/1131600

Geronimus, A. T., Hicken, M., Keene, D., & Bound, J. (2006). "Weathering" and age patterns of allostatic load scores among blacks and whites in the United States. *American Journal of Public Health, 96*(5), 826–833. doi:10.2105/AJPH.2004.060749

Glaser, R., & Kiecolt-Glaser, J. K. (2005). Stress-induced immune dysfunction: Implications for health. *Nature Reviews Immunology, 5*, 243–251. doi:10.1038/nri1571

Glaser, R., & Kiecolt-Glaser, J. K. (Eds.). (2014). *Handbook of human stress and immunity*. San Diego, CA: Academic Press.

Gonzales, N. A., Germán, M., & Fabrett, F. C. (2012). US Latino youth. In E. Chang & C. Downey (Eds.), *Handbook of race and development in mental health* (pp. 259–278). New York: Springer.

Gonzales, N. A., & Kim, L. (1997). Stress and coping in an ethnic minority context: Children's cultural ecologies. In S. A. Wolchik & I. N. Sandler (Eds.), *Handbook of children's coping: Linking theory and intervention* (pp. 481–511). New York: Plenum.

Gonzales, P. M., Blanton, H., & Williams, K. J. (2002). The effects of stereotype threat and double-minority status on the test performance of Latino women. *Personality and Social Psychology Bulletin, 28*(5), 659–670. doi:10.1177/0146167202288010

Guan, S. S. A., Bower, J. E., Almeida, D. M., Cole, S. W., Dahl, R. E., Irwin, M. R., … & Fuligni, A. J. (2016). Parental support buffers the association of depressive symptoms with cortisol and C-reactive protein during adolescence. *Brain, Behavior, and Immunity, 57*, 134–143. doi:10.1016/j.bbi.2016.03.007

Hagan, M. J., Roubinov, D. S., Mistler, A. K., & Luecken, L. J. (2014). Mental health outcomes in emerging adults exposed to childhood maltreatment: The moderating role of stress reactivity. *Child Maltreatment, 19*(3–4), 156–167. doi:10.1177/1077559514539753

Helms, J. E. (1994). The conceptualization of racial identity and other "racial" constructs. In E. J. Trickett, R. J. Watts, & D. Birman (Eds.), *Human diversity: Perspectives on people in context* (pp. 285–311). San Francisco, CA: Jossey-Bass.

Hill, L. K., Hoggard, L. S., Richmond, A. L., Gray, D. L., Williams, D. P., & Thayer, J. F. (2017). Examining the associations between perceived discrimination and heart rate variability in African Americans. *Cultural Diversity and Ethnic Minority Psychology, 23*(1), 5–14. doi:10.1037/cdp0000076

Hoyt, L. T., Zeiders, K. H., Ehrlich, K. B., & Adam, E. K. (2016). Positive upshots of cortisol in everyday life. *Emotion, 16*(4), 431–435. doi:10.1037/emo0000174

Jaramillo, J., Mello, Z. R., & Worrell, F. C. (2016). Ethnic identity, stereotype threat, and perceived discrimination among Native American adolescents. *Journal of Research on Adolescence, 26*(4), 769–775. doi:10.1111/jora.12228

Jewell, S. L., Luecken, L. J., Gress-Smith, J., Crnic, K. A., & Gonzales, N. A. (2015). Economic stress and cortisol among postpartum low-income Mexican American women: Buffering influence of family support. *Behavioral Medicine, 41*(3), 138–144. doi:10.1080/08964289.2015.1024603

John-Henderson, N. A., Rheinschmidt, M. L., Mendoza-Denton, R., & Francis, D. D. (2014). Performance and inflammation outcomes are predicted by different facets of SES under stereotype threat. *Social Psychological and Personality Science, 5*(3), 301–309. doi:10.1177/1948550613494226

Kaufman, J. S., Cooper, R. S., & McGee, D. L. (1997). Socioeconomic status and health in blacks and whites: The problem of residual confounding and the resiliency of race. *Epidemiology, 8*, 621–628. doi:10.1097/00001648-199710000-00002

Kershaw, K. N., Lewis, T. T., Diez Roux, A. V., Jenny, N. S., Liu, K., Penedo, F. J., & Carnethon, M. R. (2016). Self-reported experiences of discrimination and inflammation among men and women: The multi-ethnic study of atherosclerosis. *Health Psychology, 35*(4), 343–350. doi:10.1037/hea0000331

Kiecolt-Glaser, J. K., Preacher, K. J., MacCallum, R. C., Atkinson, C., Malarkey, W. B., & Glaser, R. (2003). Chronic stress and age-related increases in the proinflammatory cytokine IL-6. *Proceedings of the National Academy of Sciences, 100*(15), 9090–9095. doi:10.1073/pnas.1531903100

Kim, H. S., Sherman, D. K., Sasaki, J. Y., Xu, J., Chu, T. Q., Ryu, C., … Taylor, S. E. (2010). Culture, distress, and oxytocin receptor polymorphism (OXTR) interact to influence emotional support seeking. *Proceedings of the National Academy of Sciences, 107*(36), 15717–15721. doi:10.1073/pnas.1010830107

Kirschbaum, C., & Hellhammer, D. H. (1989). Salivary cortisol in psycho-biological research: An overview. *Neuropsychobiology, 22*, 150–169. doi:10.1159/000118611

Laurent, H. K., Lucas, T., Pierce, J., Goetz, S., & Granger, D. A. (2016). Coordination of cortisol response to social evaluative threat with autonomic and inflammatory responses is moderated by stress appraisals and affect. *Biological Psychology, 118*, 17–24. doi:10.1016/j.biopsycho.2016.04.066

Lazarus, R. S., & Folkman, S. (1984). *Stress, appraisal, and coping*. New York: Springer Publishing Company.

Lê-Scherban, F., Albrecht, S. S., Bertoni, A., Kandula, N., Mehta, N., & Roux, A. V. D. (2016). Immigrant status and cardiovascular risk over time: Results from the Multi-Ethnic Study of Atherosclerosis. *Annals of Epidemiology, 26*(6), 429–435. doi:10.1016/j.annepidem.2016.04.008

Levy, D. J., Heissel, J., Richeson, J. A., & Adam, E. K. (2016). Psychological and biological responses to race-based social stress as pathways to disparities in educational outcomes. *American Psychologist, 71*(6), 455–473. doi:10.1037/a0040322

Lewis, T. T., Aiello, A. E., Leurgans, S., Kelly, J., & Barnes, L. L. (2010). Self-reported experiences of everyday discrimination are associated with elevated C-reactive protein levels in older African-American adults. *Brain, Behavior, and Immunity, 24*(3), 438–443. doi:10.1016/j.bbi.2009.11.011

Lewis, T. T., Williams, D. R., Tamene, M., & Clark, C. R. (2014). Self-reported experiences of discrimination and cardiovascular disease. *Current Cardiovascular Risk Reports, 8*(1), 1–15. doi:10.1007/s12170-013-0365-2

Li, S. (2003). Biocultural orchestration of developmental plasticity across levels: The interplay of biology and culture in shaping the mind and behavior across the lifespan. *Psychological Bulletin, 129*(2), 171–194. doi:10.1037/0033-2909.129.2.171

Lovallo, W., & Thomas, T. (2000). Stress hormones in psychophysiological research. In J. Cacioppo, L. Tassinary, & G. Bernston (Eds.), *Handbook of Psychophysiology* (2nd ed., pp. 342–367). Cambridge: Cambridge University Press.

Luecken, L. J., & Gallo, L. C. (Eds.). (2008). *Handbook of physiological research methods in health psychology*. Thousand Oaks, CA: Sage Publications.

Mangold, D., Mintz, J., Javors, M., & Marino, E. (2012). Neuroticism, acculturation and the cortisol awakening response in Mexican American adults. *Hormones and Behavior, 61*(1), 23–30. doi:10.1016/j.yhbeh.2011.09.009

Mangold, D., Wand, G., Javors, M., & Mintz, J. (2010). Acculturation, childhood trauma and the cortisol awakening response in Mexican-American adults. *Hormones and Behavior, 58*(4), 637–646. doi:10.1016/j.yhbeh.2010.06.010

Marin, T. J., Chen, E., Munch, J. A., & Miller, G. E. (2009). Double-exposure to acute stress and chronic family stress is associated with immune changes in children with asthma. *Psychosomatic Medicine, 71*(4), 378–384. doi:10.1097/PSY.0b013e318199dbc3

Mattei, J., Demissie, S., Falcon, L. M., Ordovas, J. M., & Tucker, K. (2010). Allostatic load is associated with chronic conditions in the Boston Puerto Rican Health Study. *Social Science and Medicine, 70*(12), 1988–1996. doi:10.1016/j.socscimed.2010.02.024

McClure, H. H., Snodgrass, J. J., Martinez, C. R., Jr, Squires, E. C., Jiménez, R. A., Isiordia, L. E., ... & Small, J. (2015). Stress, place, and allostatic load among Mexican immigrant farmworkers in Oregon. *Journal of Immigrant and Minority Health, 17*(5), 1518–1525. doi:10.1007/s10903-014-0066-z

McDade, T. W. (2005). The ecologies of human immune function. *Annual Review of Anthropology, 34,* 495–521. doi:10.1146/annurev.anthro.34.081804.120348

McDade, T. W., Stallings, J., & Worthman, C. M. (2000). Culture change and stress in Western Samoan youth: Methodological issues in the cross-cultural study of stress and immune function. *American Journal of Human Biology, 12,* 792–802. doi:10.1002/1520-6300(200011/12)12:6<792::AID-AJHB7>3.0.CO;2-F

McDade, T. W., & Worthman, C. M. (2004). Socialization ambiguity in Samoan adolescents: A model for human development and stress in the context of culture change. *Journal of Research on Adolescence, 14*(1), 49–72. doi:10.1111/j.1532-7795.2004.01401003.x

McEwen, B. S. (1998). Stress, adaptation, and disease: Allostasis and allostatic load. *Annals of the New York Academy of Sciences, 840,* 33–44. doi:10.1111/j.1749-6632.1998.tb09546.x

McEwen, B. S. (2000). Allostasis and allostatic load: Implications for neuropsychopharmacology. *Neuropsychopharmacology, 22*(2), 108–124. doi:10.1016/S0893-133X(99)00129-3

McEwen, B. S., & Seeman, T. (1999). Protective and damaging effects of mediators of stress: Elaborating and testing the concepts of allostasis and allostatic load. *Annals of the New York Academy of Sciences, 896*(1), 30–47. doi:10.1111/j.1749-6632.1999.tb08103.x

Mendes, W. B., & Jamieson, J. (2011). Embodied stereotype threat: Exploring brain and body mechanisms underlying performance impairments. In M. Inzlicht & T. Schmader (Eds.), *Stereotype threat: Theory, process, and application* (pp. 51–68). New York: Oxford University Press.

Mozaffarian, D., Benjamin, E. J., Go, A. S., Arnett, D. K., Blaha, M. J., Cushman, M., ... & Fullerton, H. J. (2016). Executive summary: Heart disease and stroke statistics – 2016 update: A report from the American Heart Association. *Circulation, 133*(4), 447–454. doi:10.1161/CIR.0000000000000366

Muhtadie, L., Koslov, K., Akinola, M., & Mendes, W. B. (2015). Vagal flexibility: A physiological predictor of social sensitivity. *Journal of Personality and Social Psychology, 109,* 106–120. doi:10.1037/pspp0000016

Myers, H. F. (2009). Ethnicity- and socio-economic status-related stresses in context: An integrative review and conceptual model. *Journal of Behavioral Medicine, 32,* 9–19. doi:10.1007/s10865-008-9181-4

Neblett, E. W., Rivas-Drake, D., & Umaña-Taylor, A. J. (2012). The promise of racial and ethnic protective factors in promoting ethnic minority youth development. *Child Development Perspectives, 6*(3), 295–303. doi:10.1111/j.1750-8606.2012.00239.x

Neblett, E. W., & Roberts, S. O. (2013). Racial identity and autonomic responses to racial discrimination. *Psychophysiology, 50*(10), 943–953. doi:10.1111/psyp.12087

Nguyen, A.-M. D., & Benet-Martinez, V. (2012). Biculturalism and adjustment: A meta-analysis. *Journal of Cross-Cultural Psychology, 44*(1), 122–159. doi:10.1177/0022022111435097

Padgett, D. A., & Glaser, R. (2003). How stress influences the immune response. *Trends in Immunology, 24*(8), 444–448. doi:10.1016/S1471-4906(03)00173-X

Pascoe, E. A., & Smart Richman, L. (2009). Perceived discrimination and health: A meta-analytic review. *Psychological Bulletin, 135*(4), 531–554. doi:10.1037/a0016059

Peek, M. K., Cutchin, M. P., Salinas, J. J., Sheffield, K. M., Eschbach, K., Stowe, R. P., & Goodwin, J. S. (2010). Allostatic load among non-Hispanic whites, non-Hispanic blacks, and people of Mexican origin: Effects of ethnicity, nativity, and acculturation. *American Journal of Public Health, 100*(5), 940–946. doi:10.2105/AJPH.2007.129312

Phillips, A. C., Ginty, A. T., & Hughes, B. M. (2013). The other side of the coin: Blunted cardiovascular and cortisol reactivity are associated with negative health outcomes. *International Journal of Psychophysiology, 90*(1), 1–7. doi:10.1016/j.ijpsycho.2013.02.002

Phinney, J. S. (1989). Stages of ethnic identity development in minority group adolescents. *Journal of Early Adolescence, 9*(1–2), 34–49. doi:10.1177/0272431689091004

Porges, S. W. (2007). The polyvagal perspective. *Biological Psychology, 74*(2), 116–143. doi:10.1016/j.biopsycho.2006.06.009

Pruessner, J. C., Kirschbaum, C., Meinlschmid, G., & Hellhammer, D. H. (2003). Two formulas for computation of the area under the curve represent measures of total hormone concentration versus time-dependent change. *Psychoneuroendocrinology, 28*(7), 916–931. doi:10.1016/S0306-4530(02)00108-7

Pruessner, J. C., Wolf, O. T., Hellhammer, D. H., Buske-Kirschbaum, A., von Auer, K., Jobst, S., … & Kirschbaum, C. (1997). Free cortisol levels after awakening: A reliable biological marker for the assessment of adrenocortical activity. *Life Sciences, 61*, 2539–2549. doi:10.1016/S0024-3205(97)01008-4

Quas, J. A., Yim, I. S., Oberlander, T. F., Nordstokke, D., Essex, M. J., Armstrong, J. M., … Boyce, W. T. (2014). The symphonic structure of childhood stress reactivity: Patterns of sympathetic, parasympathetic, and adrenocortical responses to psychological challenge. *Development and Psychopathology, 26*, 963–982. doi:10.1017/S0954579414000480

Rogoff, B. (2003). *The cultural nature of cognitive development*. New York: Oxford University Press.

Ruiz, R. J., Pickler, R. H., Marti, C. N., & Jallo, N. (2013). Family cohesion, acculturation, maternal cortisol, and preterm birth in Mexican-American women. *International Journal of Women's Health, 5*, 243–252. doi:10.2147/IJWH.S42268

Sabogal, F., Marín, G., Otero-Sabogal, R., Marín, B. V., & Perez-Stable, E. J. (1987). Hispanic familism and acculturation: What changes and what doesn't? *Hispanic Journal of Behavioral Sciences, 9*(4), 397–412. doi:10.1177/07399863870094003

Schwartz, S. J., Weisskirch, R. S., Hurley, E. A., Zamboanga, B. L., Park, I. J., Kim, S. Y., … & Greene, A. D. (2010). Communalism, familism, and filial piety: Are they birds of a collectivist feather? *Cultural Diversity and Ethnic Minority Psychology, 16*(4), 548–560. doi:10.1037/a0021370

Seeman, T. E., Gruenewald, T. L., Cohen, S., Williams, D. R., & Matthews, K. A. (2014). Social relationships and their biological correlates: Coronary Artery Risk Development in Young Adults (CARDIA) study. *Psychoneuroendocrinology, 43*, 126–138. doi:10.1016/j.psyneuen.2014.02.008

Sellers, R. M., Copeland-Linder, N., Martin, P. P., & Lewis, R. L. (2006). Racial identity matters: The relationship between racial discrimination and psychological functioning in African American adolescents. *Journal of Research on Adolescence, 16*(2), 187–216.

Sladek, M. R., & Doane, L. D. (2015). Daily diary reports of social connection, objective sleep, and the cortisol awakening response during adolescents' first year of college. *Journal of Youth and Adolescence, 44*, 298–316. doi:10.1007/s10964-014-0244-2

Smart Richman, L. S., & Jonassaint, C. (2008). The effects of race-related stress on cortisol reactivity in the laboratory: Implications of the Duke lacrosse scandal. *Annals of Behavioral Medicine, 35*(1), 105–110. doi:10.1007/s12160-007-9013-8

Smart Richman, L., Pek, J., Pascoe, E., & Bauer, D. J. (2010). The effects of perceived discrimination on ambulatory blood pressure and affective responses to interpersonal stress modeled over 24 hours. *Health Psychology, 29*(4), 403–411. doi:10.1037/a0019045

Spencer, S. J., Logel, C., & Davies, P. G. (2016). Stereotype threat. *Annual Review of Psychology, 67*(1), 415–437. doi:10.1146/annurev-psych-073115-103235

Steele, C. M., & Aronson, J. (1995). Stereotype threat and the intellectual test performance of African Americans. *Journal of Personality and Social Psychology, 69*(5), 797–811. doi:10.1037/0022-3514.69.5.797

Steffen, P. R., Smith, T. B., Larson, M., & Butler, L. (2006). Acculturation to Western society as a risk factor for high blood pressure: A meta-analytic review. *Psychosomatic Medicine, 68*(3), 386–397. doi:10.1097/01.psy.0000221255.48190.32

Sterling, P. (2004). Principles of allostasis: Optimal design, predictive regulation, pathophysiology, and rational therapeutics. In J. Schulkin (Ed.), *Allostasis, homeostasis, and the costs of adaptation* (pp. 17–64). Cambridge: Cambridge University Press.

Sterling, P., & Eyer, J. (1988). Allostasis: A new paradigm to explain arousal pathology. In S. Fisher & J. Reason (Eds.), *Handbook of life stress, cognition and health* (pp. 629–649). New York: Wiley.

Suárez-Orozco, C., & Suárez-Orozco, M. (1995). *Transformations: Immigration, family life, and achievement motivation among Latino adolescents.* Stanford, CA: Stanford University Press.

Sue, D. W., Capodilupo, C. M., Torino, G. C., Bucceri, J. M., Holder, A., Nadal, K. L., & Esquilin, M. (2007). Racial microaggressions in everyday life: Implications for clinical practice. *American Psychologist, 62*(4), 271–286. doi:10.1037/0003-066X.62.4.271

Thayer, J. F., & Lane, R. D. (2000). A model of neurovisceral integration in emotion regulation and dysregulation. *Journal of Affective Disorders, 61*(3), 201–216. doi:10.1016/S0165-0327(00)00338-4

Thompson, H. S., Kamarck, T. W., & Manuck, S. B. (2002). The association between racial identity and hypertension in African-American adults: Elevated resting and ambulatory blood pressure as outcomes. *Ethnicity and Disease, 12*(1), 20–28.

Tomfohr, L. M., Pung, M. A., & Dimsdale, J. E. (2016). Mediators of the relationship between race and allostatic load in African and White Americans. *Health Psychology, 35*(4), 322–332. doi:10.1037/hea0000251

Torres, A., & Bowens, L. (2000). Correlation between the internalization theme of racial identity attitude survey-B and systolic blood pressure. *Ethnicity and Disease, 10*(3), 375–383.

Trawalter, S., Adam, E. K., Chase-Lansdale, P. L., & Richeson, J. A. (2012). Concerns about appearing prejudiced get under the skin: Stress responses to interracial contact in the moment and across time. *Journal of Experimental Social Psychology, 48*, 682–693. doi:10.1016/j.jesp.2011.12.003

Triandis, H. C. (1995). Attributes of individualism and collectivism. In *Individualism & collectivism* (pp. 43–80). Boulder, CO: Westview Press.

Umaña-Taylor, A. J., Quintana, S. M., Lee, R. M., Cross, W. E., Rivas-Drake, D., Schwartz, S. J., … Sellers, R. M. (2014). Ethnic and racial identity during adolescence and into young adulthood: An integrated conceptualization. *Child Development, 85*(1), 21–39. doi:10.1111/cdev.12196

Umaña-Taylor, A. J., Yazedjian, A., & Bámaca-Gómez, M. Y. (2004). Developing the Ethnic Identity Scale using Eriksonian and social identity perspectives. *Identity, 4*(1), 9–38. doi:10.1207/S1532706XID0401_2

Webster, J. I., Tonelli, L., & Sternberg, E. M. (2002). Neuroendocrine regulation of immunity. *Annual Review of Immunology, 20*(1), 125–163. doi:10.1146/annurev.immunol.20.082401.104914

Williams, D. R., Neighbors, H. W., & Jackson, J. S. (2003). Racial/ethnic discrimination and health: Findings from community studies. *American Journal of Public Health, 93*, 200–208. doi:10.2105/AJPH.93.2.200

Wommack, J. C., Ruiz, R. J., Marti, C. N., Stowe, R. P., Brown, C. E., & Murphey, C. (2013). Interleukin-10 predicts preterm birth in acculturated Hispanics. *Biological Research for Nursing, 15*(1), 78–85. doi:10.1177/1099800411416225

Worthman, C. M., & Costello, E. J. (2009). Tracking biocultural pathways to health disparities: The use of biomarkers. *Annals of Human Biology, 36*, 281–297. doi:10.1080/03014460902832934

Zeiders, K. H., Hoyt, L. T., & Adam, E. K. (2014). Associations between self-reported discrimination and diurnal cortisol rhythms among young adults: The moderating role of racial–ethnic minority status. *Psychoneuroendocrinology, 50*, 280–288. doi:10.1016/j.psyneuen.2014.08.023

11

Relations among Culture, Poverty, Stress, and Allostatic Load

Stacey N. Doan and Gary W. Evans

In the United States, 14.8% of the population lives in poverty, which is defined in 2016, by the US Census Bureau, as having an annual income of less than $28,960 for a family of five. This amounts to approximately 46.7 million people living in extraordinary circumstances. Globally more than 1.5 billion people live on less than $1 a day (Milanovic, 2013). Poverty is associated with a host of deleterious outcomes, including negative effects on behavioral health (Yoshikawa, Aber, & Beardslee, 2012) and physical health (Miller & Chen, 2013), and impaired brain development (Johnson, Riis, & Noble, 2016; Luby et al., 2013). Attempting to understand the mechanisms by which poverty affects health outcomes, a large body of work has focused on the idea that poverty leads to increased negative affect and stress – defined as an organism's reaction to environmental demands exceeding its regulatory capacity – and that these have both direct and indirect effects on physical health and psychological functioning (Selye, 2013).

However, it is only recently that researchers have begun to look at the relations among stress, physiological factors, and health through a cultural lens. Culture, race, and ethnicity shape both endogenous factors (e.g., coping strategies) and exogenous factors (e.g., exposure to discrimination), which have important implications for how we understand the relations among poverty, stress, and health outcomes. In the current chapter, we start by discussing a recent conceptualization of chronic physiological stress, namely allostatic load (AL). Next, we review the literature that establishes allostatic load as a potentially powerful mediator in the relations between poverty and physical and psychological health. Finally, we

The Handbook of Culture and Biology, First Edition. Edited by José M. Causadias, Eva H. Telzer and Nancy A. Gonzales.

summarize the literature that examines the extent to which patterns of poverty and allostatic load may be shaped by culture, race, and ethnicity.

Allostatic Load: Reconceptualizing the Consequences of Stress

In the early 1990s, McEwen (1998) proposed the necessity of taking a multisystem approach when investigating the physiological consequences of stress, rather than looking at singular indicators. Central to McEwen's proposal were the concepts of allostasis and allostatic load. Allostasis, in contrast to homeostasis, emphasizes that a healthy system is dynamically changing and adapting in response to variable environmental demands, being flexible enough to regulate responses to environmental demands upward and downward as needed (McEwen, 1998, 2012). Thus, the hormones associated with stress are necessary, and even adaptive in the short run, as they ready the system to respond. However, under repeated activation or challenges to the regulatory system, as in the context of chronic stressors, the system becomes dysregulated. Allostatic load is the "wear and tear" on the body as a consequence of repeated exposure to stressors; it is the cumulative physiological consequence of adaptive responses to environmental demands.

Since the original conceptualization of allostasis and allostatic load, a large body of research has begun to document the utility of allostatic load as both a consequence of stress and a predictor for a range of outcomes. With regard to the former, neighborhood risk (Theall, Drury, & Shirtcliff, 2012), early childhood risk exposure (Evans & Kim, 2013), minority status (Geronimus, Hicken, Keene, & Bound, 2006), low perceived social status (Seeman, Merkin, Karlamangla, Koretz, & Seeman, 2014) and age (Crimmins, Johnston, Hayward, & Seeman, 2003) have all been associated with higher allostatic load. Just as importantly, allostatic load has also been found to be an important predictor of a range of outcomes. Higher allostatic load is associated with lower baseline functioning, poorer cognitive performance, and compromised physical performance (Doan & Evans, 2011; Seeman, Singer, Rowe, Horwitz, & McEwen, 1997). McEwen also posited that elevated allostatic load compromises the ability to mount a robust response to environmental challenges and to efficiently recover to baseline functioning when the stressor is removed (McEwen, 2000). Furthermore, higher allostatic load augments the risk of incident cardiovascular disease (Seeman et al., 1997), as well as of mortality (Karlamangla,

Singer, & Seeman, 2006), and has consequences for mental health (Ganzel, Morris, & Wethington, 2010).

Poverty and Allostatic Load

Poverty researchers have capitalized on the allostatic load framework to understand the "biological embedding of poverty." Research investigating socioeconomic status (SES) and allostatic load has found a negative relationship between SES and the overall allostatic index, as well as subscales of inflammatory, metabolic, and cardiovascular risks (Seeman et al., 2004). For example, lower household income (Singer & Ryff, 1999), lower education levels (Kubzansky, Kawachi, & Sparrow, 1999) and neighborhood poverty are all associated with greater AL (Theall, Drury, & Shirtcliff, 2012). Cumulative socioeconomic disadvantage is related to allostatic load in both women and men (Gustafsson, Janlert, Theorell, Westerlund, & Hammarstrom, 2011). Allostatic load is higher among those with greater SES adversity during both childhood and adulthood, as well as cumulatively across the course of their life (Evans, 2003; Gruenwald et al., 2012).

While a large body of work demonstrates a relationship between SES and allostatic load, few studies have explored the underlying mechanisms, other than the poverty-associated cumulative risk exposure (Evans & Kim, 2012) (for an exception see Hawkley, Lavelle, Berntson, & Cacioppo, 2011). Even more importantly, while studies may demonstrate racial/ethnic differences with regard to allostatic load, there is virtually no work that has attempted to explain these differences. Thus, we have very little understanding of how cultural values, beliefs and practices may moderate these effects. In the next section, we provide a working definition of culture, race, and ethnicity. After that we review the literature on allostatic load that has adopted a cross-cultural/ethnic perspective.

Culture and Allostatic Load

Despite the impressive body of work demonstrating associations between poverty and allostatic load, surprisingly few studies have systematically investigated racial/ethnic differences in allostatic load, and even fewer have considered cultural mechanisms. This is surprising, since the concept of allostatic load may help towards an understanding of health disparities

(Carlson & Chamberlain, 2005). The current extant data suggest that, in general, minorities have worse outcomes than their White counterparts. Data from the National Health and Nutrition Examination Survey (NHANES) indicate that Blacks in general have higher scores on allostatic load than Whites, and the probability of a higher score was true at all ages, but particularly at 35–64 years (Geronimus et al., 2006). Interestingly, racial differences were not explained by poverty. Importantly, the score differentials between Blacks and Whites increased with age adjusted for SES. Moreover, Black women accrued higher allostatic load at younger ages, suggesting that Black women are at a significant health disadvantage (Chyu & Upchurch, 2011; Geronimus et al., 2006).

Latinos also have more biological risk factors than Whites, but fewer risk factors than Blacks (Crimmins, Kim, Alley, Karlamangla, & Seeman, 2007). Differences between Hispanics and Whites disappeared when SES was controlled for, which suggests that SES was a pivotal driver of the difference. However, this result was only true for foreign-born Mexican Americans. In an investigation of ethnic differences in allostatic load in a population-based sample of adults, consistently with previous work Blacks were found to have the highest total allostatic load scores, but foreign-born Mexicans were the least likely group to be in the higher allostatic-load categories (Peek et al., 2010). Estimates indicate that, consistently with the immigrant health paradox, 45–60-year-old Mexican immigrants have lower allostatic load scores upon arrival than US-born Mexican Americans, non-Hispanic Whites and non-Hispanic Blacks, and that this health advantage attenuates with duration of residence in the United States (Kaestner, Pearson, Keene, & Geronimus, 2009). Consistently with this finding, Mexican-American women who were not born in the United States had lower predicted AL scores than those born in the US (Chyu & Upchurch, 2011). Finally, for foreign-born Blacks, length of stay and age were powerful predictors of allostatic load scores. Among US-born Blacks, being older, or widowed, divorced, or separated, was associated with higher allostatic load (Doamekpor & Dinwiddie, 2015).

In sum, the overall data suggest that ethnic-minority status in the US generally confers additional risks with regard to allostatic load. Few studies have focused on the mechanisms that would explain why these differences exist. In the final section of this chapter we discuss possible mechanisms that underlie poverty and allostatic load. This model is not meant to be exhaustive, but to highlight variables that have been associated with poverty and allostatic load, and, more importantly, are influenced by cultural values and beliefs.

Mechanisms Underlying Poverty and Allostatic Load: The Influence of Culture, Race, and Ethnicity

In the following sections, we articulate three main interrelated pathways by which poverty gets under the skin to influence health and well-being, which are (1) perceived stress and stress exposure, (2) psychosocial influences, specifically parenting and social support, and (3) individual regulatory processes and coping skills. From this perspective, we can see that poverty has an effect at both the societal and the individual levels. Similarly, we argue that culture and race/ethnicity are pervasive, and color how an individual experiences the circumstances and challenges of poverty. Figure 11.1 illustrates our conceptualization of the mechanisms underlying poverty and allostatic load. We highlight culture by arguing that it can shape these factors through both endogenous and exogenous influences. More specifically, cultural factors moderate the relationship between poverty and allostatic load, as well as the link between allostatic load and health. Certain factors may exacerbate the negative effects of poverty and allostatic load, while others may serve as a protective mechanism. Understanding the underlying mechanisms would help us to see the extent to which cultural, racial and ethnic factors can either exacerbate or mitigate the effects of SES and allostatic load.

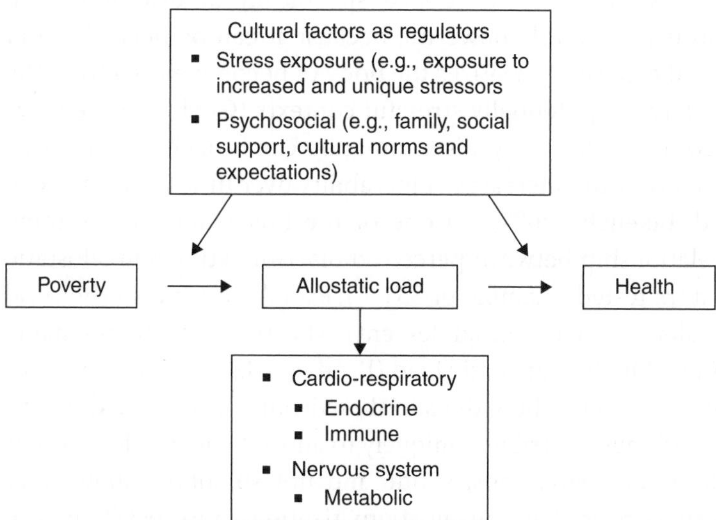

Figure 11.1 Culture and race/ethnicity influence stress exposure and moderate the relationship between stress and allostatic load

Stress Exposure

When we consider the impact of culture, race, and ethnicity on exposure to stress, we see that minorities inhabit environments that expose them to types of stressors that are both quantitatively and qualitatively different. Ethnic-minority status is associated with increased stress exposure (Slopen et al., 2010), as well as with increased exposure to unique stressors that are not applicable to the White majority (Acevedo-Garcia, Osypuk, McArdle, & Williams, 2008; Mays, Cochran, & Barnes, 2007). Concerning the sheer number of stressful events, classic work has demonstrated that both frequency and severity of stress exposure were greater for Blacks than for Whites (Dohrenwend & Dohrenwend, 1969; Uhlenhuth & Paykel, 1973). More recent studies have generally found that Blacks report higher levels of all stressful events than do non-Hispanic Whites (Turner & Avison, 2003), as well as the highest mean lifetime count of major stressful life events (Turner & Lloyd, 2004). Lu and Chen (2004) found that African-American women reported more stressful events in the past year in a wide variety of domains than did non-Hispanic Whites.

Race/ethnicity also influences the type of stressors that one experiences. The stressors that are uncontrollable and unpredictable are the most detrimental to health (Williams & Mohammed, 2009). Along these lines, a large body of research has focused on unique, uncontrollable stressors that are associated with ethnic-minority status. From this perspective, a significant body of work has looked specifically at discrimination. Discrimination is particularly powerful, because it can be pervasive and because repeated exposure sensitizes the body to become more physically reactive in stressful or potentially stressful contexts (Guyll, Matthews, & Bromberger, 2001). Additionally, discrimination can be a chronic stressor that erodes resources and increases vulnerability over time (Gee, Spencer, Chen, Yip and Takeuchi, 2007). In one of the first studies to examine the possible relationship between perceived discrimination and allostatic load, investigators tested a sample of 331 African Americans in the rural South; the results revealed that adolescents who report high and stable discrimination had higher allostatic load (Brody et al., 2014). Experiences of discrimination highlight how the social environment may be different for minorities and thus contribute uniquely to allostatic load. More recent work on racial microaggressions, subtle and not so subtle, shows that actions and experiences that convey stigmatization cause psychological distress (Torres, Driscoll, & Burrow, 2010) and increases in AL (Ong, Williams, Nwizu, & Gruenewald, 2017) that we predict would also, especially if continuously experienced, elevate allostatic load.

Increasingly, research has highlighted the fact that, in addition to the social environment, the physical environment differs for minorities, independently of SES. Neighborhood cumulative disadvantage, for example, has been associated with higher levels of allostatic load (Gustafsson et al., 2014). Residential segregation leads to racial and socioeconomic disparities in pivotal neighborhood conditions, which have important implications for health (Reardon, Fox, & Townsend, 2015). Of the number of adolescents living in very high-risk neighborhoods, 85% are minority children (Theall et al., 2012). Poverty that affects Blacks is more isolating and concentrated (Jargowsky, 2015). This is consistent with data demonstrating that Black and Hispanic families need much higher incomes than Whites to live in comparably wealthy neighborhoods (Reardon et al., 2015). Finally, the effects of neighborhood quality on allostatic load are particularly strong for Black participants, as compared to Mexican Americans and Whites (Merkin et al., 2009).

In sum, ethnic-minority status has important implications at the societal level for allostatic load. Not only are ethnic minorities exposed to a larger number of stressors, but some of the types of stressors they experience are also unique. In our overview of stress exposure, it is important to acknowledge that our discussion is not nearly complete. For example, we have not discussed acculturative stress or systemic inequities in health care access, because we chose to look at examples where relationships with allostatic load have been investigated. Importantly, as work in the field progresses, consideration of the unique stressors ethnic-minority populations have to contend with will be crucial to understanding racial and ethnic health disparities. In the next section we move from the societal to the familial level, and discuss how poverty can influence psychosocial factors.

Social and Family Processes

Psychosocial influences, such as family, communities and even larger societies, play a pivotal role in how poverty and its associated stressors are experienced. In this section we focus on two social processes that may differ at the cultural level and are likely to moderate the relationships among poverty, stress and allostatic load, namely parenting and social support.

Parenting Processes

Poverty can affect allostatic load through the sheer number of stressors it imposes. In addition, it influences important psychosocial processes that impact the development of the stress response, and disrupts parenting responses that offer protection against the effect of stressors. Here we take a life-course perspective and focus on parenting competencies and how they shape the developing stress system. From a developmental perspective, we discuss the importance of parenting behaviors early in development that are influential in shaping physiological stress reactivity (Gunnar & Quevedo, 2007), and their implications for allostatic load. We also discuss the importance of high-quality parenting as a buffer for the effects of poverty on allostatic load. We conclude with a discussion of how cultural differences in parenting practices may influence these pathways.

Parenting is compromised in a variety of ways in the context of poverty, including through harsher interactions, less responsivity, and poor modeling of stress regulation (Conger & Donnellan, 2007). These parenting behaviors directly shape children's stress physiology (Gunnar & Quevedo, 2007), and hence their allostatic load. Indeed, a large body of work argues that a primary mechanism by which poverty influences children's physical and mental health outcomes is through parenting (Conger & Donnellan, 2007). Parents from low-income families are more likely to engage in harsher and less responsive interactions with their children (Bradley & Corwyn, 2002). This parenting style may have direct effects on children's stress physiology as well as increasing certain types of psychological characteristics, such as vigilance and hostility, in children, which would have important ramifications for allostatic load. Investigators have demonstrated neuropsychological correlates of parenting in the brain that appear sensitive to experiences of childhood poverty (Kim, Ho, Evans, Liberzon, & Swain, 2015). The interplay between disadvantage, parenting and brain development is a ripe area for investigation of cultural and ethnic moderators, as parenting norms vary with background and, as indicated above, influence children's health and development.

While to the best of our knowledge no study has looked specifically at family conflict and allostatic load, a large body of work has examined physiological outcomes associated with family conflict. Children from high-conflict homes display higher levels of urinary catecholamines and higher blood pressure (Ballard, Cummins, & Larkin, 1993; Gottman & Katz, 1989). They also exhibit elevated cardiovascular reactivity (El-Sheikh & Harger, 2001), as well as elevated basal cortisol (Flinn & England, 1995) and parasympathetic withdrawal (Salomon, Matthews, & Allen, 2000). Data also suggest that children with parents who score highly on psychological control, using techniques such as guilt induction and love withdrawal to discipline children, have higher levels of cortisol (Doan et al., 2016). On the other hand, positive parent–child relations can buffer the impacts of childhood poverty on children's well-being. For example, cumulative risk is associated with greater levels of allostatic load, but only in children experiencing low maternal responsiveness (Evans, Kim, Ting, Tesher, & Shannis, 2007). Moreover, the effects of allostatic load on cognitive outcomes are moderated by levels of maternal responsiveness (Doan & Evans, 2011).

Social Support

While parenting styles and behaviors are pivotal during childhood, social support networks become influential later on in development. Higher SES is positively associated with higher rates of social cohesion (Coleman, 1988), and individuals from low-SES groups tend to have lower levels of social support (Berkman & Breslow, 1983). The role of social support in relation to health is powerful: people with lower levels of social support have substantially higher mortality rates (Kawachi, Kennedy, Lochner, & Prothrow-Stith, 1997) and more physical (Uchino, 2004) and mental (Cohen & Wills, 1985) health issues. Additionally, the combination of weak social networks, low social position, and poor coping abilities was linked to greater allostatic load (Glei, Goldman, Chuang, & Weinstein, 2007) in adults. Among elderly Taiwanese, robust social ties were associated with lower levels of AL (Seeman, Glei et al., 2004).

Culture may affect parenting and social support in multiple ways. Culture influences when and how parents care for children, the extent to which parents permit children freedom to explore, and parenting styles (nurturing or more authoritarian), behaviors, and practices. It can also influence the values parents hold, and hence the socialization strategies they use (Bornstein, 1991). One's culture can also shape one's understanding of oneself in relation to others (Kagitcibasi, 2005), and hence in essence who cares for children and in what ways. These factors may help to explain the extent to which culture influences how parenting in the context of poverty affects child physiological outcomes. For example, African Americans and Mexican Americans who are employed are much more likely than White American mothers to use members of the extended family to help raise their children (Uttal, 1999). This help from family members can buffer the effects of parental stress on child outcomes. Relatedly, familism, which encompasses loyalty to and reciprocity and solidarity with family members (Keller et al., 2006), could moderate the impact of poverty. For example, Latino families which endorse higher degrees of familism are characterized by positive interpersonal familial relationships, high family unity and social support, and close proximity with extended family members (Gaines et al., 1997; Keefe, 1984; Rueschenberg & Buriel, 1989; Sabogal, Marin, Otero-Sabogal, Marin, & Perez-Stable, 1987; Zayas & Solari, 1994).

Importantly, positive health outcomes, including health behaviors ranging from stopping smoking to taking up mammogram screening, have also been associated with higher levels of familism (Coonrod, Balacazar, Brady, Garcia, & Van Tine, 1999; Gil, Vega, & Biafora, 1998; Gil, Wagner, & Vega, 2000; Pabon, 1998; Suarez, 1994; Unger, Ritt-Olson, Teran, Huang, Hoffman, & Palmer, 2002). However, familism can be a double-edged sword. The obligations associated with higher levels of familism can lead, in certain contexts, to higher levels of stress (Kim, Knight, & Longmire, 2007). For example, if familism leads to increased "social obligations" rather than to voluntary ties, it may not confer health benefits. In addition to specific cultural values, culture imbues behaviors with meaning, so that the same behavior may have very different consequences across cultures (Lansford, Deater-Deckard, Dodge, Bates, & Pettit, 2004). If we look at corporal punishment, for example, there is some evidence to suggest that its normative use moderates its impact, so that in cultures where corporal punishment is common its negative effects are reduced (Lansford et al., 2005). In sum, cultural context shapes the availability of social resources.

Self-Regulatory and Coping Processes

There is tremendous variability across individuals with regard to exposure to stress, as well as to *the experience* of stress. Important factors that moderate whether an event is experienced as stressful, and thus moderate the stress and health link, are self-regulation and coping skills. Self-regulation, often defined as the capacity to modulate or inhibit one's behavior and emotions (Raffaelli, Crockett, & Shen, 2005), shapes how an individual experiences and responds to stress. Relatedly, coping is often defined as "changing cognitive and behavioral efforts to manage specific external and/or internal demands that are appraised as taxing or exceeding the resources of the person" (Lazarus & Folkman, 1984: 141).

Poverty disrupts self-regulatory processes such as emotion regulation, influences coping strategies (in press; Wadsworth & Santiago, 2008), and interferes with the ability to persist, to delay gratification and to activate working memory (Blair, 2010; Blair & Raver, 2012; Doan & Evans, 2011). The impact of poverty on the brain areas associated with self-regulatory processes is extensive (Hackman, Farah, & Meaney, 2010). Self-regulatory processes have direct effects on stress and physiological functioning, but also lead to maladaptive health behaviors that have negative effects on physiological functioning (Doan, Fuller-Rowell, & Evans, 2012).

One's culture, race, and ethnicity are likely to impact these cognitive and affective processes in multiple ways. First, the increased stress brought about by living in a minority in the US is likely to disrupt the development of self-regulation (Blair, 2010). Additionally, persistence in the context of adversity can come at a cost. In a recent study, for example, Brody and colleagues (2013) demonstrated a fascinating paradox. They looked at Black youth living in the rural South, and examined the relationships among self-regulation, adjustment, and allostatic load. Results revealed that under conditions of high risk, those who had lower levels of adjustment problems also had higher levels of allostatic load. These results suggest that psychosocial competence comes at a physiological cost (Brody et al., 2013). This style of high-effort coping is also thought to explain ethnic differences in allostatic load (Geronimus et al., 2006). Poverty and stress can also lead to disengagement coping styles, which in turn can have consequences for allostatic load (Fernandez et al., 2015).

While minority status may be a risk factor, certain cultural values may enhance self-regulatory abilities and thus have the potential to buffer against the effects of stress. For example, cultures that value interdependence, in which conformity to societal rules and the suppression of potential divisive emotion are important, are likely to socialize children in a way that emphasizes higher levels of self-control and provides children with ample opportunities to practice and exercise these abilities. Consistently with this perspective, data suggest that Asian children, for example, have higher levels of self-control than their European-American peers (Lan, Legare, Ponitz, Li, & Morrison, 2011; Sabbagh, Xu, Carlson, Moses, & Lee, 2006). However, the extent to which these improved self-control abilities influence how children from different cultural backgrounds handle stress has yet to be determined.

Finally, culture influences types of coping styles. There is some support for the idea that individuals from cultures which value interdependence are more likely to use passive (Bjorck, Cuthbertson, Thurman, & Lee, 2001) and avoidant (Ting-Toomey et al., 1991; Trubisky, Ting-Toomey, & Lin, 1991) coping, whereas individuals from cultures that value independence are more likely to engage in problem-focused coping (Essau & Trommsdorff, 1996). Utsey, Bolden, Lanier, and Williams (2007) investigated African Americans' culture-specific coping skills, as well as traditional resilience factors. Their results demonstrated that, above and beyond traditional predictive factors, spiritual and collective coping were significant predictors of quality-of-life outcomes. These different types of coping styles may affect health and allostatic load. For example, in a sample of African Americans, use of a disengagement coping style was associated with higher allostatic load in females (Fernandez et al., 2015).

Another implication of cultural variation in the degree of collectivism–individualism for research on poverty and chronic stress may be the importance of relative deprivation in these different cultural contexts. An emerging line of work in both medicine and the social sciences argues that relative deprivation, or how one's own or one's family's social status compares with that of one's community or a larger aggregate (for example the nation), may be more critical than absolute material deprivation (Wilkinson & Pickett, 2009). Although there are weaknesses in this argument (for example, relative inequality in income alone ignores other critical variables such as education), the role of individual and community adherence to collectivist rather than individualist beliefs could be a powerful influence on the degree to which one's views of oneself relative to others shapes one's experiences and one's responses to disadvantage.

Conclusions and Future Directions

Recent conceptualizations of stress and health have used the allostatic load framework to explain how psychosocial factors may become biologically embedded and affect mental and physical health. This body of work, however, has mostly ignored the role of culture, race, and ethnicity. In this chapter, we have discussed how culture gives meaning to the social worlds in which people live their lives, and is therefore central to defining and structuring the social determinants of health. One's culture and ethnic background shape both the nature of exposure to stress and how it is experienced.

Our review also highlights the limitations of research that examines how culture, race and ethnicity influence the experience of poverty and hence stress and allostatic load. This is particularly problematic because minorities are overrepresented in the context of poverty. We highlight several important dimensions that may shape the relationship between poverty and allostatic load. In particular, we argue that ethnic minority status and one's cultural background confer important risk and protective factors. Specifically, while ethnic minority status may affect the number of stressors as well as their influence, certain cultural values and systems of meaning may *attenuate* the impact of stress. Research on allostatic load that took the cultural framework into account would improve our understanding of the universality and generalizability of the model, and provide valuable insights into the extent to which interventions should be culturally tailored.

Importantly, the work is also limited by the fact that very few studies have looked at allostatic load in countries outside of the US, which makes it extremely difficult to generalize the pattern of findings. The few that have suggest that the results may vary as a function of country. Hu and colleagues found no direct results of SES on allostatic load after controlling for sex and age (Hu, Wagle, Goldman, Weinstein, & Seeman, 2007). Moreover, contrary to the research that focuses on US participants (Seeman, Crimmins et al., 2004), studies using Taiwanese participants did not find that allostatic load played a mediating role in explaining the SES gradient in health outcomes (Dowd & Goldman, 2006). These data suggest that a different pathway may link SES and health in Taiwan than in the US.

Another limitation of the current research is that few studies have delineated mechanisms to explain why and how poverty leads to allostatic load. It is unclear whether poverty leads to a dysregulated stress response; perhaps the link is through maladaptive health behaviors. In particular, we have focused on the mechanisms that have been most extensively studied in the literature as well as having a theoretical or empirical basis for explaining the influence of culture. Yet at the same time this area of research is still underexplored; future research should focus on factors such as health behaviors, including sleep, physical activity, alcohol consumption and smoking, which are likely to be influenced by poverty as well as shaped by social norms. Greater understanding of both specific mechanisms, as well as of the ways in which cultural factors may exacerbate or mitigate the effects of poverty on allostatic load, would lead to more effective and culturally sensitive interventions.

References

Acevedo-Garcia, D., Osypuk, T. L., McArdle, N., & Williams, D. R. (2008). Toward a policy-relevant analysis of geographic and racial/ethnic disparities in child health. *Health Affairs, 27*(2), 321–333. doi:10.1377/hlthaff.27.2.321

Ballard, M. E., Cummings, E. M., & Larkin, K. (1993). Emotional and cardiovascular responses to adults' angry behavior and to challenging tasks in children of hypertensive and normotensive parents. *Child Development, 64*(2), 500–515. doi:10.1111/j.1467-8624.1993.tb02924.x

Bradley, R. H., & Corwyn, R. F. (2002). Socioeconomic status and child development. *Annual Review of Psychology, 53*(1), 371–399. doi:10.1146/annurev.psych.53.100901.135233

Berkman, L. F., & Breslow, L. (1983). *Health and ways of living: The Alameda County study*. New York: Oxford University Press.

Bjorck, J. P., Cuthbertson, W., Thurman, J. W., & Lee, Y. S. (2001). Ethnicity, coping, and distress among Korean Americans, Filipino Americans, and Caucasian Americans. *Journal of Social Psychology, 141*(4), 421–442. doi:10.1080/00224540109600563

Blair, C. (2010). Stress and the development of self-regulation in context. *Child Development Perspectives, 4*(3), 181–188. doi:10.1111/j.1750-8606.2010.00145.x

Blair, C., & Raver, C. C. (2012). Child development in the context of adversity: Experiential canalization of brain and behavior. *American Psychologist, 67*(4), 309–318. doi:10.1037/a0027493

Bornstein, M. H. (1991). *Cultural approaches to parenting*. Hillsdale, NJ: Psychology Press. doi:10.1080/15295192.2012.683359

Brody, G. H., Lei, M. K., Chae, D. H., Yu, T., Kogan, S. M., & Beach, S. R. (2014). Perceived discrimination among African American adolescents and allostatic load: A longitudinal analysis with buffering effects. *Child Development, 85*(3), 989–1002. doi:10.1111/cdev.12213

Brody, G. H., Yu, T., Chen, E., Miller, G. E., Kogan, S. M., & Beach, S. R. (2013). Is resilience only skin deep? Rural African Americans' socioeconomic status–related risk and competence in preadolescence and psychological adjustment and allostatic load at age 19. *Psychological Science, 24*(7), 1285–1293. doi:10.1177/0956797612471954

Carlson, E. D., & Chamberlain, R. M. (2005). Allostatic load and health disparities: A theoretical orientation. *Research in Nursing and Health, 28*(4), 306–315. doi:10.1002/nur.20084

Chyu, L., & Upchurch, D. M. (2011). Racial and ethnic patterns of allostatic load among adult women in the United States: Findings from the National Health and Nutrition Examination Survey 1999–2004. *Journal of Women's Health, 20*(4), 575–583. doi:10.1089/jwh.2010.2170

Cohen, S., & Wills, T. A. (1985). Stress, social support, and the buffering hypothesis. *Psychological Bulletin, 98*(2), 310–357. doi:10.1037/a0032501

Coleman, J. S. (1988). Social capital in the creation of human capital. *American Journal of Sociology, 94*, Supplement: Organizations and institutions: Sociological and economic approaches to the analysis of social structure, S95–S120.

Conger, R. D., & Donnellan, M. B. (2007). An interactionist perspective on the socioeconomic context of human development. *Annual Review of Psychology, 58*, 175–199. doi:10.1146/annurev.psych.58.110405.085551

Coonrod, D. V., Balcazar, H., Brady, J., Garcia, S., & Van Tine, M. (1999). Smoking, acculturation and family cohesion in Mexican-American women. *Ethnic Discourse, 9*(3), 434–440.

Crimmins, E. M., Johnston, M., Hayward, M., & Seeman, T. (2003). Age differences in allostatic load: An index of physiological dysregulation. *Experimental Gerontology, 38*(7), 731–734. doi:10.1016/S0531-5565(03)00099-8

Crimmins, E. M., Kim, J. K., Alley, D. E., Karlamangla, A., & Seeman, T. (2007). Hispanic paradox in biological risk profiles. *American Journal of Public Health, 97*(7), 1305–1310. doi:10.2105/AJPH.2006.091892

Doamekpor, L. A., & Dinwiddie, G. Y. (2015). Allostatic load in foreign-born and US-born Blacks: Evidence from the 2001–2010 National Health and Nutrition Examination Survey. *American Journal of Public Health, 105*(3), 591–597. doi:10.2105/AJPH.2014.302285

Doan, S. N., & Evans, G. W. (2011). Maternal responsiveness moderates the relationship between allostatic load and working memory. *Development and Psychopathology, 23*(3), 873–880. doi:10.1017/S0954579411000368

Doan, S. N., Fuller-Rowell, T. E., & Evans, G. W. (2012). Cumulative risk and adolescent's internalizing and externalizing problems: The mediating roles of maternal responsiveness and self-regulation. *Developmental Psychology, 48*(6), 1529–1539. doi:10.1037/a0027815

Doan, S. N., Tardif, T., Miller, A., Olson, S., Kessler, D., Felt, B., & Wang, L. (2016). Consequences of "tiger" parenting: A cross-cultural study of maternal psychological control and children's cortisol stress response. *Developmental Science*. Advance online publication. doi:10.1111/desc.12404

Dohrenwend, B. P., & Dohrenwend, B. S. (1969). *Social status and psychological disorder: A causal inquiry*. New York: Wiley-Interscience.

Dowd, J. B., & Goldman, N. (2006) Do biomarkers of stress mediate the relation between socioeconomic status and health? *Journal of Epidemiological and Community Health, 60*, 633–639. doi:10.1136/jech.2005.040816

El-Sheikh, M., & Harger, J. (2001). Appraisals of marital conflict and children's adjustment, health, and physiological reactivity. *Developmental Psychology, 37*(6), 875–885. doi:10.1037/0012-1649.37.6.875

Essau, C. A., & Trommsdorff, G. (1996). Coping with university-related problems: A cross-cultural comparison. *Journal of Cross-Cultural Psychology, 27*(3), 315–328. doi:10.1177/0022022196273004

Evans, G. W. (2003). A multimethodological analysis of cumulative risk and allostatic load among rural children. *Developmental Psychology, 39*(5), 924–933. doi:10.1037/0012-1649.39.5.924

Evans, G. W., & Kim, P. (2012). Childhood poverty and young adults' allostatic load: The mediating role of childhood cumulative risk exposure. *Psychological Science, 23*(9), 979–983. doi:10.1177/0956797612441218

Evans, G. W., & Kim, P. (2013). Childhood poverty, chronic stress, self-regulation and coping. *Child Development Perspectives, 7*, 43–48. doi:10.1111/cdep.12013

Evans, G. W., Kim, P., Ting, A. H., Tesher, H. B., & Shannis, D. (2007). Cumulative risk, maternal responsiveness, and allostatic load among young adolescents. *Developmental Psychology, 43*(2), 341–351. doi.org/10.1037/0012-1649.43.2.341

Fernandez, C. A., Loucks, E. B., Arheart, K. L., Hickson, D. A., Kohn, R., Buka, S. L., & Gjelsvik, A. (2015). Evaluating the effects of coping style on allostatic load, by sex: The Jackson Heart Study, 2000–2004. *Preventing Chronic Disease, 12*. doi:10.5888/pcd12.150166

Flinn, M. V., & England, B. G. (1995). Childhood stress and family environment. *Current Anthropology, 36*(5), 854–866.

Gaines, S. O., Jr, Marelich, W. D., Bledsoe, K. L., Steers, W. N., Henderson, M. C., Granrose, C. S., … & Page, M. S. (1997). Links between race/ethnicity and cultural values as mediated by racial/ethnic identity and moderated by gender. *Journal of Personality and Social Psychology, 72*(6), 1460–1476. doi:10.1037/0022-3514.72.6.1460

Ganzel, B. L., Morris, P. A., & Wethington, E. (2010). Allostasis and the human brain: Integrating models of stress from the social and life sciences. *Psychological Review, 117*, 134–174. doi:10.1037/a0017773

Gee, G. C., Spencer, M., Chen, J., Yip, T., & Takeuchi, D. T. (2007). The association between self-reported racial discrimination and 12-month DSM-IV mental disorders among Asian Americans nationwide. *Social Science and Medicine, 64*(10), 1984–1996. doi:10.1016/j.socscimed.2007.02.013

Geronimus, A. T., Hicken, M., Keene, D., & Bound, J. (2006). "Weathering" and age patterns of allostatic load scores among Blacks and Whites in the United States. *American Journal of Public Health, 96*(5), 826–833. doi:10.2105/AJPH.2004.060749

Gil, A. G., Vega, W. A., & Biafora, F. (1998). Temporal influences of family structure and family risk factors on drug use initiation in a multiethnic sample of adolescent boys. *Journal of Youth and Adolescence, 27*, 373–393. doi:10.1023/A:1022807221074

Gil, A. G., Wagner, E. F., & Vega, W. A. (2000). Acculturation, familism and alcohol use among Latino adolescent males: Longitudinal relations. *Journal of Community Psychology, 28*, 443–458. doi:10.1002/1520-6629(200007)28:4<443::AID-JCOP6>3.0.CO;2-A

Glei, D. A., Goldman, N., Chuang, Y. L., & Weinstein, M. (2007). Do chronic stressors lead to physiological dysregulation? Testing the theory of allostatic load. *Psychosomatic Medicine, 69*(8), 769–776. doi:10.1097/PSY.0b013e318157cba6

Gottman, J. M., & Katz, L. F. (1989). Effects of marital discord on young children's peer interaction and health. *Developmental Psychology, 25*(3), 373–381. doi:10.1037/0012-1649.25.3.373

Gruenewald, T. L., Karlamangla, A. S., Hu, P., Stein-Merkin, S., Crandall, C., Koretz, B., & Seeman, T. E. (2012). History of socioeconomic disadvantage and allostatic load in later life. *Social Science and Medicine, 74*(1), 75–83. doi:10.1016/j.socscimed.2011.09.037

Gunnar, M. R., & Quevedo, K. M. (2007). Early care experiences and HPA axis regulation in children: A mechanism for later trauma vulnerability. *Progress in Brain Research, 167*, 137–149. doi:10.1016/S0079-6123(07)67010-1

Gustafsson, P. E., Janlert, U., Theorell, T., Westerlund, H., & Hammarström, A. (2011). Socioeconomic status over the life course and allostatic load in adulthood: Results from the Northern Swedish Cohort. *Journal of Epidemiology and Community Health, 65*(11), 986–992. doi:10.1136/jech.2010.108332

Gustafsson, P. E., San Sebastian, M., Janlert, U., Theorell, T., Westerlund, H., & Hammarström, A. (2014). Life-course accumulation of neighborhood disadvantage and allostatic load: Empirical integration of three social determinants of health frameworks. *American Journal of Public Health, 104*(5), 904–910. doi: 10.2105/AJPH.2013.301707F

Guyll, M., Matthews, K. A., & Bromberger, J. T. (2001). Discrimination and unfair treatment: Relationship to cardiovascular reactivity among African American and European American women. *Health Psychology, 20*(5), 315–325. doi:10.1037/0278-6133.20.5.315

Hackman, D. A., Farah, M. J., & Meaney, M. J. (2010). Socioeconomic status and the brain: Mechanistic insights from human and animal research. *Nature Reviews Neuroscience, 11*(9), 651–659. doi:10.1038/nrn2897

Hawkley, L. C., Lavelle, L. A., Berntson, G. G., & Cacioppo, J. T. (2011). Mediators of the relationship between socioeconomic status and allostatic load in the Chicago Health, Aging, and Social Relations Study (CHASRS). *Psychophysiology, 48*(8), 1134–1145. doi:10.1111/j.1469-8986.2011.01185.x

Hu, P., Wagle, N., Goldman, N., Weinstein, M., & Seeman, T. E. (2007). The associations between socioeconomic status, allostatic load and measures of health in older Taiwanese persons: Taiwan social environment and biomarkers of aging study. *Journal of Biosocial Science, 39*, 545–56. doi:10.1017/S0021932006001556

Jargowsky, P. (2015). Architecture of segregation: Civil unrest, the concentration of poverty, and public policy. Race and Inequality Report, The Century Foundation.

Johnson, S. G., Riis, J. L., & Noble, K. G. (2016). State of the art review: Poverty and the developing brain. *Pediatrics, 137*, e20153075

Kaestner, R., Pearson, J. A., Keene, D., & Geronimus, A. T. (2009). Stress, allostatic load, and health of Mexican immigrants. *Social Science Quarterly, 90*(5), 1089–1111. doi:10.1111/j.1540-6237.2009.00648.x

Kagitcibasi, C. (2005). Autonomy and relatedness in cultural context implications for self and family. *Journal of Cross-Cultural Psychology, 36*(4), 403–422. doi:10.1177/0022022105275959

Karlamangla, A. S., Singer, B. H., & Seeman, T. E. (2006). Reduction in allostatic load in older adults is associated with lower all-cause mortality risk: MacArthur studies of successful aging. *Psychosomatic Medicine, 68*(3), 500–507. doi:10.1097/01.psy.0000221270.93985.82

Kawachi, I., Kennedy, B. P., Lochner, K., & Prothrow-Stith, D. (1997). Social capital, income inequality, and mortality. *American Journal of Public Health, 87*(9), 1491–1498. doi:10.2105/AJPH.87.9.1491

Keefe, S. E. (1984). Real and ideal extended familism among Latinos and Anglo Americans: On the meaning of "close" family ties. *Human Organization, 43*, 65–70. doi:10.17730/humo.43.1.y5546831728vn6kp

Keller, H., Lamm, B., Abels, M., Yovsi, R., Borke, J., Jensen, H., … & Su, Y. (2006). Cultural models, socialization goals, and parenting ethnotheories: A multicultural analysis. *Journal of Cross-Cultural Psychology, 37*(2), 155–172. doi:10.1177/0022022105284494

Kim, J. H., Knight, B. G., & Longmire, C. V. F. (2007). The role of familism in stress and coping processes among African American and White dementia caregivers: Effects on mental and physical health. *Health Psychology, 26*(5), 564–576. doi:10.1037/0278-6133.26.5.564

Kim, P., Evans, G. W., Chen, E., Miller, G. E., & Seeman, T. E. (in press). How socioeconomic disadvantages get under the skin and into the brain across the lifespan. In N. Halfon, C. Forrest, R. Lerner, & E. Faustman (Eds.), *The handbook of life course health development*. New York: Springer.

Kim, P., Ho, S. S., Evans, G. W., Liberzon, I., & Swain, J. E. (2015). Childhood social inequalities influence neural processes in young adult caregiving. *Developmental Psychobiology, 57*, 948–960. doi:10.1002/dev.21325

Kim, P., Neuendorf, C., Bianco, H., & Evans, G. W. (in press). Exposure to childhood poverty and mental health symptomatology in adolescence: A role of coping strategies. *Stress and Health.*

Kubzansky, L. D., Kawachi, I., & Sparrow, D. (1999). Socioeconomic status, hostility, and risk factor clustering in the Normative Aging Study: Any help from the concept of allostatic load? *Annals of Behavioral Medicine, 21*, 330–338. doi:10.1007/BF02895966

Lan, X., Legare, C. H., Ponitz, C. C., Li, S., & Morrison, F. J. (2011). Investigating the links between the subcomponents of executive function and academic achievement: A cross-cultural analysis of Chinese and American preschoolers. *Journal of Experimental Child Psychology, 108*(3), 677–692. doi:10.1016/j.jecp.2010.11.001

Lansford, J. E., Chang, L., Dodge, K. A., Malone, P. S., Oburu, P., Palmérus, K., … & Tapanya, S. (2005). Physical discipline and children's adjustment: Cultural normativeness as a moderator. *Child Development, 76*(6), 1234–1246. doi:10.1111/j.1467-8624.2005.00847.x

Lansford, J. E., Deater-Deckard, K., Dodge, K. A., Bates, J. E., & Pettit, G. S. (2004). Ethnic differences in the link between physical discipline and later adolescent externalizing behaviors. *Journal of Child Psychology and Psychiatry, 45*(4), 801–812. doi:10.1111/j.1469-7610.2004.00273.x

Lazarus, R. S., & Folkman, S. (1984). *Stress, appraisal, and coping.* New York: Springer.

Lu, M. C., & Chen, B. (2004). Racial and ethnic disparities in preterm birth: The role of stressful life events. *American Journal of Obstetrics and Gynecology, 191*(3), 691–699. doi:10.1016/j.ajog.2004.04.018

Luby, J., Belden, A., Botteron, K., Marrus, N., Harms, M. P., Babb, C., … & Barch, D. (2013). The effects of poverty on childhood brain development: The mediating effect of caregiving and stressful life events. *JAMA Pediatrics, 167*(12), 1135–1142. doi:10.1001/jamapediatrics.2013.3139.

Mays, V. M., Cochran, S. D., & Barnes, N. W. (2007). Race, race-based discrimination, and health outcomes among African Americans. *Annual Review of Psychology, 58*, 201–225. doi:10.1146/annurev.psych.57.102904.190212

McEwen, B. S. (1998). Stress, adaptation, and disease: Allostasis and allostatic load. *Annals of the New York Academy of Sciences, 840*(1), 33–44. doi:10.1111/j.1749-6632.1998.tb09546.x

McEwen, B. S. (2000). The neurobiology of stress: From serendipity to clinical relevance. *Brain Research, 886*(1), 172–189. doi:10.1016/S0006-8993(00)02950-4

McEwen, B.S. (2012). Brain on stress: How the social environment gets under the skin. *Proceedings of the National Academy of Sciences, 109,* 17180–17185. doi:10.1073/pnas.1121254109

Merkin, S. S., Basurto-Dávila, R., Karlamangla, A., Bird, C. E., Lurie, N., Escarce, J., & Seeman, T. (2009). Neighborhoods and cumulative biological risk profiles by race/ethnicity in a national sample of US adults: NHANES III. *Annals of Epidemiology, 19*(3), 194–201. doi:10.1016/j.annepidem.2008.12.006

Milanovic, B. (2013). Global income inequality in numbers: In history and now. *Global Policy, 4*(2), 198–208. doi:10.1111/1758-5899.12032

Miller, G. E., & Chen, E. (2013). The biological residue of childhood poverty. *Child Development Perspectives, 7*(2), 67–73. doi: 10.1111/cdep.12021

Ong, A. D., Williams, D. R., Nwizu, U., & Gruenewald, T. (2017). Everyday unfair treatment and multisystem biological dysregulation in African American adults. *Cultural Diversity and Ethnic Minority Psychology, 23*(1), 27–35.

Pabon, E. (1998). Hispanic adolescent delinquency and the family: A discussion of sociocultural influences. *Adolescence, 33*(132), 941–955.

Peek, M. K., Cutchin, M. P., Salinas, J. J., Sheffield, K. M., Eschbach, K., Stowe, R. P., & Goodwin, J. S. (2010). Allostatic load among non-Hispanic whites, non-Hispanic Blacks, and people of Mexican origin: Effects of ethnicity, nativity, and acculturation. *American Journal of Public Health, 100*(5), 940–946. doi: 10.2105/AJPH.2007.129312

Raffaelli, M., Crockett, L. J., & Shen, Y. L. (2005). Developmental stability and change in self-regulation from childhood to adolescence. *Journal of Genetic Psychology, 166*(1), 54–76. doi: 10.3200/GNTP.166.1.54-76

Reardon, S.F., Fox, L., & Townsend, J. (2015). Neighborhood income composition by race and income, 1990–2009. *Annals of the American Academy of Political and Social Science, 660,* 78–97.

Rueschenberg E., & Buriel, R. (1989). Mexican American family functioning and acculturation: A family systems perspective. *Hispanic Journal of Behavioral Sciences, 11*(3), 232–244. doi:10.1177/07399863890113002

Sabbagh, M. A., Xu, F., Carlson, S. M., Moses, L. J., & Lee, K. (2006). The development of executive functioning and theory of mind: A comparison of Chinese and US preschoolers. *Psychological Science, 17*(1), 74–81. doi:10.1111/j.1467-9280.2005.01667.x

Sabogal, F., Marin, G., Otero-Sabogal, R., Marin, B. V., & Perez-Stable, E. J. (1987). Hispanic familism and acculturation: What changes and what doesn't? *Hispanic Journal of Behavioral Sciences, 9*(4), 397–412. doi:10.1080/13607860802224227

Salomon, K., Matthews, K. A., & Allen, M. T. (2000). Patterns of sympathetic and parasympathetic reactivity in a sample of children and adolescents. *Psychophysiology, 37*(6), 842–849. doi:10.1111/1469-8986.3760842

Seeman, T. E., Crimmins, E., Huang, M.-H., Singer, B., Bucur, A., Gruenewald, T. … & Reuben, D. B. (2004). Cumulative biological risk and socio-economic differences in mortality: MacArthur studies of successful aging. *Social Science and Medicine, 58*(10), 1985–1997. doi:10.1016/S0277-9536(03)00402-7

Seeman, T., Glei, D., Goldman, N., Weinstein, M., Singer, B., & Lin, Y. H. (2004). Social relationships and allostatic load in Taiwanese elderly and near elderly. *Social Science and Medicine, 59*(11), 2245–2257. doi:10.1016/j.socscimed.2004.03.027

Seeman, M., Merkin, S. S., Karlamangla, A., Koretz, B., & Seeman, T. (2014). Social status and biological dysregulation: The "status syndrome" and allostatic load. *Social Science and Medicine, 118*, 143–151. doi:10.1016/j.socscimed.2014.08.002

Seeman, T. E., Singer, B. H., Rowe, J. W., Horwitz, R. I., & McEwen, B. S. (1997). Price of adaptation – allostatic load and its health consequences: MacArthur studies of successful aging. *Archives of Internal Medicine, 157*(19), 2259–2268. doi:10.1001/archinte.1997.00440400111013

Selye, H. (2013). *Stress in health and disease.* Boston, MA: Butterworths.

Singer, B., & Ryff, C. D. (1999). Hierarchies of life histories and associated health risks. *Annals of the New York Academy of Sciences, 896*(1), 96–115. doi:10.1111/j.1749-6632.1999.tb08108.x

Slopen, N., Lewis, T. T., Gruenewald, T. L., Mujahid, M. S., Ryff, C. D., Albert, M. A., & Williams, D. R. (2010). Early life adversity and inflammation in African Americans and whites in the midlife in the United States survey. *Psychosomatic Medicine, 72*(7), 694–701. doi:10.1097/PSY.0b013e3181e9c16f

Suarez, L. (1994). Pap smear and mammogram screening in Mexican-American women: The effects of acculturation. *American Journal of Public Health, 84*(5), 742–746. doi:10.2105/AJPH.84.5.742

Theall, K. P., Drury, S. S., & Shirtcliff, E. A. (2012). Cumulative neighborhood risk of psychosocial stress and allostatic load in adolescents. *American Journal of Epidemiology, 176* (suppl. 7), S164–S174. doi:10.1093/aje/kws185

Ting-Toomey, S., Gao, G., Trubisky, P., Yang, Z., Kim, H., S. Lin, S. L., & Nishida, T. (1991). Culture, face maintenance, and styles of handling interpersonal conflict: A study in five cultures. *International Journal of Conflict Management, 2*(4), 275–296. doi:10.1108/eb022702

Torres, L., Driscoll, M. W., & Burrow, A. L. (2010). Microaggressions and psychological functioning among high achieving African-Americans: A mixed-methods approach. *Journal of Social and Clinical Psychology, 29*(10), 1074–1099.

Trubisky, P., Ting-Toomey, S., & Lin, S. L. (1991). The influence of individualism–collectivism and self-monitoring on conflict styles. *International Journal of Intercultural Relations, 15*(1), 65–84. doi:10.1016/0147-1767(91)90074-Q

Turner, R. J., & Avison, W. R. (2003). Status variations in stress exposure: Implications for the interpretation of research on race, socioeconomic status, and gender. *Journal of Health and Social Behavior, 44*(5), 488–505.

Turner, R. J., & Lloyd, D. A. (2004). Stress burden and the lifetime incidence of psychiatric disorder in young adults: Racial and ethnic contrasts. *Archives of General Psychiatry, 61*(5), 481–488.

Uchino, B. N. (2004). *Social support and physical health: Understanding the health consequences of relationships.* New Haven, CT: Yale University Press.

Uhlenhuth, E. H., & Paykel, E. S. (1973). Symptom intensity and life events. *Archives of General Psychiatry, 28*(4), 473–477. doi:10.1001/archpsyc.1973.01750340015002

Unger, J. B., Ritt-Olson, A., Teran, L., Huang, T., Hoffman, B. R., & Palmer, P. (2002). Cultural values and substance use in a multiethnic sample of California adolescents. *Addiction Research and Theory, 10*(3), 257–279. doi: 10.1080/16066350211869

Utsey, S., Bolden, M., Lanier, Y., & Williams, O. (2007). Examining the role of culture-specific coping as a predictor of resilient outcomes in African Americans from high-risk urban communities. *Journal of Black Psychology, 33*, 75–83. doi:10.1177/0095798406295094

Uttal, L. (1999). Using kin for child care: Embedment in the socioeconomic networks of extended families. *Journal of Marriage and Family, 61*(4), 845–857. doi:10.2307/354007

Wadsworth, M. E., & Santiago, C.D. (2008). Risk and resiliency processes in ethnically diverse families in poverty. *Journal of Family Psychology, 22*, 399–410. doi:10.1037/0893-3200.22.3.399

Williams, D. R., & Mohammed, S. A. (2009). Discrimination and racial disparities in health: Evidence and needed research. *Journal of Behavioral Medicine, 32*(1), 20–47. doi:10.1007/s10865-008-9185-0

Wilkinson, R. G., & Pickett, K. (2009). *The spirit level: Why greater equality makes societies stronger*. London: Allen Lane.

Yoshikawa, H., Aber, J. L., & Beardslee, W. R. (2012). The effects of poverty on the mental, emotional, and behavioral health of children and youth: Implications for prevention. *American Psychologist, 67*(4), 272. doi:10.1037/a0028015

Zayas, L. H., & Solari, F. (1994). Early childhood socialization in Hispanic families: Context, culture, and practice implications. *Professional Psychology: Research and Practice, 25*(3), 200–206. doi:10.1037/0735-7028.25.3.200

12

Biological Consequences of Unfair Treatment: A Theoretical and Empirical Review

Anthony D. Ong, Saarang Deshpande, and David R. Williams

A substantial body of evidence implicates self-reported discrimination or unfair treatment as important determinants of mental and physical health. Summative reviews of the literature provide consistent evidence that repeated exposure to unfair treatment disrupts goal pursuit, undermines psychological well-being, and contributes to broad-based morbidity and mortality (Lewis, Cogburn, & Williams, 2015; Schmitt, Branscombe, Postmes, & Garcia, 2014; Williams & Mohammed, 2009). Whereas *lifetime unfair treatment* refers to acute, major experiences of discrimination across a variety of life domains, such as being unfairly denied a promotion or prevented from moving into a neighborhood, *everyday unfair treatment* captures the range of chronic, day-to-day experiences of discrimination, such as being followed around in stores or being treated with less courtesy or respect than others (Pascoe & Smart Richman, 2009; Williams & Mohammed, 2009).

Although earlier reviews have discussed the relation between unfair treatment and broad mental and physical health outcomes (Pascoe & Smart Richman, 2009; Williams & Mohammed, 2009), growing evidence suggests that coping with chronic, everyday mistreatment triggers a cascade of specific physiological responses that over time may place demands on the body's ability to respond to challenges effectively (Lewis et al., 2015; Mays, Cochran, & Barnes, 2007). For example, studies have found unfair treatment and discrimination to be associated with dysregulated blood pressure (Beatty & Matthews, 2009), excess adiposity (Hunte, 2011), coronary artery calcification (Troxel, Matthews, Bromberger, & Sutton-Tyrrell, 2003), and inflammation (Lewis, Aiello, Leurgans, Kelly, & Barnes, 2010).

The Handbook of Culture and Biology, First Edition. Edited by José M. Causadias, Eva H. Telzer and Nancy A. Gonzales.

Thus, a growing body of research suggests that experiences of discrimination are a form of psychosocial stress that has important biological consequences.

The primary aim of this chapter is to summarize the current state of the science on the biological correlates of unfair treatment. Building on earlier qualitative syntheses (Lewis et al., 2015; Williams & Mohammed, 2009) and meta-analytic findings (Pascoe & Smart Richman, 2009; Schmitt et al., 2014), we focus on what is known about the relationship between unfair treatment and markers of biological health, giving emphasis to the major approaches, empirical findings, and methodological gaps that currently exist in the literature.

Conceptualizing the Role of Unfair Treatment in Health

How might experiences of unfair treatment "get under the skin" to affect health and disease outcomes? Experiences of unfair treatment can arise from multiple sources, including racial/ethnic, gender, and age discrimination. Additionally, similarly to other forms of psychosocial stress, discriminatory stressors can be acute or chronic, occur across the life span, and have an adverse impact on both mental and physical health (Lewis et al., 2015). Pascoe and Smart Richman (2009) detailed three models or pathways through which discriminatory experiences may affect health. First, perceptions of unfair treatment can have a direct effect on health. This hypothesis is supported by extensive evidence that chronic exposure to unfair treatment increases the risk of premature morbidity and mortality (Lewis et al., 2015; Mays et al., 2007; Williams & Mohammed, 2009). Second, the relationship between unfair treatment and health can be mediated through key regulatory physiological systems (e.g., cardiovascular activity, stress hormones, immune responses) that, in turn, impact health and disease outcomes. This is consistent with the argument that chronic experiences of discrimination may increase physiological arousal and thus exacerbate underlying disease states (Mays et al., 2007). Finally, and consistently with the *cardiovascular reactivity hypothesis* (Krantz & Manuck, 1984), perceptions of unfair treatment may accentuate the effects of stressful events by decreasing resilience and depleting coping resources. Accordingly, unfair treatment may affect health by exacerbating the effects of short-term stressors and hastening long-term illness. In this review, we examine the relationship between unfair treatment and three regulatory physiological systems: cardiovascular, neuroendocrine, and immune function.

Defining and Measuring Biological Pathways

Cardiovascular Function

Blood pressure (BP) and heart rate (HR) are indicators of cardiovascular functioning. Temporary increases in BP and HR are natural and normal responses to ongoing demands and challenges. However, recurrent or prolonged activation of the cardiovascular system can result in levels of response (e.g., arterial calcification and inelasticity) that have the potential to increase the risk of adverse cardiovascular outcomes, including stroke and coronary heart disease (Blascovich & Katkin, 1993).

Neuroendocrine Function

The hypothalamic-pituitary-adrenal (HPA) axis is a primary neuroendocrine pathway. The hormones produced by the HPA axis influence a wide range of physiological, behavioral, and health outcomes and are considered key mediators of the association between psychological factors and physical health (McEwen, 1998). In particular, activation of the HPA axis involves a cascade of signals that results in the release of adrenocorticotropic hormone (ACTH) from the pituitary and of cortisol from the adrenal cortex. Dysregulation of the HPA axis contributes to processes that play a role in hypertension, atherosclerosis, and coronary heart disease. Our review focuses on diurnal cortisol rhythm and acute cortisol responses to unfair treatment, two key surrogate endpoints related to cardiovascular disease.

Immune Function

Experiences of unfair treatment can get under the skin to influence immunity via inflammation, which is the body's immediate response to infection and injury. Several inflammatory markers, including C-reactive protein (CRP), interleukin-6 (IL-6), and fibrinogen, have been examined as indicators of chronic disease risk. Persistent inflammation contributes to accumulating damage in tissues that surround sites of chronic infection and has been implicated as a central mechanism explaining how psychosocial factors can contribute to chronic disease, including atherosclerosis and cancer (Miller, Chen, & Cole, 2009).

Scope of the Review

In this chapter, we review evidence that examines the relationship between unfair treatment and biological pathways. To promote greater insight into the role of unfair treatment in biological health, the review is narrative rather than quantitative. Studies are organized according to the key regulatory physiological system: cardiovascular, neuroendocrine, or immune. To provide greater detail than is presented in the text, the review includes tables of lists of all the cross-sectional, longitudinal, ambulatory, and experimental studies that were located in the literature review. Cross-sectional studies examine the extent to which unfair treatment is associated with biological outcomes. Longitudinal studies explore whether previous levels of unfair treatment predict subsequent levels of physiological responses across more extended periods of time. Ambulatory studies, in comparison, use intensive repeated-measures methodology (e.g., momentary experience sampling) across several days or weeks to examine how within-person variation in unfair treatment and discrimination relates to biological processes. Finally, experimental studies simulate exposure to unfair treatment (e.g., films depicting racism) and evaluate whether induced transient states create alterations in physiological responses.

Database Sources and Study Screening

A comprehensive search for all available research on the topic was performed in four electronic bibliographic databases (MEDLINE in PubMed, PsycINFO, CINAHL, Web of Science). The search strategy included keywords drawn from commonly used instruments for measuring unfair treatment and discrimination, and a comprehensive list of biological health outcomes generated by the authors. Additional studies were identified through cited reference searching of included articles and known reviews. Full-text screening was performed on potentially relevant studies that were identified to meet inclusion criteria or for which criteria could not be established. To be included, a study had to (1) be a published empirical study (rather than a meta-analysis or theoretical review), (2) involve more than a single human subject, (3) include, as an independent variable, a measure of unfair treatment or discrimination or an experimental manipulation of unfair treatment (e.g., racial stressor, social rejection/social exclusion), and (4) include, as a dependent variable, an objective measure of biological functioning. Studies were excluded if they (1) used a single-case research design (e.g., a clinical case study), (2) assessed only the contemporaneous correlation between unfair treatment and physiological responses, or (3) examined only the effect of physiological functioning on unfair treatment or mean differences in unfair treatment between physiologically impaired and non-impaired samples.

Data Extraction and Study Characteristics

From the retrieved articles, 167 titles and abstracts were identified as potentially relevant and full texts were screened to determine eligibility. Eighty-two articles fulfilled the inclusion criteria and were therefore included. The 82 studies recruited a total of 63,303 respondents. The average age of the participants in each study ranged from 24 to 49 years old. Of the studies that reported gender composition, 15 (18.3%) had only female participants and five (6.1%) had only male participants. The majority of included studies were cross-sectional (n = 33, 40.2%), followed by experimental (n = 18, 22%) and ambulatory (n = 18, 22%) studies. In addition, we retrieved 13 (15.9%) longitudinal studies.

Unfair Treatment and Cardiovascular Functioning

Table 12.1 presents cross-sectional, longitudinal, ambulatory, and experimental studies that address the potential impact of unfair treatment on cardiovascular outcomes in healthy populations. Cross-sectional evidence linking unfair treatment to cardiovascular functioning has been reported in 29 previous studies. The majority of studies conceptualized unfair treatment by using single-administration, paper-and-pencil questionnaires. Among the cross-sectional studies reviewed, 11 (37.9%) controlled for potential psychological confounding factors, such as perceived stress or depressive symptoms, whereas the remainder (n = 18, 62.1%) did not control for psychological covariates when examining the association between unfair treatment and cardiovascular outcomes. Of note, 16 (55.2%) cross-sectional studies reported null findings (Akdeniz et al., 2014; Albert et al., 2008; Barksdale, Farrug, & Harkness, 2009; Brown, Matthews, Bromberger, & Chang, 2006; Chae, Lincoln, Adler, & Syme, 2010; R. Clark,

Table 12.1 Summary of unfair treatment and cardiovascular end points

Study	Unfair treatment	Endpoint	Covariates	Findings
Ambulatory studies				
Beatty & Matthews (2009)	Everyday unfair treatment	BP	Gender, race, BMI	Interaction of more unfair treatment and race is associated with higher night/day DBP ratio.
Beatty Moody et al. (2016)	Perceived ethnic discrimination	SBP and DBP	Gender, race, BMI, education, poverty level, cynical hostility, life stressors, smoking, caffeine and alcohol consumption	Greater perceived ethnic discrimination and older age predicted higher DBP.
Brondolo et al. (2008)	Perceived ethnic discrimination	ABP	Age, gender, race	Perceived racism and nocturnal ABP were positively associated.
R. Clark (2000)	Perceived racism	SBP, DBP, and recovery	Task-induced anxiety and anger, task and general stress, baseline DBP	Perceived racism positively predicted DBP changes, early recovery, and late recovery.
Gregoski et al. (2013)	Everyday discrimination	SBP and DBP nocturnal dipping	Age, gender, BMI, ethnicity	Interaction of everyday discrimination, endothelin-1 gene polymorphism, and ethnicity negatively predicted SBP and DBP nocturnal dipping.
Hill et al. (2007)	Perceived racism	SBP and DBP	Gender, BMI	Perceived racism in academic setting positively predicted daytime and night-time DBP.
Kaholokula et al. (2012)	Felt oppression	SBP and DBP	Age, sex, BMI, marital status, education, psychological stress, ethnicity, generational status	Felt oppression was positively correlated with SBP.

Matthews et al. (2005)	Perceived unfair treatment	SBP and DBP	Race, sex, BMI, study location, BP measurement position, physical activity, consumption	Mistreatment attributed to physical appearance was positively associated with ABP. No significant correlation of racial discrimination with ABP.
Richman et al. (2007)	Perceived discrimination	SBP, DBP, and HR	Age, gender, SES, BMI	Interaction of discrimination (past year) and discrimination (lifetime) with cynicism and optimism was associated with higher reactivity and slower recovery. The effect was larger for Blacks.
Singleton et al. (2008)	Perceived racism	SBP and DBP	Coping, BDI	Interaction of perceived racism and passive coping (avoidance) was positively correlated with overall and daytime SBP and DBP.
Smart Richman et al. (2010)	Perceived discrimination	SBP, DBP, and HR	Age, BMI, hostility, neuroticism	Perceived discrimination positively predicted slopes from SBP and DBP and negatively predicted nocturnal dipping in HR.
Tomfohr et al. (2010)	Everyday discrimination	SBP and DBP	Gender, race, BMI, SES, social desirability, hostility, marital status, alcohol consumption, smoking	Discrimination negatively predicted nocturnal SBP and DBP dipping.
Wagner et al. (2013)	Racial discrimination	Endothelial function	Baseline flow-mediated dilation, fasting glucose, lipid medication	Lifetime racial discrimination was negatively associated with recovery of endothelial function.

(*continued*)

Table 12.1 *(Continued)*

Study	Unfair treatment	Endpoint	Covariates	Findings
Cross-sectional studies				
Akdeniz et al. (2014)	Perceived discrimination	HR	Socio-demographic and task performance characteristics	No significant difference in HR for ethnic minorities and controls.
Albert et al. (2008)	Perceived racial/ethnic discrimination	Aortic plaque area, aortic wall thickness, and CAC	Age, HTN, type 2 diabetes, smoking, cholesterol, BMI, education, physical activity	No association of perceived racial or ethnic discrimination with aortic plaque area, aortic wall thickness, or CAC.
Barksdale et al. (2009)	Perceived racism	SBP and DBP	Frustration, sadness	No correlation between perceived racial discrimination and SBP or DBP.
Brown et al. (2006)	Everyday discrimination	SBP and DBP	Age, BMI, BP medication use, education, family HTN history	No significant correlation between discrimination and SBP. Low-magnitude, significant correlation between discrimination and DBP.
Chae et al. (2010)	Major experiences of discrimination	CVD history	Racial group attitudes	No significant relationship between more situations of racial discrimination and history of CVD.
Chae et al. (2012)	Major experiences of discrimination	CVD history	Mood disorder history	Interaction of racial discrimination with mood disorder history predicts history of CVD.
R. Clark (2006b)	Everyday discrimination	SBP and DBP	Age, BMI, gender	Interaction of perceived racism and trait anger positively predicts SBP and DBP.

R. Clark, Benkert, & Flack (2006)	Racism-related vigilance	LAE	Gender	No independent prediction of LAE and LAE reactivity by racism-related vigilance.
R. Clark & Gochett (2006)	Everyday discrimination	SBP and DBP	Age, BMI, coping response	No independent prediction of SBP or DBP by perceived racism. High perceived racism and high acceptance coping predicted lower SBP in Black youths.
Cooper et al. (2009)	Perceived discrimination	ET-1 levels	Resting MAP, BMI, social desirability, exercise	Interaction of discrimination and ethnicity significantly predicted ET-1 levels.
Din-Dziethamet al. (2004)	Race-based discrimination at work	SBP and DBP	Age, marital status, SES, BMI, coping	No association between race-based discrimination at work and SBP or DBP.
Eliezer et al. (2011)	Perceived personal gender discrimination	SBP and DBP	General anxiety, system-justifying beliefs	No independent prediction of SBP or DBP by perceived personal discrimination. Interaction of perceived personal discrimination and system-justifying beliefs predicted SBP and DBP.
Goosby et al. (2015)	Everyday discrimination	SBP and DBP	Age, gender, BMI, waist circumference, mother's education	Daily discrimination positively predicts SBP and DBP.
Hicken et al. (2014)	Racism-related vigilance	HTN by BP measurement	Age, gender, immigrant generation, SES, education	Interaction of racism-related vigilance with ethnicity was positively associated with hypertension prevalence.

(*continued*)

Table 12.1 *(Continued)*

Study	Unfair treatment	Endpoint	Covariates	Findings
Krieger et al. (2013)	Experiences of discrimination and structural discrimination	SBP	Age, gender, poverty level, education, social desirability, waist and hip circumference, smoking	No significant association between experiences of discrimination or structural discrimination and SBP.
Lepore et al. (2006)	Racial stressor	SBP, DBP, and HR	Age, BMI, smoking, immigrant status	Racial stressors were associated with DBP reactivity and marginally associated with SBP reactivity in Black women, compared with non-racial stressors.
McClure et al. (2010)	Discrimination-related stress	SBP and DBP	Age, BMI, waist circumference	Discrimination-related stress predicted higher SBP in men but not in women.
Nadimpalli, Cleland et al. (2016)	Everyday discrimination	SBP and DBP	Age, gender, employment, years in US, health insurance, income, education	No significant association between self-reported discrimination and SBP or DBP.
Nadimpalli, Dulin-Keita et al. (2016)	Everyday discrimination	SBP	Age, sex, education, workplace, household income, marital status, depressive symptoms, years in US, cultural beliefs, social support, English proficiency	No significant association between everyday discrimination and SBP.
Neblett & Carter (2012)	Racial discrimination	SBP, DBP, and MAP	Age, sex, study location, BMI, parent education, SES, physical and mental health	Interaction between discrimination and racial identity was negatively correlated with DBP. No significant correlation between racial discrimination and SBP, DBP, or MAP.

Ong et al. (2017)	Everyday discrimination	SBP, DBP, and HR	Age, gender, education, medication use, smoking, alcohol, depression, perceived stress	Everyday discrimination is positively associated with cardiovascular regulation outcomes.
Peters (2006)	Racial discrimination	SBP and DBP	Education, SES, trait anxiety and depression, emotional approach coping, trait anger	No significant relationship between perceived racism and SBP or DBP.
Poston et al. (2001)	Perceived racism	HTN by BP measurement	Age, BMI, birthplace	No significant association between perceived racism and HTN.
Roberts et al. (2008)	Perceived discrimination	HTN by BP measurement	BMI, education, occupation, psychosocial well-being, gender	Non-racial discrimination in women was significantly associated with HTN. No significant association between racial discrimination and HTN.
Ryan et al. (2006)	Perceived racial/ethnic discrimination	SBP and DBP	Age, gender, SES, education, employment, BMI, smoking, health insurance status, exercise, HTN medication use	Discrimination is significantly related to SBP in a U-shaped manner. The mean assessment of discrimination predicts the lowest SBP.
Sims et al. (2012)	Everyday, lifetime, and burden of discrimination	HTN by BP measurement	Age, gender, SES, BMI, CV risk factors	Lifetime discrimination and burden from discrimination were positively associated with HTN prevalence.
Troxel et al. (2003)	Unfair treatment	Intima-media thickness	Age, SBP composite stress, BMI, cholesterol, waist–hip ratio	Unfair treatment positively predicted intima-media thickness in Black women.
Tull et al. (1999)	Internalized racism	SBP and DBP	Age, education, anxiety, depression	No independent relation of internalized racism to SBP or DBP.

(*continued*)

Table 12.1 *(Continued)*

Study	Unfair treatment	Endpoint	Covariates	Findings
Utsey & Hook (2007)	Race-related stress	HR variability	Gender, psychological distress	No significant correlation between individual or institutional racism and HR variability.
Experimental studies				
Blascovich et al. (2001)	Stereotype threat	MAP	Baseline MAP, Remote Associates Test score	High stereotype threat led to a significant increase in MAP in Blacks.
R. Clark (2006a)	Racism	SBP and DBP	Age, BMI, smoking, income, HR, caffeine and alcohol consumption, task-induced anger and cynicism	Perceived racism positively predicts SBP.
V. R. Clark et al. (2005)	Racial profiling	SV and CO		Private regard (Black-oriented) positively predicted SV and CO.
Fang & Myers (2001)	Racial stressor	DBP and DBP reactivity	Ethnicity, order of tasks, BMI, resting SBP and DBP	Racial stressors significantly increased DBP and DBP reactivity compared with neutral stimuli.
Guyll et al. (2001)	Discrimination	SBP, DBP, and HR	Age, BMI, smoking, medication use	Discrimination was positively associated with baseline HR and DBP reactivity.
McNeilly et al. (1995)	Racist provocation	SBP, DBP, and HR	Height, weight, family HTN history, education	Racist provocation caused increased SBP, DBP, and HR.
Mendes et al. (2008)	Social rejection	CO, TPR, ventricular contractility	Race, evaluator race, negative emotion, performance	Social rejection significantly affected CO and TPR but not ventricular contractility.

Merritt et al. (2006)	Perceived racism	SBP, DBP, and HR	Age, BMI, smoking	Interaction of perceived racism with non-racist provocation caused increased DBP.
Salomon & Jagusztyn (2008)	Perceived ethnic discrimination	SBP, DBP, and HR	BMI, waist–hip ratio, US born, education, income, parents' education	Past discrimination was associated with higher SBP in Latinos and lower SBP in Whites. Interaction of ethnicity and attribution of discrimination to ethnicity predicted resting SBP and SBP reactivity.
Sawyer et al. (2012)	Prejudice and racism-related vigilance	SBP, DBP, MAP, HR, CO, TPR, pre-ejection period	Trait anxiety, depression, optimism	Prejudice (anticipation) caused increased SBP, DBP, MAP, and HR and decreased pre-ejection period. Prejudice (interaction) caused increased HR and decreased pre-ejection period.
Longitudinal studies				
Brody et al. (2014)	Racist events	SBP and DBP	SES, perceived stress, unhealthy behavior	Perceived discrimination predicts higher SBP. Interaction of perceived discrimination and emotional support predicts lower SBP and DBP.
De Vogli et al. (2007)	Unfairness	Incident coronary events	Age, gender, baseline physical functioning	Unfairness independently predicted increased coronary events.

(*continued*)

Table 12.1 *(Continued)*

Study	Unfair treatment	Endpoint	Covariates	Findings
Everage et al. (2012)	Racial discrimination	CAC	Age, gender, SEP, psychosocial variables, CHD risk factors	Racial discrimination and CAC were inversely associated.
Everson-Rose et al. (2015)	Lifetime discrimination	SBP	Age, race, sex, education, marital status, income, smoking, alcohol consumption	Lifetime discrimination was negatively correlated with SBP.
Lewis et al. (2006)	Everyday discrimination	CAC	Age, education, BMI	Chronic exposure to everyday discrimination was positively associated with the presence of CAC.
Peterson et al. (2016)	Everyday discrimination	Intima-media thickness and adventitial diameter	Age, race, SES, BMI, health behaviors, medication use	Discrimination was significantly related to intima-media thickness and adventitial diameter in Caucasian women but in no other demographic.

Benkert, & Flack, 2006; R. Clark & Gochett, 2006; Din-Dzietham, Nembhard, Collins, & Davis, 2004; Eliezer, Townsend, Sawyer, Major, & Mendes, 2011; Krieger et al., 2013; Nadimpalli, Cleland et al., 2016; Nadimpalli, Dulin-Keita, Salas, Kanaya, & Kandula, 2016; Peters, 2006; Poston et al., 2001; Tull et al., 1999; Utsey & Hook, 2007). Despite a limited set of studies ($n = 6$), longitudinal investigations provisionally support a link between unfair treatment and cardiovascular risk, demonstrating that this association holds even when the two variables are measured many years (ranging from 2 to 15) apart. Among the studies reviewed, four were consistent with theoretical predictions (Brody et al., 2014; De Vogli, Ferrie, Chandola, Kivimaki, & Marmot, 2007; Lewis et al., 2006; Peterson, Matthews, Derby, Bromberger, & Thurston, 2016) and two studies reported findings that opposed theoretical predictions (Everage, Gjelsvik, McGarvey, Linkletter, & Loucks, 2012; Everson-Rose et al., 2015). For example, in one study that followed more than 8,000 British civil servants aged 35–55 years for an average of 11 years, unfair treatment was a predictor of increased coronary events and impaired health functioning, independently of established risk factors of coronary heart disease (De Vogli et al., 2007).

Evidence linking transient (state-level) unfair treatment and cardiovascular outcomes has been reported in short-term longitudinal or ambulatory studies. Of the 13 studies identified, all reported a unique independent or interactive association between unfair treatment and cardiovascular risk (Beatty, Matthews, Bromberger, & Brown, 2014; Beatty Moody et al., 2016; Brondolo et al., 2008; R. Clark, 2000; Gregoski et al., 2013; Hill, Kobayashi, & Hughes, 2007; Kaholokula, Grandinetti, Keller, Nacapoy, & Mau, 2012; Matthews, Salomon, Kenyon, & Zhou, 2005; Richman, Bennett, Pek, Siegler, & Williams, 2007; Singleton, Robertson, Robinson, Austin, & Edochie, 2008; Smart Richman, Pek, Pascoe, & Bauer, 2010; Tomfohr, Cooper, Mills, Nelesen, & Dimsdale, 2010; Wagner, Tennen, Finan, Ghuman, & Burg, 2013). For example, in a study of 189 healthy White and African-American adolescents (aged 14–16 years), Beatty and Matthews (2009) found that greater unfair treatment was associated with a higher night/day diastolic blood pressure ratio among African Americans. Finally, of the ten studies that examined the effects of laboratory-induced unfair treatment on cardiovascular outcomes, all found significant causal effects (Blascovich, Spencer, Quinn, & Steele, 2001; R. Clark, 2006a; V. R. Clark, Cobb, Hopkins, & Smith, 2005; Fang & Myers, 2001; Guyll, Matthews, & Bromberger, 2001; McNeilly et al., 1995; Mendes, Major, McCoy, & Blascovich, 2008; Merritt, Bennett, Williams, Edwards, & Sollers, 2006; Salomon & Jagusztyn, 2008; Sawyer, Major,

Casad, Townsend, & Mendes, 2012). For example, among healthy African-American men between the ages of 18 and 47, those reporting high levels of perceived racism showed larger increases in blood pressure across a laboratory stress-challenge task that contained blatantly discriminatory versus neutral stimuli (Fang & Myers, 2001). Overall, findings indicate that higher levels of self-reported unfair treatment are uniquely associated with cardiovascular risk in non-clinical samples.

Unfair Treatment and Neuroendocrine Endpoints

Cross-sectional investigations of the role of unfair treatment in neuroendocrine functioning have been described in three previous studies: one found an association consistent with theoretical predictions (Ong, Williams, Nwizu, & Gruenewald, 2017) and two reported null findings (Akdeniz et al., 2014; Ratner, Halim, & Amodio, 2013). For example, in a study of 60 Blacks and Latinos between the ages of 18 and 44, Ratner et al. (2013) found that greater perceptions of everyday discrimination were not associated with higher basal IL-6. Of the three longitudinal studies reviewed (ranging from 3 months to 20 years), two were consistent with theoretical predictions (Adam et al., 2015; Thayer & Kuzawa, 2015) and one reported null findings (Brody et al., 2014). In a prospective study of 331 rural African Americans between the ages of 16 and 18 years, Brody et al. (2014) found a non-significant association between perceived discrimination and cortisol. Among the six ambulatory studies identified, five reported a unique association between unfair treatment and neuroendocrine risk (Doane & Zeiders, 2014; Fuller-Rowell, Doan, & Eccles, 2012; Huynh, Guan, Almeida, McCreath, & Fuligni, 2016; Kaholokula et al., 2012; Zeiders, Hoyt, & Adam, 2014). In contrast, in a study of 179 preadolescent youth, Martin, Bruce, and Fisher (2012) found that diurnal salivary cortisol rhythms were unrelated to perceptions of perceived discrimination. Finally, of the five experimental studies identified (see Table 12.2), four found effects of laboratory-induced unfair treatment on neuroendocrine outcomes (Hatzenbuehler & McLaughlin, 2014; Richman & Jonassaint, 2008; Townsend, Major, Gangi, & Mendes, 2011; Weik, Maroof, Zöller, & Deinzer, 2010), while one study did not (Zöller, Maroof, Weik, & Deinzer, 2010). For example, Hatzenbuehler and McLaughlin (2014) examined cortisol reactivity to a laboratory challenge among 74 lesbian, gay, and bisexual young adults and found that LGB young adults who were raised in highly stigmatizing environments as adolescents evidenced

Table 12.2 Summary of unfair treatment and neuroendocrine endpoints

Study	Unfair treatment	Endpoint	Covariates	Findings
Ambulatory studies				
Doane & Zeiders (2014)	Perceived discrimination	Salivary cortisol	Social support, negative affect, gender, caffeine, oral contraceptive use, race, ethnicity, parents' education	Perceived discrimination was negatively correlated with cortisol awakening response.
Fuller-Rowell et al. (2012)	Daily discrimination	Diurnal cortisol rhythm	Age, gender, SES, smoking, medication	Perceived discrimination is associated with a flatter diurnal cortisol slope in Whites, but a steeper slope in Blacks.
Huynh et al. (2016)	Perceived everyday racism	Salivary cortisol	Age, gender, race, height, weight	Discrimination was positively correlated with total cortisol output and bedtime cortisol and negatively correlated with waking cortisol. Discrimination was associated with a flatter daily decline.
Kaholokula et al. (2012)	Attributed oppression	Salivary cortisol	Age, sex, BMI, marital status, education, psychological stress, ethnicity, Hawaiian ancestry	Attributed oppression was negatively correlated with diurnal cortisol levels.
Martin et al. (2012)	Perceived racial/ethnic discrimination	Salivary cortisol	Age, gender, sleep, wake time, race, SES, psychosocial risk	No correlation between perceived discrimination and cortisol slope coefficient or levels.
Zeiders et al. (2014)	Everyday discrimination	Salivary cortisol	Age, gender, SES, neuroticism, hours of sleep, oral contraceptive use, exercise, alcohol and caffeine use	Discrimination predicted a less negative diurnal cortisol slope for racial and ethnic minorities.

(*continued*)

Table 12.2 *(Continued)*

Study	Unfair treatment	Endpoint	Covariates	Findings
Cross-sectional studies				
Akdeniz et al. (2014)	Perceived discrimination	Salivary cortisol	Socio-demographic and task performance characteristics	No significant difference in salivary cortisol for ethnic minorities and controls.
Ong et al. (2017)	Everyday discrimination	Epinephrine, nor-epinephrine, cortisol, and DHEA sulfate	Age, gender, education, medication use, smoking, alcohol, depression, perceived stress	Everyday discrimination is positively associated with epinephrine, norepinephrine, cortisol, and DHEA sulfate levels.
Ratner et al. (2013)	Perceived stigmatization	DHEA and salivary cortisol	Age, income, perceived stress	No significant correlation between discrimination and DHEA or mid-afternoon cortisol levels.
Experimental studies				
Hatzenbuehler & McLaughlin (2014)	Structural and perceived stigma	Salivary cortisol	Age, gender, race, smoking, exercise, caffeine use	State-level structural stigma, but not perceived stigma, was positively associated with cortisol reactivity.
Richman & Jonassaint (2008)	Race-related stress	Salivary cortisol	Gender	Race-related stress was positively associated with cortisol levels.
Townsend et al. (2011)	Social identity threat	Cortisol reactivity	Age, menstrual cycle, anxiety, depression, perceptions of personal control	Interaction of sexist discrimination and chronic perceptions of sexism positively predicted cortisol reactivity.

Weik et al. (2010)	Social exclusion	Salivary cortisol	Perceived social support, locus of control, baseline cortisol, oral contraceptive use, anger, depression	Social exclusion results in a blunted cortisol response to stress in women but not in men.
Zöller et al. (2010)	Social exclusion	Salivary cortisol	Age, self-esteem, social support, neuroticism, oral contraceptive use, baseline cortisol	No significant effect of social exclusion on cortisol secretion in women.
Longitudinal studies				
Adam et al. (2015)	Perceived racial discrimination	Salivary cortisol	Time of waking, birth control use, smoking, depressive symptoms	Greater perceived racial discrimination predicted flatter diurnal cortisol slopes and lower cortisol awakening response. Effects are more prominent in Blacks.
Brody et al. (2014)	Racist events	Cortisol, epinephrine, and nor-epinephrine levels	SES, perceived stress, unhealthy behavior	No significant association between perceived discrimination and cortisol, epinephrine, and norepinephrine levels. Interaction of perceived discrimination and emotional support predicts lower cortisol levels.
Thayer & Kuzawa (2015)	Everyday discrimination	Salivary cortisol	Ethnicity, age, SES, BMI	Discrimination was positively associated with evening cortisol and positively predicted cortisol reactivity of infant offspring.

blunted cortisol responses to laboratory stress compared with those from low-stigma environments. Taken together, studies that investigated the association between unfair treatment and neuroendocrine endpoints (e.g., acute and diurnal changes in salivary cortisol levels) demonstrate that perceptions of unfair treatment are associated with neuroendocrine risk, even when the effects of perceived stress and depressive symptomatology are controlled for.

Unfair Treatment and Immune Functioning

Table 12.3 presents cross-sectional, longitudinal, ambulatory and experimental studies that address the role of unfair treatment in immune outcomes. Of the eight cross-sectional studies identified, six reported an association between discrimination or unfair treatment and immune function (Doyle & Molix, 2014; Goosby, Malone, Richardson, Cheadle, & Williams, 2015; Kershaw et al., 2016; Lewis et al., 2010; McClure et al., 2010; Ong et al., 2017) while the remaining two did not (Albert et al., 2008; Ratner et al., 2013). Additionally, four (50%) controlled for potential confounding factors, such as perceived stress or depressive symptoms, whereas the remainder did not. Among the longitudinal studies reviewed (ranging from 10 months to 14 years), five were consistent with theoretical predictions (Beatty et al., 2014; Brody, Yu, Miller, & Chen, 2015; Christian, Iams, Porter, & Glaser, 2012; Cunningham et al., 2012; Friedman, Williams, Singer, & Ryff, 2009), and one reported null findings (Brody et al., 2014). For example, in a study that followed a community sample of 160 African Americans aged 17–19 years for an average of three years, youth exposed to high levels of racial discrimination evidenced elevated cytokine levels three years later (Brody et al., 2015). Finally, experimental studies of unfair treatment and immune functioning find that laboratory-induced unfair treatment significantly predicts immune outcomes (John-Henderson, Rheinschmidt, Mendoza-Denton, & Francis, 2014; John-Henderson, Stellar, Mendoza-Denton, & Francis, 2015; Stetler, Chen, & Miller, 2006). For example, John-Henderson and colleagues (2015) examined inflammatory cytokine interleukin-6 (IL-6) levels in response to social-evaluative threat induced in the laboratory among a sample of 190 college students. Findings suggest that participants reporting low subjective social class showed greater increases in IL-6 responses to laboratory stress. Overall, unfair treatment tends to be associated with elevated levels of inflammation (e.g., IL-6, CRP, fibrinogen). However, most studies in this area

Table 12.3 Summary of unfair treatment and immune endpoints

Study	Unfair treatment	Endpoint	Covariates	Findings
Cross-sectional studies				
Albert et al. (2008)	Perceived racial/ethnic discrimination	MCP-1, CRP and IL-18 levels	Age, HTN, type 2 diabetes, smoking, cholesterol, BMI, education, physical activity	No significant association between perceived racial or ethnic discrimination and MCP-1, CRP or IL-18.
Doyle & Molix (2014)	Perceived discrimination	IL-6, E-selectin, and CRP levels	Stressor appraisal	Perceived discrimination was positively correlated with IL-6 and E-selectin levels but not CRP levels.
Goosby et al. (2015)	Everyday discrimination	CRP levels	Age, gender, BMI, waist circumference, mother's education	Daily discrimination positively predicts CRP levels.
Kershaw et al. (2016)	Everyday and lifetime discrimination	IL-6 and CRP levels	Age, education, employment, recent infection, smoking, BMI, anti-inflammatory use, hormone replacement therapy	Everyday discrimination was negatively related to IL-6 levels in men. Lifetime discrimination was positively related to IL-6 levels in women. No significant association between discrimination and CRP levels.
Lewis et al. (2010)	Everyday discrimination	CRP levels	Age, sex, education, depressive symptoms, smoking, BP, diabetes	Everyday discrimination is positively associated with CRP levels.

(*continued*)

Table 12.3 *(Continued)*

Study	Unfair treatment	Endpoint	Covariates	Findings
McClure et al. (2010)	Discrimination-related stress	Antibody levels	Age, BMI, waist circumference	Discrimination-related stress predicted higher Epstein–Barr virus antibody levels in men and marginally predicted higher antibody levels in women.
Ong et al. (2017)	Everyday discrimination	CRP, IL-6, E-selectin, fibrinogen, ICAM-1 levels	Age, gender, education, medication use, smoking, alcohol, depression, perceived stress	Everyday discrimination is positively associated with inflammation endpoints.
Ratner et al. (2013)	Perceived stigmatization	IL-6 levels	Age, income, perceived stress	No significant correlation between discrimination and IL-6 levels.
Experimental studies				
John-Henderson et al. (2014)	Stereotype threat	IL-6 levels	SES, BMI, baseline inflammation	SES-based stereotype threat positively predicted post-stressor inflammation.
John-Henderson et al. (2015)	Social-evaluative threat	IL-6 levels	Gender, BMI, sleep, ethnicity	Social-evaluative stress is positively associated with IL-6 levels.
Stetler et al. (2006)	Racism experience	Antibody response	Age, gender, education, income, oral contraceptive use, smoking, alcohol consumption	Racism experience disclosure negatively predicted antibody levels to an influenza vaccine.

Longitudinal studies				
Beatty et al. (2014)	Everyday discrimination	CRP levels	Age, race, education, smoking, alcohol consumption, physical activity, SBP, cholesterol, BMI	Interaction of everyday discrimination and BMI predicts CRP levels.
Brody et al. (2014)	Racist events	CRP levels	SES, perceived stress, unhealthy behavior	No significant association between perceived discrimination and CRP levels.
Brody et al. (2015)	Racial discrimination	Inflammation composite	SES, life stress, depressive symptoms, BMI	Racial discrimination positively predicted future inflammation levels.
Christian et al. (2012)	Experiences of discrimination	Antibody levels	Race, pregnancy trimester	Greater Epstein–Barr virus antibody levels in Black women than in White women. Racial discrimination in Blacks increased the magnitude of this association.
Cunningham et al. (2012)	Discrimination	CRP levels	Age, education, cholesterol, SBP	Discrimination negatively predicted CRP levels in Black men and women. Discrimination positively predicted CRP levels in White women.
Friedman et al. (2009)	Chronic discrimination	E-selectin	Age, marital status, education, race, smoking, alcohol and caffeine use	Major discrimination and chronic everyday discrimination positively predicted levels of circulating E-selectin in men but not in women.

assessed unfair treatment via self-report, which may inflate the strength of the association by shared methods. Experimental and longitudinal studies provide preliminary evidence that unfair treatment may have proximal and long-term implications for inflammation risk, but additional research directly assessing the effect of unfair treatment on inflammatory markers is needed to determine whether interventions can alter immune responses.

Conclusions and Future Directions

Although findings from the studies reviewed support a link between unfair treatment and biological correlates, the majority of included studies contained basic methodological weaknesses. Of primary concern is the limited number of longitudinal and experimental studies. Indeed, studies to date have largely been cross-sectional, making it difficult to infer the causal significance of associations. Overall, perhaps one of the most striking findings is just how few studies have addressed issues related to causality and the direction of association between unfair treatment and regulatory physiological systems.

Other methodological challenges concern the measurement of unfair treatment. As reviewed in Lewis et al. (2015), there are two common approaches to assessing discrimination experiences. One approach asks specifically about attributions about unfair treatment (the one-stage approach). A second approach inquires about discriminatory experiences as a form of unfair treatment more broadly and then follows up with a question about attribution after a general response has been endorsed (the two-stage approach). These two approaches make different assumptions about how best to query respondents, and thus have unique limitations and strengths. With the one-stage approach, the intent of the question is clearly focused on attribution. In contrast, a strength of the two-stage approach is that it does not require respondents to engage in the challenging cognitive task of attributing cause at the same time as they recall and report experiences of discrimination (Williams & Mohammed, 2009).

To date, so few longitudinal investigations of unfair treatment and biological endpoints have been conducted that conclusions must be drawn cautiously. Moreover, the vast majority of included studies relied upon self-report measures of mistreatment; very few studies examined the effects of simulated exposure to discrimination on biological processes. Considering the significant heterogeneity across studies in measures of unfair treatment and physiological outcomes, measurement error remains an issue that may contribute to biases associated with effect estimation. In addition, the inclusion of confounding variables, such as perceived stress or psychological distress symptoms, varied widely across studies. Given that depressive and anxiety symptoms may covary with perceived discrimination (Lewis et al., 2015), attention to potential confounding by negative arousal states is critical.

Finally, we note that the risk of publication bias is inherent in any systematic review of empirical evidence. Publication bias can cause studies that report null associations between unfair treatment and biological outcomes to remain unpublished. It should be noted that such a bias may also result in a failure to publish inconclusive or disconfirming evidence. This problem might be addressed in future meta-analyses by including methods for detecting, quantifying and adjusting for publication bias associated with effect estimation (e.g., funnel plots).

Overall, the limitations in the existing data provide an important impetus for future work. First, reciprocal or bidirectional links between unfair treatment and physiological responses have rarely been examined in previous work. In addition to providing a more rigorous assessment of mechanistic pathways, prospective, multi-wave, longitudinal studies are critically important in advancing the science of unfair treatment and biology because they (1) allow for tests of theoretical models that assume stability of relations over time, (2) help address questions regarding duration of unfair treatment and whether sustained mistreatment over time is associated with biological outcomes above and beyond a single report, and (3) provide evidence against reverse-causality arguments, which posit that individuals who are physiologically reactive may also report more mistreatment. Similarly, as noted earlier, controlled experimental studies that investigate the effect of unfair treatment on physiological responses are especially scarce. Thus, prospective and experimental studies that address the causal relationship between discrimination and biological heath are urgently needed.

Second, although many studies have investigated the relationship between reported experiences of unfair treatment and health among African Americans (for reviews, see Mays et al., 2007; Williams & Mohammed, 2009), few have related unfair treatment to multisystem functioning. Rather, most studies have focused on individual physiological indicators or preclinical endpoints of poor health. Given that the effects of chronic stress are typically non-specific (Segerstrom & Miller, 2004), such single-system studies cannot adequately capture the cumulative impact of exposure to everyday unfair treatment. In comparison, a multisystem approach is consistent with evidence that many people, particularly at later ages, suffer from multiple, co-occurring chronic conditions which are likely to contribute to increased risks of morbidity and mortality (Yancik et al., 2007). The concept of allostatic load (AL), introduced by McEwen and Stellar (1993), reflects the cumulative "wear and tear" of chronic stress on the body. According to the allostatic framework, chronic stressors can cause dysregulation of interrelated physiological systems, which if prolonged may ultimately lead to disease. Such dysregulation is characterized by elevated (or reduced) physiological activity across multiple regulatory systems, including the sympathetic nervous system, the HPA axis, the immune system, and cardiovascular and metabolic processes. Future studies should investigate the association between everyday unfair treatment and a multisystem index of cumulative biological "wear and tear" or AL.

Third, we find that the literature contains plausible accounts of physiological mechanisms associated with unfair treatment and health but, with few exceptions, it includes few published studies that provide formal tests of mechanistic hypotheses. In addition to biological mediators, it is likely that other behavioral or physiological pathways are in play. Given research demonstrating that unfair treatment is associated with lower levels of health care seeking (for a review, see Williams & Mohammed, 2009) and access to health care explains a significant amount of variance in ethnic/racial disparities in health (Williams & Rucker, 2000), future studies should examine the role of medical care and healthcare-seeking behaviors (e.g., interactions with health care providers, adherence to treatment advice) as potential pathways linking everyday unfair treatment and health.

Finally, it is possible that vulnerability to the health consequences of mistreatment may be a function of the frequency of exposure rather than the attribution of the type of discrimination experienced (Beatty & Matthews, 2009). Research on "intersectionalities" (Lewis et al., 2015) suggests that occupying multiple disadvantaged statuses (e.g., African-American and female) may shape both the experiences and the consequences of everyday unfair treatment. It is noteworthy that this work has largely focused on subjective, self-reported health. Thus, studies examining the impact of multiple group identities on objective physical health outcomes are an important priority for future research.

In conclusion, the extant evidence indicates that perceptions of unfair treatment are associated with downstream biological processes (immune, neuroendocrine, cardiovascular) that are implicated in the pathogenesis of disease. Although there is growing support for an association between unfair treatment and biological outcomes, full understanding of the phenomenon is far from complete. The main issues limiting the validity and generalizability of the results include inadequate control of confounders, insufficient information regarding study design, small heterogeneous samples and a paucity of longitudinal and experimental studies. To the extent that progress can be made on these issues, efforts to combat mistreatment and discrimination, particularly among ethnic and racial minorities and other marginalized groups, may play an important role in improving well-being, minimizing chronic illness, and prolonging life.

Abbreviations

ABP ambulatory blood pressure
ACC anterior cingulate cortex
BDI Beck depression inventory
BMI body mass index
CAC Coronary artery calcium
CHD coronary heart disease
CO cardiac output
CRP C-reactive protein
CV cardiovascular
CVD cardiovascular disease
DBP diastolic blood pressure
DHEA dehydroepiandrosterone
ET-1 endothelin 1
HPA hypothalamic-pituitary-adrenal
HR heart rate
HTN hypertension
IL-6 interleukin 6
LAE large arterial elasticity
MAP mean arterial pressure
MCP-1 monocyte chemoattractant protein 1
SBP systolic blood pressure
SEP socioeconomic position
SES socioeconomic status
SV stroke volume
TPR total peripheral resistance

References

Adam, E. K., Heissel, J. A., Zeiders, K. H., Richeson, J. A., Ross, E. C., Ehrlich, K. B., … & Malanchuk, O. (2015). Developmental histories of perceived racial discrimination and diurnal cortisol profiles in adulthood: A 20-year prospective study. *Psychoneuroendocrinology, 62*, 279–291. doi:10.1016/j.psyneuen.2015.08.018

Akdeniz, C., Tost, H., Streit, F., Haddad, L., Wüst, S., Schäfer, A., … & Meyer-Lindenberg, A. (2014). Neuroimaging evidence for a role of neural social stress processing in ethnic minority-associated environmental risk. *JAMA Psychiatry, 71*(6), 672–680. doi:10.1001/jamapsychiatry.2014.35

Albert, M. A., Ravenell, J., Glynn, R. J., Khera, A., Halevy, N., & de Lemos, J. A. (2008). Cardiovascular risk indicators and perceived race/ethnic discrimination in the Dallas Heart Study. *American Heart Journal, 156*(6), 1103–1109. doi:10.1016/j.ahj.2008.07.027

Barksdale, D. J., Farrug, E. R., & Harkness, K. (2009). Racial discrimination and blood pressure: Perceptions, emotions, and behaviors of black American adults. *Issues in Mental Health Nursing, 30*(2), 104–111. doi:10.1080/01612840802597879

Beatty, D. L., & Matthews, K. A. (2009). Unfair treatment and trait anger in relation to nighttime ambulatory blood pressure in African American and white adolescents. *Psychosomatic Medicine, 71*(8), 813–820. doi:10.1097/PSY.0b013e3181b3b6f8

Beatty, D. L., Matthews, K. A., Bromberger, J. T., & Brown, C. (2014). Everyday discrimination prospectively predicts inflammation across 7-years in racially diverse midlife women: Study of women's health across the nation. *Journal of Social Issues, 70*(2), 298–314. doi:10.1111/josi.12061

Beatty Moody, D. L., Waldstein, S. R., Tobin, J. N., Cassells, A., Schwartz, J. C., & Brondolo, E. (2016). Lifetime racial/ethnic discrimination and ambulatory blood pressure: The moderating effect of age. *Health Psychology, 35*(4), 333–342. doi:10.1037/hea0000270

Blascovich, J., & Katkin, E. S. (Eds.). (1993). *Cardiovascular reactivity to psychological stress and disease*. Washington, DC: American Psychological Association.

Blascovich, J., Spencer, S. J., Quinn, D., & Steele, C. (2001). African Americans and high blood pressure: The role of stereotype threat. *Psychological Science, 12*(3), 225–229. doi:10.1111/1467-9280.00340

Brody, G. H., Lei, M. K., Chae, D. H., Yu, T., Kogan, S. M., & Beach, S. R. (2014). Perceived discrimination among African American adolescents and allostatic load: A longitudinal analysis with buffering effects. *Child Development, 85*(3), 989–1002. doi:10.1111/cdev.12213

Brody, G. H., Yu, T., Miller, G. E., & Chen, E. (2015). Discrimination, racial identity, and cytokine levels among African-American adolescents. *Journal of Adolescent Health, 56*(5), 496–501. doi:10.1016/j.jadohealth.2015.01.017

Brondolo, E., Libby, D. J., Denton, E. G., Thompson, S., Beatty, D. L., Schwartz, J., … & Gerin, W. (2008). Racism and ambulatory blood pressure in a community sample. *Psychosomatic Medicine, 70*(1), 49–56. doi:10.1097/PSY.0b013e31815ff3bd

Brown, C., Matthews, K. A., Bromberger, J. T., & Chang, Y. (2006). The relation between perceived unfair treatment and blood pressure in a racially/ethnically diverse sample of women. *American Journal of Epidemiology, 164*(3), 257–262. doi:10.1093/aje/kwj196

Chae, D. H., Lincoln, K. D., Adler, N. E., & Syme, S. L. (2010). Do experiences of racial discrimination predict cardiovascular disease among African American men? The moderating role of internalized negative racial group attitudes. *Social Science and Medicine, 71*(6), 1182–1188. doi:10.1016/j.socscimed.2010.05.045

Chae, D. H., Nuru-Jeter, A. M., Lincoln, K. D., & Arriola, K. R. J. (2012). Racial discrimination, mood disorders, and cardiovascular disease among black Americans. *Annals of Epidemiology, 22*(2), 104–111. doi:10.1016/j.annepidem.2011.10.009

Christian, L. M., Iams, J. D., Porter, K., & Glaser, R. (2012). Epstein–Barr virus reactivation during pregnancy and postpartum: Effects of race and racial discrimination. *Brain, Behavior, and Immunity, 26*(8), 1280–1287. doi:10.1016/j.bbi.2012.08.006

Clark, R. (2000). Perceptions of interethnic group racism predict increased vascular reactivity to a laboratory challenge in college women. *Annals of Behavioral Medicine, 22*(3), 214–222.

Clark, R. (2006a). Perceived racism and vascular reactivity in black college women: Moderating effects of seeking social support. *Health Psychology, 25*(1), 20–25. doi:10.1037/0278-6133.25.1.20

Clark, R. (2006b). Interactive but not direct effects of perceived racism and trait anger predict resting systolic and diastolic blood pressure in black adolescents. *Health Psychology, 25*(5), 580–585. doi:10.1037/0278-6133.25.5.580

Clark, R., Benkert, R. A., & Flack, J. M. (2006). Large arterial elasticity varies as a function of gender and racism-related vigilance in black youth. *Journal of Adolescent Health, 39*(4), 562–569. doi:10.1016/j.jadohealth.2006.02.012

Clark, R., & Gochett, P. (2006). Interactive effects of perceived racism and coping responses predict a school-based assessment of blood pressure in black youth. *Annals of Behavioral Medicine, 32*(1), 1–9. doi:10.1207/s15324796abm3201_1

Clark, V. R., Cobb, R., Hopkins, R., & Smith, C. (2005). Black racial identity as a mediator of cardiovascular reactivity to racism in African-American college students. *Ethnicity and Disease, 16*(1), 108–113.

Cooper, D. C., Mills, P. J., Bardwell, W. A., Ziegler, M. G., & Dimsdale, J. E. (2009). The effects of ethnic discrimination and socioeconomic status on endothelin-1 among blacks and whites. *American Journal of Hypertension, 22*(7), 698–704. doi:10.1038/ajh.2009.72

Cunningham, T. J., Seeman, T. E., Kawachi, I., Gortmaker, S. L., Jacobs, D. R., Kiefe, C. I., & Berkman, L. F. (2012). Racial/ethnic and gender differences in the association between self-reported experiences of racial/ethnic discrimination and inflammation in the CARDIA cohort of 4 US communities. *Social Science and Medicine, 75*(5), 922–931. doi:10.1016/j.socscimed.2012.04.027

De Vogli, R., Ferrie, J. E., Chandola, T., Kivimaki, M., & Marmot, M. G. (2007). Unfairness and health: Evidence from the Whitehall II Study. *Journal of Epidemiological and Community Health, 61*(6), 513–518. doi:10.1136/jech.2006.052563

Din-Dzietham, R., Nembhard, W. N., Collins, R., & Davis, S. K. (2004). Perceived stress following race-based discrimination at work is associated with hypertension in African–Americans. The metro Atlanta heart disease study, 1999–2001. *Social Science and Medicine, 58*(3), 449–461. doi:10.1016/s0277-9536(03)00211-9

Doane, L. D., & Zeiders, K. H. (2014). Contextual moderators of momentary cortisol and negative affect in adolescents' daily lives. *Journal of Adolescent Health, 54*(5), 536–542. doi:10.1016/j.jadohealth.2013.10.007

Doyle, D. M., & Molix, L. (2014). Perceived discrimination as a stressor for close relationships: Identifying psychological and physiological pathways. *Journal of Behavioral Medicine, 37*(6), 1134–1144. doi:10.1007/s10865-014-9563-8

Eliezer, D., Townsend, S. S. M., Sawyer, P. J., Major, B., & Mendes, W. B. (2011). System-justifying beliefs moderate the relationship between perceived discrimination and resting blood pressure. *Social Cognition, 29*(3), 303–321. doi:10.1521/soco.2011.29.3.303

Everage, N. J., Gjelsvik, A., McGarvey, S. T., Linkletter, C. D., & Loucks, E. B. (2012). Inverse associations between perceived racism and coronary artery calcification. *Annals of Epidemiology, 22*(3), 183–190. doi:10.1016/j.annepidem.2012.01.005

Everson-Rose, S. A., Lutsey, P. L., Roetker, N. S., Lewis, T. T., Kershaw, K. N., Alonso, A., & Diez Roux, A. V. (2015). Perceived discrimination and incident cardiovascular events: The multi-ethnic study of atherosclerosis.

American Journal of Epidemiology, 182(3), 225–234. doi:10.1093/aje/kwv035

Fang, C. Y., & Myers, H. F. (2001). The effects of racial stressors and hostility on cardiovascular reactivity in African American and Caucasian men. *Health Psychology, 20*(1), 64–70. doi:10.1037/0278-6133.20.1.64

Friedman, E. M., Williams, D. R., Singer, B. H., & Ryff, C. D. (2009). Chronic discrimination predicts higher circulating levels of E-selectin in a national sample: The MIDUS study. *Brain, Behavior, and Immunity, 23*(5), 684–692. doi:10.1016/j.bbi.2009.01.002

Fuller-Rowell, T. E., Doan, S. N., & Eccles, J. S. (2012). Differential effects of perceived discrimination on the diurnal cortisol rhythm of African Americans and Whites. *Psychoneuroendocrinology, 37*(1), 107–118. doi:10.1016/j.psyneuen.2011.05.011

Goosby, B. J., Malone, S., Richardson, E. A., Cheadle, J. E., & Williams, D. T. (2015). Perceived discrimination and markers of cardiovascular risk among low-income African American youth. *American Journal of Human Biology, 27*(4), 546–552. doi:10.1002/ajhb.22683

Gregoski, M. J., Buxbaum, S. G., Kapuku, G., Dong, Y., Zhu, H., Davis, M., … & Treiber, F. A. (2013). Interactive influences of ethnicity, endothelin-1 gene, and everyday discrimination upon nocturnal ambulatory blood pressure. *Annals of Behavioral Medicine, 45*(3), 377–386. doi:10.1007/s12160-013-9472-z

Guyll, M., Matthews, K. A., & Bromberger, J. T. (2001). Discrimination and unfair treatment: Relationship to cardiovascular reactivity among African American and European American women. *Health Psychology, 20*(5), 315–325. doi:10.1037/0278-6133.20.5.315

Hatzenbuehler, M. L., & McLaughlin, K. A. (2014). Structural stigma and hypothalamic–pituitary–adrenocortical axis reactivity in lesbian, gay, and bisexual young adults. *Annals of Behavioral Medicine, 47*(1), 39–47. doi:10.1007/s12160-013-9556-9

Hicken, M. T., Lee, H., Morenoff, J., House, J. S., & Williams, D. R. (2014). Racial/ethnic disparities in hypertension prevalence: Reconsidering the role of chronic stress. *American Journal of Public Health, 104*(1), 117–123. doi:10.2105/AJPH.2013.301395

Hill, L. K., Kobayashi, I., & Hughes, J. W. (2007). Perceived racism and ambulatory blood pressure in African American college students. *Journal of Black Psychology, 33*(4), 404–421. doi:10.1177/0095798407307042

Hunte, H. E. (2011). Association between perceived interpersonal everyday discrimination and waist circumference over a 9-year period in the Midlife

Development in the United States cohort study. *American Journal of Epidemiology, 173*(11), 1232–1239. doi:10.1093/aje/kwq463

Huynh, V. W., Guan, S.-S. A., Almeida, D. M., McCreath, H., & Fuligni, A. J. (2016). Everyday discrimination and diurnal cortisol during adolescence. *Hormones and Behavior, 80*, 76–81. doi:10.1016/j.yhbeh.2016.01.009

John-Henderson, N. A., Rheinschmidt, M. L., Mendoza-Denton, R., & Francis, D. D. (2014). Performance and inflammation outcomes are predicted by different facets of SES under stereotype threat. *Social Psychological and Personality Science, 5*(3), 301–309. doi:10.1177/1948550613494226

John-Henderson, N. A., Stellar, J. E., Mendoza-Denton, R., & Francis, D. D. (2015). The role of interpersonal processes in shaping inflammatory responses to social-evaluative threat. *Biological Psychology, 110*, 134–137. doi:10.1016/j.biopsycho.2015.07.011

Kaholokula, J. K., Grandinetti, A., Keller, S., Nacapoy, A. H., & Mau, M. K. (2012). Association between perceived racism and physiological stress indices in Native Hawaiians. *Journal of Behavioral Medicine, 35*(1), 27–37. doi:10.1007/s10865-011-9330-z

Kershaw, K. N., Lewis, T. T., Diez Roux, A. V., Jenny, N. S., Liu, K., Penedo, F. J., & Carnethon, M. R. (2016). Self-reported experiences of discrimination and inflammation among men and women: The multi-ethnic study of atherosclerosis. *Health Psychology, 35*(4), 343–350. doi:10.1037/hea0000331

Krantz, D. S., & Manuck, S. B. (1984). Acute psychophysiologic reactivity and risk of cardiovascular disease: A review and methodologic critique. *Psychological Bulletin, 96*, 435–464.

Krieger, N., Waterman, P. D., Kosheleva, A., Chen, J. T., Smith, K. W., Carney, D. R., ... & Freeman, E. R. (2013). Racial discrimination & cardiovascular disease risk: My body my story study of 1005 US-born black and white community health center participants (US). *PLoS One, 8*(10), e77174. doi:10.1371/journal.pone.0077174

Lepore, S. J., Revenson, T. A., Weinberger, S. L., Weston, P., Frisina, P. G., Robertson, R., ... & Cross, W. (2006). Effects of social stressors on cardiovascular reactivity in Black and White women. *Annals of Behavioral Medicine, 31*(2), 120–127. doi:10.1207/s15324796abm3102_3

Lewis, T. T., Aiello, A. E., Leurgans, S., Kelly, J., & Barnes, L. L. (2010). Self-reported experiences of everyday discrimination are associated with elevated C-reactive protein levels in older African-American adults. *Brain, Behavior and Immunity, 24*(3), 438–443. doi:10.1016/j.bbi.2009.11.011

Lewis, T. T., Cogburn, C. D., & Williams, D. R. (2015). Self-reported experiences of discrimination and health: Scientific advances, ongoing controversies, and emerging issues. *Annual Review of Clinical Psychology, 11*, 407–440.

Lewis, T. T., Everson-Rose, S. A., Powell, L. H., Matthews, K. A., Brown, C., Karavolos, K., … & Wesley, D. (2006). Chronic exposure to everyday discrimination and coronary artery calcification in African-American women: The SWAN Heart Study. *Psychosomatic Medicine, 68*(3), 362–368. doi:10.1097/01.psy.0000221360.94700.16

Martin, C. G., Bruce, J., & Fisher, P. A. (2012). Racial and ethnic differences in diurnal cortisol rhythms in preadolescents: The role of parental psychosocial risk and monitoring. *Hormones and behavior, 61*(5), 661–668. doi:10.1016/j.yhbeh.2012.02.025

Matthews, K. A., Salomon, K., Kenyon, K., & Zhou, F. (2005). Unfair treatment, discrimination, and ambulatory blood pressure in black and white adolescents. *Health Psychology, 24*(3), 258–265. doi:10.1037/0278-6133.24.3.258

Mays, V. M., Cochran, S. D., & Barnes, N. W. (2007). Race, race-based discrimination, and health outcomes among African Americans. *Annual Review of Psychology, 58*, 201–225.

McClure, H. H., Martinez, C. R., Snodgrass, J. J., Eddy, J. M., Jiménez, R. A., Isiordia, L. E., & McDade, T. W. (2010). Discrimination-related stress, blood pressure and Epstein–Barr virus antibodies among Latin American immigrants in Oregon, US. *Journal of Biosocial Science, 42*(4), 433–461. doi:10.1017/S0021932010000039

McEwen, B. S. (1998). Protective and damaging effects of stress mediators. *New England Journal of Medicine, 338*(3), 171–179. doi:10.1056/NEJM199801153380307

McEwen, B. S., & Stellar, E. (1993). Stress and the individual: Mechanisms leading to disease. *Archives of Internal Medicine, 153*, 2093–2101.

McNeilly, M. D., Robinson, E. L., Anderson, N. B., Pieper, C. F., Shah, A., Toth, P. S., … & Gerin, W. (1995). Effects of racist provocation and social support on cardiovascular reactivity in African American women. *International Journal of Behavioral Medicine, 2*(4), 321–338. doi:10.1207/s15327558ijbm0204_3

Mendes, W. B., Major, B., McCoy, S., & Blascovich, J. (2008). How attributional ambiguity shapes physiological and emotional responses to social rejection and acceptance. *Journal of Personality and Social Psychology, 94*(2), 278–291. doi:10.1037/0022-3514.94.2.278

Merritt, M. M., Bennett, G. G., Jr., Williams, R. B., Edwards, C. L., & Sollers, J. J., III. (2006). Perceived racism and cardiovascular reactivity and recovery to personally relevant stress. *Health Psychology, 25*(3), 364–369. doi:10.1037/0278-6133.25.3.364

Miller, G., Chen, E., & Cole, S. W. (2009). Health psychology: Developing biologically plausible models linking the social world and physical health. *Annual Review of Psychology, 60*, 501–524.

Nadimpalli, S. B., Cleland, C. M., Hutchinson, M. K., Islam, N., Barnes, L. L., & Van Devanter, N. (2016). The association between discrimination and the health of Sikh Asian Indians. *Health Psychology, 35*(4), 351–355. doi:10.1037/hea0000268

Nadimpalli, S. B., Dulin-Keita, A., Salas, C., Kanaya, A. M., & Kandula, N. R. (2016). Associations between discrimination and cardiovascular health among Asian Indians in the United States. *Journal of Immigrant and Minority Health*. doi:10.1007/s10903-016-0413-3

Neblett, E. W., Jr., & Carter, S. E. (2012). The protective role of racial identity and Africentric worldview in the association between racial discrimination and blood pressure. *Psychosomatic Medicine, 74*(5), 509–516. doi:10.1097/PSY.0b013e3182583a50

Ong, A. D., Williams, D. R., Nwizu, U., & Gruenewald, T. (2017). Everyday unfair treatment and multisystem biological dysregulation in African-American adults. *Cultural Diversity and Ethnic Minority Psychology, 23*(1), 27–35.

Pascoe, E. A., & Smart Richman, L. (2009). Perceived discrimination and health: A meta-analytic review. *Psychological Bulletin, 135*(4), 531–554. doi:10.1037/a0016059

Peters, R. M. (2006). The relationship of racism, chronic stress emotions, and blood pressure. *Journal of Nursing Scholarship, 38*(3), 234–240. doi:10.1111/j.1547-5069.2006.00108.x

Peterson, L. M., Matthews, K. A., Derby, C. A., Bromberger, J. T., & Thurston, R. C. (2016). The relationship between cumulative unfair treatment and intima media thickness and adventitial diameter: The moderating role of race in the study of women's health across the nation. *Health Psychology, 35*(4), 313–321. doi:10.1037/hea0000288

Poston, W. C., Pavlik, V., Hyman, D., Ogbonnaya, K., Hanis, C., Haddock, C., … & Foreyt, J. (2001). Genetic bottlenecks, perceived racism, and hypertension risk among African Americans and first-generation African immigrants. *Journal of Human Hypertension, 15*(5), 341–351.

Ratner, K. G., Halim, M. L., & Amodio, D. M. (2013). Perceived stigmatization, ingroup pride, and immune and endocrine activity evidence from a community sample of Black and Latina women. *Social Psychological and Personality Science, 4*(1), 82–91. doi:10.1177/1948550612443715

Richman, L. S., Bennett, G. G., Pek, J., Siegler, I., & Williams, R. B., Jr (2007). Discrimination, dispositions, and cardiovascular responses to stress. *Health Psychology, 26*(6), 675–683. doi:10.1037/0278-6133.26.6.675

Richman, L. S., & Jonassaint, C. (2008). The effects of race-related stress on cortisol reactivity in the laboratory: Implications of the Duke lacrosse scandal. *Annals of Behavioral Medicine, 35*(1), 105–110. doi:10.1007/s12160-007-9013-8

Roberts, C. B., Vines, A. I., Kaufman, J. S., & James, S. A. (2008). Cross-sectional association between perceived discrimination and hypertension in African-American men and women: The Pitt County Study. *American Journal of Epidemiology, 167*(5), 624–632. doi:10.1093/aje/kwm334

Ryan, A. M., Gee, G. C., & Laflamme, D. F. (2006). The association between self-reported discrimination, physical health and blood pressure: Findings from African Americans, Black immigrants, and Latino immigrants in New Hampshire. *Journal of Health Care for the Poor and Underserved, 17*(2), 116–132. doi:10.1353/hpu.2006.0079

Salomon, K., & Jagusztyn, N. E. (2008). Resting cardiovascular levels and reactivity to interpersonal incivility among Black, Latina/o, and White individuals: The moderating role of ethnic discrimination. *Health Psychology, 27*(4), 473–481. doi:10.1037/0278-6133.27.4.473

Sawyer, P. J., Major, B., Casad, B. J., Townsend, S. S., & Mendes, W. B. (2012). Discrimination and the stress response: Psychological and physiological consequences of anticipating prejudice in interethnic interactions. *American Journal of Public Health, 102*(5), 1020–1026. doi:10.2105/AJPH.2011.300620

Schmitt, M. T., Branscombe, N., Postmes, T., & Garcia, A. (2014). The consequences of perceived discrimination for psychological well-being: A meta-analytic review. *Psychological Bulletin, 140*, 921–948.

Segerstrom, S. C., & Miller, G. E. (2004). Psychological stress and the human immune system: A meta-analytic study of 30 years of inquiry. *Psychological Bulletin, 130*(4), 601–630.

Sims, M., Diez-Roux, A. V., Dudley, A., Gebreab, S., Wyatt, S. B., Bruce, M. A., … & Taylor, H. A. (2012). Perceived discrimination and hypertension among African Americans in the Jackson Heart Study. *American Journal of Public Health, 102*(S2), S258–S265. doi:10.2105/Ajph.2011.300523

Singleton, G. J., Robertson, J., Robinson, J. C., Austin, C., & Edochie, V. (2008). Perceived racism and coping: Joint predictors of blood pressure in Black Americans. *Negro Educational Review, 59*(1–2), 93–113.

Smart Richman, L., Pek, J., Pascoe, E., & Bauer, D. J. (2010). The effects of perceived discrimination on ambulatory blood pressure and affective responses to interpersonal stress modeled over 24 hours. *Health Psychology, 29*(4), 403–411.

Stetler, C., Chen, E., & Miller, G. E. (2006). Written disclosure of experiences with racial discrimination and antibody response to an influenza vaccine. *International Journal of Behavioral Medicine, 13*(1), 60–68. doi:10.1207/s15327558ijbm1301_8

Thayer, Z. M., & Kuzawa, C. W. (2015). Ethnic discrimination predicts poor self-rated health and cortisol in pregnancy: Insights from New Zealand. *Social Science and Medicine, 128*, 36–42. doi:10.1016/j.socscimed.2015.01.003

Tomfohr, L., Cooper, D. C., Mills, P. J., Nelesen, R. A., & Dimsdale, J. E. (2010). Everyday discrimination and nocturnal blood pressure dipping in black and white Americans. *Psychosomatic Medicine, 72*(3), 266–272. doi:10.1097/PSY.0b013e3181d0d8b2

Townsend, S. S., Major, B., Gangi, C. E., & Mendes, W. B. (2011). From "in the air" to "under the skin": Cortisol responses to social identity threat. *Personality and Social Psychology Bulletin, 37*(2), 151–164. doi:10.1177/0146167210392384

Troxel, W. M., Matthews, K. A., Bromberger, J. T., & Sutton-Tyrrell, K. (2003). Chronic stress burden, discrimination, and subclinical carotid artery disease in African American and Caucasian women. *Health Psychology, 22*(3), 300–309. doi:10.1037/0278-6133.22.3.300

Tull, S., Wickramasuriya, T., Taylor, J., Smith-Burns, V., Brown, M., Champagnie, G., … & Walker, S. (1999). Relationship of internalized racism to abdominal obesity and blood pressure in Afro-Caribbean women. *Journal of the National Medical Association, 91*(8), 447–452.

Utsey, S. O., & Hook, J. N. (2007). Heart rate variability as a physiological moderator of the relationship between race-related stress and psychological distress in African Americans. *Cultural Diversity and Ethnic Minority Psychology, 13*(3), 250–253. doi:10.1037/1099-9809.13.3.250

Wagner, J. A., Tennen, H., Finan, P. H., Ghuman, N., & Burg, M. M. (2013). Self-reported racial discrimination and endothelial reactivity to acute stress in women. *Stress and Health, 29*(3), 214–221. doi:10.1002/smi.2449

Weik, U., Maroof, P., Zöller, C., & Deinzer, R. (2010). Pre-experience of social exclusion suppresses cortisol response to psychosocial stress in women but not in men. *Hormones and Behavior, 58*(5), 891–897. doi:10.1016/j.yhbeh.2010.08.018

Williams, D. R., & Mohammed, S. A. (2009). Discrimination and racial disparities in health: Evidence and needed research. *Journal of Behavioral Medicine, 32*, 20–47.

Williams, D. R., & Rucker, T. D. (2000). Understanding and addressing racial disparities in health care. *Health Care Financing Review, 21*(4), 75–90.

Yancik, R., Ershler, W. B., Satariano, W., Hazzard, W., Cohen, H. J., & Ferrucci, L. (2007). Report of the national aging task force on comorbidity. *Journal of Gerontology: Medical Sciences, 62*, 275–280.

Zeiders, K. H., Hoyt, L. T., & Adam, E. K. (2014). Associations between self-reported discrimination and diurnal cortisol rhythms among young adults: The moderating role of racial–ethnic minority status. *Psychoneuroendocrinology, 50*, 280–288. doi:10.1016/j.psyneuen.2014.08.023

Zöller, C., Maroof, P., Weik, U., & Deinzer, R. (2010). No effect of social exclusion on salivary cortisol secretion in women in a randomized controlled study. *Psychoneuroendocrinology, 35*(9), 1294–1298. doi:10.1016/j.psyneuen.2010.02.019

13

Cultural Experiences, Social Ties, and Stress: Focusing on the HPA Axis

Shu-wen Wang and Belinda Campos

Human beings are social animals, existing in webs of interpersonal connections that shape their experiences and influence their physical and mental health. Relatedness, or feeling belongingness or connectedness with others, has been described as a basic psychological need (Ryan & Deci, 2000), and social relationships across multiple contexts have been examined in terms of their impact on social, psychological, and physiological functioning. The sensitivity of the hypothalamic-pituitary-adrenal (HPA) axis, and its end product cortisol, to social experiences makes it an ideal biomarker for studying cultural influences on interpersonal processes and stress physiology. This is especially true since the norms, beliefs, and practices surrounding social behavior are shaped by the cultural context in which they are embedded, with implications for health and well-being (Soto, Chentsova-Dutton, & Lee, 2013). This chapter will review the state of the literature examining how culture – broadly defined as shared systems of values, norms, behaviors, and products that shape the mind and the brain in a cycle of mutual constitution (Markus & Kitayama, 1991, 2010; Ryder, Ban, & Chentsova-Dutton, 2011) – modulates the connection between social experiences, emotion regulation, and the HPA axis. We also extend recommendations for the field on how better to tap the potential in studying the cultural shaping of socio-emotional experiences and their links with the HPA axis.

The Handbook of Culture and Biology, First Edition. Edited by José M. Causadias, Eva H. Telzer and Nancy A. Gonzales.

The HPA Axis and the "Stress Hormone" Cortisol

The HPA axis is one of the body's key stress regulatory systems, whose activation culminates in the release of the hormone cortisol (Lovallo & Thomas, 2000). When the brain detects a threat or a challenge, or is otherwise under stress, the hypothalamus produces corticotropin-releasing hormone (CRH), which triggers the release of adrenocorticotropic hormone (ACTH) from the anterior pituitary, which stimulates the adrenal cortex to secrete glucocorticoids, primarily cortisol in humans, into the bloodstream. Glucocorticoids play an inhibitory role that signals the body to shut down the stress response. This cascade of effects comprises a system that supports a wide range of normal physiological functions, such as helping the body to maintain homeostasis, growth, and reproductive function, and is also involved in regulating other vital systems, including the immune and cardiovascular systems (Lovallo & Thomas, 2000; Sapolsky, Romero, & Munck, 2000; Saxbe, 2008).

The HPA axis has attracted particular interest amongst researchers because of its role as a "mobilizer" of energy resources to meet the short-term metabolic demands of stress and the health implications of system dysregulation. HPA-axis dysregulation, whether through chronic hyperactivity or hyporeactivity, is associated with a host of negative health effects, including hypertension, cardiovascular disease, dysregulations in inflammatory and immune processes, and deficits in cognitive and emotional functioning (Sapolsky et al., 2000). The allostatic-load model (McEwen, 1998) posits that repeated stressful experiences can lead to an accumulation of physiological "hits" that cause wear and tear on the body's self-regulatory systems. Dysregulation of the HPA axis is considered to be an indicator of allostatic load resulting from chronic overactivation of the stress system (McEwen, 1998). Thus, cortisol – as the hormonal end product of the HPA axis – has attracted substantial attention as a biomarker for subjective and objective stress, and as a potential mediator between stressful experiences and physical health outcomes (Saxbe, 2008).

The HPA Axis and Its Sensitivity to Social Experience

Researchers have wondered whether the HPA axis is more sensitive to certain kinds of stressful experiences. The answer is a definite yes. A meta-analysis of 208 laboratory studies of acute psychological stressors concluded that tasks containing social-evaluative threat (i.e., an important aspect of the self is or could be negatively judged by others), especially under uncontrollable conditions (when participants feel they cannot escape negative consequences), were associated with the largest cortisol changes (Dickerson & Kemeny, 2004). Evidence from naturalistic daily studies on social experiences also shows that indicators of poorer relationship quality are linked with dysregulated cortisol functioning (Adam & Gunnar, 2001; Barnett, Steptoe, & Gareis, 2005; Slatcher, Robles, Repetti, & Fellows, 2010). While negative social experiences, such as social evaluation or conflict, may be studied as sources of threat or stress, there is also a large literature showing that positive social experiences – such as social support – can have a range of direct beneficial effects, as well as protecting against the deleterious effects that stress can have on health and well-being (Cohen, 2004; Hennessy, Kaiser, & Sachser, 2009; Seeman, 1996; Taylor, 2007). For example, greater perceptions of overall support (Abercrombie, Giese-Davis, Sephton, Epel, Turner-Cobb, & Spiegel, 2004; Sjögren, Leanderson, & Kristenson, 2006) and higher ratings of relationship satisfaction (Saxbe, Repetti, & Nishina, 2008; Vedhara, Tuinstra, Miles, Sanderman, & Ranchor, 2006) predict more favorable diurnal cortisol rhythms, with further evidence that being in a more satisfying relationship (Saxbe et al., 2008) and perceiving (Burton, Bonanno, & Hatzenbuehler, 2014) or actually receiving (Ditzen, Hoppmann, & Klumb, 2008; Kirschbaum, Klauer, Filipp, & Hellhammer, 1995) more social support reduces cortisol responding to stressors, in the form of both acute reactivity to laboratory stressors and diurnal cortisol slopes.

Cortisol Parameters

While several parameters are used in cortisol studies, we highlight two general approaches in this review. First, short-term cortisol reactivity in response to acute laboratory stressors permits the study of stress responding in a controlled setting where the nature of the stressor is clearly identifiable (Dickerson & Kemeny, 2004). The cortisol reactivity variable is typically calculated as a change score between a baseline measure and a post-stressor measure of cortisol, and cortisol recovery variables can similarly be calculated with subsequent assessment timepoints after the stressor. One of the most widely used and best-researched laboratory stressor paradigms is the Trier Social Stress Test (TSST; Frisch, Hausser, & Mojzisch, 2015; Kirschbaum, Pirke, & Hellhammer, 1993), which involves mental arithmetic and speech tasks in front of an unresponsive audience (i.e., under social-evaluative threat), a situation that has reliably been shown to trigger cortisol and psychological stress responses (Dickerson &

Kemeny, 2004). Research employing the TSST has examined how specific social variables buffer the neuroendocrine stress reaction in response to social-evaluative threat (Frisch et al., 2015). In this line of questioning the cortisol response to the TSST is the main dependent variable, as researchers examine the kinds of factors (e.g., sex, culture, social support, personality) that moderate the stress–cortisol association.

Second, basal cortisol rhythms provide a naturalistic perspective on HPA-axis functioning in everyday life. Cortisol is released in a diurnal rhythm, peaking within the first hour of awakening, declining steeply over the morning hours, and then gradually tapering off in the afternoon and evening before reaching its night-time low (Saxbe, 2008). According to the allostatic load model (McEwen, 1998), steeper diurnal slopes represent more favorable HPA-axis functioning, and blunted or flattened diurnal slopes, typically due to a sustained elevation in cortisol, reflect dysregulated HPA-axis functioning linked with chronic stress (Miller, Chen, & Zhou, 2007; Saxbe, 2008). Consequently, steeper diurnal slopes are generally associated with better psychosocial functioning, whereas flatter slopes are linked with poorer relationship functioning, and worse mental and physical health (see, e.g., Bhattacharyya, Molloy, & Steptoe, 2008; Miller et al., 2007; Sephton, Sapolsky, Kraemer, & Spiegel, 2000; Sjögren, et al., 2006). Researchers sometimes focus just on the cortisol awakening response (CAR), the rapid rise shown by salivary cortisol within the first 30–45 minutes after waking (Pruessner, Kirschbaum, & Hellhammer, 1995). According to the "boost hypothesis" (Adam, Hawkley, Kudielka, & Cacioppo, 2006), the CAR signals an adaptive effort to cope with the day's anticipated challenges; thus, a larger-than-average or a smaller-than-average CAR may reflect poor adaptation to chronic stress (Saxbe, 2008). Researchers also sometimes derive an area-under-the-curve (AUC) parameter based on multiple timepoints of daily cortisol levels that reflects the total amount of daily circulating cortisol (Saxbe, 2008). These various cortisol parameters provide different glimpses into the naturally occurring associations between chronic levels of stress and basal cortisol profiles, as well as moderating factors that influence those links. The selection of the parameter impacts what "view" of that process is obtained.

The Broad Reach of Culture and Ethnicity: Key Constructs and Why Culture Matters

Culture and ethnicity are central to shaping social experience, including the social experiences to which the HPA axis system is responsive. Among laypeople and researchers alike, there is often confusion over the degree to which culture and ethnicity are distinct, overlapping, or interchangeable constructs. Although the answer may depend on the specific context in question, culture and ethnicity are best thought of as distinct constructs that can have overlap. Culture includes the knowledge acquired through social learning that equips an individual to proficiently navigate the rules, norms, and expectations of their society (Dressler, 2004; Heine, 2012). Ethnicity is one's membership in a coherent social group that shares a name and often, but not always, language, food and celebration traditions, and historical memories. Members of ethnic groups often share socially learned worldviews that reflect real or perceived common culture. For this reason, ethnicity captures elements of culture, and thus is frequently used by researchers as a surrogate for culture. However, the use of demographic variables, such as ethnicity and associated pan-ethnic labels, as sole proxies for culture has been criticized by scholars who note problems, such as construct validity and assumptions of homogeneity within groups (DiPietro & Bursik, 2012; Priem, Lyon, & Dess, 1999). Thus, culture variables and measures of cultural constructs that aim to promote an understanding of experience, worldview, or belief are often considered to have greater utility than group membership.

One of the powerful roles that culture plays in human life is in shaping the social environment that people experience. Cultural practices, actions that reflect agreed-upon social knowledge, are embedded in every aspect of our social environments. For example, in some cultures people share physical space with others: they may co-sleep with their infants and live in households that include parents, children and extended family members (e.g., Campos & Kim, in press; Markus & Kitayama, 1991). In other cultures, people may prepare separate bedrooms for their infants before they are born and prefer nuclear family households. In either context, people typically feel that their own practices are normal and desirable ways to organize their lives. Engaging in these practices further reinforces those beliefs. Overall, our expectations of how people *should* be are cultural, and reflect, shape, and reinforce socially learned views of what is valued and normal. In turn, these expectations become the map that guides our social interactions, the emotions we feel, our relationship experiences and our responses to stressors.

Cultural psychology has produced two prominent theoretical frameworks that have been used to examine the cultural influences on social ties and emotion process that are relevant to social functioning. The first of these, individualism–collectivism, describes a cultural orientation broadly characteristic of a group of people that is reflected in a pattern of shared attitudes, beliefs, norms, and values (Hofstede, 1980; Schweder & Bourne, 1984; Triandis, 1995). While individualistic cultures define the self as independent and autonomous, with personal goals taking priority over the goals of collectives, collectivistic cultures view the self as one aspect of a larger social unit in which personal goals are subordinated to the goals of the larger group. Similarly, the second cultural framework of independent–interdependent construals of the self (that is, how an individual views the self or how the self is subjectively organized; Markus & Kitayama, 1991, 2010) also depicts two divergent approaches to understanding human social relationships. Independent self-construals represent the self as distinct, autonomous and self-contained, motivated primarily to express and assert its own internal attributes (i.e., attitudes, traits, and preferences), which are considered unique and fixed. Interdependent self-construals, on the other hand, interpret the self primarily as a participant in a larger social unit. While the "self in relation to specific others" also has internal attributes, these attributes are thought to be context-dependent, and thus subject to regulation in the service of adjusting and accommodating to others (Markus & Kitayama, 1991: 227). Thus, the individualism–collectivism and independence–interdependence constructs reflect human variation in the degree to which people see themselves as being *separate* from or *connected* with others. While researchers have often worked on the broad assumption from early studies (e.g., Hofstede, 1980) that individualism characterizes Western, English-speaking, industrialized cultures (e.g., the US, Canada, the UK, Australia) and collectivism characterizes the remaining majority of the world's population, the distinctions are sometimes murky and there is great nuance and complexity in the individualism–collectivism literature. Scholars have called for a conceptual refinement of individualism–collectivism that allows for a more dynamic and developmentally informed view of those constructs that uses better measurement methods (Causadias, 2013), and indeed, while ethnic minority groups in the US are often broadly painted as collectivistic, a meta-analysis of cross-national and within-US differences has found that ethnic minority groups are not uniformly more collectivistic than European-American majority groups, and nor are European Americans necessarily more individualistic than all ethnic minorities (Oyserman, Coon, & Kemmelmeier, 2002).

Nevertheless, it is this separateness-or-connection distinction that arguably most shapes social ties, and subsequently their links with the HPA axis. Emotion regulation processes, particularly as they pertain to how emotions are perceived and regulated in social settings, are also germane to social functioning. The primacy of family and social relationships is reflected in their various incarnations across different cultural groups. Differentially termed *familism* (among Latinos), *communalism* (among African Americans and Caribbean Blacks), and *filial piety* (among Asians), these constructs have been found to load onto a common collectivistic factor that prioritizes social relations (Schwartz, Weisskirch et al., 2010). Indeed, the importance given to the social unit versus the individual as the primary organizing factor for psychological processes governs human social behavior in nuanced and multifaceted ways. This cascade of cultural effects on social processes can lead to profound differences in health outcomes. For example, the associations of familism (or familialism) with greater social support and lower stress were significantly stronger among pregnant Latinas than among pregnant European Americans, and this greater social support predicted higher infant birth weight specifically for the children of foreign-born Latinas, a group for whom familism is very highly endorsed (Campos et al., 2008).

Although we may speak about normative individualistic and collectivistic cultural scripts for social ties and behavior, recognition is growing of the diversity and nuance in those scripts even within their larger cultural frameworks. Campos and Kim (in press) describe culture as a multilevel construct that captures broad distinctions at the most fundamental level (e.g., individualism–collectivism), then branches out into more precise components applied in differing constellations (or *cultural packages*) that are specific to certain cultural contexts. For example, Campos and Kim delineate two distinct forms of collectivism that govern East Asian and Latino cultural contexts: *harmony collectivism* in East Asian cultures – a priority on preventing potential social ruptures and conflict and preserving social harmony through the control of emotion expression and behavior – and *convivial collectivism* in Latino cultures, in which interdependent relationships are established through positive emotion expression, warmth, and polite behavior, which contribute to smooth and pleasant social interaction. Relatedly, research on Eastern Europeans has identified a form of *practical interdependence* in which face concerns and social harmony are de-emphasized, but mutual responsibility for solving problems is heightened (Chentsova-Dutton & Vaughn, 2012; Michailova & Hutchings, 2006). In this context, problem-focused advice giving is interpreted as very supportive, regardless of whether the advice was solicited (versus unsolicited or imposed), a finding that differs from the negative effects of threat to personal autonomy conferred by unsolicited support in European-American samples (Chentsova-Dutton, 2012; Chentsova-Dutton & Vaughn, 2012). Thus, even within cultural contexts broadly construed as collectivistic, different cultural packages shape the values, beliefs, and social practices that determine what specific kinds of social interactions are experienced as positive and helpful in particular cultural settings.

Culture and the HPA Axis

There is a limited, but quickly growing, body of work that examines the links between various aspects or operationalizations of culture and the HPA axis.

Acculturation

One of the few areas in which the links of cultural processes with HPA axis activity have been studied is in the context of people who are adapting from one cultural context to another. This process of adaptation, termed acculturation, has long been thought to have implications for health (e.g., Schwartz, Unger, Zamboanga, & Szapocznik, 2010), and more recently for physiological processes implicated in health (Mangold, Mintz, Javors, & Marino, 2012; Nicholson, Miller, Schwertz, & Sorokin, 2013). At least two studies have examined the extent to which the acculturative process itself is a stressor that may lead to the dysregulation of the HPA axis. For example, Mangold and colleagues (2012) examined the association of US acculturation, measured by self-reported comfort with the English language and with English-language music, books, and television, as well as with English-speaking European-American friends, with the cortisol awakening response (CAR). They found that a higher level of acculturation to the US was associated with an attenuated CAR in a sample of Mexican-descent adults (18–38 age range). The CAR was most strongly attenuated among the participants who were both highly US-acculturated and high in neuroticism, a personality trait characterized by sensitivity to stress. Similarly, Nicholson and colleagues (2013) examined the association of US acculturation, as indexed by comfort with the English language, in a sample of husbands and wives (44–78 age range) who had migrated to the US from the former Soviet Union. Unlike Mangold and colleagues (2012), Nicholson and colleagues (2013) found no association of acculturation with the CAR. However, Nicholson and colleagues (2013) did find that higher US acculturation was associated with higher levels of daily circulating cortisol (area-under-the-curve derived from four samples taken on one weekday) in women but not in men.

Ethnicity

Because ethnicity is often used by researchers as a surrogate for culture, the link of ethnicity with HPA-axis activity may have implications for cultural variation. At least three studies have sought to examine ethnic variation in diurnal cortisol (Cohen et al., 2006; DeSantis et al., 2007; Karlamangla, Friedman, Seeman, Stawksi, & Almeida, 2013). The study by DeSantis and colleagues (2007) sampled young people of African-American, Latino-American, Asian-American, European-American, and multiracial backgrounds (16–18 age range) and found that African-American and Latino-American youth, but not Asian-American youth, had flatter slopes across their waking days than their European-American counterparts. This pattern is consistent with that found for the African-American samples of the other two studies (Cohen et al., 2006; Karlamangla et al., 2013), but the sample in DeSantis and colleagues (2007) was more diverse. However, scholars should be cautious about interpreting these findings as indicative of cultural processes. Culture and ethnicity can overlap, but when a particular feature of culture is not specifically measured ethnic variation may reflect other processes. These include culture- or ethnicity-related intergroup processes (stereotype threat, marginalized ethnic identities) or societal and structural inequalities that adversely affect ethnic minorities, which are addressed in other chapters of this book (e.g., chapter 9, Doan and Evans on culture and poverty, and chapter 12, Ong, Deshpande, and Williams on the neurobiology of microaggressions). Indeed, other studies have found that the cortisol output of the HPA axis is responsive to the quality of intergroup interactions (Page-Gould, Mendoza-Denton, Alegre, & Siy, 2010; Page-Gould, Mendoza-Denton, & Tropp, 2008). Moreover, a key goal of studies that examine ethnic variation in diurnal cortisol rhythms has been to identify physiological pathways that might explain racial disparities in health outcomes.

"Other" Forms of Culture

Importantly, however, culture is not constrained by ethnicity, and many forms of culture (e.g., religion, social class, regional cultures within a nation) are quite separate from ethnicity. Some of the work in this area has also found associations with the HPA axis. For example, research on a "culture of honor" in the American South has found that Southerners react with more angry emotion and elevated levels of cortisol and testosterone than Northerners in response to perceived insults and slights from a research confederate in a laboratory setting (Cohen, Nisbett, Bowdle, & Schwarz, 1996). Socioeconomic status research has found that when a university's mission statement emphasized norms more consistent with the independent values reflected in the middle class (e.g., participating in independent research, expressing ideas and opinions) than with the interdependent values found in the working class (e.g., participating in collaborative research, connecting with students and faculty), first-generation students experienced greater increases in cortisol and showed more negative emotions during speeches they were asked to give about their college goals (Stephens, Townsend, Markus, & Phillips, 2012).

Cultural Shaping of the Links between Social Ties and the HPA Axis

Most of the work on the cultural shaping of social ties has focused on social support as an interpersonal process, in which the provider communicates to the recipient that he or she is valued, cared for, and part of a reciprocal relationship (Cobb, 1976; Cohen & Wills, 1985). While research has widely documented the many relational and health benefits of social support (Cohen, 2004; Cohen & Wills, 1985; Seeman, 1996; Taylor, 2007), including links with steeper diurnal cortisol slopes and reduced reactivity to acute stressors (e.g., Abercrombie et al., 2004; Burton et al., 2014; Ditzen et al., 2008; Kirschbaum et al., 1995; Sjögren et al., 2006), a quickly growing body of research has now uncovered extensive cultural variation in the degree, nature, and effectiveness of the support that is preferentially used in different cultural settings (see Kim, Sherman, & Taylor, 2008, for a review). This includes cultural differences in whether social support is even viewed as a desired form of coping (Burleson & Mortenson, 2003; Mortenson, 2006; Taylor et al., 2004), the frequency, likelihood, and effectiveness of support use (Kim, Sherman, Ko, & Taylor, 2006; Taylor et al., 2004; Wang, Shih, Hu, Louie, & Lau, 2010), and the kinds of relationships that are preferentially accessed for support (Chang, Chen, & Alegria, 2014; Wang et al., 2010; Wang & Lau, 2015). Across studies, the cultural disincentive to mobilize support has been found for East Asian/Asian-American groups, who use support less and perceive support to be less helpful than do their European-American counterparts, a finding that has been attributed to relationship concerns such as group harmony (Chang, 2015; Kim et al., 2006; Taylor et al., 2004; Wang et al., 2010).

Fewer studies have directly examined cultural patterns in the association between social ties and cortisol activity. Some of these studies have utilized the Trier Social Stress Test (TSST) to elicit a stress reaction in the laboratory (e.g., Wang & Lau, 2015). Much of the research is predicated on the notion of *cultural fit*, which posits that a match between an individual's own personal attitudes and behaviors and those of the culture in which they are embedded is linked with health and well-being (Soto et al., 2013). The primary assumption in this experimental research is that better cultural fit with an experimental condition mitigates an acute cortisol response to a stressor, but poorer fit is linked with greater cortisol reactivity. Other studies take the approach of using correlational designs to examine specific cultural moderator variables that are thought to modulate the association between support activation and stress responding (e.g., Holland, Thompson, Tzuang, & Gallagher-Thompson, 2010). The few studies that investigate cultural differences in the association between social experiences and cortisol activity are reviewed below and summarized in Table 13.1.

In an early study that adopted the TSST, Taylor, Welch, Kim, and Sherman (2007) examined cultural differences between European Americans and Asian Americans in cortisol and negative mood reactivity. Participants engaged in writing tasks that activated either implicit support (i.e., they were asked to reflect on valued social groups and their importance without disclosure of a problem), explicit support (i.e., they were asked to disclose a problem via a direct request for help), or no support. Researchers hypothesized that explicit support – the common operationalization of support – is a better cultural fit for individualistic cultures that foster independence, assertion, and self-expression in drawing upon relationships to get one's needs met, whereas implicit support presents a better cultural match for collectivistic cultures that encourage interdependence and the preservation of group harmony over personal needs (Taylor et al., 2007). Indeed, smaller cortisol and negative mood changes were found for European Americans activating explicit (rather than implicit) support, whereas Asian Americans experienced the protective benefits of implicit (versus explicit) support (Taylor et al., 2007).

Wang and Lau (2015) also examined cultural fit by investigating whether perceptions that relationships were characterized by mutual or non-mutual support could mitigate some of the stressfulness of explicit support activation. They reasoned that mutual support, characterized by the interdependent sharing of help and comfort between relationship partners, presented a better cultural fit for East Asians/Asian Americans by offsetting fears of disrupting group harmony and imposing a disproportional burden on relationships, whereas the mutuality or non-mutuality of support should not have as much influence on the experiences of European

Table 13.1 Key published studies that examine culture, social ties and the HPA axis

Citation	Sample	Method/design	Key findings
Campos et al. (2014), Study 2 (drawn from same dataset as Campos, et al. (under review))	37 Latinas and 22 non-Latina females	Examined neuroticism as a moderator on the between-subject associations between culture and stress responses to the Trier Social Stress Test. Nine salivary cortisol samples were taken over 90 minutes. The outcome variable includes cortisol responding over 90 minutes.	Neuroticism was generally associated with more blunted cortisol responding, but neuroticism predicted less blunted cortisol responding in Latinas than in non-Latinas.
Holland et al. (2010)	47 female Chinese-American caregivers of older dementia patients	Examined the associations of different sociocultural variables (belief in traditional Asian values, depression, perceived self-efficacy, coping strategies) with diurnal cortisol slopes. Three salivary cortisol samples (wake, 5pm, 9pm) collected on each of two days. The outcome variable includes diurnal cortisol slope.	Belief in traditional Asian values was the only variable found to buffer the effects of stress; caregivers who endorsed higher levels of traditional Asian values showed steeper diurnal cortisol slopes.

Campos et al. (under review) (drawn from same dataset as Campos et al. (2014))	50 Latino males and females and 35 non-Latino males and females	Examined mediation and moderation with familism and perceived support in the between-subject associations between culture and stress responses to the Trier Social Stress Test. Nine salivary cortisol samples were taken over 90 minutes. The outcome variable includes cortisol responding over 90 minutes.	Familism buffered cortisol responding through its association with perceived support for Latinos (but not for non-Latinos).
Mangold et al. (2012)	59 Mexican-American males and females	Examined the association of acculturation and neuroticism on the cortisol awakening response. Four salivary cortisol samples were taken at awakening and 30, 45 and 60 minutes after awakening.	Higher US acculturation was associated with an attenuated CAR. Higher US acculturation and high neuroticism in interaction were associated with an attenuated CAR.
Nicholson et al. (2013)	68 husbands and 69 wives who had emigrated to the US from the former Soviet Union	Examined AUC derived from four salivary cortisol samples (wake, 40 minutes after wake, before lunch, before dinner) taken on one weekday.	There was no association of acculturation with the CAR. However, higher US acculturation was associated with higher levels of daily circulating cortisol in women but not in men.

(*continued*)

Table 13.1 (*Continued*)

Citation	Sample	Method/design	Key findings
Taylor et al. (2007)	41 Asian/Asian-American males and females, and 40 European-American males and females	Examined implicit and explicit support. 2 (cultural groups) × 3 (social-support conditions) between-subject design using the Trier Social Stress Test. Three salivary cortisol samples were taken over 45 minutes. The dependent variables include cortisol reactivity, heart rate, blood pressure and psychological stress.	Asians/Asian Americans showed lower cortisol and psychological distress responses in the implicit support condition, whereas European Americans showed lower cortisol and psychological distress responses in the explicit support condition.
Wang & Lau (2015)	41 Asian/Asian-American males and females, and 41 European-American males and females	Examined mutual and non-mutual support. 2 (cultural groups) × 2 (social-support conditions) between-subject design using the Trier Social Stress Test. Two salivary cortisol samples were taken at baseline and post stressor. The dependent variables include cortisol reactivity, psychological distress (negative mood) and observed anxious behavior.	Asians/Asian Americans in the mutual support condition showed lower cortisol, negative mood, and observed anxious-behavior responses, whereas European Americans showed either no difference or a beneficial response in the non-mutual support condition.

Americans who are socialized to freely draw on their networks for help. Consistent findings across cortisol, negative mood, and behavioral indicators of stress reactivity supported this hypothesis, showing smaller amounts of reactivity for East Asians/Asian Americans in the mutual versus non-mutual support condition, but no differences for European Americans.

Studies have also moved beyond imaginal activations of social support in the laboratory via writing tasks to examining how different modes of social support in real-life friendship dyads may impact stress reactivity processes. Guan and colleagues (under review) investigated the effects of different formats of support (face-to-face, computer-mediated, or no support) on stress reactivity processes, using an ethnically diverse sample of young adult females; they found that self-reported independence, but not interdependence, moderated the effect of support format on cortisol reactivity. Specifically, those higher on independence had smaller cortisol reactivity scores for both formats of support, face-to-face and computer-mediated, than for no support, which indicates that holding an independent – but not interdependent – self-construal helped participants reap additional benefit from both explicit support contexts.

Whereas the previous studies examined cultural fit by using experimental designs to manipulate support conditions as an independent variable, other studies have examined culturally rooted variables that moderate general stress reactivity to the TSST in diverse samples. A study by Campos and colleagues (2014) examined the role of neuroticism, a dispositional sensitivity to stress or negative affect associated with blunted diurnal cortisol slopes (Lahey, 2009), in stress reactivity processes in the laboratory as well as in support perceptions outside of the laboratory. Using a sample of European-American, East-Asian, and Latina females, the multi-study paper first established that Latinas's perceived support did not vary by neuroticism, whereas European Americans and East Asians felt less supported if they were high on neuroticism. The examination of cortisol reactivity and prolonged recovery over time from the TSST acts as an individual-difference variable indicative of diurnal cortisol rhythms, which differs from a focus on short-term reactivity. Those results revealed that while higher neuroticism generally predicted a more blunted cortisol response, a significant interaction with cultural group indicated that neuroticism predicted less blunted cortisol reactivity and recovery in Latinas than in non-Latinas. The authors suggest that the Latino context – with an emphasis on interdependence, close physical proximity, social support and positive emotionality – may mitigate the costs of neuroticism (Campos et al., 2014). In another study that targeted familism as the cultural moderator, results showed that familism buffered cortisol responses to the TSST, via its association with perceived support, in US Latinos, but not in those of Asian or European background (Campos, Yim, & Busse, under review). Thus, a worthwhile future direction in research would be the examination of how specific cultural values such as familism may facilitate relationship processes in ways that help shield people from the effects of stress on the HPA axis.

The common thread of the aforementioned studies is the examination of short-term HPA-axis reactivity to acute stressors in the laboratory using the TSST. While diurnal cortisol studies have identified ethnic differences in cortisol slopes, they typically do not directly test cultural factors as mediating variables in the ethnicity–cortisol relationship. An exception comes from a growing literature on caregiver experiences and their links with subjective as well as objective health and well-being. Most of this work has shown that caregivers, like other chronically stressed groups, show more elevated and blunted diurnal cortisol slopes (Gallagher-Thompson et al., 2006; Kim & Knight, 2008), although this is not the case for all groups: Kenyan Luo elders caring for orphaned grandchildren do not show this association (Ice, Sadruddin, Vagedes, Yogo, & Juma, 2012). Caregiving presents a particularly interesting context since it is an intimate social process characterized by great emotional, psychological and physical demands, but its experience is also greatly shaped by cultural justifications for caregiving. In a study on Chinese-American female caregivers of older dementia patients, Holland and colleagues (2010) demonstrated that strong endorsement of traditional Asian values, which include the Confucian tradition of filial piety or children's responsibility to care for parents, was correlated not only with less depression and greater caregiving self-efficacy, but also with a steeper diurnal cortisol slope pattern. Thus, cultural beliefs that prioritize relational roles and responsibilities may be protective for the burdens and demands of caregiving on the psychology and physiology of the caregiver.

Conclusions and Future Directions

The literature covered above sprawls across several disparate areas, and includes few papers that converge at the core juncture of culture, social experience, and the HPA axis. We believe that this area is on the verge of tremendous growth, noting that most of those select papers were published in just the last few years and that other projects are currently in progress. These studies build on the strengths of their primary areas, but also bridge across to related areas, both theoretically and methodologically, to shed new light on the complex interplay of culture, relationships and physiological functioning.

Cultural research has articulated, or presumed, broad individualistic–collectivistic or independent–interdependent cultural differences in psychological and health processes, which have generally manifested as examinations of East–West differences. As the state of the science develops and attention turns to better understanding the nuanced "cultural packages" that comprise different forms of collectivism and even individualism (Campos & Kim, in press), the field will become increasingly sophisticated in its understanding of how specific processes are shaped by certain cultural factors that apply for particular people. And as this operationalization of "culture" becomes more and more refined, the identification and assessment of candidate physiological systems, and the specific parameters used to measure those systems, will become more adept and targeted.

As researchers delve more deeply into the cultural shaping of HPA-axis functioning, emotion regulation will need to be better studied. The emotion regulation strategies that people employ in coping with stressful events influence cortisol reactivity (Lam, Dickerson, Zoccola, & Zaldivar, 2009). Culture is central to shaping how emotions are regulated, including preferences for experiencing certain kinds of emotions, for seeking situations that are congruent with preferred emotions, and for managing emotions when coping with stress (e.g., Mesquita, 2001; Ruby, Falk, Heine, & Villa, 2012; Safdar et al., 2009; Soto, Levenson, & Ebling, 2005; Su, Tsai, & Lai, under review; Tsai, 2007; Tsai, Chiang, & Lau, 2015). It also shapes the extent to which everyday social interactions are experienced as either emotionally positive or as posing threats to the self that are emotionally negative. For example, Campos, Keltner, Beck, Gonzaga, and John (2007) found that teasing, an everyday social practice that benefits relational bonds at the expense of the self, is more threatening to European Americans than to Asian Americans. Similarly, there is cultural variation in the extent to which people benefit from expressing their negative emotions, including in the context of trauma (Butler, Lee, & Gross, 2007; Knowles, Wearing, & Campos, 2011; Soto, Perez, Kim, Lee, & Minnick, 2011). These variations, which shape the emotions that people experience in their everyday social interactions and in their responses to highly stressful or traumatic events, may have implications for HPA-axis activation.

We have focused this chapter on the HPA axis because it is a key system for understanding the connection between social experience and physiological processes. Of course, other systems closely linked to the HPA axis – such as the immune system – are also well suited to illuminating how culture and social experience intersect to affect health. For example, a study examining the links between social ties and proinflammatory cytokine interleukin-6 (IL-6) found that social strain was linked with higher levels of IL-6 for European Americans, but not for Asian Americans, whereas perceiving more supportive friendships was marginally associated with elevated levels of IL-6 for Asian Americans, but not for European Americans (Chiang, Saphire-Bernstein, Kim, Sherman, & Taylor, 2013). These findings dovetail with the culture and cortisol research, which indicates that the aspects of relationships that present poor cultural fit for a certain group take a coordinated toll on the immune and stress-regulatory systems.

However, the HPA axis, with its sensitivity to social experiences in particular, is ideally suited for research on culture, social ties and health. Yet there is much that remains unknown, and potential that remains untapped, in this area. Studies examining short-term reactivity to laboratory stressors, such as the TSST, which activates social-evaluative threat, provide a close-up view of stress reactivity in a controlled environment, whereas research that investigates diurnal cortisol profiles illuminates the effects of chronic stress burden on HPA-axis functioning. There is especially a lack of research into cultural influences on diurnal cortisol profiles and their sensitivity to everyday social experiences; this relationship is an understudied (compared with reactions to acute stressors in the laboratory) but key component of understanding health processes (Repetti, Wang, & Saxbe, 2011). A logical next step would be to draw on the strengths of both approaches to better understand the cultural shaping of naturalistic stress reactivity, that is, momentary reactivity to acute stressors that take place in everyday contexts. Additionally, studies have yet to venture beyond the level of the individual to directly measure dyadic processes. Naturalistic observational research has demonstrated that everyday stressors can shape social behaviors (Wang & Repetti, 2014; Wang, Repetti, & Campos, 2011), yet the operationalization of the social variables in the studies reviewed here has relied upon self-reports or imaginal manipulations of social support. Research that directly observed interpersonal process as it relates to HPA-axis activity, for example by using laboratory observation of social support behavior coupled with ambulatory measurement of diurnal cortisol rhythms, would provide a much-needed perspective on how enacted behaviors are associated with stress physiology. Given the growing body of work on co-regulation of the HPA-axis in couples (Saxbe & Repetti, 2010), dyadic analyses that look at partner associations are potentially fruitful areas for future work.

While the burgeoning work in this area has predominantly treated culture or cultural group as the primary moderator in the link between social experiences and health, much can be learned by taking approaches that emphasize multiple moderation. We encourage further targeted exploration of specific cultural values (e.g., familism, harmony values) that move beyond broad independence–interdependence or individualism–collectivism strokes, and extend beyond the immediate sociocultural environment to examine how other factors, such as those that vary between individuals (e.g., neuroticism in Campos et al., 2014), all converge and interact to shape culture, social ties, and HPA-axis processes. A focus on mediation analyses to identify the mechanisms by which culture works (e.g., familism and perceived support; Campos et al., under review) would also advance the field.

In closing, we encourage future research to home in on the study of cultural experiences, social ties, and the HPA axis. As research methods for studying cortisol – both in its collection and assay and in the statistical modeling of different cortisol parameters – become more advanced, accessible and convenient, and as the theory behind the influence of culture on social ties becomes increasingly nuanced, rich, and varied, the time is ripe to capitalize on this unique stress biomarker to illuminate the role of the long arm of culture in modulating how social experiences "get under the skin."

References

Abercrombie, H. C., Giese-Davis, J., Sephton, S., Epel, E. S., Turner-Cobb, J. M., & Spiegel, D. (2004). Flattened salivary cortisol rhythms in metastatic breast cancer patients. *Psychoneuroendocrinology, 29*, 1082–1092. doi:10.1016/j.psyneuen.2003.11.003

Adam, E. K., & Gunnar, M. R. (2001). Relationship functioning and home and work demands predict individual differences in diurnal cortisol patterns in women. *Psychoneuroendocrinology, 26*, 189–208.

Adam, E. K., Hawkley, L. C., Kudielka, B. M., & Cacioppo, J. T. (2006). Day-to-day dynamics of experience–cortisol associations in a population-based sample of older adults. *Proceedings of the National Academy of Sciences, 103*, 17058–17063. doi:10.1073/pnas.0605053103

Barnett, R. C., Steptoe, A., & Gareis, K. C. (2005). Marital-role quality and stress-related psychobiological indicators. *Annals of Behavioral Medicine, 30*(1), 36–43. 10.1207/s15324796abm3001_5

Bhattacharyya, M. R., Molloy, G. J., & Steptoe, A. (2008). Depression is associated with flatter cortisol rhythms in patients with coronary artery disease. *Journal of Psychosomatic Research, 65*, 107–113. doi:10.1016/j.jpsychores.2008.03.012

Burleson, B. R., & Mortenson, S. (2003). Explaining cultural differences in evaluations of emotional support behaviors: Exploring the mediating influences of value systems and interaction goals. *Communication Reports, 15*, 43–55. doi:10.1177/0093650202250873

Burton, C. L, Bonanno, G. A., & Hatzenbuehler, M. L. (2014). Familiar social support predicts a reduced cortisol response to stress in sexual minority young adults. *Psychoneuroendocrinology, 47*, 241–245. doi:10.1016/j.psyneuen.2014.05.013

Butler, E. A., Lee, T. L., & Gross, J. J. (2007). Emotion regulation and culture: Are the social consequences of emotion suppression culture-specific? *Emotion, 7*, 30–48. doi:10.1037/1528-3542.7.1.30

Campos, B., Busse, D., Yim, I. S., Dayan, A., Chevez, L., & Schoebi, D. (2014). Are the costs of neuroticism inevitable? Evidence of attenuated effects in U.S. Latinas. *Cultural Diversity and Ethnic Minority Psychology, 20*(3), 430–440. doi:10.1037/a0035329

Campos, B., Dunkel Schetter, C., Abdou, C. M., Hobel, C. J., Glynn, L. M., & Sandman, C. A. (2008). Familialism, social support, and stress: Positive implications for pregnant Latinas. *Cultural Diversity and Ethnic Minority Psychology, 14*(2), 155–162. doi:10.1037/1099-9809.14.2.155

Campos, B., Keltner, D., Beck, J. M., Gonzaga, G. C., & John, O. P. (2007). Culture and teasing: The relational benefits of reduced desire for positive self-differentiation. *Personality and Social Psychology Bulletin, 33*, 3–16. doi:10.1177/0146167206293788

Campos, B., & Kim, H. S. (in press). Culture, relationships and health: Incorporating the cultural diversity of family and close relationships into our understanding of health. *American Psychologist.*

Campos, B., Yim, I. S., & Busse, D. (under review). Culture as a pathway to maximizing the stress-buffering role of social support.

Causadias, J. M. (2013). A roadmap for the integration of culture into developmental psychopathology. *Development and Psychopathology, 25*, 1375–1398. doi:10.1017/S0954579413000679

Chang, J. (2015). The interplay between collectivism and social support processes among Asian and Latino American college students. *Asian American Journal of Psychology, 6*, 4–14. doi:10.1037/a0035820

Chang, J., Chen, C.-N., & Alegria, M. (2014). Contextualizing social support: Pathways to help seeking in Latinos, Asian Americans, and Whites. *Journal of Social and Clinical Psychology, 22*, 1–13. doi:10.1521/jscp.2014.33.1.1

Chentsova-Dutton, Y. (2012). Butting in versus being a friend: Cultural differences and similarities in the evaluation of imposed social support. *Journal of Social Psychology, 152*(4), 493–509. doi:10.1080/00224545.2011.642025

Chentsova-Dutton, Y., & Vaughn, A. (2012). Let me tell you what to do: Cultural differences in advice-giving. *Journal of Cross-Cultural Psychology, 43*(5), 687–703. doi:10.1177/0022022111402343

Chiang, J., Saphire-Bernstein, S., Kim, H. S., Sherman, D. K., & Taylor, S. E. (2013). Cultural differences in the link between supportive relationships and proinflammatory cytokines. *Social Psychological and Personality Science, 4*, 511–520. doi:10.1177/1948550612467831

Cobb, S. (1976). Social support as a moderator of life stress. *Psychosomatic Medicine, 38*, 300–314. doi:10.1097/00006842-197609000-00003

Cohen, D., Nisbett, R. E., Bowdle, B. F., & Schwarz, N. (1996). Insult, aggression, and the Southern culture of honor: An experimental ethnography. *Journal of Personality and Social Psychology, 70*, 945–960. doi:10.1037/0022-3514.70.5.945

Cohen, S. (2004). Social relationships and health. *American Psychologist, 59*, 676–684. doi:10.1037/0003-066X.59.8.676

Cohen, S., Schwartz, J. E., Epel, E., Kirschbaum, C., Sidney, S., & Seeman, T. (2006). Socioeconomic status, race, and diurnal cortisol decline in the Coronary Artery Risk Development in Young Adults (CARDIA) Study. *Psychosomatic Medicine, 68*, 41–50. doi:10.1097/01.psy.0000195967.51768.ea

Cohen, S., & Wills, T. A. (1985). Stress, social support, and the buffering hypothesis. *Psychological Bulletin, 98*, 310–357. doi:10.1037/0033-2909.98.2.310

DeSantis, A. S., Adam, E. K., Doane, L. D., Mineka, S., Zinbarg, R. E., & Craske, M. G. (2007). Racial/ethnic differences in cortisol diurnal rhythms in a community sample of adolescents. *Journal of Adolescent Health, 41*, 3–13. doi:10.1016/j.jadohealth.2007.03.006

Dickerson, S. S., & Kemeny, M. E. (2004). Acute stressors and cortisol responses: A theoretical integration and synthesis of laboratory research. *Psychological Bulletin, 130*(3), 355–391. doi:10.1037/0033-2909.130.3.355

DiPietro, S. M., & Bursik, R. J. (2012). Studies of the new immigration: The new dangers of pan-ethnic classifications. *Annals of the American Academy of Political and Social Science, 641*, 247–267. doi:10.1177/0002716211431687

Ditzen, B., Hoppmann, C., & Klumb, P. (2008). Positive couple interactions and daily cortisol: On the stress-protecting role of intimacy. *Psychosomatic Medicine, 70,* 883–889. doi:10.1097/PSY.0b013e318185c4fc

Dressler, W. W. (2004). Culture and the risk of disease. *British Medical Bulletin, 69,* 21–31. doi:10.1093/bmb/ldh020

Frisch, J. U., Hausser, J. A., & Mojzisch, A. (2015). The Trier Social Stress Test as a paradigm to study how people respond to threat in social interactions. *Frontiers in Psychology, 6,* 1–15. doi:10.3389/fpsyg.2015.00014

Gallagher-Thompson, D., Shurgot, G. R., Rider, K., Gray, H. L., McKibbin, C. L., Kraemer, H. C., … & Thompson, L. W. (2006). Ethnicity, stress, and cortisol function in Hispanic and non-Hispanic white women: A preliminary study of family dementia caregivers and noncaregivers. *American Journal of Geriatric Psychiatry, 14*(4), 334–342. doi:10.1097/01.JGP.0000206485.73618.87

Guan, S.-S. A., Chiang, J., Sherman, L. E., Nguyen, J., Tsui, Y., & Robles, T. F. (under review). Culture moderates the effect of social support across communication contexts in young adult females.

Heine, S. J. (2012). *Cultural psychology* (2nd ed.). New York: W. W. Norton & Company.

Hennessy, M. B., Kaiser, S., & Sachser, N. (2009). Social buffering of the stress response: Diversity, mechanisms, and functions. *Frontiers in Neuroendocrinology, 30,* 470–482. doi:10.1016/j.yfrne.2009.06.001

Hofstede, G. (1980). *Culture's consequences: International differences in work-related values.* London: Sage.

Holland, J. M., Thompson, L. W., Tzuang, M., & Gallagher-Thompson, D. (2010). Psychosocial factors among Chinese American women dementia caregivers and their association with salivary cortisol: Results of an exploratory study. *Ageing International, 35,* 109–127. doi:10.1007/s12126-010-9057-0

Ice, G. H., Sadruddin, A. F. A., Vagedes, A., Yogo, J., & Juma, E. (2012). Stress associated with caregiving: An examination of the stress process model among Kenyan Luo elders. *Social Science and Medicine, 74,* 2020–2027. doi:10.1016/j.socscimed.2012.02.018

Karlamangla, A. S., Friedman, E. M., Seeman, T. E., Stawksi, R. S., & Almeida, D. M. (2013). Daytime trajectories of cortisol: Demographic and socioeconomic differences – findings from the National Study of Daily Experiences. *Psychoneuroendocrinology, 38*(11), 2585–2597. doi:10.1016/j.psyneuen.2013.06.010

Kim, H. S., Sherman, D. K., Ko, D., & Taylor, S. E. (2006). Pursuit of comfort and pursuit of harmony: Culture, relationships, and social support seeking.

Personality and Social Psychology Bulletin, 32, 1595–1607. doi:10.1177/0146167206291991

Kim, H. S., Sherman, D. K., & Taylor, S. E. (2008). Culture and social support. *American Psychologist, 63*, 518–526. doi:10.1037/0003-066X

Kim, J.-H., & Knight, B. G. (2008). Effects of caregiver status, coping styles, and social support on the physical health of Korean American caregivers. *The Gerontologist, 48*, 287–299. doi:10.1093/geront/48.3.287

Kirschbaum, C., Klauer, T., Filipp, S.-H., & Hellhammer, D. H. (1995). Sex-specific effects of social support on cortisol and subjective responses to acute psychological stress. *Psychosomatic Medicine, 57*, 23–31. doi:10.1097/00006842-199501000-00004

Kirschbaum, C., Pirke, K. M., & Hellhammer, D. H. (1993). The Trier Social Stress Test: A tool for investigating psychobiological stress responses in a laboratory setting. *Neuropsychobiology, 28*, 76–81. doi:10.1159/000119004

Knowles, E., Wearing, J., & Campos, B. (2011). Culture and the health benefits of expressive writing. *Social Psychological and Personality Science, 2*, 408–415. doi:10.1177/1948550610395780

Lahey, B. B. (2009). Public health significance of neuroticism. *American Psychologist, 64*, 241–256. doi:10.1037/a0015309

Lam, S., Dickerson, S. S., Zoccola, P. M., & Zaldivar, F. (2009). Emotion regulation and cortisol reactivity to a social-evaluative speech task. *Psychoneuroendocrinology, 34*, 1355–1362. doi:10.1016/j.psyneuen.2009.04.006

Lovallo, W. R., & Thomas, T. L. (2000). Stress hormones in psychophysiological research: Emotional, behavioral and cognitive implications. In J. T. Cacioppo, L. G. Tassinary, & G. G. Berntson (Eds.), *Handbook of psychophysiology* (pp. 342–367). Cambridge: Cambridge University Press.

Mangold, D., Mintz, J., Javors, M., & Marino, E. (2012). Neuroticism, acculturation and the cortisol awakening response in Mexican American adults. *Hormones and Behavior, 61*, 23–30. doi:10.1016/j.yhbeh.2011.09.009

Markus, H. R., & Kitayama, S. (1991). Culture and the self: Implications for cognition, emotion, and motivation. *Psychological Review, 98*(2), 224–253. doi:10.1037/0033-295X.98.2.224

Markus, H. R., & Kitayama, S. (2010). Cultures and selves: A cycle of mutual constitution. *Perspectives on Psychological Science, 5*, 420–430. doi:10.1177/1745691610375557

McEwen, B. S. (1998). Stress, adaptation, and disease: Allostasis and allostatic load. *Annals of the New York Academy of Sciences, 840*, 33–44. doi:10.1111/j.1749-6632.1998.tb09546.x

Mesquita, B. (2001). Emotions in collectivist and individualists contexts. *Journal of Personality and Social Psychology, 80,* 68–74. doi:10.1037/0022-3514.80.1.68

Michailova, S., & Hutchings, K. (2006). National cultural influences on knowledge sharing: A comparison of China and Russia. *Journal of Management Studies, 43,* 383–405. doi:10.1111/j.1467-6486.2006.00595.x

Miller, G. E., Chen, E., & Zhou, E. S. (2007). If it goes up, must it come down? Chronic stress and the hypothalamic-pituitary-adrenocortical axis in humans. *Psychological Bulletin, 133*(1), 25–45. doi:10.1037/0033-2909.133.1.25

Mortenson, S. (2006). Cultural differences and similarities in seeking social support as a response to academic failure: A comparison of American and Chinese college students.*Communication Education, 55,* 127–147. doi:10.1080/03634520600565811

Nicholson, L. M., Miller, A. M., Schwertz, D., & Sorokin, O. (2013). Gender differences in acculturation, stress, and salivary cortisol response among former Soviet immigrants. *Journal of Immigrant and Minority Health, 15,* 540–552. doi:10.1007/s10903-012-9752-x

Oyserman, D., Coon, H. M., & Kemmelmeier, M. (2002). Rethinking individualism and collectivism: Evaluation of theoretical assumptions and meta-analyses. *Psychological Bulletin, 128,* 3–72. doi:10.1037/0033-2909.128.1.3

Page-Gould, E., Mendoza-Denton, R., Alegre, J. M., & Siy, J. O. (2010). Understanding the impact of cross-group friendship on interactions with novel outgroup members. *Journal of Personality and Social Psychology, 98,* 775–793. doi:10.1037/a0017880

Page-Gould, E., Mendoza-Denton, R., & Tropp, L. (2008). With a little help from my cross-group friend: Reducing anxiety in intergroup contexts through cross-group friendship. *Journal of Personality and Social Psychology, 95,* 1080–1094. doi:10.1037/0022-3514.95.5.1080

Priem, R. L., Lyon, D. W., & Dess, G. G. (1999). Inherent limitations of demographic proxies in top management team heterogeneity research. *Journal of Management, 25,* 935–953. doi:10.1177/014920639902500607

Pruessner, J. C., Kirschbaum, C., & Hellhammer, D. (1995). Waking up – the first stressor of the day? Free cortisol levels double within minutes after awakening. *Journal of Psychophysiology, 9,* 365.

Repetti, R. L., Wang, S., & Saxbe, D. (2011). Adult health in the context of everyday life. *Annals of Behavioral Medicine, 42*(3), 285–293. doi:10.1007/s12160-011-9293-x

Ruby, M. B., Falk, C. F., Heine, S. J., & Villa, C. (2012). Not all collectivisms are equal: Opposing preferences for ideal affect between East Asians and Mexicans. *Emotion, 12,* 1206–1209. doi:10.1037/a0029118

Ryan, R. M., & Deci, E. L. (2000). Self-determination theory and the facilitation of intrinsic motivation, social development, and well-being. *American Psychologist, 55,* 68–78. doi:10.1037/0003-066X.55.1.68

Ryder, A. G., Ban, L. M., & Chentsova-Dutton, Y. E. (2011). Towards a cultural–clinical psychology. *Social and Personality Psychology Compass, 5*(12), 960–975. doi:10.1111/j.1751-9004.2011.00404.x

Safdar, S., Friedlmeier, W., Matsumoto, D., Yoo, S. H., Kwantes, C. T., Kakai, H., & Shigemasu, E. (2009). Variations of emotional display rules within and across cultures: A comparison between Canada, USA, and Japan. *Canadian Journal of Behavioral Science, 41,* 1–10. doi:10.1037/a0014387

Sapolsky, R. M., Romero, L. M., & Munck, A. U. (2000). How do glucocorticoids influence stress responses? Integrating permissive, suppressive, stimulatory, and preparative actions. *Endocrine Reviews, 21,* 55–89. doi:10.1210/er.21.1.55

Saxbe, D. E. (2008). A field (researcher's) guide to cortisol: Tracking HPA axis functioning in everyday life. *Health Psychology Review, 2,* 163–190. doi:10.1080/17437190802530812

Saxbe, D. E., & Repetti, R. L. (2010). For better or worse? Co-regulation of couples' cortisol levels and mood states. *Journal of Personality and Social Psychology, 98,* 92–103. doi:10.1037/a0016959

Saxbe, D. E., Repetti, R. L., & Nishina, A. (2008). Marital satisfaction, recovery from work, and diurnal cortisol among men and women. *Health Psychology, 27*(1), 15–25. doi:10.1037/0278-6133.27.1.15

Schwartz, S. J., Unger, J. B., Zamboanga, B. L., & Szapocznik, J. (2010). Rethinking the concept of acculturation: Implications for theory and research. *American Psychologist, 65,* 237–251. doi:10.1037/a0019330

Schwartz, S. J., Weisskirch, R. S., Hurley, E. A., Zamboanga, B. L., Park, I. J., Kim, S. Y., … & Greene, A. D. (2010). Communalism, familism, and filial piety: Are they birds of a collectivist feather? *Cultural Diversity and Ethnic Minority Psychology, 16,* 548–560. doi:10.1037/a0021370

Seeman, T. E. (1996). Social ties and health: The benefits of social integration. *Annals of Epidemiology, 6,* 442–451. doi:10.1016/S1047-2797(96)00095-6

Sephton, S. E., Sapolsky, R. M., Kraemer, H. C., & Spiegel, D. (2000). Diurnal cortisol rhythm as a predictor of breast cancer survival. *Journal of National Cancer Institute, 92,* 994–1000. doi:10.1093/jnci/92.12.994

Shweder, R. A., & Bourne, E. J. (1984). Does the concept of the person vary cross-culturally? In R. A. Shweder & R. A. LeVine (Eds.), *Culture theory:*

Essays on mind, self, and emotion (pp. 158–199). Cambridge: Cambridge University Press.

Sjögren, E., Leanderson, P., & Kristenson, M. (2006). Diurnal saliva cortisol levels and relations to psychosocial factors in a population sample of middle-aged Swedish men and women. *International Journal of Behavioral Medicine, 13*(3), 193–200. doi:10.1207/s15327558ijbm1303_2

Slatcher, R. B., Robles, T. F., Repetti, R. L., & Fellows, M. D. (2010). Momentary work worries, marital disclosure, and salivary cortisol among parents of young children. *Psychosomatic Medicine, 72*, 887–896. doi:10.1097/PSY.0b013e3181f60fcc

Soto, J. A., Chentsova-Dutton, Y., & Lee, E. A. (2013). The role of cultural fit in the connection between health and social relationships. In M. L. Newman and N. A. Roberts (Eds.), *Health and social relationships: The good, the bad, and the complicated* (pp. 189–212) Washington, DC: American Psychological Association.

Soto, J. A., Levenson, R. W., & Ebling, R. (2005). Cultures of moderation and expression: Emotional experience, behavior, and physiology in Chinese Americans and Mexican Americans. *Emotion, 5*, 154–165. doi:10.1037/1528-3542.5.2.154

Soto, J. A., Perez, C. R., Kim, Y. H., Lee, E. A., & Minnick, M. R. (2011). Is expressive suppression always associated with poorer psychological functioning? A cross-cultural comparison between European Americans and Hong Kong Chinese. *Emotion, 11*, 1450–1455. doi:10.1037/a0023340

Stephens, N. M., Townsend, S. S. M., Markus, H. R., & Phillips, L. T. (2012). A cultural mismatch: Independent cultural norms produce greater increases in cortisol and more negative emotions among first-generation college students. *Journal of Experimental Social Psychology, 48*, 1389–1393. doi:10.1016/j.jesp.2012.07.008

Su, J. C.-Y., Tsai, H.-T., & Lai, W.-S. (under review). When the means justify the end: The role of regulatory fit in emotion regulation.

Taylor, S. E. (2007). Social support. In H. S. Friedman & R. C. Silver (eds), *Foundations of health psychology* (pp. 145–171). New York: Oxford University Press.

Taylor, S. E., Sherman, D. K., Kim, H. S., Jarcho, J., Takagi, K., & Dunagan, M. S. (2004). Culture and social support: Who seeks it and why? *Journal of Personality and Social Psychology, 87*, 354–362. doi:10.1037/0022-3514.87.3.354

Taylor, S. E., Welch, W. T., Kim, H. S., & Sherman, D. K. (2007). Cultural differences in the impact of social support on psychological and biological stress responses. *Psychological Science, 18*, 831–837.

Triandis, H. C. (1995). *Individualism & collectivism*. Boulder, CO: Westview Press.

Tsai, J. L. (2007). Ideal affect: Cultural causes and behavioral consequences. *Perspectives on Psychological Science, 2*, 242–259. doi:10.1111/j.1745-6916.2007.00043.x

Tsai, W., Chiang, J. J., & Lau, A. S. (2015). The effects of self-enhancement and self-improvement on recovery from stress differ across cultural groups. *Social Psychological and Personality Science, 7*, 21–28. doi:10.1177/1948550615598380

Vedhara, K., Tuinstra, J., Miles, J. N. V., Sanderman, R. B., & Ranchor, A. V. (2006). Psychosocial factors associated with indices of cortisol production in women with breast cancer and controls. *Psychoneuroendocrinology, 31*, 299–311. doi:10.1016/j.psyneuen.2005.08.006

Wang, S., & Lau, A. S. (2015). Mutual and non-mutual social support: Cultural differences in the psychological, behavioral, and biological effects of support-seeking. *Journal of Cross-Cultural Psychology, 46*(7), 916–929. doi:10.1177/0022022115592967

Wang, S. W., Shih, J. H., Hu, A. W., Louie, J. Y., & Lau, A. S. (2010). Cultural differences in daily support experiences. *Cultural Diversity and Ethnic Minority Psychology, 16*(3), 413–420. doi:10.1037/a0019885

Wang, S., & Repetti, R. L. (2014). Psychological well-being and job stress predict marital support behavior: A naturalistic observation study of dual-earner couples in their homes. *Journal of Personality and Social Psychology, 107*(5), 864–878. doi:10.1037/a0037869

Wang, S., Repetti, R. L., & Campos, B. (2011). Job stress and family social behavior: The moderating role of neuroticism. *Journal of Occupational Health Psychology, 16*(4), 441–456. doi:10.1037/a0025100

14

Cultural Influences on Parasympathetic Activity

LaBarron K. Hill and Lori S. Hoggard

The last two decades have seen a tremendous increase in efforts to identify and understand the pathways underlying disparities in disease and health among minority populations in the US (Adler & Stewart, 2010; Steptoe & Marmot, 2002). Indeed, this shift is reflected in the progression of one of the broad aims of the US Department of Health and Human Services' Healthy People initiative; from 2000 to the current iteration of Healthy People 2020, the goal to merely reduce health disparities has transformed into a more potent mission to eliminate disparities in health, and to attain health equity and health improvement not only for specific populations but for all Americans (US Department of Health and Human Services, 2011). This objective has been one of the motivating factors driving transdisciplinary research aimed at enhancing our understanding of the biobehavioral pathways and mechanisms that can be leveraged to develop effective prevention and intervention programs (Jones & Neblett, 2016a, 2016b; Townsend & Belgrave, 2009).

Inherent in the biobehavioral perspective on health disparities is increasing recognition that interactions among biological, psychological, social, environmental, and other factors play a tremendous role in disease risk and etiology (Clark, Anderson, Clark, & Williams, 1999). Culture has come to the forefront as a prominent factor determining disease risk and etiology, and has increasingly informed efforts to eliminate disparities (Thomas, Fine, & Ibrahim, 2004). Amid numerous definitions, culture may be broadly conceptualized as the complex lens through which one's perceptions, behaviors, and attitudes towards the world are shaped. Culture provides collective group identification built on shared meanings, history, and symbols (Parham, 2009). Further, culture is an inextricable element of

The Handbook of Culture and Biology, First Edition. Edited by José M. Causadias, Eva H. Telzer and Nancy A. Gonzales.

ethnicity, which has been further defined as the sense of identification with or belonging to a specific group that one derives not only from physical characteristics (e.g., race) and self-perceptions, but also from the perceptions of others (Fernando, 2010). Central to this designation is the notion that it is not only an individual's worldview, but also how one is viewed, and thus reacted to by others, that has the potential to influence health. Scholars have long argued that the systematic denigration, persecution and socioeconomic disenfranchisement of minority groups based on perceived cultural, ethnic, or racial differences is one the most salient pathways underlying disparities in health (Clark et al., 1999).

To date, a significant amount of research has focused on the role of the sympathetic nervous system (SNS) as the predominate means of documenting the relationships among ethnicity, biobehavioral factors, and health. In contrast, there has been a recent proliferation of research examining the role of the parasympathetic nervous system (PNS), and in particular its regulation of the heart, as a means of better understanding the deleterious effects of biobehavioral factors on health and disease risk. In the present chapter we provide a review of an emerging body of research that links ethnicity and discrimination to heart rate variability (HRV), a potent biomarker of parasympathetic activity. We begin with an overview of autonomic nervous system regulation of the heart and a definition of HRV. Next, we describe a regulatory model linking HRV to health and disease. Thereafter, we review the current literature linking ethnicity[1] and discrimination to HRV and provide considerations that may be useful in guiding future thinking on the relationship between cultural influences and parasympathetic activity. We end the chapter with a brief discussion of intervention and prevention programs that may promote more adaptive physiological functioning (e.g., increased heart rate variability) and promote health equity for racial/ethnic groups.

Heart Rate Variability: The Wandering Biomarker

One of the many ways in which researchers have attempted to decipher the multifaceted and complex influences of cultural and biobehavioral factors on mental and physical health has been through the examination of biomarkers (Miller, Chen, & Cole, 2009; Szanton, Gill, & Allen, 2005; Worthman & Costello, 2009). While typically non- or minimally invasive, biomarkers are quantifiable biological or physiological measures associated with the functional or dysfunctional activity of one or more organ systems (Djuric et al., 2008). Amid an ever-growing number of surrogate endpoints, ranging from biochemical markers found in blood, saliva, and hair to polymorphic variations in genes, heart rate and blood pressure remain perhaps the best-known and widely studied biomarkers (Gerin et al., 2000). This is not surprising, as cardiovascular activity has long been considered a general indicator of physiological arousal in response to acute and chronic stressors encountered in one's environment (Cannon, 1922; Selye, 1950).

Both blood pressure (BP) and heart rate are largely reflexively governed by the autonomic nervous system (ANS). The ANS has been described as the "first line of defense" in response to environmental stressors (Hill et al., 2017; Palatini & Julius, 2009), with ANS-mediated changes in heart rate and blood flow to the large muscle groups preceding the full neuroendocrine and hormonal cascade of the hypothalamic-pituitary axis (HPA). The ANS is further subdivided into two complementary branches, the sympathetic and the parasympathetic branch. Classical conceptualizations as well as contemporary models have largely emphasized the role of the sympathetic branch. In particular, BP is near-exclusively regulated by SNS activity, and models of disease etiology and progression have emphasized heightened or dysregulated SNS activity and diminished PNS activity as the predominate pattern of numerous disease states, including hypertension. In contrast, the heart, which is a potent codeterminant of BP, is dually influenced by the sympathetic and parasympathetic branches. Via the stellate ganglion, SNS influence of the heart is primarily excitatory, leading to an increase in heart rate, and subsequently in BP, in response to increased metabolic demand. Parasympathetic regulation of heart rate is primarily inhibitory, working to slow heart rate following periods of arousal and promoting energy conservation and restorative functions. Although parasympathetic activity is mediated through other cranial nerves, the vagus (i.e., the 10th cranial nerve, or the *wandering* nerve) accounts for approximately 75% of all PNS nerve fibers, which innervate the entire thorax and abdomen with projections to the lungs, the esophagus, the stomach, the small intestine, the liver, the gallbladder and the pancreas, in addition to the heart (Guyton & Hall, 2000).

Although fluctuations in heart rate are typically quantified in terms of beats per minute, parasympathetic influences on the heart occur at a near-instantaneous frequency, on an order of magnitude of milliseconds (ms). By comparison, sympathetic influences on the heart can range from seconds to minutes. As this important distinction in time course indicates, PNS modulation of the heart is much more responsive, and thus also more sensitive to changes in one's environment. Importantly, when heart rate is measured continuously, the variations in time from one heart beat to the next can be recorded, quantified and transformed, yielding heart rate variability.[2] Broadly, when the body is at rest, HRV is typically high and resting heart rate is low, a pattern that reflects a low degree of metabolic demand or arousal (e.g., "rest and digest"). Conversely, an increase in arousal will generally produce a corresponding reduction in HRV and subsequently, though not necessarily, an increase in heart rate (e.g., "fight or flight"; Appelhans & Luecken, 2006). Although we have to this point spoken of SNS and PNS regulation of the heart in purely reciprocal terms, it should be noted that the dynamic interplay of these two systems is indeed more complex, as additional and alternative modes or patterns of non-reciprocal and co-activation have been described (Berntson, Cacioppo, & Quigley, 1991; Berntson, Norman, Hawkley, & Cacioppo, 2008; Paton, Boscan, Pickering, & Nalivaiko, 2005). Nonetheless, regulation of the heart is dominated by parasympathetic activity (Saul, 1990). Notably, PNS activity has also been linked to other key processes (e.g., inflammation, HPA-axis functioning and glucose regulation; Thayer & Sternberg, 2006) implicated in cumulative models (e.g., allostatic load; see Doane, Sladek, & Adam, chapter 10 in this volume) of disease onset, which further demonstrates the importance of the PNS in regulating health and biological functioning.

Heart Rate Variability: From Stressor to Brain and Body

It has long been theorized that interconnectivity between the heart and brain is an important pathway linking experience of the external world to alterations in the body (for an overview see Thayer & Lane, 2009). Accordingly, any factor that influences the heart will have a discernible effect on the activity of the brain, and vice versa. Importantly, HRV has been proposed as an index of this bidirectional link, and scholars have further outlined the structural and functional mechanisms that facilitate this communication (Thayer & Siegle, 2002). In particular, the process underlying the transmission of psychosocial stressors to alterations in physiological functioning has been termed *neurovisceral integration* (NI). One of the central tenets of the NI model is that through inhibition of the reflexive and largely automatic tendencies of older, lower brain structures, the neocortex facilitates broader evaluation and processing of visual and other environmental information that might otherwise register as ambiguous or threatening, thereby activating the fight-or-flight response. For example, one can imagine encountering a snake during a hike in the woods. The classic and appropriate response in this situation is to flee (i.e., see snake, run), although in some instances, individuals may also exhibit a vigilance (freezing) response, characterized by slowed movement and heightened sensitivity to visual, auditory and other cues. In contrast, when one sees a replica of a snake in a toyshop, contextual information allows one to process that the snake is not "real," thereby pre-empting the physiological sequelae of the stress response and maintaining a situationally appropriate mode of functioning.

Although much more complex and nuanced, a basic interpretation of the NI perspective is that individuals with higher HRV may have better health because of greater cognitive and emotional flexibility and adaptability to changes in the environment. In contrast, individuals with low HRV are more likely to be characterized by poorer health, putatively as a result of dysregulated stress responses, culminating in disease onset. In support of this general view of HRV, a number of reviews and meta-analytic studies have documented the association between lower HRV and a host of physical and mental health outcomes, including cardiovascular disease (Thayer, Yamamoto, & Brosschot, 2010), diabetes and the metabolic syndrome (da Silva et al., 2016; Stuckey, Tulppo, Kiviniemi, & Petrella, 2014), pulmonary disease (Roque et al., 2014), normal and disordered sleep (Stein & Pu, 2012; Tobaldini et al., 2013), depression (Bassett, 2016) and anxiety (Chalmers, Quintana, Abbott, & Kemp, 2014; Friedman, 2007; Tully, Cosh, & Baune, 2013) among several other patho-physiological and psychological conditions.

Under the NI perspective, HRV is considered not only a biomarker of somatic and psychological health, but also a marker of the integrity of the functional pathway between the autonomic and the central nervous systems. Others have characterized HRV as a common mechanism connecting mental and physical health (Larsen & Christenfeld, 2009), or more broadly as an index of biopsychosocial well-being (Kemp & Quintana, 2013). Given these and other well-known conceptualizations of the importance of HRV (e.g., PolyVagal Theory; for an overview see Porges, 2009), it is surprising that so little research has considered the relationship between race/ethnicity and HRV. Of the existing work in this area, much of the focus has been on (1) ethnic differences in HRV, predominately between Whites and African Americans, (2) the relationship between perceived discrimination and HRV, and (3) socioeconomic status and HRV. Thus the following review should be considered more descriptive than exhaustive in nature.

The Paradox of Ethnicity/Race and Heart Rate Variability

Given the well-documented and pervasive disparities, particularly in rates of cardiovascular disease (CVD), among African Americans, one would expect any comparative examination of ethnicity and HRV to reveal a distinct and consistent pattern of low HRV in this group. Indeed, researchers have previously suggested that lower HRV among African Americans may, in fact, reflect a central mechanism underlying the excessive burden of CVD in African Americans (Lampert, Ickovics, Horwitz, & Lee, 2005). Yet a preponderance of studies in this small but growing literature has shown that African Americans tend to exhibit higher, not lower, HRV than Whites.

Although efforts to systematically examine the relationship between ethnicity and HRV have only recently appeared, evidence of higher HRV among African Americans has existed for over 20 years. In perhaps the first study to examine ethnic differences in HRV, Liao and colleagues (1995) examined age, race, and sex differences in autonomic function in a large ($N > 1{,}900$) sample of middle-aged (age range 45–64) adults, randomly selected from the Atherosclerotic Risk in Communities (ARIC) study. In analyses adjusted for age and gender, these researchers found African Americans to have higher HRV than Whites. In a later study, Urbina, Bao, Pickoff, and Berenson (1998) examined autonomic responses to several laboratory stressor tasks (standing, hand grip, Valsalva maneuver and cold pressor), in a sample of African-American and White males (mean age 14) drawn from the Bogalusa Heart Study. These researchers found that across all study tasks, African-American males, despite displaying a pattern of greater resting and ambulatory blood pressure, exhibited higher HRV than White males. In addition, data has also suggested that African Americans may exhibit higher HRV than members of other ethnic groups. For example, Ohira and colleagues (2008) reported that African Americans displayed higher HRV than White, Hispanic, and Chinese participants in an analysis of data from the Multi-Ethnic Study of Atherosclerosis (MESA) study.

Despite these indications, other research has shown an opposite pattern, of lower HRV among African Americans than among Whites and others. For example, Lampert and colleagues (2005) reported lower HRV among African Americans than among Whites, in a middle-aged ($M = 48$, $SD = 17$) outpatient sample undergoing 24-hour heart rate monitoring. A study by Zion and colleagues (2003) also reported significantly lower HRV in young, healthy, African-American men than in an age-matched group of European-, Hispanic-, and Asian-American men. Further, in a subsample of data from the ARIC study, Choi and colleagues (2006) reported that African Americans exhibit a pattern of lower HRV more typical of that observed among older Whites. In addition to these inverse findings, some studies have also indicated no differences in HRV between African Americans and Whites (Arthur, Katkin, & Mezzacappa, 2004; Franke, Lee, Buchanan, & Hernandez, 2004; Stein et al., 1997).

In the context of these mixed and contradictory findings, a meta-analysis summarized the available literature on ethnic differences in HRV (Hill et al., 2015). In a final sample of 17 studies encompassing a total of over 11,000 participants, Hill and colleagues (2015) reported that African Americans exhibited higher HRV than Whites, an effect which equated to a difference of nearly one standard deviation (Hedges' $g = 0.93$, 95% confidence interval = 0.25–1.62).[3] Moreover, this pattern held even after several potential confounds, including age, sex, and differences in the health status of participants, were accounted for. Although these findings have seemingly limited scope with respect to other ethnic groups, there is some indication that non-White ethnicity may be broadly associated with higher HRV. For instance, Martin and colleagues (2010) examined associations among sex, ethnicity, HRV, and Type D personality, and found female sex and African-, Hispanic-, and Asian-American ethnicity to be associated with higher HRV at rest. Another study, of post-menopausal women participating in an exercise intervention study, revealed a trend toward higher HRV among Hispanic women than among White women (Earnest, Lavie, Blair, & Church, 2008). More recently, a study by Kemp and colleagues (2016) evaluated differences in HRV among a sample of Brazilian civil service employees ($N = 11{,}989$). In this sample, participants defined their race as either Black, Brown, or White, a pattern consistent with national census approaches in Brazil. Interestingly, these researchers found that self-identified Black participants exhibited higher HRV than both Brown and White participants. In addition, Brown participants also displayed higher HRV than White participants. These authors further note that their findings for HRV parallel those reported by Hill and colleagues (2015), as Blacks in Brazil also face a greater cardiovascular disease and mortality burden.

At first glance, evidence of higher HRV among ethnic groups with typically greater disease risk profiles appears to raise many more questions than it provides answers. Given the broad consensus regarding the meaning of higher HRV in general, it is paramount to determine whether higher HRV among African Americans, and potentially other groups, is indeed beneficial or advantageous for mental and physical health. In addition, although findings seem to indicate that this pattern is consistent in men and women, research in the larger HRV literature has indicated that women tend to exhibit higher HRV than men (Koenig & Thayer, 2016), and one study has shown that ethnic differences in HRV may be more robust among women than among men (Fuller-Rowell et al., 2013). Thus, it will also be essential to examine more closely the impact of gender on ethnic differences in HRV. One clear indication from the current work is that additional research, including longitudinal investigations to assess whether and how HRV changes over time in African Americans, is needed to fully elucidate not only the meaning, but also the origins, of this conundrum. For instance, it has previously been shown that ethnic differences in HRV between African Americans and Whites may be observable as early as in the first six months of life (Propper et al., 2008). Still other research has shown that prenatal factors, such as a maternal history of depression and a greater number of life stressors, were associated with lower HRV among African-American newborns (Jacob, Byrne, & Keenan, 2009). As illustrated by these examples, both between- and within-group approaches are needed to better identify other factors that may be driving the association between ethnicity and HRV.

Racism, Discrimination, and Heart Rate Variability

Over 25 years ago, researchers proposed that racism and racial discrimination negatively affect health through increased sympathetic nervous system activity (Anderson, McNeilly, & Myers, 1992). Several years later, a broader biopsychosocial model was proposed in which the experience of racism and racial discrimination across multiple domains (structural, institutional, and interpersonal) was conceptualized as a unique form of chronic psychosocial stress contributing to the dysregulation of multiple biological systems (Clark et al., 1999). Other research suggested that racism and discrimination achieve their negative impact on health not only through heightened SNS activity but also through low or diminished HRV (Brosschot & Thayer, 1998). In one of the first studies to explore this association empirically, Dorr, Brosschot, Sollers, and Thayer (2007) examined both hemodynamic and autonomic cardiovascular recovery following a debate task involving a racial or non-racial topic in a sample of African-American and White men. Interestingly, these researchers found that African-American men who had been instructed to express versus inhibit their anger following the debate exhibited blunted HRV recovery during the 10-minute post-debate period. Using a different experimental paradigm, Neblett and Roberts (2013) also found that African Americans exhibited decreases in HRV while completing a blatantly racist imaginal task. This pattern was partially moderated by private regard, or the extent to which one has positive feelings towards one's racial group, and the race of the perpetrator, so that individuals with moderate levels of private regard exhibited a greater decrease in HRV during the blatantly racist imaginal task when the perpetrator was White versus Black. There is also modest evidence that the impact of discrimination on HRV may extend to other groups: a study by Wagner, Lampert, Tennen, and Feinn (2015) found an inverse association between lifetime discrimination and HRV assessed during a stressful speech task in a sample of White and African-American women.

More recently, Hoggard, Hill, Gray, and Sellers (2015) considered the effects of intergroup and intragroup discrimination on HRV assessed across two days in a sample of African-American women. These researchers found that racial discrimination involving an African-American confederate who posed as the perpetrator of racist statements was paradoxically associated with an increase in HRV during the 20-minute period following the interaction. In contrast, racial discrimination involving a White perpetrator was associated with no change in HRV. On day 2 of the study, those participants who had experienced discrimination from the White perpetrator exhibited lower HRV and higher HR than those who had experienced discrimination involving the African-American perpetrator on day 1. The researchers posited that merely returning to the environment in which one had previously experienced discrimination may have served as a salient trigger causing a shift in cardiac autonomic functioning. Findings from another investigation seem to support this notion. Notably, Hill and colleagues (2017) explored the relationship between differing facets of perceived ethnic discrimination, including social exclusion, stigmatization, discrimination at work or school, threats or acts of harm, and a global measure of discrimination across the lifetime, and HRV in a sample of African Americans. These researchers found that lifetime discrimination was associated with lower HRV. When the subdomains were considered, only discrimination related to perceived threats or the experience of actual acts of harm was significantly associated with lower HRV. Previous research has indicated that discrimination related to threats or the experience of actual harassment or harm may have an especially potent and detrimental impact on health (Brondolo et al., 2008; Hill et al., 2017). Subject to replication, these findings nonetheless suggest that discrimination – attributed to ethnicity or the anticipation or experience of harm – is associated with a more adverse pattern of lower HRV.

While there has been limited study of the relationship between discrimination and HRV, overall there is also some indication of the potentially protective role of HRV on mental health and well-being among African Americans. For instance, Utsey and Hook (2007) assessed resting-state HRV as a psychophysiological moderator on the association between race-related stress and psychological distress in 215 African-American college students. Higher levels of perceived institutional racism were associated with greater psychological distress for all participants; however, the strength of this pattern was weaker among men with higher basal HRV. Cooper, Thayer, and Waldstein (2014) have also shown that higher HRV may be associated with a more positive psychological profile. In particular, these researchers examined the association between hemodynamic and autonomic cardiovascular function and the use of prayer as a preferred means of coping with discrimination in a sample of 81 African-American women. These investigators found that prayer coping was positively and significantly associated with HRV assessed during the recovery period following the racism recall task.

Although the results from this small corpus of studies are broadly consistent with the expectations posed by the NI perspective, other recent evidence indicates that the relationship between discrimination and HRV may be more nuanced. Notably in the study by Kemp and colleagues (2016), the relationship between race and HRV was partially mediated by discrimination. That is, discrimination was associated with the higher HRV observed in Black and Brown Brazilians. At least one other study has reported a similarly paradoxical pattern in African Americans. Notably, Keen, Turner, Mwendwa, Callender, and Campbell (2015) observed a positive association between HRV and self-reported depressive symptoms in a sample of middle-aged African Americans. While interpretation of these findings is largely speculative at this point, some insight may be drawn from the research by Cooper and colleagues (2014). In particular, prayer as a coping response to discrimination was associated with higher HRV, and a growing body of research has characterized HRV as an index of self- and emotion-regulation capacity (for reviews see Beauchaine, 2015; Beauchaine & Thayer, 2015; McCraty & Shaffer, 2015; Segerstrom & Nes, 2007). Drawing on these conceptualizations, researchers have argued that the broader pattern of higher HRV among African Americans may indeed represent a physiological adaptation, putatively as the result of frequent attempts to cope with racial discrimination (Hill et al., 2015; Hill et al., 2017; Kemp et al., 2016). Future work that employs ecological momentary assessment approaches and ambulatory HRV monitoring will be invaluable to the examination of this *compensation hypothesis*. Importantly, as others (Brondolo, 2015; Jones & Neblett, 2016a, 2016b) have noted, studies that allow a more detailed examination of contextual factors (e.g., the frequency of discrimination exposure, the compounding effects of neighborhood and other background stressors) are an essential next step in refining current mechanistic models of racial health disparities and ultimately improving the efficacy of interventions aimed at reducing them.

Socioeconomic Status and HRV

As researchers attempt to elucidate the influence of culture on HRV, it is also important to focus on social class or socioeconomic position. Social class/socioeconomic position is "a multifaceted system of stratification and meaning-making that takes into account socioeconomic status (SES), cultural capital, and social networks, as well as beliefs, values, and behaviors associated with these material and social resources" (Webb, 2014, p. 15). The literature documenting the association between socioeconomic status (SES) and health is vast. Autonomic dysfunction has been characterized as one of the mechanisms potentially linking low SES to racial disparities in health (Boylan, Jennings, & Matthews, 2016; Fuller-Rowell et al., 2013; Lampert et al., 2005; Sloan et al., 2005). Although a full review of this literature is warranted, the breadth of such an undertaking exceeds the scope of the present work (for a discussion on culture, poverty, stress, and allostatic load, see Doan and Evans, chapter 11 in this volume).

There is evidence of a general trend of low SES being associated with lower basal HRV (Lampert et al., 2005; Sloan et al., 2005), and impaired recovery in HRV following stressful tasks (Fuller-Rowell et al., 2013; Steptoe et al., 2002). For example, Sloan and colleagues (2005) examined whether HRV might be a significant pathway in linking SES to health in over 700 African-American and White adults from the Coronary Artery Risk Development in Young Adults (CARDIA) study. Irrespective of race, moderate and high levels of SES (i.e., income) were associated with higher HRV in a relative dose–response fashion, although the magnitude of differences appeared to be more robust among Whites. In a later study, Fuller-Rowell and colleagues (2013) examined race- and age-related patterns in

HRV at rest and the change in HRV following a set of laboratory stressor tasks in an age-diverse (age range = 25–74) sample of African-American and White participants from the Midlife in the United States (MIDUS) study. In addition to baseline HRV, these researchers examined basal HRV reactivity, or the difference between HRV at rest and HRV recorded during the stressor task. Results indicated that PNS modulation of the heart following the experience of stressors may decline more rapidly with increasing age among African Americans and individuals with lower SES. These findings suggest that lower SES may be a risk factor for diminished HRV, but also that the relationship between SES and HRV may vary as a function of whether HRV is assessed at rest or during stress. Findings from another study suggest that even the relationship between SES and stressor-related HRV may not be so straightforward. In particular, Boylan and colleagues (2016) examined the relationship between child- and adulthood SES and HRV during completion of a series of stressor tasks, and in the following recovery period, in a sample of 246 African-American and White men (age range 30–34) followed longitudinally since 1988 as part of the Pittsburgh Youth Study. Importantly, while these researchers found no association between childhood SES and stress-related HRV, they observed a significant inverse association between adulthood SES and HRV during post-stress recovery. Although ethnicity did not appear to account for these researchers' findings, it is interesting to consider whether there may indeed be similar divergence between SES and HRV to that observed for ethnicity and discrimination.

It is widely held that differences in health among minorities are largely attributable to social and economic inequalities (Nazroo, 2003), which influence nearly every aspect of daily life, including education and employment opportunities, access to adequate healthcare and medical treatment, and environmental factors such as exposure to toxic food, water, and living conditions. Other work has shown that ethnic differences in numerous health outcomes were largely diminished or completely attenuated when African Americans and Whites living in similar social and economic conditions were compared (LaVeist, Pollack, Thorpe, Fesahazion, & Gaskin, 2011). These contrasting views, along with the findings briefly outlined above, underscore the need for additional research to better characterize the relationship between SES and HRV and to determine the consistency of this relationship with respect to age and ethnicity. It is also important that future research endeavors to focus on SES assessed at both the community and individual levels.

Conclusions and Future Directions

The goal of this chapter was to provide an introductory overview of heart rate variability and to characterize emerging research that demonstrates its unique association with ethnicity and discrimination. Scholars have long theorized the importance of the autonomic nervous system in transmitting the deleterious effects of racism and discrimination on health. Given its position at the forefront of the stress response, HRV may provide a more exact lens for examining the interaction of the biopsychosocial factors that underlie and drive racial disparities in health.

Despite a proliferation of interest in HRV and an ever-growing body of research, there has been comparatively little examination of its role in accounting for ethnic differences in health. While modest in comparison to the broader HRV literature, the studies reviewed here underscore the need to consider not only whether HRV is universally informative as a relative marker of physical and mental health, but also whether cultural factors may uniquely interact with HRV to mitigate or exacerbate disease risk. Importantly, it appears that the paradox posed by higher HRV among African Americans may extend from the first months of life at least into middle age. This raises important questions regarding the potential benefit of higher HRV. Indeed, if higher HRV among African Americans does reflect a type of physiological adaptation, what are its origins? And, what factors are associated with the erosion of this, putatively, protective mechanism? While there is evidence that discrimination is associated with lower HRV, there also is some indication that this relationship is influenced by additional factors, including whether experiences of discrimination are accompanied by threats or actual harm, the race of the perpetrator, and individual differences in how one copes with racism and discrimination. In addition, while the conceptualization of SES is inherently complex, an implication from previous work is that assessing measures of HRV during stress may provide additional context for understanding variations in HRV as a function of ethnicity. Stress-related measurements may also be useful in evaluating the potential compensatory functions of HRV. For instance, are individuals with higher HRV more or less reactive to stressors in daily life? The implications of this hypothesis are particularly relevant to the discussion of the frequency, chronicity, and seeming persistence of the effects of discrimination on health.

Although the current zeitgeist in biobehavioral health disparities research is seemingly characterized by a focus on multisystems approaches, there is an essential need for additional research on HRV in diverse populations. Indeed, HRV is already an integrated component of some studies that examine cumulative changes in health (e.g., MIDUS), and, given its potential role as a mediator of other stress processes, research examining changes in the association of HRV with other biomarkers over time will be especially illuminative. Prospective longitudinal data is also needed to explain whether observed ethnic differences in HRV change over the life course and to allow the assessment of the role of gender in accounting for these differences. Also, while the paradoxical relationship of HRV with ethnicity has been described and examined predominately in terms of physical health, the ramifications of this pattern in relation to mental health outcomes among African Americans and other diverse groups remains largely unexplored.

As a potential target for intervention, HRV may indeed be malleable: previous research has shown that exercise interventions, in particular, are associated with improvements in HRV (e.g., Routledge, Campbell, McFetridge-Durdle, & Bacon, 2010). There is also evidence that psychotherapeutic treatment, particularly cognitive behavioral therapy (CBT), and biofeedback, may contribute to modest improvements in HRV among individuals with depression and mild anxiety (for an overview see Kemp & Quintana, 2013). Racial discrimination is associated with an increased risk of depression among African Americans (for a review see Lewis, Cogburn, & Williams, 2015). In addition, African Americans with depressive symptoms, who also experience race-related stress, may be more prone to employ maladaptive coping strategies such as rumination (Hoggard, Byrd, & Sellers, 2015). Further, there are parallels between the anticipatory stress (vigilance) associated with past experiences and expectations of future discrimination, and hypervigilance, a well-documented feature of generalized anxiety disorder (GAD) and post-traumatic stress disorder (PTSD). Growing research in this area (e.g., Graham, West, Martinez, & Roemer, 2016; Hicken, Lee, Ailshire, Burgard, & Williams, 2013) will have important implications for examinations of the utility of psychotherapeutic interventions, including culturally tailored approaches (for a detailed overview see Jones & Neblett, 2016a, 2016b) such as Africultural coping (Utsey, Adams, & Bolden, 2000), social support seeking (Harrell, 2000), and racial and ethnic identity development (Banks, Kohn-Wood, & Spencer, 2006), not only in addressing discrimination-related distress, but also, potentially, in enhancing HRV.

Although effective prevention and intervention are overarching aims in the effort to eliminate health disparities, the research discussed here further emphasizes the importance of, and the continued need for, further explication of the mechanisms and pathways through which disparities arise. We recommend that future research studies move beyond comparative methods and employ person-centered approaches that may account for the role of multiple overlapping identities (gender, religious, social class); this person-centered and intersectional approach would allow scholars to consider more closely the rich heterogeneity within ethnic and cultural groups as a means of better understanding the origins of differences in health. Ultimately, excavating mechanisms and pathways and capturing the rich heterogeneity within ethnic and cultural groups will provide opportunities to identify additional leverage points for interventions, including individual-level interventions as well as structural-level interventions that redistribute wealth, resources, and opportunities.

Notes

1 We note that our review of this literature primarily focuses on African Americans/Blacks, as the extant literature largely focuses on African Americans/Blacks. We also note that we have used the terms African American and Black interchangeably throughout the chapter. Our decision to use African American versus Black was, in part, based on whether certain citations dictated the use of one or the other.

2 We acknowledge that HRV can refer to a multitude of measures obtained from the analysis of interbeat-interval data reflecting primarily parasympathetic, but also a mixture of parasympathetic and sympathetic, influences. For parsimony, our use of the term HRV throughout this chapter is in reference to findings based on measures of parasympathetic (i.e., vagally mediated) HRV.

3 Hedges' *g* is a standardized measure of effect size that may be interpreted similarly to Cohen's *d*.

References

Adler, N. E., & Stewart, J. (2010). Preface to the biology of disadvantage: Socioeconomic status and health. *Annals of the New York Academy of Sciences, 1186*, 1–4. doi:10.1111/j.1749-6632.2009.05385.x

Anderson, N. B., McNeilly, M., & Myers, H. (1992). Toward understanding race difference in autonomic reactivity. In J. R. Turner, A. Sherwood, & K. C. Light (Eds.), *Individual differences in cardiovascular response to stress* (pp. 125–145). New York: Springer.

Appelhans, B. M., & Luecken, L. J. (2006). Heart rate variability as an index of regulated emotional responding. *Review of General Psychology, 10*(3), 229–240.

Arthur, C. M., Katkin, E. S., & Mezzacappa, E. S. (2004). Cardiovascular reactivity to mental arithmetic and cold pressor in African Americans, Caribbean Americans, and white Americans. *Annals of Behavioral Medicine, 27*(1), 31–37.

Banks, K. H., Kohn-Wood, L. P., & Spencer, M. (2006). An examination of the African American experience of everyday discrimination and symptoms of psychological distress. *Community Mental Health Journal, 42*(6), 555–570.

Bassett, D. (2016). A literature review of heart rate variability in depressive and bipolar disorders. *Australian and New Zealand Journal of Psychiatry, 50*(6), 511–519.

Beauchaine, T. P. (2015). Respiratory sinus arrhythmia: A transdiagnostic biomarker of emotion dysregulation and psychopathology. *Current Opinion in Psychology, 3,* 43–47. doi:10.1016/j.copsyc.2015.01.017

Beauchaine, T. P., & Thayer, J. F. (2015). Heart rate variability as a transdiagnostic biomarker of psychopathology. *International Journal of Psychophysiology, 98*(2 Pt 2), 338–350. doi:10.1016/j.ijpsycho.2015.08.004

Berntson, G. G., Cacioppo, J. T., & Quigley, K. S. (1991). Autonomic determinism: The modes of autonomic control, the doctrine of autonomic space, and the laws of autonomic constraint. *Psychological Review, 98*(4), 459–487.

Berntson, G. G., Norman, G. J., Hawkley, L. C., & Cacioppo, J. T. (2008). Cardiac autonomic balance versus cardiac regulatory capacity. *Psychophysiology, 45*(4), 643–652. doi:10.1111/j.1469-8986.2008.00652.x

Boylan, J. M., Jennings, J. R., & Matthews, K. A. (2016). Childhood socioeconomic status and cardiovascular reactivity and recovery among Black and White men: Mitigating effects of psychological resources. *Health Psychology, 35*(9), 957–966. doi:10.1037/hea0000355

Brondolo, E. (2015). Racial and ethnic disparities in health: Examining the contexts that shape resilience and risk. *Psychosomatic Medicine, 77*(1), 2–5. doi:10.1097/PSY.0000000000000149

Brondolo, E., Brady, N., Thompson, S., Tobin, J. N., Cassells, A., Sweeney, M., … & Contrada, R. J. (2008). Perceived racism and negative affect: Analyses of trait and state measures of affect in a community sample. *Journal of Social and Clinical Psychology, 27*(2), 150–173.

Brosschot, J. F., & Thayer, J. F. (1998). Anger inhibition, cardiovascular recovery, and vagal function: A model of the link between hostility and cardiovascular disease. *Annals of Behavioral Medicine, 20*(4), 326–332.

Cannon, W. B. (1922). New evidence for sympathetic control of some internal secretions. *American Journal of Psychiatry, 79*(1), 15–30.

Chalmers, J. A., Quintana, D. S., Abbott, M. J., & Kemp, A. H. (2014). Anxiety disorders are associated with reduced heart rate variability: A meta-analysis. *Frontiers in Psychiatry, 5*, 80. doi:10.3389/fpsyt.2014.00080

Choi, J. B., Hong, S., Nelesen, R., Bardwell, W. A., Natarajan, L., Schubert, C., & Dimsdale, J. E. (2006). Age and ethnicity differences in short-term heart-rate variability. *Psychosomatic Medicine, 68*(3), 421–426. doi:10.1097/01.psy.0000221378.09239.6a

Clark, R., Anderson, N. B., Clark, V. R., & Williams, D. R. (1999). Racism as a stressor for African Americans. A biopsychosocial model. *American Psychologist, 54*(10), 805–816.

Cooper, D. C., Thayer, J. F., & Waldstein, S. R. (2014). Coping with racism: The impact of prayer on cardiovascular reactivity and post-stress recovery in African American women. *Annals of Behavioral Medicine, 47*(2), 218–230. doi:10.1007/s12160-013-9540-4

da Silva, F., Kastelianne, A., de Rezende Barbosa, P. D. C., Marques Vanderlei, F., Destro Christofaro, D. G., Vanderlei, M., & Carlos, L. (2016). Application of heart rate variability in diagnosis and prognosis of individuals with diabetes mellitus: Systematic review. *Annals of Noninvasive Electrocardiology, 21*(3), 223–235. doi:10.1111/anec.12372

Djuric, Z., Bird, C. E., Furumoto-Dawson, A., Rauscher, G. H., Ruffin, M. T. t., Stowe, R. P., … & Masi, C. M. (2008). Biomarkers of psychological stress in health disparities research. *Open Biomarkers Journal, 1*, 7–19. doi:10.2174/1875318300801010007

Dorr, N., Brosschot, J. F., Sollers, J. J., III, & Thayer, J. F. (2007). Damned if you do, damned if you don't: The differential effect of expression and inhibition of anger on cardiovascular recovery in black and white males. *International Journal of Psychophysiology, 66*(2), 125–134. doi:10.1016/j.ijpsycho.2007.03.022

Earnest, C. P., Lavie, C. J., Blair, S. N., & Church, T. S. (2008). Heart rate variability characteristics in sedentary postmenopausal women following six months of exercise training: The DREW study. *PLoS One, 3*(6), e2288. doi:10.1371/journal.pone.0002288

Fernando, S. (2010). *Mental health, race and culture* (3rd ed.). Basingstoke/New York: Palgrave Macmillan.

Franke, W. D., Lee, K., Buchanan, D. B., & Hernandez, J. P. (2004). Blacks and whites differ in responses, but not tolerance, to orthostatic stress. *Clinical Autonomic Research, 14*(1), 19–25. doi:10.1007/s10286-004-0155-5

Friedman, B. H. (2007). An autonomic flexibility–neurovisceral integration model of anxiety and cardiac vagal tone. *Biological Psychology, 74*(2), 185–199. doi:10.1016/j.biopsycho.2005.08.009

Fuller-Rowell, T. E., Williams, D. R., Love, G. D., McKinley, P. S., Sloan, R. P., & Ryff, C. D. (2013). Race differences in age-trends of autonomic nervous system functioning. *Journal of Aging and Health, 25*(5), 839–862. doi:10.1177/0898264313491427

Gerin, W., Pickering, T. G., Glynn, L., Christenfeld, N., Schwartz, A., Carroll, D., & Davidson, K. (2000). An historical context for behavioral models of hypertension. *Journal of Psychosomatic Research, 48*(4–5), 369–377.

Graham, J. R., West, L. M., Martinez, J., & Roemer, L. (2016). The mediating role of internalized racism in the relationship between racist experiences and anxiety symptoms in a Black American sample. *Cultural Diversity and Ethnic Minority Psychology, 22*(3), 369–376. doi:10.1037/cdp0000073

Guyton, A., & Hall, J. (2000). *Textbook of medical physiology* (10th ed.). Philadelphia, PA: W. B. Saunders.

Harrell, S. P. (2000). A multidimensional conceptualization of racism-related stress: Implications for the well-being of people of color. *American Journal of Orthopsychiatry, 70*(1), 42–57. doi:10.1037/h0087722

Hicken, M. T., Lee, H., Ailshire, J., Burgard, S. A., & Williams, D. R. (2013). "Every shut eye, ain't sleep": The role of racism-related vigilance in racial/ethnic disparities in sleep difficulty. *Race and Social Problems, 5*(2), 100–112. doi:10.1007/s12552-013-9095-9

Hill, L. K., Hoggard, L. S., Richmond, A. S., Gray, D. L., Williams, D. P., & Thayer, J. F. (2017). Examining the association between perceived discrimination and heart rate variability in African Americans. *Cultural Diversity and Ethnic Minority Psychology, 23*(1), 5–14.

Hill, L. K., Hu, D. D., Koenig, J., Sollers, J. J., III, Kapuku, G., Wang, X., … & Thayer, J. F. (2015). Ethnic differences in resting heart rate variability: A systematic review and meta-analysis. *Psychosomatic Medicine, 77*(1), 16–25. doi:10.1097/PSY.0000000000000133

Hoggard, L. S., Byrd, C. M., & Sellers, R. M. (2015). The lagged effects of racial discrimination on depressive symptomology and interactions with racial identity. *Journal of Counseling Psychology, 62*(2), 216–225. doi:10.1037/cou0000069

Hoggard, L. S., Hill, L. K., Gray, D. L., & Sellers, R. M. (2015). Capturing the cardiac effects of racial discrimination: Do the effects "keep going"? *International Journal of Psychophysiology, 97*(2), 163–170. doi:10.1016/j.ijpsycho.2015.04.015

Jacob, S., Byrne, M., & Keenan, K. (2009). Neonatal physiological regulation is associated with perinatal factors: A study of neonates born to healthy African American women living in poverty. *Infant Mental Health Journal, 30*(1), 82–94. doi:10.1002/imhj.20204

Jones, S. C., & Neblett, E. W. (2016a). Future directions in research on racism-related stress and racial-ethnic protective factors for Black youth. *Journal of Clinical Child and Adolescent Psychology*, 1–13. doi:10.1080/15374416.2016.1146991

Jones, S. C., & Neblett, E. W. (2016b). Racial-ethnic protective factors and mechanisms in psychosocial prevention and intervention programs for Black youth. *Clinical Child and Family Psychology Review, 19*(2), 134–161. doi:10.1007/s10567-016-0201-6

Keen, L., II, Turner, A. D., Mwendwa, D., Callender, C., & Campbell, A., Jr. (2015). Depressive symptomatology and respiratory sinus arrhythmia in a non-clinical sample of middle-aged African Americans. *Biological Psychology, 108*, 56–61. doi:10.1016/j.biopsycho.2015.03.008

Kemp, A. H., Koenig, J., Thayer, J. F., Bittencourt, M. S., Pereira, A. C., Santos, I. S., … & Lotufo, P. A. (2016). Race and resting-state heart rate variability in Brazilian civil servants and the mediating effects of discrimination: An ELSA–Brasil cohort study. *Psychosomatic Medicine, 78*(8), 950–958. doi:10.1097/PSY.0000000000000359

Kemp, A. H., & Quintana, D. S. (2013). The relationship between mental and physical health: Insights from the study of heart rate variability. *International Journal of Psychophysiology, 89*(3), 288–296. doi:10.1016/j.ijpsycho.2013.06.018

Koenig, J., & Thayer, J. F. (2016). Sex differences in healthy human heart rate variability: A meta-analysis. *Neuroscience and Biobehavioral Reviews, 64*, 288–310.

Lampert, R., Ickovics, J., Horwitz, R., & Lee, F. (2005). Depressed autonomic nervous system function in African Americans and individuals of lower social class: A potential mechanism of race- and class-related disparities in health outcomes. *American Heart Journal, 150*(1), 153–160. doi:10.1016/j.ahj.2004.08.008

Larsen, B. A., & Christenfeld, N. J. (2009). Cardiovascular disease and psychiatric comorbidity: The potential role of perseverative cognition. *Cardiovascular Psychiatry and Neurology*, 2009, 791017. doi:10.1155/2009/791017

LaVeist, T., Pollack, K., Thorpe, R., Jr., Fesahazion, R., & Gaskin, D. (2011). Place, not race: Disparities dissipate in southwest Baltimore when Blacks and Whites live under similar conditions. *Health Affairs, 30*(10), 1880–1887. doi:10.1377/hlthaff.2011.0640

Lewis, T. T., Cogburn, C. D., & Williams, D. R. (2015). Self-reported experiences of discrimination and health: Scientific advances, ongoing controversies, and emerging issues. *Annual Review of Clinical Psychology, 11*, 407–440.

Liao, D., Barnes, R. W., Chambless, L. E., Simpson, R. J., Jr., Sorlie, P., & Heiss, G. (1995). Age, race, and sex differences in autonomic cardiac function measured by spectral analysis of heart rate variability: The ARIC study. *American Journal of Cardiology, 76*(12), 906–912. doi:10.1016/S0002-9149(99)80260-4

Martin, L. A., Doster, J. A., Critelli, J. W., Lambert, P. L., Purdum, M., Powers, C., & Prazak, M. (2010). Ethnicity and Type D personality as predictors of heart rate variability. *International Journal of Psychophysiology, 76*(2), 118–121. doi:10.1016/j.ijpsycho.2010.03.001

McCraty, R., & Shaffer, F. (2015). Heart rate variability: New perspectives on physiological mechanisms, assessment of self-regulatory capacity, and health risk. *Global Advances in Health and Medicine, 4*(1), 46–61. doi:10.7453/gahmj.2014.073

Miller, G., Chen, E., & Cole, S. W. (2009). Health psychology: Developing biologically plausible models linking the social world and physical health. *Annual Review of Psychology, 60*, 501–524. doi:10.1146/annurev.psych.60.110707.163551

Nazroo, J. Y. (2003). The structuring of ethnic inequalities in health: Economic position, racial discrimination, and racism. *American Journal of Public Health, 93*(2), 277–284.

Neblett, E. W., Jr., & Roberts, S. O. (2013). Racial identity and autonomic responses to racial discrimination. *Psychophysiology, 50*(10), 943–953. doi:10.1111/psyp.12087

Ohira, T., Diez Roux, A. V., Prineas, R. J., Kizilbash, M. A., Carnethon, M. R., & Folsom, A. R. (2008). Associations of psychosocial factors with heart rate and its short-term variability: Multi-ethnic study of atherosclerosis. *Psychosomatic Medicine, 70*(2), 141–146. doi:10.1097/PSY.0b013e318160686a

Palatini, P., & Julius, S. (2009). The role of cardiac autonomic function in hypertension and cardiovascular disease. *Current Hypertension Reports, 11*(3), 199–205. doi: 10.1007/s11906-009-0035-4

Parham, T. A. (2009). Foundations for an African American psychology: Extending roots to an ancient Kemetic past. In H. A. Neville, B. M. Tynes, & S. O. Utsey (Eds.) *Handbook of African American psychology* (pp. 3–18). Thousand Oaks, CA: Sage Publications.

Paton, J. F., Boscan, P., Pickering, A. E., & Nalivaiko, E. (2005). The yin and yang of cardiac autonomic control: Vago-sympathetic interactions revisited. *Brain Research Reviews, 49*(3), 555–565. doi:10.1016/j.brainresrev.2005.02.005

Porges, S. W. (2009). The polyvagal theory: New insights into adaptive reactions of the autonomic nervous system. *Cleveland Clinic Journal of Medicine, 76*(Suppl 2), S86–S90.

Propper, C., Moore, G. A., Mills-Koonce, W. R., Halpern, C. T., Hill-Soderlund, A. L., Calkins, S. D., … & Cox, M. (2008). Gene–environment contributions to the development of infant vagal reactivity: The interaction of dopamine and maternal sensitivity. *Child Development, 79*(5), 1377–1394. doi:10.1111/j.1467-8624.2008.01194.x

Roque, A. L., Valenti, V. E., Massetti, T., da Silva, T. D., Monteiro, C. B., Oliveira, F. R., … & Ferreira, C. (2014). Chronic obstructive pulmonary disease and heart rate variability: A literature update. *International Archives of Medicine, 7*, 43. doi:10.1186/1755-7682-7-43

Routledge, F. S., Campbell, T. S., McFetridge-Durdle, J. A., & Bacon, S. L. (2010). Improvements in heart rate variability with exercise therapy. *Canadian Journal of Cardiology, 26*(6), 303–312. doi:10.1016/S0828-282X(10)70395-0

Saul, J. P. (1990). Beat-to-beat variations of heart rate reflect modulation of cardiac autonomic outflow. *Physiology, 5*(1), 32–37.

Segerstrom, S. C., & Nes, L. S. (2007). Heart rate variability reflects self-regulatory strength, effort, and fatigue. *Psychological Science, 18*(3), 275–281. doi:10.1111/j.1467-9280.2007.01888.x

Selye, H. (1950). Stress and the general adaptation syndrome. *British Medical Journal, 1*(4667), 1383–1392.

Sloan, R. P., Huang, M.-H., Sidney, S., Liu, K., Williams, O. D., & Seeman, T. (2005). Socioeconomic status and health: Is parasympathetic nervous system activity an intervening mechanism? *International Journal of Epidemiology, 34*(2), 309–315.

Stein, P. K., Freedland, K. E., Skala, J. A., Carney, R. M., Davila-Roman, V., Rich, M. W., & Kleiger, R. E. (1997). Heart rate variability is independent of age, gender, and race in congestive heart failure with a recent acute exacerbation. *American Journal of Cardiology, 79*(4), 511–512.

Stein, P. K., & Pu, Y. (2012). Heart rate variability, sleep and sleep disorders. *Sleep Medicine Reviews, 16*(1), 47–66. doi:10.1016/j.smrv.2011.02.005

Steptoe, A., Feldman, P. J., Kunz, S., Owen, N., Willemsen, G., & Marmot, M. (2002). Stress responsivity and socioeconomic status: A mechanism for increased cardiovascular disease risk? *European Heart Journal, 23*(22), 1757–1763.

Steptoe, A., & Marmot, M. (2002). The role of psychobiological pathways in socio-economic inequalities in cardiovascular disease risk. *European Heart Journal, 23*(1), 13–25. doi:10.1053/euhj.2001.2611

Stuckey, M. I., Tulppo, M. P., Kiviniemi, A. M., & Petrella, R. J. (2014). Heart rate variability and the metabolic syndrome: A systematic review of the literature. *Diabetes/Metabolism Research and Reviews, 30*(8), 784–793. doi:10.1002/dmrr.2555

Szanton, S. L., Gill, J. M., & Allen, J. K. (2005). Allostatic load: A mechanism of socioeconomic health disparities? *Biological Research for Nursing, 7*(1), 7–15. doi:10.1177/1099800405278216

Thayer, J. F., & Lane, R. D. (2009). Claude Bernard and the heart–brain connection: Further elaboration of a model of neurovisceral integration. *Neuroscience and Biobehavioral Reviews, 33*(2), 81–88. doi:10.1016/j.neubiorev.2008.08.004

Thayer, J. F., & Siegle, G. J. (2002). Neurovisceral integration in cardiac and emotional regulation. *IEEE Engineering in Medicine and Biology Magazine, 21*(4), 24–29.

Thayer, J. F., & Sternberg, E. (2006). Beyond heart rate variability: Vagal regulation of allostatic systems. *Annals of the New York Academy of Sciences, 1088*, 361–372. doi:10.1196/annals.1366.014

Thayer, J. F., Yamamoto, S. S., & Brosschot, J. F. (2010). The relationship of autonomic imbalance, heart rate variability and cardiovascular disease risk factors. *International Journal of Cardiology, 141*(2), 122–131. doi:10.1016/j.ijcard.2009.09.543

Thomas, S. B., Fine, M. J., & Ibrahim, S. A. (2004). Health disparities: The importance of culture and health communication. *American Journal of Public Health, 94*(12), 2050.

Tobaldini, E., Nobili, L., Strada, S., Casali, K. R., Braghiroli, A., & Montano, N. (2013). Heart rate variability in normal and pathological sleep. *Frontiers in Physiology, 4*, 294. doi:10.3389/fphys.2013.00294

Townsend, T. G., & Belgrave, F. Z. (2009). Eliminating health disparities: Challenges for African American psychologists. *Journal of Black Psychology, 35*(2), 146–153. doi:10.1177/0095798409333605

Tully, P. J., Cosh, S. M., & Baune, B. T. (2013). A review of the affects of worry and generalized anxiety disorder upon cardiovascular health and coronary heart disease. *Psychology Health & Medicine, 18*(6), 627–644. doi:10.1080/13548506.2012.749355

Urbina, E. M., Bao, W. H., Pickoff, A. S., & Berenson, G. S. (1998). Ethnic (black–white) contrasts in heart rate variability during cardiovascular reactivity testing in male adolescents with high and low blood pressure:

The Bogalusa Heart Study. *American Journal of Hypertension, 11*(2), 196–202. doi:10.1016/S0895-7061(97)00314-2

US Department of Health and Human Services (2011). *Healthy people 2020.* Washington, DC: Office of Disease Prevention and Health Promotion, US Department of Health and Human Services.

Utsey, S. O., Adams, E. P., & Bolden, M. (2000). Development and initial validation of the Africultural Coping Systems Inventory. *Journal of Black Psychology, 26*(2), 194–215.

Utsey, S. O., & Hook, J. N. (2007). Heart rate variability as a physiological moderator of the relationship between race-related stress and psychological distress in African Americans. *Cultural Diversity and Ethnic Minority Psychology, 13*(3), 250–253. doi:10.1037/1099-9809.13.3.250

Wagner, J., Lampert, R., Tennen, H., & Feinn, R. (2015). Exposure to discrimination and heart rate variability reactivity to acute stress among women with diabetes. *Stress Health, 31*(3), 255–262. doi:10.1002/smi.2542

Webb, F. R. (2014). The role of social class identity: Implications for African American and White college students' psychological and academic outcomes. Doctoral dissertation, University of Michigan.

Worthman, C. M., & Costello, E. J. (2009). Tracking biocultural pathways in population health: The value of biomarkers. *Annals of Human Biology, 36*(3), 281–297. doi:10.1080/03014460902832934

Zion, A. S., Bond, V., Adams, R. G., Williams, D., Fullilove, R. E., Sloan, R. P., … & De Meersman, R. E. (2003). Low arterial compliance in young African-American males. *American Journal of Physiology – Heart and Circulatory Physiology, 285*(2), H457–H462. doi:10.1152/ajpheart.00497.2002

15

Neurobiology of Stress and Drug Use Vulnerability in Culturally Diverse Communities

Ezemenari M. Obasi, Kristin A. Wilborn, Lucia Cavanagh, Sandra Yan, and Ewune Ewane

Ethnic and cultural disparities related to stress exposure provide a unique framework from which we examine drug use vulnerability. There is a long-standing history of social oppression and explicit and implicit biases contributing to alterations in the HPA axis, which have been implicated in drug use vulnerability. This chapter will focus on outlining those oppressions and demonstrating the risks for racial/ethnic communities in connection with unique stressors as a risk factor for disparate rates of drug and alcohol use and misuse. To understand the unique dynamics of drug use vulnerability in these communities, we will first briefly discuss stress, the relationship between stress and the HPA axis, and the HPA axis as it relates to drug use vulnerability. We will then examine several racial/ethnic communities in the United States and discuss unique risks and protective factors that are related to stress and drug use in these populations.

What Is Stress?

Hans Selye's work has played a large role in the operationalization of stress. His definition of stress as the "non-specific neuroendocrine response of the body" (Selye, 1936, 1956) helped shape the way we understand stress today. Selye is well known for introducing a physiologically based model for the stress response, known as General Adaptation Syndrome (GAS). This model explained the stress response in three stages. The first stage was alarm. This is the time during which the body activates the "fight or flight" response. The second stage was resistance. During this stage, the

The Handbook of Culture and Biology, First Edition. Edited by José M. Causadias, Eva H. Telzer and Nancy A. Gonzales.

body remains in an alerted state, ready to respond when needed. The third stage was exhaustion. If the body stays in the resistance phase, physiological resources become depleted, putting the organism at risk of disease and even death. While we have moved beyond Selye's work, his efforts greatly changed the course of stress research (for a review, see Selye, 1976). Indeed, much research on stress still relates to the neuroendocrine system and the fight-or-flight response.

Before one can understand the process by which the body responds to stressors, there needs to be an understanding of the difference between a stressor, which is the event or stimulus, and stress, which is the body's reaction to that stressor. A stressor may be identified as the action and stress as the response. These broad definitions may lend themselves to overgeneralizing (citing every experience as a stressor) or over-restrictive (only including the most traumatic of events) definitions. Consequently, context and individual appraisal of stressors, combined with stress reactions, are central to the understanding of the stress response.

Defining Stressors

It is critical to recognize that, as a construct, a stressor can be either positive or negative, of short duration or chronic. Major stressors are important life events that cause significant distress, such as a death in the family or being laid off. Daily hassles, on the other hand, are happenings within one's life that are irritating, frustrating, and distressing. While daily hassles tend to occur with some frequency, major stressors generally occur more infrequently and tend to be more severe in nature (Blankstein & Flett, 1992). Daily hassles have been found to be a better predictor of psychological and physical symptoms, such as overall health status, somatic symptoms, and energy levels, than are major stressors, probably because of their chronicity (DeLongis, Coyne, Dakof, Folkman, & Lazarus, 1982). This is especially relevant to communities of color, as they are more likely than their European-American counterparts to experience chronic stressors, such as acculturative stress and discrimination.

Similarly, it is important to recognize that stress is an everyday occurrence and is healthy and adaptive. Manageable levels of stress appear, in fact, to promote physiological and psychological health and balance (Seery, Leo, Lupien, Kondrak, & Almonte, 2013). In a similar vein, some stressors can be motivating. Performance tends to follow an inverted U shape in relation to exposure to stressors: low levels of stressors present as under the radar and so do not stimulate the necessary motivation, or high levels are over the threshold and lead to high anxiety and physiological responses that interfere with performance (Seery et al., 2013).

Stress and the Hypothalamic-Pituitary-Adrenal (HPA) Axis

As is often the case in research, much of the focus within stress has been on what is abnormal or problematic, even though there is a healthy function of the human stress response. To understand when a stress response is maladaptive, we must first understand how a stress response is adaptive. The sympathetic arm of the autonomic nervous system is activated as an adaptive response to a perceived stressor. This stimulates the adrenal glands to release epinephrine, which causes an increased heart rate, increased breathing, and a release of glucose to help meet the metabolic needs of the physical response to stress. Almost simultaneously, there is a signal to the paraventricular nucleus of the hypothalamus to trigger activity in the hypothalamic-pituitary-adrenal (HPA) axis (Kolb & Whishaw, 2005; McEwen, 1998). The hypothalamus is located near the brainstem and is responsible, among other things, for controlling endocrine functions and helping to maintain homeostasis. Additionally, the hypothalamus connects areas of the brain responsible for emotional responses and decision making, namely the frontal cortex and the amygdala, parts of the limbic system that contribute to the regulation of the HPA axis and, in turn, are impacted by glucocorticoid flooding in times of excess stress (Lovallo, 2005).

In response to a perceived stressor, the hypothalamus releases corticotrophin-releasing hormone (CRH), which binds to the corticotrophin-releasing hormone receptor CRHR1, which then releases corticotrophin in the anterior pituitary (Bittencourt & Sawchenko, 2000). Specifically, CRH targets the release of adrenocorticotrophic hormone (ACTH) from the pituitary corticotrophs, which are located in the anterior pituitary. ACTH is released and binds to the adrenal cortex, which subsequently releases the glucocorticoid cortisol. Deactivation of the HPA system occurs when cortisol binds to hypothalamic receptors (Kolb & Whishaw, 2005). One role of cortisol is to bring the body back to homeostasis after a stressor through negative feedback inhibition (negative feedback loop), which inhibits the secretion of glucocorticoids, thereby limiting the duration of tissue exposure and minimizing the potentially adverse physical and psychological effects (Longenbaker, 2011).

Chronic Stress and Drug Use Vulnerability

McEwen's (2006) concept of allostasis, maintaining stability in the context of change, provides a theoretical viewpoint for understanding the deleterious effects of being chronically exposed to stressors. Specifically, allostasis characterizes the individual as capable of adapting or changing to meet the demands of a changing environment or social context. As the individual is consistently exposed to that environment over time, the inherent variability may become less malleable. The individual's regulatory capacities are marked by (1) stable trajectories, including long-term maturational and age-related shifts as well as "setpoints," and (2) short-term changes to meet the demands of the proximate social context. Hormones are important, since hormonal changes provide insight into the match of our biology with our social context. Hormones are remarkably responsive to the environment, constantly changing in response to our physical, social and emotional world. Yet hormones are also the platform for the genetic blueprint of the individual: they activate genes nearly everywhere in the human body. Hormones allow gene expression to vary across time, social context, physical environments and developmental stage (Gottlieb, 1996). Allostasis frames the interplay between genetic, neural, behavioral, and environmental forces as a developmental phenomenon, with social contextual cues shaping the phenotypic expression of the genetic and biological building blocks. Chronic activation of stress-responsive systems by ongoing experiences of racism, violence, crime, unemployment, financial strain, and low-to-no socioeconomic status can cause "wear and tear" on regulatory systems by way of allostatic load (McEwen, 1998). Allostasis does not provide a simple prediction for unidirectional alterations: both hypo- and hyper-arousal result from extreme environmental input. Salient stressful experiences may alter the "setpoint" for stress regulation along hypo- or hyper-arousal trajectories. A dysregulated stress system, in turn, may contribute to drug use and abuse (Koob & Le Moal, 2001).

Research that examines the relationship between the dysregulation of the HPA axis and drug addiction has led to mixed research findings; significantly little of it focuses on communities of color. Previous research has found HPA activity to fluctuate significantly following substance use. Animal models suggest that sensitivity to stress, recovery from stress, and the uncontrollability of stressors are strong predictors of drug use and abuse (Goeders, 2002; Goeders & Guerin, 1994). For example, there may be a propensity to use drugs during times of stress because of increased activation of addiction-related neurocircuitry by CRH (Takahashi, Rako,

Takano-Shimizu, Hoffmann, & Lee, 2010). The activation of the HPA axis and enhanced expression of CRH have been observed during acute phases of withdrawal in drug-dependent animal models. Because drug withdrawal is both psychologically and physically stressful, it has been suggested that increased CRH neurotransmission plays a role in coping with withdrawal and continued drug use (Skelton, Nemeroff, & Owens, 2004). CRH antagonists have been found to decrease the chronically activated HPA axis that is exhibited in drug-dependent individuals (Contoreggi et al., 2003). This suggests that targeting CRH may be beneficial in treating stress-related drug addictions.

A growing body of literature links stress dysregulation and drug use vulnerability. Some research has demonstrated how the CRHR1 genotype interacts with stress in the environment to increase alcohol-seeking behavior in rats (Hansson et al., 2006; Hansson, Cippitelli, Wolfgang, Ciccocioppo, & Heilig, 2007). CRHR1 has been implicated in the down-regulation of the withdrawal symptoms of alcohol (Hansson et al., 2007) and cocaine (Koylu, Balkan, Kuhar, & Pogun, 2006). Additionally, rats with an up-regulated expression of the CRHR1 gene were found to be more susceptible to excessive alcohol self-administration when subjected to stress (Hansson et al., 2006). Further, increased activity at CRHR1 receptors in the post-dependent state has been found to inhibit heavy drinking and reduce relapse risk (Sommer et al., 2008). In human studies, CRHR1 has been linked to basal cortisol levels and mental health outcomes (Bradley et al., 2008; Obasi et al., 2015; Wasserman, Wasserman, Rozanov, & Solowski, 2009).

The directionality in the relationship between stress and drug use remains unclear. There is a dearth of human-based longitudinal investigations into trajectories of HPA regulation as a predictor of drug use vulnerability across time. That being said, we are currently investigating this phenomenon in the Hwemudua Addictions and Health Disparities Laboratory (HAHDL; National Institute for Drug Abuse grant R01DA034739) in a sample of African Americans. We believe this work needs to be carried out across a diverse range of populations and social contexts in order to articulate clear mechanisms that can serve as targets for data-driven prevention and intervention efforts. The rest of the chapter, consequently, examines the African-American, American Indian/Alaskan Native, Asian, and Latino communities in the United States and how their unique experiences and exposure to stressors may influence distinct drug use vulnerabilities. A cultural viewpoint on this topic is particularly important, as many perspectives are derived from a typical European-American, Protestant tradition and ignore the historical and cultural context of underserved and marginalized communities.

Stress and Drug Use in Racially Diverse Communities

The Black/African-American Community

People of African descent represent approximately 13.3% of the US population (US Census Bureau, 2015), yet are disproportionately exposed to chronic stress (e.g. racism, discrimination, violence, crime, neighborhood disorganization, unemployment, and financial strain; Clark, Anderson, Clark, & Williams, 1999). Consistently with the model outlined above, African Americans show dysregulation of the HPA axis following exposure to chronic stress, and this dysregulation seems to be consistent with increased risk of drug and alcohol use in African Americans (Obasi et al., 2015).

Stressors in the Black Community

People of African descent are often overrepresented in residentially segregated neighborhoods and more likely to live in conditions characterized by poverty and violence, known stressors that negatively affect psychosocial well-being (US Department of Health and Human Services, 2001). These communities often suffer from limited access to community resources such as health services, and from poor-quality schools, limited employment opportunities, and food deserts. In addition to their social context, it is critical to acknowledge the incessant exposure to racism and daily microaggressions. For example, in a population of African-American males, nearly 86% reported experiencing racial discrimination from police or the court system and almost 73% reported job discrimination (Chae et al., 2014).

The chronic nature of racial discrimination within the US has been identified as a major risk factor for African Americans. According to Jones (1997), the experience of racism is multidimensional and can be viewed as a tripartite typology that comprises individual racism (which occurs on a personal level), institutional racism and cultural racism. Institutional racism is experienced by the group by way of social and institutional policies that differentially target and discriminate against communities according to their phenotypic racial attributes, while cultural racism has largely replaced biological racism by pointing out differences in culture to posit superiority. Although less overt than biological racism, cultural racism continues to perpetuate stereotypes and create systemic instances of injustice, and is often used as a tool to exercise dominance, superiority, and control over marginalized communities (Ben-Eliezer, 2004).

Institutional racism can be exemplified in our educational system, which continues to disadvantage African Americans. Spring (2016) suggested that the No Child Left Behind Act of 2001 reinstitutionalized the sentiment of separate but equal. Rather than continuing with successful desegregation efforts, which were balancing learning opportunities, these policies created a shift in our educational system toward more racially and economically segregated schools, which perpetuates socioeconomic imbalances by disallowing proper educational opportunities for children from low-income families, specifically at a disproportionate rate for African-American children. Furthermore, examples of cultural racism can be found in the overt manner in which historical African-American contributions are ignored, which leads to the marginalization of the community. Cultural racism can also be exemplified by the ways in which standardized test scores are used to differentially constrain educational opportunities for African Americans (for a review, see Jencks & Phillips, 1998). Steele (1997) suggested that stereotype threat exists for any member of a group that is viewed negatively in a particular domain. That member then performs more poorly in that domain because of anxiety about confirming the stereotype, creating a self-fulfilling prophecy.

Another major source of stress for African Americans is financial burden. Overall, a disproportionate number of African-American families live with severe, chronic economic stress that has the potential to take a toll on emerging adults. Residents in these communities experience many of the risk factors associated with drug abuse: mental illness, personality traits (impulsivity, aggression, dependence), familial risk (a history of pathology, drug abuse, physical or mental abuse, divorce, a chaotic home environment), a deprived social environment (racism, discrimination, neighborhood disorganization, unemployment, drug availability, acculturative stress, affiliation with deviant peers, and lack of involvement in cultural activities), substandard education (poor performance and dropping out), and positive attitudes toward drug use (Hawkins, Catalano, & Miller, 1992). In spite of the long list of stressors and risk factors, African-American rates of drug use do not always follow predicted trajectories.

As previously discussed, while there is certainly a relationship between HPA-axis dysregulation and drug use, the directionality of that relationship is still unclear. It may be that African Americans use alcohol, tobacco, and illicit drugs at a higher rate to reduce stress. While there are some theoretical and empirical insights into the perceived stress reduction properties of substance use, we know that substance use activates the HPA axis and contributes to allostatic load and disparate rates of disease in the African-American community (Jackson, Knight, & Rafferty, 2010; Obasi, Tackett, Shirtcliff, & Cavanagh, 2016; Obasi et al., 2015).

Drug Use in the Black Community

The fact that African Americans initiate drug use later in life and experience greater drug-use morbidity than national trends is a major paradox in addictions research, especially given their exposure to the aforementioned risk factors. In 2014, African Americans between the ages of 12 and 25 used illicit drugs at below the national average rate when use was measured over the lifetime, in the past year, and in the past month. While African Americans had used marijuana in the past year at a greater rate than the general population in this age group, those who were 18–25 and those who were 26 and older used at a lesser lifetime rate. Interestingly, African Americans aged 26 and older had used crack and cocaine at a greater rate than the national average in the past year and the past month, but still used hallucinogens and inhalants at a lesser rate than the national average over the lifetime, in the past year, and in the past month (SAMHSA, 2016b). This divergence of drug use trends has been termed the "racial crossover effect"; this is the interaction of race and age in substance use, whereby African Americans are less likely to use substances during adolescence, but exhibit higher rates of drinking and drug use problems by the age of 35 (Watt, 2008). It is not clear at what age this begins, but data suggest that it is between 18 and 21 years of age (Trinidad, Gilpin, Lee, & Pierce, 2004). The timing of this increase in drug use coincides with a challenging transition for African-American emerging adults.

Protective Factors in the Black Community

A growing body of literature is investigating protective factors as a way of understanding within-group variation in risk and incidents of health outcomes in the Black community. Some of the most commonly studied protective factors include genetics, spirituality, religiosity, traditional beliefs and behaviors, effective parenting, extended kin networks, social support, academic success, and the possession of skill sets for coping with stress (Hawkins et al., 1992).

One of the most widely assessed protective factors for African Americans is religiosity. While the majority of this body of literature characterizes this protective factor as spirituality, more often than not church attendance (or religiosity) is used as a proxy. For example, a relationship has been found between total abstinence or lower levels of alcohol consumption and frequent church attendance and religious participation amongst African Americans (Bazargan, Sherkat, & Bazaragan, 2004; Steinman & Zimmerman, 2004). A meta-analysis found religious coping to be moderately beneficial for managing psychological adjustment to stress (Ano & Vasconcelles, 2005). For example, Ellison, Musick, and Henderson (2008) found that both attendance and the use of religious guidance had buffering effects on psychological distress.

Maintaining traditional African-American beliefs and cultural practices may be considered a promotive factor, which differs from a protective factor in that promotive factors not only protect against adversity, but increase the likelihood of competency in a particular behavior (Causadias, Salvatore, & Sroufe, 2012; Causadias, 2013). For example, African Americans who employed a traditionalist acculturation strategy were found to exhibit higher rates of abstinence (Klonoff & Landrine, 1999) and lower psychological distress (Obasi & Leong, 2009). This is consistent with the finding that African Americans who reported being involved in African-American social networks and showed political awareness consumed less alcohol than others (Herd & Grube, 1996).

The American Indian/Alaskan Native Community

Of the many indigenous communities in the United States today, American Indian/Alaskan Native (AIAN) groups have a long-standing history of trauma and subjugation. While sociocultural differences exist between AIAN communities, there are some similarities that stem from their shared historical past. It is with this understanding that we cautiously provide a general overview of this underserved and understudied population.

Stressors in the AIAN Community

One of the main sources of stress in the AIAN community is the historical treatment of AIAN individuals. From the introduction of disease, which resulted in an enormous reduction of the population, to separation and inadequate treatment, numerous examples contribute to AIAN peoples' legacy of mistrust of "White people" and the "White man's medicine" (Thompson, Walker, & Silk-Walker, 1993). Whitbeck, Chen, Hoyt, and Adams (2004) demonstrated that historical losses and traumas are frequently revisited by both adults and children in the AIAN community.

These populations face additional burdens in the form of poverty. Approximately a quarter of people of AIAN descent are from families in which no adult has graduated from high school. Additionally, about 55% of AIAN families live with incomes 200% below the national poverty level (Zuckerman, Haley, Roubideaux, & Lillie-Blanton, 2004). Similarly, one in three AIAN children were considered poor in 2006–2010. Interestingly, children in sovereign areas were the most likely to be poor: 39% of the total (Pettit et al., 2014). Monetary considerations are a form of stress for adults, children, and adolescents. Adolescents from a Cherokee-Keetoowah community named finding work as one of their greatest sources of stress (Kelley & Lowe, 2012). As well as having the obvious added stressors that come with being economically disadvantaged, those in lower classes appear to use positive coping strategies inadequately.

AIAN women also experience more interpersonal violence than any other racial group. For example, according to the US Department of Justice, AIAN women are more likely to suffer from domestic violence than White, African-American, or Asian-American women (18.2% compared with 6.3%, 8.2%, and 1.5% respectively; Catalano, 2007). Additionally, AIAN women in New York City report high rates of childhood trauma (28.2%), domestic violence (40%), and rape (48%) in comparison to national norms (Evans-Campbell, Lindhorst, Huang, & Walters, 2006). Furthermore, weapons are used in domestic violence incidents involving AIAN women more frequently than in any other group (Malcoe, Duran, & Montgomery, 2004; Wood & Magen, 2009). It is theorized that the loss of culture and traditional practices, followed by forced assimilation, has increased the pervasiveness of mental disorders and dysfunctional family life, which have led to an increased risk of familial abuse (Duran & Duran, 1995).

Furthermore, racial discrimination continues to be a major source of stress for AIAN communities. For example, this marginalized group is the only major ethnic group toward whom overt racism is still accepted in their country (for example, the use of caricatures in sports teams, the use of derogatory language), and discrimination remains a risk factor for substance use among American Indian adolescents and is both directly and indirectly associated with alcohol abuse in AIAN individuals (Whitbeck et al., 2004). Additionally, American Indian children who attend elementary school outside of their tribal community often hear that their customs are directly opposed to those of the dominant culture, which leads to truancy and alcohol abuse (Horejsi, Craig, & Pablo, 1992). Unfortunately, there is a lack of peer-reviewed studies on the effects of racial discrimination on Native Americans (Currie et al., 2013). Similarly, studies of the effects of discrimination, the HPA axis, and drug and alcohol abuse would greatly contribute to the understanding of risk factors in this community.

Drug Use in the AIAN Community

The experience of significant stressors at such alarming rates has been associated with AIAN using licit/illicit substances as a negative coping strategy. The rate of past-month illicit drug use among AIAN ages 12 or older was 14.9% in 2014 (compared to the national average of 10.2%), and in 2010 AIANs had the highest rate of drug-induced deaths (SAMHSA, 2016a). AIAN teens tend to have an earlier onset of use of illicit substances and are more likely to combine substances.

Again, although we are limited by a dearth of information on the AIAN communities, most sources describe high rates of alcohol use among both children and adults. Horejsi and colleagues (1992) estimate that 100% of individuals in the AIAN community are affected either directly or indirectly by alcoholism. Again, although misrepresentation of arrest and morbidity rates, and the limited number of studies, prescribe caution, substance use remains a major problem in the AIAN community and significantly contributes to preventable deaths in the community (Snipp, 1997). Seemingly a familial issue, youth rates of alcoholism are attributed both to childhood trauma as a result of parental drug and alcohol abuse and to peer pressure within the family (Wall, Garcia-Andrade, Wong, Lau, & Elhers, 2000).

Given the several types of stressors unique to this community, it is not surprising that many are related to an increased risk of drug and alcohol abuse. Those who had exposure to at least three types of childhood trauma (for example, witnessing intimate partner violence against their mother, emotional abuse, physical abuse) showed a four-times increased risk of high alcohol and marijuana use in a sample of Native American emerging adults. Given that 78% of participants in that sample had experienced at least one type of childhood trauma, this is a particularly important source of stress in this population (Brockie, Dana-Sacco, Wallen, Wilcox, & Campbell, 2015). In a similar study of a sample with comparable rates of exposure to childhood trauma, Koss and colleagues (2003) demonstrated an increased risk of alcohol dependence in American Indian adults. Similarly, associations with historical loss increased the risk of drug and alcohol use, as did experiences of discrimination (Brockie et al., 2015; Whitbeck et al., 2004).

Protective Factors in the AIAN Community

Although there are high rates of substance use and abuse among AIANs, it is important to recognize protective factors that support positive health trajectories. For example, knowledge of one's native tongue seems to be an important protective factor in several communities. This commands respect and honor amongst individuals. Additionally, attending cultural ceremonies seems to be protective, as it helps one to feel proud and to get an individual "back on the right track" (Mmari, Blum, & Teufel-Shone, 2010).

Interestingly, in the midst of forced assimilation, returning to the roots of their tribes seem to be the most efficacious resource available to AIANs. Regarding traditional therapy, Traveling Thunder expressed displeasure at the continuing attempts at assimilation: "Go [to the] white psychiatrists in the Indian Health Service and say, rid me of my history, my past, and brainwash me forever so I can be like a Whiteman" (Gone, 2007). Unfortunately, there are few studies examining the efficacy of indigenous techniques in treating mental illness and substance abuse. It is important to note that some steps have been taken to address these issues. For example, the Native American Health Center has opened several locations to provide mental, physical, spiritual, and social services to help restore balance and health through mental illness and substance abuse treatment (Native American Health Center, 2016). Additionally, treatment groups are being created that provide traditional healing within the community, such as a drumming-assisted recovery therapy developed to help with substance use disorders (Dickerson, Robichaud, Teruya, Nagaran, & Hser, 2012).

The Asian Community

Historically, the Asian community has been stereotypically viewed as a "model" minority group. Dubbed the "model minority myth" because of its association with Asian Americans and the embodiment of the American dream, this stereotype is beginning to gain more momentum in the literature. Implicit in this misrepresentation is an assumption that they do not experience problems related to psychological health, medical comorbidity, or addictions. However, the Asian community as a whole has been largely underrepresented in psychological research and professional service delivery. An example of this can be seen in the meta-analysis by Fong and Tsuang (2007), which found that Asian Americans are significantly underrepresented in addictions treatment across a wide range of different clinical settings. Furthermore, these disproportionate statistics appear to be enduring, as recent studies have reported that little progress is being made in eliminating these disparities in regard to Asian Americans' underutilization of mental health services (Sue, Yan Cheng, Saad, & Chu, 2012). Several theories have been proposed, which range from historical oversight to unique sociocultural factors such as "losing face" (Fong & Tsuang, 2007).

In addition, it has been found that the Asian community has a wide range of intra-ethnic variability when it comes to substance abuse prevalence rates, help-seeking behaviors, and the types of social support systems that are readily available to them (Fong & Tsuang, 2007; Singh, McBride, & Kak, 2015). For example, over 50% of Japanese Americans and Korean Americans were found to have used alcohol in the past month, compared with 25% in other Asian subgroups (Price, Risk, Wong, & Klingle, 2002). Thus, care should be taken not to overgeneralize data across people of Asian descent.

Stress in the Asian Community

A major cause of stress for people of Asian descent in the US is acculturative stress. This includes multiple facets, such as social isolation, lack of familiarity with American customs, guilt about leaving family and friends behind, communication difficulties, employment difficulties, legal status stress, and race or language discrimination (Singh et al., 2015). As a result, negative outcomes such as psychological distress, depressive symptoms, and poor physiological health have been linked to acculturative stress (Lui, 2015; Singh et al., 2015; Xu & Chi, 2013).

The acculturation gap-distress theory argues that generational effects stem from the intergenerational cultural conflict between the collectivist traditional heritage and the individualistic American mainstream (Lui, 2015). Acculturation mismatch was found to be positively associated with intergenerational cultural conflict and internalizing problems, and negatively correlated with offspring mental health, educational outcomes and adaptive functioning (Lui, 2015).

Drug Use in the Asian Community

Several studies have suggested that Asian Americans exhibit lower rates of alcohol, stimulants, marijuana, and heroin substance use disorders than the national averages (Kim, Ziedonis, Chen, 2007; Price et al., 2002). The 2015 Substance Abuse and Mental Health Services Administration (SAMHSA, 2016b) survey found that only 9% of Asian-American adults used illicit drugs in the past year, exhibiting the lowest rate of all racial groups (Price et al., 2002). Kim and colleagues (2007) found that this population also exhibits significantly lower rates of smoking – approximately 17% compared to the estimated 21% for the general population. However, Asian Americans who smoke routinely have been shown to smoke more cigarettes per day than any other ethnic group, averaging close to 17 cigarettes per day (Kim et al., 2007).

Protective Factors in the Asian Community

Overall, Asian Americans tend to utilize coping strategies which reflect behaviors consistent with their holistic culture, such as the use of religion–spirituality, acceptance, reframing, striving, family support, avoidance and detachment, private emotional outbursts, and sense of coherence. Sense of coherence can be defined as an enduring attitude of how people view life, manage tension and identify and mobilize their external and internal resources, together with an ability to cope effectively and resolve tension in a health-promoting manner (Eriksson & Lindström, 2007). Some studies have found that family/social support, religion–spirituality, and a sense of coherence acted as partial mediators and buffers in the relationship between acculturative stress and life satisfaction (Singh et al., 2015; Xu & Chi, 2013).

In addition, Nguyen (2015) demonstrated that racial identity, particularly acceptance and appreciation of one's own culture, may serve as a protective factor against depression and is positively associated with psychological well-being. Conversely, risk factors associated with Asian Americans include enculturation-related aspects, including stigmatization of mental illness, fear of loss of face, and filial piety, which were all negatively associated with help-seeking behaviors (Lin, 2015).

The Latino Community

The Latino community has seen a steady increase in the US over the past 40 years, with projective estimates suggesting that Latinos will make up 30% of the US population by 2050 (see Stepler & Brown, 2016 for a review). Despite its increasing presence, the Latino community remains understudied and underserved in many respects. Moreover, the heterogeneity within ethnic groups of Latino descent further complicates our understanding of the unique stressors associated with this group.

Stressors in the Latino Community

The Latino community faces multiple sources of stress in the US, including those related to acculturation and language barriers, immigration status and documentation, as well as numerous sociocultural inequities including underemployment, low educational attainment and experiences of racism and discrimination. Among the Latino community, acculturative stress can be marked by pressures to adapt to mainstream culture, balance dichotomized cultural experiences (e.g., speaking Spanish at home and English at school), and manage feelings of inferiority and perceived discrimination (Berry, 1997). Acculturative stress is linked to an array of negative outcomes for Latinos, including increased alcohol and cigarette use (Lorenzo-Blanco & Cortina, 2012; Lorenzo-Blanco & Unger, 2015). Undocumented immigrants may also be more vulnerable to experiencing acculturative conflict (Schwartz et al., 2015). Differences in levels of assimilation between family members can also be a source of stress within the family unit. Indeed, differential acculturation strategies and levels of assimilation within Latino families have been associated with increased substance use, risky sexual behavior, and depressive symptoms among Latino adolescents (Schwartz et al., 2012).

Relatedly, lack of proficiency in English can be a notable source of stress in the Latino community. Language barriers can be limiting in access to health care, education and socioeconomic attainment. Within the health care sector, Latinos are more frequently misdiagnosed and undertreated, and many report experiences of distrust, discrimination, and culturally insensitive practices that contribute to such miscommunication (SAMHSA, 2012). Health insurance coverage is also substantially lower in the Latino community (23.7% are uninsured compared with 12% of people of all races), which places additional limits on access to health care (Stepler & Brown, 2016). Lack of language proficiency in the majority language can also impact educational attainment. Approximately 21% of Latino adults do not have a high school diploma, compared with just 5.8% of the general population. Moreover, the vast majority of these individuals never attain a General Educational Development (GED) credential (considered equivalent to the high school diploma), which in turn can limit occupational and socioeconomic attainment. Indeed, Latinos tend to be overrepresented in rates of poverty, unemployment, and substandard housing.

Finally, immigration status presents a distinctive source of stress for the Latino community. Approximately 35% of Latinos in the US are foreign-born, and only 11% of those have obtained US citizenship, leaving a large component of the Latino community undocumented (Stepler & Brown, 2016). Because of this, about half of Latinos express having daily concerns that they, a family member or a close friend will be deported. Lack of legal status poses its own set of hardships, as undocumented workers often exist in a low-paid, unskilled labor pool, and may be particularly vulnerable to being taken advantage of because of their undocumented status. Even among documented immigrants, stressors such as severed ties to family and friends, loss of supportive resources, language inadequacy and difficulty finding employment can function to agitate chronic stress among Latino immigrants. Sociopolitical factors, such as anti-immigration sentiments at the national level, further contribute to perceived discrimination and feelings of inferiority at the individual level (Zagefka, González, & Brown, 2011).

Although the Latino community shares many characteristics, it is important to recognize its within-group heterogeneity. The Latino community is from a variety of countries of origin, and European, African, and Asian immigration throughout the span of Latin American history has resulted in a wide range of phenotypes (Comas-Diaz, 2012). The mixed heritage and heterogeneity of the Latino community can pose difficult questions of ethnic identity. While ethnic identity can foster a sense of belonging and group membership, the diversity within the Latino community often challenges the notion of belonging to one distinct ethnic group. Thus, many Latino youth self-identify by their ancestral country of origin (e.g., Mexican, Puerto Rican). As is the case for most other racial minority groups, there is a lack of information regarding the link between these distinct stressors and how changes to the HPA axis due to these stressors may influence drug use vulnerability in the Latino community.

Drug Use in the Latino Community

Given the sociopolitical climate in the US regarding Latino immigration, the impact of cultural stress on health and drug use outcomes is a particularly relevant factor to investigate. While drug use prevalence rates for Latinos generally mirror those of the general population, rates of use are quickly increasing in the Latino community. In 2014, the rate of illicit drug use – during the past month – among Latinos aged 12 to 17 was 10.5%, compared to 8.7% in 2013 (SAMHSA, 2015). Notably, the percentage for Whites, Blacks, and Asians did not change significantly, suggesting a unique trend within the Latino community.

Latino adolescents were also more likely than Black or Asian adolescents to have initiated alcohol or cigarette use in the past year. Moreover, Latinos who initiate drug use may be more vulnerable to developing dependency than other ethnic groups in the US. Latinos aged 12 and older were more likely than non-Latino Whites to have needed substance use treatment in the past year (9.9% versus 9.2%), and the rate of chemical dependency admissions was higher among Latinos than among non-Latino Whites. Despite a greater need for treatment, Latinos tend to be less likely than non-Latino Whites to receive treatment (9.0% versus 10.5%). Among Latinos who do receive treatment, a lack of culturally tailored substance abuse interventions can contribute to observed higher rates of treatment drop-out (Gil & Vega, 2001). Latinos may also experience greater negative consequences of drug and alcohol use, including intimate partner violence, incarceration, homelessness, and medical problems (Amaro, Arevalo, Gonzalez, Szapocznik, & Iguchi, 2006). On the other hand, despite seemingly increasing rates of illicit drug use within the Latino community, a significant decrease in cigarette use has been observed among Latino adolescents (from 7.9% in 2010 to 3.98% in 2014). Additionally, a growing focus on training culturally competent health care providers, providing bilingual services, and developing culturally tailored intervention programs suggests a more optimistic picture for the future (Alvarez, Jason, Olson, Ferrari, & Davis, 2007).

Protective Factors in the Latino Community

If these disparities in drug use are to be addressed effectively, culture-specific protective factors should be considered. Strong family ties and family obligation values have been associated with lower substance use among Latino adolescents (Gil, Wagner, & Vega, 2000; Telzer, Gonzalez, & Fuligni, 2014). A central value in the Latino culture is the development and maintenance of interpersonal relationships. *Personalismo* is the deeply personal communication style displayed by many Latinos, which emphasizes interdependence, mutual respect, and cooperation. Such personal communication styles are complemented by a relational disposition (the quality of being *simpático*) among Latinos that aims to create a hospitable and gracious atmosphere. Perhaps the apex of interpersonal relations within the Latino community can be seen within the family dynamic. An emphasis on family unity and respect (*familismo*) among many Latino subgroups typically plays out in affectionate and respectful relationships among large networks of immediate and extended family (Antshel, 2002). For many Latinos, the family network extends to close friends, godparents, clergy members, and neighbors. Because of these strong familial and social relationships, emotional, social, and economic support is often readily available, and open disclosure with parents and other family members is more common. A trend in Latino families of having large households with hierarchical structures further provides accessible support and defined role functions, which can enhance an individual's sense of stability and personal identity.

Finally, an emphasis on spiritual and religious values within the Latino culture often provides an adaptive and accessible coping strategy. Catholicism is a common, though not the only, religious practice among Latino communities. Prayers to patron saints can provide a source of comfort during specific hardships. Religiosity also provides a context for finding meaning in stressful experiences and reframing stressful events into growth opportunities (Ano & Vasconcelles, 2005; Schwartz et al., 2015). Religious forgiveness can also be useful for developing a sense of resilience to and acceptance of perceived transgressions and personal mistakes. The protective effects of such positive religious coping have been demonstrated thorough its association with multiple positive physical and mental health outcomes, including decreased alcohol use (Schwartz et al., 2015).

Conclusions and Future Directions

To give greater insights into the neurobiology of the dynamic interplay between stress physiology and drug use vulnerability in diverse populations, five critical areas need to be addressed in future research. (1) There needs to be a concerted effort to fund research that focuses on diverse populations suffering from health disparities. Given the changing demographics of the US, we can no longer feel comfortable overgeneralizing from innovative research studies that are largely driven by European-American samples of convenience. (2) Greater dialogue needs to take place between animal and human researchers. While animal models provide an opportunity to investigate the progression of addictions within a shorter time span, efforts to explore the applicability of these models to more complex human phenomena have been very limited. (3) Culture needs to be at the center of research designs and paradigm development. Often, cultural phenomena are relegated to exploratory aims or distal moderators. In order to achieve real breakthroughs, the scientific community desperately needs greater precision in the measurement of culture-specific phenomena and to understand its central importance to every research question that is formulated. (4) As mentioned above, longitudinal studies are needed to shed light on the directionality of the relationship between the neurobiology of stress dysregulation and drug use vulnerability. Given the high level of exposure to chronic stress that diverse ethnic communities endure, it is imperative that we begin to understand how social stressors "get under the skin" and have a deleterious effect on health and the progression of drug abuse disorders. (5) Finally, the field needs to move beyond the use of a single indicator of stress physiology (i.e., cortisol) and simplistic models of allostatic load that add biomarkers while assuming they all have an equal bearing on health outcomes. How does the HPA axis affect the hypothalamus-pituitary-gonadal axis, the hypothalamus-pituitary-growth hormone axis, the hypothalamus-pituitary-thyroid axis, and basic immunology across time? Ultimately, more sophisticated analytic strategies, in conjunction with a broader range of theoretically supported biomarkers, are needed to provide greater insights into a complex public health problem – drug addictions in the US.

References

Alvarez, J., Jason, L. A., Olson, B. D., Ferrari, J. R., & Davis, M. I. (2007). Substance abuse prevalence and treatment among Latinos and Latinas. *Journal of Ethnicity and Substance Abuse, 6*(2), 115–141. doi:10.1300/J233v06n02_08

Amaro, H., Arévalo, S., Gonzalez, G., Szapocznik, J., & Iguchi, M. Y. (2006). Needs and scientific opportunities for research on substance abuse treatment among Hispanic adults. *Drug and Alcohol Dependence, 84*(Supp.), S64–S75. doi:10.1016/j.drugalcdep.2006.05.008

Ano, G. G., & Vasconcelles, E. B. (2005). Religious coping and psychological adjustment to stress: A meta-analysis. *Journal of Clinical Psychology, 61*(4), 461–480. doi:10.1002/jclp.20049

Antshel, K. M. (2002). Integrating culture as a means of improving treatment adherence in the Latino population. *Psychology, Health and Medicine, 7*(4), 435–449. doi:10.1080/13548500210000015258

Bazargan, S., Sherkat, D. E., & Bazaragan, M. (2004). Religion and alcohol use among African American and Hispanic inner-city emergency care patients. *Journal for the Scientific Study of Religion, 43*, 419–428. doi:10.1111/j.1468-5906.2004.00244.x

Ben-Eliezer, U. (2004). Becoming a black Jew: Cultural racism and anti-racism in contemporary Israel. *Social Identities, 10*(2), 245–266. doi:10.1080/1350463042000227371

Berry, J. W. (1997). Immigration, acculturation, and adaptation. *Applied Psychology, 46*, 5–68. doi:10.1111/j.1464-0597.1997.tb01087.x

Bittencourt, J. C., & Sawchenko, P. E. (2000). Do centrally administered neuropeptides access cognate receptors? An analysis in the central corticotropin-releasing factor system. *Journal of Neuroscience, 20*, 1142–1156.

Blankstein, K. R., & Flett, G. L. (1992). Specificity in the assessment of daily hassles: Hassles, locus of control, and adjustment in college students. *Canadian Journal of Behavioural Science/Revue canadienne des sciences du comportement, 24*(3), 382–398. doi:10.1037/h0078738

Bradley, R. G., Binder, E. B., Epstein, M. P., Tang, Y., Nair, H. P. Liu, W., … & Ressler, K. J. (2008). Influence of child abuse on adult depression: Moderation by the corticotropin-releasing hormone receptor gene. *Archives of General Psychiatry, 65*, 190–200. doi:10.1001/archgenpsychiatry.2007.26

Brockie, T. N., Dana-Sacco, G., Wallen, G. R., Wilcox, H. C., & Campbell, J. C. (2015). The relationship of adverse childhood experiences to PTSD, depression, poly-drug use and suicide attempt in reservation-based Native American adolescents and young adults. *American Journal of Community Psychology, 55*, 411–421. doi:10.1007/s10464-015-9721-3

Catalano, S. (2007). Intimate partner violence in the United States. Bureau of Justice Statistics, Washington, DC. Retrieved from https://www.bjs.gov/content/pub/pdf/ipvus.pdf (accessed July 12, 2017).

Causadias, J. M. (2013). A roadmap for the integration of culture into developmental psychopathology. *Development and Psychopathology, 25*, 1375–1398. doi:10.1017/s0954579413000679

Causadias, J. M., Salvatore, J. E., & Sroufe, L. A. (2012). Early patterns of self-regulation as risk and promotive factors in development: A longitudinal study from childhood to adulthood in a high-risk sample. *International Journal of Behavioral Development*, 1–10. doi:10.1177/0165025412444076

Chae, D. H., Nuru-Jeter, A. M., Adler, N. E., Brody, G. H., Lin, J., Blackburn, E. H., & Epel, E. S. (2014). Discrimination, racial bias, and telomere length in African-American men. *American Journal of Preventative Medicine, 46*, 103–111. doi:10.1016/j.amepre.2013.10.020

Clark, R., Anderson, N. B., Clark, V. R., & Williams, D. R. (1999). Racism as a stressor for African Americans: A biopsychosocial model. *American Psychologist, 54*, 805–816. doi:10.1037/0003-066X.54.10.805

Comas-Diaz, L. (2012). *Multicultural care: A clinician's guide to cultural competence*. Washington, DC: American Psychological Association.

Contoreggi, C., Herning, R. I., Na, P., Gold, P. W., Chrousos, G., Negro, P. J., … & Cadet, J. L. (2003). Stress hormone responses to corticotropin-releasing hormone in substance abusers without severe comorbid psychiatric disease. *Biological Psychiatry, 54*, 873–882. doi:10.1016/S0006-3223(03)00167-7

Currie, C. L., Wild, T. C., Schopflocher, D. P., Laing, L., Veugelers, P., & Parlee, B. (2013). Racial discrimination, post traumatic stress, and gambling problems among urban Aboriginal adults in Canada. *Journal of Gambling Studies, 29*(3), 393–415. doi:10.1007/s10899-012-9323-z

DeLongis, A., Coyne, J. C., Dakof, G., Folkman, S., & Lazarus, R. S. (1982). Relationships of daily hassles, uplifts, and major life events to health status. *Health Psychology, 1*, 119–136. doi:10.1037/0278-6133.1.2.119

Dickerson, D., Robichaud, F., Teruya, C., Nagaran, K., & Hser, Y. (2012). Utilizing drumming for American Indians/Alaska Natives with substance use disorders: A focus group. *American Journal of Drug and Alcohol Abuse, 38*, 505–510. doi:10.3109/00952990.2012.699565

Duran, E., & Duran, B. (1995). *Native American postcolonial psychology*. Albany, NY: State University of New York Press.

Ellison, C. G., Musick, M. A., & Henderson, A. K. (2008). Balm in Gilead: Racism, religious involvement, and psychological distress among African-American adults. *Journal for the Scientific Study of Religion, 47*(2), 291–309. doi:10.1111/j.1468-5906.2008.00408.x

Eriksson, M., & Lindström, B. (2007). Antonovsky's sense of coherence scale and its relation with quality of life: A systematic review. *Journal of Epidemiology and Community Health, 61*, 938–344. doi:10.1136/jech.2006.056028

Evans-Campbell, T., Lindhorst, T., Huang, B., & Walters, K. L. (2006). Interpersonal violence in the lives of urban American Indian and Alaska Native women: Implications for health, mental health, and help-seeking. *American Journal of Public Health, 96*(8), 1416–1422. doi:10.2105/AJPH.2004.054213

Fong, T. W., & Tsuang, J. (2007). Asian-Americans, addictions, and barriers to treatment. *Psychiatry (Edgmont), 4*(11), 51–59.

Gil, A. G., & Vega, W. A. (2001). Latino drug use, scope, risk factors and reduction strategies. In M. Aguire-Molina, C. W. Molina, & R. E. Zambrana (Eds.). *Health issues in the Latino community* (pp. 435–458). San Francisco, CA: Jossey-Bass.

Gil, A. G., Wagner, E. F., & Vega, W. A. (2000). Acculturation, familism, and alcohol use among Latino adolescent males: Longitudinal relations. *Journal of Community Psychology, 28*(4), 443–458. doi:10.1002/1520-6629(200007)28:4<443::AID-JCOP6>3.0.CO;2-A

Goeders, N. E. (2002). Stress and cocaine addiction. *Journal of Pharmacological and Experimental Therapeutics, 301*, 785–789. doi:10.1124/jpet.301.3.785

Goeders, N. E., & Guerin, G. F. (1994). Non-contingent electric footshock facilitates the acquisition of intravenous cocaine self-administration in rats. *Psychopharmacology, 114,* 63–70. doi:10.1007/BF02245445

Gone, J. P. (2007). "We never was happy living like a Whiteman": Mental health disparities and the postcolonial predicament in American Indian communities. *American Journal of Community Psychology, 40,* 290–300. doi:10.1007/s10464-007-9136-x

Gottlieb, G. (1996). Developmental psychobiological theory. In R. B. Cairns, G. H. Elder, & E. J. Costello (Eds.) *Developmental science* (pp. 63–77). Cambridge: Cambridge University Press.

Hansson, A. C., Cippitelli, A., Sommer, W. H., Fedeli, A., Björk, K, Soverchia, L., … & Ciccocioppo, R. (2006). Variation at the rat *Crhr1* locus and sensitivity to relapse into alcohol seeking induced by environmental stress. *Proceedings of the National Academy of Sciences, 103,* 15236–15241. doi:10.1073/pnas.0604419103

Hansson, A. C., Cippitelli, A., Wolfgang, H. S., Ciccocioppo, R., & Heilig, M. (2007). Region-specific down-regulation of *Crhr1* gene expression in alcohol-preferring msP rats following *ad lib* access to alcohol. *Addiction Biology, 12*(1), 30–34. doi:10.1111/j.1369-1600.2007.00050.x

Hawkins, J. D., Catalano, R. F., & Miller, J. Y. (1992). Risk and protective factors for alcohol and other drug problems in adolescence and early adulthood: Implications for substance abuse prevention. *Psychological Bulletin, 112*(1), 64–105.

Herd, D., & Grube, J. (1996). Black identity and drinking in the US: A national study. *Addiction, 91*(6), 845–857. doi:10.1046/j.1360-0443.1996.91684510.x

Horejsi, C., Craig, B. H., & Pablo, J. (1992). Reactions by Native American parents to child protection agencies: Cultural and community factors. *Child Welfare, 71,* 329–342.

Jackson, J. S., Knight, K. M., & Rafferty, J. A. (2010). Race and unhealthy behaviors: Chronic stress, the HPA axis, and physical and mental health disparities over the life course. *American Journal of Public Health, 100*(5), 933–939. doi:10.2015/AJPH.2008.143446

Jencks, C., & Phillips, M. (Eds.) (1998). *The Black-White Test Score Gap.* Washington, DC: Brookings Institution Press.

Jones, J. M. (1997). *Prejudice and racism* (2nd ed.). New York: McGraw-Hill.

Kelley, M., & Lowe, J. (2012). The health challenge of stress experienced by Native American adolescents. *Archives of Psychiatry Nursing, 26,* 71–73. doi:10.1016/j.apnu.2011.10.001

Kim, S. S., Ziedonis, D., & Chen, K. W. (2007). Tobacco use and dependence in Asian Americans: A review of the literature. *Nicotine and Tobacco Research*, *9*(2), 169–184. doi:10.1080/14622200601080323

Klonoff, E. A., & Landrine, H. (1999). Acculturation and alcohol use among blacks: The benefits of remaining culturally traditional. *Western Journal of Black Studies*, *23*, 211.

Kolb, B., & Whishaw, I. Q. (2005). *An introduction to brain and behavior* (2nd ed.). New York: Worth Publishers.

Koob, G. F., & Le Moal, M. (2001). Drug addiction, dysregulation of reward, and allostasis. *Neuropsychopharmacology*, *24*, 97–129. doi:10.1016/S0893-133X(00)00195-0

Koss, M. P., Yuan, N. P., Dightman, D., Prince, R. J., Polacca, M., Sanderson, B., & Goldman, D. (2003). Adverse childhood exposures and alcohol dependence among seven Native American tribes. *American Journal of Preventive Medicine*, *25*, 238–244. doi:10.1016/s0749-3797(03)00195-8

Koylu, E. O., Balkan, B., Kuhar, M. J., & Pogun, S. (2006). Cocaine and amphetamine regulated transcript (CART) and the stress response. *Peptides*, *27*(8), 1956–1969. doi:10.1016/j.peptides.2006.03.032

Lin, R. (2015). Asian American acculturation and psychological help-seeking attitudes: Meta-analysis. Doctoral dissertation, Wheaton College. Retrieved from http://gradworks.umi.com/36/42/3642799.html (accessed July 13, 2017).

Longenbaker, S. N. (2011). *Mader's Understanding human anatomy and physiology* (7th edn). New York: McGraw-Hill.

Lorenzo-Blanco, E. I., & Cortina, L. M. (2012). Latino/a depression and smoking: An analysis through the lenses of culture, gender, and ethnicity. *American Journal of Community Psychology*, *51*(3–4), 332–346. doi:10.1007/s10464-012-9553-3

Lorenzo-Blanco, E. I., & Unger, J. B. (2015). Ethnic discrimination, acculturative stress, and family conflict as predictors of depressive symptoms and cigarette smoking among Latina/o youth: The mediating role of perceived stress. *Journal of Youth and Adolescence*, *44*(10), 1984–1997. doi:10.1007/s10964-015-0339-4

Lovallo, W. R. (2005). Cardiovascular reactivity: Mechanisms and pathways to cardiovascular disease. *International Journal of Psychophysiology*, *58*, 119–132. doi:10.1016/j.ijpsycho.2004.11.007

Lui, P. P. (2015). Intergenerational cultural conflict, mental health, and educational outcomes among Asian and Latino/a Americans: Qualitative and meta-analytic review. *Psychological Bulletin, 141*(2), 404–446. doi:10.1037/a0038449

Malcoe, L. H., Duran, B. M., & Montgomery, J. M. (2004). Socioeconomic disparities in intimate partner violence against Native American women: A cross-sectional study. *BCM Medicine, 2*(1), 20. doi:10.1186/1741-7015-2-20

McEwen, B. S. (1998). Protective and damaging effects of stress mediators. *New England Journal of Medicine, 338*, 171–179. doi:10.1016/j.ijpsycho.2004.11.007

McEwen, B. S. (2006). Protective and damaging effects of stress mediators: Central role of the brain. *Dialogues in Clinical Neuroscience, 8*, 367–381. PMCID: PMC3181832

Mmari, K. N., Blum, R. W., & Teufel-Shone, N. (2010). What increases risk and protection for delinquent behaviors among American Indian youth? Findings from three tribal communities. *Youth and Society, 41*(3), 382–413. doi:10.1177/0044118X09333645

Native American Health Center (2016, March 18). Clinical behavioral health. Retrieved from http://www.nativehealth.org/content/community-wellness.

Nguyen, T. H. (2015). Southeast Asian American racial identity: A protective factor against psychological distress. *Dissertation Abstracts International, 75*.

Obasi, E. M., & Leong, F. L. (2009). Psychological distress, acculturation, and mental health-seeking attitudes among people of African descent in the United States: A preliminary investigation. *Journal of Counseling Psychology, 56*, 227–238. doi:10.1037/a0014865

Obasi, E. M., Shirtcliff, E. A., Brody, G. H., MacKillop, J., Pittman, D. M., Cavanagh, L., & Philibert, R. A. (2015). The relationship between alcohol consumption, perceived stress, and CRHR1 genotype on the hypothalamic–pituitary–adrenal axis in rural African Americans. *Frontiers in Psychology, 6*, 832. doi:10.3389/fpsyg.2015.00832

Obasi, E. M., Tackett, J. L., Shirtcliff, E. A., & Cavanagh, L. (2016). The effects of alcohol and cigarette consumption on dehydroepiandrosterone (DHEA) in rural African Americans. *Journal of Black Psychology*. doi:10.1177/0095798416665742.

Pettit, K. L., Kingsley, G. T., Biess, J., Bertumen, K., Pindus, N., Narducci, C., & Budde, A. (2014). Continuity and change: Demographic, socioeconomic, and housing conditions of American Indians and Alaska Natives. US Department of Housing and Urban Development, Office of Policy Development and Research. Retrieved from https://www.huduser.gov/portal//publications/pdf/housing_conditions.pdf (accessed April 15, 2017).

Price, R. K., Risk, N. K., Wong, M. M., & Klingle, R. S. (2002). Substance use and abuse by Asian Americans and Pacific Islanders: Preliminary results from four national epidemiologic studies. *Public Health Reports, 117*(Suppl. 1), S39–S50. PMCID: PMC1913701

SAMHSA (Substance Abuse and Mental Health Services Administration), Center for Behavioral Health Statistics and Quality (2012). *The NSDUH Report: Need for and Receipt of Substance Use Treatment among Hispanics.* 25 October. Rockville, MD. Retrieved from: https://www.samhsa.gov/data/sites/default/files/NSDUH117/NSDUH117/NSDUHSR117HispanicTreatmentNeeds2012.htm (accessed May 31, 2017).

SAMHSA (Substance Abuse and Mental Health Services Administration), Center for Behavioral Health Statistics and Quality (2015). *2014 National Survey on Drug Use and Health: Detailed Tables.* Rockville, MD.

SAMHSA (Substance Abuse and Mental Health Services Administration) (2016a). Racial and ethnic minority populations. February. Retrieved from http://www.samhsa.gov/specific-populations/racial-ethnic-minority (accessed April 15, 2017).

SAMHSA (Substance Abuse and Mental Health Services Administration), Center for Behavioral Health Statistics and Quality (2016b). *Results from the 2015 National Survey on Drug Use and Health.* (HHS Publication No. SMA 15-4927, NSDUH Series H-50). Retrieved from http://www.samhsa.gov/data/sites/default/files/NSDUH-DetTabs-2015/NSDUH-DetTabs-2015/NSDUH-DetTabs-2015.pdf (accessed 31 May, 2017).

Schwartz, S. J., Unger, J. B., Baezconde-Garbanati, L., Zamboanga, B. L., Lorenzo-Blanco, E. I., Des Rosiers, S. E., … & Piña-Watson, B. M. (2015). Trajectories of cultural stressors and effects on mental health and substance use among Hispanic immigrant adolescents. *Journal of Adolescent Health, 56*(4), 433–439. doi:10.1016/j.jadohealth.2014.12.011

Schwartz, S. J., Unger, J. B., Des Rosiers, S. E., Huang, S., Baezconde-Garbanati, L., Lorenzo-Blanco, E. I., … & Szapocznik, J. (2012). Substance use and sexual behavior among recent Hispanic immigrant adolescents: Effects of parent–adolescent differential acculturation and communication. *Drug and Alcohol Dependence, 125*, S26–S34. doi:10.1016/j.drugalcdep.2012.05.020

Seery, M. D., Leo, R. J., Lupien, S. P., Kondrak, C. L., & Almonte, J. L. (2013). An upside to adversity? Moderate cumulative lifetime adversity is associated with resilient responses in the face of controlled stressors. *Psychological Science, 24*, 1181–1189. doi:10.1177/0956797612469210

Selye, H. (1936). A syndrome produced by diverse nocuous agents. *Nature, 138*(3479), 32–32. doi:10.1038/138032a0

Selye, H. (1956). *The stress of life*. New York: McGraw-Hill.

Selye, H. (1976). *Stress in health and disease*. Boston, MA: Butterworths.

Singh, S., McBride, K., & Kak, V. (2015). Role of social support in examining acculturative stress and psychological distress among Asian American immigrants and three sub-groups: Results from NLAAS. *Journal of Immigrant and Minority Health, 17*, 1597–1606. doi:10.1007/s10903-015-0213-1

Skelton, K. H., Nemeroff, C. B., & Owens, M. J. (2004). Spontaneous withdrawal from the triazolobenzodiazepine alprazolam increases cortical corticotropin-releasing factor mRNA expression. *Journal of Neuroscience, 24*, 9303–9312. doi:http://dx.doi.org/10.1523/JNEUROSCI.1737-04.2004

Snipp, M. (1997). Some observations about racial boundaries and the experiences of American Indians. *Ethnic and Racial Studies, 20*, 668–689. doi:10.1080/01419870.1997.9993984

Sommer, W. H., Rimondini, R., Hansson, A. C., Hipskind, P. A., Gehlert, D. R., Barr, C. S., & Heilig, M. A. (2008). Upregulation of voluntary alcohol intake, behavioral sensitivity to stress, and amygdala Crhr1 expression following a history of dependence. *Biological Psychiatry, 63*, 139–145. doi:http://dx.doi.org/10.1016/j.biopsych.2007.01.010

Spring, J. (2016). *Deculturalization and the struggle for equality: A brief history of the education of dominated cultures in the United States* (8th ed.). New York: Routledge.

Steele, C. M. (1997). A threat in the air: How stereotypes shape intellectual identity and performance. *American Psychologist, 52*, 613–629. doi:10.1037/0003-66X.52.6.613

Steinman, K. J., & Zimmerman, M. A. (2004). Religious activity and risk behavior among African American adolescents: Concurrent and developmental effects. *American Journal of Social Psychology, 33*, 151–161. doi:10.1023/B:AJCP.0000027002.93526.bb

Stepler, R., & Brown, A. (2016). Statistical portrait of Hispanics in the United States. Pew Research Center. Retrieved from http://www.pewhispanic.org/2016/04/19/statistical-portrait-of-hispanics-in-the-united-states/.

Sue, S., Yan Cheng, J. K., Saad, C. S., & Chu, J. P. (2012). Asian American mental health: A call to action. *American Psychologist, 67*(7), 532–544. doi:10.1037/a0028900

Takahashi, K. H., Rako, L., Takano-Shimizu, T., Hoffmann, A. A., & Lee, S. F. (2010). Effects of small *Hsp* genes on developmental stability and microenvironmental canalization. *BCM Evolutionary Biology, 10*, 284. doi:10.1186/1471-2148-10-284

Telzer, E. H., Gonazalez, N., & Fuligni, A. J. (2014). Family obligation values and family assistance behaviors: Protective and risk factors for Mexican-American adolescents' substance use. *Journal of Youth and Adolescence, 43*, 270–283. doi:10.1007/s10964-013-9941-5

Thompson, J. W., Walker, R. D., & Silk-Walker, P. (1993). Psychiatric care of American Indians and Alaska Natives. In A. C. Gaw (ed.), *Culture, ethnicity, and mental illness* (pp. 189–243). Washington, DC: American Psychiatric Press.

Trinidad, D. R., Gilpin, E. A., Lee, L., & Pierce, J. P. (2004). Do the majority of Asian-Americans and African-Americans smokers start as adults? *American Journal of Preventative Medicine, 26*(2), 156–158. doi:http://dx.doi.org.ezproxy.lib.uh.edu/10.1016/j.amepre.2003.10.008

US Census Bureau (2015). QuickFacts. Retrieved from https://www.census.gov/quickfacts/table/PST045215/00 (accessed April 15, 2017).

US Department of Health and Human Services (2001). Mental health: Culture, race, and ethnicity – A supplement to Mental health: A report of the Surgeon General. Rockville, MD: US Department of Health and Human Services, Substance Abuse and Mental Health Services Administration, Center for Mental Health Services. Retrieved from https://www.ncbi.nlm.nih.gov/books/NBK44243/ (accessed April 15, 2017).

Wall, T. L., Garcia-Andrade, C., Wong, V., Lau, P., & Ehlers, C. L. (2000). Parental history of alcoholism and problem behaviors in Native-American children and adolescents. *Alcoholism: Clinical and Experimental Research, 24*(1), 30–34. doi:10.1111/j.1530-0277.2000.tb04549.x

Wasserman, D., Wasserman, J., Rozanov, V., & Sokolowski, M. (2009). Depression in suicidal males: Genetic risk variants in the *CRHR1* gene. *Genes, Brain and Behavior, 8*, 72–79. doi:10.1111/j.1601-183X.2008.00446.x

Watt, T. (2008). The race/ethnic age crossover effect in drug use and heavy drinking. *Journal of Ethnicity in Substance Abuse, 7*(1), 93–114. doi:10.1080/15332640802083303

Whitbeck, L. B., Chen, X., Hoyt, D. R., & Adams, G. W. (2004). Discrimination, historical loss and enculturation: Culturally specific risk and resiliency factors for alcohol abuse among American Indians. *Journal of Studies on Alcohol and Drugs, 65*(4), 409–418.

Wood, D. S., & Magen, R. H. (2009). Intimate partner violence against Athabaskan women residing in interior Alaska: results of a victimization survey. *Violence against Women, 15*, 497–507. doi:10.1177/1077801208331245

Xu, L., & Chi, I. (2013). Acculturative stress and depressive symptoms among Asian immigrants in the United States: The roles of social support and negative interaction. *Asian American Journal of Psychology, 43,* 217–266. doi:10.1037/a0030167

Zagefka, H., González, R., & Brown, R. (2011). How minority members' perceptions of majority members' acculturation preferences shape minority members' own acculturation preferences: Evidence from Chile. *British Journal of Social Psychology, 50*(2), 216–233. doi:10.1348/014466610X512211

Zuckerman, S., Haley, J., Roubideaux, Y., & Lillie-Blanton, M. (2004). Health service access, use, and insurance coverage among American Indian/Alaska Natives and Whites: What role does the Indian Health Service play? *American Journal of Public Health, 94,* 53–59. doi:10.2105/AJPH.94.1.53

Part V

Cultural Neuroscience

16

An Introduction to Cultural Neuroscience

Lynda C. Lin and Eva H. Telzer

This chapter's goal is to serve as a brief introduction to the emerging field of cultural neuroscience. It does not intend to provide an extensive review but rather a brief overview of the field. We start by defining cultural neuroscience and follow by providing important reasons for doing research in this field. Next we explain some key terms and methodologies. We then highlight important studies in the field and provide recommendations for designing a study. Finally, we make suggestions for future directions. Throughout this chapter, we choose a few specific examples to illustrate ways in which cultural neuroscience researchers have utilized the concepts and tools described here.

What Is Cultural Neuroscience?

Cultural neuroscience is an emerging interdisciplinary field that combines theories and methods from cultural and social psychology, anthropology, and social and cognitive neuroscience to investigate the interactions between culture, psychological processes, brain, and genes at different timescales (for reviews, see Chiao, Cheon, Pornpattananangkul, Mrazek, & Blizinsky, 2013; Han et al., 2013; Kim & Sasaki, 2014). Because of the broad interdisciplinary nature of the field, describing all of the different ways in which cultural neuroscientists do research in this area is beyond the scope of this chapter. Here we will be focusing on the most common method, which is representations in the brain through neuroimaging techniques.

Because this field lies at the intersection of many areas of study, we begin by describing how cultural neuroscience derives from each of these

The Handbook of Culture and Biology, First Edition. Edited by José M. Causadias, Eva H. Telzer and Nancy A. Gonzales.

disciplines. First, it borrows from anthropology and cultural and social psychology by assuming that people's sociocultural environments largely shape how they think and behave. Second, it takes tools and theories from social and cognitive neuroscience to investigate neural mechanisms of social and cognitive phenomena in different contexts (Ochsner & Lieberman, 2001). Taken together, cultural neuroscience combines findings and methods from these various fields to study sociocultural variations in cognitive and social processes and how they are represented in the brain. It aims to uncover how repeated engagement in different sociocultural environments might influence the brain (Kitayama & Uskul, 2011).

It is important to note that cultural neuroscience does not intend to be a way of classifying people into categories. In other words, its goal is not to show that differences in brain activity among cultural groups are hard-wired; instead, it demonstrates the opposite: how our brain is shaped by and responds to our sociocultural environment, how malleable and flexible it is in response to its surroundings (Han et al., 2013). In addition, it is important to point out that cultural neuroscience does not necessarily look at neural similarities and differences between races and nationalities but rather at those between cultures (Chiao & Ambady, 2007; Chiao et al., 2010). Indeed, some cultural neuroscience studies have looked at differences in neural activity between people of the same race and same nationality but who come from distinct sociocultural backgrounds, such as people of different religions (Han et al., 2008; Han et al., 2010), socioeconomic backgrounds (Varnum, Blais, Hampton, & Brewer, 2015), or cultural values (Ray et al., 2010). It is clear that a more exact definition of these different constructs is needed, and so we expand on this issue in the following sections.

Why Study Cultural Neuroscience?

One of the main strengths of cultural neuroscience is that it helps bridge the gap between culture and biology (culture–biology interplay; see Causadias, Telzer, & Gonzales, chapter 1 in this volume). Integrating the study of culture with neurobiological processes improves our understanding of the relationship between brain and behavior. Using neuroscience to understand cultural influences on the brain is also advantageous because much of culture rests outside of conscious awareness, and so using brain-imaging techniques allows researchers to get at processes that are not readily available at the conscious level through self-reports.

Another reason to study cultural neuroscience is to get a better understanding of the extent to which psychological processes and their associated neural activity are universal or culture-specific. To date, most psychology and neuroimaging studies have been conducted with Western samples. Indeed, about 90% of fMRI studies have come from countries of Western origin (Chiao, 2009). Furthermore, most psychological studies have been conducted with Westerners, who only account for about 12% of the world population (Arnett, 2008). As many of the studies in the field of cultural neuroscience have already shown, there exist variations in psychological and neural processes between people from different cultural groups. Thus, cultural neuroscience studies can provide a more complete view of the universality of psychological and neural processes.

In an increasingly global and multicultural world, it is important to investigate differences in issues related to cultural diversity, such as discrimination, prejudice, and racism. Learning how culture can influence people's perceptions of and interactions with others at both behavioral and neural levels could lead to greater understanding and improved relationships among intercultural groups. Studying cultural neuroscience can increase our understanding of how explicit and implicit beliefs, values, and behaviors shape the neural mechanisms that underlie differences in psychological processes and behaviors across cultures, and may ultimately reduce intergroup conflict.

Key Terms and Methods

Measuring the Brain

One of the main interests of cultural neuroscientists is determining the patterns of brain activity that underlie sociocultural differences in cognitive, affective, and behavioral processes. A common way to do this is to measure neural activity in two groups of subjects who were brought up in different sociocultural environments and then compare and contrast their brain activity in response to a certain task. The assumption is that differences in sociocultural environments might result in divergent cognitive, affective, and behavioral processes, and that these variations might be reflected in the brain in distinct ways.

Advances in technology in the past few decades have given rise to various ways to measure brain activity. For example, different methods of looking at brain activity include the use of functional magnetic resonance imaging (fMRI), electroencephalography (EEG), transcranial magnetic stimulation (TMS), and functional near-infrared spectroscopy (fNIRS). Each technique measures brain activity in a different way, such as by tracking changes in blood flow (fMRI) or measuring electrical activity in the brain (EEG), and each method has its strengths and limitations. fMRI has advantages and disadvantages compared with other methods of measuring neural activity. On the one hand, one of its strengths is that it has relatively high spatial resolution and is non-invasive. On the other hand, one of its weaknesses is that because the hemodynamic response (see next paragraph for clarification) is very slow (it reaches its peak about 5–6 seconds after the onset of a neural stimulus), its temporal resolution is low compared to that of other techniques such as EEG, which allows millisecond temporal resolution. Of the various techniques available to measure brain activity, this chapter focuses on the method most commonly used by cultural neuroscientists: fMRI.

fMRI is a functional neuroimaging technique that measures changes in blood flow in the brain. The basic idea is that when the brain performs a certain task during a brain scan, more blood will flow into the areas of the brain that are being recruited for the task at hand or, in some cases, fMRI can measure changes in blood flow in a resting brain void of any task demands. One of the most common ways in which changes in blood flow are measured is by keeping track of the levels of oxygenation and deoxygenation in the blood, a contrast known as the blood-oxygen-level-dependent (BOLD) signal. When blood flows to a certain area of the brain, it indicates that those brain cells are being used. This is known as the brain's hemodynamic response, which serves as a proxy for areas of the brain that become active. The activation brain maps produced by fMRI can then be analyzed by means of a variety of techniques, including univariate (looking at overall mean differences in activation between conditions) and multivariate (looking at distributed patterns of brain activation between groups and conditions) analyses.

Key Terms for Regions of the Brain in Cultural Neuroscience

Some neuroscience terms are commonly used when we discuss the brain (see Table 16.1 and Figure 16.1). Researchers refer to frontal parts of the brain using terms such as anterior and rostral, while areas towards the back of the brain are referenced by words such as posterior and caudal. Superior and dorsal areas are towards the top of the brain, while inferior and ventral areas are towards the bottom. Brain images may be displayed in

Table 16.1 Abbreviations and jargon used in cultural neuroscience

Term	Meaning
MPFC	medial prefrontal cortex
pSTS	posterior superior temporal sulcus
VS	ventral striatum
TPJ	temporoparietal junction
FFA	fusiform "face" area
ACC	anterior cingulate cortex
VLPFC	ventrolateral prefrontal cortex
anterior	towards the front of the brain
posterior	towards the back of the brain
rostral	towards the front of the brain
caudal	towards the back of the brain
dorsal	towards the top of the brain
ventral	towards the bottom of the brain
superior	towards the top of the brain
inferior	towards the bottom of the brain
lateral	away from the middle of the brain
medial	towards the middle of the brain

an axial, coronal, or sagittal plane (see Figure 16.1). Specific brain regions are usually associated with certain psychological processes. For example, areas frequently activated when thinking about others (or mentalizing) include the temporoparietal junction (TPJ), the posterior superior temporal sulcus (pSTS), and the dorsomedial prefrontal cortex (dMPFC) (Frith & Frith, 2006). An area commonly associated with thinking about the self is the medial prefrontal cortex (MPFC; Johnson et al., 2002; Kelley et al., 2002; see Varnum & Hampton, chapter 18 in this volume). The ventral striatum (VS) is commonly implicated in reward processing, including the receipt and anticipation of primary and secondary rewards (Delgado, 2007). Finally, the amygdala is involved in emotion processing: it detects salient cues in the environment, and is activated by both threatening and positive emotional stimuli (Hamann, Ely, Hoffman, & Kilts, 2002; see Figure 16.2). Meta-analyses and sources such as the website Neurosynth.org (Yarkoni, Poldrack, Nichols, Van Essen, & Wager, 2011), which synthesizes results from multiple neuroimaging studies, are helpful for identifying

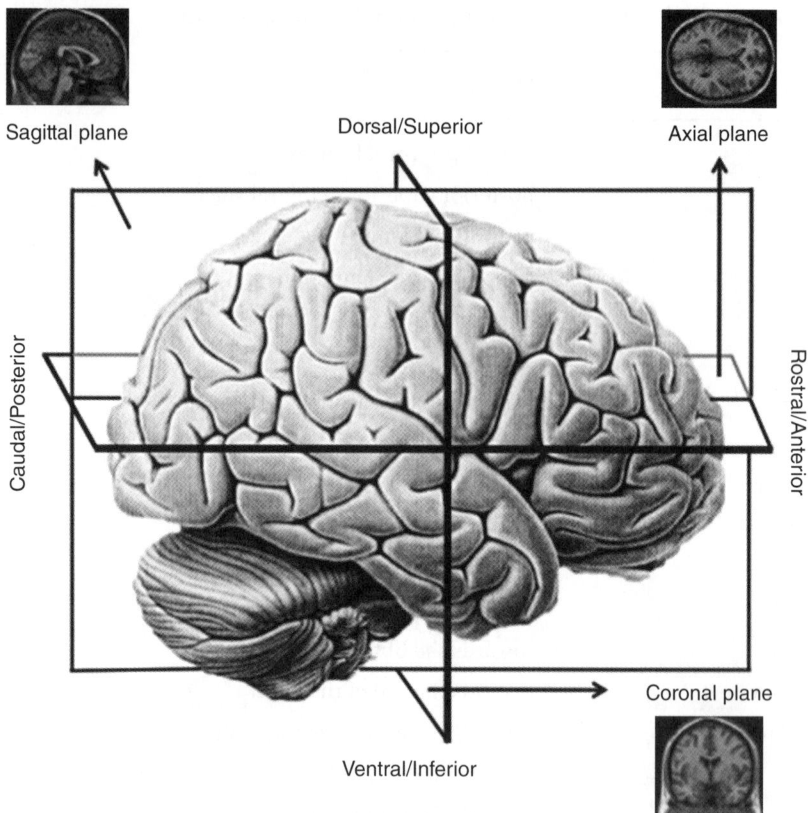

Figure 16.1 Terms commonly used for different parts of the brain

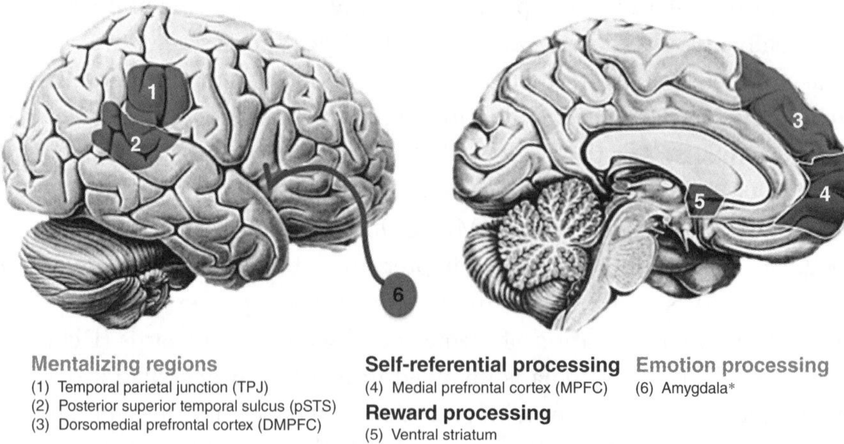

Figure 16.2 Brain regions commonly activated when the brain performs mentalizing, self-referential, and reward- and emotion-processing tasks. *Indicates subcortical structure

regions that might be associated with the psychological process of interest. In some cases, more exploratory analyses might be done in which there are no *a priori* hypotheses about which regions might be activated.

Defining Culture

It is important to define culture and make the distinction between culture, nationality, and race. Culture has long been an issue of debate and has been defined in many different ways (Kroeber & Kluckhohn, 1952), but in the social-psychological sense it can be construed as ideas, values, beliefs, and practices shared by a group of people (Chiao et al., 2010). "Nationality," on the other hand, refers to shared membership based on belonging to the same state or nation. People may be of the same nationality (for example, one is native-born and the other has naturalized citizenship) but not necessarily share ideas, values, practices, and beliefs. Likewise, people of the same race, usually categorized as sharing external physical characteristics like skin color and facial features, may have similar ethnic backgrounds but not necessarily share common cultural experiences. For example, Chinese and Chinese Americans belong to the same race but they might not share the same ideas, values, beliefs, and practices (Han et al., 2013).

Measuring and Manipulating Cultural Constructs of Interest

Because of the differentiations between culture, nationality, and race, and because there are similarities between the three concepts, it is important that studies in cultural neuroscience measure the cultural constructs of interest, such as values or beliefs, that are thought to differ between two cultural groups (Han et al., 2013). One way to do this is to use well-validated self-report measures to look at differences between two cultural groups and then test whether there is a relationship between these values and neural responses. For example, self-construal is a construct that has been found to be different in Western and East Asian societies. On the one hand, East Asians tend to have an idea of the self that is interdependent. That is, the self is thought of as encompassing not just the person itself but also close others. On the other hand, Western societies tend to have a more independent view of the self, where the self is thought of as very different from others (Markus & Kitayama, 1991). Thus, a well-validated measure that gets at individual differences in independent and interdependent self-construals, such as the Self-Construal Scale (Singelis, 1994), can be used to measure cultural values. Measuring the cultural construct of interest, rather than assuming that people from the same nationality or race share similar cultural experiences, may allow researchers to address both the within and the between variability shown by members of the same and different cultural groups. Because people from the same culture might adhere to certain cultural values more than others, evaluating cultural values helps researchers measure within- and between-group individual differences and is one way to disentangle culture from other concepts such as race and nationality.

A method commonly used in cultural neuroscience to assess the relationship between cultural values and neural activity is cultural priming. Cultural priming rests on the assumption that individuals can possess awareness of multiple cultural systems at the same time. Through cultural priming, researchers can temporarily heighten awareness of one cultural value over another (explicitly or implicitly) by using contextual cues (Hong, Morris, Chiu, & Benet-Martinez, 2000), which leads individuals to use mindsets and behaviors that are more consistent with the primed culture. Researchers can then test the effects of this manipulation on behavior and neural processes. For example, priming individuals to have a more independent or interdependent self-construal can result in participants' using different cognitive processes related to each construct. Because different cultural priming techniques have different effects on cognitive and social processes, it is important to use a manipulation that is appropriate to the task at hand (Chiao, 2009; Oyserman & Lee, 2008). One way to use this technique in cultural neuroscience is to prime participants with a cultural value, such as self-construal, before they perform a task in the fMRI scanner (see Meyer, chapter 17 in this volume). For example, Sui and Han (2007) used self-construal priming (they asked participants to read essays and count the number of independent pronouns, such as "I," and the number of interdependent pronouns, such as "we," in them) to examine the resulting neural activity while making face orientation judgments about their own faces and familiar faces. They found that a certain area of the brain (the prefrontal cortex) was activated more when the subject was making self versus familiar judgments, and that this difference was even greater after independent than after interdependent self-construal priming, illustrating how cultural priming can modulate neural activity of self-awareness related to recognition of one's own face. This kind of paradigm illustrates the dynamic nature of culture and can help researchers make more causal inferences regarding the relationship between cultural values and neural activity. However, when using priming paradigms one should also be careful to utilize well-validated priming techniques; this is especially important in neuroscience studies because the effects can sometimes be too small to be detected using fMRI (Powers & Heatherton, 2013).

Making Cross-Cultural Comparisons

The vast majority of studies in cultural neuroscience look at whether behavioral similarities and differences between cultural groups might reveal dissimilar underlying patterns of brain activity. There are various ways in which this might be shown. For example, two different cultural groups may use different brain regions to perform similar behavioral tasks. To illustrate, Tang and colleagues (2006) found that native English speakers used language-related regions, such as the left perisylvian cortices, and native Chinese speakers utilized more vision- and space-related regions, such as visuo-premotor areas, to perform the same arithmetic task. This example demonstrates how two groups may show similar outcomes at the behavioral level but dissimilar patterns at the neural level, highlighting how biological encoding of numbers is shaped by sociocultural differences in learning strategies and educational systems. Alternatively, two cultural groups may use the same brain regions but in opposite ways. For example, Telzer, Masten, Berkman, Liberman, and Fuligni (2010) found that although Latino and White participants contributed to their families at similar rates in a donation task, Latino participants had increased reward-related brain activity when giving to their family while White participants showed more activation in the same regions when gaining money for themselves. This example illustrates how each group might present with different neural activation in the same brain region, despite the similar behavioral outcome. These findings suggest that the sociocultural meaning or value of the behavior is different across cultural groups: whereas Latino youth may find contributing to their family a rewarding and culturally important behavior, White youth may find the same behavior less rewarding and personally meaningful. These kinds of neural findings complement and support our understanding of how culture might modulate the relationship between brain and behavior.

There are several factors to take into consideration when making cross-cultural comparisons in neuroscience research. For example, it is ideal if all of the data are collected using the same scanner to prevent the possibility that differences in scanner properties or scanning environments influence results. Thus, if data collection is done at two or more different locations, one should be careful to make sure that the fMRI scanner properties at each site allow the data collected at all the places to be comparable. Chiao and colleagues (2010) provide a list of suggestions for reducing cross-site variations in data collection. They suggest that one should (1) use fMRI scanners from the same vendor with the same protocols, (2) conduct inter-scanner reliability and calibration tests to compare signal-to-noise ratio across sites, (3) use the same presentation software and hardware at each site, (4) match the scanning and training environments as closely as possible, (5) utilize culturally appropriate scripts, and (6) run quality assurance tests on the collected data. It is important to take the steps above in order to be sure that any differences found across groups are due not to scanner differences but to functional differences in brain activation between participants.

It is also important to control for other factors that might explain differences seen between cultural groups, including age, gender, education, and socioeconomic status (Han et al., 2013). In addition, when possible, the participants' native languages should be used to minimize the potential confounds of language processing. This is especially important in cultural neuroscience studies, because neural regions that might be activated when performing a task might correspond not to the task effects in which researchers are mainly interested, but to regions related to language comprehension. For example, if a certain region is activated when participants from Culture A, but not those from Culture B, perform a task, the difference in activation might not be a reflection of the different cultural ways in which participants from each group are performing the task, but due to differences in language comprehension or to differences in task difficulty that result from differences in language comprehension. In order to disentangle these two possibilities and eliminate potential noise signals unrelated to the main issues of interest, one should use a participant's native language when possible.

Behavioral and Neural Findings

This section illustrates some ways in which researchers have studied how cultural factors influence psychological processes and their corresponding neural activity. Studies in cultural neuroscience have found cultural differences in neural activation in different psychological domains, including visual perception (Goh et al., 2010; Jenkins, Yang, Goh, Hong, & Park, 2010), attention (Hedden, Ketay, Aron, Markus, & Gabrieli, 2008), mentalizing (Adams et al., 2010; Kobayashi, Glover, & Temple, 2006), and empathy (de Greck et al., 2012). We highlight four studies that demonstrate how cultural neuroscientists have explored brain and culture interactions in the areas of self, emotion, perception, and prosocial behavior. Through these examples, we also illustrate how these empirical studies have used the methods described throughout this chapter.

In the first example, Zhu, Zhang, Fan, and Han (2007) were interested in studying the neural correlates of self-representations between subjects from East Asian (Chinese) and Western (English, American, Australian, and Canadian) backgrounds. Using previous findings that self-representations differ between these two cultures, with East Asians showing a more interdependent view of the self, while Westerners possess a more independent view, Zhu and colleagues (2007) hypothesized that neural regions related to thinking about the self, such as the MPFC, might show similar activation when East Asian participants thought about themselves and about their mother, but that Western participants might show distinct neural activation when thinking about the same targets. To this end, they had participants judge personal trait adjectives about themselves, their mother, or a public person (e.g., former American president Bill Clinton for the Western subjects and former Chinese premier Zhu Rongji for the East Asian subjects) while undergoing a brain scan. They found that when thinking about themselves rather than the public figure, both groups recruited the MPFC, a key region that is involved in self-representation. However, when thinking about their mother rather than the public figure, Chinese participants also recruited the MPFC but Western participants did not (Zhu et al., 2007). These results suggest that culture influences self-representations in the brain, with Chinese individuals recruiting the MPFC to represent both the self and the mother and Western participants recruiting the MPFC solely to represent the self. These findings provide evidence that differences in self-representation between East Asian (Chinese in this case) and Western (English, American, Australian and Canadian in this study) individuals can be seen not only at the behavioral level but also at the neural level (for further discussion on culture and self–other overlap in neural circuits, see Varnum & Hampton, chapter 18 in this volume).

Another area of interest in cultural neuroscience is the study of emotions. Previous research has shown that culture shapes ideal affect, or the ideal state people would like to feel (Tsai, Knutson, & Fung, 2006). On the one hand, Hong Kong Chinese value low-arousal positive states, such as feeling calm and relaxed, more than do European Americans. On the other hand, European Americans value more high-arousal positive states, such as feeling excited and enthusiastic, more than do Hong Kong Chinese (Tsai et al., 2006). Using these findings, Park, Tsai, Chim, Blevins, and Knutson

(2016) hypothesized that, compared with Chinese participants, European Americans might find faces displaying excited expressions more rewarding than those showing calm expressions. In order to test this, they presented European-American and Chinese participants with faces that showed calm and excited expressions as part of an fMRI task. Their results supported their hypothesis: they found that, compared with Chinese participants, European-American participants showed higher activation in the ventral striatum and caudate, areas related to reward processing, when viewing excited versus calm faces. These neural findings supplement behavioral findings that culture influences the positive affective states that people ideally want to feel and demonstrate that, indeed, the valuation and reward associated with each culture's ideal affective state seems to be reflected in the brain.

In another example, Freeman, Rule, Adams, and Ambady (2009) were interested in studying how the observed behavioral differences in the ways American and Japanese cultures reinforce dominant and subordinate behaviors respectively would be reflected in the brain. To this end, they used fMRI to measure brain activity while American and Japanese participants viewed images that exhibited a dominant or a subordinate posture. They found the same brain regions firing for different stimuli: Americans showed increased reward-related activity in the striatum and the MPFC for dominant versus submissive postures, while Japanese showed the same pattern of activation but for submissive versus dominant postures. In addition, the magnitude of brain activity positively correlated with how much participants valued dominance and submissiveness. In other words, the more a participant self-reported a tendency towards more dominance (or submissiveness), the more reward-related activity was present for the dominant (or submissive) figures. This study serves as an example of how the same stimuli can elicit different activation in the same brain regions, depending on the values reinforced by each culture.

In another study, Telzer, Ichien, and Qu (2015) explored the neural correlates of prosocial behaviors in an intergroup context. They designed an fMRI task in which European-American and Chinese participants were given the option to donate money to a European-American or Chinese confederate. They found that across both cultural groups participants showed increased reward-related activation in the VS when donating to their in-group as opposed to their out-group, which suggests that both groups found it more rewarding to be prosocial towards the in-group than toward the out-group. In addition, they found that those with higher group identity, and Chinese participants more so than American ones, showed more activation in areas commonly related to self-control (VLPFC, ACC) and mentalizing (TPJ, DMPFC) when donating to the out-group as opposed to the in-group. This study illustrates how one can study universal similarities as well as culture-specific differences between groups.

Suggestions for Steps in Designing a Study

This section provides a general guide to the design of cultural neuroscience studies involving fMRI. The first step in designing a study is to identify a psychological process of interest. Some examples of these are emotion, cognition, perception, motivation, decision making, representations of the self, and intergroup relations. For example, one might be interested in testing whether people from different sociocultural backgrounds have different representations of the self. Once the psychological process of interest has been identified, the second step is to hypothesize whether it might vary depending on the cultural construct of interest. For example, Hofstede (2001) provides a list of dimensions by which cultures can be differentiated and that affect human behavior, including power distance, uncertainty avoidance, individualism versus collectivism, masculinity versus femininity, and long-term versus short-term orientation. Cultures also tend to differ in their cognitive styles of thinking. For instance, East Asian cultures tend to engage in more holistic thinking, meaning that they pay attention to the context and how the parts of a whole might be related to each other. In contrast, Western cultures have a more analytic style of thinking, where each part of the whole is independent of the others and of the context (Nisbett, Peng, Choi, & Norenzayan, 2001). In this second step, one theorizes how some of these cultural factors might influence the psychological process of interest. This stage can be informed by theories and findings from cultural psychology. For example, say the psychological process of interest is self-representation. It has been found that representations of the self differ between East Asian and Western societies, the former having a more interdependent self-construal and the latter a more independent view of the self (Markus & Kitayama, 1991), so it is important to make sure that the groups the researchers are comparing differ in the cultural construct of interest, and not to assume that people from the same sociocultural context have the same cultural values. Thus it is important to find and administer a well-validated questionnaire that measures the cultural construct of interest, which in this example is independence–interdependence.

A third step is to hypothesize which neural systems might be involved in the psychological process of interest. For example, if one is interested in cultural differences in self-representation, one might think that there would be differences in MPFC activation when participants from two different cultures engage in a self-referential task. If one is interested instead in how cultures place different value on what they find rewarding, perhaps one would expect to see differential VS activation between cultural groups.

A fourth step is to design a task that gets at the psychological process of interest. For example, if we are interested in studying how people perceive the self in relation to others, we might create a study that asks participants to think about themselves and about others. However, special considerations are necessary when designing an fMRI task, to ensure that the task is getting at the psychological process of interest, which in this case is self-referential processing. To illustrate, if we give participants 10 seconds to think about themselves, they might spend the first 2 seconds doing what they are asked to, but then spend 8 seconds thinking about something else, such as homework (see Figure 16.3). In that case, we end up measuring neural activity induced by something completely unrelated to what we

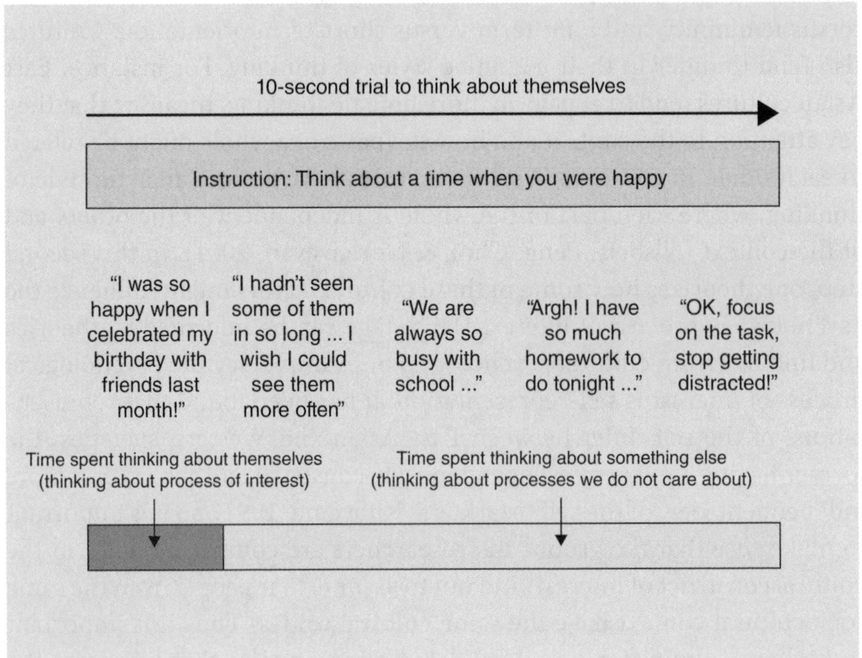

Figure 16.3 Considerations when designing an fMRI task. This example illustrates that it can be hard to isolate the psychological process of interest

want to study. In addition, it is important to make sure the conditions and stimuli we are contrasting are comparable in most dimensions except for one – the one we are interested in. For example, if we would like to examine how people from different cultures might empathize with their in-groups differently, we could present participants from Culture A and Culture B with pictures of their in-groups and ask them to empathize with the people in the picture. In this case, we should ensure that the pictures being presented to the two cultural groups are matched for details such as valence, arousal and background. Otherwise, if one sees differences in brain activation between cultural groups, it might not be because participants from each culture empathized differently with their own in-groups, but rather because the pictures from Culture A were more interesting than those from Culture B and so might activate more attention-related regions than empathy-related regions. These examples illustrate the challenges associated with isolating the psychological process of interest and highlight that a task must be designed with care in order to eliminate the potential confounds presented by processes we are not interested in. Careful thought when designing the fMRI paradigm will increase the validity of the results by ensuring that we are measuring what we are intending to measure, and will also lead to more accurate interpretation of results.

The final step is to analyze the data and interpret the findings. After data collection is done, fMRI data are preprocessed in a series of steps that correct for individual variability to make the data comparable across subjects. Different statistical analyses are then performed to infer if there is differential activation between conditions of interest. As mentioned earlier, before data collection, one might hypothesize which brain regions might be activated by the psychological processes of interest. However, once data are ready for analyses, one should be careful about reverse inferences (Poldrack, 2006), or inferring that because a certain brain region gets activated a particular cognitive function is engaged. In other words, the activation of a region when a certain task is performed does not necessarily mean that the psychological process in which we are interested is involved. For example, if we see MPFC activation in participants from Culture A but not in participants from Culture B when they are doing a self-referential task, we cannot conclude that participants from Culture A engaged in self-referential processing but participants in Culture B did not. All we can say is that there were differences in activation between the two groups in a brain region commonly associated with self-referential processing, and we have to interpret the neuroimaging findings with caution (Schwartz, Lilienfeld, Meca, & Sauvigné, 2016). As with other psychological studies, one should also be aware of possible issues related to statistical power and inflated correlations (Yarkoni, 2009).

Conclusions and Future Directions

Cultural neuroscience has already provided many insights into the relationship between culture and the brain, and has raised several interesting questions for moving forward. However, there is still much to be done. Here we describe some promising avenues for future research.

One of the current limitations in the field of cultural neuroscience is that the vast majority of studies have focused on East Asian and Western samples. While this has given us a very rich understanding of the differences between these two groups, there is still much to be explored about other cultures around the world. In addition, more studies should examine how sociocultural variability and socio-ecological factors, such as residential mobility, might relate to cultural differences within a nation (Ng, Morris, & Oishi, 2013). Inclusion of the study of more cultures within and across nations will provide a more comprehensive view of the behavioral and neural mechanisms that are specific to each culture versus those that are universal.

Another limitation in the field is that most studies in cultural neuroscience have been done on adult samples. Thus, one methodological future direction would be to conduct developmental and longitudinal studies. As previously illustrated, studies in cultural neuroscience have shown that the brain adjusts to its sociocultural context. But the question arises as to whether there is a sensitive period for individuals to become attuned to their sociocultural environment. Are there certain developmental periods when the brain is more receptive to its sociocultural environment than others? And if culture shapes patterns of brain activity early in life, can these patterns be changed later in life? Developmental and longitudinal studies would help answer these kinds of questions by giving us more insights into when and how culture and brain shape each other. For further discussion of developmental considerations in cultural neuroscience, see Miller and Kinsbourne (2012) and Qu and Telzer, chapter 19 in this volume.

Another future direction would be to use different techniques to analyze fMRI data. The most prevalent way in which fMRI data is currently analyzed is through univariate methods, in which the overall mean activations in brain regions between conditions of interest are compared. However, given that brain regions do not operate in isolation, it is also important to look at how different regions are connected to each other and how they function together. In other words, it is important to focus not just on a single brain region but on brain networks. For example, it is possible that two cultures show similar overall brain activation in two regions, but use those regions differently at the network level. That is, the way the two regions are interconnected and communicate with each other might differ between cultures. Another way to study culture and brain interactions, which has not been done extensively in the field, is to look at the connectivity between brain structures rather than at brain function. One way to study this would be to examine the neural connectivity in structural white matter tracts between groups by using techniques such as diffusor tensor imaging (DTI), or to examine functional connectivity by using task-free resting-state scans.

An area of research that is also part of the field of cultural neuroscience but is not explored as much as brain activity is neurogenetics (Chiao & Ambady, 2007), or the study of how genes influence the formation of the nervous system. Doing more research in this area can help us understand how genes can regulate brain development across cultures, which would give us a deeper understanding of how culture can influence not only our neural activity but also our biochemistry. Cultures differ in the frequency of alleles, or variants of a gene (Chiao & Blizinsky, 2010; Luo & Han, 2014), and evidence has shown that these differences can even have an influence on cultural values and neural activity depending on the variant of the gene (Ma et al., 2014). Thus, combining neuroimaging and neurogenetics approaches might give us a greater understanding of how biology and culture interact and give rise to social behaviors, and can also help disentangle the effects that are cultural from those that are genetic (Hyde, Tompson, Creswell, & Falk, 2015). Moreover, imaging genetics has important implications for physical and mental health outcomes (Chiao, 2009), and thus future studies should consider how culture–gene interactions influence neural processes and their potential links to population health (Chiao, 2009; Chiao et al., 2013). For a discussion of culture and genetics, see Causadias and Korous, chapter 7 in this volume.

In conclusion, this chapter introduces readers to some of the most commonly used concepts and methods in the field of cultural neuroscience, and highlights ways in which cultural neuroscientists have studied cultural influences on neural activity. One of the greatest strengths of this field is that it sheds light on the interplay between culture and biology. Given the interdisciplinary nature of cultural neuroscience, we believe that a stronger integration among fields, including cognitive neuroscience, developmental psychology and neurogenetics, will lead to a greater understanding of the bidirectional influences of culture and brain. These future directions would give us a more complete picture of how culture and biology interact to shape the mind and the brain.

References

Adams, R. B., Jr, Rule, N. O., Franklin, R. G., Jr, Wang, E., Stevenson, M. T., Yoshikawa, S., … & Ambady, N. (2010). Cross-cultural reading the mind in the eyes: An fMRI investigation. *Journal of Cognitive Neuroscience, 22*(1), 97–108. doi:10.1162/jocn.2009.21187

Arnett, J. J. (2008). The neglected 95%: Why American psychology needs to become less American. *American Psychologist, 63*(7), 602–614. doi:10.1037/0003-066X.63.7.602

Chiao, J. Y. (2009). Cultural neuroscience: A once and future discipline. *Progress in Brain Research, 178*, 287–304. doi:10.1016/S0079-6123(09)17821-4

Chiao, J. Y., & Ambady, N. (2007). Cultural neuroscience: Parsing universality and diversity across levels of analysis. In S. Kitayama & D. Cohen (Eds.), *Handbook of cultural psychology* (pp. 237–254). New York: Guilford Press.

Chiao, J. Y., & Blizinsky, K. D. (2010). Culture–gene coevolution of individualism–collectivism and the serotonin transporter gene. *Proceedings of the Royal Society B: Biological Sciences, 277*(1681), 529–537. doi:10.1098/rspb.2009.1650

Chiao, J. Y., Cheon, B. K., Pornpattananangkul, N., Mrazek, A. J., & Blizinsky, K. D. (2013). Cultural neuroscience: Progress and promise. *Psychological Inquiry, 24*(1), 1–19. doi:10.1080/1047840X.2013.752715

Chiao, J. Y., Hariri, A. R., Harada, T., Mano, Y., Sadato, N., Parrish, T. B., & Iidaka, T. (2010). Theory and methods in cultural neuroscience. *Social Cognitive and Affective Neuroscience, 5*(2–3), 356–361. doi:10.1093/scan/nsq063

de Greck, M., Shi, Z., Wang, G., Zuo, X., Yang, X., Wang, X., … & Han, S. (2012). Culture modulates brain activity during empathy with anger. *NeuroImage, 59*(3), 2871–2882. doi:10.1016/j.neuroimage.2011.09.052

Delgado, M. R. (2007). Reward-related responses in the human striatum. *Annals of the New York Academy of Sciences, 1104*(1), 70–88. doi:10.1196/annals.1390.002

Freeman, J. B., Rule, N. O., Adams, R. B., Jr, & Ambady, N. (2009). Culture shapes a mesolimbic response to signals of dominance and subordination that associates with behavior. *Neuroimage, 47*(1), 353–359. doi:10.1016/j.neuroimage.2009.04.038

Frith, C. D., & Frith, U. (2006). The neural basis of mentalizing. *Neuron, 50*(4), 531–534. doi10.1016/j.neuron.2006.05.001

Goh, J. O., Leshikar, E. D., Sutton, B. P., Tan, J. C., Sim, S. K., Hebrank, A. C., & Park, D. C. (2010). Culture differences in neural processing of faces and houses in the ventral visual cortex. *Social Cognitive and Affective Neuroscience, 5*(2–3), 227–235. doi:10.1093/scan/nsq060

Hamann, S. B., Ely, T. D., Hoffman, J. M., & Kilts, C. D. (2002). Ecstasy and agony: Activation of the human amygdala in positive and negative emotion. *Psychological Science, 13*(2), 135–141. doi:10.1111/1467-9280.00425

Han, S., Gu, X., Mao, L., Ge, J., Wang, G., & Ma, Y. (2010). Neural substrates of self-referential processing in Chinese Buddhists. *Social Cognitive and Affective Neuroscience, 5*(2–3), 332–339. doi:10.1093/scan/nsp027

Han, S., Mao, L., Gu, X., Zhu, Y., Ge, J., & Ma, Y. (2008). Neural consequences of religious belief on self-referential processing. *Social Neuroscience, 3*(1), 1–15. doi:10.1080/17470910701469681

Han, S., Northoff, G., Vogeley, K., Wexler, B. E., Kitayama, S., & Varnum, M. E. (2013). A cultural neuroscience approach to the biosocial nature of the human brain. *Annual Review of Psychology, 64*, 335–359. doi:10.1146/annurev-psych-071112-054629

Hedden, T., Ketay, S., Aron, A., Markus, H. R., & Gabrieli, J. D. (2008). Cultural influences on neural substrates of attentional control. *Psychological Science, 19*(1), 12–17. doi:10.1111/j.1467-9280.2008.02038.x

Hofstede, G. (2001). *Culture's consequences: Comparing values, behaviors, institutions, and organizations across nations.* Thousand Oaks, CA: Sage Publications.

Hong, Y.-y., Morris, M. W., Chiu, C.-y., & Benet-Martinez, V. (2000). Multicultural minds: A dynamic constructivist approach to culture and cognition. *American Psychologist, 55*(7), 709–720. doi:10.1037/0003-066X.55.7.709

Hyde, L. W., Tompson, S., Creswell, J. D., & Falk, E. B. (2015). Cultural neuroscience: New directions as the field matures. *Culture and Brain, 3*(2), 75–92. doi:10.1007/s40167-014-0024-6

Jenkins, L. J., Yang, Y.-J., Goh, J., Hong, Y.-Y., & Park, D. C. (2010). Cultural differences in the lateral occipital complex while viewing incongruent scenes. *Social Cognitive and Affective Neuroscience, 5*(2–3), 236–241. doi:10.1093/scan/nsp056

Johnson, S. C., Baxter, L. C., Wilder, L. S., Pipe, J. G., Heiserman, J. E., & Prigatano, G. P. (2002). Neural correlates of self-reflection. *Brain, 125*(8), 1808–1814. doi:10.1093/brain/awf181

Kelley, W. M., Macrae, C. N., Wyland, C. L., Caglar, S., Inati, S., & Heatherton, T. F. (2002). Finding the self? An event-related fMRI study. *Journal of Cognitive Neuroscience, 14*(5), 785–794. doi:10.1162/08989290260138672

Kim, H. S., & Sasaki, J. Y. (2014). Cultural neuroscience: Biology of the mind in cultural contexts. *Annual Review of Psychology, 65*, 487–514. doi:10.1146/annurev-psych-010213-115040

Kitayama, S., & Uskul, A. K. (2011). Culture, mind, and the brain: Current evidence and future directions. *Annual Review of Psychology, 62*, 419–449. doi:10.1146/annurev-psych-120709-145357

Kobayashi, C., Glover, G. H., & Temple, E. (2006). Cultural and linguistic influence on neural bases of “theory of mind”: An fMRI study with Japanese bilinguals. *Brain and Language, 98*(2), 210–220. doi:10.1016/j.bandl.2006.04.013

Kroeber, A. L., & Kluckhohn, C. (1952). *Culture: A critical review of concepts and definitions*. Cambridge, MA: Harvard University Press.

Luo, S., & Han, S. (2014). The association between an oxytocin receptor gene polymorphism and cultural orientations. *Culture and Brain, 2*(1), 89–107. doi:10.1007/s40167-014-0017-5

Ma, Y., Wang, C., Li, B., Zhang, W., Rao, Y., & Han, S. (2014). Does self-construal predict activity in the social brain network? A genetic moderation effect. *Social Cognitive and Affective Neuroscience, 9*(9), 1360–1367. doi:10.1093/scan/nst125

Markus, H. R., & Kitayama, S. (1991). Culture and the self: Implications for cognition, emotion, and motivation. *Psychological Review, 98*(2), 224–253. doi:10.1037/0033-295X.98.2.224

Miller, J. G., & Kinsbourne, M. (2012). Culture and neuroscience in developmental psychology: Contributions and challenges. *Child Development Perspectives, 6*(1), 35–41. doi:10.1111/j.1750-8606.2011.00188.x

Ng, B. W., Morris, J. P., & Oishi, S. (2013). Cultural neuroscience: The current state of affairs. *Psychological Inquiry, 24*(1), 53–57. doi:10.1080/1047840X.2013.766569

Nisbett, R. E., Peng, K., Choi, I., & Norenzayan, A. (2001). Culture and systems of thought: Holistic versus analytic cognition. *Psychological Review, 108*(2), 291–310. doi:10.1037/0033-295X.108.2.291

Ochsner, K. N., & Lieberman, M. D. (2001). The emergence of social cognitive neuroscience. *American Psychologist, 56*(9), 717–734. doi:10.1037/0003-066X.56.9.717

Oyserman, D., & Lee, S. W. (2008). Does culture influence what and how we think? Effects of priming individualism and collectivism. *Psychological Bulletin, 134*(2), 311–342. doi:10.1037/0033-2909.134.2.311

Park, B., Tsai, J. L., Chim, L., Blevins, E., & Knutson, B. (2016). Neural evidence for cultural differences in the valuation of positive facial expressions. *Social Cognitive and Affective Neuroscience, 11*(2), 243–252. doi:10.1093/scan/nsv113

Poldrack, R. A. (2006). Can cognitive processes be inferred from neuroimaging data? *Trends in Cognitive Sciences, 10*(2), 59–63. doi:10.1016/j.tics.2005.12.004

Powers, K. E., & Heatherton, T. F. (2013). Implicitly priming the social brain: Failure to find neural effects. *PloS One, 8*(2), e56596. doi:10.1371/journal.pone.0056596

Ray, R. D., Shelton, A. L., Hollon, N. G., Matsumoto, D., Frankel, C. B., Gross, J. J., & Gabrieli, J. D. (2010). Interdependent self-construal and neural representations of self and mother. *Social Cognitive and Affective Neuroscience, 5*(2–3), 318–323. doi:10.1093/scan/nsp039

Schwartz, S. J., Lilienfeld, S. O., Meca, A., & Sauvigné, K. C. (2016). The role of neuroscience within psychology: A call for inclusiveness over exclusiveness. *American Psychologist, 71*(1), 52–70. doi:10.1037/a0039678

Singelis, T. M. (1994). The measurement of independent and interdependent self-construals. *Personality and Social Psychology Bulletin, 20*(5), 580–591. doi:10.1177/0146167294205014

Sui, J., & Han, S. (2007). Self-construal priming modulates neural substrates of self-awareness. *Psychological Science, 18*(10), 861–866. doi:10.1111/j.1467-9280.2007.01992.x

Tang, Y., Zhang, W., Chen, K., Feng, S., Ji, Y., Shen, J., … & Liu, Y. (2006). Arithmetic processing in the brain shaped by cultures. *Proceedings of the National Academy of Sciences, 103*(28), 10775–10780. doi:10.1073/pnas.0604416103

Telzer, E. H., Ichien, N., & Qu, Y. (2015). The ties that bind: Group membership shapes the neural correlates of in-group favoritism. *NeuroImage, 115*, 42–51. doi:10.1016/j.neuroimage.2015.04.035

Telzer, E. H., Masten, C. L., Berkman, E. T., Lieberman, M. D., & Fuligni, A. J. (2010). Gaining while giving: An fMRI study of the rewards of family assistance among White and Latino youth. *Social Neuroscience, 5*(5–6), 508–518. doi:10.1080/17470911003687913

Tsai, J. L., Knutson, B., & Fung, H. H. (2006). Cultural variation in affect valuation. *Journal of Personality and Social Psychology, 90*(2), 288–307. doi:10.1037/0022-3514.90.2.288

Varnum, M. E., Blais, C., Hampton, R. S., & Brewer, G. A. (2015). Social class affects neural empathic responses. *Culture and Brain, 3*(2), 122–130. doi:10.1007/s40167-015-0031-2

Yarkoni, T. (2009). Big correlations in little studies: Inflated fMRI correlations reflect low statistical power – Commentary on Vul et al. (2009). *Perspectives on Psychological Science, 4*(3), 294–298. doi:10.1111/j.1745-6924.2009.01127.x

Yarkoni, T., Poldrack, R. A., Nichols, T. E., Van Essen, D. C., & Wager, T. D. (2011). Large-scale automated synthesis of human functional neuroimaging data. *Nature Methods, 8*(8), 665–670. doi:10.1038/nmeth.1635

Zhu, Y., Zhang, L., Fan, J., & Han, S. (2007). Neural basis of cultural influence on self-representation. *Neuroimage, 34*(3), 1310–1316. doi:10.1016/j.neuroimage.2006.08.047

17

Neurobiological Causes and Consequences of Cultural Differences in Social Cognition

Meghan L. Meyer

Individuals from different cultures vary in how they perceive, think about and respond to the social world. A prominent view is that environmental factors, such as the prevalence of infectious disease threats, may promote certain social cognitive processes that facilitate survival (Fincher & Thornhill, 2008; Schaller & Duncan, 2007). Thus, cultures across the globe vary in ideologies, such as collectivism versus individualism, in part because environmental factors vary across regions of the world. However, the underlying neurobiological mechanisms that link environmental factors, like threat of infection, to differences in cultural ideologies remains unknown. Another mystery is how our cultural background spontaneously shapes our responses to the social environment. Specifically, while it is well known that cultural background influences many of our social reactions, to date it remains unclear *how* cultural backgrounds (1) guide our responses from moment to moment and (2) mold our social learning and memory. The goal of the present chapter is to review neuroscience research that may offer new insight into these lingering questions.

How Do Environmental Factors Influence Cultural Ideologies? The Parasite Stress Theory of Sociality

Given that infectious disease threats vary regionally, cultures around the world may foster different cultural ideologies in part to cope with the disease threats posed by the region. In particular, the parasite stress theory of sociality suggests that the threat of infectious and parasitic diseases fosters social cognitive processes that prioritize assortative sociality, such as

The Handbook of Culture and Biology, First Edition. Edited by José M. Causadias, Eva H. Telzer and Nancy A. Gonzales.

strong feelings of connection to in-group members and avoidance of out-group members (Fincher & Thornhill, 2012; Fincher, Thornhill, Murray, & Schaller, 2008; Schaller & Duncan, 2007). The logic of the parasite stress theory of sociality is that connection to in-group members and avoidance of out-group members should minimize the possibility of infection from novel pathogens (Faulkner, Schaller, Park, & Duncan, 2004; Fincher & Thornhill, 2008; Navarrete & Fessler, 2006; Navarrete, Fessler, & Eng, 2007; Park, Schaller, & Crandall, 2007; Schaller & Duncan, 2007; Schaller & Murray, 2008).

Support for the parasite stress theory of sociality comes from evidence that cultural differences in assortative sociality scale with infectious disease prevalence (Fincher & Thornhill, 2012; cf. Currie & Mace, 2012; van de Vliert & Postmes, 2012). For example, a common component of collectivism (versus individualism) is amplified in-group/out-group divisions, in which in-group cohesion and out-group avoidance are heightened (Iyengar, Lepper, & Ross, 1999; Markus & Kitayama, 2010; Meyer et al., 2015; Triandis, 1972, 1989). Interestingly, pathogen prevalence across regions of the world positively correlates with the degree to which collectivistic ideologies are endorsed by cultures in those regions. In fact, this relationship exists with historical as well as with contemporary levels of pathogen prevalence (Fincher et al., 2008). Pathogen prevalence has also been linked to a variety of other cultural ideologies relevant to assortative sociality, such as religiosity, conservatism, and the importance of family ties (Fincher & Thornhill, 2008).

Of course, there are benefits associated with interacting with out-group members, such as access to new trade goods and mate options. Computational modeling approaches have addressed this tradeoff by showing that disease threat tips the cost–benefit ratio of connecting with out-group members. Specifically, spontaneously formed groups will preferentially form connections with agents distant from their local social network when the threat of infection is low. However, when the threat of infection is high, groups prefer more local and less global social network connections (Brown, Fincher, & Walasek, 2016).

While provocative, the parasite stress theory of sociality relies on correlational data, and more recently computational modeling, for support. Thus it remains unclear how – in terms of underlying biological mechanisms – threat of infection influences cultural ideologies. Research from social neuroscience suggests that inflammation, the body's first line of defense against infection, may be a mechanism by which threat of infection promotes assortative sociality. This work finds that inflammation not only defends the body from physical threats, but also heightens neural sensitivity to social threats.

Research on how inflammation influences social cognition often uses neuropharmacological manipulations to systematically induce inflammation, and subsequently measures neural and behavioral responses to social threats and rewards. In these paradigms, participants are randomly assigned to receive either endotoxin (0.4–0.8 ng/kg), which induces inflammation in a safe and time-limited manner, or a placebo. Two hours later, when endotoxin-induced inflammation is at its peak (Krabbe et al., 2005; Reichenberg et al., 2001; Suffredini, Hochstein, & McMahon, 1999; Wright, Strike, Brydon, & Steptoe, 2005), participants complete psychological tasks of interest.

For example, in one study, participants were randomly assigned to receive endotoxin or a placebo and subsequently underwent functional magnetic resonance imaging (fMRI). During their fMRI scan, participants alternated between viewing photographs of (1) socially threatening strangers (e.g., an angry face), (2) socially non-threatening strangers (e.g., a smiling face), (3) non-social threatening images (e.g., a snake), and (4) non-social, non-threatening images (e.g., a cup). Results showed that activity in the amygdala, a region previously associated with threat responding (Green & Phillips, 2004; Phan, Fitzgerald, Nathan, & Tancer, 2006), preferentially increased in participants who had received endotoxin when they viewed threatening strangers (Inagaki, Muscatell, Irwin, Cole, & Eisenberger, 2012). Thus, inducing inflammation, the body's response to physical threats in the environment, enhances sensitivity to social threats in the environment. Therefore, inflammation may amplify the threat of out-group strangers, and so facilitate assortative sociality.

Other work that combines endotoxin administration with fMRI scanning finds that inflammation also increases neural sensitivity to social acceptance. Muscatell and colleagues (2016) found that when participants received negative (versus neutral) social feedback, endotoxin (versus placebo) increased activity in the neural regions associated with threat and distress (the amygdala, the dorsal anterior cingulate cortex) (Adolphs, 2001; Amaral et al., 2003). Alternatively, when participants received positive (versus neutral) social feedback, endotoxin (versus placebo) increased activity in brain regions associated with reward (the ventral striatum and the ventromedial prefrontal cortex; Cador, Robbins, & Everitt, 1989; Gläscher, Hampton, & O'Doherty, 2009; Kable & Glimcher, 2007; Knutson, Taylor, Kaufmann, Peterson, & Glover, 2005; O'Doherty, Deichman, Critchley, & Dolan, 2002; Padoa-Schioppa & Assad, 2006;

Sabatinelli, Bradley, Lang, Costa, & Versace, 2007). Moreover, another study found that the participants with the greatest inflammatory response to endotoxin exposure showed the greatest activity in distress-related neural regions during social exclusion (Eisenberger, Inagaki, Rameson, Mashal, & Irwin, 2009). Together, these findings suggest that inflammation heightens sensitivity to social acceptance, another process that may be relevant to assortative sociality.

Interestingly, animal and human research has shown that inflammation also increases affiliation with familiar others, a process that is probably key to the in-group-connection component of assortative sociality. For example, in both rats and non-human primates, inducing an inflammatory response increases the amount of close contact with familiar cagemates (Dantzer, 2001; Willette, Lubach, & Coe, 2007; Yee & Prendergast, 2010). Piggybacking on this work, a study in humans found that administration of endotoxin (versus placebo) increased participants' self-reported desire to spend time with close others (Inagaki et al., 2015). When these participants underwent fMRI scanning, individuals who received endotoxin (versus placebo) also showed greater activity in the ventral striatum, a region key to reward processing (Cador et al., 1989; Knutson et al., 2005; O'Doherty et al., 2002), when they viewed photographs of a close other compared to photographs of a gender-, age-, and race-matched non-close other. Furthermore, the participants with the greatest inflammatory response showed the greatest ventral striatum activity in response to observing photographs of their close other. Thus, inflammation may increase the reward value of close others, motivating the desire to affiliate with them.

Inflammation also influences "mentalizing," or the process of thinking about people's personality traits, intentions, and emotions (Frith & Frith, 2006; Kullmann et al., 2014; Moieni et al., 2015; Muscatell et al., 2016). When participants think about other people's mental states in the fMRI scanner, prior administration of endotoxin (versus placebo) increases neural activity in the two brain regions most consistently implicated in mentalizing – the temporoparietal junction and the medial prefrontal cortex (Frith & Frith, 2006; Saxe & Kanwisher, 2003; Spunt, Satpute, & Lieberman, 2011). In one study, after administration of endotoxin (versus placebo), participants completed the "Reading the Mind in the Eyes" task, which requires them to determine what a photographed person is thinking on the basis of limited information expressed in the photographed person's eyes (Kullmann et al., 2013). Participants who were administered endotoxin (versus placebo) showed increased activity in the temporoparietal junction during the Reading the Mind in the Eyes task. Meanwhile, another study using a different mentalizing task, in which participants consider what other people think of them, found that administration of endotoxin (versus placebo) increased activity in the medial prefrontal cortex (Muscatell et al., 2016). Together, these studies suggest that inflammation may enhance mentalizing neural mechanisms.

In connection with the parasite stress theory of sociality, collectivistic ideologies also influence mentalizing (de Greck et al., 2012; Harada, Li, & Chaoi, 2010; Meyer et al., 2015; Wang et al., 2012; Zhu, Zhang, Fan, & Han, 2007), particularly mentalizing about in-group and out-group members. For example, one study found that greater endorsement of collectivistic ideology simultaneously correlated with (1) greater activity in the medial prefrontal cortex when mentalizing about an in-group member and (2) less activity in the medial prefrontal cortex when mentalizing about an out-group member (Meyer et al., 2015). In other words, interdependent self-construal was associated with a mentalizing tradeoff in the medial prefrontal cortex for in-group versus out-group members. Given that inflammation influences mentalizing neural responses, and that mentalizing neural responses to in-group and out-group members vary as a function of collectivism, inflammation may also trigger mentalizing patterns important to the development and maintenance of collectivistic ideologies. That said, this suggestion is preliminary and requires empirical testing in future research.

To date, only a handful of studies have begun to explore the role of inflammation in social and affective processes, and even fewer have begun to link inflammation to differences in cultural ideologies. However, two pieces of evidence suggest this may be a fruitful area to probe the parasite stress theory of sociality. First, it has been shown that simply viewing diseased-looking people is sufficient to increase inflammation (Schaller, Miller, Gervais, Yager, & Chen, 2010), which suggests that the immune system may respond similarly to threats of infection and real infection. Second, a study has found that, after observing photographs of diseased-looking people, participants with collectivistic ancestral backgrounds (versus individualistic ancestral backgrounds) showed significant increases from baseline in immunoglobulin A (IgA) (Brown, Ikeuchi, & Lucas, 2014), which is used by the immune system to counteract pathogens (Carter & Curran, 2011). Thus, a promising direction for future cross-cultural neuroscience research may be to examine whether inflammation triggers threat-related neural circuitry in response to out-group members and reward responses to in-group members (see Figure 17.1A–B), which may in turn

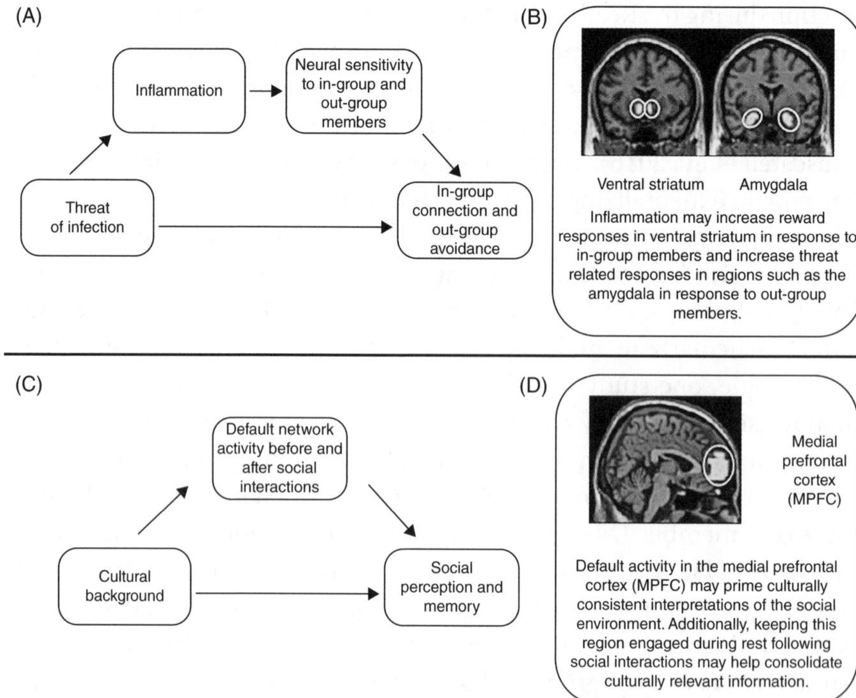

Figure 17.1 Potential mechanisms by which threat of infection leads to in-group preference and out-group avoidance (A–B) and cultural background shapes social perception and memory (C–D)

promote assortative sociality common to regions of the world with known threats of infection.

What Nudges Culturally Consistent Interpretations of the Social World?

Cross-cultural psychology research has shown that cultural ideologies influence how people think about the social environment (Markus & Kitayama, 1991, 2010). For example, among individuals from individualistic cultures, behavior is often interpreted as driven by personal dispositions (Ross & Nisbett, 2011). In contrast, individuals from collectivistic cultures interpret the same behavior as driven by social contextual factors (Choi, Nisbett, & Norenzayan, 1999). Collectivism and individualism also shape how we perceive ourselves. Collectivistic cultures tend to foster interdependent self-construals, which incorporate the values, goals and traits of other people in their social group. In contrast, individualistic cultures tend to foster independent self-construals, in which the self is defined by its uniqueness from others (see Markus & Kitayama, 1991, 2010 for reviews). Taken together, such findings suggest that collectivistic and individualistic cultural ideologies foster different patterns of self- and other-processing.

Cultural differences in self- and other-processing can be traced to different patterns of brain activity in the medial prefrontal cortex (e.g., Harada, Li, & Choi, 2010; Zhu et al., 2007). Portions of the medial prefrontal cortex are known to support various mentalizing processes about the self and others, including impression formation, trait judgments, and mental state inference (Denny, Kober, Wager, & Ochsner, 2012; Van Overwalle, 2009). Consistently with past cross-cultural psychology findings, a quantitative meta-analysis showed that East Asians from collectivistic cultures (versus Western samples from individualistic cultures) show greater activity in a dorsal portion of the medial prefrontal cortex (the dorsomedial prefrontal cortex) across a variety of social cognition tasks (see Han & Ma, 2014). The dorsomedial prefrontal cortex engages when participants are instructed to mentalize about people's intentions and states of mind (Denny et al., 2012; Mitchell, Banaji, & Macrae, 2005; Mitchell, Macrae, & Banaji, 2005; Spunt, Falk, & Lieberman, 2010; Spunt & Lieberman, 2012; Spunt et al., 2011; Van Overwalle, 2009), a process that may be more common among individuals from collectivistic cultures. Indeed, participants from collectivistic cultures (Chinese nationals) show equivalent medial prefrontal cortex activity when thinking about themselves and about close others, whereas participants from individualistic cultures (Caucasians from England, America, Australia, and Canada) more selectively recruit medial prefrontal cortex specifically for thinking about themselves (Zhu et al., 2007).

While this past work has localized "where" cultural differences in self- and other-processing exist in the brain, it remains unknown "how" different patterns of neural activity in these regions drive culturally influenced interpretations of the social world. The next section suggests that understanding an important physiological property of the medial prefrontal cortex – that it is part of the brain's neural baseline – may shed new insight into how cultural differences in self- and other-processing frame perceptions and responses to the social environment.

The medial prefrontal cortex is part of a larger neurocognitive network, which includes the precuneus, the temporoparietal junction and the temporal poles, known to engage whenever our mind is free (Raichle & Snyder, 2007). While other networks of the brain show reduced neural engagement when participants are not required to perform an experimental task, the default network engages whenever participants are not instructed to perform any task at all. This observation is so robust that it even led cognitive neuroscientists to term this network the "default network," because it appears to consistently engage by default (Binder et al., 1999; Greicius, Krasnow, Reiss, & Menon, 2003; Mayozer et al., 2001; Raichle, 2010; Raichle et al., 2001; Shulman et al., 1997). The default network engages during "resting-state scans," in which participants rest and relax in the scanner (typically for 5–8 minutes) as well as during brief mental breaks (typically 10–30 seconds) that occur in between experimental conditions. One study found that even during very brief rest periods (2 seconds), participants increase default network activity, including activity in the medial prefrontal cortex (Meyer, Spunt, & Lieberman, 2017). Thus, the tendency to engage the default network during mental breaks happens immediately, as soon as people are left to their own mental devices.

Priming Hypothesis

One way to think of the default network is that these regions comprise the baseline neural activity with which we enter new situations. Given that culturally specific responses during social processing are represented in the medial prefrontal cortex and that these regions engage reflexively by default, it is possible that moment-to-moment activity in the medial prefrontal cortex primes individuals to think and behave more or less consistently with their belief system (see Figure 17.1C–D).

Support for this possibility comes from studies that examine how neural activity during brief periods of rest (6–9 seconds) just before a self- and other-judgment task influences the speed (or ease) with which participants respond to these tasks (Meyer & Lieberman, 2017; Spunt, Meyer, & Lieberman, 2015). For example, in one study, participants shifted between 6–9-second rest periods and making trait judgments about themselves (e.g., "Are you funny?"), a well-known person (e.g., "Is Barack Obama charming?"), and a well-known non-social object (e.g., "Is the Grand Canyon dry?"; Meyer et al., 2017). Neural activity in the medial prefrontal cortex during each rest period corresponded with faster reaction time specifically on subsequent self-judgment trials. In contrast, neural activity in the dorsomedial prefrontal cortex during each rest period corresponded with faster reaction time on subsequent other-person (Barack Obama) trials. Meanwhile, no region of the brain during rest periods that preceded Grand Canyon trials corresponded with faster reaction time on these non-self and non-social judgments. Thus, medial and dorsomedial prefrontal cortex activity at rest may preferentially prime self- and other-processing, respectively. Consistently with this suggestion, dorsomedial prefrontal cortex activity seconds before reasoning about other people's mental states also led participants to identify more quickly the mental states driving a person's behavior (Spunt, Meyer, & Lieberman, 2015).

Medial and dorsomedial priming effects may relate to cultural differences in social cognition in at least two ways. First, if the medial prefrontal cortex primes self-referential processing, then individuals with interdependent self-construals may show this effect not only for themselves, but also for close others who are incorporated into their self-concepts. Cultural neuroscience paradigms often exogenously prime interdependent and independent self-construals and subsequently measure neural responses during self- and other-processing trials. While this approach has been useful for understanding how different self-construals influence social cognition, it does not explain how everyday social cognition is influenced – endogenously – by self-construal. Neural priming paradigms like the ones reviewed above suggest that medial prefrontal cortex activity at rest may be an endogenous prime that inclines individuals towards interdependent versus independent thinking.

Second, given past findings that individualism fosters dispositional attributions of behavior whereas collectivism fosters contextual attributions of behavior (Choi et al., 1999; Ross & Nisbett, 2011), and that the dorsomedial prefrontal cortex supports mental state reasoning (Denny et al., 2012; Mitchell, Banaji, & Macrae, 2005; Mitchell, Macrae, & Banaji, 2005; Spunt, Falk, & Lieberman, 2010; Spunt & Lieberman, 2012; Spunt, Satpute, & Liberman, 2011; Van Overwalle, 2009), different neural patterns within the dorsomedial prefrontal cortex at rest may prime people toward dispositional versus contextual attributions.

Thus, priming mechanisms in both the medial and the dorsomedial prefrontal cortices may nudge people to perceive the environment through, for example, a more collectivistic or individualistic lens, depending on their cultural background.

Consistently with these ideas, differences in interdependent self-construal and independent self-construal can be traced to differences in medial prefrontal cortex activity at rest. During a 7-minute resting-state scan, Chinese nationals with stronger interdependent self-construal showed greater connectivity (e.g., correlated changes in neural activity over time) between the medial prefrontal cortex and the dorsomedial prefrontal cortex, the region associated with thinking about other people's intentions and states of mind (Wang, Oyserman, Liu, Li, & Han, 2013). In contrast, individuals with stronger independent self-construal showed greater functional connectivity between the medial prefrontal cortex and the precuneus, a region associated with autobiographical and episodic memory (Addis, McIntosh, Moscovitch, Crawley, & McAndrews, 2004; Cavanna & Trimble, 2006; Svoboda, McKinnon, & Levine, 2006). Thus, interdependent self-construal mechanisms in the medial prefrontal cortex may link to mechanisms in the dorsomedial prefrontal cortex associated with thinking about other people, whereas independent self-construal mechanisms in the medial prefrontal cortex may link to other forms of self-processing, such as thinking about oneself in the past. Future work may reveal whether these different connectivity profiles at rest nudge different neural, cognitive, and behavioral responses known to vary between individuals from collectivistic and individualistic cultures.

How Does Cultural Background Influence How We Remember the Social World?

In addition to influencing how we respond to the present social context, cultural ideologies shape how we remember past social events. For example, one study found that individuals from China and the United States vary in the social content they remember from their own personal lives (Conway, Wang, Hanyu, & Haque, 2005). That is, participants from China mentioned other people (besides themselves) more often, and described more than twice as many social interactions than participants from the United States, when prompted to describe autobiographical memories. In contrast, participants from the United States (versus China), described more memories with personal themes (e.g., personal success).

These cultural differences in memory may be related to what social psychologists have termed "the self-reference effect" in memory: information that is encoded as relevant to the self is better recalled than information unrelated to the self (Rogers, Kuiper, & Kirker, 1977; Symons & Johnson, 1997). One possibility is that Chinese individuals (and perhaps individuals from other collectivistic cultures) are more likely than individuals in the United States (and perhaps individuals from other individualistic cultures) to consider information about people in the social environment as self-relevant. In line with this hypothesis, the self-reference effect extends to close others among individuals from Chinese culture, but not to individuals from Western cultures (e.g., Americans, Australians, and

Canadians; Klein, Loftus, & Burton, 1989; Lord, 1980; Zhu et al., 2007; Zhu & Zhang, 2002). While some work has shown that engaging the medial prefrontal cortex during the encoding of self-relevant information is associated with the self-reference effect in memory (Macrae, Moran, Heatherton, Banfield, & Kelley, 2004; Zhu et al., 2007), to date no work has explored how, in terms of neural mechanisms, self-relevant information is consolidated (i.e., committed to memory after encoding).

Consolidation Hypothesis

In connection with the possibility that collectivistic versus individualistic cultural background may influence what is remembered from the social environment, another function of default medial prefrontal cortex activity during rest may be to consolidate newly acquired social information (see Figure 17.1C–D). This hypothesis stems from animal research that found that, during sleep and waking rest, neural reactivation helps consolidate new information (Foster & Wilson, 2006; Hoffman & McNaughton, 2002; Ji & Wilson, 2007; Qin, McNaughton, Skaggs, & Barnes, 1997). Given that the medial prefrontal cortex is already engaged by default when participants rest in the scanner, a similar process could occur during human rest: the medial prefrontal cortex may work with other default network regions during mental breaks to consolidate social information.

To enable researchers to explore this possibility, participants underwent fMRI scanning and formed impressions of various people and locations (Meyer et al., 2017). During impression formation trials, participants observed either a person's face (social impression condition) or a location (non-social impression formation condition) and two traits that had been used to describe the person or location in the past. These two tasks were interleaved with resting-state scans that occurred before (baseline) and after each impression formation task. After their scan, participants completed a surprise memory task requiring them to identify which traits were presented with which faces and locations. The medial prefrontal cortex showed greater connectivity with other portions of the default network associated with social cognition (e.g., the temporoparietal junction) during the rest period that occurred after the participants had formed impressions of people than in the baseline rest period, as well as in the rest period that followed location impression formation. Moreover, greater connectivity between the medial prefrontal cortex and the temporoparietal junction during the rest that occurred after the participants had formed social impressions predicted better associative memory for the traits paired with faces (but not those paired with locations). Together, these findings are consistent with the idea that one function of medial prefrontal cortex and temporoparietal junction activity during rest may be that they work together to consolidate newly acquired social information. Given that default network connectivity during rest consolidates social information, it is possible that different forms of social consolidation occur during rest as a function of cultural ideologies.

Conclusions and Future Directions

Cultural ideologies influence our responses to the social environment. Cultural ideologies may evolve, in part, to help people cope with certain environmental factors, such as pathogen prevalence. This chapter presented research that suggests that inflammation – the body's first line of defense against infection – may be a mechanism through which the threat of infection influences cultural ideologies. Once cultural ideologies are formed, they may go on to influence how we perceive the social world and what we learn from it via default activity in portions of the medial prefrontal cortex. Future research should test these possibilities directly and ultimately aim to develop a model of the neurobiological causes and consequences of cultural ideologies.

Such a model would not only inform how culture "gets under the skin" and influences behavior, but may also help predict how cultural ideologies develop, spread, and change. For example, while it is well known that cultures vary in their ideologies, the neurocognitive mechanisms through which these ideologies and their related cultural norms develop and spread across individuals remains unknown. Interestingly, the medial prefrontal cortex has been associated (in Western samples) with social norms newly learned in adolescence (Welborn et al., 2016) and adulthood (Zaki, Schirmer, & Mitchell, 2011). Moreover, medial prefrontal cortex activity while encoding culturally relevant ideas (e.g., beliefs about the consequences of smoking) predicts the tendency to endorse and spread the ideas communicated in the message (Falk, Morelli, Welborn, Dambacher, & Lieberman, 2013). Future research that extends this literature to the cultural neuroscience arena may reveal interesting information about the development and spread of culture. As mentioned earlier in this chapter, the medial prefrontal cortex communicates with other portions of the default network during rest to consolidate newly acquired social information (Meyer et al., 2017). Thus, rest may be a time in which the medial prefrontal cortex solidifies, or consolidates, social norms.

Additionally, while most cultural neuroscience research to date maps existing cultural ideologies to areas of the brain, far less is known about how culturally influenced neural mechanisms can change with exposure to new environments. Acculturation is the process of learning cultural practices and beliefs when one joins a new culture, for example when relocating from one culture to another. While this is a very common phenomenon, relatively little is known about the brain basis of acculturation. It is known, however, that individuals with bicultural identities from Eastern and Western cultures can reflexively recruit the medial prefrontal cortex in response to thinking about the self independently or interdependently, depending on the cultural ideology with which they are primed (Chiao et al., 2010). Moreover, changes in cultural identity after migrating to another culture also reveal changes in medial prefrontal cortex responses to the self and close others (Chen, Wagner, Kelley, & Heatherton, 2015). Interestingly, both of these studies examined samples aged 19–27 years old, suggesting that self-construal in the medial prefrontal cortex appears to be flexible and susceptible to cultural changes even in young adulthood. Given that moving to new cultures is a common occurrence, research on these questions should yield theoretically and practically relevant information about the brain basis of acculturation.

In conclusion, cultural neuroscience has made great strides in understanding how cultural backgrounds influence social cognition. However, many questions remain unanswered. Future research that incorporates new methods, such as inducing inflammation and examining neural activity during rest, may shed new insight into the multifaceted relationships between neurobiology, cultural ideologies, and social cognition.

References

Addis, D. R., McIntosh, A. R., Moscovitch, M., Crawley, A. P., & McAndrews, M. P. (2004). Characterizing spatial and temporal features of autobiographical memory retrieval networks: A partial least squares approach. *Neuroimage, 23*(4), 1460–1471. doi:10.1016/j.neuroimage.2004.08.007

Adolphs, R. (2001). The neurobiology of social cognition. *Current Opinion in Neurobiology, 11*(2), 231–239. doi:0959-4388/01

Amaral, D. G., Bauman, M. D., Capitanio, J. P., Lavenex, P., Mason, W. A., Mauldin-Jourdain, M. L., & Mendoza, S. P. (2003). The amygdala: Is it an essential component of the neural network for social cognition? *Neuropsychologia, 41*(4), 517–522.

Binder, J. R., Frost, J. A., Hammeke, T. A., Bellgowan, P. S. F., Rao, S. M., & Cox, R. W. (1999). Conceptual processing during the conscious resting state: A functional MRI study. *Journal of Cognitive Neuroscience, 11*(1), 80–93. doi:10.1162/089892999563265

Brown, D. A., Fincher, C. L., & Walasek, L. (2016). Personality, parasites, political attitudes, and cooperation: A model of how infection prevalence influences openness and social group formation. *Topics in Cognitive Science, 8*, 98–117. doi:10.1111/tops.12175.

Brown, S. G., Ikeuchi, R. K., & Lucas, D. R., III (2014). Collectivism/individualism and its relationship to behavioral and physiological immunity. *Health Psychology and Behavioral Medicine: An Open Access Journal, 2*(1), 653–664. doi:10.1080/21642850.2014.916218

Cador, M., Robbins, T. W., & Everitt, B. J. (1989). Involvement of the amygdala in stimulus–reward associations: Interaction with the ventral striatum. *Neuroscience, 30*(1), 77–86. doi:10.1016/0306-4522(89)90354-0

Carter, N. J., & Curran, M. P. (2011). Live attenuated influenza vaccine (FluMist®; Fluenz™): A review of its use in the prevention of seasonal influenza in children and adults. *Drugs, 71*(12), 1591–1622. doi:10.2165/11206860-000000000-00000

Cavanna, A. E., & Trimble, M. R. (2006). The precuneus: A review of its functional anatomy and behavioural correlates. *Brain, 129*(3), 564–583. doi:10.1093/brain/awl004

Chen, P. H. A., Wagner, D. D., Kelley, W. M., & Heatherton, T. F. (2015). Activity in cortical midline structures is modulated by self-construal changes during acculturation. *Culture and Brain, 3*(1), 39–52. doi:10.1007/s40167-015-0026-z

Chiao, J. Y., Harada, T., Komeda, H., Li, Z., Mano, Y., Saito, D., … & Iidaka, T. (2010). Dynamic cultural influences on neural representations of the self. *Journal of Cognitive Neuroscience, 22*(1), 1–11. doi:10.1162/jocn.2009.21192

Choi, I., Nisbett, R. E., & Norenzayan, A. (1999). Causal attribution across cultures: Variation and universality. *Psychological Bulletin, 125*(1), 47–63. doi:10.1037/0033-2909.125.1.47

Conway, M. A., Wang, Q., Hanyu, K., & Haque, S. (2005). A cross-cultural investigation of autobiographical memory: On the universality and cultural variation of the reminiscence bump. *Journal of Cross-Cultural Psychology, 36*(6), 739–749. doi:10.1177/0022022105280512

Currie, T. E., & Mace, R. (2012). Analyses do not support the parasite-stress theory of human sociality. *Behavioral and Brain Sciences, 35*(2), 83–85. doi:10.1017/S0140525X11000963

Dantzer, R. (2001). Cytokine-induced sickness behavior: Where do we stand? *Brain, Behavior, and Immunity, 15*(1), 7–24. doi:10.1006/brbi.2000.0613

de Greck, M., Shi, Z., Wang, G., Zuo, X., Yang, X., Wang, X., ... & Han, S. (2012). Culture modulates brain activity during empathy with anger. *NeuroImage, 59*(3), 2871–2882. doi:10.1016/j.neuroimage.2011.09.052

Denny, B. T., Kober, H., Wager, T. D., & Ochsner, K. N. (2012). A meta-analysis of functional neuroimaging studies of self- and other judgments reveals a spatial gradient for mentalizing in medial prefrontal cortex. *Journal of Cognitive Neuroscience, 24*(8), 1742–1752. doi:10.1162/jocn_a_00233

Eisenberger, N. I., Inagaki, T. K., Rameson, L. T., Mashal, N. M., & Irwin, M. R. (2009). An fMRI study of cytokine-induced depressed mood and social pain: The role of sex differences. *Neuroimage, 47*(3), 881–890. doi:10.1016/j.neuroimage.2009.04.040

Falk, E. B., Morelli, S. A., Welborn, B. L, Dambacher, K., & Lieberman, M. D. (2013). Creating buzz: The neural correlates of effective message propagation. *Psychological Science, 24*(7), 1234–1242. doi:10.1177/0956797612474670

Faulkner, J., Schaller, M., Park, J. H., & Duncan, L. A. (2004). Evolved disease-avoidance mechanisms and contemporary xenophobic attitudes. *Group Processes and Intergroup Relations, 7*(4), 333–353. doi:10.1177/1368430204046142

Fincher, C. L., & Thornhill, R. (2008). Assortative sociality, limited dispersal, infectious disease and the genesis of the global pattern of religion diversity. *Proceedings of the Royal Society B, 275*(1651), 2587–2594. doi:10.1098/rspb.2008.0688

Fincher, C. L., & Thornhill, R. (2012). Parasite-stress promotes in-group assortative sociality: The cases of strong family ties and heightened religiosity. *Behavioral and Brain Sciences, 35*(2), 61–79. doi:10.1017/S0140525X11000021

Fincher, C. L., Thornhill, R., Murray, D. R., & Schaller, M. (2008). Pathogen prevalence predicts human cross-cultural variability in individualism/collectivism. *Proceedings of the Royal Society B, 275*(1640), 1279–1285. doi:10.1098/rspb.2008.0094

Foster, D. J., and Wilson, M.A. (2006). Reverse replay of behavioural sequences in hippocampal place cells during the awake state. *Nature, 440,* 680–683. doi:10.1038/nature04587

Frith, C. D., & Frith, U. (2006). The neural basis of mentalizing. *Neuron, 50*(4), 531–534. doi:10.1016/j.neuron.2006.05.001

Gläscher, J., Hampton, A. N., & O'Doherty, J. P. (2009). Determining a role for ventromedial prefrontal cortex in encoding action-based value signals during reward-related decision making. *Cerebral Cortex, 19*(2), 483–495. doi:10.1093/cercor/bhn098

Green, M. J., & Phillips, M. L. (2004). Social threat perception and the evolution of paranoia. *Neuroscience and Biobehavioral Reviews, 28*(3), 333–342. doi:10.1016/j.neubiorev.2004.03.006

Greicius, M. D., Krasnow, B., Reiss, A. L., & Menon, V. (2003). Functional connectivity in the resting brain: A network analysis of the default mode hypothesis. *Proceedings of the National Academy of Sciences, 100*(1), 253–258. doi:10.1073/pnas.0135058100

Han, S., & Ma, Y. (2014). Cultural differences in human brain activity: A quantitative meta-analysis. *NeuroImage, 99,* 293–300. doi:10.1016/j.neuroimage.2014.05.062

Harada, T., Li, Z., & Chiao, J. Y. (2010). Differential dorsal and ventral medial prefrontal representations of the implicit self modulated by individualism and collectivism: An fMRI study. *Social Neuroscience, 5*(3), 257–271. doi:10.1080/17470910903374895

Hoffman, K. L., & McNaughton, B. L. (2002). Coordinated reactivation of distributed memory traces in primate neocortex. *Science, 297*(5589), 2070–2073. doi:10.1126/science.1073538

Inagaki, T. K., Muscatell, K. A., Irwin, M. R., Cole, S. W., & Eisenberger, N. I. (2012). Inflammation selectively enhances amygdala activity to socially threatening images. *Neuroimage, 59*(4), 3222–3226. doi:10.1016/j.neuroimage.2011.10.090

Inagaki, T. K., Muscatell, K. A., Irwin, M. R., Moieni, M., Dutcher, J. M., Jevtic, I., … & Eisenberger, N. I. (2015). The role of the ventral striatum in inflammatory-induced approach toward support figures. *Brain, Behavior, and Immunity, 44,* 247–252. doi:10.1016/j.bbi.2014.10.006

Iyengar, S. S., Lepper, M. R., & Ross, L. (1999). Independence from whom? Interdependence with whom? Cultural perspectives on ingroups versus outgroups. In D. A. Prentice & D. T. Miller (Eds.), *Cultural divides: Understanding and overcoming group conflict* (pp. 273–301). New York: Russell Sage Foundation.

Ji, D., & Wilson, M. A. (2007). Coordinated memory replay in the visual cortex and hippocampus during sleep. *Nature Neuroscience, 10*(1), 100–107. doi:10.1038/nn1825

Kable, J. W., & Glimcher, P. W. (2007). The neural correlates of subjective value during intertemporal choice. *Nature Neuroscience, 10*(12), 1625–1633. doi:10.1038/nn2007

Klein, S. B., Loftus, J., & Burton, H. A. (1989). Two self-reference effects: The importance of distinguishing between self-descriptiveness judgments and autobiographical retrieval in self-referent encoding. *Journal of Personality and Social Psychology, 56*(6), 853–865. doi:10.1037/0022-3514.56.6.853

Knutson, B., Taylor, J., Kaufman, M., Peterson, R., & Glover, G. (2005). Distributed neural representation of expected value. *Journal of Neuroscience, 25*(19), 4806–4812. doi:10.1523/JNEUROSCI.0642-05.2005

Krabbe, K. S., Reichenberg, A., Yirmiya, R., Smed, A., Pedersen, B. K., & Bruunsgaard, H. (2005). Low-dose endotoxemia and human neuropsychological functions. *Brain, Behavior, and Immunology, 19*(5), 453–460. doi:10.1016/j.bbi.2005.04.010

Kullmann, J. S., Grigoleit, J.-S., Wolf, O. T., Engler, H., Oberbeck, R., Elsenbruch, S., … & Gizewski, E. R. (2014). Experimental human endotoxemia enhances brain activity during social cognition. *Social Cognitive and Affective Neuroscience, 9*(6), 786–793. doi:10.1093/scan/nst049

Lord, C. G. (1980). Schemas and images as memory aids: Two modes of processing social information. *Journal of Personality and Social Psychology, 38*(2), 257–269. doi:10.1037/0022-3514.38.2.257

Macrae, C. N., Moran, J. M., Heatherton, T. F., Banfield, J. F., & Kelley, W. M. (2004). Medial prefrontal activity predicts memory for self. *Cerebral Cortex, 14*(6), 647–654. doi:10.1093/cercor/bhh025

Markus, H., & Kitayama, S. (1991). Culture and self: Implications for cognition, emotion, and motivation. *Psychological Review, 98*(2), 224–253. doi:10.1037/0033-295X.98.2.224

Markus, H. R., & Kitayama, S. (2010). Cultures and selves: A cycle of mutual constitution. *Perspectives on Psychological Science, 5*(4), 420–430. doi:10.1177/1745691610375557

Mazoyer, B., Zago, L., Mellet, E., Bricogne, S., Etard, O., Houde, O., … & Tzourio-Mazoyer, N. (2001). Cortical networks for working memory and executive functions sustain the conscious resting state in man. *Brain Research Bulletin, 54*(3), 287–298. doi:10.1016/S0361-9230(00)00437-8

Meyer, M. L. & Lieberman, M. D. (2017). Medial prefrontal cortex (MPFC) activity during rest primes self-referential processing. Manuscript in preparation.

Meyer, M. L., Masten, C. L., Ma, Y., Wang, C., Shi, Z., Eisenberger, N. I., … & Han, S. (2015). Differential neural activation to friends and strangers links interdependence to empathy. *Culture and Brain, 3*(1), 21–38. doi:10.1007/s40167-014-0023-7

Meyer, M. L., Spunt, R. P., & Lieberman, M. D. (2017). Default network regions consolidate social information. Manuscript in preparation.

Mitchell, J. P., Banaji, M. R., & Macrae, C. N. (2005). General and specific contributions of the medial prefrontal cortex to knowledge about mental states. *Neuroimage, 28*(4), 757–762. doi:10.1016/j.neuroimage.2005.03.011

Mitchell, J. P., Macrae, C. N., & Banaji, M. R. (2005). Forming impressions of people versus inanimate objects: Social-cognitive processing in the medial prefrontal cortex. *Neuroimage, 26*(1), 251–257. doi:10.1016/j.neuroimage.2005.01.031

Moieni, M. A., Irwin, M. R., Jevtic, I., Breen, E. C., Cho, H. J., Arevalo, J. M. G., … & Eisenberger (2015). Trait sensitivity to social disconnection enhances pro-inflammatory responses to a randomized controlled trial of endotoxin. *Psychoneuroendocrinology, 62,* 336–342. doi:10.1016/j.psyneuen.2015.08.020

Muscatell, K. A., Moieni, M., Inagaki, T. K., Dutcher, J. M., Jevtic, I., Breen, E. C., … & Eisenberger, N. I. (2016). Exposure to an inflammatory challenge enhances neural sensitivity to negative and positive social feedback. *Brain, Behavior, and Immunity, 57,* 21–29. doi:10.1016/j.bbi.2016.03.022

Navarrete, C. D., & Fessler, D. M. (2006). Disease avoidance and ethnocentrism: The effects of disease vulnerability and disgust sensitivity on intergroup attitudes. *Evolution and Human Behavior, 27*(4), 270–282. doi:10.1016/j.evolhumbehav.2005.12.001

Navarrete, C. D., Fessler, D. M., & Eng, S. J. (2007). Elevated ethnocentrism in the first trimester of pregnancy. *Evolution and Human Behavior, 28*(1), 60–65. doi:10.1016/j.evolhumbehav.2006.06.002

O'Doherty, J. P., Deichmann, R., Critchley, H. D., & Dolan, R. J. (2002). Neural responses during anticipation of a primary taste reward. *Neuron, 33*(5), 815–826. doi:10.1016/S0896-6273(02)00603-7

Padoa-Schioppa, C., & Assad, J. A. (2006). Neurons in the orbitofrontal cortex encode economic value. *Nature, 441*(7090), 223–226. doi:10.1038/nature04676

Park, J. H., Schaller, M., & Crandall, C. S. (2007). Pathogen-avoidance mechanisms and the stigmatization of obese people. *Evolution and Human Behavior, 28*(6), 410–414. doi:10.1016/j.evolhumbehav.2007.05.008

Phan, K. L., Fitzgerald, D. A., Nathan, P. J., & Tancer, M. E. (2006). Association between amygdala hyperactivity to harsh faces and severity of social anxiety in generalized social phobia. *Biological Psychiatry, 59*(5), 424–429. doi:10.1016/j.biopsych.2005.08.012

Qin, Y. L., McNaughton, B. L., Skaggs, W. E., & Barnes, C. A. (1997). Memory reprocessing in corticocortical and hippocampocortical neuronal ensembles. *Philosophical Transactions of the Royal Society B, 352*(1360), 1525–1533. doi:10.1098/rstb.1997.0139

Raichle, M. E. (2010). Two views of brain function. *Trends in Cognitive Sciences, 14*(4), 180–190. doi:10.1016/j.tics.2010.01.008

Raichle, M. E., MacLeod, A. M., Snyder, A. Z., Powers, W. J., Gusnard, D. A., & Shulman, G. L. (2001). A default mode of brain function. *Proceedings of the National Academy of Sciences, 98*(2), 676–682. doi:10.1073/pnas.98.2.676

Raichle, M. E., & Snyder, A. Z. (2007). A default mode of brain function: A brief history of an evolving idea. *Neuroimage, 37*(4), 1083–1090. doi:10.1016/j.neuroimage.2007.02.041

Reichenberg, A., Yirmiya, R., Schuld, A., Kraus, T., Haack, M., Morag, A., & Pollmächer, T. (2001). Cytokine-associated emotional and cognitive disturbances in humans. *Archives of General Psychiatry, 58*(5), 445–452. doi:10.1001/archpsyc.58.5.445

Rogers, T. B., Kuiper, N. A., & Kirker, W. S. (1977). Self-reference and the encoding of personal information. *Journal of Personality and Social Psychology, 35*(9), 677–688. doi:10.1037/0022-3514.35.9.677

Ross, L., & Nisbett, R. E. (2011). *The person and the situation: Perspectives of social psychology*. London: Pinter & Martin.

Sabatinelli, D., Bradley, M. M., Lang, P. J., Costa, V. D., & Versace, F. (2007). Pleasure rather than salience activates human nucleus accumbens and medial prefrontal cortex. *Journal of Neurophysiology, 98*(3), 1374–1379. doi:10.1152/jn.00230.2007

Saxe, R., & Kanwisher, N. (2003). People thinking about thinking people: The role of the temporo-parietal junction in "theory of mind." *Neuroimage, 19*(4), 1835–1842. doi:10.1016/S1053-8119(03)00230-1

Schaller, M., & Duncan, L. A. (2007). The behavioral immune system: Its evolution and social psychological implications. In J. P. Forges, M. G. Haselton, & W. Von Hippel (Eds.), *Evolution and the social mind:*

Evolutionary psychology and social cognition (pp. 293–307). New York: Psychology Press.

Schaller, M., Miller, G. E., Gervais, W. M., Yager, S., & Chen, E. (2010). Mere visual perception of other people's disease symptoms facilitates a more aggressive immune response. *Psychological Science, 21*(5), 649–652. doi:10.1177/0956797610368064

Schaller, M., & Murray, D. R. (2008). Pathogens, personality, and culture: Disease prevalence predicts worldwide variability in sociosexuality, extraversion, and openness to experience. *Journal of Personality and Social Psychology, 95*(1), 212–221. doi:10.1037/0022-3514.95.1.212

Shulman, G. L., Fiez, J. A., Corbetta, M., Buckner, R. L., Miezin, F. M., Raichle, M. E., & Petersen, S. E. (1997). Common blood flow changes across visual tasks: II. Decreases in cerebral cortex. *Journal of Cognitive Neuroscience, 9*(5), 648–663. doi:10.1162/jocn.1997.9.5.648

Spunt, R. P., Falk, E. B., & Lieberman, M. D. (2010). Dissociable neural systems support retrieval of *how* and *why* action knowledge. *Psychological Science, 21*(11), 1593–1598. doi:10.1177/0956797610386618

Spunt, R. P., & Lieberman, M. D. (2012). Dissociating modality-specific and supramodal neural systems for action understanding. *Journal of Neuroscience, 32*(10), 3575–3583. doi:10.1523/JNEUROSCI.5715-11.2012

Spunt, R. P., Meyer, M. L., & Lieberman, M. D. (2015). The default mode of human brain function primes the intentional stance. *Journal of Cognitive Neuroscience, 27*(6), 1116–1124. doi:10.1162/jocn_a_00785

Spunt, R. P., Satpute, A. B., & Lieberman, M. D. (2011). Identifying the what, why, and how of an observed action: An fMRI study of mentalizing and mechanizing during action observation. *Journal of Cognitive Neuroscience, 23*(1), 63–74. doi:10.1162/jocn.2010.21446

Suffredini, A. F., Hochstein, H. D., & McMahon, F. G. (1999). Dose-related inflammatory effects of intravenous endotoxin in humans: Evaluation of a new clinical lot of Escherichia coli O: 113 endotoxin. *Journal of Infectious Diseases, 179*(5), 1278–1282. doi:10.1086/314717

Svoboda, E., McKinnon, M. C., & Levine, B. (2006). The functional neuroanatomy of autobiographical memory: A meta-analysis. *Neuropsychologia, 44*(12), 2189–2208. doi:10.1016/j.neuropsychologia.2006.05.023

Symons, C. S., & Johnson, B. T. (1997). The self-reference effect in memory: A meta-analysis. *Psychological Bulletin, 121*(3), 371–394. doi:10.1037/0033-2909.121.3.371

Triandis, H. C. (1972). *The analysis of subjective culture.* New York: Wiley.

Triandis, H. C. (1989). The self and social behavior in differing cultural contexts. *Psychological Review, 96*(3), 506–520. doi:10.1037/0033-295X.96.3.506

Van de Vliert, E., & Postmes, T. (2012). Climato-economic livability predicts societal collectivism and political autocracy better than parasitic stress does. *Behavioral and Brain Sciences, 35*(2), 94–95. doi:10.1017/S0140525X11001075

Van Overwalle, F. (2009). Social cognition and the brain: A meta-analysis. *Human Brain Mapping, 30*(3), 829–858. doi:dx.doi.org/10.1002/hbm.20547

Wang, C., Oyserman, D., Liu, Q., Li, H., & Han, S. (2013). Accessible cultural mind-set modulates default mode activity: Evidence for the culturally situated brain. *Social Neuroscience, 8*(3), 203–216. doi:10.1080/17470919.2013.775966

Wang, G., Mao, L., Ma, Y., Yang, X., Cao, J., Liu, X., … & Han, S. (2012). Neural representations of close others in collectivistic brains. *Social Cognitive and Affective Neuroscience, 7*, 222–229. doi:10.1093/scan/nsr002

Welborn, B. L., Lieberman, M. D., Goldenberg, D., Fuligni, A. J., Galván, A., & Telzer, E. H. (2016). Neural mechanisms of social influence in adolescence. *Social Cognitive and Affective Neuroscience, 11*(1), 100–109. doi:10.1093/scan/nsv095

Willette, A. A., Lubach, G. R., & Coe, C. L. (2007). Environmental context differentially affects behavioral, leukocyte, cortisol, and interleukin-6 responses to low doses of endotoxin in the rhesus monkey. *Brain, Behavior, and Immunity, 21*(6), 807–815. doi:10.1016/j.bbi.2007.01.007

Wright, C. E., Strike, P. C., Brydon, L., & Steptoe, A. (2005). Acute inflammation and negative mood: Mediation by cytokine activation. *Brain, Behavior, and Immunity, 19*(4), 345–350. doi:10.1016/j.bbi.2004.10.003

Yee, J. R., & Prendergast, B. J. (2010). Sex-specific social regulation of inflammatory responses and sickness behaviors. *Brain, Behavior, and Immunity, 24*(6), 942–951. doi:10.1016/j.bbi.2010.03.006

Zaki, J., Schirmer, J., & Mitchell, J. P. (2011). Social influence modulates the neural computation of value. *Psychological Science, 22*(7), 894–900. doi:10.1177/0956797611411057

Zhu, Y., & Zhang, L. (2002). An experimental study on the self-reference effect. *Science in China Series C: Life Sciences, 45*(2), 120–128. doi:10.1360/02yc9014

Zhu, Y., Zhang, L., Fan, J., & Han, S. (2007). Neural basis of cultural influence on self-representation. *Neuroimage, 34*(3), 1310–1316. doi:10.1016/j.neuroimage.2006.08.047

18

Culture and Self–Other Overlap in Neural Circuits

Michael E. W. Varnum and Ryan S. Hampton

A fundamental feature that distinguishes human cultural groups from each other is the extent to which the self is viewed as distinct and separate from others (independent) versus encompassing and overlapping with close others (interdependent) (Markus & Kitayama, 1991; Triandis, 1989; Varnum, Grossmann, Kitayama, & Nisbett, 2010). Cultural differences along this dimension, self-construal, have been linked to differences in other psychological processes ranging from analytic versus holistic modes of attention and reasoning (Nisbett, Peng, Choi, & Norenzayan, 2001; Varnum et al., 2010), to emotion regulation (Murata, Moser, & Kitayama, 2013), to conformity (Bond & Smith, 1996; Snibbe & Markus, 2005). Differences in self-construal have been observed across national and ethnic groups and also as a function of social class, region, religion, and political orientation (Cohen & Varnum, 2016). Variations in self-construal across human cultural groups have been hypothesized to have their roots in variations in a number of features of socio-ecology, and today there is evidence that a number of such features, including the prevalence of infectious disease (Fincher & Thornhill, 2012), climatic stress (van de Vliert, 2013), modes of subsistence (Talhelm, Zhang, Oishi, Shimini, Duan, Lan, & Kitayama, 2014; Uskul, Kitayama, & Nisbett, 2008), the predominance of white collar employment (Grossmann & Varnum, 2015), residential mobility (Oishi, 2010), and the settling of frontiers (Kitayama, Ishii, Imada, Takemura, & Ramaswamy, 2006; Varnum & Kitayama, 2011), may ultimately underlie these group differences.

The current chapter focuses on studies that use neural measures to address whether culture affects vicarious mental experience. Before we review the evidence, it is worth considering why neural measures may be

The Handbook of Culture and Biology, First Edition. Edited by José M. Causadias, Eva H. Telzer and Nancy A. Gonzales.

especially suited to addressing this question. Compared with traditional social-psychological and cognitive methods (questionnaires, implicit tests, behavioral observation, reaction time, etc.), methods like EEG and fMRI are more expensive, more time-consuming, and require a greater amount of training on the part of experimenters. However, there are a number of reasons why such methods may be advantageous: (1) neural measures provide more proximate access to mental activity, (2) such measures are often more sensitive than conventional measures, and (3) such measures may capture differences in cognition in the absence of differences in downstream behavioral responses and in the absence of behavioral responses altogether. In addition to these advantages, neural measures also help avoid a number of common pitfalls in cross-cultural research, including (1) social desirability (a tendency to give responses that are viewed positively in one's society or cast the self in a good light), (2) lack of insight (the fact that people are often unaware of many of their mental processes; Bargh, 1989; Nisbett & Wilson, 1977), (3) response biases (the fact that individuals and cultural groups use response scales differently; Hamamura, Heine, & Paulhaus, 1999), and (4) the reference group effect (the fact that people rate themselves in comparison with others in their society rather than with humanity at large; Heine, Lehman, Peng, & Greenholtz, 2002). At the same time there is good reason to believe that psychology as a field is strongest when it includes both more traditional approaches and neuroscience methods (for a detailed discussion see Schwartz, Lilienfeld, Meca, & Sauvigné, 2016).

A large body of work has thus attempted to answer questions regarding the distal mechanisms which lead human cultural groups to vary in how they think about and experience the self. At the same time, a new field, cultural neuroscience, has emerged which uses techniques including EEG (electroencephalogram), ERP (event-related potentials) and fMRI (functional magnetic resonance imaging) to try to understand the proximate neural mechanisms through which such differences are instantiated, as well as to uncover new effects which more traditional measures may not be as well suited to capturing (for extensive reviews see Kitayama & Uskul, 2011 and Han et al., 2013). EEG and ERP capture electrical activity in the brain, recorded at the scalp, produced by the firing of neurons. EEG provides information on the oscillatory dynamics of these neural signals, and ERP provides information regarding the magnitude and time course of such signals in response to stimuli or behaviors. fMRI provides information on activation in the brain by measuring changes in its magnetic fields, at less fine-grained temporal resolution but with excellent spatial resolution, enabling researchers to localize neural activation to various brain structures. The present chapter reviews common problems with study designs used to evaluate cultural differences in vicarious mental experiences and provides neural evidence that helps to disambiguate such experiences, including (1) self-representation, (2) positive self and other views, (3) empathy, (4) vicarious reward/loss, and (5) motor resonance (Figure 18.1). The chapter concludes by positing future questions and challenges for the field of cultural neuroscience.

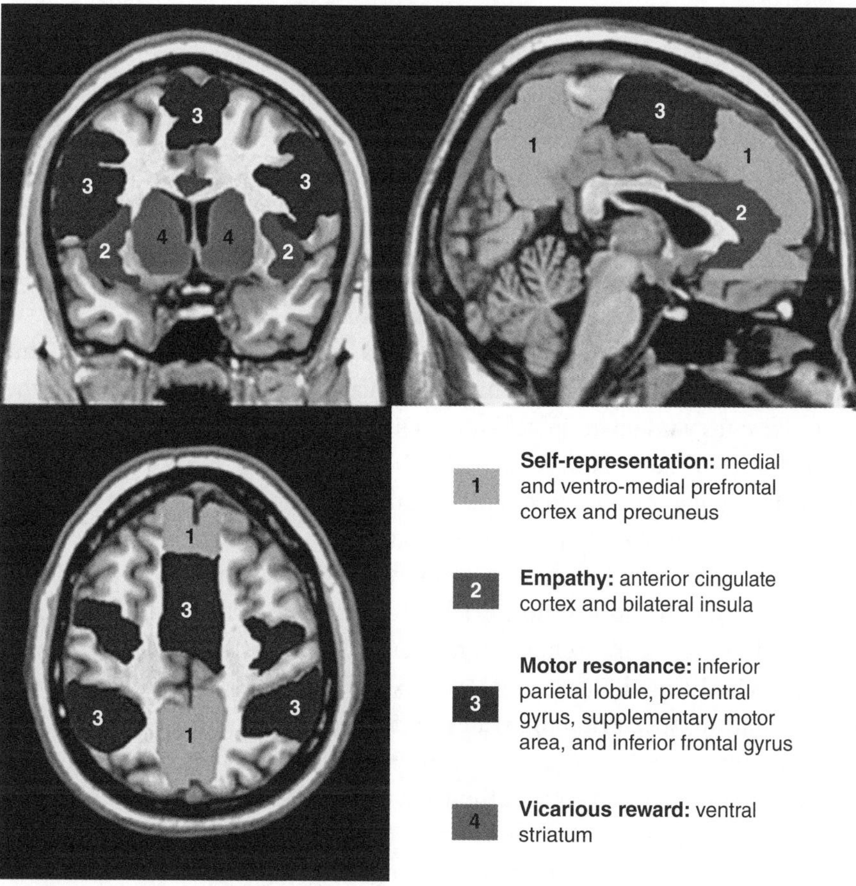

Figure 18.1 Brain regions involved in culturally modulated vicarious mental experience. Figure created using automated anatomical labeling (AAL; Tzourio-Mazoyer et al., 2002) areas derived from study coordinates of cultural effects, displayed at MNI coordinates (3/8/51). Reproduced with permission of Elsevier

Self-Representation

Representation of the self and others as distinct or overlapping is most frequently assessed across cultures using self-report surveys such as the Singelis Self-Construal Scale (Singelis, 1994). Such measures are susceptible to a number of response biases and have yielded somewhat inconsistent results. Alternatives like the Inclusion of Others in the Self scale (IOS) provide more direct tests of self–other overlap (Aron, Aron, & Smollan, 1992). The IOS uses a set of seven pairs of overlapping circles, ranging from completely separate to almost completely overlapping, which participants use to indicate their sense of overlap with others such as close family or friends. Research using the IOS type of measure to compare different cultures tend to find that collectivistic cultures like China and India unsurprisingly rate their overlap with close others higher than more individualistic cultures like Canada (Li, 2002; Li, Zhang, Bhatt, & Yum, 2006). Still, these relationships are not so simple as the singular vague construct of "overlap" with others. In a study across five cultures, Uleman, Rhee, Bardoliwalla, Semin, and Toyama (2000) documented subtle differences in the way that people from different cultures feel they overlap with others in specific areas like reputation, emotions, similarity, and harmony.

One of the earliest studies in cultural neuroscience addressed this question in a far more direct manner by measuring the extent to which the neural circuitry involved in self-representation may differ as a function of culture (Zhu, Zhang, Fan, & Han, 2007). In this fMRI study, Chinese and Western participants were cued to make judgments regarding whether trait adjectives applied to one self, one's mother, or a famous stranger. The results were consistent with the notion that for East Asians the self includes close others (such as one's mother) whereas for Westerners it includes only the individual: the researchers found that East Asians showed comparable activation in the medial prefrontal cortex (mPFC), a region involved in self-representation, when making trait judgments about both themselves and their mothers, whereas Westerners showed greater activation in this region when making judgments about themselves versus their mothers. A follow-up study further showed that Chinese participants also show common activation in these areas when performing trait judgments for the self and their spouse or child as opposed to a celebrity (Han, Ma, & Wang, 2016). Priming Western versus East Asian cultural symbols among a bicultural sample (Hong Kong Chinese) produced similar results: priming Western culture led to greater differentiation between self and mother in the ventral mPFC when judgments were made regarding traits, whereas priming

Chinese culture led to comparable activation when judgments regarding oneself and one's mother were made (Ng, Han, Mao, & Lai, 2010). In a similar vein, in a study with bicultural participants (Asian-American students) Chiao and colleagues (2009) found that priming individualistic values led to greater activation in the mPFC and the posterior cingulate cortex (PCC) when subjects made general versus contextual judgments about themselves, whereas priming collectivist values led to greater activation in these regions when participants made more contextual judgments about the self. Taken together these findings suggest that the brain may store and process information related to self-concept in a manner that is shaped by culture, and that the extent to which other people are included in one's self-concept is reflected in self–other overlap in activation of these neural regions.

Positive Views of the Self and Others

Apart from the question of inclusion of others into the self-concept, cross-cultural researchers have argued for years about whether different cultures have different levels of implicitly positive views of their self. Among claims that positive self views are universal (Sedikides, Gaertner, & Toguchi, 2003; Sedikides, Gaertner, & Vevea, 2005, 2007) or constrained to predominantly Western cultures (Heine & Hamamura, 2007; Heine, Kitayama, & Lehman, 2001; Heine, Lehman, Markus, & Kitayama, 1999), there are a number of complicating artifacts and confounds that make it difficult to assess which theory is correct.

Comparing positive self views across cultures necessitates consideration of several factors that have been identified as potential confounds in self-report questionnaires, such as differences in socially desirable responding (Dudley, McFarland, Goodman, Hunt, & Sydell, 2005) and differences in response styles (C. Chen, Lee, & Stevenson, 1995). Furthermore, studies demonstrating a lack of positive self views in East Asian cultures have been criticized for focusing on traits or "selves" that are inherently more valued in Western cultures than in Eastern cultural contexts. For example, Sedikides et al. (2003) found that Japanese participants self-enhanced for culturally relevant collectivistic traits, and Brown and Kobayashi (2002) demonstrated that Japanese participants have more positive views of their close friends than of others. In this cultural context, it may be more desired to exaggerate culturally relevant traits, and more appropriate, given cultural norms about modesty, to enhance a close other as a proxy for the self.

Finally, a study with bicultural Hong Kong Chinese showed that participants self-enhanced more when participating in English than in Mandarin Chinese (Lee, Oyserman, & Bond, 2010), implicating language as a cultural prime.

Many of these flaws coincide with the limitations of traditional self-report and behavioral studies outlined above, but cultural neuroscience has since helped to shed light on this question. Research utilizing the N400 component (which indexes semantic association) has demonstrated more association between positive trait words and the self than between these words and an unfamiliar other for Westerners (Watson, Dritschel, Obonsawin, & Jentzsch, 2007) and for Chinese (Y. Chen et al., 2013) separately, but not in a direct comparison. Using a different paradigm, Cai, Wu, Shi, Gu, and Sedikides (2016) concluded that there was no difference in implicit positive self views between Chinese and Westerners, using the late positive potential (LPP). However, this study did not use the more common N400 paradigm, and the researchers based their conclusions on a non-significant three-way interaction with a sample size underpowered to detect such an effect.

Another study, which used a word pair N400 paradigm similar to one used in previous work (Y. Chen et al., 2013; Watson et al., 2007), attempted to test this question while controlling for several potential confounds such as language, different self-construals, and cultural value of traits (Hampton & Varnum, 2016). Across self-report, behavioral, and ERP measures, they found that Americans associated the personal self with positive traits while Chinese participants did not. Furthermore, Chinese participants, regardless of language, actually associated positive traits with unfamiliar others whereas Americans did not. Interestingly, the two groups equally associated positive traits with their own mother. Considering these findings in the N400 framework outlined by Kutas & Federmeier (2011), it is likely that culture shapes the way that "self" and "other" networks in the brain include positive and negative concepts.

Empathy

Given that East Asian and Western cultural groups differ in whether they take a more bounded or a more inclusive view of the self, one might expect that empathic neural responses would be stronger among East Asians, given their more interdependent self-construals. Typical social-psychological research has nonetheless provided mixed results. One study found that ego-focused "pride" advertisements were actually more appealing than other-focused "empathy" ads to people from a collectivist culture and that this trend was reversed for those from an individualistic culture (Aaker & Williams, 1998). Although a large-scale cross-national examination of empathy per se has not been undertaken to our knowledge, conscientiousness, a correlate of empathy, tends to be lower in Eastern cultures (McCrae & Terracciano, 2005), a finding corroborated by other national comparisons (Schmitt, Allik, McCrae, & Benet-Martinez, 2007). However, Mottus and colleagues (2012) demonstrated that measuring conscientiousness across national borders is problematic when it comes to extreme or neutral response styles, and showed that controlling for such response styles could drastically change the ranking of countries in conscientiousness.

Surprisingly, cross-cultural neuroscience studies of empathy have not tended to yield baseline differences across cultural groups (Jiang, Varnum, Hou, & Han, 2014). Instead, people show fairly robust in-group biases in empathic neural responses (Cheon et al., 2011; Mathur, Harada, Lipke, & Chiao, 2010; Sheng & Han, 2012). Interestingly, priming independence appears to reduce neural empathic P2 responses to images of strangers in pain among Westerners, but not among Chinese, whereas priming interdependence reduces such responses among Chinese but not among Westerners (Jiang et al., 2014). Furthermore, among Chinese participants interdependence is positively related to increased neuro-empathic responses in the dorsal anterior cingulate cortex (dACC) and the anterior insula for a friend in a social-exclusion scenario, but is actually negatively correlated with such neural indicators of empathy for strangers (Meyer et al., 2014), suggesting that trait-level interdependence may be related to increased empathic ability, but also a stronger preference for close others than for strangers. Another recent study using fMRI and a Chinese sample explored how self-construal may affect racial in-group bias, finding that priming independence resulted in enhanced racial in-group bias in insula response to images of others in pain, whereas priming independence reduced racial in-group bias in insula response (Wang et al., 2015).

Other forms of culture may have more straightforward effects on neural empathic responses. For example, in a recent ERP study Varnum, Blais, Hampton, and Brewer (2015) showed that although higher socioeconomic status (SES) participants self-reported higher empathy, lower SES was associated with enhanced P200 (an ERP component that indexes early attentional responses) to images of others expressing pain. This finding is consistent with prior work showing that the self-construal of working-class people tends to be more interdependent (Grossmann & Varnum, 2011; Na, Grossmann, Varnum, Kitayama, Gonzalez, & Nisbett, 2010) and that they are more attuned to others' emotional states (Kraus, Côté, & Keltner, 2010). Thus the ways in which culture may cause us to experience others' emotions as our own are complicated, and different forms of culture (nationality/ethnicity versus class) appear to have somewhat different effects. It seems then that Western and East Asian cultures do not show clear evidence of baseline differences in neural empathic responses; however, there is consistent evidence of in-group bias in such responses, and social class (another form of culture) does appear linked to baseline differences in neural empathic responses.

Vicarious Reward and Loss

In addition to abstract representations of the self and empathic responses to pain, cultural factors also appear to modulate the extent to which we experience others' outcomes as our own. For example, when playing a game in which points could be won to purchase items for oneself or a friend, participants from East Asian cultural backgrounds showed comparable ERN (an ERP component seen in response to errors) when they made mistakes in trials that were played for oneself and for a friend; however, European Americans showed stronger ERN when making errors that affected outcomes for oneself than for a friend (Kitayama & Park, 2013). Similarly, using an fMRI paradigm, Varnum, Shi, Chen, Qiu, and Han (2014) found that priming interdependence led to comparable activation of the ventral striatum (part of the brain's reward network) in response to winning money for both oneself and a friend, whereas priming independence led to stronger responses to winning money for oneself. In addition, Telzer, Ichien, and Qu (2015) have shown that Americans and East Asians exhibit an in-group bias in responses in the ventral striatum when donating money to a cultural in-group versus an out-group member. Taken together these findings suggest that culture shapes the extent to which we process others' outcomes as our own.

Motor Resonance

Finally, culture appears to shape vicarious experience in even more fundamental and visceral ways; that is, culture modulates motor resonance (the experience of others' actions and bodies as one's own). For example, lower SES is associated with stronger mu suppression (an EEG correlate of activation of the mirror neuron system) when the subject is observing others' action (Varnum, Blais, & Brewer, 2016). Manipulations of individuals' perceived status have been shown to yield parallel effects in a study using a combined transcranial magnetic stimulation/electromyograms (TMS/EMG) paradigm, an approach in which electrical impulses sent from the brain to the muscles are measured at the muscles (Hogeveen & Obhi, 2012). Further, individual differences in self-reported interdependence are positively correlated with the strength of mu suppression (Varnum et al., 2016). In addition, priming interdependence enhances motor resonance when observing others' movements, whereas priming independence decreases this response (Obhi, Hogeveen, & Pascual-Leone, 2011). To date, however, East–West comparisons of motor resonance have not been conducted. In summary, studies using a variety of paradigms suggest that culture may influence the degree to which we experience others' actions as our own.

Conclusions and Future Directions

A growing body of research is unveiling the ways in which culture modulates self–other overlap in neural circuits. The studies highlighted in this chapter have demonstrated cultural influences on the extent to which we incorporate others into abstract self-schemas, on how we view those self-schemas, and on how we experience others' emotions as our own, experience their outcomes as our own, and experience their movements as our own. These findings highlight the fact that cultural differences in views of the self not only are linked to different values and beliefs but also appear to lead to more basic and visceral differences in the experience of the self.

The research we have summarized highlights growing evidence that the extent to which others are included in the self, in terms of how the brain stores and processes information ranging from higher-order self-representations to motor movements, is modulated by the extent to which different cultures emphasize more bounded versus inclusive notions of the self. However, a number of key questions have yet to be answered regarding how culture influences neural self–other overlap. One such question is how we acquire the ways of experiencing the self that are typical in our cultural group. To date, the vast majority of research in cultural neuroscience has focused on adult samples, and typically convenience samples consisting of university students. We know very little about how the process of enculturation takes place at the level of the brain. We do not know, for example, whether critical periods exist for this type of enculturation, nor do we know how this process may play out over the life course. To answer these questions we will have to expand our samples to include children, and adults of varying ages. Ideally, longitudinal research could be conducted in this vein as well (see Qu & Telzer, chapter 19 in this volume).

In addition to using neural methods to understand how enculturation affects the self, it would be useful to turn our focus on acculturation as well. According to the United Nations (2005), 191 million people migrated to a different country in 2005; 232 million did so in 2013 (United Nations, 2013). Many of these people have moved from cultural contexts where one type of self-construal is predominant to contexts where another type is predominant. Yet we know little about how acculturation affects the brain (but see P.-H. Chen, Wagner, Kelley, & Heatherton, 2015 for an exception). Using neural measures to systematically study acculturation will allow us to understand how moving to a culture with a different type of self-construal might shape vicarious mental experience and provide insight into the extent to which the neural circuits that underpin these tendencies are malleable versus canalized. In addition, such work might reveal the extent to which neural markers of acculturation (as opposed to more traditional measures of identification with a new culture) may predict important outcomes including well-being, adjustment, and health.

Another limitation of the current body of knowledge regarding how culture affects neural self–other overlap is that it tends to come from a limited number of cultural groups, primarily consisting of samples from North America, Western Europe, and East Asia. These groups have been the focus of most cross-cultural research in recent decades. By expanding the database, so to speak, to include other cultural groups from different regions (e.g., Latin America, the Middle East, Africa) we will not only provide a fuller picture of how culture impacts vicarious mental experience but will also enable the testing of more hypotheses regarding the ultimate sources of cultural variation in these phenomena. It would also be worthwhile to begin to gather such data among smaller-scale societies, given that industrialized and small-scale societies appear to differ on a host of psychological tendencies (Henrich, Heine, & Norenzayan, 2010). It is also worth noting that meta-analyses of the effects of culture on neural self–other overlap are largely lacking (with the exception of Han & Ma, 2014).

There are other types of vicarious mental experiences that are likely to be culturally influenced. For example, cultural neuroscientists might expand upon work that shows that culture influences the extent to which we process others' experiences and feelings as our own, by exploring emotional contagion (Hatfield, Cacioppo, & Rapson, 1993). Research on susceptibility to emotional contagion has provided evidence that it differs as a function of gender and gender roles (Doherty, Orimoto, Singelis, Hatfield, & Hebb, 1995; Hatfield et al., 1993), as well as cultural collectivism and interdependence (Singelis, 1995). Functional MRI and dual brain studies could shed light on reliable signals of emotional contagion (rather than relying on self-report or facial coding as in previous research) and may reveal neural coupling related to contagion effects. We might expect then that, when these paradigms are used, people from more interdependent cultural contexts will show greater evidence of emotional contagion than those from more independent cultural contexts.

Cultural neuroscientists may also turn their attention to another way in which culture may lead to differences in self–other overlap, namely memory. People tend to show a bias towards remembering more self-relevant information than other types of information as a functional part of a Self-Memory System (Conway & Pleydell-Pearce, 2000; Conway, Singer, & Tagini, 2004). However, if others are included in one's self-concept one should also show a bias for information about close others. Preliminary findings in this domain suggest that cultures differ in the extent to which self- and non-self-relevant information enhances or interferes with task-relevant stimuli (Sui, Liu, & Han, 2012) and task-irrelevant stimuli (Liu, Liu, Zhu, Wang, Rotshtein, & Sui, 2015). Specifically, British participants responded faster and showed a stronger N2 (a component related to perceptual salience) when they saw task-relevant self-information than when they saw non-self-information, and were slower (i.e., more distracted) when the self-information was not related to the task. Chinese participants, on the other hand, showed neither enhancement effects of task-relevant self-information nor interference effects of task-irrelevant self-information, and their N2 responses suggested a perceptual bias favoring a familiar other over the self.

Certain EEG techniques could be employed to detect whether or not this is indeed the case, and, further, to help differentiate whether any such cultural differences are due to encoding or retrieval. The difference due to memory (Dm) ERP (neural activity occurring during the study phase of a memory experiment at central and parietal sites; Paller, Kutas, & Mayes, 1987; Paller, McCarthy, & Wood, 1988) is a broad relative positivity at approximately 400–800 ms post-stimulus onset that arises when two waveforms are compared, one for correctly remembered items and one for incorrectly remembered items. This could be used to compare self-relevant items against stranger-relevant items or important other-relevant items: a Dm effect would suggest differences in encoding. For retrieval, the old/new effect (Wilding & Rugg, 1996) is a left-parietal positivity from 600 ms that tends to appear in response to retrieval probes that are correctly identified as old (having been previously presented) or new (not having been previously presented). For this ERP, one might test whether the old/new effect varies for self-relevant information, again compared with close other-relevant information or stranger-relevant information, to see if culture modulates retrieval rather than encoding.

Another promising avenue for understanding how culture affects neural processes involved in self–other overlap lies in exploring the interplay between culture and genes. For example, a recent study tested the association between individualism–collectivism and the allelic frequency of the serotonin transporter functional polymorphism (5-HTTLPR) across world cultures (Chiao & Blizinsky, 2010). Countries that were higher in collectivism were more likely to have higher concentrations of people with the short (S) allele of the serotonin transporter gene. Further, the prevalence of the short allele predicted fewer instances of anxiety and mood disorders, which was mediated by the presence of collectivistic cultural values. Similarly, Mrazek, Chiao, Blizinsky, Lun, and Gelfand (2013) found a link between the short allele of the same serotonin transporter gene and tightness–looseness orientations and strictness of norms across 21 nations. Frequency of the short allele correlated with ecological threat, and susceptibility to ecological threat was correlated with tightness–looseness, but this relationship was mediated by a high frequency of S allele carriers. The oxytocin receptor gene polymorphism (OXTR rs53576) has also been implicated in national differences in collectivistic cultural values and, specifically, serves as a potent mediator between pathogen prevalence and collectivistic values, so that both historical and contemporary pathogen prevalence predicted higher presence of the oxytocin polymorphism, which then predicted greater collectivism (Luo & Han, 2014). Other research on the oxytocin receptor gene has suggested that culture moderates the relationship between OXTR genotype and loneliness, so that among European Americans G-allele carriers had higher levels of loneliness than those with the A-allele, whereas this effect was not present (and in fact the opposite trend was observed) among Japanese. That is, the same genotype may be expressed differently as a function of cultural context (Kim & Sasaki, 2014). In fact a study has found that differences in self-construal between European Americans and East Asians were present only among those who carried variants of DRD4 (2-repeat and 7-repeat alleles) that are associated with greater dopaminergic signaling, not among those carrying the 4-repeat allele (Kitayama et al., 2014).

Finally, with the advent of methods for simultaneously measuring neural activity in the brains of two or more interacting participants, there is the opportunity to expand our inquiry beyond vicarious neural experience to the study of shared experience. These techniques are in their infancy, but assessing correlations in neural activity among multiple interacting brains provides a new avenue of inquiry that, while related to vicarious experience, is conceptually distinct. Given that we are an inherently social species and spend most of our waking hours interacting with conspecifics who make up our cultural groups, it would be worthwhile to begin to explore how culture may modulate the ways in which we experience phenomena including cooperation, competition, and shared responses to events and cultural products.

Previous 2-brain studies have used EEG hyperscanning to measure brain signals simultaneously, calculating a phase-locking value (PLV) that measures phase covariance at a specific frequency, so that if waveform onsets and offsets covary to a high degree, their PLV is high (Lachaux, Rodriguez, Martinerie, & Varela, 1999). Studies have shown that spontaneous behavioral synchrony in a simple hand movement paradigm is accompanied by oscillatory synchrony (Dumas, Nadel, Soussignan, Martinerie, & Garnero, 2010), and that increased phase-locking is also found among the neural responses of guitarists playing together (Lindenberger, Li, Gruber, & Müller, 2009; Müller, Sänger, & Lindenberger, 2013). In fact, in some 2-brain studies oscillations in an area of one person's brain are sometimes more correlated with those of their interaction partner than with their own oscillations in other areas of the brain (Müller et al., 2013). Adapting these methods for cultural comparisons could potentially evaluate differences in neural synchrony with in-group versus out-group members as moderated by cultural differences in in-group/out-group permeability. In the same vein, it could help to shed light on the question of neural coupling with others who are integrated or not integrated into one's self-concept by examining PLV while people engage in social interaction with a stranger versus a close other.

Culture influences the extent to which we include others in the self. These effects extend beyond lay theories, beliefs, and values; they are also seen in a number of neural circuits underpinning a variety of vicarious mental experiences, including self-representation, emotion, reward/loss, and our sense of our bodies. Methods such as fMRI and EEG/ERP provide valuable tools that have enabled us to capture these effects of culture at the level of the brain. Numerous challenges remain for the field of cultural neuroscience, and new techniques represent new opportunities for growth and discovery in this new field.

References

Aaker, J. L., & Williams, P. (1998). Empathy versus pride: The influence of emotional appeals across cultures. *Journal of Consumer Research, 25*(3), 241–261. doi:10.1086/209537

Aron, A., Aron, E. N., & Smollan, D. (1992). Inclusion of Other in the Self Scale and the structure of interpersonal closeness. *Journal of Personality and Social Psychology, 63*(4), 596–612. doi:10.1037/0022-3514.63.4.596

Bargh, J. A. (1989). Conditional automaticity: Varieties of automatic influence in social perception and cognition. In J. S. Uleman & J. A. Bargh (Eds.), *Unintended thought* (pp. 3–51). New York: Guilford Press.

Bond, R., & Smith, P. B. (1996). Culture and conformity: A meta-analysis of studies using Asch's (1952b, 1956) line judgment task. *Psychological Bulletin, 119*(1), 111–137. doi:10.1037//0033-2909.119.1.111

Brown, J. D., & Kobayashi, C. (2002). Self-enhancement in Japan and America. *Asian Journal of Social Psychology, 5*, 145–167.

Cai, H., Wu, L., Shi, Y., Gu, R., & Sedikides, C. (2016). Self-enhancement among Westerners and Easterners: A cultural neuroscience approach. *Social Cognitive and Affective Neuroscience, 11*(10), 1569–1578. doi:10.1093/scan/nsw072

Chen, C., Lee, S., & Stevenson, H. W. (1995). Response style and cross-cultural comparisons of rating scales among East Asian and North American students. *Psychological Science, 6*(3), 170–175. doi:10.1111/j.1467-9280.1995.tb00327.x

Chen, P.-H. A., Wagner, D. D., Kelley, W. M., & Heatherton, T. F. (2015). Activity in cortical midline structures is modulated by self-construal changes during acculturation. *Culture and Brain, 3*(1), 39–52. doi:10.1007/s40167-015-0026-z

Chen, Y., Zhong, Y., Zhou, H., Zhang, S., Tan, Q., & Fan, W. (2013). Evidence for implicit self-positivity bias: An event-related brain potential study. *Experimental Brain Research, 232*, 985–998. doi:10.1007/s00221-013-3810-z

Cheon, B. K., Im, D. M., Harada, T., Kim, J. S., Mathur, V. A., Scimeca, J. M., … & Chiao, J. Y. (2011). Cultural influences on neural basis of intergroup empathy. *NeuroImage, 57*(2), 642–650.

Chiao, J. Y., & Blizinsky, K. D. (2010). Culture–gene coevolution of individualism–collectivism and the serotonin transporter gene. *Proceedings of the Royal Society B, 277*(1681), 529–537. doi:10.1098/rspb.2009.1650

Chiao, J. Y., Harada, T., Komeda, H., Li, Z., Mano, Y., Saito, D., ... & Iidaka, T. (2009). Neural basis of individualistic and collectivistic views of self. *Human Brain Mapping, 30*(9), 2813–2820. doi:10.1002/hbm.20707

Cohen, A. B., & Varnum, M. E. W. (2016). Beyond East vs. West: Social class, region, and religion as forms of culture. *Current Opinion in Psychology, 8*, 5–9.

Conway, M. A., & Pleydell-Pearce, C. W. (2000). The construction of autobiographical memories in the self-memory system. *Psychological Review, 107*(2), 261–288. doi:10.1037//0033-295X.107.2.261

Conway, M. A., Singer, J. A., & Tagini, A. (2004). The self and autobiographical memory: Correspondence and coherence. *Social Cognition, 22*(5), 491–529. doi:10.1521/soco.22.5.491.50768

Doherty, R. W., Orimoto, L., Singelis, T. M., Hatfield, E., & Hebb, J. (1995). Emotional contagion: Gender and occupational differences. *Psychology of Women Quarterly, 19*(3), 355–371. doi:10.1111/j.1471-6402.1995.tb00080.x

Dudley, N. M., McFarland, L. A., Goodman, S. A., Hunt, S. T., & Sydell, E. J. (2005). Racial differences in socially desirable responding in selection contexts: Magnitude and consequences. *Journal of Personality Assessment, 85*(1), 50–64. doi:10.1207/s15327752jpa8501_05

Dumas, G., Nadel, J., Soussignan, R., Martinerie, J., & Garnero, L. (2010). Inter-brain synchronization during social interaction. *PLoS One, 5*(8), e12166. doi:10.1371/journal.pone.0012166

Fincher, C. L., & Thornhill, R. (2012). Parasite-stress promotes in-group assortative sociality: The cases of strong family ties and heightened religiosity. *Behavioral and Brain Sciences, 35*(2), 61–79. doi:10.1017/S0140525X11000021

Grossmann, I., & Varnum, M. E. W. (2011). Social class, culture, and cognition. *Social Psychological and Personality Science, 2*(1), 81–89. doi:10.1177/1948550610377119

Grossmann, I., & Varnum, M. E. W. (2015). Social structures, infectious diseases, disasters, secularism and cultural change in America. *Psychological Science, 26*, 311–324. doi:10.1177/0956797614563765

Hamamura, T., Heine, S. J., & Paulhus, D. L. (2008). Cultural differences in response styles: The role of dialectical thinking. *Personality and Individual Differences, 44*(4), 932–942.

Hampton, R. S., & Varnum, M. E. W. (2016) Do cultures vary in self-enhancement? ERP, behavioral, and self-report evidence. Manuscript submitted for publication.

Han, S., & Ma, Y. (2014). Cultural differences in human brain activity: A quantitative meta-analysis. *NeuroImage, 99,* 293–300.

Han, S., Ma, Y., & Wang, G. (2016). Shared neural representations of self and conjugal family members in Chinese brain. *Culture and Brain, 4,* 72–86. doi:10.1007/s40167-016-0036-5

Han, S., Northoff, G., Vogeley, K., Wexler, B. E., Kitayama, S., & Varnum, M. E. W. (2013). A cultural neuroscience approach to the biosocial nature of the human brain. *Annual Review of Psychology, 64,* 335–359.

Hatfield, E., Cacioppo, J. T., & Rapson, R. L. (1993). Emotional contagion. *Current Directions in Psychological Science, 2*(3), 96–99. doi:10.1111/1467-8721.ep10770953

Heine, S. J., & Hamamura, T. (2007). In search of East Asian self-enhancement. *Personality and Social Psychology Review, 11*(1), 4–27. doi:10.1177/1088868306294587

Heine, S. J., Kitayama, S., & Lehman, D. R. (2001). Cultural differences in self-evaluation: Japanese readily accept negative self-relevant information. *Journal of Cross-Cultural Psychology, 32*(4), 434–443. doi:10.1177/0022022101032004004

Heine, S. J., Lehman, D. R., Markus, H. R., & Kitayama, S. (1999). Is there a universal need for positive self-regard? *Psychological Review, 106*(4), 766–794. doi:10.1037/0033-295X.106.4.766

Heine, S. J., Lehman, D. R., Peng, K., & Greenholtz, J. (2002). What's wrong with cross-cultural comparisons of subjective Likert scales? The reference-group effect. *Journal of Personality and Social Psychology, 82*(6), 903–918.

Henrich, J., Heine, S. J., & Norenzayan, A. (2010). The weirdest people in the world? *Behavioral and Brain Sciences, 33*(2–3), 61–83; discussion 83–135. doi:10.1017/S0140525X0999152X

Hogeveen, J., & Obhi, S. S. (2012). Social interaction enhances motor resonance for observed human actions. *Journal of Neuroscience, 32*(17), 5984–5989. doi:10.1523/JNEUROSCI.5938-11.2012

Jiang, C., Varnum, M. E. W., Hou, Y., & Han, S. (2014). Distinct effects of self-construal priming on empathic neural responses in Chinese and Westerners. *Social Neuroscience, 9*(2), 130–138.

Kim, H. S., & Sasaki, J. Y. (2014). Cultural neuroscience: Biology of the mind in cultural contexts. *Annual Review of Psychology, 65,* 487–514.

Kitayama, S., Ishii, K., Imada, T., Takemura, K., & Ramaswamy, J. (2006). Voluntary settlement and the spirit of independence: Evidence from Japan's

"Northern frontier." *Journal of Personality and Social Psychology, 91*(3), 369–384. doi:10.1037/0022-3514.91.3.369

Kitayama, S., King, A., Yoon, C., Tompson, S., Huff, S., & Liberzon, I. (2014). The dopamine D4 receptor gene (DRD4) moderates cultural difference in independent versus interdependent social orientation. *Psychological Science, 25*(6), 1169–1177.

Kitayama, S., & Park, J. (2013). Error-related brain activity reveals self-centric motivation: Culture matters. *Journal of Experimental Psychology: General.* doi:10.1037/a0031696

Kitayama, S., & Uskul, A. K. (2011). Culture, mind, and the brain: Current evidence and future directions. *Annual Review of Psychology, 62,* 419–449. doi:10.1146/annurev-psych-120709-145357

Kraus, M. W., Côté, S., & Keltner, D. (2010). Social class, contextualism, and empathic accuracy. *Psychological Science, 21*(11), 1716–1723. doi:10.1177/0956797610387613

Kutas, M., & Federmeier, K. D. (2011). Thirty years and counting: Finding meaning in the N400 component of the event-related brain potential (ERP). *Annual Review of Psychology, 62,* 621–647. doi:10.1146/annurev.psych.093008.131123

Lachaux, J. P., Rodriguez, E., Martinerie, J., & Varela, F. J. (1999). Measuring phase synchrony in brain signals. *Human Brain Mapping, 8*(4), 194–208. doi:10.1002/(SICI)1097-0193(1999)8:4<194::AID-HBM4>3.0.CO;2-C

LeClair, J., Sasaki, J. Y., Ishii, K., Shinada, M., & Kim, H. S. (2016). Gene–culture interaction: Influence of culture and oxytocin receptor gene (OXTR) polymorphism on loneliness. *Culture and Brain, 4*(1), 21–37.

Lee, S. W. S., Oyserman, D., & Bond, M. H. (2010). Am I doing better than you? That depends on whether you ask me in English or Chinese: Self-enhancement effects of language as a cultural mindset prime. *Journal of Experimental Social Psychology, 46*(5), 785–791. doi:10.1016/j.jesp.2010.04.005

Li, H. Z. (2002). Culture, gender and self–close-other(s) connectedness in Canadian and Chinese samples. *European Journal of Social Psychology, 32*(1), 93–104.

Li, H. Z., Zhang, Z., Bhatt, G., & Yum, Y.-O. (2006). Rethinking culture and self-construal: China as a middle land. *Journal of Social Psychology, 146*(5), 591–610. doi:10.3200/SOCP.146.5.591-610

Lindenberger, U., Li, S.-C., Gruber, W., & Müller, V. (2009). Brains swinging in concert: Cortical phase synchronization while playing guitar. *BMC Neuroscience, 10,* 22. doi:10.1186/1471-2202-10-22

Liu, M., Liu, C. H., Zhu, Y., Wang, R., Rotshtein, P., & Sui, J. (2015) Self-related information interfere with task performances: A cross-cultural investigation. *Culture and Brain, 3,* 112–121. doi:10.1007/s40167-015-0030-3

Luo, S., & Han, S. (2014). The association between an oxytocin receptor gene polymorphism and cultural orientations. *Culture and Brain, 2,* 89–107. doi:10.1007/s40167-014-0017-5

Markus, H. R., & Kitayama, S. (1991). Culture and the self: Implications for cognition, emotion, and motivation. *Psychological Review, 98*(2), 224–253. doi:10.1037/0033-295X.98.2.224

Mathur, V. A., Harada, T., Lipke, T., & Chiao, J. Y. (2010). Neural basis of extraordinary empathy and altruistic motivation. *Neuroimage, 51*(4), 1468–1475.

McCrae, R. R., & Terracciano, A. (2005). Personality profiles of cultures: Aggregate personality traits. *Journal of Personality and Social Psychology, 89*(3), 407–425. doi:10.1037/0022-3514.89.3.407

Meyer, M. L., Mastern, C. L., Ma, Y., Wang, C., Shi, Z., Eisenberger, N. I., … & Han, S. (2014). Differential neural activation to friends and strangers links interdependence to empathy. *Culture and Brain, 3,* 21–38. doi:10.1007/s40167-014-0023-7

Mottus, R., Allik, J., Realo, A., Rossier, J., Zecca, G., Ah-Kion, J., … & Johnson, W. (2012). The effect of response style on self-reported conscientiousness across 20 countries. *Personality and Social Psychology Bulletin, 38*(11), 1423–1436. doi:10.1177/0146167212451275

Mrazek, A. J., Chiao, J. Y., Blizinsky, K. D., Lun, J., & Gelfand, M. J. (2013). The role of culture–gene coevolution in morality judgment: Examining the interplay between tightness–looseness and allelic variation of the serotonin transporter gene. *Culture and Brain, 1,* 1–18. doi:10.1007/s40167-013-0009-x

Müller, V., Sänger, J., & Lindenberger, U. (2013). Intra- and inter-brain synchronization during musical improvisation on the guitar. *PLoS One, 8*(9). doi:10.1371/journal.pone.0073852

Murata, A., Moser, J. S., & Kitayama, S. (2013). Culture shapes electrocortical responses during emotion suppression. *Social Cognitive and Affective Neuroscience, 8*(5), 595–601. doi:10.1093/scan/nss036

Na, J., Grossmann, I., Varnum, M. E. W., Kitayama, S., Gonzalez, R., & Nisbett, R. E. (2010). Cultural differences are not always reducible to individual differences. *Proceedings of the National Academy of Sciences, 107*(14), 6192–6197. doi:10.1073/pnas.1001911107

Ng, S. H., Han, S., Mao, L., & Lai, J. C. L. (2010). Dynamic bicultural brains: fMRI study of their flexible neural representation of self and significant others in response to culture primes. *Asian Journal of Social Psychology, 13*(2), 83–91. doi:10.1111/j.1467-839X.2010.01303.x

Nisbett, R. E., Peng, K., Choi, I., & Norenzayan, A. (2001). Culture and systems of thought: Holistic versus analytic cognition. *Psychological Review, 108*(2), 291–310. doi:10.1037/0033-295X.108.2.291

Nisbett, R. E., & Wilson, T. D. (1977). Telling more than we can know: Verbal reports on mental processes. *Psychological Review, 84*(3), 231–259.

Obhi, S. S., Hogeveen, J., & Pascual-Leone, A. (2011). Resonating with others: The effects of self-construal type on motor cortical output. *Journal of Neuroscience, 31*(41), 14531–14535. doi:10.1523/JNEUROSCI.3186-11.2011

Oishi, S. (2010). The psychology of residential mobility: Implications for the self, social relationships, and well-being. *Perspectives on Psychological Science, 5*(1), 5–21. doi:10.1177/1745691609356781

Paller, K., Kutas, M., & Mayes, A. (1987). Neural correlates of encoding in an incidental learning paradigm. *Electroencephalography and Clinical Neurophysiology, 67*, 360–371.

Paller, K., McCarthy, G., & Wood, C. (1988). ERPs predictive of subsequent recall and recognition performance. *Biological Psychology, 26*, 269–276.

Schmitt, D. P., Allik, J., McCrae, R. R., & Benet-Martínez, V. (2007). The geographic distribution of Big Five personality traits: Patterns and profiles of human self-description across 56 nations. *Journal of Cross-Cultural Psychology, 38*(2), 173–212. doi:10.1177/0022022106297299

Schwartz, S. J., Lilienfeld, S. O., Meca, A., & Sauvigné, K. C. (2016). The role of neuroscience within psychology: A call for inclusiveness over exclusiveness. *American Psychologist, 71*(1), 52–70.

Sedikides, C., Gaertner, L., & Toguchi, Y. (2003). Pancultural self-enhancement. *Journal of Personality and Social Psychology, 84*(1), 60–79. doi:10.1037/0022-3514.84.1.60

Sedikides, C., Gaertner, L., & Vevea, J. L. (2005). Pancultural self-enhancement reloaded: A meta-analytic reply to Heine (2005). *Journal of Personality and Social Psychology, 89*(4), 539–551. doi:10.1037/0022-3514.89.4.539

Sedikides, C., Gaertner, L., & Vevea, J. L. (2007). Inclusion of theory-relevant moderators yield [sic] the same conclusions as Sedikides, Gaertner, and Vevea (2005): A meta-analytical reply to Heine, Kitayama, and Hamamura (2007). *Asian Journal of Social Psychology, 10*(2), 59–67. doi:10.1111/j.1467-839X.2007.00212.x

Sheng, F., & Han, S. (2012). Manipulations of cognitive strategies and intergroup relationships reduce the racial bias in empathic neural responses. *NeuroImage, 61*(4), 786–797.

Singelis, T. M. (1994). The measurement of independent and interdependent self-construals. *Personality and Social Psychology Bulletin, 20*(5), 580–591. doi:10.1177/0146167294205014

Singelis, T. M. (1995). The effects of culture, gender, and self-construal on emotional contagion. Doctoral dissertation, University of Hawaii. Available from ProQuest Dissertations & Theses Global: Social Sciences (304197921).

Snibbe, A. C., & Markus, H. R. (2005). You can't always get what you want: Educational attainment, agency, and choice. *Journal of Personality and Social Psychology, 88*(4), 703–720. doi:10.1037/0022-3514.88.4.703

Sui, J., Liu, C. H., Han, S. (2012) Cultural difference in neural mechanisms of self-recognition. *Social Neuroscience, 4*(5), 402–411. doi: 10.1080/17470910802674825

Talhelm, T., Zhang, X., Oishi, S., Shimini, C., Duan, D., Lan, X., & Kitayama, S. (2014). Large-scale psychological differences within China explained by rice versus wheat agriculture. *Science, 344*, 603–608.

Telzer, E. H., Ichien, N., & Qu, Y. (2015). The ties that bind: Group membership shapes the neural correlates of in-group favoritism. *NeuroImage, 115*, 42–51.

Triandis, H. C. (1989). The self and social behavior in differing cultural contexts. *Psychological Review, 96*(3), 506–520. doi:10.1037/0033-295X.96.3.506

Tzourio-Mazoyer, N., Landeau, B., Papathanassiou, D., Crivello, F., Etard, O., Delcroix, N., … & Joliot, M. (2002). Automated anatomical labeling of activations in SPM using a macroscopic anatomical parcellation of the MNI MRI single-subject brain. *NeuroImage, 15*(1), 273–89. doi:10.1006/nimg.2001.0978

Uleman, J. S., Rhee, E., Bardoliwalla, N., Semin, G., & Toyama, M. (2000). The relational self: Closeness to ingroups depends on who they are, culture, and the type of closeness. *Asian Journal of Social Psychology, 3*(1), 1–17. doi:10.1111/1467-839X.00052

United Nations (2005). International migration facts and figures. Retrieved from http://www.un.org/esa/population/migration/hld/Text/Migration_factsheet.pdf (accessed April 17, 2017).

United Nations (2013). The number of international migrants worldwide reaches 232 million. *Population Facts No. 2013/2.* Retrieved from http://esa.un.org/unmigration/documents/the_number_of_international_migrants.pdf (accessed April 17, 2017).

Uskul, A. K., Kitayama, S., & Nisbett, R. E. (2008). Ecocultural basis of cognition: Farmers and fishermen are more holistic than herders.

Proceedings of the National Academy of Sciences, 105(25), 8552–8556. doi:10.1073/pnas.0803874105

van de Vliert, E. (2013). Climato-economic habitats support patterns of human needs, stresses, and freedoms. *Behavioral and Brain Sciences, 36*(5), 465–480. doi:10.1017/S0140525X12002828

Varnum, M. E. W., Blais, C., & Brewer, G. A. (2016). Social class affects Mu-suppression during action observation. *Social Neuroscience, 11*(4), 449–454.

Varnum, M. E. W., Blais, C., Hampton, R. S., & Brewer, G. A. (2015). Social class affects neural empathic responses. *Culture and Brain, 3*(2), 122–130. doi:10.1007/s40167-015-0031-2

Varnum, M. E. W., Grossmann, I., Kitayama, S., & Nisbett, R. E. (2010). The origin of cultural differences in cognition: The social orientation hypothesis. *Current Directions in Psychological Science, 19*, 9–13. doi:10.1177/0963721409359301

Varnum, M. E. W., & Kitayama, S. (2011). What's in a name? Popular names are less common on frontiers. *Psychological Science, 22*(2), 176–183. doi:10.1177/0956797610395396

Varnum, M. E. W., Shi, Z., Chen, A., Qiu, J., & Han, S. (2014). When "Your" reward is the same as "My" reward: Self-construal priming shifts neural responses to own vs. friends' rewards. *NeuroImage, 87*, 164–169. doi:10.1016/j.neuroimage.2013.10.042

Wang, C., Wu, B., Liu, Y., Wu, X., & Han, S. (2015). Challenging emotional prejudice by changing self-concept: Priming independent self-construal reduces racial in-group bias in neural responses to other's pain. *Social Cognitive and Affective Neuroscience, 10*(9), 1195–1201. doi:10.1093/scan/nsv005

Watson, L. A., Dritschel, B., Obonsawin, M. C., & Jentzsch, I. (2007). Seeing yourself in a positive light: Brain correlates of the self-positivity bias. *Brain Research, 1152*(2002), 106–110. doi:10.1016/j.brainres.2007.03.049

Wilding, E., & Rugg, M. (1996). An event-related potential study of recognition memory with and without retrieval of source. *Brain, 119*, 889–906.

Zhu, Y., Zhang, L., Fan, J., & Han, S. (2007). Neural basis of cultural influence on self-representation. *NeuroImage, 34*(3), 1310–6. doi:10.1016/j.neuroimage.2006.08.047

19

Developmental Cultural Neuroscience: Progress and Prospect

Yang Qu and Eva H. Telzer

Cultural diversity in mind and behavior has received much attention from psychologists, philosophers, anthropologists, and sociologists. With rapid progress in neuroimaging techniques, the past decade has witnessed a number of theoretical and empirical advances in the field of cultural neuroscience (for reviews see, e.g., Chiao & Ambady, 2007; Han & Northoff, 2008; Kim & Sasaki, 2014; Kitayama & Uskul, 2011), which focuses on examining how culture plays a role in neurobiological processes (Chiao & Ambady, 2007). This line of research has documented cultural differences in the neural basis that underlies a variety of psychological processes, such as face perception, language, memory, self-judgment, emotion, and perspective taking (e.g., Freeman, Rule, & Ambady, 2009; Zhu, Zhang, Fan, & Han, 2007). Such compelling evidence suggests that cultural experience can lead to changes in the structure and function of the human brain.

Although cultural neuroscience has revealed the important role of culture in shaping the brain, little is known about *how* such cultural differences in neurobiological processes gradually emerge in the process of children's development. Research on cultural neuroscience has almost exclusively compared adults from different cultures, without taking into consideration how the culturally wired brain develops from childhood into adolescence and adulthood. This is a lacuna, in that the transmission of culture remains unclear without an understanding of the developmental process. For decades, theories and studies in developmental psychology highlight the key role of social inputs in shaping children's cognition, motivation, emotion, and behavior (e.g., Bronfenbrenner, 1979; Collins & Steinberg, 2006). Therefore, the study of culture and biology needs to

The Handbook of Culture and Biology, First Edition. Edited by José M. Causadias, Eva H. Telzer and Nancy A. Gonzales.

incorporate a developmental perspective, in order to better explain how diverse cultural environments influence the development of children's minds, brains, and behaviors.

What Is Developmental Cultural Neuroscience?

In this chapter, we propose *developmental cultural neuroscience* – the intersection of developmental psychology, cross-cultural psychology, and neuroscience (Figure 19.1). Developmental cultural neuroscience is an emerging interdisciplinary field that investigates cultural similarities and differences in brain, psychological, and behavioral development across the lifespan using a neuroimaging approach along with observation, survey, and experimental approaches. For decades, researchers have extensively investigated each of the intersections of two of these fields: the intersection of cultural psychology and neuroscience (cultural neuroscience), the intersection of developmental psychology and neuroscience (developmental neuroscience), and the intersection of developmental psychology and

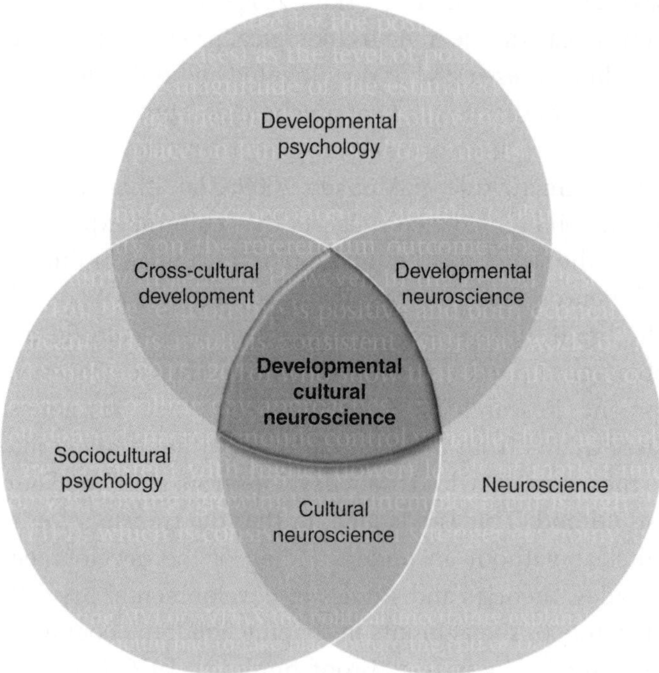

Figure 19.1 Developmental cultural neuroscience as a unique intersection of developmental psychology, cross-cultural psychology, and neuroscience

cultural psychology (developmental cultural psychology). However, the intersection of all three of these fields has received little attention.

Decades of research in developmental psychology, cultural psychology, and neuroscience have provided valuable lessons for this interdisciplinary field. For example, developmental psychology highlights the importance of examining developmental populations across the life span. By employing longitudinal assessments, researchers can carefully examine the developmental trajectories of children's and adolescents' functioning over either a short or a long period of time. Moreover, examining individual differences in these developmental trajectories can shed light on the unique or collaborative impact of social environments, such as family, peer groups, and school. Over the past 30 years, cultural psychology has identified key cultural values that guide individuals' motivation, cognition, and emotion in different cultures (e.g., Markus & Kitayama, 1991; Triandis, 1995). For example, the best-known cultural value that differs between the West and East Asia is independence versus interdependence (Markus & Kitayama, 1991), which provides important insights into individual and group behavior in Western and East Asian cultures. Accumulated evidence in cultural psychology emphasizes the necessity of examining psychological and behavioral phenomena in cross-cultural settings to unpack the role of culture. With the advent of sophisticated brain-imaging tools (e.g., functional magnetic resonance imaging (fMRI), electroencephalograms (EEG)), the field of psychology has witnessed a huge influx of neuroscience research in the past two decades. For example, statistical modeling in fMRI allows researchers to examine not only how activation in a specific brain region underlies psychological processes, but also how brain regions interact with other regions during these processes.

Why Study Developmental Cultural Neuroscience?

Developmental cultural neuroscience is a novel empirical approach to the examination of the neural mechanisms that underlie cultural differences and similarities in psychological processes across development. There are three key reasons to study this interdisciplinary field.

First, developmental cultural neuroscience provides *cultural psychology* with information about the process through which culture shapes behavior. Decades of research on cultural psychology has documented cultural differences in how people think, feel, and behave by using a variety of approaches, such as survey, observation, and experimental paradigms

(Kitayama & Cohen, 2007). As evidence of cultural differences accumulates, there have been calls to move from simply documenting cultural differences to unpacking how culture exerts its influence (e.g., Bond, 2002; Bukowski & Sippola, 1998; Heine & Norenzayan, 2006). Echoing these calls, endeavors in developmental cultural neuroscience provide a new approach to identifying the underlying mechanisms. Incorporating perspectives from developmental psychology and neuroscience, researchers can examine how culture shapes children's neurobiological processes over time, and how this contributes to cultural differences in their psychological adjustment.

Second, developmental cultural neuroscience provides *developmental psychology* with information about how social environments lead to cultural diversity in children's functioning. Social environments, such as parent–child interactions, peer socialization, and school structure, shape and are shaped by children's behavioral and psychological adjustment. Past research in developmental psychology has highlighted the role of culturally rooted social practices in the developmental process through which cultural values and norms are transmitted to children. Developmental cultural neuroscience can provide new understanding about the process of cultural socialization. For example, this line of research will elucidate how parenting practices in different cultures affect trajectories of children's brain development, leading to culturally distinct neurobiological processes and behavior over time. Moreover, this field can help us understand how children's neurobiological systems interact with their culturally rooted social environment.

Third, developmental cultural neuroscience provides *neuroscience* with knowledge about brain plasticity and neural function. Advances in developmental cultural neuroscience inspire empirical investigation into how cultural inputs affect brain development, which may support the accumulating evidence of the brain's malleability from childhood to adulthood. Moreover, research on developmental cultural neuroscience may identify the culturally unique or shared neural mechanisms that underlie children's behavior, and explore how neural structure and function are linked to children's psychological processes in different cultures. This line of research will provide a comprehensive understanding of the brain's plasticity.

The developmental cultural neuroscience approach provides a holistic perspective on how culture influences child development, and broadens our understanding of cultural transmission and neural plasticity. Instead of treating cultural influence as static, this approach captures the dynamic process of cultural transmission over time. Children's neural development serves as a key mechanism through which culturally rooted social practices contribute to divergent developmental trajectories. Thus, children's brain development provides a window on how culture influences children's beliefs, feelings, and behaviors. By examining children's neural functioning, we can elucidate the process through which cultural values are transmitted from social environment to children, across generations. Moreover, the accumulation of empirical evidence can help us understand better when, how, and why there are cultural differences in individuals' adjustment over the course of development. In addition to depicting different trajectories of children's brain development across cultures, development cultural neuroscience can help us identify key social practices that contribute to such differences in children's neural development, providing empirical explanations for cultural differences in child functioning. Finally, developmental cultural neuroscience equips us with valuable tools to examine the underlying neural mechanisms by which social environments and practices shape child development. This knowledge can be used in future interventions that aim to promote children's learning and psychological adjustment.

Framework of Developmental Cultural Neuroscience

To further our understanding of the complex relationships between culture and children's development, we propose an overarching framework of developmental cultural neuroscience that takes into account the reciprocal link between culture, social practices, child biology, and child adjustment, elucidating how cultural and biological factors interact in the process of child development. In particular, this framework highlights the fact that culturally rooted social practices shape children's neural development, which has implications for cultural differences in children's adjustment.

A key aspect of the developmental cultural neuroscience framework is to point out the reciprocal relations between cultural environment, brain, and child development. Theories in cultural psychology argue that culture and individuals' adjustment are mutually constituted (Markus & Kitayama, 2010). On the one hand, sociocultural contexts shape individuals' cognition, emotion, and behavior by providing sociocultural meanings and practices. On the other hand, as highlighted by Markus and Kitayama (2010), individuals' thoughts, feelings, and actions reinforce, and sometimes change, sociocultural meanings and practices. This idea of mutual constitution is echoed in the developmental psychology field, and much attention has been paid to how children's social environment and behavior influence each other over time. For example, decades of research suggest that parents' practices shape and are shaped by children's psychological adjustment (for reviews, see Belsky, 1984; Sanson & Rothbart, 1995). As a potential mechanism linking the two, children's brain development may also play a role in this reciprocal process.

Culturally Rooted Social Practices Affect Children's Brain Development

As Kitayama and Uskul (2011) have suggested, cultural values and beliefs may be hard to observe. However, they are embedded in a rich array of social practices, such as parent–child interaction, peer communication, and teaching practices. For example, in East Asian and Latino families, emphasis is placed on family obligation, which entails children and adolescents supporting the family, assisting their parents, and making sacrifices for the family (e.g., Chao & Tseng, 2002; Ho, 1996; Suárez-Orozco & Suárez-Orozco, 1995). This distinctive aspect of family relationships deeply shapes East Asian and Latino children's social practices in the family. It is important to note that parent–child interaction is not the only pathway in the process of cultural transmission and that it is likely that multiple forces are involved. Culture can be transmitted from many social agents (peers, teachers, media) via either conscious or unconscious (e.g., modeling) processes. For example, Chen (2012) has elaborated how peer groups can serve as important socialization agents in the process of cultural transmission, guiding children towards cultural beliefs and practices.

These culturally rooted social practices play a key role in shaping children's neural functioning across cultures. A pioneering study conducted by Telzer, Masten, Berkman, Liberman, and Fuligni (2010) examined cultural differences in Latino- and European-American youth's neural activation when making financial decisions in which young people and their families gain or lose money. Latino youth – whose social environments place more importance on helping the family – showed more neural activation in the mesolimbic reward system when making decisions to contribute to their family that involved self-sacrifice. In contrast, European-American youth showed more mesolimbic reward activation when gaining for themselves and not their family. This suggests that cultural differences in family obligation values and behaviors contribute to divergent neural functioning in Latino- and European-American adolescents, leading Latino adolescents to see making sacrifices for the family as personally rewarding. Therefore, research using a developmental cultural neuroscience approach can elucidate how culturally rooted practices shape children's neural functioning.

Culturally Shaped Brain Processes Underlie Children's Real-Life Functioning

Children's brain development (e.g., neural function and structure), which is shaped by culturally rooted practices, plays a key role in children's behavioral and psychological adjustment. The reason for studying children's brain development in cross-cultural settings is not just to document how culture influences brain development, but also to examine how the brain serves as a mechanism that contributes to differences in children's and adolescents' adjustment. Therefore, the developmental cultural neuroscience framework emphasizes the importance of understanding the link between neural functioning and real-life adjustment. Without an understanding of the *function* and the long-term implications of neural activation in a specific region for each cultural group, the mean difference in neural activation between cultural groups is less meaningful. Therefore, it is important to link culturally shaped neural activation with children's real-life functioning, such as learning, school engagement, risk-taking behavior, and emotional well-being.

Guided by this framework, Telzer, Fuligni, Lieberman, and Gálvan (2013a) examined the impact of family obligation – a distinctive family relationship among Latino families – on Latino adolescents' neural processes, with attention to the implication for their real-life functioning. Adolescents who reported greater family obligation values showed decreased activation in reward regions during risk taking and increased activation in cognitive control regions during behavioral inhibition. Importantly, such culturally shaped neural functioning played a role in Latino adolescents' adjustment. Specifically, the decreased reward activation was associated with less real-life risk-taking behavior, and increased cognitive control activation was associated with better decision-making skills. In another study, Telzer, Fuligni, Lieberman, and Gálvan (2013b) followed adolescents longitudinally and found that Latino youth who showed heightened mesolimbic reward activation when making self-sacrifices for their family showed longitudinal declines in risk-taking behaviors. Taken together, these findings suggest that engaging in social relationships that allow adolescents to put the needs of others before their own may alter activation in neural regions involved in reward sensitivity and cognitive control, and that such culturally shaped neural functioning may facilitate the development of skills and motivations to avoid risk taking.

Identifying cultural differences in children's neural processes can also help us understand why cultural differences in children's adjustment occur. For example, there is much evidence that, compared with their East Asian counterparts, American children and adolescents tend to show poorer performance in a variety of academic subjects (e.g., PISA, 2013; Stevenson, Chen, & Lee, 1993; US Department of Education, 2011). Understanding why East Asian children may do better at school could provide insight into how to promote American children's learning and academic achievement. Given that children's executive function consistently predicts their school engagement and academic achievement (Blair & Razza, 2007; McClelland & Cameron, 2011), executive function may play a key role in creating such differences. Indeed, East Asian children tend to perform better than their age-matched Western peers in a variety of executive function tasks (e.g., Lan, Legare, Ponitz, Li, & Morrison, 2011; Sabbagh, Xu, Carlson, Moses, & Lee, 2006). Therefore, a key question is whether children's brain functioning underlies cultural differences in executive function. To address this issue, Lahat, Todd, Mahy, Lau, and Zelazo (2010) examined cultural differences in the neural correlates of executive function by recording high-density EEG data. In the context of a Go/NoGo task, Chinese-Canadian children showed larger N2 amplitudes than European-Canadian children, with larger N2 amplitudes associated with better performance (i.e., faster reaction time). Larger N2 amplitudes among Chinese-Canadian children seem to be driven by their greater activation in dorsomedial, ventromedial, and ventrolateral prefrontal regions than in their European-Canadian counterparts (Lahat et al., 2010). Therefore, children's brain development may serve as a key mechanism underlying differences in their executive function across cultures and ultimately contributing to cultural differences in children's learning and academic achievement.

Progress

In this section, we present emerging findings regarding developmental cultural neuroscience. Although this nascent field includes very few studies that incorporate all three subfields (culture, development, and neuroscience), evidence is emerging and accumulating. We provide a review of the few studies which have incorporated a developmental cultural neuroscience approach, or which have included two of the three subfields but have implications for the third. While the field is extremely new, emerging research has addressed different topics using a developmental cultural neuroscience framework, including race perception, family relationships and cultural stereotypes of adolescence.

Race Perception

A well-documented phenomenon in the field of race perception is the differentiation between faces of own versus other ethnic groups. Because they have greater exposure to faces from their own culture, people are better at perceiving and recognizing the facial expressions of individuals from their own races than those of other races, a phenomenon called the other-race effect or in-group advantage (Elfenbein & Ambady, 2002; Kelly et al., 2007; Scott & Monesson, 2009; Vogel, Monesson, & Scott, 2012). Neuroimaging research examines the neural processes that underlie in-group versus out-group perception. A key neural region involved in this process is the amygdala, which is consistently involved in face perception and emotion processing (e.g., Anderson & Phelps, 2001; Hamann, Ely, Hoffman, & Kilts, 2002). Specifically, the amygdala shows greater activation to racial out-groups and unfamiliar faces than to racial in-groups and familiar faces (DuBois et al., 1999; Hart et al., 2000; Rule et al., 2010). For example, both American and Japanese individuals show a stronger amygdala response to cultural out-group faces than to cultural in-group faces (Rule et al., 2010).

The developmental process underlying this in-group/out-group bias has remained elusive. There is scarce evidence of when and how culture exerts its influences on children's neurodevelopment of race perception. Developmental research suggests that infants less than 1 year old can categorize faces by race and are sensitive to in-group versus out-group faces in their environment (for a review, see Shutts, 2015). The exclusive exposure to in-group faces in early postnatal development may modulate children's neurodevelopment and influence their neural response to in-group/out-group faces later in life. To investigate how culture exerts its influence on children's neural development of race perception, Telzer, Flannery, and colleagues (2013) examined this issue, using an international adoption design. In this study, children were raised in orphanage care in either East Asia or Eastern Europe as infants and later adopted by families in the United States. This experience limits children's exposure to faces of other cultures in early life (e.g., they have exclusive exposure to Asian faces or European faces), which is considered a form a deprivation, and also provides a natural way of quantifying the length of deprivation (that is, the age of adoption and initial exposure to other-race faces is known). Findings suggest that deprivation of other-race faces in infancy disrupts recognition of emotion and results in heightened amygdala response to other-race faces during adolescence. More importantly, greater length of deprivation (that is, a later age of adoption) is associated with greater neural activation to other-race faces. This research not only elucidates how changes in cultural environments (e.g., deprivation of other-race faces) influence children's neural function over time, but also informs developmental theories on early postnatal development, suggesting that this period of development may be a sensitive period for neural development of race perception.

In addition to resulting in differentiation between own- and other-race faces, culture shapes children's neurodevelopment of race perception in other ways. Notably, culture conveys knowledge and biases about specific races (e.g., stereotypes of these races). For example, implicit negative stereotypes about African Americans are still evident in American society. Such stereotypes and biases may be reflected in neural activation during perception of that racial group. Indeed, neuroimaging research in American adults has consistently found that perception of African-American (versus European-American) faces is associated with increased amygdala activity (e.g., Cunningham et al., 2004; Lieberman, Hariri, Jarcho, Eisenberger, & Bookheimer, 2005), suggesting that African American faces hold significant saliency in adulthood, probably because of a lifetime of learned associations about black versus white. Importantly, both European-American and African-American adults show greater amygdala response while viewing African-American than European-American faces (Lieberman et al., 2005), suggesting that learned associations are shared across racial groups. Given that the internalization of stereotypes is a process of cultural learning, it is important to examine when this cultural bias is reflected in differential neural reactivity over development and whether the social environment can attenuate such differentiation. To address these issues, Telzer, Humphreys, Shapiro, and Tottenham (2013) examined age-related differences in amygdala sensitivity to race by recruiting children aged from four to sixteen years. Interestingly, differential amygdala sensitivity to African-American (versus European-American) faces was not present in childhood, but emerged over adolescence, a time when children begin to explore the meaning of race and are aware of racial stereotypes (Apfelbaum, Pauker, Ambady, Sommers, & Norton, 2008; Roberts et al., 1999). Moreover, children from European-American and African-American backgrounds showed similar developmental trajectories in amygdala response to African-American faces, suggesting that they are exposed to similar messages about race in society. Children's social environment also modulates the amygdala response to race: greater peer diversity is associated with attenuated amygdala response to African-American faces, suggesting that greater contact with individuals from diverse backgrounds can reduce the neural salience of race.

Taken together, studies that use a developmental cultural neuroscience approach to examine race perception inform us about how culture exerts its influences on children's race perception. First, culture may play a role in children's neural development to race perception during early postnatal development. The international adoption study conducted by Telzer, Flannery, and colleagues (2013) suggests that even later exposure to other-race faces (e.g., adoption into a new culture) cannot attenuate heightened neural activation to other-race faces. Second, cultural knowledge and biases about races may have an impact on children's neurodevelopment. For example, developmental changes in children's neural reactivity to African-American faces suggest that the neural biases observed among adults do not reflect innate processes (Telzer, Humphreys et al., 2013). Rather, such neural biases emerge during adolescence, reflecting children's increasing internalization of cultural norms and biases. Third, greater exposure to diverse peers attenuates the amygdala response to race, highlighting the importance of diversity in youths' lives and underscoring how plastic the amygdala response is. In each of these studies, findings indicate that culture may influence children's neural functioning of race perception during a critical developmental period.

Family Relationships

As children's most proximal social environment, the family serves as a core mechanism through which cultural values and beliefs are transmitted to children. The emphasis placed on family relationships varies across different cultures. As discussed above, Latin American cultures place a significant emphasis on fulfilling family obligation (Suárez-Orozco & Suárez-Orozco, 1995). Specifically, children and adolescents are expected to support, assist, and take into account the needs and wishes of the family, for example by caring for siblings, doing household chores, and providing financial assistance (Fuligni & Pedersen, 2002; Telzer & Fuligni, 2009). Family obligation has consistently been identified as the most distinctive aspect of relationships within families from Mexican backgrounds in the United States, and it conveys unique cultural meanings and values. Indeed, compared with youth from European backgrounds, youth from Mexican backgrounds spend almost twice as much time helping their family each day, and assist their family 5–6 days per week on average, suggesting that family assistance is a meaningful daily routine for these adolescents (Telzer & Fuligni, 2009). Further, young adults from Mexican backgrounds make greater financial contributions to their families than their peers from European backgrounds (Fuligni & Pedersen, 2002), and those from second and third generations continue to maintain a strong sense of family obligation (Fuligni, Tseng, & Lam, 1999).

The culturally rooted family practices that children and adolescents are engaged in may modulate their neural functioning across cultures. Specifically, the practices that fulfill family obligation often require Latino youth to sacrifice their time and money to help their family. Although these practices can be demanding, Latino youth may begin to internalize the heightened cultural value of family obligation and perceive such behavior as personally and socially rewarding. As described above, Telzer and colleagues (2010) examined Latino-American and European-American youth's neural activation when they made sacrifices for their family at a cost to themselves, a behavior that closely approximates family obligation behaviors. Compared with their European-American counterparts, Latino-American youth showed greater activation in the mesolimbic reward system (i.e., the ventral striatum) when making a donation to the family that involved self-sacrifice, suggesting that Latino youth see such behaviors as personally rewarding. Importantly, the extent of reward activity when contributing to their family varied, depending on the young person's family obligation values: youth who reported greater family obligation values showed the highest reward activation when contributing to their family (Telzer, Fuligni, & Gálvan, 2016), which suggests that family relationships that are culturally meaningful can modulate youth's neural functioning.

Family obligation values may be a cultural resource, protecting youth from maladaptive outcomes such as risk taking and depression. Indeed, Mexican-origin youth with higher family obligation values show lower rates of substance use and association with deviant peers (Telzer, Gonzales, & Fuligni, 2014), as well as longitudinal declines in depression and greater self-reported meaning in life (Telzer, Tsai, Gonzales, & Fuligni, 2015). To test whether the rewarding nature of family obligation explains this protective effect, Telzer, Fuligni, Lieberman, and Gálvan (2013b, 2014) scanned a sample of Mexican youth as they completed a family obligation task during which they made financial sacrifices for their family. Results indicated that Mexican youth who showed greater ventral striatum activation (i.e., greater reward-related activation) when providing assistance to their family showed longitudinal declines in risk-taking behaviors and depressive symptoms across the high-school years. These data suggest that the meaningful and rewarding nature of family obligation is protective for Mexican-origin youth. Taken together, these findings suggest that culturally rooted family practices, such as practices that fulfill family obligation, affect adolescents' neural functioning, which plays a role in their real-life functioning.

Cultural Stereotypes of Adolescence

As anthropologists have long noted, culture shapes how youth navigate the teen years (e.g., Mead, 1928; Schlegel & Barry, 1991). Compared with their counterparts in Western countries, youth in non-Western countries appear to be less prone to the "storm and stress" of adolescence (for a review, see Arnett, 1999). For example, American youth often view school as less valuable as they enter adolescence, becoming less engaged in academics over time (e.g., Eccles et al., 1993). In contrast, research in China does not reveal such a trend: Chinese youth maintain their engagement in school over early adolescence (e.g., Wang & Pomerantz, 2009). Moreover, American youth engage in more risk taking than their Chinese counterparts (e.g., Greenberger, Chen, Beam, Whang, & Dong, 2000).

Research suggests that cultural stereotypes about adolescence differ in the United States and China, creating differences in the pathways youth take over this phase of development. For example, American youth view the teenage years in a more negative light – as fighting with their parents, being rebellious, and disengaging from school (e.g., Buchanan & Hughes, 2009; Qu, Pomerantz, Wang, Cheung, & Cimpian, 2016). In contrast, because of the key role of filial piety in Chinese culture, which involves children repaying parents and bringing honor to their family, adolescence in China is viewed as a time of fulfilling responsibilities to the family and working hard at school (Qu et al., 2016). Importantly, differences in how youth view adolescence contribute to their adjustment. For example, the more youth see the teenage years (as compared with younger children) as a time of disregarding family responsibilities, the less they are engaged with school and the more they take part in risky activities (e.g., cheating or fighting; Qu et al., 2016; Qu, Pomerantz, Wang, & Ng, in preparation). Therefore, these findings not only identify differences in how adolescence is viewed in different cultures, but also highlight how such differences contribute to divergent trajectories as youth navigate the early adolescent years.

Guided by the developmental cultural neuroscience framework, Qu, Pomerantz, McCormick, and Telzer (in preparation) further examined how cultural stereotypes about teens – seeing adolescence in a negative way – contribute to changes in American youth's neural processes that accompany their adjustment during adolescence. Using a three-wave longitudinal neuroimaging design, they found that youth with more negative conceptions about the teen years showed greater increases in risk taking over the transition from middle to high school (8th to 9th grade, which occurs around age 14 to 15). Moreover, youth who viewed the teen years more negatively also showed longitudinal increases in activation of the bilateral ventrolateral prefrontal cortex (VLPFC), a brain region involved in cognitive control. This suggests that youth who see the teen years in a negative light may engage in more effortful control in order to regulate their impulsive behavior effectively over time, as they need to recruit more neural resources to do so. Notably, such neural increases were related to longitudinal increases in young people's risk taking over the transition from middle to high school. Taken together, these findings highlight neural plasticity during adolescence and underscore the detrimental role of cultural stereotypes of teens in shaping youth's neural and psychological development at this stage.

Conclusions and Future Directions

Most of the studies in developmental cultural neuroscience to date have exclusively used cross-sectional designs, which compare children in different cultural groups at a single time point or examine how individual differences in cultural experiences correlate with neural processing. Although some studies have examined how the neural processing of cultural values relates to longitudinal changes in adolescents' internalizing and externalizing symptoms (e.g., Telzer, Fuligni, Lieberman, & Gálvan, 2013b, 2014), to the best of our knowledge no study so far has utilized longitudinal neuroimaging scans to examine how culture and brain correlations change over development.

Conceptually, cross-sectional designs treat childhood and adolescence as a snapshot in time (Kraemer, Yesavage, Taylor, & Kupfer, 2000). This static perspective cannot capture both the dynamic nature of brain development and longitudinal relationships between brain and behavior. Statistically, although cross-sectional studies aim to provide information on mean-level differences in terms of neural activation across different cultural groups, it is impossible to know, from only a single time point, if children's neural systems develop in the same direction or at the same rate in different cultures. For example, although children in two cultures may show the same neural activation at the mean level, children in one culture may be in the upward trajectories and children in the other culture may be in the downward trajectories. Such differences would not be observable in children's mean-level activation at a single time point. Therefore, many scholars highlight the importance of applying longitudinal approaches to research in developmental neuroscience (e.g., Dahl, 2011).

Longitudinal studies on adolescent brain development have revealed striking neural changes as children navigate the teen years (Braams, van Duijvenvoorde, Peper, & Crone, 2015; Pfeifer et al., 2011; Qu, Galván, Fuligni, Lieberman, & Telzer, 2015). While all these studies have been conducted with Western samples, the results provide initial evidence for how the brain is changing across development, underscoring significant neural changes that occur during the adolescent years. In fact, neural processing may be more variable and sensitive to the social and cultural environment during adolescence than during childhood or adulthood, as evidenced by greater variability and less stability in neural processing across 3-month intervals (van den Bulk et al., 2013), as well as by greater sensitivity to the social context in adolescence (Chein, Albert, O'Brien, Uckert, & Steinberg, 2011). This line of research suggests that culture may exert greater influence on children's brain development during this period of development. Therefore, future studies should employ a longitudinal neuroimaging approach to investigate how culture contributes to divergent trajectories of children's brain development and how such different neural trajectories lead to different changes in children's adjustment over time. This can inform our understanding of how culture is internalized at the neural level and how that changes across time. Moreover, longitudinal neuroimaging enables us to examine the reciprocal relationships between culture, brain, and child functioning.

A second important future direction is to design culturally relevant tasks that capture culture-specific values and practices. These tasks need to meet two criteria. First, they need to reflect specific cultural values or knowledge. By capturing key cultural values in the tasks, investigators can measure the neural processes that are shaped by such cultural values. However, this does not mean that the task design needs to be complicated. Differences in cultural values can be reflected in a variety of areas, ranging from low-level sensory/perceptual processing to high-level social cognitive processing and decision making. Therefore, the usefulness of tasks depends on whether cultural values play a role in the design paradigm. Second, tasks need to be developmentally appropriate. The latter may be particularly important when researchers plan to examine neural functioning longitudinally or across different developmental groups. This requires that participants of different ages are able to understand and perform the task, so that the comparison is meaningful.

A good example of culturally relevant tasks is the family donation task developed by Telzer and colleagues (2010). The key purpose of this task was to capture family obligation in Latino-American families. In this task, youth can earn money for themselves and contribute money to their family. In particular, they can contribute money to their family at a cost to themselves, a behavior that closely approximates family obligation behaviors. Although it embodies a relatively complex psychological construct, the task is ecologically valid for several reasons. First, meaningful cultural group differences emerged, so that Latino and European youth showed distinct neural signals during the task (Telzer et al., 2010). Second, activation during the task was correlated with meaningful behaviors and values, including how fulfilled they felt in their daily lives when helping their family (Telzer et al., 2010) and how much they valued family obligation (Telzer et al., 2016). Third, neural activation during the task had significant predictive validity across time, predicting trajectories of psychological functioning (Telzer, Fuligni, Lieberman, & Gálvan, 2013b, 2014). Finally, the task is widely used across samples and age groups (Telzer et al., 2010, 2016).

In conclusion, numerous empirical studies in adults have demonstrated that individuals in different cultures show different neurobiological processes underlying a variety of psychological functioning, such as face perception, language, memory, self-judgment, emotion, and perspective taking (e.g., Chiao & Ambady, 2007; Freeman et al., 2009; Kim & Sasaki, 2014; Zhu et al., 2007). However, without systematic examination of the developmental process, little is known about how culture influences the brain as individuals develop from childhood to adulthood, and how such brain development underlies cultural differences in psychological adjustment across time. Developmental cultural neuroscience provides researchers with a unique approach to investigating *when*, *how*, and *why* children in different cultures show divergent neural, psychological, and behavioral trajectories in the course of development. Advances in this promising field may provide valuable insights into cultural transmission and neuroplasticity, with implications for promoting children's learning and mental health in diverse cultures.

References

Anderson, A. K., & Phelps, E. A. (2001). Lesions of the human amygdala impair enhanced perception of emotionally salient events. *Nature, 411*(6835), 305–309. doi:10.1038/35077083

Apfelbaum, E. P., Pauker, K., Ambady, N., Sommers, S. R., & Norton, M. I. (2008). Learning (not) to talk about race: When older children underperform in social categorization. *Developmental Psychology, 44*, 1513–1518. doi:10.1037/a0012835

Arnett, J. J. (1999). Adolescent storm and stress, reconsidered. *American Psychologist, 54*, 317–326. doi:10.1037/0003-066X.54.5.317

Belsky, J. (1984). The determinants of parenting: A process model. *Child Development, 55*(1), 83–96. doi:10.2307/1129836

Blair, C., & Razza, R. P. (2007). Relating effortful control, executive function, and false belief understanding to emerging math and literacy ability in kindergarten. *Child Development, 78*, 647–663. doi:10.1111/j.1467-8624.2007.01019.x

Bond, M. H. (2002). Reclaiming the individual from Hofstede's ecological analysis – A 20-year odyssey: Comment on Oyserman et al. (2002). *Psychological Bulletin, 128*, 73–77. doi:10.1037/0033-2909.128.1.73

Braams, B. R., van Duijvenvoorde, Anna C. K., Peper, J. S., & Crone, E. A. (2015). Longitudinal changes in adolescent risk-taking: A comprehensive study of neural responses to rewards, pubertal development, and risk-taking behavior. *Journal of Neuroscience, 35*, 7226–7238. doi:10.1523/JNEUROSCI.4764-14.2015

Bronfenbrenner, U. (1979). *The ecology of human development: Experiments by nature and design*. Cambridge, MA: Harvard University Press.

Buchanan, C. M., & Hughes, J. L. (2009). Construction of social reality during early adolescence: Can expecting storm and stress increase real or perceived storm and stress? *Journal of Research on Adolescence, 19*, 261–285. doi:10.1111/j.1532-7795.2009.00596.x

Bukowski, W. M., & Sippola, L. K. (1998). Diversity and the social mind: Goals, constructs, culture, and development. *Developmental Psychology, 34*, 742–746. doi:10.1037/0012-1649.34.4.742

Chao, R., & Tseng, V. (2002). Parenting of Asians. In M. H. Bornstein (Ed.), *Handbook of parenting. Volume 4: Social conditions and applied parenting* (2nd ed., pp. 59–93). Mahwah, NJ: Lawrence Erlbaum Associates.

Chein, J., Albert, D., O'Brien, L., Uckert, K., & Steinberg, L. (2011). Peers increase adolescent risk taking by enhancing activity in the brain's reward circuitry. *Developmental Science, 14*(2), 10. doi:10.1111/j.1467-7687.2010.01035.x

Chen, X. (2012). Culture, peer interaction, and socioemotional development. *Child Development Perspectives, 6*, 27–34. doi:10.1111/j.1750-8606.2011.00187.x

Chiao, J. Y., & Ambady, N. (2007). Cultural neuroscience: Parsing universality and diversity across levels of analysis. In S. Kitayama & D. Cohen (Eds.), *Handbook of cultural psychology* (pp. 237–254). New York: Guilford Press.

Collins, W. A., & Steinberg, L. (2006). Adolescent development in interpersonal context. In N. Eisenberg (Ed.), *Handbook of child psychology. Volume 3: Social, emotional, and personality development* (6th ed., pp. 1003–1067). Hoboken, NJ: Wiley.

Cunningham, W. A., Johnson, M. K., Raye, C. L., Gatenby, J. C., Gore, J. C., & Banaji, M. R. (2004). Separable neural components in the processing of Black and White faces. *Psychological Science, 15*, 806–813. doi:10.1111/j.0956-7976.2004.00760.x

Dahl, R. (2011). Understanding the risky business of adolescence. *Neuron, 69*(5), 837–839. doi:10.1016/j.neuron.2011.02.036

Dubois, S., Rossion, B., Schiltz, C., Bodart, J. M., Michel, C., Bruyer, R., & Crommelinck, M. (1999). Effect of familiarity on the processing of human faces. *NeuroImage, 9*, 278–289. doi:10.1006/nimg.1998.0409

Eccles, J. S., Midgley, C., Wigfield, A., Buchanan, C. M., Reuman, D., Flanagan, C., & Mac Iver, D. (1993). Development during adolescence: The impact of stage-environment fit on young adolescents' experiences in schools and in families. *American Psychologist, 48*, 90–101. doi:10.1037/0003-066X.48.2.90

Elfenbein, H. A., & Ambady, N. (2002). On the universality and cultural specificity of emotion recognition: A meta-analysis. *Psychological Bulletin, 128*(2), 203–235. doi:10.1037/0033-2909.128.2.203

Freeman, J. B., Rule, N. O., Ambady, N. (2009). The cultural neuroscience of person perception. *Progress in Brain Research, 178*, 191–201. doi:10.1016/S0079-6123(09)17813-5

Fuligni, A. J., & Pedersen, S. (2002). Family obligation and the transition to young adulthood. *Developmental Psychology, 38*(5), 856–868. doi:10.1037/0012-1649.38.5.856

Fuligni, A. J., Tseng, V., & Lam, M. (1999). Attitudes toward family obligations among American adolescents from Asian, Latin American, and European backgrounds. *Child Development, 70*, 1030–1044. doi:10.1111/1467-8624.00075

Greenberger, E., Chen, C., Beam, M., Whang, S., & Dong, Q. (2000). The perceived social contexts of adolescents' misconduct: A comparative study of youths in three cultures. *Journal of Research on Adolescence, 10*, 365–388. doi:10.1207/SJRA1003_7

Hamann, S. B., Ely, T. D., Hoffman, J. M., & Kilts, C. D. (2002). Ecstasy and agony: Activation of human amygdala in positive and negative emotion. *Psychological Science, 13*(2), 135–141. doi:10.1111/1467-9280.00425

Han, S., & Northoff, G. (2008). Culture-sensitive neural substrates of human cognition: A transcultural neuroimaging approach. *Nature Reviews Neuroscience, 9*(8), 646–654. doi:10.1038/nrn2456

Hart, A. J., Whalen, P. J., Shin, L. M., McInerney, S. C., Fischer, H., & Rauch, S. L. (2000). Differential response in the human amygdala to racial outgroup vs ingroup face stimuli. *NeuroReport, 11*(11), 2351–2355. doi:10.1097/00001756-200008030-00004

Heine, S. J., & Norenzayan, A. (2006). Toward a psychological science for a cultural species. *Perspectives on Psychological Science, 1*, 251–269. doi:10.1111/j.1745-6916.2006.00015.x

Ho, D. Y. F. (1996). Filial piety and its psychological consequences. In M. H. Bond (Ed.), *Handbook of Chinese psychology* (pp. 155–165). New York: Oxford University Press.

Kelly, D. J., Quinn, P. C., Slater, A. M., Lee, K., Ge, L., & Pascalis, O. (2007). The other-race effect develops during infancy: Evidence of perceptual narrowing. *Psychological Science, 18*(12), 1084–1089. doi:10.1111/j.1467-9280.2007.02029.x

Kim, H. S., & Sasaki, J. Y. (2014). Cultural neuroscience: Biology of the mind in cultural contexts. *Annual Review of Psychology, 65*, 487–514. doi:10.1146/annurev-psych-010213-115040

Kitayama, S., & Cohen, D. (2007). *Handbook of cultural psychology*. New York: Guilford Press.

Kitayama, S., & Uskul, A. K. (2011). Culture, mind, and the brain: Current evidence and future directions. *Annual Review of Psychology, 62*, 419–449. doi:10.1146/annurev-psych-120709-145357

Kraemer, H. C., Yesavage, J. A., Taylor, J. L., & Kupfer, D. (2000). How can we learn about developmental processes from cross-sectional studies, or can we? *American Journal of Psychiatry, 157*, 163–171. doi:10.1176/appi.ajp.157.2.163

Lahat, A., Todd, R. M., Mahy, C. E. V., Lau, K., & Zelazo, P. D. (2010). Neurophysiological correlates of executive function: A comparison of European-Canadian and Chinese-Canadian 5-year-old children. *Frontiers in Human Neuroscience, 3*, 1–10. doi:10.3389/neuro.09.072.2009

Lan, X., Legare, C. H., Ponitz, C. C., Li, S., & Morrison, F. J. (2011). Investigating the links between the subcomponents of executive function and academic achievement: A cross-cultural analysis of Chinese and American preschoolers. *Journal of Experimental Child Psychology, 108*(3), 677–692. doi:10.1016/j.jecp.2010.11.001

Lieberman, M. D., Hariri, A., Jarcho, J. M., Eisenberger, N. I., & Bookheimer, S. Y. (2005). An fMRI investigation of race-related amygdala activity in African American and Caucasian American individuals. *Nature Neuroscience, 8*, 720–722. doi:10.1038/nn1465

Markus, H. R., & Kitayama, S. (1991). Culture and the self: Implications for cognition, emotion, and motivation. *Psychological Review, 98*(2), 224–253. doi:10.1037/0033-295X.98.2.224

Markus, H. R., & Kitayama, S. (2010). Cultures and selves: A cycle of mutual constitution. *Perspectives on Psychological Science, 5*(4), 420–430. doi:10.1177/1745691610375557

McClelland, M. M., & Cameron, C. E. (2011). Self-regulation and academic achievement in elementary school children. *New Directions for Child and Adolescent Development, 2011*, 29–44. doi:10.1002/cd.302

Mead, M. (1928). *Coming of age in Samoa: A psychological study of primitive youth for Western civilization*. New York: William Morrow.

Pfeifer, J. H., Masten, C. L., Moore, W. E., Oswald, T. M., Mazziotta, J. C., Iacoboni, M., & Dapretto, M. (2011). Entering adolescence: Resistance to peer influence, risky behavior, and neural changes in emotion reactivity. *Neuron, 69*, 1029–1036. doi:10.1016/j.neuron.2011.02.019

PISA (2013). PISA 2012 results. Retrieved from http://www.oecd.org/pisa/keyfindings/PISA-2012-results-snapshot-Volume-I-ENG.pdf (accessed May 15, 2014).

Qu, Y., Galván, A., Fuligni, A. J., Lieberman, M. D., & Telzer, E. H. (2015). Longitudinal changes in prefrontal cortex activation underlie declines in adolescent risk taking. *Journal of Neuroscience, 35*, 11308–11314. doi:10.1523/JNEUROSCI.1553-15.2015

Qu, Y., Pomerantz, E. M., McCormick, E. M., & Telzer, E. H. (in preparation). "Oh no, here come the teen years!" Conceptions of adolescence predict changes in the prefrontal cortex and risk taking.

Qu, Y., Pomerantz, E. M., Wang, M., Cheung, S., & Cimpian, A. (2016). Conceptions of adolescence: Implications for differences in engagement in school over early adolescence in the United States and China. *Journal of Youth and Adolescence, 45*, 1512–1526. doi:10.1007/s10964-016-0492-4

Qu, Y., Pomerantz, E. M., Wang, Q., & Ng, F. (in preparation). Conceptions of adolescence in Mainland China and Hong Kong: Implications for differences in risk taking over early adolescence.

Roberts, R. E., Phinney, J. S., Masee, L. C., Chen, R., Roberts, C. R., & Romero, A. (1999). The structure of ethnic identity of young adolescents from diverse ethnocultural groups. *Journal of Early Adolescence, 19*, 301–322.

Rule, N. O., Freeman, J. B., Moran, J. M., Gabrieli, J. D. E., Adams, R. B., Jr., & Ambady, N. (2010). Voting behavior is reflected in amygdala response across cultures. *Social Cognitive and Affective Neuroscience, 5*(2–3), 349–355. doi:10.1177/0272431699019003001

Sabbagh, M. A., Xu, F., Carlson, S. M., Moses, L. J., & Lee, K. (2006). The development of executive functioning and theory of mind: A comparison of Chinese and U.S. preschoolers. *Psychological Science, 17*(1), 74–81. doi:10.1111/j.1467-9280.2005.01667.x

Sanson, A. V., & Rothbart, M. K. (1995). Child temperament and parenting. In M. H. Bornstein (Ed.), *Handbook of parenting. Volume 4: Applied and practical parenting* (pp. 299–321). Hillsdale, NJ: Lawrence Erlbaum Associates.

Schlegel, A., & Barry, H., III. (1991). *Adolescence: An anthropological inquiry*. New York: Free Press.

Scott, L. S., & Monesson, A. (2009). The origin of biases in face perception. *Psychological Science, 20*(6), 676–680. doi:10.1111/j.1467-9280.2009.02348.x

Shutts, K. (2015). Young children's preferences: Gender, race, and social status. *Child development perspectives, 9*(4), 262–266. doi:10.1111/cdep.12154

Stevenson, H. W., Chen, C., & Lee, S. (1993). Mathematics achievement of Chinese, Japanese, and American children: Ten years later. *Science, 259*, 53–58. doi:10.1126/science.8418494

Suárez-Orozco, C., & Suárez-Orozco, M. M. (1995). *Transformations: Immigration, family life, and achievement motivation among Latino adolescents*. Stanford, CA: Stanford University Press.

Telzer, E. H., Flannery, J., Shapiro, M., Humphreys, K. L., Goff, B., Gabard-Durman, L., Gee, D. G., & Tottenham, N. (2013). Early experience shapes amygdala sensitivity to race: An international adoption design. *Journal of Neuroscience, 33*, 13484–13488. doi:10.1523/JNEUROSCI.1272-13.2013

Telzer, E. H., & Fuligni, A. J. (2009). Daily family assistance and the psychological well-being of adolescents from Latin American, Asian, and European backgrounds. *Developmental Psychology, 45*, 1177–1189. doi:10.1037/a0014728

Telzer, E. H., Fuligni, A. J., & Gálvan, A. (2016). Identifying a cultural resource: Neural correlates of familial influence on risk taking among

Mexican-origin adolescents. In J. Y. Chiao, S.-C. Li, R. Seligman, & R. Turner (Eds.), *The Oxford handbook of cultural neuroscience* (pp. 209–222). New York: Oxford University Press.

Telzer, E. H., Fuligni, A. J., Lieberman, M. D., & Gálvan, A. (2013a). Meaningful family relationships: Neurocognitive buffers of adolescent risk taking. *Journal of Cognitive Neuroscience, 25*, 374–387. doi:10.1162/jocn_a_00331

Telzer, E. H., Fuligni, A. J., Lieberman, M. D., & Gálvan, A. (2013b). Ventral striatum activation to prosocial rewards predicts longitudinal declines in adolescent risk taking. *Developmental Cognitive Neuroscience, 3*, 45–52. doi:10.1016/j.dcn.2012.08.004

Telzer, E. H., Fuligni, A. J., Lieberman, M. D., & Gálvan, A. (2014). Neural sensitivity to eudaimonic and hedonic rewards differentially predict adolescent depressive symptoms over time. *Proceedings of the National Academy of Sciences, 111*, 6600–6605. doi:10.1073/pnas.1323014111

Telzer, E. H., Gonzales, N., & Fuligni, A. J. (2014). Family obligation values and family assistance behaviors: Protective and risk factors for adolescent substance use. *Journal of Youth and Adolescence, 43*, 270–283. doi:10.1007/s10964-013-9941-5

Telzer, E. H., Humphreys, K., Shapiro, M., & Tottenham, N. L. (2013). Amygdala sensitivity to race is not present in childhood but emerges in adolescence. *Journal of Cognitive Neuroscience, 25*, 234–244. doi:10.1162/jocn_a_00311

Telzer, E. H., Masten, C. L., Berkman, E. T., Lieberman, M. D., & Fuligni, A. J. (2010). Gaining while giving: An fMRI study of the rewards of family assistance among White and Latino youth. *Social Neuroscience, 5*, 508–518. doi:10.1080/17470911003687913

Telzer, E. H., Tsai, K. M., Gonzales, N., & Fuligni, A. J. (2015). Mexican-American adolescents' family obligation values and behaviors: Links to internalizing symptoms across time and family context. *Developmental Psychology, 51*, 75–86. doi:10.1037/a0038434.

Triandis, H. C. (1995). *Individualism & collectivism*. Boulder, CO: Westview Press.

US Department of Education (2011). Trends in International Mathematics and Science Study: Mathematics achievement of fourth- and eighth-graders in 2011. Retrieved from https://nces.ed.gov/TIMSS/results11_math11.asp (accessed May 15, 2014).

van den Bulk, B. G., Koolschijn, P. C. M. P., Meens, P. H. F., van Lang, N. D. J., van der Wee, N. J. A., Rombouts, S. A. R. B., … & Crone, E. A. (2013). How stable is activation in the amygdala and prefrontal cortex in adolescence? A study of emotional face processing across three measurements. *Developmental Cognitive Neuroscience, 4*, 65–76. doi:10.1016/j.dcn.2012.09.005

Vogel, M., Monesson, A., & Scott, L. S. (2012). Building biases in infancy: The influence of race on face and voice emotion matching. *Developmental Science, 15*(3), 359–372. doi:10.1111/j.1467-7687.2012.01138.x

Wang, Q., & Pomerantz, E. M. (2009). The motivational landscape of early adolescence in the United States and China: A longitudinal investigation. *Child Development, 80*(4), 1272–1287. doi:10.1111/j.1467-8624.2009.01331.x

Zhu, Y., Zhang, L., Fan, J., & Han, S. (2007). Neural basis of cultural influence on self-representation. *Neuroimage, 34*(3), 1310–1316. doi:10.1016/j.neuroimage.2006.08.047

Index

Note: Page numbers in **bold type** indicate Figures, and those in *italic* indicate Tables.

The Handbook of Culture and Biology, First Edition. Edited by José M. Causadias, Eva H. Telzer and Nancy A. Gonzales.

C

g

h

o

p

t

V

W

Index compiled by Frank Pert